LIFE AFTER DEATH

*The Viola da Gamba in Britain
from Purcell to Dolmetsch*

Music in Britain, 1600–1900

ISSN 1752–1904

Series Editors:
RACHEL COWGILL & PETER HOLMAN

This series provides a forum for the best new work in this area; it takes a deliberately inclusive approach, covering immigrants and emigrants as well as native musicians. Contributions on all aspects of seventeenth-, eighteenth- and nineteenth-century British music studies are welcomed, particularly those placing music in its social and historical contexts, and addressing Britain's musical links with Europe and the rest of the globe.

Proposals or queries should be sent in the first instance to Professor Rachel Cowgill, Professor Peter Holman or Boydell & Brewer at the addresses shown below. All submissions will receive prompt and informed consideration.

Professor Rachel Cowgill, School of Music, Cardiff University,
31 Corbett Road, Cardiff, CF10 3EB
email: CowgillRE@cardiff.ac.uk

Professor Peter Holman, School of Music, University of Leeds, Leeds, LS2 9JT
email: p.k.holman@leeds.ac.uk

Boydell & Brewer, PO Box 9, Woodbridge, Suffolk, IP12 3DF
email: editorial@boydell.co.uk

Previously published volumes are listed opposite

Thomas Gainsborough, *Karl Friedrich Abel* (*c.* 1765)

LIFE AFTER DEATH

❧

The Viola da Gamba in Britain from Purcell to Dolmetsch

Peter Holman

THE BOYDELL PRESS

The right of Peter Holman to be identified as the author of this
work has been asserted in accordance with sections 77 and 78
of the Copyright, Designs and Patents Act 1988

First published 2010
The Boydell Press, Woodbridge
Reprinted in paperback 2013

ISBN 978 1 84383 574 5 hardback
ISBN 978 1 84383 820 3 paperback

The Boydell Press is an imprint of Boydell & Brewer Ltd
PO Box 9, Woodbridge, Suffolk IP12 3DF, UK
and of Boydell & Brewer Inc.
668 Mt Hope Avenue, Rochester, NY 14620–2731, USA
website: www.boydellandbrewer.com

A CIP catalogue record of this publication is available
from the British Library

The publisher has no responsibility for the continued existence
or accuracy of URLs for external or third-party internet websites
referred to in this book, and does not guarantee that any content on
such websites is, or will remain, accurate or appropriate.

Papers used by Boydell & Brewer are natural, recyclable products
made from wood grown in sustainable forests

Designed and typeset in Adobe Minion Pro by
David Roberts, Pershore, Worcestershire

Printed and bound in the United States of America

Contents

Illustrations

ILLUSTRATIONS IN THE TEXT

Music Examples

Abbreviations

GENERAL ABBREVIATIONS
(in addition to those in *GMO*)

CC	copy (copies) consulted
comp.	compiled (by)
illus.	illustration; illustrated (in)
intro.	introduction (by)
ME	modern edition(s)
R	(pagination or foliation) of a volume reversed
repr.	reprinted (by); reproduced (by)
WM	(date on) watermark

BIBLIOGRAPHICAL ABBREVIATIONS

BDA	*A Biographical Dictionary of Actors, Actresses, Musicians, Dancers, Managers, and other Stage Personnel in London, 1660–1800*, ed. P. H. Highfill jr. *et al.*, 16 vols. (Carbondale and Edwardsville, IL, 1973–93)
BDECM	*A Biographical Dictionary of English Court Musicians, 1485–1714*, comp. A. Ashbee, D. Lasocki *et al.*, 2 vols. (Aldershot, 1998)
BLIC	*The British Library Integrated Catalogue* (http://catalogue.bl.uk)
BMB	J. D. Brown and S. S. Stratton, *British Musical Biography: a Dictionary of Musical Artists, Authors and Composers Born in Britain and its Colonies* (Birmingham, 1897)
BurneyH	C. Burney, *A General History of Music* (London, 1776–89), ed. F. Mercer (London, 1935)
DA	*The Daily Advertiser*
DC	*The Daily Courant*
DP	*The Daily Post*
DUR	*The Daily Universal Register*
ECCO	*Eighteenth-Century Collections Online* (www.gale.cengage.com)
ECM	*Eighteenth-Century Music*
EEBO	*Early English Books Online* (eebo.chadwyck.com)
EM	*Early Music*
EMP	*Early Music Performer*

GA	*The General Advertiser*
GMO	*Grove Music Online*, ed. D. L. Root (www.oxfordmusiconline.com), all accessed 12/2009
Grove 1	*A Dictionary of Music and Musicians*, ed. G. Grove, 4 vols. (London, 1878–90)
GSJ	*The Galpin Society Journal*
GZ	*The Gazeteer and London Daily Advertiser*; *The Gazeteer and New Daily Advertiser*
HawkinsH	J. Hawkins, *A General History of the Science and Practice of Music* (London, 1776; 2/1853; repr. 1963)
HWV	Händel-Werke-Verzeichnis, in *Händel-Handbuch*, ed. W. and M. Eisen, 4 vols. (Kassel, 1978–86)
IGI	*The International Genealogical Index* (www.familysearch.org)
JAMS	*Journal of the American Musicological Society*
JRMA	*Journal of the Royal Musical Association*
JVdGSA	*Journal of the Viola da Gamba Society of America*
LSJ	*The Lute Society Journal*
MB	Musica Britannica
MC	*The Morning Chronicle and London Advertiser*; *The Morning Chronicle*
MGG2	*Die Musik in Geschichte und Gegenwart: allgemeine Enzyklopädie der Musik, begründet von Friedrich Blume. Zweite, neuerarbeitete Ausgabe*, ed. L. Finscher, 28 vols. (Kassel, 1994–2008)
MH	*The Morning Herald*
ML	*Music & Letters*
MLE	Music for London Entertainment, 1660–1800
MO	*The Musical Opinion*
MP	*The Morning Post and Daily Advertiser*; *The Morning Post*
MQ	*The Musical Quarterly*
MS	*The Musical Standard*
MT	*The Musical Times*
MW	*The Musical World*
OED	*The Oxford English Dictionary* (www.oed.com)
PA	*The Public Advertiser*
P(R)MA	*Proceedings of the (Royal) Musical Association*
RECM	*Records of English Court Music*, comp. A. Ashbee, 9 vols. (Snodland and Aldershot, 1986–96)
RISM	Répertoire International des Sources Musicales
Rm	*Revue musicale*
RMARC	*Royal Musical Association Research Chronicle*

RRMBE   Recent Researches in the Music of the Baroque Era
RRMCE   Recent Researches in the Music of the Classical Era
TilmouthC M. Tilmouth, 'A Calendar of References to Music in Newspapers
           Published in London and the Provinces (1660–1719)', *RMARC*, 1
           (1960), whole vol. 2 (1961), 1–15
VdGS   *The Viola da Gamba Society Thematic Index of Music for Viols*,
           comp. G. Dodd and A. Ashbee ([York], 6/1992, 7/2002) (www.vdgs.
           org.uk/publications-ThematicIndex.html)
VdGSIM   *The Viola da Gamba Society Index of Manuscripts Containing
           Consort Music*, 2 vols., comp. A. Ashbee, R. Thompson, and
           J. Wainwright (Aldershot, 2001, 2007)
VdGSJ   *The Viola da Gamba Society Journal* (www.vdgs.org.uk/
           publications-Journal.html)
WKO   W. Knape, *Bibliographisch-thematisches Verzeichnis der
           Kompositionen von Karl Friedrich Abel (1723–1787)* (Cuxhaven, 1971)
Z   F. B. Zimmerman, *Henry Purcell, 1659–1695: an Analytical
           Catalogue of his Music* (London, 1963)

LIBRARY SIGLA

(following the RISM system used in *GMO*)

Austria

A-LA   Lambach, Benediktiner-Stift Lambach, Bibliothek
A-Wn   Österreichische Nationalbibliothek, Musiksammlung

Australia

AUS-NLwm   Nedlands, Wigmore Music Library, University of Western
           Australia

Belgium

B-Bc   Brussels, Conservatoire Royal de Musique, Bibliothèque /
           Koninklijk Conservatorium, Bibliotheek
B-Br   Brussels, Bibliothèque Royale Albert 1.er

Czech Republic

CZ-Pnm   Prague, Narodní Muzeum

Germany

D-B	Berlin, Staatsbibliothek zu Berlin Preußischer Kulturbesitz, Musikabteilung
D-Dl	Dresden, Sächische Landesbibliothek, Staats- und Universitätsbibliothek Dresden
D-DS	Darmstadt, Universitäts- und Landesbibliothek Darmstadt
D-Hs	Hamburg, Staats- und Universitätsbibliothek Carl von Ossietzky, Musikabteilung
D-Kl	Kassel, Landesbibliothek und Murhardsche Bibliothek der Stadt Kassel
D-ROu	Rostock, Universitätsbibliothek, Fachgebiet Musik
D-SÜN	Sünching, Schloß
D-ZL	Leutkirch, Fürstlich Waldburg-Zeil'sches Archiv

Denmark

DK-Kk	Copenhagen, Det Kongelige Bibliotek Slotsholmen
DK-Km	Copenhagen, Musikhistorisk Museum og Carl Claudius samlings

France

F-Pn	Paris, Bibliothèque nationale de France, Département de la Musique

Great Britain

GB-BEcr	Bedford, Bedfordshire and Luton Archives and Records Service
GB-Bp	Birmingham, Public Libraries
GB-Cfm	Cambridge, Fitzwilliam Museum
GB-Ckc	Cambridge, Rowe Music Library, King's College
GB-Cmc	Cambridge, Magdalene College
GB-Cu	Cambridge, University Library
GB-DRc	Durham, Cathedral Library
GB-DU	Dundee, Public Libraries
GB-En	Edinburgh, National Library of Scotland
GB-Er	Edinburgh, Reid Music Library of the University of Edinburgh
GB-Eu	Edinburgh, University Library
GB-HAdolmetsch	Haslemere, Dolmetsch Library
GB-HU	Hull, University of Hull Library
GB-Lam	London, Royal Academy of Music, Library
GB-Lbbc	London, British Broadcasting Corporation, Music Library
GB-Lbl	London, The British Library

GB-Lcm	London, Royal College of Music
GB-Lfom	London, The Foundling Museum
GB-Lhh	London, The Handel House Museum
GB-Lml	London, Museum of London
GB-Lna	London, The National Archives
GB-Lu	London, University of London, Senate House Library
GB-Lv	London, Victoria & Albert Museum Library
GB-LEbc	Leeds, University of Leeds, Brotherton Library
GB-NH	Northampton, Record Office
GB-NTu	Newcastle upon Tyne, University Library
GB-Ob	Oxford, Bodleian Library

The Netherlands

NL-DHa	The Hague, Koninklijk Huisarchief
NL-DHgm	The Hague, Gemeentemuseum

Russia

RUS-Mrg	Moskva, Rossijskaja Gosudarstvennaja biblioteka

United States of America

US-AUS	Austin, TX, University of Texas at Austin, The Harry Ransom Humanities Research Center
US-CAh	Cambridge, MA, Harvard University, Houghton Library
US-Cn	Chicago, IL, Newberry Library
US-NH	New Haven, CT, Yale University, Irving S. Gilmore Music Library
US-NHub	New Haven, CT, Yale University, Beinecke Rare Book and Manuscript Library
US-NYp	New York, NY, New York Public Library at Lincoln Center, Music Division
US-SM	San Marino, CA, Henry E. Huntingdon Library & Art Gallery
US-U	Urbana, IL, University of Illinois at Urbana-Champaign, Music Library
US-WC	Washington, DC, Library of Congress, Music Division

Note to the Reader

PRIMARY sources have been transcribed without changing spelling, capitalisation or punctuation, though readers should be alert to the possibility that quotations taken from secondary sources might have been modernised more radically. Music examples have been edited with a minimum of editorial intervention, though obvious errors and inconsistencies have been corrected without comment. Pitches are indicated using the system in which the open strings of the bass viol and the violin are rendered as $D–G–c–e–a–d'$ and $g–d'–a'–e''$ respectively. I have modernised the English system of reckoning the year from Lady Day (25 March). Until 1752 England used the 'Old Style' or Julian calendar, which was ten days (eleven after 1700) behind the 'New Style' or Gregorian calendar used in Scotland and most continental European countries; Englishmen may or may not have used the Gregorian calendar while abroad. I have retained the old system of English currency: there were twelve pence (*d.*) to the shilling (*s.*), and twenty shillings to the pound (*£*). All printed books mentioned in the main text were published in London unless otherwise stated. To save space I have not included routine footnote references to biographies in *BDA*, *GMO*, *MGG2*, and the *Oxford Dictionary of National Biography* (www.oxforddnb.com). Those providing, or drawing attention to, particular sources are acknowledged in brackets in the footnotes.

For Mark

Preface

As its title indicates, this book is a study of an instrument in decline. For much of the seventeenth century the viol and its contrapuntal consort repertory was particularly associated with England – it was one of those 'Inventions … wherin we excelled other nations', as John Evelyn put it (ch. 1). Thus the book is concerned with the viol 'after the golden age', beginning with its decline during the Restoration period – a significant moment being 31 August 1680, the date of Henry Purcell's last complete fantasia – and ending with its revival at the end of nineteenth century – a landmark being 21 November 1890, the first appearance of Arnold Dolmetsch's viol consort.

I have four main objectives in writing this book. First, to document a remarkable thread of musical history that has been largely ignored by scholars and performers. My research has revealed a sizeable repertory of attractive viola da gamba music written or arranged in eighteenth-century Britain. Late viola da gamba music has aroused a good deal of interest in recent years, with scholars such as Michael O'Loghlin, Fred Flassig and Bettina Hoffmann and players such as Jordi Savall, Christophe Coin and Vittorio Ghielmi providing the European context for developments in Britain. After focusing initially on the eighteenth century, I decided to extend the study to include the nineteenth century, partly to disprove the oft-repeated assertion that Abel was the last gamba player in Britain. I will show that there was always at least one person playing the instrument in London throughout the nineteenth century.

Second, I use the viola da gamba and related instruments to make the point that instruments (the 'hardware') often remain essentially the same, while their function and the music written and arranged for them (the 'software') changes radically. Thus, after about 1720 the gamba ceased to be a consort instrument or the bass instrument of mixed ensembles with its music written in the bass clef, becoming a solo instrument in the alto or tenor register with its music written mostly in the alto and treble clefs (ch. 2). At the same time the name of the six- or seven-string fretted instrument changed from 'bass viol' to 'viola da gamba' or some Anglicised equivalent such as 'viol di gambo'. 'Bass viol' remained in use, particularly in parish church music, as the name of four-string unfretted cello-like instruments. For the rest of the eighteenth century the gamba was associated with up-to-date music; it was only in the middle of the nineteenth century that it became associated with the developing early music revival.

Third, the book is a group portrait of more than 150 individuals, male, female, amateur and professional, who owned, played, wrote for, or wrote about the gamba in the eighteenth and nineteenth centuries. It was not a mainstream instrument, and the amateurs who played it tended to be distinctive and interesting people; they included aristocrats and politicians such as Sir Edward Walpole, Elizabeth, Countess of Pembroke, and Benjamin Franklin, writers and intellectuals such as Daniel Defoe, Conyers Middleton, and Laurence Sterne, and painters such as Thomas Jones, Thomas Gainsborough, and John Cawse. My research has revealed a good deal about their musical activities which I hope will be of general interest to musicologists and cultural historians. Nearly all the professional musicians who played the gamba at the time were cellists first and foremost, and most of them were immigrants. One thread of my work is to try to understand why, despite the fact that they were in most respects representatives of modernity in eighteenth-century Britain, they chose to play an obsolete and rare instrument (ch. 3, 8). Of course, the distinction between amateur and professional musicians is not without its problems at a period when socially ambitious musicians often aspired to leave the music profession behind them, and when amateurs were sometimes as accomplished as professionals. I have chosen to restrict the word 'professional' to those who essentially earned their living from playing instruments, including the gamba. Thus John Gostling, a court singer and clergyman, could be thought of as a professional musician, but seems to have played the gamba for pleasure.

This brings me to my fourth objective: to make some observations about eighteenth- and nineteenth-century British musical culture from an unexpected vantage-point, the study of a supposedly 'marginal' instrument. One is concerned with musical education for amateurs, and the role of universities and music clubs in the process (ch. 2). I argue that musical life in the early eighteenth century owed more than has been recognised to members of the professions – doctors, lawyers and clergymen – who received musical instruction at Oxford and Cambridge and later became mainstays of music clubs around the country. Another theme is the fashion for exotic musical instruments in mid-eighteenth-century England, and, in particular, the ways that they illustrate the change from an Italianate musical culture to one increasingly dominated by German music and musicians, and the parallel change from a culture dominated by vocal music to a more modern one focussed on instruments and instrumental music (ch. 4). I argue that German musical instrument makers such as John Frederick Hintz were more important in this process than has been recognised. Ch. 5 and 6 are concerned with Charles Frederick Abel, the greatest eighteenth-century gamba player and the most prolific contemporary composer for the instrument. New light is thrown on his life, his activities as a performer, and his gamba music. In ch. 7 I examine the connection between the gamba and the sensibility cult, at its height around 1760. The leading exponent of the cult, Laurence Sterne, seems to have played the gamba, as did Ann Ford, who moved audiences to tears with her public performances. I argue that the association of the gamba with sensibility helps to explain its appeal to intellectuals and aristocrats. The last two chapters concern the gamba in the nineteenth century. Ch. 8 deals with Abel's legacy and the continued use of the instrument as an exotic but essentially contemporary instrument, used to play modern or relatively recent music. Ch. 9 deals with its role in the nineteenth-century early music revival. The early music movement in eighteenth-century England was largely concerned with old vocal music. This has also been true of research into the subject in modern times: little work has been done on the revival of old instruments and old instrumental music. I show that the process sometimes involved misrepresentation and forgery, including the composition of fake old music; that the reception of J. S. Bach's music in England acted as an important stimulus from the 1860s; and that Arnold Dolmetsch's activities in the 1890s were not so ground-breaking as has been supposed.

An additional objective is to demonstrate the range of primary documentary sources available to the music historian interested in eighteenth- and nineteenth-century Britain, including newspapers, periodicals, letters, diaries, financial documents, and the biographical sources used by family historians. I began by using traditional paper-based sources, but soon realised that my project was ideally suited to exploit the on-line resources that have become available during the last few years, including *British Periodicals*, *Early English Books Online*, *Eighteenth-Century Collections Online*, *Nineteenth-Century British Library Newspapers*, *Nineteenth-Century UK Periodicals*, and *Seventeenth-Eighteenth-Century Burney Collections Newspapers*. They led me to many sources that I otherwise would have missed, and made it easier to place my work in the social and cultural contexts of the time – an essential project for anyone interested in the history of instruments and instrumental music.

Acknowledgements

A PROJECT of this sort inevitably owes much to the work of others and to the help of friends and colleagues. Mark Caudle's enthusiasm for the repertory, demonstrated in performance and in conversation, fired my own interest in it; I dedicate the book to him as a long-standing friend and colleague. I began serious research in the late 1990s when Ian Davies drew my attention to a set of gamba sonatas apparently compiled in England around 1730 in a manuscript now at GB-Lu (ch. 3, 7). At an early stage Ian Woodfield generously made the files he had assembled on the subject available to me. Searching for those making, playing, buying, selling, and composing for the gamba was greatly aided by the databases of newspaper references assembled by Rosamond McGuinness (*Computer Register of Musical Data in London Newspapers, 1660–1800*) and Simon McVeigh (*Calendar of London Concerts, 1750–1800*), and kindly made available to me. I was enabled to complete the book by a period of research leave funded partly by the Arts and Humanities Research Council and partly by the University of Leeds; I am grateful to Laurence Dreyfus for acting as my Nominated Reviewer for the application. Ch. 3, 5, 7, and 9 contain material that first appeared in articles written for the journals *Early Music, Eighteenth-Century Music*, and *Ad Parnassum*. I am grateful to Andrew Woolley for setting the music examples for me, to my daughter Louise for helping me with the index, and to the Music & Letters Trust for a grant towards the costs of production.

I would also like to thank the following for reading drafts of the book in whole or part: Andrew Ashbee, Lanie Graf, Ben Hebbert, Bettina Hoffmann, Thomas MacCracken, Michael O'Loghlin, David Pinto, Robert Rawson, Stephen Roe, Susan Sloman, and Robert Thompson. I have benefited greatly from their advice and criticism. In addition, the following provided me with information or helped me in various ways (with apologies to anyone forgotten): Ann van Allen-Russell, Patxi del Amo, Cassie Barber, Olive Baldwin, Jonathan Barry, Johannes Boer, John Catch, Jane Clark, Colin Coleman, Tim Crawford, John Cunningham, Simon Dickinson, Jeanne Dolmetsch, Sally Drage, Katharine Ellis, Tassilo Erhardt, Michael Fleming, Ian Gammie, Chris Gammon, John Greenacombe, Nancy Hadden, Ian Harwood, Susanne Heinrich, the late Anthony Hicks, Simon Hill, Kerry Houston, James Hume, David Hunter, Joan Jeffery, the late David Johnson, Harry Johnstone, Richard King, Lowell Lindgren, Richard Luckett, Charles Medlam, Triona O'Hanlon, Samantha Owens, Mike Parker, David Ransome, Robert Rawson, David Rhodes, Michael Robertson, John Robinson, Lucy Roe, Ann Royle, Roz Southey, Arne Spohr, Matthew Spring, Richard Sutcliffe, Nicholas Temperley, Teri Noel Towe, Peter Ward-Jones, Bryan White, Philip White, Thelma Wilson, Andrew Woolley, and Günter von Zadow.

Peter Holman,
Colchester,
December 2009.

Origins and Contexts

I T is now generally accepted that the viol family came into being in the 1490s, when the Valencian viol, a single-size bowed instrument played in chords in the medieval manner, was imported into northern Italy from Catalonia, fitted with an arched bridge, and developed in several sizes for polyphonic music.[1] From the first, viols were thought to be particularly suitable for accompanying the voice or for playing contrapuntal music; the earliest repertories seem to have been the polyphonic frottola and French and Flemish 'songs without words' transmitted in Italian sources.[2] The first known viol consort was commissioned by Isabella d'Este for the Mantuan court; she played the viol herself, as did her brother Alfonso d'Este, Duke of Ferrara, and other members of their circle.[3] It was the only socially acceptable ensemble instrument for much of the sixteenth century, played by 'gentlemen, merchants, and other persons of culture' ('les gentilz hommes, marchantz, & autre gens de vertuz'), as the Lyons composer Philibert Jambe de Fer put it in 1556.[4] However, it was also played by professional instrumentalists as an alternative to violins or wind instruments, and its rapid spread across Europe in the early sixteenth century probably owed much to groups from Italy that settled, for instance, in Paris in the 1520s, in London in 1540, in Munich in the 1550s, or in Vienna in the 1560s.[5]

Around 1600 the viol consort declined in mainland Europe in the face of the increasing popularity of the violin and the fashion for mixed ensembles. Vincenzo Giustiniani wrote in 1628 that 'the uniformity of the sound' of single-

---

[1] I. Woodfield, *The Early History of the Viol* (Cambridge, 1984); P. Holman, *Four and Twenty Fiddlers: the Violin at the English Court, 1540–1690* (Oxford, 2/1995), 14–17.

[2] See esp. W. F. Prizer, 'The Frottola and the Unwritten Tradition', *Studi musicali*, 15 (1986), 3–37; L. Litterick, 'On Italian Instrumental Ensemble Music of the late Fifteenth Century', in *Music in Medieval and Early Modern Europe: Patronage, Sources and Texts*, ed. I. Fenlon (Cambridge, 1981), 117–30.

[3] See esp. W. F. Prizer, 'Isabella d'Este and Lorenzo da Pavia, "Master Instrument Maker"', *Early Music History*, 2 (1982), 87–127.

[4] Facs. in F. Lesure, '*L'Épitome musical* de Philibert Jambe de Fer (1556)', *Annales musicologiques*, 6 (1958–63), 341–86, at [377].

[5] Woodfield, *The Early History of the Viol*, 191–227; Holman, *Four and Twenty Fiddlers*, 19–21, 70–87.

sonority ensembles such as viols and flutes became 'tiresome rather quickly' and was 'an incentive to sleep' on a hot afternoon.[6] Viol consorts are occasionally encountered later in sophisticated musical circles, such as the Barberini household in Rome in the 1630s, written for by Cherubino Waesich,[7] or as an occasional change from violins, as in 'Ad cor: Vulnerasti cor meum', BuxWV 75, from Buxtehude's cycle 'Membra Jesu nostri',[8] or the aria in Vivaldi's oratorio *Juditha triumphans* (1716) with a 'concerto di viole all'inglese' – apparently a consort of viols.[9] Only a few later examples of amateur viol consorts in continental Europe are known: the Huygens family cultivated them at The Hague in the late 1630s and 40s,[10] and members of the family of Duke August the younger of Brunswick-Wolfenbüttel appear in Albert Freyse's mid-seventeenth-century painting playing six viols with a spinet.[11]

Things were different in England. Viol playing was well established from the 1530s among court musicians and those in noble households,[12] though large numbers of amateurs only began to take it up around 1600 just as their counterparts elsewhere were abandoning it. The English sixteenth-century consort repertory was apparently intended essentially for professionals, be they court string players, waits, or members of the Chapel Royal and other collegiate choirs. It may not all have been intended for viols: wind instruments and wordless voices have been

---

[6] Adapted from V. Giustiniani, *Discorso sopra la Musica (1628)*, trans. C. MacClintock, Musicological Studies and Documents, 9 (Rome, 1962), 79–80.

[7] F. Grampp, 'A Little-Known Collection of Canzonas Rediscovered: the *Canzoni a cinque da sonarsi con le viole da gamba* by Cherubino Waesich (Rome, 1632)', *Chelys*, 32 (2004), 21–44.

[8] K. J. Snyder, *Dieterich Buxtehude, Organist in Lübeck* (New York, 1987), esp. 368–9. See also pieces listed in D. P. and P. Walker, *German Sacred Polyphonic Vocal Music between Schütz and Bach: Sources and Critical Editions* (Warren, MI, 1992).

[9] For Vivaldi and the *viola all'inglese*, see V. Ghielmi, 'An Eighteenth-Century Italian Treatise and other Clues to the History of the Viola da Gamba in Italy', in *The Italian Viola da Gamba: Proceedings of the International Symposium on the Italian Viola da Gamba, Magnano, Italy, 29 April-1 May 2000*, ed. S. Orlando (Solignac, 2002), 73–85, at 83–4; M. Talbot, 'Vivaldi and the English Viol', *EM*, 30 (2002), 381–94; B. Hoffmann, 'Il violoncello all'inglese', *Studi Vivaldiani*, 4 (2004), 43–51.

[10] T. Crawford, 'Constantijn Huygens and the 'Engelsche Viool', *Chelys*, 18 (1989), 41–60, at 43–5.

[11] Braunschweig, Landesmuseum, VM3278. A detail is illus. in A. Otterstedt, *The Viol: History of an Instrument*, trans. H. Reiners (Kassel, 2002), 107.

[12] See esp. Woodfield, *The Early History of the Viol*, 210–12; Holman, *Four and Twenty Fiddlers*, 123–4.

proposed as alternatives.[13] It consists mostly of contrapuntal fantasias and pieces with a plainsong *cantus firmus* in four, five, six, and occasionally seven parts, modelled on (and sometimes based on) sacred music, and composed mostly by court and church composers such as Christopher Tye, Robert White, Robert Parsons, Alfonso Ferrabosco senior, and William Byrd.[14]

In the reign of James I the repertory was transformed by a new generation of court composers, including Alfonso Ferrabosco junior, John Coprario, Orlando Gibbons, Thomas Lupo, Thomas Tomkins, and John Ward, most of them working in the household of Prince Charles, Prince of Wales 1617–25. Their models tended to be Italian madrigals rather than sacred music, and they were stimulated by a fashion for the viol among amateurs, led by Prince Charles, who could 'play his part exactly well on the *Bass-Viol*, especially of those Incomparable Fancies of Mr. *Coperario* to the *Organ*', according to John Playford.[15] From about 1620 consort music was routinely accompanied by a chamber organ, the player essentially doubling the string parts by reading from score or a written-out part.[16]

Later in the century the traditional repertory of viol consort music, 'our *Grave Musick, Fancies* of 3, 4, 5, and 6 *Parts* to the *Organ*' as Thomas Mace put it,[17] was added to by John Jenkins, William Lawes, Richard Mico, John Hingeston, Simon Ives, and others, and was expanded to include dance music – Mace's '*Pavins, Allmaines, Solemn, and Sweet Delightful Ayres*'. New scorings and genres were increasingly popular. Lupo, Gibbons and Coprario introduced the violin into contrapuntal consort, while Coprario created the three-movement fantasia-suite (usually fantasia–almand–galliard or corant), a genre to which Lawes, Jenkins, Hingeston, Christopher Simpson, Christopher Gibbons, Matthew Locke, and

---

[13] W. Edwards, 'The Performance of Ensemble Music in Elizabethan England', *PRMA*, 97 (1970–1), 113–23; P. Doe, 'The Emergence of the In Nomine: some Notes and Queries on the Work of Tudor Church Musicians', in *Modern Musical Scholarship*, ed. E. Olleson (Stocksfield, 1980), 79–92.

[14] ME: *Elizabethan Consort Music: I, II*, ed. P. Doe, MB, 44, 45 (London, 1979, 1988).

[15] J. Playford, *An Introduction to the Skill of Musick* (London, 10/1683), Preface; CC: *EEBO*, Wing P2482. See esp. C. D. S. Field, 'Consort Music I: up to 1660', in *The Seventeenth Century*, ed. I. Spink, The Blackwell History of Music in Britain, 3 (Oxford, 1992), 197–244. Little has been written about the development of amateur viol playing in England and the 'new' consort repertory, but see C. Monson, *Voices and Viols in England, 1600–1650: the Sources and the Music* (Ann Arbor, MI, 1982); A. Ashbee, 'Manuscripts of Consort Music in London, *c.* 1600–1625: some Observations', *VdGSJ*, 1 (2007), 1–19.

[16] See P. Holman, '"Evenly, Softly, and Sweetly Acchording to All": the Organ Accompaniment of English Consort Music', in *John Jenkins and his Time: Studies in English Consort Music*, ed. A. Ashbee and Holman (Oxford, 1996), 353–82.

[17] T. Mace, *Musick's Monument* (London, 1676; repr. 1968), 234.

others contributed until the 1660s. Most fantasia-suites are for one or two violins, bass viol and organ (now often obbligato as well as doubling), though Jenkins seems to have preferred the treble viol to the violin, and used some new scorings: treble and two basses, two trebles and two basses, and three trebles (probably violins), bass and organ.[18]

Another Jacobean innovation, possibly invented by Ferrabosco or Coprario, was music for two or three lyra viols – small bass viols played from tablature using variant tunings to facilitate the playing of chords in different keys. Lawes, Jenkins, Ives, and others contributed to the repertory, and Jenkins and Simpson were among those who wrote lyra consorts for violin or treble viol, lyra viol, bass viol, and harpsichord, with or without theorbo.[19] Other novel mixed ensembles were Lawes's harp consorts, for violin, harp (probably the Irish wire-strung type), bass viol, and theorbo, and his Royal Consorts, for two violins, two bass viols, and two theorboes.[20] A third Jacobean innovation was the development of music for one or two solo bass viols with organ. Its repertory included airs by Ward and fantasias by Coprario, though most of it consisted of divisions (or variations) on ground basses or the bass parts of dances or polyphonic vocal music. Early composers were Ferrabosco, Maurice Webster, Daniel Norcombe, and Henry Butler; the genre was codified in Simpson's *The Division-Violist* (1659).[21] Lawes and Jenkins contributed to it in the 1630s, and at the same time began to incorporate divisions into contrapuntal consort music, in the process creating a lively, sectionalised type of fantasia akin to (but not necessarily derived from) the Italian sonata. The only English viol players to write sonatas before the late seventeenth century, Henry Butler (d. 1652) and William Young (d. 1662), worked abroad, in Madrid and Innsbruck.

It used to be thought that the Puritans were against music, and that the art suffered badly during the Interregnum.[22] It is true that the court broke up in

---

[18] See esp. C. D. S. Field, 'The English Consort Suite of the Seventeenth Century', (PhD diss., U. of Oxford, 1970); A. Ashbee, *The Harmonious Musick of John Jenkins*, ii: *Suites, Airs and Vocal Music* (forthcoming), ch. 1–6.

[19] See esp. I. H. Stoltzfus, 'The Lyra Viol in Consort with other Instruments' (PhD diss., Louisiana State U., 1983); J. Cunningham, *The Consort Music of William Lawes, 1602–1645* (Woodbridge, 2010), ch. 3; Ashbee, *The Harmonious Musick of John Jenkins*, ii, ch. 13.

[20] See esp. D. Pinto, *For ye Violls: the Consort and Dance Music of William Lawes* (London, 1995), 34–69; Cunningham, *The Consort Music of William Lawes*, ch. 4, 7.

[21] See esp. J. M. Richards, 'A Study of Music for Bass Viol Written in England in the Seventeenth Century' (PhD diss., U. of Oxford, 1961).

[22] First challenged in P. Scholes, *The Puritans and Music in England and New England* (Oxford, 1934; repr. 1969).

1642, leaving the royal musicians to fend for themselves, and that the Parliamentary authorities closed the theatres and disbanded cathedral choirs. But they had nothing against instrumental music, and the upheavals of the 1640s provided a suitable environment for its intensive cultivation in private; as the writer Roger North put it in a memorable phrase, 'many chose rather to fidle at home, than to goe out, and be knockt on the head abroad'.[23] At that period viol playing was particularly associated with country house society, such as the L'Estrange family at Hunstanton in Norfolk,[24] the Norths at Kirtling in Cambridgeshire,[25] and the Hattons at Kirby Hall in Northamptonshire.[26]

❧ Decline and Fall

IN fact, consort music suffered more from the restoration of the monarchy in 1660, partly because the return of musicians to the court caused the decline of music-making elsewhere (such as the important music meetings in Commonwealth Oxford),[27] and partly because composers were once more preoccupied with vocal music, needed in the theatres and in the Chapel Royal and other collegiate foundations. There was also the question of Charles II's musical taste. North wrote that, although Charles was 'a professed lover of musick', he had 'an utter detestation of Fancys', the more so after Sir Joseph Williamson, an under-secretary of state at Whitehall, had invited him to hear 'a successless entertainment of that kind'; as a result 'the King (as his way was) could not forbear whetting his witt upon the subject of the Fancy-musick, and its patron the Secretary'.[28] North added that Charles 'could not bear any musick to which he could not keep the time' – that is, he only liked music he could beat time to. Locke and Jenkins seem to have written fantasia-suites for the court Broken Consort (the successor to the group that played contrapuntal consort before the Civil War) soon after the Restoration,[29] though it was disbanded in 1663 after the death of the German virtuoso violinist Thomas Baltzar, and it was soon replaced in the Privy Chamber

[23] *Roger North on Music*, ed. J. Wilson (London, 1959), 294.

[24] *VdGSIM*, i. 6–7, and the works cited there.

[25] *VdGSIM*, i. 11–12, and the works cited there.

[26] J. P. Wainwright, *Musical Patronage in Seventeenth-Century England: Christopher, First Baron Hatton (1605–1670)* (Aldershot, 1997); *VdGSIM*, i. 3–4.

[27] B. Bellingham, 'The Musical Circle of Anthony Wood in Oxford during the Commonwealth and Restoration', *JVdGSA*, 19 (1982), 6–70; Holman, *Four and Twenty Fiddlers*, 267–75; P. Gouk, 'Music', in *The History of the University of Oxford*, iv: *Seventeenth-Century Oxford*, ed. N. Tyacke (Oxford, 1997), 621–40.

[28] *Roger North on Music*, ed. Wilson, 350.

[29] Holman, *Four and Twenty Fiddlers*, 275–81.

(the private apartments at Whitehall) by a section of the Twenty-Four Violins, presumably playing dance music that Charles could beat time to.[30]

Not surprisingly, this change caught the attention of contemporary writers. For Roger North it was 'the grand metamorfosis of musick' that resulted in 'the old way of consorts' being replaced at court by 'an establishment, after a French model, of 24 violins'; or, as he put it in another essay: 'after the manner of France he [Charles II] set up a band of 24 violins to play at his dinners, which disbanded all the old English musick at once'.[31] In similar vein, Anthony Wood wrote that 'before the restoration of K. Charles 2, and especially after, viols began to be out of fashion and only violins used, as treble violin, tenor and bass-violin'.[32] Thomas Mace blamed the decline of '*Those Choice Consorts, to Equally-Seiz'd Instruments, (Rare Chests of Viols)*' on 'new *Modes* and *Fashions*' that set up 'a *Great Idol* in their Room': a '*High-Priz'd Noise*' of '10 or 20 *Violins*, &c.' playing '*Some-Single-Soul'd Ayre*; it may be of 2 or 3 *Parts*'.[33] In fact, things were not that simple. Charles II's 'High-Priz'd Noise' was not new in 1660: it was a revived and enlarged version of the pre-war court violin band, an institution that went back to 1540, not long after viols had first arrived in England.[34] If the 'old English musick' was the Broken Consort, as is likely, then the Twenty-Four Violins replaced a mixed ensemble of two or three violins, one or two bass viols and continuo, not a viol consort. There was no court viol consort after 1660, though viol players continued to be employed at court throughout Charles II's reign and beyond (Ch. 1).

The perception among contemporary writers was that amateur consort playing declined rapidly after the Restoration. North wrote that 'gentlemen, following also the humour of the Court, fell in *pesle mesle*, and soon thrust out the treble viol', and he implied that the repertory had ended with Jenkins and Locke: 'after M[r] Jenkens I know but one poderose [i.e. *poderosa*, strong or mighty] consort of that kind composed, which was M[r] M. Locke's 4 parts, worthy to bring up the 'rere, after which we may expect no more of that style'.[35] And again: Locke composed 'a magnifick consort of 4 parts, after the old style, which was the last of the kind that hath bin made'.[36] Locke's Consort of Four Parts was probably

---

[30] Ibid., 281, 284–6.

[31] *Roger North on Music*, ed. Wilson, 300, 349.

[32] J. D. Shute, 'Anthony à Wood and his Manuscript Wood D19 (4) at the Bodleian Library, Oxford, an Annotated Transcription', 2 vols. (PhD diss., International Institute for Advanced Studies, Clayton, MO, 1979), ii. 99.

[33] Mace, *Musick's Monument*, 236.

[34] Holman, *Four and Twenty Fiddlers*, esp. ch. 3, 4, 12.

[35] *Roger North on Music*, ed. Wilson, 301.

[36] Ibid., 349.

written during the 1650s.[37] North wrote around 1695 that 'the late improvements of Musick have bin the ruin, and almost the banishment of it [the viol consort] from the nation', while by 1697 the treble viol was 'much out of Doors, since the Violin came so much in request', according to the Revd William Turner.[38]

Despite his spirited defence of the viol consort, Mace admitted that 'Very Little of *This so Eminent Musick* do we hear of in *These Times*, (the *Less* the *Greater Pity*.)'.[39] Perhaps he (or his publisher John Carr) anticipated a revival following the publication of his *Musick's Monument* in 1676, for the next year Carr advertised two complete chests of viols:

> There is also Two *Chests of* VIALS to be sold; one made by Mr. *John Ross*, who formerly lived in *Bridewel*, containing Two Trebles, Three Tenors, One Basse; The Chest was made in the Year 1598. / The other Chest being made by Mr. *Henry Smith*, who formerly lived over against *Hatton-House* in *Holbourn*, containing Two Trebles, Two Tenors, Two Basses; The Chest was made in the Year 1633. / *Both these Chests are very Curious Work*.[40]

Mace had recommended chests of viols by Rose, Smith and others in *Musick's Monument*, adding that 'we chiefly *Value Old Instruments*, before *New*; for by *Experience*, they are found to be far the *Best*'.[41] However, Carr rather undermined the case for them by inserting his advertisement into *Tripla concordia*, a collection of fashionable three-part violin dance music in the French style – just the sort of thing Mace was complaining about.

Significantly, all the viols purchased for court use in the Restoration period were basses or lyra viols rather than trebles and tenors (Ch. 1), and a similar pattern can be seen in the surviving instruments: a few English late seventeenth-century treble viols survive, though they are heavily outnumbered by basses. Of more than fifty extant viol-family instruments by, or attributed to, Barak Norman, the most prominent London maker around 1700, all but two are basses.[42]

---

37 M. Locke, *Chamber Music II*, ed. M. Tilmouth, MB, 32 (London, 1972), xv.

38 *Roger North on Music*, ed. Wilson, 11; W. Turner, *A Compleat History of the Most Remarkable Providences, both of Judgment and Mercy, which have Hapned in this Present Age*, 3 vols. (London, 1697), iii. 8; CC: *EEBO*, Wing T3345. See also M. Tilmouth, 'Some Improvements in Music Noted by William Turner in 1697', *GSJ*, 10 (1957), 57–9.

39 Mace, *Musick's Monument*, 236.

40 J. Carr, *Tripla concordia, or A Choice Collection of New Airs, in Three Parts, for Treble and Basse-Violins* (London, 1677), prelims; CC: *EEBO*, Wing T2286A.

41 Mace, *Musick's Monument*, 245.

42 B. Hebbert, 'A Catalogue of Surviving Instruments by, or Ascribed to, Barak Norman', *GSJ*, 54 (2001), 285–329. See also P. Tourin, *Viollist: a Comprehensive*

This could be an accident of survival: bass viols continued to be used throughout the eighteenth century, while trebles and tenors would have had to have been converted into violins or violas to remain useful.[43] Nevertheless, a census of surviving viols by Henry Jaye, Norman's early seventeenth century counterpart, lists twelve trebles against ten basses, suggesting that there was a real change of makers' priorities during the century.[44]

The sources of viol consort music present a slightly different picture. Recent research has shown that manuscripts containing portions of the repertory were copied or were in use rather later than was once thought. For example, Francis Withy, a singing man at Christ Church in Oxford from 1670, owned and used two early seventeenth-century sets of part-books, GB-Ob, MSS Mus. Sch. E.415–18 and E.437–42.[45] He annotated the former, a collection of five-part pavans and other dances by Tomkins, Ferrabosco junior, Mico, Young, John Withy (Francis's father), and others, and edited and added to the latter, a large collection of fantasias and related works in three to six parts by Lupo, Jenkins, Ferrabosco junior, Coprario, Ward, Gibbons, and others. GB-Lbl, Add. MS 31423, fols. 1–75, containing four-part fantasias and dances by Mico, Brewer, Ferrabosco junior, Child, and John Withy, was copied probably in the late 1680s by someone (once thought to be John Jenkins) who may have been associated with the North family.[46]

Sale catalogues also list manuscripts of the older repertory. John Playford promised in 1681 that 'all such as desire to be accommodated with such choice Consorts of Music for Violins and Viols as were Composed by Dr Colman, Mr William Laws, Mr John Jenkins, Dr Benjamin Rogers, Mr Matthew Locke and divers others, may have them fairly and true Prick'd'.[47] A 1690 catalogue issued by his son Henry includes collections of this sort, including some that seem to be

Catalogue of Historical Viole da Gamba in Public and Private Collections (Duxbury. VT, 1979).

[43] B. Hebbert, 'William Borracleffe, Nathaniel Cross, and a Clutch of Tudor Viols', *GSJ*, 51 (2003), 69–76, esp. 71.

[44] M. Fleming, T. MacCracken, and K. Martius, *Jaye Project* (www.vdgs.org.uk/information-JayeProject.html).

[45] J. Irving, 'Consort Playing in mid-Seventeenth-Century Worcester', *EM*, 12 (1984), 337–44; Ashbee, *The Harmonious Musick of John Jenkins*, i: *The Fantasias for Viols* (Surbiton, 1992), 148, 156–7; R. Thompson, 'Some Late Sources of Music by John Jenkins', in *John Jenkins and his Time*, ed. Ashbee and Holman, 271–307, at 285; *VdGSIM*, ii. 10–12, 178–81, 198–206.

[46] P. Willetts, 'Autograph Music by John Jenkins', *ML*, 48 (1967), 124–6; Thompson, 'Some Late Sources', 290; *VdGSIM*, ii. 13–14, 77–8, 82–5.

[47] R. Thompson, 'Manuscript Music in Purcell's London', *EM*, 23 (1995), 605–18, at 613.

lost: 'Mr. *Lawes* 2 and 3 parts, Fancies, Almanis, and Galliards for 2 Trebles, and Basses to the Organ, in Folio, fairly prick'd'; 'Coperarios 2 parts, Treble and Bass, fairly prick'd'; 'Mr. *Lawes* Consort for 2 Lyra's, a Violin and Theorbo, prick'd in quarto'; 'Mr. *Lawes* Harp-Consort, and his Little Consort, in 4 parts, quarto, fairly pr[icked]', and 'Mr. *Lawes* and *Dr. Rogers* Airs of 4 parts, in quarto, fairly prick'd'.[48] The instrumental items in Henry Playford's 1697 catalogue are mostly more modern, though it includes 'Mr. *Jenkins*'s Royal Consort, fairly Prick'd' and '*Fantazies* Ayres, &c. in 5 Parts, by Mr. *Lock*'.[49] The former was perhaps one of Jenkins's late sets of fantasia suites, written at court in the early 1660s, while the latter could have been a copy of the Consort of Four Parts with an added continuo part.[50]

However, the fact that people continued to copy and collect viol consort collections does not necessarily mean that they played them, or if they did, that they played them entirely on viols. The antiquarian impulse was already taking hold among English musicians,[51] and evidence that parts conceived for treble viols were later played on violins is provided by the collection acquired by the Oxford Music School in 1667 from the North household at Kirtling; Jenkins worked at Kirtling in the 1660s as tutor to the children, including Roger, grandson of Dudley, 3rd Lord North.[52] According to Roger North, Jenkins was 'an accomplished master of the viol' and only tried to 'compass the Violin in his old age', inspired like others by Thomas Baltzar's playing, while Dudley North 'played on that antiquated instrument called the treble viol'; at Kirtling the consorts were 'usually all viols to the organ or harpsicord' and the violin 'came in late, and

---

[48] H. Playford, *A Curious Collection of Musick-Books, both Vocal and Instrumental* (London, 1690); CC: GB-Lbl, Harley MS 5936, fol. 421. Anthony Wood's copy, GB-OB, Wood E 22, no. 9, is repr. in J. Bergsagel, 'Music in Oxford in Holberg's Time', in *Hvad Fatter gjør … boghistoriske, litteraere ok musikalske essays tilegnet Erik Dal*, ed. H. Glahn *et al.* (Herning, 1982), 34–61, at 46–57. See also W. C. Smith, 'Playford: some Hitherto Unnoticed Catalogues of Early Music', *MT*, 67 (1926), 636–9, 701–4; A. H. King, 'Fragments of Early Printed Music in the Bagford Collection', *ML*, 40 (1959), 269–73; L. Coral, 'Music in English Auction Sales, 1676–1750' (PhD diss., U. of London, 1974), esp. 32–8, 53–5.

[49] H. Playford, *A General Catalogue of all the Choicest Musick-Books in English, Latin, Italian and French, both Vocal and Instrumental* (London, *c.* 1697); CC: GB-Lbl, Harley MS 5936/422.

[50] Thompson, 'Manuscript Music in Purcell's London', 615.

[51] W. Weber, *The Rise of Musical Classics in Eighteenth-Century England: a Study in Canon, Ritual, and Ideology* (Oxford, 1992), esp. 23–56.

[52] Ashbee, *The Harmonious Musick of John Jenkins*, i. 71–5, 94–9. See also M. Crum, 'The Consort Music from Kirtling, Bought for the Oxford Music School from Anthony Wood, 1667', *Chelys*, 4 (1972), 3–10.

imperfectly'.[53] Most of the upper parts of the Kirtling copies are labelled just 'treble', including copies of several sets of Jenkins fantasia suites, though in the 1682 catalogue of the Music School collection they are listed as 'for one Base Viol & Violin to ye Organ' and 'Two Violins & one Base [to ye Organ]' – suggesting that they were played with violins in Restoration Oxford.[54]

This, of course, is relevant to Purcell's fantasias. These matchless works, mostly written in 1680, became part of the core viol consort repertory in the twentieth century,[55] though, as we have seen, Roger North thought that Locke had composed the last set of viol consorts. He evidently did not know of Purcell's fantasias, despite being acquainted with the composer, probably because they did not circulate widely (the few secondary sources were mostly copied directly from the autograph, GB-Lbl, Add MS 30930), and only one copy, an early version of the three-part fantasy z733, is in parts rather than score.[56] I have argued that Purcell wrote them as part of an intensive self-imposed programme of study devoted to mastering contrapuntal techniques.[57] Most of them may never have been performed until the modern revival of viol music, and if they were the upper parts are likely to have been played on violins.[58] Be that as it may, Purcell's last-known fantasia, z743 in four parts dated Tuesday 31 August 1680, effectively brought the great tradition of English viol consort music to a close.[59]

[53] *Roger North on Music*, ed. Wilson, 10–11, 298, 345.

[54] M. Crum, 'Early Lists of the Oxford Music School Collection', *ML*, 48 (1967), 23–34, at 28.

[55] L. Robinson, 'Purcell's Fantasias: the Jewel in the Crown of English Consort Music', *EM*, 26 (1998), 357–9.

[56] R. Shay and R. Thompson, *Purcell Manuscripts: the Principal Musical Sources* (Cambridge, 2000), esp. 84–113. ME: H. Purcell, *Works*, 31: *Fantazias and Miscellaneous Instrumental Music*, ed. T. Dart, rev. M. Tilmouth, A. Browning, and P. Holman (London, 2/1990), 3–4.

[57] P. Holman, *Henry Purcell* (Oxford, 1994), esp. 74–6.

[58] The first known revivals, by Arnold Dolmetsch and his associates, were of an unidentified three-part fantasia at 6 Keppel Street, Bloomsbury on 29/11/1895, and the Fantasia upon One Note, z745, at the Portman Rooms on 20/12/1895 (Jeanne Dolmetsch, Brian Blood and Tim Crawford); see also *The Times*, 21/12/1895, p. 6. A successful recording using violins and viols is in *Henry Purcell: Complete Chamber Music*, Musica Amphion / Pieter-Jan Belder, Brilliant Classics, 93647 (rec. 2006–7).

[59] z744, an incomplete piece in the same manuscript dated 'Feb. ye 24 1682/3', edited in Purcell, *Fantazias and Miscellaneous Instrumental Music*, ed. Dart, rev. Tilmouth *et al.*, 99, is usually thought of as an unfinished fantasia, though its writing with two equal and crossing treble parts and its relatively straightforward counterpoint with an Italianate canzona-style subject suggests that it is for violins rather than viols. Perhaps it is the fugal section of an overture.

1 Title-page of Carolus Hacquart, *Chelys*, op. 3 (The Hague, 1686)

2 Frederick Kerseboom or Causabon, *Sir John Langham* (1683)

3 Title-page of G. F. Handel, *Giulio Cesare* (London, 1724), published by John Cluer

4 *(left)* John Frederick Hintz, tenor-size viola da gamba (1762)
5 *(right)* John Frederick Hintz, alto-size viola da gamba (undated)

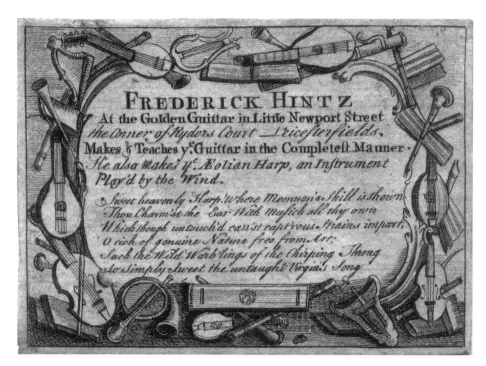

6, 7 John Frederick Hintz, trade cards

8 *(above)* A Concert in Cambridge, etching by Sir Abraham Hume after Thomas Orde

9 *(left)* John Nixon, 'A Solo on the Viola da Gamba, Mr Abel' (1787)

10 Thomas Gainsborough, preparatory drawing for *Karl Friedrich Abel* (*c.* 1765)

11 Thomas Gainsborough, *Karl Friedrich Abel* (1777)

12 C. F. Abel, autograph cartouche, US-NYp, Drexel MS 5871, flyleaf

13 C. F. Abel's autograph, US-NYp, Drexel MS 5871, p. 1

14 C. F. Abel's autograph

15 Thomas Gainsborough, *Portrait of Miss Ann Ford, later Mrs. Philip Thicknesse* (1760)

16 Susanna Duncombe, *Miss Ford /
Mrs Thicknesse*

17 The title-page of Elisabetta de Gambarini, *Lessons for the Harpsichord*, op. 2 (London, 1748)

18 Thomas Gainsborough, *A Perspective View of a Cottage belonging to Philip Thicknesse Esqr. near Languard Fort in Suffolk* (1753–4)

19 Thomas Gainborough, unfinished portrait of Margaret Gainsborough

Flauto.

TROIS
QUINTETTOS
Pour
FLUTE, VIOLON,
DEUX ALTO VIOLE
et
VIOLONCELLE.
Composés
Par
A. LIDEL.
OEUVRE V.

N.º 441.   Prix f 3 .10.

Chés J. J. HUMMEL, à Berlin avec Privilége du Roi;
à Amsterdam au Grand Magazin de Musique et aux Adresses Ordinaires.

20 The title-page of the Hummel edition of Andreas Lidel, *Three Quintettos*, op. 5

21 John Cawse, *On her Spanish Guitar she Played a Ditty which Lulled her Old Guardian to Sleep*

22 The Brousil Family of Prague (*c. 1857*)

23 Transcription for 'Viol de Gamba' of Robert Schumann, 'Abendlied',
op. 85, no. 12 (1849) in the hand of Edward Payne

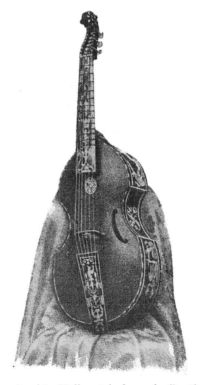

24 Joachim Tielke, viola da gamba (?1718),

25 Arnold, Elodie and Hélène Dolmetsch in costume, *c.* 1895

26 Arnold Dolmetsch holding a viola d'amore attributed to Testore, studio photograph *c.* 1888

CHAPTER 1

'Musitians on the Viol de Gamba':
Professional Players in Restoration England

❧ *The Viol at Court*

IN 1660 the royal music was revived with the rest of the court more or less exactly as it had stood in 1642. At least ten viol players were given places: Thomas Bates, Paul Francis Bridges, Charles Coleman senior and junior (sharing a place), William Gregory junior, Henry Hawes, John Hingeston, John Smith, Dietrich (Theodore) Stoeffken (Steffkins), and his son Frederick William (also sharing a place).[1] In addition, John Jenkins and John Lillie, famous virtuoso viol players, were employed as lutenists.[2] They all served in the Private Music except for Bates and Gregory, who were assigned to the Chapel Royal, probably to support the bass of the choir.[3] Significantly, treble or tenor viols are not mentioned in Restoration court payments. Dietrich Stoeffken was paid for a bass viol on 16 July 1661 and lyra viols on 14 May 1663 and 14 March 1671,[4] while Smith, Bates, Bridges, Hawes, and Gregory were paid for bass viols on 4 September, 22 October and 18 November 1662, 17 June 1664, and 7 February 1665 respectively.[5] Hingeston provided 'a Base Vyall for the Private Musicke' in 1661–2.[6]

Two related trends are observable during Charles II's reign. There was a reduction in the number of posts for viol players as individuals died or surrendered their places, and new appointees were increasingly likely to double up as members of the Twenty-Four Violins – where they presumably played violin-family instruments rather than viols. Of the players appointed in 1660, Coleman senior died in 1664, leaving his son in sole possession of the place; Dietrich Stoeffken died in 1673 while on court business in Cologne, also leaving his son in sole possession. Hawes was succeeded by the violinist Joseph Fashion in 1679; and Gregory, who

---

[1] For the revival of the royal music in 1660, see Holman, *Four and Twenty Fiddlers: the Violin at the English Court, 1540–1690* (Oxford, 2/1995), esp. 282. See also *BDECM*, i. 126–8, 192–3, 271–4, 523–5, 553, 574–6; ii. 1027–8, 1049–53.

[2] *BDECM*, ii. 623–5, 725–6.

[3] Holman, *Four and Twenty Fiddlers*, esp. 403.

[4] *RECM*, i. 19, 45, 103.

[5] *RECM*, i. 36, 37, 39, 55, 60.

[6] *RECM*, v. 119.

had inherited Bates's place in 1679, was not reappointed at the beginning of James II's reign in 1685. Bridges and Smith lost their posts in 1673 because they were Catholics and were therefore banned from the court by the provisions of the Test Act, passed in that year.[7] Bridges was replaced by John Young, described as 'viol de Gambo' when he was sworn in on 13 May 1674, though Young was replaced by a violinist, William Hall, at his death in 1679.[8] Smith's replacement, Francis Cruys, was probably a viol player, though he was also a member of the 'Band of Violins' that accompanied William III to the Netherlands in 1691; Robert Carr, who replaced Hingeston in 1683, was probably a violinist.[9]

Thus there may have been only one specialist viol player in the royal music by the start of James II's reign in 1685: Coleman junior (d. 1694) ('Base Viol') and Henry Purcell ('Harpsicall') appear with a group of solo singers in an initial list of James's reformed Private Music, suggesting that they formed the group's continuo team.[10] However, Frederick William Steffkins (d. 1709) continued to serve in the main Private Music (a reformed version of the old Twenty-Four Violins), and he was joined in 1689 by his brother Christian Leopold (d. 1714). Frederick was left a 'violin in a firr' in Hingeston's will,[11] and both brothers played in the violin band that went to the Netherlands in 1691, though they continued to play the viol. Frederick advertised in the winter of 1703–4 that he could set the frets of viols 'in perfect proportions' using 'the proportions of Notes and half Notes' calculated by Thomas Salmon; he offered to give directions 'for the use of the Fingerboard, so as to play the Notes perfect, or else to find out the best bearing in every Key and Tuning, the Frets reaching quite [a]cross the Neck of the Viol, and being moveable according to the present practice'.[12] The brothers demonstrated the system (unequal temperament) to the Royal Society on 3 July 1705, playing a sonata for two viols and another in which Gasparo Visconti played 'upon the Violin in Consort with them, wherin the most compleat Harmony was heard'.[13] The latter was by Corelli, played with two violins and two

---

[7] Holman, *Four and Twenty Violins*, 299.

[8] For Hall and Young, see *BDECM*, i. 536–7; ii. 1183–4.

[9] *RECM*, ii. 38–9. For Carr and Cruys, see *BDECM*, i. 233, 325–6.

[10] *RECM*, ii. 122; see also Holman, *Four and Twenty Fiddlers*, 415–20.

[11] *BDECM*, i. 575–6.

[12] *The Postman*, 15/1/1704; see also TilmouthC, 52.

[13] [The Royal Society of London], *The Philosophical Transactions (from the Year 1700 to the Year 1720), Abrig'd and Dispos'd under Several Heads*, ed. H. Jones, 2 vols. (London, 2/1731), i. 469–74, at 470; CC: ECCO, ESTC T103707; see also S. Pollens, 'A Viola da Gamba Temperament Preserved by Antonio Stradivari', *ECM*, 3 (2006), 125–32.

viols.[14] No sonatas for two viols by the brothers have survived, though there is a suite for solo viol by Frederick in GB-DRc, MS Mus. A27, pp. 249–52.[15] Visconti married Christian's daughter Ebenezar or Cristina on 22 April 1704 at St Antholin, Budge Row in London and they subsequently settled in Cremona. She too was a viol player: there is a template by Stradivarius for 'the neck-length of Signorina Cristina Visconti's viol made in 1707' ('Manico della longezza della viola della Sig[nori]na Cristina Visconta fatta li 1707').[16]

❧ Visitors and Immigrants

FOR much of the seventeenth century the viol was particularly associated with England, much as the lute was thought to be French, the violin Italian, and the harp Irish. In a letter to Samuel Pepys on 7 July 1680 John Evelyn listed 'Musitians on the Viol de Gamba' among 'Inventions … wherin we exceeded other Nations'.[17] Roger North wrote that during that period 'there was a great flocking together hither of forrein masters', and: 'Here came over many Germans, cheifly violists, as Scheiffare, Vogelsang, and of other names to fright one.'[18] The gamba player Wilhelm Ludwig Vogelsang (d. 1707) is first recorded at the Berlin court in 1671, reappearing in 1677 when it was noted that he had 'undertaken long journeys to England and other countries to complete his studies' ('der zu seiner Perfection grosse Reisen nach England und anderen Ländern gethan').[19] Nothing is known of 'Scheiffare', unless North misremembered his name and was actually thinking of the Augsburg composer Jakob Scheiffelhut (1647–1709) – a name that might well have frightened him. As a town musician Scheiffelhut would probably have played the viol as well as a violin-family instrument, and he published several sets of suites for three- and four-part strings.

Other viol players are known to have visited England from Germany. David Adams (b. 1641–3), the son of the English harper Edward Adams, received

---

14 L. Miller and A. Cohen, *Music in the Royal Society of London, 1660–1806* (Detroit, MI, 1987), 66–7, 207; P. Gouk, *Music, Science and Natural Magic in Seventeenth-Century England* (New Haven, CT, 1999), esp. 62–3.

15 *VdGSIM*, ii. 51.

16 See esp. M. Herzog, 'Stradivari's Viols', *GSJ*, 57 (2004), 183–94, at 189–91.

17 *Particular Friends: the Correspondence of Samuel Pepys and John Evelyn*, ed. G. de la Bédoyère (Woodbridge, 2/2005), 104–5 (Michael Fleming).

18 *Roger North on Music*, ed. J. Wilson (London, 1959), 302, 351.

19 L. Schneider, 'Geschichte der churfürstlich und königlich Preussichen Capelle', *Geschichte der Oper und des königlichen Opernhauses in Berlin* (Berlin, 1852), 12; C. Sachs, *Musik und Oper am Kurbrandenburgischen Hof* (Berlin, 1910), 55, 170, 230.

permission and funding from the Berlin court in 1661 'to go on a three-year journey to complete his study on the viola da gamba and harp' ('3 Jahre auf Reisen zu
gehen um sich auf der Viol de Jambe [sic] und Harfe zu perfectioniren'), and travelled to England in 1672,[20] while Paul Kreß (1635–94) requested permission from
the Stuttgart court in 1662 to study 'the viola da gamba which is flourishing there'
('Viol de Gamba welche dort in flor') – that is, in England.[21] When Peter Grecke
applied for a post as a Lübeck town musician on 24 February 1672 he stated that
he had studied in Italy, had spent time in Germany, England and Holland, and
played the *violdegambe, Bassviolone* vnd *violone*' among other instruments.[22]
GB-Ob, MS Mus. Sch. D.253 has four suites for two bass viols by him (Ch. 2).

The most important visitor was August Kühnel (b. 1645). After studying in
Paris he worked at the court of Moritz, Duke of Saxony-Zeitz. He seems to have
travelled to England towards the end of 1682: in October he wrote from Zeitz to
a Munich court official that he was going 'on a journey to England to find out
what viola da gamba players there were in that country from which the viola da
gamba had come' ('eine Reiße in Engellandt zu thun, vmb zu erfahren waß vor
Viol d'gambisten /: weil die Viol d'gamba auß Engellandt her kombt').[23] Unfortunately, the most eminent players active in England in the 1660s and 70s – Christopher Simpson, Dietrich Stoeffken, John Lillie, and John Jenkins – were dead
by then. Nevertheless, Kühnel made the journey and announced in London in
November 1685 that 'Several Sonata's, composed after the Italian way, for one
and two Bass-Viols, with a Thorough-Basse' would be 'Engraven upon Copper
Plates', published by subscription, and demonstrated on Thursdays at the Dancing School in Walbrook and on Saturdays at the Dancing School in York Buildings.[24] The publication is lost, if it was ever published, and it is unclear whether
the pieces were the same as those published by Kühnel in 1698.[25]

Kühnel would have needed another player to demonstrate his sonatas
for two bass viols, and there is circumstantial evidence that he was Gottfried

[20] Schneider, 'Geschichte der churfürstlich und königlich Preussichen Capelle', 11;
Sachs, *Musik und Oper*, 48, 55, 169–70.

[21] J. Sittard, *Zur Geschichte der Musik und des Theaters am Württembergischen
Hofe*, 2 vols. (Stuttgart, 1890–1; repr. 1970), i. 58. See also U. Siegele, 'Johann
Albrecht Kreß', MGG2, x, col. 868.

[22] C. Stiehl, 'Gesuch des Peter Grecke um Verleihung einer Rathsmusikantenstelle',
Monatshefte für Musik-Geschichte, 20 (1888), 111–12.

[23] J. K. Kerll, *Ausgewählte Werke Erster Theil*, ed. A. Sandberger, Denkmäler der
Tonkunst in Bayern, II/2 (Leipzig, 1901), lxxxii–lxxxiii.

[24] DC, 19/11/1685. See also TilmouthC, 7.

[25] A. Kühnel, *Sonate ô partite ad una ô due viole da gamba con il basso continuo*
([Kassel], 1698; repr. 1998); RISM A/I K 2060.

Finger (*c.* 1655–1730).[26] Finger and Kühnel both seem to have been in Munich in 1682, and the 1685 advertisements mentioned that Kühnel would give 'some performance upon the Barritone'; Finger also probably played the baryton (the variant of the bass viol with plucked strings running under the fingerboard): he wrote seven suites for baryton and gamba and provided information about the 'Barytone Viol' for James Talbot's manuscript treatise on instruments, compiled in the 1690s.[27] Furthermore, GB-Ob, MS Mus. Sch. D.249, no. 16/2 (fols. 86–95v), an arrangement for violin, bass viol and continuo of Kühnel's Sonata no. 3 in G minor for two bass viols and continuo, is in the hand of James Sherard. Finger probably taught Sherard and supplied much of the gamba music in his collection (Ch. 2); perhaps he also made this arrangement.

Kühnel soon went back to Germany – he joined the Darmstadt court in 1686 – but Finger remained in England and joined James II's Catholic chapel at Whitehall, opened on Christmas Day 1686; he was one of nine instrumentalists appointed by a warrant dated 5 July 1687.[28] Dedicating his *Sonatae XII. pro diversis instrumentis*, op. 1 (1688) to the king, Finger stated that his sole ambition was for it to 'serve the Chapel Royal' ('haec Musica CAPELLAE REGIAE inserviat').[29] The first three sonatas are for violin, gamba and continuo, and may therefore have been played by the composer with one of the violinists employed in the chapel, such as William Hall or Thomas Farmer. The chapel was closed after James II was replaced by William and Mary in 1689, so Finger started a new career in London's theatres and public concerts. He promoted concerts during the 1690s at York Buildings in Villiers Street, London's first proper concert hall: a weekly 'consort' on Thursdays was announced on 18 April 1689, and Finger's weekly series was first advertised on 23 November 1693.[30] There is no record of him in London for nearly two years, between 8 April 1697, when a dialogue by him was sung at York Buildings, and 17 February 1699, when 'a Consort of Vocal

---

[26] For Finger, see esp. *BDECM*, i. 418–21; R. Rawson, 'From Olomouc to London: the Early Music of Gottfried Finger (*c.* 1655–1730)', 2 vols. (PhD diss., Royal Holloway, U. of London, 2002) [RI].

[27] Rawson, 'From Olomouc to London', esp. 121–30, 185–203; C. A. Gartrell, *A History of the Baryton and its Music, King of Instruments, Instrument of Kings* (Lanham, MD, 2009), 39–48.

[28] See esp. *RECM*, v. 84, 86–7.

[29] RISM A/I F 845; CC: GB-Lbl, K.1.i.15; ME: *Three Centuries of Music in Score*, ed. K. Cooper and S. T. Sommer, 8, *Chamber Music II: Trio Sonatas, Part 1* (New York, 1990), 111–81.

[30] TilmouthC, 8, 14. For York Buildings, see esp. M. Tilmouth, 'Chamber Music in England, 1675–1720' (PhD diss., U. of Cambridge, 1960), 17–37.

and Instrumental Musick, after the Italian manner' was performed in his benefit concert, also at York Buildings.[31]

Finger left England for good in 1701 after coming last in the competition to set Congreve's masque *The Judgement of Paris*, though he left behind a large collection of music that was advertised between November 1704 and April 1705.[32] According to the sale catalogue it was 'a Choice Collection of greatest *Italian* Masters; brought over from *Italy*, by *Mr. FINGER*' (which tells us where he went in 1697), and it includes a list of '*Mr.* Finger's *Great Pieces for his Consort in* York-Buildings', which gives an idea of what was performed.[33] He clearly had sizeable forces: most of the parts are said to have been '*prick'd* 3 *times over*' and the pieces include 'A Consort for 4 Trumpets, a Kettle-Drum, 2 Hautboys, 2 Violins, Tenors and bass', '3 Full Sonata's for 2 Chorus's', '3 sonata's for 4 Flutes [i.e. recorders] and basses', '3 sonatas for 2 Flutes, and 2 Hautboys in 2 Chorus's', and '2 sonatas, and a Ground, in 18 books, for Trumpets, Hautboys, violins, Tenors, and basses, with several Airs'.

Finger's library also contained solo and trio sonatas, including those by him 'for a Flute and *Viol de Gamba*' and 'for a violin and *Viol de Gamba*'. Among the other music was Antonio Veracini's *Sonate da camera*, op. 3 (Modena, 1696), with the original 'violone, ò arcileuto' part described as for 'Viol' (interesting evidence that Italian parts for *violone* (i.e. bass violin) were allocated to the bass viol in England),[34] and a manuscript of '6 *Italian* sonatas for a Violin, bass-viol, and Thorough-bass' – which may also have been taken from the Italian repertory for violin, *violone* and continuo. Of more than seventy-five instrumental pieces in the catalogue by Finger, fifty-two are described as sonatas, suggesting that the developing popularity of the genre in England was connected with the rapid development of concert life in the 1690s. The type of sonata used by Finger, combining virtuosity with ear-tickling sonorities, was just what was required at a time when music lovers were becoming accustomed to listening to music rather than playing it themselves.

---

[31] TilmouthC, 19, 26.

[32] TilmouthC, 57–8.

[33] H. Playford, *A Catalogue of Vocal and Instrumental Musick, Printed and Written, being a Choice Collection of the Greatest Italian Masters, Brought over from Italy by Mr. Finger, as also several Excellent Pieces of his own Composition* (London, 1705); CC: GB-Lbl, c.127.i.1.(4); see P. Holman, 'The Sale Catalogue of Gottfried Finger's Music Library: New Light on London Concert Life in the 1690s', *RMARC*, 43 (2010), 23–38.

[34] RISM A/I V 1201. For the meanings of *violone*, see esp. B. Hoffmann, 'The Nomenclature of the Viol in Italy', trans. R. Carter and J. Steedman, *VdGSJ*, 2 (2008), 1–16, at 7–9.

Another visitor was the Dutch composer and gamba player Carolus Hacquart (b. *c.* 1640). The only evidence of his presence in London is a document dated 16 July 1697 granting 'Charles Hakert, native of Holland' a pass to return home.[35] There is no trace of him in the Netherlands after 1686; he was probably one of the Dutchmen who came to England after the Glorious Revolution. We have no idea of what he did in England, though the fact that Finger owned a copy of his *Chelys*, op. 3 (The Hague, 1686) suggests that they worked together in London; it is the only collection of solo gamba music in Finger's sale catalogue.[36] Significantly, the catalogue gives his first name in an Anglicised form, 'Mr. *Charles Hacquart*', rather than 'CAROLO HACQUART', the form used on the title-page – which includes a presumed portrait of the composer (Plate 1).

Only one copy of the gamba part of *Chelys* survives, GB-DRc, Mus. C92, once owned by the clergyman Philip Falle (Ch. 2). The bass part is lost, but it is listed in Finger's sale catalogue ('2 Books for a Viol *da Gambo*, and a Thorough-Bass'), and in an advertisement for the 1703 Roger reprint.[37] Falle copied thirty-six of its pieces into GB-DRc, MS Mus. A27, including the bass for nine of them.[38] Sherard also included the bass in his copy of the dances from Suite no. 8 in E minor, GB-Ob, MS. Mus. Sch. D.249, no. 27 (fols. 145v–148v), possibly from Finger's copy of the print. Another souvenir of Hacquart's time in England may be the four suites for solo gamba by his younger brother Philip (b. 1645) in GB-Ob, MSS Mus. Sch. F.573 and F.574.[39] The manuscripts are not in Carolus's hand, though the spellings of the titles suggest that they were written by someone who spoke Dutch, and they have connections with the Hacquart family: MS Mus. Sch. F.574, p. 76, contains a simple minuet for two bass viols by a certain Lartigue entitled 'Menuet desdie â mademoiselle Joanna Hacquart'; Joanna (b. 1675) was Philip's daughter.[40]

35 *Calendar of State Papers, Domestic Series, of the Reign of William III, 1 January – 31 December 1697*, ed. W. J. Hardy (London, 1927), 254. For Hacquart, see P. Andriessen, *Carel Hacquart (c. 1640–1701?): een biografische bijdrage, het werk* (Brussels, 1974).

36 RISM A/I H 36. See Andriessen, *Carel Hacquart*, 118–37, 174–80.

37 F. Lesure, *Bibliographie des éditions musicales publiées par Estienne Roger et Michel-Charles le Cène (Amsterdam, 1696–1743)* (Paris, 1969), 43, 68.

38 *VdGSIM*, ii. 43–53. ME of the gamba part of Suite no. 1: Andriessen, *Carel Hacquart*, 243–5.

39 ME: P. Hacquart, *The Complete Works for Solo Viola da Gamba*, ed. F.-P. Goy (Albany, CA, 1999).

40 For the manuscripts, see P. Holman, 'Thomas Baltzar (?1631–1663), the "Incomperable *Lubicer* on the Violin"', *Chelys*, 13 (1984), 3–38, at 26–9; Hacquart, *The Complete Works*, ed. Goy, i–ii.

❧ *New Genres*

NORTH wrote that the Germans with 'names to fright one' introduced 'many solos for the viol and the violin, being rough and unaiery devisions, but for the active part they were coveted'.[41] This probably refers to the type of trio sonata for violin, bass viol and continuo cultivated mainly in German-speaking areas of Europe as an alternative to the standard types with two violins. It was surprisingly popular in England, perhaps because it was compatible with the existing repertory of fantasia suites for violin, bass viol and organ. English manuscripts contain more than thirty examples, by composers ranging from Antonio Bertali, Heinrich Schmelzer and William Young in Austria and Henry Butler in Spain to Dietrich Becker in Hamburg and Philippe van Wichel, Giuseppe Zamponi and the expatriate Jesuit priest Anthony Poole in the Netherlands.[42] In several manuscripts they appear with Jenkins's most sonata-like and virtuosic fantasias for treble, bass and organ, VdGS, Group IV.[43]

In most cases we do not know how this repertory was transmitted to England. North implied that the visiting German viol players were responsible, and that may be so in some cases, though Paul Francis Bridges and Dietrich Stoeffken were also on the Continent during the Civil War and Commonwealth.[44] Some of the copies must be relatively early. GB-Ob, MS Mus. Sch. c.80, which starts with a sonata by Bertali and includes six sets of divisions on a ground for treble (viol or violin), bass viol and continuo possibly by Jenkins, is in the hand of Edward Lowe, professor of music at Oxford (d. 1682).[45] Most of the repertory is found in three related manuscripts: GB-DRc, MS Mus. D2, apparently compiled and copied for the Hampshire landowner Sir John St Barbe in the 1670s and later owned by Philip Falle; GB-Lbl, Add. MS 31423, Set 6 (fols. 216–263), seemingly copied by someone (once thought to be Jenkins) associated with the North family; and

---

[41] *Roger North on Music*, ed. Wilson, 302.

[42] M. Caudle, 'The English Repertory for Violin, Bass Viol and Continuo', *Chelys*, 6 (1975–6), 69–75.

[43] See A. Ashbee, 'Music for Treble, Bass and Organ by John Jenkins', *Chelys*, 6 (1975–6), 25–42, at 27–37; A. Ashbee, *The Harmonious Musick of John Jenkins*, ii: *Suites, Airs and Vocal Music* (forthcoming), ch. 4. ME: J. Jenkins, *Fantasia in D minor*, ed. P. Evans (London, 1958); J. Jenkins, *Two Fantasia Suites for Treble Viol (Violin), Bass Viol and Organ*, ed. A. Ashbee (Albany, CA, 1991).

[44] For a discussion of how a sonata seemingly by Bertali might have reached England, see T. Erhardt, 'Revisiting a Buxtehude Curiosity Once Again', *EMP*, 24 (June 2009), 16–21.

[45] ME: *Eight Symphonies for Bass and Treble (Violino o Treble Viol e Viola da Gamba)*, ed. C. Contadin and M. Pelliciari (Albese con Cassano, 2005).

GB-HAdolmetsch, MS II.c.25.[46] The last two are a little later than D2: they were written on paper made around 1680 and they include music from Philippe van Wichel's *Fasciculus dulcedinis*, op. 1 (Brussels, 1678). B-Bc, MS XY 24.910, three composite part-books assembled by an unidentified Englishman, contains a related repertory. The six sections range in date from the middle of the seventeenth century (autographs by Christopher Simpson) to after 1700 (a set of trio sonatas including some from Finger's op. 5 (1702)), and includes six airs in division style by Anthony Poole for violin, bass viol and continuo, a sonata by him for violin and two bass viols, and autograph parts of a suite by George Loosemore (1619–82) for treble, lyra viol and bass.[47]

A parallel repertory, continental music for two bass viols, is also found in D2 and two of Falle's other manuscripts, GB-DRc, MSS Mus. D4 and D10 (Ch. 2), as well as GB-Lbl, Add. MS 31430, Set 1 (fols. 1–13), copied by the North family associate.[48] It includes pieces by the Stuttgart composer Johann Michael Nicolai, 'P. [?Pater] Poul' (probably Anthony Poole), William Young, 'G. Schultz' (probably the Nuremberg gamba player Gabriel Schütz), and others. As with the violin and bass viol repertory, it had its counterpart in an English genre of dances, fantasias and divisions that went back to the reign of James I, and was copied alongside pieces by Jenkins – though the more sonata-like ones attributed to him are now thought to be by Nicolai and Young.[49] The two-bass repertory was initially smaller than that for violin and bass viol, though it was later enlarged by pieces by Finger, Benjamin Hely, Marais, and others. Both repertories mix pieces in two parts, where the continuo shadows the lowest string part, with those in three, with a partially or wholly independent continuo.

❧ *Finger's Viol Music*

WE have more than fifty surviving pieces by Finger with solo or obbligato gamba parts, either attributed to him, in unascribed autograph copies, or

[46] R. Thompson, 'Some Late Sources of Music by John Jenkins', in *John Jenkins and his Time: Studies in English Consort Music*, ed. A. Ashbee and P. Holman (Oxford, 1996), 271–307; *VdGSIM*, ii. esp. 54–9, 70–6, 80–1, 93–4.

[47] Information from Andrew Ashbee and Patxi del Amo.

[48] Thompson, 'Some Late Sources', 280, 287–9; *VdGSIM*, ii. 60–1, 64–9.

[49] The former VdGS, Jenkins, nos. 51–9, are now VdGS, Nicolai, nos. 3–10. The Fantasia in D minor, formerly VdGS, Jenkins, no. 40, is now VdGS, Young, no. 23. For the repertory, see esp. J. M. Richards, 'A Study of Music for Bass Viol Written in England in the Seventeenth Century' (PhD diss., U. of Oxford, 1961); J. Cunningham, *The Consort Music of William Lawes, 1602–1645* (Woodbridge, 2010), ch. 8.

likely to be by him by virtue of their style.[50] The largest source is a mostly auto-graph pair of part-books, D-SÜN, MS 12, containing twenty-five pieces for two viols and seven suites for gamba and baryton, all probably with missing bass parts.[51] Of the eighteen pieces in English sources currently accepted as by Finger (eight of which are related to pieces in D-SÜN, MS 12),[52] all but two are in the collection of manuscripts owned by James Sherard: the Prelude in E minor for solo gamba, RI115 (GB-DRc, MS Mus. A27, p. 123), copied by Philip Falle,[53] and the G minor divisions, RI140 (GB-Ob, MS Mus. Sch. c.61, pp. 57–56 rev), copied by Francis Withy.[54] Sherard's Finger manuscripts, now in GB-Ob, MSS Mus. Sch. c.93, D.228 and D.249, include seven sonatas and a suite for gamba and continuo, RI141–1149,[55] only five of which have surviving bass parts; a sonata and three suites for two bass viols, RI59, 74, 76, 77, all of which may originally had continuo parts; the Chaconne in G major, RI154, for two gambas and bass; the Pastorale in A major, RI173, for three gambas and continuo; and the Suite in A major, RI174, for violin or gamba, gamba and continuo. There is also the 'Lesson' in A major, RI196, for 'violetta', gamba and continuo. All are in Sherard's hand except for the copies of the solo part of the six sonatas, RI141, 143–6, 148 (D.228, fols. 99–105v), the Suites in E minor, RI77, and A major for two viols, RI74 (D.228, nos. 11, 12, fols. 62–69v), and part of the Suite in D major, RI76 (D.249, no. 12, fols. 66–69v), which are autograph.

Finger was the most important viol player in late seventeenth-century Eng-land. He was a prolific but uneven composer: some of the pieces he published for amateurs are simple and rather uninteresting, leading Burney to describe him as 'more feeble, but more polished [than Thomas Baltzar], and like Bassani and Corelli'.[56] However, much of his solo viol music, presumably written for his own use, is complex, ambitious, and virtuosic. He was born at Olmütz in Moravia (now Olomouc in the Czech Republic), the probable son of the trumpeter Georg Finger, and as a young man he was apparently in the service of the bishop of

[50] A. Marshall, 'The Viola da Gamba Music of Godfrey Finger', *Chelys*, 1 (1969), 16–26; Rawson, 'From Olomouc to London', esp. i. 83–90; ii. 159, 173–203, 219–24, 231–6, 240–5; G. Finger, *The Music for Solo Viol*, ed. R. Rawson and P. Wagner (London, 2009).

[51] F. Flassig, *Die soloistische Gambenmusik in Deutschland im 18. Jahrhundert* (Göttingen, 1998), 59–72, 257–60; Rawson, 'From Olomouc to London', esp. i. 31–6.

[52] Rawson, 'From Olomouc to London', i. 33.

[53] ME: Finger, *The Music for Solo Viol*, ed. Rawson and Wagner, no. 12.

[54] ME: ibid., no. 3.

[55] ME: ibid., nos. 4–11.

[56] BurneyH, ii. 462.

Olmütz, Karl Liechtenstein-Castelcorno: there are pieces in his hand in the bishop's music collection at nearby Kremsier (now Kroměříž).[57] There he would have come into contact with Heinrich Biber, who was in Liechtenstein-Castelcorno's service in the 1660s.[58] Biber was a gamba player as well as a violinist, and may have taught Finger.

Finger's more old-fashioned gamba sonatas have many features in common with Biber's violin sonatas, and may therefore have been written while he was still in Moravia. Like them, they mix three main types of material: improvisatory free passagework often changing speed and affect (a version of what Kircher, Mattheson and others called the *stylus phantasticus*),[59] more tuneful and structured sections, often cast in the form of a ground bass or an aria with variations, and lively passages in dance rhythms. For instance, the D major sonata, RI146, no. 2 of the set of six (D.228, no. 17, fols. 100v–101), begins with a *stylus phantasticus* passage in six contrasted sections, has a melodious central aria with two variations, and, after an *adagio* passage in chords and broken chords, ends with two linked dance-like passages, in minuet and jig rhythm respectively. The bass part of this fine sonata is lost, though the chords in the gamba part and the repeated harmonies in the aria make reconstructing one relatively straightforward.[60] Another excellent piece, also missing its bass part, is the extended Sonata or Suite in D major for two bass viols, RI76 (D.249, no. 12, fols. 66–69v).[61] It has an unconventional but highly effective structure: after an allemande and a gigue the work mostly consists of a massive ground bass (a major-mode variant of the *passacaglia* chord sequence) which emerges out of a *stylus phantasticus* passage. It is interrupted in the middle by a passage of chromatic counterpoint outlining the same harmonies (Ex. 1.1), and it concludes with an Adagio that also alludes to them. Subtle links of this sort between sections are characteristic of Biber's music.

Biber's influence on Finger can also be heard in the details of the solo writing, such as the use of rapid scale passages over a (sometimes presumed) pedal

---

[57] Rawson, 'From Olomouc to London', esp. ii. 348–9; J. Sehnal, *Pavel Vejvanovský and the Kroměříž Music Collection: Perspectives on Seventeenth-Century Music in Moravia* (Olomouc, 2008), esp. 167–8.

[58] E. T. Chafe, *The Church Music of Heinrich Biber* (Ann Arbor, MI, 1987), 2, 7–11.

[59] P. Collins, *The 'Stylus Phantasticus' and Free Keyboard Music of the North German Baroque* (Aldershot, 2005), esp. 29–89.

[60] Reconstruction in the ME, Finger, *The Music for Solo Viol*, ed. Rawson and Wagner, no. 7. Another, by Mark Caudle, is recorded on *The Noble Bass Viol*, The Parley of Instruments, Hyperion, CDA 67088 (1998).

[61] ME: G. Finger, *Suite in E minor and Suite in D major for Two Bass Viols*, ed. A. Marshall (Ottawa, 1981). Mark Caudle's edition, with a reconstruction of the bass part, is recorded on *The Noble Bass Viol*.

Ex. 1.1 Gottfried Finger, Sonata or Suite in D major, R176, bb. 116–31

point, staccato notes under a slur, and *scordatura* – variant tunings that facilitate the playing of chords in particular keys and alter the sonority of the instrument. *Scordatura* was applied to the violin in the early seventeenth century and was commonly used by Austrian and central European composers. Biber exploited its potential to the full in his famous Mystery or Rosary Sonatas, written in Salzburg in the 1670s.[62] English viol players also used variant tunings in the lyra-viol repertory, but with the music notated in tablature. Tablature tells the player where to place the fingers rather than which note to play, side-stepping the need to learn each tuning. The 'hand-grip' notation of *scordatura* achieves a similar result by rather cruder means: the music is in staff notation but is organised so that the correct notes sound when the player reads the notation as if the instrument was tuned normally.

Finger was just about the only gamba composer to use *scordatura*, presumably inspired by Biber.[63] Five of his pieces in GB-Ob use it: the Suite in E minor, R177 (D.228, no. 11, fols. 62–65v) is for two viols tuned $E-G-B-e-a-d'$, while the rest are in A major and use an instrument tuned $E-A-c\sharp-e-a-c\sharp'$: the Suite R1149 for gamba and continuo (D.249, no. 26, fols. 142–145v); the Suite R174 for two viols (D.228, no. 12, fols. 66–69v); the Suite R1174 for violin or gamba, gamba and continuo (D.249, no. 15, fols. 82–85v; no. 28, fols. 149–152v); and the Sonata R1144 for gamba and continuo (D.228, no. 20, fols. 103v–104; D.249, no. 29, fols. 153–156v). The continuo part of R1144 is in B♭ major, suggesting that the sounding pitch was a semitone higher or that the continuo instrument was tuned a semitone lower than normal.[64]

R1174 is particularly interesting because the alternative violin part requires the tuning $a-e'-a'-e''$, commonly used by central European composers to obtain sonorous effects in A major; Finger presumably thought of $E-A-c\sharp-e-a-c\sharp'$ as its viol equivalent.[65] Both tunings were listed by James Talbot, $E-G-B-e-a-d'$ as a tuning for the 'consort bass viol' and $E-A-c\sharp-e-a-c\sharp'$ as the 'Common tuning Sharp' for the lyra viol. However, the 'Common tuning Sharp' (expressed

---

[62] See esp. Chafe, *The Church Music of Heinrich Biber*, 185–92; D. Glüxam, *Die Violinskordatur und ihre Rolle in der Geschichte des Violinspieles: unter besonderer Berücksichtigung der Quellen der erzbischöflichen Musiksammlung in Kremsier* (Tutzing, 1999).

[63] There are also ten *scordatura* pieces, probably by Anthony Poole, in F-Pn, Vm⁷ 137.323, fols. 5v–6v, 9–11, 21, 30, 78v–79 (Patxi del Amo).

[64] ME of R1149 and R1144: Finger, *The Music for Solo Viol*, ed. Rawson and Wagner, nos. 4 and 10, where R1149 is labelled 'Balletti Scordati' and the gamba part of R1144 is transcribed in B♭ major.

[65] For an incomplete list of pieces using the tuning, see Glüxam, *Die Violinskordatur*, 428. It is not included in ibid., 80, a list of lyra viol tunings and their violin equivalents.

as *efdef*) is hardly common: it is only found in two English lyra viol sources, while *E–G–B–e–a–d'* (*fffed*) is used in only one.[66] R1174 is also of interest because it has *doubles* or variations on the repeats in the dances for both solo instruments. Perhaps Finger came across similar written-out variations in dances by Jenkins, such as the almands and corants of the fantasia-suites in A minor and G minor, VdGS, Group IV. Another work with *doubles* is the so-called 'Lesson' or Suite in A major, R1196 (D.249, no. 9, fols. 49–54v) for *violetta*, gamba and continuo. The *violetta* part is written in the treble clef and has a range similar to Finger's violin parts, $A–c\sharp'''$, which presumably rules out the ordinary viola even though solo viola parts were often given that label in Germany at the time.[67] An obvious possibility is the treble viol, which Finger clearly knew since he was the source of the little information on it in the Talbot manuscript.[68] However, I wonder whether he really intended the viola d'amore, which was fashionable in Austria and Central Europe in the late seventeenth century; Biber wrote several works for it and a variant was known as the *Englisch violet* in the eighteenth century.[69]

There are several other interesting Finger works at Oxford, and they illustrate other aspects of his Moravian musical heritage. The Sonata in D minor, R1147, for gamba and continuo (D.249, no. 10, fols. 55–57v), copied by Sherard, turns out to be an arrangement of a violin sonata by the Italian violinist Ignazio Albertini (c. 1644–85), published posthumously in 1692.[70] Albertini worked at the Viennese court but is first heard of in a letter of 6 July 1671 from Karl Liechtenstein-Castelcorno to Johann Heinrich Schmelzer, which shows that he was known to the bishop.[71] Finger may have obtained a copy of his sonata at that time. The published violin version has several more sections than the gamba version, so either Finger shortened it when he made the arrangement or the published version is an expanded revision of the original.

[66] F. Traficante, 'Lyra Viol Tunings: "All Ways Have Been Tryed to Do It"', *Acta musicologica*, 42 (1970), 183–205, 256, at 199, 202; R. Donington, 'James Talbot's Manuscript: Bowed Strings', *Chelys*, 6 (1975–6), 43–60, at 43, 48, 49.

[67] H. M. Brown and S. Bonta, 'Violetta', *GMO*.

[68] Donington, 'James Talbot's Manuscript', 43, 46.

[69] M. and D. Jappe, *Viola d'amore Bibliographie* (Winterthur, 1997); M. Rônez, 'Aperçus sur la viola d'amour en Allemagne du Sud vers 1700', in *Amour et sympathie* (Limoges, 1995), 223–71; Chafe, *The Church Music of Heinrich Biber*, 23–4, 241–2, 250; M. Rosenblum, 'English Violet', *GMO*.

[70] I. Albertini, *Sonatinae XII Violino Solo* (Vienna and Frankfurt, 1692), no. 1; RISM A/I A 686; ME of the gamba arrangement: Finger, *The Music for Solo Viol*, ed. Rawson and Wagner, no. 2.

[71] P. Nettl, 'Die Wiener Tanzkomposition in der zweiten Hälfte des siebzehnten Jahrhunderts', *Studien der Musikwissenschaft*, 8 (1921), 45–175, at 169–70.

The Pastorale in A major, RI57 (D.249, no. 17, fols. 96–103v), for three bass viols and continuo belongs to a genre of central-European pieces that quote Christmas songs and use programmatic ideas to illustrate episodes in the Christmas story; they were presumably performed during midnight mass.[72] It has several sections in common with a longer pastorella by Finger for two bass viols (with a missing bass) in D-SÜN, MS 12, and it also shares ideas with other Christmas pieces, including Schmelzer's Pastorella for two violins and continuo and Biber's for violin and continuo; the latter is also in A major, a common key for Christmas pieces.[73] A work of this sort would have had no function in Protestant England (except possibly in James II's Catholic chapel), and it is unlikely that Sherard understood all the allusions: the tunes quoted include 'Parvule pupule', 'Joseph adstabit' and 'Resonet in laudibus', and there are passages that seem to illustrate the Christmas story, including the shepherds hastening to Bethlehem and the rocking of the crib (Ex. 1.2).

Not of all of Finger's gamba sonatas conform to the Biber type. Three of the set of six, no. 3 in A major RI141 (D.228, no. 18, fols. 101v–102), no. 4 in D minor RI148 (D.228, no. 19, fols. 102v–103; D.249, no. 24, fols. 134–137v), and no. 6 in A minor RI143 (D.228, no. 21, fols. 104v–105), are more modern and were presumably written in England.[74] There is a trend towards separate movements rather than *stylus phantasticus* sequences, with clear-cut themes and Italianate harmonic patterns, rather simpler solo writing with a minimum of chords, and the use (or implied use: RI147 is the only one with a surviving continuo part) of an active bass that takes part in the musical argument rather than just providing a simple accompaniment. RI140, the G minor divisions, also seems to date from Finger's time in England. Its ground bass, a distinctive five-bar version of the *passacaglia*, was popularised in England by Lully's song 'Scocca pur', LWV76/3.[75] A fine keyboard setting was probably made by Henry Purcell, and Purcell used its bass for his great ground for two violins and bass, Z807, no. 6 of his *Sonata's in Four Parts*. Francis Withy was clearly interested in it: he copied (and perhaps composed) a setting for two violins and bass in MS Mus. Sch. C.61, pp. 59–58 rev, a few pages before RI140. Finger's gamba setting comes immediately after a piece

---

[72] R. Rawson, 'Gottfried Finger's Christmas Pastorellas', *EM*, 33 (2005), 591–606. ME: G. Finger, *Pastoralle 'Resonet in Laudibus'*, ed. K. Ruhland (Magdeburg, 2004).

[73] Chafe, *The Church Music of Heinrich Biber*, 3–5, 245; Rawson, 'Gottfried Finger's Christmas Pastorellas', esp. 594–6.

[74] ME: Finger, *The Music for Solo Viol*, ed. Rawson and Wagner, nos. 8, 9, 11.

[75] R. Klakowich, '"Scocca pur": Genesis of an English Ground', *JRMA*, 116 (1991), 63–77.

Ex. 1.2 Gottfried Finger, Pastorale in A major, R157, bb. 91–9

Withy dated 'July 30 [16]92', so it probably dates from around then, and may have been written for Withy.[76]

Despite their quality and their interest for us today, Finger's solo gamba works do not seem to have made much of an impression. No other gamba composer in England used *scordatura*, and his version of the Biber type of sonata does not seem to have been imitated. However, his three sonatas for violin, bass viol and continuo in op. 1 do seem to have had some influence, probably simply because

---

[76] *VdGSIM*, ii. 143.

Ex. 1.3 Gottfried Finger, Sonata in A major, R1197, op. 1, no. 3, Adagio, bb. 1–5

they were available in print. They are more modern and straightforward than most of his solo gamba works. No. 1 in D minor, R1198, is in three separate movements, Fast–Slow–Fast, while no. 3 in A major, R1197, follows the Slow–Fast–Slow–Fast pattern, though with a return to the opening idea at the end – a nice touch. No. 2 in F major, R1199, is more old-fashioned: in the middle there are separate solos for the gamba and the violin, each consisting of several short contrasted sections, as in many mid-century German sonatas. In these sonatas the gamba part is mostly independent of the bass, making three real parts. In the central Adagio of R1197 bow vibrato is indicated by slurs over repeated notes; the slurs are also in the continuo part, probably meaning that Finger intended a second bowed bass instrument to play the part (Ex. 1.3). This is another modern feature: in earlier sonatas with obbligato bass viol the continuo mostly shadows the viol part, so that a second bowed bass is not required.[77] R1199 is more old-fashioned in this respect than the others, so may be the earliest of the three. R1197 is the most attractive, with a well-developed first Allegro using neat invertible counterpoint, and a second Allegro in 6/4 with some Purcellian descending sequences and some nice ambiguous rhythms, mixing three beats in the bar with two (Ex. 1.4).

There are two works for violin, bass viol and continuo by English composers that seem to relate to these sonatas. The more obvious case is William Corbett's

[77] P. Allsop, 'The Role of the Stringed Bass as a Continuo Instrument in Italian Seventeenth-Century Instrumental Music', *Chelys*, 8 (1978–9), 31–7.

Ex. 1.4 Gottfried Finger, Sonata in A major, RI197, op. 1, no. 3, Allegro, bb. 31–8

Sonata in D major, *XII Sonate à tre*, op. 1, no. 1 (Amsterdam, 1700; repr. 2003); its scoring is given as 'Violino e Viola di Gamba Col B C'.[78] Corbett (?1680–1748) may have studied with Finger as a teenager in London in the 1690s: his op. 1, no. 12, a Sonata in C major for trumpet (or violin), oboe (or violin), violoncello and continuo, seems to have been modelled on Finger's C major sonata, RI170, for the same combination, and he included two Finger sonatas in his op. 2, also published in Amsterdam. Finger's influence presumably explains why Estienne Roger, Europe's leading music publisher, took on an unknown and inexperienced English composer; Finger had begun to publish with Roger in 1698.[79] Corbett's sonata is fairly close to Finger in style, particularly in the sonorous opening Adagio, where the gamba's chords fill out in the textures, and in the central Adagio, where the flatwards lurch of the tune and the varied repeat and extension

---

[78] RISM A/I C 3640; Lesure, *Bibliographie des éditions musicales*, 63.

[79] Lesure, *Bibliographie des éditions musicales*, 36.

of the phrase are characteristic touches (Ex. 1.5). However, Corbett's gamba part mostly decorates the bass in the older fashion, and it is printed in the violoncello part-book rather than the second violin book, so it looks as if he did not intend the continuo to be doubled by a second string bass. The sonata has a few awkward moments, though it is effective enough. Perhaps Finger helped the young violinist with the gamba part (which is idiomatic and grateful to play), and performed it with him in London concerts.

The other work is Henry Purcell's Sonata in G minor, z780.[80] This fine piece is sometimes described as a violin sonata because the only source, copied by the York cleric Edward Finch into a manuscript last seen at Sotheby's in 1935, is (or was) on two staves, for violin and bass; luckily it was published several times in violin and piano versions before the manuscript disappeared.[81] However, Thurston Dart realised that a number of the imitative bass entries in the fast movements were missing or incomplete, and that it was possible to reinstate them by adding an obbligato gamba part along the lines of those in the German repertory, so that the continuo becomes a typical 'shadowing' part (Ex. 1.6). The sonata is more modern than all but two of Purcell's printed trio sonatas (1697, nos. 9 and 10), and may therefore date from the late 1680s – that is, around the time Finger published his op. 1. Hawkins's anecdote about Purcell disliking the gamba will be discussed in Chapter 2, though we should note here that his two sets of trio sonatas require it: the title-page of the 1683 set just specified 'TWO VIOLLINS And BASSE: To the Organ or Harpsecord', but a contemporary advertisement described the bass part more precisely as 'Bass-Viol'.[82] As with Italian à tre sonatas (or for that matter some trio sonatas by other composers written in Restoration England), the string bass participates fully in the musical discussion, with the continuo frequently shadowing it in simplified form.

It is noteworthy that Finger does not seem to have used the bass viol to play ordinary bass parts, at least in his later music. In the Oxford version of the Pastorale, R157, the third viol essentially doubles the continuo, but in the tavola of his op. 1 the bass part of nos. 4–6 is listed as 'Viola di Basso' (i.e. bass violin or violoncello); nos. 7–9 and 10–12 do not have string bass parts because they are in four parts, and the bass part-book is required for the third violin and the viola parts respectively. For this reason, presumably, the copy in the sale catalogue of Finger's library included '3 written Basses'. Finger probably played the

---

[80] ME: H. Purcell, *Works*, 31: *Fantazias and Miscellaneous Instrumental Music*, ed. T. Dart, rev. M. Tilmouth, A. Browning, and P. Holman (London, 2/1990), 100–5.

[81] R. Illing, *Henry Purcell: Sonata in G minor for Violin and Continuo: an Account of its Survival from both the Historical and Technical Points of View* (Bedford Park, South Australia, 1975).

[82] P. Holman, *Henry Purcell* (Oxford, 1994), 85–6.

Ex. 1.5 William Corbett, Sonata in D major, op. 1, no. 1, Adagio, bb. 1–16

bass violin or violoncello as well as the gamba in the York Buildings concerts, perhaps acting as a continuo team with the harpsichordist J. G. Keller (d. 1704). Finger's trio sonatas op. 5 (*c.* 1702) and opp. 4 and 6 (1703), specify *violoncello* on the bass line,[83] and op. 5, no. 10, R1201, is a sonata for violin, 'Violone o Fagotto'

---

83 Rawson, 'From Olomouc to London', ii. 340–2.

Ex. 1.6 Henry Purcell, Sonata in G minor, z780, Allegro, bb. 1–5

obbligato and continuo.[84] He may have abandoned the gamba in later life: he was described at Innsbruck in 1717 as 'a good bassoonist, reportedly plays *Baß* and *Bassetl* as well as trumpet' ('ein guter Fagottist, spiele Baß und Bassettl sowie Trompete').[85] Leopold Mozart wrote that the *Bassel* or *Bassette* 'also goes under the name *Violoncell*, from the Italian *violoncello*'.[86]

Keller was closely connected with Finger: he wrote in an almost identical style, their music appeared in several joint publications, and he purchased Finger's music collection in conjunction with John Banister junior. The catalogue includes '*an excellent Double Bass, 2 bass-viols (one of them made by* Jay) 2 *Spinnets, 2 violins and an Harpsichord (all of them the late Mr. Keller's Instruments)*'; we know from his will (in which he left his 'best fiddle and spinnett' to his son Godfrey) that he died between 11 and 23 November 1704, when it was made and proved respectively.[87] The double bass and the viols had presumably previously belonged to Finger. There is one work by Keller with an obbligato gamba part, a 'Ciaccona' in D minor for violin, 'Viola di Basso' (with gamba-like writing and

---

[84] ME: G. Finger, *Sonata in C, opus 5, no. 10*, ed. P. Holman (London, 1980).

[85] W. Senn, *Musik und Theater am Hof zu Innsbruck: Geschichte der Hofkapelle vom 15. Jahrhundert bis zu deren Auflösung im Jahre 1748* (Innsbruck, 1954), 319 (Robert Rawson).

[86] J. Webster, 'Violoncello and Double Bass in the Chamber Music of Haydn and his Contemporaries, 1750–1780', *JAMS*, 29 (1976), 413–38, esp. 414–17.

[87] GB-Lna, PROB 11/479, fols. 104v–105.

a six-note chord at the end), and continuo in autograph parts, GB-Ob, MS Mus. Sch. c.44, fols. 75, 76b, 77. Edward Lowe copied it and some other Keller pieces into his 'New Consort Books' (GB-Ob, MSS Mus. Sch. E. 443, pp. 74–5; E. 445, p. 66; E. 446, p. 57) around 1680, so it dates from before Finger came to England.

❧ Other Professional Players around 1700

BENJAMIN Hely (d. 1699) was the most prominent native gamba player in the 1690s, though little is known of his life. He was described as 'the late famous Mr Benjamin Hely' when John Hare's anthology *The Compleat Violist* was advertised on 20 April 1699, and was called '*ye late famous Master*' on its title-page, confirming that he was a professional musician.[88] An inventory of his possessions, taken for probate purposes on 6 October 1699, includes four viols (by Pitts, Hoskins and two 'supposed to be Hoskins'), as well as a violin, 'an old Gittar of Mundon', and 'an old flute of Scotney', suggesting that he taught the violin, recorder and Baroque guitar as well as the bass viol.[89] The music he owned included 'his owne sonatas', the first two books of Matteis's *Ayrs for the Violin*, Corelli's trio sonatas opp. 1, 2 and 4, a set of Finger sonatas, a Lully opera, 'Vilalias [?Vitali's] Sonatas', and 'Simsons Division Violist'. '5 Gittar's and Cases Damaged in their Return from Barbadoes' suggest that he spent some time in the Caribbean. He could be the Benjamin Hely whose children Benjamin, Joseph and Mary were baptised at St Mary's Aylesbury on 5 September 1680, 20 May 1683 and 4 February 1690.[90]

Hely's most important music is his set of six sonatas for two solo bass viols and 'a Thorow Bass for ye Harpsicord or Bass Violl'. They survive in three sets of parts in GB-Ob: MS Mus. Sch. c.78, an autograph to judge from the 'BH' monograms worked into the terminal decorations; MS Mus. Sch. D.251, a copy in an unidentified hand from Sherard's collection; and MS Mus. Sch. E.428, the two solo parts in Francis Withy's hand with the sonatas in a different order.[91] The last suggests that c.78 – perhaps 'his owne sonatas' listed in the 1699 inventory – had already reached Oxford by the early eighteenth century, or that Withy had access to them while the composer was still alive. At the end of c.78 another hand added an A major sonata for violin, bass viol and continuo, which has led to the suggestion

---

[88] TilmouthC, 28. CC: GB-Ob, Mus. Sch. F.588.

[89] London, Guildhall Library, MS 19504/52/10 (Ben Hebbert).

[90] IGI.

[91] VdGSIM, ii. 182–3; ME: B. Hely, *Sonatas ... for Two Bass Viols and Continuo or Three Bass Viols*, ed. I. Graham-Jones, 3 vols. (St Albans, n.d.). I am grateful to Ian Graham-Jones for providing me with scores of the sonatas.

that it too is by Hely, though it is attributed more convincingly to Dietrich Becker in an early eighteenth-century score, GB-Lbl, Add. MS 64965, no. 4, fols. 13–17.

Hely's sonatas are effectively Purcellian trio sonatas with the upper parts put down the octave. They all start, as most Purcell sonatas do, with a homophonic duple-time Grave, which leads to a contrapuntal Allegro in canzona style. There is subsequently at least one triple-time movement, either in a flowing 3/2 marked Largo or in a dance-like 3/4. In one case, in no. 1 in G minor, a homophonic 3/2 Largo leads to a contrapuntal section in the same rhythm marked Allegro, a favourite device of Purcell (Ex. 1.7). Unfortunately, Hely was no Purcell: the movements are short-winded and the part-writing is sometimes clumsy, though he knew how to write idiomatically for his instrument, and the combination of three bass viols and harpsichord is pleasingly rich, particularly in those passages where he hit on a vein of Purcellian harmony, such as the concluding Adagio of Sonata no. 3 in B♭, which dives into the tonic minor (Ex. 1.8).

There are three other works by Hely: an F major suite for two bass viols, GB-Cfm, MU. MS 634, and solo suites in A minor and A major in *The Compleat Violist*, pp. 13–16.[92] The solo suites are also in GB-Cfm, MU. MS 641, but with an extra movement, suggesting that they were not copied from the print. Both manuscripts came from the library of the Ferrar family of Little Gidding in Huntingdonshire, and MU. MS 641 seems to be in the hand of Edward Ferrar, a Huntingdon attorney and perhaps a Hely pupil (Ch. 2). The bass viol duet was a conservative genre, so it is not surprising that Hely's suite is more old-fashioned than his sonatas, with some effective contrapuntal writing in the first three movements, a Prelude, Air and Almand, seemingly influenced by Locke's duets.[93] The two solo suites, each consisting (in the print) of conventional sequences of Almand, Corant, Saraband and Jig are also attractive, with effective *style brisé* writing ranging across the instrument and some sonorous chords.

Matthew Novell's life is equally mysterious. Virtually everything we know about him comes from his twelve *Sonate da camera, or Chamber Musick* (1704) for two violins and bass; the bass is labelled 'Theorbo-lute Spinett or Harpsicord' on the title-page but 'Violone o Cimbalo' at the top of each page.[94] In the dedication to Henry Somerset, Duke of Beaufort he wrote that he 'lately had the Honour to be made one of your Graces Servants', presumably at Badminton in Gloucestershire, and mentions his 'Forreign Travels' – in Italy, to judge from the style of his music. According to the title-page it was engraved by Thomas

---

[92] ME: B. Hely, *Two Solo Suites*, ed. I. Graham Jones (St Albans, n.d.).

[93] The first viol part of the Sarabande was copied into both part-books, so the second part is lost.

[94] RISM A/I N 799; CC: US-Wc, M.412.4.N9 (Case) (Andrew Woolley).

Ex. 1.7 Benjamin Hely, Sonata no. 1 in G minor, Largo–Allegro, bb. 18–32

Cross, was 'Printed for the Author', and was 'sold by him at Mr Crouches at the three Lutes in Princes-street Covent Garden' – the address of the music seller and publisher John Crouch.[95] Novell is relevant here because he is probably the person listed as 'Novelle. Viol-di-gambist' in the address-book section of

95 TilmouthC, 54; C. Humphries and W. C. Smith, *Music Publishing in the British Isles* (Oxford, 2/1970), 123.

Ex. 1.8 Benjamin Hely, Sonata no. 3 in B♭ major, 4th movement, bb. 15–21

J. S. Cousser's commonplace book.[96] Cousser (1660–1727) arrived in London on Christmas Day 1704, remaining there until he left for Dublin in 1707; he eventually became master of the Irish state music.[97] Novell belongs to a group of English composers, including John Ravenscroft, William Topham, William Corbett and James Sherard, who published imitations of Corelli's trio sonatas, though he was unusual in concentrating on the *da camera* type.[98] His sonatas are competent but unenterprising in everything but the choice of keys, which include E major, F♯ minor and B major.

William Gorton (d. 1711) was a member of the Private Music from 1696 until his death, possibly acting as a deputy to George Bingham from 1689, though he is discussed here because he there is no evidence that he played the viol at court.[99] He styled himself 'Organist of the Parrish Church at Greenwich' on the title-page of *A Choice Collection of New Ayres, Compos'd and Contriv'd for Two Bass-*

96 US-NHub, Osborn MS 16, p. 26 (Samantha Owens).

97 See esp. H. Samuel, 'Johann Sigismond Cousser in London and Dublin', *ML*, 61 (1980), 158–71; H. Samuel, 'Johann Sigismond Cousser Comes to London in 1704', *MT*, 122 (1981), 591–3; D. Hunter, 'The Irish State Music from 1716 to 1742 and Handel's Band in Dublin', *Göttinger Händel-Beiträge*, 11 (2006), 171–98, at 173–5, 187–9.

98 W. S. Newman, *The Sonata in the Baroque Era* (Chapel Hill, NC, 1959), 311–12; Tilmouth, 'Chamber Music in England', 295–7, 301–3, 320–3; M. Tilmouth, 'James Sherard, an English Amateur Composer', *ML*, 47 (1966), 313–22.

99 *BDECM*, i. 150–1, 497.

Viols (1701),[100] was appointed organist of St Clement Eastcheap in 1702,[101] and published two instruction books in 1704 (Ch. 2). *A Choice Collection* was published by 'John Young Musical-Instrument Seller',[102] probably a relative of the court viol player, and consists of two engraved part-books containing thirteen pieces for two viols in four suites, together with a D major prelude for solo viol – the last filling a vacant space on the first page of the second part, which otherwise just has the ground bass of the first duet, a simple set of divisions. Nos. 4, 5, 7, 8 and 9 are also in Gorton's autograph score, GB-Lbl, Add. MS 17850, fols. 3, 22, 24, apparently in pre-publication versions, though with readings that help correct the numerous errors in the print. The duets are unpretentious but effective, with idiomatic writing including chords and much swapping of roles between the viols. They are the sort of thing he would have needed as a London music teacher. Like Hely's duet, they bring together older idioms reminiscent of Locke, such as the almands in the second, third and fourth suites (nos. 5, 7, 10), with 'new ayres', such as the minuet-like movements (nos. 3, 8) using the fashionable dotted idiom of French dance music.

John Moss is also known mainly for a single publication, *Lessons for the Basse-Viol* (1671).[103] He seems to be the person who petitioned unsuccessfully for a place in St Paul's Cathedral choir at the Restoration, for he mentioned then that he was 'bred upp all his tyme in the liberall Science of Musick vocall and instrumentall in the Quire of Wells; and hath gotten his livelihood some part of the late troubles by teaching such schollars as were willing to learne both to play and sing in this Citie'.[104] Property in Wells and elsewhere in Somerset is mentioned in his will – which also tells us that he died on 5 July 1707.[105] The John Moss who was a vicar choral at Wells and was buried there on 9 July 1679 was presumably his father. Since Moss junior wrote lyra-viol music he presumably played the instrument, though he was also an organist: he petitioned Christ's Hospital for the post of music master on 17 December 1675 (also unsuccessfully because he was married and the post required a single man), 'declaring his skill in playing upon the organ and other instruments of musick'; he was organist of St Mary Woolnoth between 1678 and 1706, doubling up at St. Dunstan in the

[100] RISM A/1 G 3027; CC: GB-Cfm, MU. 1002–3; ME: W. Gorton, *Twelve Airs for Two Bass Viols, 1701*, ed. D. Beecher and B. Gillingham (Ottawa, 1979); W. Gorton, *Prelude for Solo Bass Viol*, ed. G. Dodd, VdGS Music, 87 (n.p., 1972, repr. 2005).

[101] D. Dawe, *Organists of the City of London, 1666–1850* (Padstow, 1983), 102.

[102] See Humphries and Smith, *Music Publishing in the British Isles*, 346, 390.

[103] RISM A/1 M 3801; CC: F-Pn, Rés. 860; ME: ed. T. Conner, 2 vols. (Hannacroix, NY, 2004–5).

[104] *BDECM*, ii. 812–13.

[105] GB-Lna, PROB 11/501, fols. 263v–265v.

East between 1683 and 1696.[106] He received Jenkins's place as a lutenist in the Private Music by a warrant dated 19 April 1678, holding it until the end of Charles II's reign; he was not reappointed under James II.[107] He presumably played all three instruments, using whichever was appropriate for teaching; in his will he described himself simply as 'of the Citty of London teacher of musick'. At the time professional musicians routinely played several instruments, doubtless finding that it made them readily employable as teachers and members of ensembles. The luxury of concentrating on a single instrument was usually the preserve of only the most celebrated virtuosos or those in the most prestigious posts.

Moss's *Lessons* are scored for lyra-viol in tablature with a staff-notation bass; there are twenty-six four-movement suites, each consisting of an alman, corant, saraband, and 'jigg-alman' – an unusual type that combines the features of both dances. As music the pieces are unadventurous and short-winded, remarkable mainly for forming the only single-composer English lyra-viol collection from the second half of the century. By 1671 the repertory was already in decline. The last publication was the 1682 edition of Playford's *Musick's Recreation on the Viol, Lyra-Way*, and the only English source later than that seems to be a manuscript from the More Molyneux family papers of Loseley Park in Surrey, now Surrey History Centre, Woking, LM/1083/91/35.[108] The Woking manuscript can be dated to 1688 or later because it includes versions of 'Siface's Farewell' (the castrato left London on 19 June 1687) and 'Lilliburlero' (a tune associated with the Glorious Revolution). English composers stopped using tablature for viol music because they stopped using variant tunings, witness the pieces already discussed by Frederick Steffkins and Hely. In 1672–3 Matthew Locke criticised Thomas Salmon for recommending the harp-way lyra-viol tunings instead of the ordinary bass viol tuning, pointing out 'the ridiculousness of confining the *Viol* to a Tuning, incapable of being used well in more than one Key, whereas the Old Way [i.e. the ordinary tuning] injoyed all'.[109] He printed an Almand of his own composition in staff notation which he claimed was impossible to play with Salmon's 'new confin'd Tuning', identifying it as harp-way sharp or *defhf* at the beginning (Illus. 1.1).[110]

[106] Dawe, *Organists of the City of London*, 128.

[107] *RECM*, i. 178, 231.

[108] J. Cunningham and A. Woolley, 'A Little-Known Source of Restoration Lyra-Viol and Keyboard Music: Surrey History Centre, Woking, LM/1083/91/35', *RMARC*, 43 (2010), 1–22.

[109] M. Locke, *The Present Practice of Musick Vindicated* (London, 1673; repr. 1974), 9; Traficante, 'Lyra Viol Tunings', 193–5, 197.

[110] Locke, *The Present Practice of Musick Vindicated*, 10.

Illus. 1.1 Matthew Locke, Almand, from *The Present Practice of Musick Vindicated*
(London, 1673)

The decline of tablature is also illustrated in GB-Lcm, c41/1 (formerly II.F.10
(2)), a manuscript appendix to a copy of Simpson's *Division-Violist* (1659).[111] It
was started not long after the publication of the book as a conventional collection
of divisions by Norcombe, Butler, Simpson, Young, Jenkins, and others, though
later hands added divisions for violin, recorder and (probably) oboe, as well as
well as some arias by the Venetian composer Carlo Pallavacino. At the end, evidently copied in the early eighteenth century – they come after recorder divisions
by Finger, one (fols. 39v–40; RI110) first published *c.* 1700 – are two suites from
the section in ordinary tuning in Moss's *Lessons* (fols. 52v–55v) copied out in two-
stave staff notation. The manuscript also includes other staff-notation solo bass
viol music, including suites in D major and E minor (fols. 33v–37) by the Lincoln
composer John Cutts (d. 1692). Another example of the same process is Philip
Falle's staff-notation transcriptions in GB-DRc, MS Mus. A27, pp. 107–8, of three
pieces for lyra viol and bass from Simpson's *Compendium of Practical Music*.[112]

Moss, like the Steffkins brothers and Gorton, belonged to the last generation
of native English professional viol players. Most of those active in London after
them were immigrants, from Italy, France or the German-speaking areas of
Europe. The exception that proves the role is the violinist Henry Eccles, though
by the second decade of the century he was a representative of imported musical

---

[111]   ME: *Eight Divisions for a Treble Instrument*, ed. S. Heinrich (Oxford, 2001); *Nineteen Divisions for Bass Viol*, ed. Heinrich (Oxford, 2001).

[112]   C. Simpson, *A Compendium of Practical Music* (London, 3/1678; repr. 2007),
172–7; *VdGSIM*, ii. 47 (Patxi del Amo).

culture as a member of the Italian opera house orchestra and then as an employee of a French aristocrat (Ch. 3). The last native professional player in the continuous tradition seems to have been Thomas Shuttleworth, the father of the composer Obadiah. Hawkins wrote that he was 'a teacher of music ... living in Spitalfields in the year 1738' who made a good living by copying Corelli's sonatas; he had 'frequent concerts at his house for the entertainment of a few select friends, in which the sons played the violin, the daughter the harpsichord, and the old gentleman the viol da gamba'.[113] They doubtless played Corelli's trio sonatas as well as Obadiah's own sonatas, now lost. With one or two exceptions, it was not until the middle of the nineteenth century that English professional musicians once again took an interest in the viol.

❧ New Roles

A N important change to the bass viol's role in the Restoration period was its increasing use as a continuo instrument, often in unfamiliar milieux such as theatre orchestras. In the lists of the performers for John Crowne's court masque *Calisto* (1675) three 'Bass Viols', Charles Coleman junior, Frederick William Steffkins and Thomas Bates, are listed separately from the thirty-one 'Violins' (the traditional collective noun included all three sizes of the family), probably because they were part of the continuo group with two harpsichords and two theorboes.[114] As we have seen, Coleman junior and Purcell seemingly provided the continuo for a group of solo singers in James II's Private Music, probably in court odes and vocal chamber music. There was a change in the style of the continuo parts of English songs in the 1680s and 90s: until then composers had provided simple functional accompaniments, suitable for the lute-family instruments that singers had traditionally learned. Following Italian practice as transmitted by immigrant singing teachers in London, they began to develop more complex and wide-ranging continuo parts, imitating the voice and often incorporating running passages.[115] This was partly because the harpsichord had begun to replace the theorbo as the normal continuo instrument. The title-pages of Restoration song-books typically specifed 'Theorbo-Lute, or Bass-Viol' until 1687, when there was a change to formulas such as 'Harpsichord, Theorbo, or Bass-Viol' or 'Theorbo-Lute, Bass-Viol, Harpsichord, or Organ'.[116]

[113] HawkinsH, ii. 675, 826.

[114] Holman, *Four and Twenty Fiddlers*, 366–73.

[115] See Holman, *Henry Purcell*, 35–6, 58–9.

[116] See the transcriptions in C. L. Day and E. B. Murrie, *English Song-Books, 1651–1702: a Bibliography* (London, 1940).

This does not necessarily mean that the bass viol was used in conjunction with the harpsichord or theorbo, as is the normal practice today. In domestic situations they were often treated as alternatives, so that the viol was used alone, with or without chords to fill out the harmony. Samuel Pepys entertained himself in this way several times in 1660: 'A great while at my Viall and voice, learning to sing [Simon Ives's song] *Fly boy, fly boy* without book' (18 February); 'Then home and sang a song to my vial' (22 February); and 'Before I went to church I sang [Henry Lawes's] *Orpheus Hymne* to my viall' (4 March).[117] Nevertheless, in elite musical circles the gamba was apparently used with continuo instruments, particularly in large-scale works. That was certainly the practice in France: in 1704 the Paris opera orchestra included a *petit chœur* consisting, apparently, of two violins, a harpsichord, two theorboes, two bass viols and two bass violins.[118] In operas the *petit chœur* had the double function of providing the continuo for the vocal sections and acting as a *concertino* to the *grand chœur*, the main orchestra. There are also references to the combination of bass viol, theorbo and harpsichord in French music. Marc-Antoine Charpentier's eight-part sonata, H548, has parts for bass viol, bass violin, theorbo and harpsichord, while in Act II, Scene 1 of Molière's *Le bourgeois gentilhomme* (1670) the *maître de musique* advises Monsieur Jourdain to have concerts in his house consisting of three voices, 'accompanied by a bass viol, a theorbo and a harpsichord for the continuo, with two violins for the ritornellos' ('accompagnées d'une basse de viole, d'un théorbe et d'un clavecin pour les basses continues, avec deux dessus de violon pour jouer les ritournelles').[119]

There is less evidence of this sort in Restoration England, but it is reasonable to assume that similar continuo groups were used in French-style dramatic works produced in London, such as Robert Cambert's opera *Ariane, ou le mariage de Bacchus* (1674) or Louis Grabu's *Albion and Albanius* (1684).[120] In the latter, published in full score in 1687, Grabu laid out the continuo in a manner derived from the Ballard scores of Lully's operas, with a separate continuo part (labelled 'The BASS continued', a translation of Ballard's *basse continue*) that is confined mostly

---

[117] S. Pepys, *The Diary*, ed. R. Latham and W. Mathews, 11 vols., i: *1660* (London, 1970), 59, 64, 76.

[118] J. de La Gorce, 'L'Académie Royale de Musique en 1704, d'après des documents inédits conservés dans les archives notariales', *Revue de musicologie*, 65 (1979), 160–91, esp. 178.

[119] J. A. Sadie, 'Bowed Continuo Instruments in French Baroque Chamber Music', *PRMA*, 105 (1978–9), 37–49, at 37–8.

[120] Holman, *Four and Twenty Fiddlers*, 343–4, 383–8. ME: L. Grabu, *Albion and Albanius*, ed. B. White, Purcell Society Edition Companion Series, 1 (London, 2007).

to the vocal sections. Grabu also used a Lullian *petit chœur*, as in the 'Concert of Venus' in Act III, where two solo violins and 'Flutes' (i.e. recorders) and continuo are contrasted with the five-part strings. Contemporary theatre works by native Englishmen, such as Blow's *Venus and Adonis* (?1683) and Purcell's *King Arthur*, z628 (1691) and *The Fairy Queen*, z629 (1692), may have used the same system, for they contain three-part passages for pairs of wind instruments or solo violins contrasted with four-part passages for the full orchestra.[121]

There is also evidence about continuo practice in the sets of parts for contemporary concerted pieces performed in Oxford. Most of them are academic odes performed in degree ceremonies each July, first in the University Church and after 1669 in the Sheldonian Theatre.[122] They show that the most common way of laying out continuo parts was the same as that used in much of continental Europe for most of the seventeenth century: the continuo instrument or instruments play throughout the work, while the string bass plays only when the upper string parts are playing.[123] Bass viols seem to have been the norm in Restoration Oxford, presumably because the bass violin – Roger North's 'very hard and harsh sounded base' – was played only by professionals.[124] A bass violin does not seem to be clearly specified in Oxford sources until William Morley's 'Let the shrill trumpet's loud alarms', apparently performed for his B.Mus. degree in the year following the 1713 Act.[125]

In the set of autograph material for Matthew Locke's motet 'Ad te levavi oculos meos', performed at the Oxford Music School on 16 November 1665, there are four parts for bass instruments: a two-stave partially-figured continuo part with leads and cues in the right hand, a partially figured single-stave bass, and two unfigured basses.[126] The first two play throughout and were probably intended

[121] ME: J. Blow, *Venus and Adonis*, ed. B. Wood, Purcell Society Edition Companion Series, 2 (London, 2008); H. Purcell, *Works*, 12: *The Fairy Queen*, ed. J. S. Shedlock, rev. A. Lewis (London, 1968); H. Purcell, *Works*, 26: *King Arthur*, ed. D. Arundell, rev. A. M. Laurie (London, 1971).

[122] P. Holman, 'Original Sets of Parts for Restoration Concerted Music at Oxford', in *Performing the Music of Henry Purcell*, ed. M. Burden (Oxford, 1996), 9–19, 265–71.

[123] See esp. G. Dixon, 'Continuo Scoring in the Early Baroque: the Role of Bowed Bass Instruments', *Chelys*, 15 (1986), 38–53; Holman, *Four and Twenty Fiddlers*, 406–7.

[124] *Roger North on Music*, ed. Wilson, 304.

[125] GB-Ob, MS Mus. Sch. c. 131, fols. 15–16v; see also H. D. Johnstone, 'Music and Drama at the Oxford Act of 1713', in *Concert Life in Eighteenth-Century Britain*, ed. S. Wollenburg and S. McVeigh (Aldershot, 2004), 199–218, at 211–12, 214.

[126] GB-Ob, MSS Mus. Sch. c.44, fols. 1, 3, 10v, 12v; ME: M. Locke, *Anthems and Motets*, ed. P. le Huray, MB, 38 (London, 1976), no. 1.

respectively for the Dallam chamber organ in the Music School and a theorbo. One of the unfigured parts has music for all the passages the violins play while the other has only the opening symphony and the last chorus. They must be for bass viols because they also include the bass viol parts of Locke's so-called 'Oxford Suite' for two violins, two bass viols and continuo, apparently written for the same occasion.[127] The more modern method of using a string bass to play throughout is first found in Richard Goodson's ode 'Quis efficaci carmine Pindarus', written in the 1690s, and is also used in Morley's ode and John Isham's 'O tuneful god', apparently also performed following the 1713 Act; the last has two continuous instrumental bass parts.[128]

There is early performing material for only one major concerted work by Purcell: GB-Ob, Tenbury MS 1309, a set of nineteen vocal and instrumental parts for the 1692 St Cecilia ode, 'Hail, bright Cecilia', z328.[129] It is in the hand of Daniel Henstridge, organist of Canterbury Cathedral 1698–1736, and may have been copied for the St Cecilia concerts that the Canterbury music club seems to have given annually from about the time Henstridge arrived there.[130] The only instrumental bass part, no. 4 in the set, is labelled 'The Thorow Bass' on the cover and 'Viol Bass' above the opening bars. It is partially figured, seemingly to be shared by a continuo player and a string bass player, the continuo player presumably at a keyboard with the string player looking over his shoulder, or playing a lute-family instrument and sharing the part with the viol player. It is strange that a viol should be the only string bass in such a heavily scored work, though the set includes only single instrumental and vocal parts, which (assuming that duplicates have not been lost) implies small-scale performances. Another possibility is that the word 'Viol' is an abbreviation for 'Violin', implying the louder bass violin – a possibility that could of course be extended to some of the other Oxford bass parts. A later and incomplete set of parts for the same work, GB-Ob, MS Mus. c.27, fols. 2–25, said to be in the hand of the Chapel Royal singer Bernard Gates (c. 1685–1773), includes two unfigured bass parts, one untitled (fols. 16–19v) and the other labelled 'Cont^r: Bass' (fols. 21–25v) – presumably meaning 'contrabass'. They include all the solo movements (except for ''Tis Nature's voice', labelled 'Solo with the Harpsichord'), which is strange if the latter really is a double bass

---

[127] ME: Locke, *Chamber Music II*, ed. Tilmouth, 100–4.

[128] GB-Ob, MSS Mus. Sch. c.134, fols. 10v–13v; c.140, 28v–34v.

[129] See the ME: H. Purcell, *Works*, 8: *Ode on St Cecilia's Day 1692*, ed. P. Dennison (Borough Green, 1978), esp. x–xi.

[130] R. Ford, 'Minor Canons at Canterbury Cathedral: the Gostlings and their Colleagues', 3 vols. (PhD diss., U. of California, Berkeley, 1984), 446–7. For Henstridge, see W. Shaw, *The Succession of Organists of the Chapel Royal and the Cathedrals of England and Wales from c. 1538* (Oxford, 1991), 47–8, 235–6.

part, though it could conceivably be intended for a large instrument played partly or wholly at written pitch.

🎜 Large Bass Instruments

THIS brings us to another new role for the viol around 1700. Instruments larger, and tuned lower, than the bass viol were used in England from about 1620: Gibbons, Coprario and George Jeffreys wrote for one going down to *AA*.[131] They labelled it 'Double Base' or 'The great Dooble Basse', and payments for great bass viols are recorded in court accounts in 1625 and 1627; another appears in a 1638 inventory of Ingatestone Hall in Essex.[132] John Hingeston left a 'great double Basse' to William Gregory junior in his will,[133] and John Blow seems to have intended an instrument of this sort in his anthem 'Lord, who shall dwell in thy tabernacle?', written for the Chapel Royal around 1680.[134] Pairs of 'Flutes' (i.e. recorders) and violins are supported respectively by a 'Base Flute' and a 'Double Base'. The bass parts go down to *CC* and *CC♯* respectively, and are presumably intended to sound at the same octave since they frequently exchange phrases. The 'Base Flute' must be the largest size of Baroque recorder, called 'Double Bass' by James Talbot,[135] and to match it the bowed 'Double Base' needs to play at sounding pitch rather than transposing all or some of the part down an octave. Thus it seems to have been a viol a size larger than the ordinary bass, akin to the early seventeenth-century instrument. Blow presumably chose it for its rich yet delicate sonority.

The use of large bowed bass instruments can also be inferred from some English concerted works from around 1700. The bass parts of Restoration orchestral music often include *BB* and *BB♭*, notes below the range of the violoncello or the six-string bass viol, indicating that they were played on bass violins tuned *BB♭–F–c–g*.[136] However, there are *AA*s in the orchestral bass parts of four works by Jeremiah Clarke: the Song on the Assumption, T202; the ode 'Tell the world', T208; the masque 'The Four Seasons, or Love in every Age', T300B, his major contribution to the semi-opera *The Island Princess*; and the Barbados Song, T204.

[131] Holman, *Four and Twenty Fiddlers*, 215–17.

[132] *RECM*, iii. 134, 138; *Examples of English Handwriting, 1150–1750*, ed. H. E. P. Grieve ([Chelmsford], 1954), 30, pl. 28.

[133] *BDECM*, i. 575–6.

[134] Holman, *Four and Twenty Fiddlers*, 408–10; ME: J. Blow, *Anthems II: Anthems with Orchestra*, ed. B. Wood, MB, 50 (London, 1984), no. 3.

[135] A. Baines, 'James Talbot's Manuscript (Christ Church Library, Music MS 1187); I: Wind Instruments', *GSJ*, 1 (1948), 9–26, at 17–18.

[136] Holman, *Four and Twenty Fiddlers*, 318–19.

The opening symphony of the Song on the Assumption, in up to thirteen parts in places, has two equal and crossing bass parts, both of which go down to *AA*, so he must have envisioned using at least two stringed instruments with that note.[137] There are also *AA*s in the bass parts of the solo sections of this work, and there is even a *GG* in the dialogue 'Must I a girl for ever be?' in 'The Four Seasons'. *GG* was readily available on theorboes and contemporary English keyboard instruments; it occurs elsewhere, for instance in a solo vocal section in Act II of the first version of Blow's *Venus and Adonis*.[138]

The problem with assessing the significance of the *AA*s is that Clarke was experimental and bold in his orchestral writing, giving the trumpets apparently unplayable non-harmonic tones in the Song on the Assumption and in 'Come, come along, for a dance and a song', T200, his ode on the death of Henry Purcell (1695), so it is not clear whether his demands were entirely realistic. If, as has been argued, the Song on the Assumption was written in memory of Queen Mary (d. 28/12/1694), it would have been written for Winchester College, where Clarke was organist from 1692 until, probably, the winter of 1695–6, when he came to London.[139] We know nothing of instrumental ensembles in Winchester, though the other three works were presumably written for mainstream London musicians. 'Tell the world', celebrating the Peace of Ryswick, was probably Clarke's 'New Pastoral on the Peace', performed at York Buildings on 16 December 1697;[140] *The Island Princess* was put on at Drury Lane in February 1699; and the Barbados Song was probably written for a meeting of its merchants at Stationers' Hall in January 1703.[141] We might dismiss Clarke's low bass notes as a personal eccentricity were it not for the fact that they also occur in the orchestral sections of William Croft's D major Te Deum and Jubilate, apparently first performed in the Chapel Royal on 17 February 1709 to celebrate the battle of Malplaquet and revised in 1715.[142] More examples will probably come to light as the concerted music of the period is investigated more fully.

What sort of stringed instrument could have played parts that go down to *AA*? The bass violin, the violoncello and the six-string bass viol can be ruled out, while

[137] For the sources of Clarke's works, see T. F. Taylor, *Thematic Catalog of the Works of Jeremiah Clarke* (Detroit, 1977) [T]. See also B. White and A. Woolley, 'Jeremiah Clarke (*c.* 1674–1707), a Tercentenary Tribute', *EMP*, 21 (November 2007), 25–36.

[138] Blow, *Venus and Adonis*, ed. Wood, 78.

[139] White and Woolley, 'Jeremiah Clarke', 29.

[140] TilmouthC, 22.

[141] White and Woolley, 'Jeremiah Clarke', 30–31.

[142] GB-Lcm, MS 840; GB-Lbl, Add. MS 17845. See also D. Burrows, *Handel and the English Chapel Royal* (Oxford, 2005), esp. 139–42.

the seven-string bass viol with an extra *AA* string only seems to have been developed in France in the late seventeenth century (apparently by Sainte-Colombe senior),[143] and is not known to have been used in England around 1700. James Talbot gave six tunings for the 'Consort Bass Viol', one with five strings and the rest with six; none has a note lower than *C*.[144] There are a few surviving English bass viols with seven strings, including several by Edward Lewis, but they all seem to have been remodelled in eighteenth-century France, perhaps by the Paris maker Claude Pierray.[145] One obvious possibility is the early seventeenth-century 'great bass viol' or 'great double bass', and another is Talbot's 'Violone or Double Bass wth 6 Strings' tuned *GG–C–F–A–d–g*; he called it 'German', and instruments of this sort were common in German-speaking areas of Europe.[146] Talbot also described a 'Double Bass wth 5 Strings' tuned either *FF–AA–D–F♯–A* or *GG–AA–D–F♯–A* that had been lent by Finger; perhaps it was the 'excellent Double Bass' in the catalogue of Finger's library. Three large bass instruments by Lewis survive with bodies shaped like bass violins but with the top of the back cut away like a bass viol. Their heads have been replaced, so we do not know how they were originally strung.[147] The Wells doctor Claver Morris (Ch. 2) owned a Lewis instrument he called variously 'the great Bass-Violin', 'a large Bass-Violin', and 'my Double-Bass'.[148] It is likely that such instruments were used to play parts mostly at pitch, perhaps in conjunction with ordinary bass violins.

The change to the more modern bass scoring with violoncellos and octave-transposing double basses seems to have followed the establishment of an Italian opera orchestra in London in 1705–6. In some lists 'Saggione' (the Italian composer Giuseppe Fedeli) was listed as the 'Double Base' alongside four 'Violoncelli', and in one list Saggione and 'Francisco' (the cellist François Goodsens) are given

---

143 J. Rousseau, *Traité de la viole* (Paris, 1687; repr. 1980), 24: 'C'est aussi à Monsieur de SAINTE COLOMBE que nous sommes obligez de la septiéme chorde qu'il a ajoûtée à la Viole, & dont il a par ce moyen augmenté l'estenduë d'une Quarte'.

144 Donington, 'James Talbot's Manuscript', 47–8.

145 Information from Ben Hebbert. For Lewis see B. Hebbert, 'The Richard Meares Viol in the Metropolitan Museum of Art Re-evaluated', *JVdGSA*, 20 (2003), 36–48.

146 Donington, 'James Talbot's Manuscript', 49–50; there are facsimiles at www.greatbassviol.com. For the *GG* viol, see esp. K. J. Snyder, *Dieterich Buxtehude, Organist in Lübeck* (New York, 1987), 371–2; J. Morton, 'The Early History and Use of the G Violone', *JVdGSA*, 36 (1999), 40–66; T. Borgir, S. Bonta and A. Planyavsky, 'Violone', *GMO*.

147 Information from Ben Hebbert.

148 H. D. Johnstone, 'Instruments, Strings, Wire and other Musical Miscellanea in the Account Books of Claver Morris (1659–1727)', *GSJ*, 60 (2007), 29–35, at 31, 33–4.

as the '2 Double Bases'.[149] Saggione (with Michel Pignolet de Montéclair) is said to have introduced the *contre basse* into the Paris opera around 1700,[150] and is listed as playing 'Violono grosso' in Cousser's commonplace book.[151] Three of the seven paintings by Marco Ricci, supposedly showing rehearsals for the 1708 London production of the opera *Pyrrhus and Demetrius* by Alessandro Scarlatti and Nicola Haym, include large double basses that look like transposing instruments.[152] J. C. Pepusch, who worked for the opera company at that time, defined *violone* in 1724 as:

> a very large Bass Violin, or Double Bass, it being as large again in every Way as a common Bass Violin, and the Strings twice as thick and twice as long, renders the Sound just an Octave lower than the common Bass Violin. This Instrument is used only in Great Consorts, as Operas, and other publick Musick.[153]

'A double Bass with a Case for it made by M^r. [John] Barrett' is in the 1720 inventory of instruments owned by the Duke of Chandos, drawn up by Pepusch.[154] The change to the new scoring was accompanied by a rise in the tessitura of the bass line (which made transposing down the octave feasible and more necessary), and the development of a more active and virtuosic style of writing – as can be seen, for instance, by comparing the orchestral bass passages of Purcell's semi-operas of the 1690s with those in the operas Handel wrote for London about twenty years later.

At the same time there was a decline in the use of the bass viol as a continuo instrument. This can be charted from the title-pages of English songbooks: after 1700 the bass viol was no longer mentioned as an alternative to lute-family instruments or keyboards in vocal collections, even when, as in the case of John Eccles's *A Collection of Songs for One, Two and Three Voices* (1704) or John Reading's *A Book of New Songs* (1710), viols are portrayed on the

---

[149] *Vice Chamberlain Coke's Theatrical Papers, 1706–1715*, ed. J. Milhous and R. D. Hume (Carbondale and Edwardsville, IL, 1982), 31, 33, 127, 159.

[150] M. Cyr, '*Basses* and *basse continue* in the Orchestra of the Paris Opéra, 1700–1764', *EM*, 10 (1982), 155–70, at 157.

[151] US-NHub, Osborn MS 16, p. 411 (Samantha Owens).

[152] See esp. R. Leppert, 'Imagery, Musical Confrontation and Cultural Difference in early Eighteenth-Century London', *EM*, 14 (1986), 323–45.

[153] G. Strahle, *An Early Music Dictionary: Musical Terms from British Sources, 1500–1740* (Cambridge, 1995), 411.

[154] *The British Violin: the Catalogue of the 1998 Exhibition '400 Years of Violin and Bow Making in the British Isles'*, ed. J. Milnes (Oxford, 2000), 34.

title-page.[155] The change is even more striking in instrumental collections: the viol is mentioned only twice on the title-pages of John Walsh's publications: *Six Sonatas and Solos, Three for a Violin and Three for the Flute, with a Thorough Bass for the Harpsicord, Theorboe or Bass-Viol* (1700) by William Croft and 'an Italian Mr' (probably Finger),[156] and the reprint of William Williams's *Six Sonata's in Three Parts, Three for Two Violins and Three for Two Flutes, with a Part for the Base-Violin or Viol* (1703).[157] In the latter 'a Part For the Base-Violin or Viol' is mentioned on the title-page but the bass part for each piece is labelled 'Violone' – that is, bass violin. After 1703 Walsh only mentioned violin-family bass instruments, whether on title-pages or in the headings in the individual parts. Examples are: 'Violono Basso', the label on the bass part for J. C. Pez's *Sonata in D♯ in 3 Parts* (1704);[158] 'Organo e violoncello', the label on the bass part for *Two Sonatas for Violins in Parts, one by Signr Caldara and the other by Signr Gabrielli* (1704);[159] and *Bononcini's Aires for Two Flutes and a Bass … with a Thorough Bass for the Harpsicord or Bass Violin* (1705).[160] Thus the viol seems to have been replaced by the bass violin or violoncello in the first decade of the century, at least in London's elite musical circles. Manuscripts of Pepusch's violin sonatas composed around this time specify bass viol on the bass part, but Walsh publications of some of them allocate the part to the bass violin (Ch. 3). Pepusch was seemingly the last composer in England to specify the bass viol as a continuo instrument.

🎵 *Conclusion*

ENGLAND was a centre of viol playing in the seventeenth century, attracting students from the Continent, though the number of native professional players declined rapidly after 1660. The most eminent player in London after

---

[155] RISM A/I E 311, R 489; D. Hunter, *Opera and Song Books Published in England, 1703–1726, a Descriptive Bibliography* (London, 1997), 30–41, 193–5.

[156] W. C. Smith, *A Bibliography of the Musical Works Published by John Walsh during the Years 1695–1720* (Oxford, 2/1968), 12, no. 28; R. L. Hardie, '"Curiously Fitted and Contriv'd": Production Strategies Employed by John Walsh from 1695 to 1712, with a Descriptive Catalogue of his Instrumental Publications' (PhD diss., U. of Western Ontario, 2000), 245, no. 7.

[157] RISM A/I W 1173; Smith, *A Bibliography*, 38–9, no. 126; Hardie, 'Curiously Fitted and Contriv'd', 269, no. 25.

[158] RISM A/I P 1690; Smith, *A Bibliography*, 48, no. 150a; Hardie, 'Curiously Fitted and Contriv'd', 284, no. 39.

[159] RISM A/I B 3622; Smith, *A Bibliography*, 53, no. 165; Hardie, 'Curiously Fitted and Contriv'd', 291, no. 46.

[160] Smith, *A Bibliography*, 56, no. 178; Hardie, 'Curiously Fitted and Contriv'd', 299, no. 51.

the 1670s was the Moravian Gottfried Finger, and after about 1710 nearly all the professional players were immigrants – a return to the situation in the first half of the sixteenth century. At the same time there were sweeping changes to the viol's role and function. Viol consort playing may have lingered on among amateurs, but there was no court viol consort after 1660, and Charles II's musical taste favoured the violin and French-style dance music. Thus there was no more call for treble and tenor viols, though the bass continued to be used as a solo and continuo instrument. In the 1690s public concerts brought the sonata to the fore as the main vehicle for instrumental virtuosity – hence the English repertories of sonatas for solo bass viol, two bass viols, or violin, bass viol, with continuo. Solo bass viol music was written in staff notation and in ordinary tuning rather than in tablature with variant tunings, and the instrument was increasingly used to play solo or obbligato parts rather than bass lines, though it seemingly had a role as a continuo instrument in Restoration concerted music until it was replaced by the violoncello early in the eighteenth century. Large viols, tuned in *AA* or *GG* and essentially playing at pitch, also seem to have been used in used in orchestras around 1700, though they were soon replaced by double basses that transposed bass parts down the octave in the modern manner.

CHAPTER 2

'The Noble Base Viol':
Amateur Players around 1700

❧ Meanings and Role

THE bass viol was still played by professionals in France and Germany in
the early eighteenth century, though in those areas it came to be associated
particularly with the aristocracy and even royalty. Players included the Regent of
France, Philippe II, Duc d'Orléans, and his son Louis; Louis XV's daughter Hen-
riette-Anne de France; Louis, Duc de Bourgogne; Friedrich Wilhelm II of Prussia; the Elector Maximilian II Emanuel of Bavaria, his children Franz Joseph,
Clemens August and Johann Theodor, and his grandson Maximilian III Joseph;
Karl Theodor, Elector of Bavaria; Joseph I of Hessen-Darmstadt; Clemens Wenzeslaus of Saxony; and Joseph von Ursenbeck-Massimi.[1] This is no surprise: the
viol had been associated with the aristocracy for more than 200 years, and its low,
plaintive and distinctive voice expressed their virtues of reticence, discernment
and exclusivity. It was also not a regular member of the orchestra, so its players could sidestep demeaning associations with the world of professional music
making. At the same time it was a versatile and flexible instrument, useful for
playing all sorts of solo and ensemble music.

Things were rather different in Britain. Many at the time commented on the
distinctive nature of British society, relatively egalitarian and unpolarised by
comparison with other European countries. As William Guthrie put it 1770: 'In
other countries, the great body of the people have little power, and consequently
meet with little respect; in Great Britain the people have their due influence, and
meet accordingly with a proper share of attention'.[2] He attributed this situation
to 'that happy constitution of government, which, towards the close of the last
century, was confirmed to us, and which makes the peculiar glory of this nation'
– that is, the political settlement following the Glorious Revolution of 1688.

---

[1] L. Robinson, 'Forqueray (1) Antoine Forqueray ['le père'], GMO; L. Robinson,
'Viol, 6: France from c. 1600', GMO; F. Flassig, Die Soloistische Gambenmusik in
Deutschland im 18. Jahrhundert (Göttingen, 1998), 162–7, 178–86, 188–9, 203–8.

[2] W. Guthrie, A New Geographical, Historical, and Commercial Grammar, and
Present State of the Several Kingdoms of the World (London, 1770), iii; CC: ECCO,
ESTC T149699. See also P. Langford, A Polite and Commercial People: England,
1727–1783 (Oxford, 1989), esp. 59–121.

He pointed out that high culture was not just available to the few: 'the great body of the people, no less than the dignified, the learned or the wealthy few, had a title to be amused, informed and edified'.

In music this seems to have had two rather different effects. The upper classes – 'the wealthy few' – seem increasingly to have regarded music as something best left to women or (preferably foreign) professionals. John Locke wrote that:

> *Musick* is thought to have some affinity with Dancing, and a good Hand, upon some Instruments, is by many People mightily valued; but it wastes so much of a young Man's time, to gain but a moderate Skill in it; and engages often in such odd Company, that many think it much better spared: And I have, amongst Men of Parts and Business, so seldom heard any one commended, or esteemed for having an Excellency in *Musick*, that amongst all these things that ever came into the List of Accomplishments, I think I may give it the last place.[3]

The 1690s was the time when fashionable society was becoming accustomed to listening to music in public concerts rather than playing it at home, and when the grand tour was giving upper-class young men a taste for Italian opera; an Italian opera house was established in London in the following decade, supported by aristocratic patronage (Ch. 3). It remained socially acceptable for men to play stringed instruments, though there was a feeling that it should not be done too well, echoing Renaissance ideas. Thus Sir John Clerk of Penicuik (1676–1755), an accomplished, harpsichordist, violinist and composer in his youth, wrote in 1750 that his brother Hugh 'play'd on the violencello with all the perfection of the Greatest Master, and rather too well for a Gentleman'.[4] Clerk even echoed Locke in his 'Advice to a Young Man who is Desirous of Making a Great Figure in the World' by stating that performing 'well on any Instrument of Musick' was 'a mean turn of mind by which a great deal of pretious time is wasted'.[5]

By contrast, the increasing thirst for music among 'the great body of the people' is shown by the development of music clubs from the late seventeenth

---

[3] J. Locke, *Some Thoughts Concerning Education* (London, 1693), 235–6; CC: *EEBO*, Wing L2762.

[4] H. Goodwill, 'The Musical Involvement of the Landed Classes in Eastern Scotland, 1685–1760' (PhD diss., U. of Edinburgh, 2000), 77. See also E. Gibson, *The Royal Academy of Music, 1719–1728: the Institution and its Directors* (New York, 1989), 40–51.

[5] Goodwill, 'The Musical Involvement', 77.

century, part of the proliferation of clubs and societies of all sorts.[6] The viol was part of this process: it was cultivated by a remarkably broad spectrum of society in the early eighteenth century, doubtless aided by the ready availability of instruments old and new, the need for bass instruments in amateur music clubs, and the development of a solo repertory, which allowed it to be used for solitary and relatively inexpensive music making. By 1710, when Richard Steele attempted to define the characters of various instruments, the bass viol had acquired down-to-earth associations:

> There is another Musical Instrument, which is more frequent in this Nation than any other; I mean your Bass-Viol, which grumbles in the Bottom of the Consort, and with a surly Masculine Sound, strengthens the Harmony, and tempers the Sweetness of the several Instruments that play along with it. The Bass-Viol is an Instrument of a quite different Nature to the Trumpet, and may signifie Men of rough Sense, and unpolished Parts, who do not love to hear themselves talk, but sometimes break out in an agreeable Bluntness, unexpected Wit, and surly Pleasantry, to the no small Diversion of their Friends and Companions. In short, I look upon every sensible true-born *Britain*, to be naturally a Bass-Viol.[7]

This attempt to equate the bass viol with 'Men of rough Sense, and unpolished Parts' is remarkable, though it is corroborated by the many ordinary viol players discussed in this chapter, and by the continued appearance of published instructions, doubtless aimed at those unable to afford regular personal tuition.

❧ *Instruction Books*

THE simplest instructions were large single sheets of paper, evidently intended for children to refer to as they practised, such as Henry Playford's 'A Table Engraven on Copper shewing any Note with the compass of the Bass-Viol; very Beneficial for Young Practitioners on that Instrument', advertised in 1694,[8] or William Gorton's 'A View of the first Rudiments of Musick for the

---

[6] See esp. M. Tilmouth, 'The Beginnings of Provincial Concert Life in England', in *Music in Eighteenth-Century England: Essays in Memory of Charles Cudworth*, ed. C. Hogwood and R. Luckett (Cambridge, 1983), 1–17; P. Borsay, *The English Urban Renaissance: Culture and Society in the Provincial Town, 1660–1770* (Oxford, 1989), 121–7, 332–5.

[7] *The Tatler*, no. 153 (1/4/1710), ed. D. F. Bond, 3 vols. (Oxford, 1987), ii. 358–62, at 360.

[8] M. Tilmouth, 'Chamber Music in England, 1675–1720' (PhD diss., U. of Cambridge, 1960), 354.

Harpsicord, Singing, Flute and Bass Viol, with all the Characters for Time and Graceing, and Proper Rules for so doing', advertised on 9 May 1704; no copy of either survives.[9] John Hare's *The Compleat Violist* (1699) also emphasised its didactic purpose. It is 'An Introduction to ye Art of Playing on ye Bass Viol', 'chiefly designed for young Practitioners', containing 'all ye necessary Rules, and ye true method to be observed in order to play well on that instrument'. However, some of the material was just simplified from Playford's *Introduction to the Skill of Musick*,[10] and it is hardly detailed enough to enable the novice to learn without a teacher. After studying the three-page introduction covering basic musical notation, tuning the viol, holding it, and using the bow, he was expected to be able to play a graded sequence of pieces, beginning with psalms and moving on to popular tunes such the famous *forlana* from Campra's *L'Europe galante* (1697) or Jeremiah Clarke's 'Prince of Denmark's March', and then to more complex dances. He would have had to play well to tackle the suites by Benjamin Hely at the end (Ch. 1).

An important feature of *The Compleat Violist* is its use of the treble clef for the first two groups. The introduction states that the 'G solreut Cliff ... is proper for the Treble Viol, or to play Airs or Tunes of songs on the Viol' (i.e. on the bass viol an octave lower), and an advertisement pointed out that it featured 'the divers manner of playing' using the treble, alto and bass clefs.[11] The treble clef was the most common way of notating gamba music in the late eighteenth century, presumably because it enabled players familiar with it to read violin music and songs down the octave; for the same reason violoncellists began to use it in the 1760s.[12] The idea probably came from vocal music. John Playford pioneered the use of the octave-transposing treble clef in his song collections, writing in *Cantica sacra* (1674) that music using it 'may properly be Sung by Men as well as Boyes or Weomen'.[13] *The Compleat Violist* is apparently the earliest source to apply it to instruments. It was used again in Walsh's *Aires and Symphonys for ye Bass Viol* (1710) and in several early eighteenth-century manuscripts (Ch. 3). England was in advance of other countries in this respect.

---

[9] TilmouthC, 55. It is not to be confused with Gorton's *Catechetical Questions in Musick* (London, 1704), CC: US-Wc, MT7.G67 (Case), which deals with notation but not ornamentation.

[10] R. Herissone, *Music Theory in Seventeenth-Century England* (Oxford, 2000), 280.

[11] *The Post Boy*, 30/11/1699.

[12] V. Walden, *One Hundred Years of Violoncello: a History of Technique and Performance Practice, 1740–1840* (Cambridge, 1998), 74–8.

[13] P. Holman, *Henry Purcell* (Oxford, 1994), 48.

At the other end of the educational process was the third edition of Christopher Simpson's *Division-Viol* (1712), published by the instrument maker and music seller Richard Meares junior.[14] Few amateur players would have been able to master Simpson's written-out divisions or could have improvised fluently according to his rules, and one wonders how many were still interested in attaining these advanced and specialised skills. Copies of the earlier editions of Simpson were still in use, often with manuscript appendices that included violin or recorder music as well as original bass viol music – a trend recognised by Meares, who appended arrangements of two Corelli violin sonatas to his edition (Ch. 3). *The Division-Viol* probably lasted so long because there were few advanced printed music treatises in English, and because it offered instruction in harmony as well as playing divisions on the viol. It was for this reason, presumably, that copies of the various editions featured twenty-eight times in auction sales up to 1750.[15]

The 1712 *Division-Viol* was the last English treatise devoted to the viol, though the instrument still featured in general instruction books. 'An Introduction to the Playing on the Bass Viol. &c.' remained essentially unchanged in Playford's *Introduction to the Skill of Musick* until the nineteenth and last edition of 1730.[16] By then the sections with the tunings of treble and tenor viols must have seemed archaic if not incomprehensible to potential players. They are still found in Thomas Brown's *The Compleat Musick-Master* (3/1722), but with the observation that they were 'much out of request in *England*, when they still preserve their Credit in *France*'.[17] The violoncello began to replace the viol in instruction books in the 1730s, beginning with Peter Prelleur's 'THE GAMUT *for the* VIOLONCELLO' (1731), reflecting its sudden popularity among amateurs.[18] But William Tans'ur still described 'The *Viol di Gambo*, or *Leg-Viol*' in his *New Musical Grammar* (1746), stating that it is 'what we call our *Bass-Viol*, having *six Strings*'.[19] In 1756 he added illustrations

[14] CC: GB-Lbl, g.299. For Meares, see esp. C. Humphries and W. C. Smith, *Music Publishing in the British Isles* (Oxford, 2/1970), 230; *The British Violin: the Catalogue of the 1998 Exhibition '400 Years of Violin and Bow Making in the British Isles'*, ed. J. Milnes (Oxford, 2000), 14, 16–17; B. Hebbert, 'Three Generations of the Meares Family in the London Music Trade, 1638–1749' (MMus diss., U. of Leeds, 2001), 27–51.

[15] L. Coral, 'Music in English Auction Sales, 1676–1750' (PhD diss., U. of London, 1974), esp. 85, 314–15.

[16] Herissone, *Music Theory in Seventeenth-Century England*, esp. 269–70.

[17] CC: *ECCO*, ESTC T160899. See also Tilmouth, 'Chamber Music in England', 152–3.

[18] Page appended to 'The Art of Playing the Violin', P. Prelleur, *The Modern Musick-Master, or The Universal Musician* (London, 2/1731; repr. 1965).

[19] W. Tans'ur, *A New Musical Grammar, or The Harmonical Spectator* (London, 1746; repr. 2004), 75.

of the notes available on each string in first position, information still retained in 1772.[20]

❧ Meanings of 'Bass Viol'

TANS'UR brings us to the problem of the meaning of 'bass viol' in what we might call vernacular musical milieux. He described himself on the title-page of *The Elements of Musick Display'd* as 'Professor, Corrector, and Teacher of CHURCH-MUSIC, above 50 Years', and aimed his publications at members of country church choirs wishing to improve their musical education. It is of interest that he refers gamba players requiring 'more LESSONS' to some two-part psalm tunes printed earlier in his book, for we shall see that the clock-maker John Harrison, a parish church musician, played the viol and mentioned playing two-part psalm tunes on viols. At least one surviving gamba may be a church instrument: it is made out of mahogany with a violoncello-like body but an original thick neck with six pegs.[21] William Gardiner wrote that a choir at the dissenting chapel in Leicester led by his father around 1760 obtained a 'bass-viol' by 'Baruch [Barak] Norman' so that the continuo part of William Croft's *Musica sacra* could be played on it; he claimed that it was 'the first instrument of its kind ever introduced into a place of worship'.[22] The gamba may occasionally have been used in churches and chapels partly because of its similarity to the psalterer, one of several simple fretted bowed instruments developed in the early eighteenth century to enable those unskilled in music to play psalm tunes or their basses from a simple letter tablature.[23]

Nevertheless, the term 'bass viol' as found in hundreds of parish church documents between the middle of the eighteenth century and the late nineteenth century usually refers to some sort of violoncello rather than the gamba, just as large violoncellos made in America, such as those by the New Hampshire maker Abraham Prescott, were conventionally called 'bass viols'.[24] Many four-string

---

[20] W. Tans'ur, *A New Musical Grammar and Dictionary, or A General Introduction to the Whole Art of Musick* (London, 3/1756), 96–7; CC: ECCO, ESTC T098064; W. Tans'ur, *The Elements of Musick Display'd* (London, 5/1772; repr. n.d.), 84–5; CC: GB-Lbl, C.16.

[21] A. Baines, *Victoria and Albert Museum, Catalogue of Musical Instruments*, ii: *Non-Keyboard Instruments* (London, 1968), 8, fig. 9, no. 172–1882.

[22] W. Gardiner, *Music and Friends, or Pleasant Recollections of a Dilettante*, 3 vols. (London, 1838), i. 3.

[23] S. Jeans, 'The Psalterer', *GSJ*, 39 (1986), 2–20.

[24] F. R. Selch, 'Bass Viol', *GMO*. See also N. Temperley, *The Music of the English Parish Church*, 2 vols. (Cambridge, 1979), i. 149–51. Many unpublished

bass instruments in British public collections are known to have come from parish churches.[25] There are also some tell-tale discrepancies in the terminology used in parish documents, for instance in the well-researched counties of Northampton and Rutland. In the Weston-by-Welland accounts there are repeated payments for '4 Bass Viol strings', as if complete sets were purchased, while at Blakesley carriage was paid for the 'Violincio' on 24 March 1833; there are three subsequent references to violoncello strings, but in 1836, 1839 and 1840 'Viol strings' reappear.[26] At Raunds there are payments for bass viol strings on 18 October 1834 and 29 April 1835 but on 16 November the 'violonchello' was repaired, while at Moulton a base viol was referred to repeatedly between 1812 and 1828 but on 27 December 1829 a new 'Violincello' bow was purchased.[27] The London violin maker John Betts repaired a 'Violoncello' for the church at Hellidon in 1819 but bass viol strings were purchased in 1841, while at Kelmarsh a 'bass viol' was purchased in 1813 but the violoncello was repaired in 1829.[28] At Oakham parish church in Rutland a violoncello appears in an 1806 inventory but '3 strings for Base Viole' were purchased in 1808.[29]

It has been suggested that this state of affairs can be explained by the Sternhold and Hopkins 'old version' of the 150th Psalm, which includes the phrase 'Praise him upon the viol',[30] though 'bass viol' may simply have been used as an abbreviation of 'bass violin'. It is also significant that the six-string fretted instrument began to be called 'viola da gamba' (or an Anglicised variant such as 'viol di gambo') rather than 'bass viol' around 1710, the time it changed from a bass instrument to a solo instrument in elite musical circles. This left 'bass viol' vacant for the bass violin or the violoncello – instruments that still played bass lines. 'Bass viol' was sometimes used in the same sense in secular music. It is unlikely that when Viscount Percival mentioned 'bass viols' among the performers of his private concerts in the early 1730s he really meant gamba players. The

references can be located by searching for 'viol' in *Access to Archives* (www.nationalarchives.gov.uk/a2a/).

[25] S. J. Weston, 'The Instrumentation and Music of the Church Choir-Band in Eastern England, with Particular Reference to Northamptonshire, during the late Eighteenth Century and early Nineteenth Centuries' (PhD diss., U. of Leicester, 1995), 243, 259, 261, 264; B. Neece, 'The Cello in Britain: a Technical and Social History', *GSJ*, 56 (2003), 77–115, at 87–8, 95–7, 99–100.

[26] Weston, 'The Instrumentation and Music of the Church Choir-Band', 294, 301.

[27] Ibid., 309, 341.

[28] H. Davidson, *Choirs, Bands and Organs: a History of Church Music in Northamptonshire and Rutland* (Oxford, 2003), 105, 110.

[29] Ibid., 184.

[30] Neece, 'The Cello in Britain', 87.

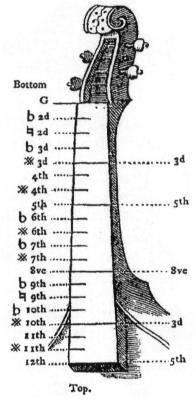

Illus. 2.1 Joshua Steele, illustration of the neck of a 'bass viol' from *Prosodia rationalis* (London, 1779)

groups seem to have been small orchestras with multiple violins in which the 'bass viols' played the bass with a harpsichord and 'great bass'. On one occasion, 9 March 1733, 'Mr. Payne, Mr. Withrington' were 'on the bass viol', while on 15 February 1734 they were listed as playing the violoncello with Andrea Caporale.[31] In attempting to use musical symbols to notate speech rhythms and pitches, Joshua Steele suggested the use of a 'bass viol', but gave it four strings (the lowest C) and later referred to as a 'violincello'.[32] An illustration shows a violoncello-like neck with the sloping shoulders of a viol (Illus. 2.1). In 1789 Benjamin Franklin wrote that the six-stringed instrument 'called *Viol de Gambo*' is 'about the Size of a Bass Viol, but is not the same' (Ch. 7). A verse description of the Holywell Music Room band in Oxford in the early 1790s refers to the cellist Robert Inchbald strumming away on his 'bass viol'.[33] There is no other evidence that he played the gamba, and even if he did it is unlikely that he would have used it in an orchestra. In the face of evidence of this sort I have been wary of assuming that references to the 'bass viol' after about 1720 refer to the gamba unless there is some sort of corroborating evidence, especially if the writer was not a knowledgeable musician or was outside elite musical circles.

[31] *Diary of Viscount Percival afterwards First Earl of Egmont*, ed. R. A. Roberts, 3 vols., *Historical Manuscripts Commission*, 63 (London, 1920, 1923), i. 342; ii. 30.

[32] J. Steele, *Prosodia rationalis, or An Essay towards Establishing the Melody and Measure of Speech, to be Expressed and Perpetuated by Peculiar Symbols* (London, 1779), 16, 37; CC: ECCO, ESTC T046009 (Simon Hill). See also J. C. Kassler, *The Science of Music in Britain, 1714–1830: a Catalogue of Writings, Lectures and Inventions*, 2 vols. (New York, 1979), ii. 974–8.

[33] *Reminiscences of Oxford by Oxford Men, 1559–1850*, ed. L. M. Quiller Couch (Oxford, 1892), 197. For Inchbald, see J. Doane, *A Musical Directory for the Year 1794* (London, 1794; repr. 1993), 36; J. H. Mee, *The Oldest Music Room in Europe: a Record of Eighteenth-Century Enterprise at Oxford* (London, 1911), 120, 121, 130.

❧ *Amateur Players*

THE rest of this chapter is devoted to investigating amateurs known to have played the viol in early eighteenth-century Britain. It is not an easy task: domestic music making is always more poorly documented than organised, public activity, which generates financial documents, advertisements, and comments in letters and diaries. Also, we often do not know whether individuals who learned the viol as children in the seventeenth century continued to do so in later life. Even those who maintained their musical interests in later life may have changed to more up-to-date instruments. For instance, Samuel Pepys (1633–1703) played the bass viol and the lyra viol in the 1660s,[34] though there is nothing for these instruments among the music manuscripts and prints in his library at GB-Cmc, collected after the Diary period.

Sir John Langham (*c.* 1671–1747) was painted aged twelve in 1683 by Frederick Kerseboom or Causabon playing what appears to be a Jaye bass viol (Plate 2).[35] His assured and relaxed posture suggests that he was a skilled player, though there does not seem to be any evidence that he continued to play after he became fourth baronet in 1701 and built Cottesbrooke Hall in Northamptonshire.[36] There are other contemporary instances of viols owned by upper-class families, though we do not know who played them or how long their interest lasted. Family tradition holds that the 1691 Barak Norman bass viol at Longford Castle near Salisbury was purchased new by the Bouverie family (later Earls of Radnor), who acquired the castle in 1717 and still own it, though how long it was used is unclear.[37] The possessions of the amateur composer Robert Orme, advertised in November and December 1711, included 'Cremona-Violins, Ross, and Jay-Viols, Flutes, Hautboys, Guitarrs, Lutes and Harpsychords, made by the best Hands: Together with an excellent Collection of BOOKS of MUSICK, containing the choicest Sonatas, Motetts, Aires, &c. purchased at great Expence, and with the

---

[34] See esp. M. Fleming, 'Instrument Makers Named Hill and Hunt in Pepys's London', *GSJ*, 55 (2002), 382–5; M. Davidson, 'Samuel Pepys and the Viol', *JVdGSA*, 42 (2005), 5–18.

[35] I am grateful to Simon Dickinson Fine Art, London for information about the painting. For the viol, see B. Hebbert, 'A Catalogue of Surviving Instruments by, or Ascribed to, Barak Norman', *GSJ*, 54 (2001), 285–329, at 325.

[36] *Access to Archives* reports 'a description of the "Viola da gamba"' in the Langham (Cottesbrooke) collection on deposit at GB-NH, L(C)899, though the Archivist, Ms Eleanor Winyard, informs me that it and other papers from the collection have now been withdrawn by the depositors and are inaccessible.

[37] Hebbert, 'A Catalogue of Surviving Instruments', 291; information from Ben Hebbert.

Advice of the most judicious Masters'.[38] There is no direct evidence that Orme played the viol himself.

🎵 Musical Education

 EARLY eighteenth-century amateur viol players can be divided roughly into three groups according to social milieu and musical upbringing. The children of upper-class families such as the Langhams and the Bouveries were probably taught by full- or part-time household musicians. An alternative, increasingly popular around 1700, was for them to be taught while on the grand tour or during a period of education in the Netherlands or France. Thus Peregrine Hyde Osborne, Viscount Dunblane (1691–1731), grandson of the Duke of Leeds, was sent to Utrecht in December 1706 with his elder brother William Henry Osborne, Earl of Danby.[39] Louis Bérard, their governor, kept accounts and sent letters back to England that show that the curriculum included languages, riding, fencing, geography, mathematics, and music. Teachers of 'the Lute & Harpsychords' were initially mentioned, and William seems to have developed into an accomplished lutenist (two lute manuscripts owned by him survive), though Peregrine took to the viol and the recorder. Bérard wrote on 27 September 1707 that he 'learns of one & the same M[aste]r, both of the Bass viole & of the flute, & has a very good stroke at both'; he had lessons three days a week on the viol and two on the recorder.[40] A 'Bass Violl & a Bow' was purchased on 1 November 1708, followed by 'a good viole for L[or]d Peregrine' on 2 July 1709, and 'a case for L[or]d Peregrine's Viole' on 22 August.[41] In the winter of 1710–11 the boys and their party visited Hanover and Hamburg, where their lessons continued, though William died of smallpox in August, shortly after their return to Utrecht. There is no sign that Peregrine played the viol in later life (he eventually became third Duke of Leeds), though '2 Bass Viols in Do. [cases]' in an 1838 inventory of Hornby Castle in Lancashire (seat of the Dukes of Leeds) suggests that he may have done.[42] The brothers evidently reached a good standard, taking part in private and public concerts with other young aristocrats and their teachers.[43]

Roger North (1651–1734) certainly came from a family that employed household

---

[38] *DC*, 3/12/1711. See also TilmouthC, 80.

[39] T. Crawford, 'Lord Danby, Lutenist of Quality', *The Lute*, 25/2 (1985), 53–68; T. Crawford, 'Lord Danby's Lute Book: a New Source of Handel's Hamburg Music', *Göttinger Händel-Beiträge*, 2 (1986), 19–50.

[40] Crawford, 'Lord Danby', 58.

[41] Ibid., 59, 60.

[42] Ibid., 67, fn. 31.

[43] Crawford, 'Lord Danby's Lute Book', 23.

musicians.[44] At various times the establishment at Kirtling Hall in Cambridge-shire included John Jenkins, the organists Henry and George Loosemore, the viol player John Lillie, and the violinist Francis White, the steward at Kirtling.[45] Roger started on the treble viol at Kirtling after he left school, apparently taught by Jenkins himself, and later transferred to the bass, using it to accompany songs and duets with his elder brother Francis; he started by playing just bass lines and progressed 'by degrees to put in cords, and at last to full harmony, as the instru-ment would afford'.[46] Later he learned the keyboard, and also played the violin: we glimpse him playing it in Purcell's 'Itallian manner'd compositions' (i.e. trio sonatas) with the composer present.[47] There is no evidence that he played the viol in later life. He wrote around 1710 that the violin had 'engross't all people's fancy to learne, and very few will touch upon any other', though in the same essay, 'The Noble Base Viol', he thought that:

> all the sublimitys of the violin – the swelling, *tremolo*, tempering, and what[ever] else can be thought admirable – have place in the use of the Base Viol, as well as drawing a noble sound; and all with such a vast compass, as expresseth upper, mean and lower parts, and in a lute way toucheth the accords, and is no less swift than the violin itself, but wonderfully more copious.[48]

At his death he left two harpsichords, two violins and two bass viols, one of which had been given to him by William Sancroft 'at his leaving Lambeth' – that is, in 1690 when Sancroft was replaced as archbishop of Canterbury for refusing to accept William and Mary's legitimacy.[49]

One portion of the North family music library was acquired for the Oxford Music School in 1667 (Introduction), and what seems to be another, evidently copied in the 1680s, is now in GB-Lbl, Add. MSS 31422–5, 31430, 31435, 31436, and GB-Lcm, MS 870.[50] It includes selections from the English viol consort

---

44 For Roger North, see esp. F. J. M. Korsten, *Roger North (1651–1734): Virtuoso and Essayist* (Amsterdam, 1981).

45 Ashbee, *The Harmonious Musick of John Jenkins*, i: *The Fantasias for Viols* (Surbiton, 1992), 74–5.

46 *Roger North on Music*, ed. J. Wilson (London, 1959), 21–2, 26.

47 Ibid., 27, 47–8.

48 Ibid., 227.

49 Ibid., xxi–xxii.

50 P. Holman, 'Suites by Jenkins Rediscovered', *EM*, 6 (1978), 25–35; R. Thompson, 'Some Late Sources of Music by John Jenkins', in *John Jenkins and his Time: Studies in English Consort Music*, ed. A. Ashbee and P. Holman (Oxford, 1996), 271–307, esp. 279–80, 289–91; *VdGSIM*, ii. 13–14, 77–103, 114, 116–24, 131–2.

repertory, sets of fantasia suites by Jenkins and Christopher Gibbons, German sonatas for two violins or violin, bass viol and continuo, sinfonias by G. B. Ferini and Stefano Landi, extracts from Lully's operas, and trio sonatas by Colista, Cazzati, Vitali, Stradella, Grossi, degli Antonii, and Franchesini. The sonatas perhaps relate to Roger's involvement with he called 'that company which introduc't the Itallian composed entertainements of musick which they call *Sonnata's*', presumably in London in the 1680s.[51] The collection was probably in his library in the 1720s, for in an essay written at that time he seemingly referred to Add. MS 31423, fols. 76–123, one of two known copies of Jenkins's fantasia suites for three violins, bass viol and continuo.[52] The *'sonata a.2 in score'* that North prepared as an example of how to engrave music on copper may have been one of the sonatas from his collection; no copies of the resulting publication survive.[53]

All in all, there is remarkably little evidence of viol playing among the English aristocracy in the early eighteenth century, especially when compared to France or German-speaking parts of Europe. Frederick Lewis, Prince of Wales is sometimes mentioned as playing the instrument, as on 10 August 1732, when Viscount Percival wrote that he was 'learning the bass-viol',[54] though we have observed Percival seemingly using 'bass viol' to mean the violoncello. The three versions of Mercier's painting *Frederick, Prince of Wales and his Sisters* (c. 1733) all show the prince playing a violoncello,[55] and Horace Walpole presented him with a 'Cremona violoncello' (Ch. 7). Frederick's teacher between 1734 and 1737 was Charles Pardini, a cellist rather than a viol player.[56] The 1730s was the time when English amateurs began to take up the violoncello, with Frederick as an

---

[51] *Roger North on Music*, ed. Wilson, 25.

[52] GB-Lbl, Add. MS 32533, fol. 138; see the letter by D. Pinto, *EM*, 6 (1978), 483. See also *VdGSIM*, ii. 15–16, 22–3, 77–8, 85–6.

[53] *Roger North on Music*, ed. Wilson, 29.

[54] *Diary of Viscount Percival*, ed. Roberts, i. 290.

[55] J. Ingamells and R. Raines, 'A Catalogue of the Paintings, Drawings and Etchings of Philip Mercier', *Walpole Society*, 46 (1978), 1–70, at 21–2, nos. 38–40; illus. in *Philip Mercier, 1689–1760*, ed. J. Ingamells and R. Raines (London, 1969), nos. 24–6. A young man playing a seven-string bass viol in Mercier's Watteauesque *A Musical Party* (c. 1725), Ingamells and Raines, 'A Catalogue', 2, 60, no. 154, illus. 1c, has traditionally been identified as Frederick, despite the fact that at the time the painter was in London and the prince in Hanover. The painting appeared at Sotheby's, 9/7/2009, lot 8 (Michael Fleming).

[56] P. E. Daub, 'Music at the Court of George II (r. 1727–1760)' (PhD diss., Cornell U., 1985), 49, 261–2, 346. For Pardini, see L. Lindgren, 'Italian Violoncellists and some Violoncello Solos Published in Eighteenth-Century Britain', in *Music in Eighteenth-Century Britain*, ed. D. W. Jones (Aldershot, 2000), 121–57, at 139–40.

important role-model. By then musical aristocrats were mostly engaged with Italian culture, represented in music by opera and the violin family. A survey of the musical activities of the directors of the Royal Academy of Music, formed in 1719–20 to revive the Italian opera company in London, does not report evidence that any of them were gamba players.[57] Things were different in the 1760s and 1770s, when Abel's example prompted a number of aristocrats to learn it (Ch. 8).

❧ Educating the Professions: Oxford

MOST early eighteenth-century amateur gamba players were members of the professions: clergy, doctors and lawyers. They were typically educated at Oxford, Cambridge or the Inns of Court in London, and it is in those places that many of them would have received musical instruction. Nathaniel Crew (1633–1721), bishop of Durham from 1674, 'played his part in concert on the viol da gamba' when he was at Oxford;[58] he studied at Lincoln College between 1653 and 1658 and continued as a fellow, becoming rector in 1668 and bishop of Oxford in 1671. Anthony Wood wrote that Crew was a member of William Ellis's music meeting in March 1659 as 'a violinist and violist, but alwaies played out of tune, as having no good eare'.[59] The antiquary Matthew Hutton (1638/9–1711), later rector of Aynho in Northamptonshire, was an undergraduate and then fellow of Brasenose College, Oxford. Wood lists him as a member of Ellis's meeting and as 'an excellent violist'.[60] Manuscripts copied by him at York Minster Library include consort music by Jenkins, Simpson and others with dates of 1667, 1668, 1671 and 1674, evidently copied and used in Oxford, as well as later vocal and instrumental music (including Purcell theatre songs from the 1690s), showing that his musical interests continued in later life.[61] Hutton's exact contemporary Narcissus Marsh (1638–1713), later archbishop of Armagh, was an undergraduate at Magdalen Hall and a fellow of Exeter College from 1658 until he left for Ireland in 1678. Marsh wrote in his diary: 'I had also before this [1664] betaken myself to the practice of Musick, especially of the Bass Viol, and after the fire of London [1666], I constantly kept a weekly consort (of instrumental musick and

[57] Gibson, *The Royal Academy of Music*, esp. 21–107.

[58] HawkinsH, ii. 806.

[59] B. Bellingham, 'The Musical Circle of Anthony Wood in Oxford during the Commonwealth and Restoration', *JVdGSA*, 19 (1982), 6–70, at 39.

[60] Ibid.; P. J. Willetts, 'Music from the Circle of Anthony Wood at Oxford', *British Museum Quarterly*, 24 (1961), 71–5.

[61] See esp. R. Charteris, 'Matthew Hutton (1638–1711) and his Manuscripts in York Minster Library', *GSJ*, 28 (1976), 2–6; *VdGSIM*, i. 4–5, 229–34.

sometimes vocal musick) in my chamber on Wednesday in the afternoon, and then on Thursday, as long as I lived in Oxford'.[62] Marsh's Library, founded in Dublin in 1701, contains some of the manuscripts of consort music he used at Oxford.[63]

Philip Falle (1656–1742), a student of Marsh, assembled a large collection of foreign music prints.[64] He came from Jersey, entered Exeter College in 1669, moved to St Alban's Hall with Marsh in 1673, and was ordained in 1679. He was a member of the delegation sent by the states of Jersey in 1692 to appeal to William III for assistance against the French. In 1698 he was chaplain to the Duke of Portland during his embassy to Paris, and on his return he became one of William's chaplains, accompanying him to the Netherlands in 1699, 1700 and 1701 – when he probably collected much of his music. He became a prebendary of Durham Cathedral in 1700, eventually bequeathing the collection to its library (GB-DRc).[65] The prints include copies of Simpson's *Division-Viol* (B12) and Rousseau's *Traité de la viole* (A31), collections of solo viol music by Gorton, Hacquart, Marais, Schenck, and a certain Mr Carolo, as well as the 1682 edition of *Musick's Recreation on the Viol, Lyra-Way* (C96), *The Compleat Violist* (C95), and *Aires & Symphonys for ye Bass Viol* (C93) – the last published in 1710 and therefore one of his last acquisitions.[66] There are also many Amsterdam and Antwerp editions of ensemble music with violins, some with obbligato viol parts; a number of them are now unique.

More evidence that Falle was a viol player is provided by five of his manuscripts. MS Mus. D2 is a set of three part-books apparently assembled from a collection of loose sheets and consisting of sonatas and other pieces for two violins and continuo, violin, bass viol and continuo, solo bass viol and continuo and two bass viols and continuo, by composers across Europe: Balthasar Richard and Giuseppe Zamponi (Brussels), Heinrich Schmelzer (Vienna), William Young (Innsbruck), Johann Michael Nicolai (Stuttgart), Clamor Heinrich Abel (Celle, Hannover and Bremen), Dietrich Becker (Hamburg), Nathaniel Schnittelbach (Lübeck), and Henry Butler (Madrid); Jenkins is the only named composer

[62] Bellingham, 'The Musical Circle', 40, 43–4.

[63] See esp. R. Charteris, 'Consort Music Manuscripts in Archbishop Marsh's Library, Dublin', *RMARC*, 13 (1976), 27–57; R. Thompson, 'A Further Look at the Consort Manuscripts in Archbishop Marsh's Library, Dublin', *Chelys*, 24 (1995), 3–18.

[64] For Falle, see esp. M. Urquhart, 'Prebendary Philip Falle (1656–1742) and the Durham Bass Viol Manuscript A.27', *Chelys*, 5 (1973–4), 7–20.

[65] R. A. Harman, *A Catalogue of the Printed Music and Books on Music in Durham Cathedral Library* (London, 1968), ix–xi.

[66] Urquhart, 'Prebendary Philip Falle', 14–15.

resident in England.[67] It seems to have been copied in the 1670s by someone working for John St Barbe of Broadlands in Hampshire. St Barbe was a pupil of Christopher Simpson and spent four years on the grand tour between 1674 and 1678 – an obvious opportunity for him to have collected the foreign music. It is not clear how Falle acquired the set, though from 1676 to 1681 he worked in the Diocese of Chichester, which included Broadlands.

Two other sets, MS Mus. D4 and D5, contain a similar repertory.[68] D4 has pieces for two bass viols and continuo by Jenkins, Young, 'P. Poul' (probably the Jesuit priest Anthony Poole), and 'G. Schults' (probably the Nuremberg gamba player Gabriel Schütz), while D5 has music for violin, bass viol and continuo and two bass viols and continuo by Schmelzer, Butler, Jenkins, Zamponi, and a certain 'S[igno]r Claussen'. Both were copied on similar paper, though by different hands, and there are indications that their copyists were German or Dutch: D4 has corrupt spellings of English names such as 'Joung' and 'Jenckings', and the Dutch-sounding name of an owner or copyist, 'A Koon', appears on the flyleaves, while the D5 hand is strongly Germanic in appearance, though he spells Jenkins and Butler correctly. A fourth manuscript, MS Mus. D10, is a small oblong score containing music by Nicolai, Butler, Young and others, mostly for one, two and three bass viols and continuo, with pieces for violin, bass viol and continuo at the end.[69] Again, the hand is Germanic in appearance, with corrupt spellings of English names such as 'Henrich Botler' and 'Maarit Webster'. Falle may have acquired these manuscripts when he was in the Netherlands or from immigrants in England – perhaps the more likely possibility given that they contain some English pieces.

They do not necessarily tell us much about Falle's musical taste or abilities, for they may all have been acquired second hand. However, MS Mus. A27, a large oblong quarto score of music for solo gamba with and without continuo, is important because it is in his hand.[70] He copied mostly from his own prints, perhaps to have favourite pieces available in a single book while travelling, though not everything comes from them: a few are marked 'Ex. mss.' or in one case 'Ex. Mss. Gallico'. Falle probably acquired some of these, including pieces by Blancourt, Marais, Dufaut, and Du Buisson, while he was in Paris in 1698 (he marked his copy of Rousseau's *Traité* 'acheté à Paris'),[71] while others throw light on possible teachers. Among the unaccompanied pieces are Finger's Prelude in E minor

---

[67] *VdGSIM*, ii. 6–7, 54–9, and the literature cited there.

[68] *VdGSIM*, ii. 60–3.

[69] *VdGSIM*, ii. 64–9.

[70] Urquhart, 'Prebendary Philip Falle'; *VdGSIM*, ii. 43–53.

[71] Urquhart, 'Prebendary Philip Falle', 11

R115 (p. 123),[72] a G major suite by Frederick Steffkins (pp. 249–52), and, most significant, all the only known pieces by 'Mr. De Ste Colombe Le Fils', including a remarkable programmatic tombeau in memory of his father (pp. 314–19).[73] A 'Mr. St. Colombe' put on a benefit concert at Hickford's Room in London on 14 May 1713,[74] and we shall see that a 'Mr. Cynelum' taught Dudley Ryder the viol in 1715 and 1716. The Sainte-Colombe who worked in Scotland was named Peter, lived and worked in Edinburgh as a musician from at least 1696, and died there in or before 5 October 1712,[75] so cannot be the same person as the London Sainte-Colombe. The latter is likely to be the composer of the pieces in A27 since Falle is not known to have visited Scotland. Falle must have been a fine player, and two pieces, Fantasie and Passacaille 'in genere Harmonico' (pp. 320–7), show that he was also a competent composer, with Marais and other French viol composers as models (Ex. 2.1).

Claver Morris (1659–1727) also studied at Oxford, at New Inn Hall from 1676, though he became a doctor rather than a clergyman. The evidence of his interest in the gamba comes from accounts and diaries he kept of his life and work in Wells and the surrounding area from the 1680s.[76] He owned a number of instruments, including two violins by John Barrett, a viola, a bass viol, a 'large Bass-Violin' or 'Double-Bass' by Edward Lewis, a recorder, an oboe, a 'Bassoon or Curtill', a two-manual harpsichord, and at least one spinet.[77] It is not clear how many of them he played himself (though there is a payment to a Mr Hall for teaching him the violin in 1686), for some of them were probably purchased for the music club he ran in Wells. But he probably played the viol: he repeatedly refers to 'his' bass viol in his accounts, he purchased strings for it, an 'Iron-Pin to hang the Viol on, in the Musick-Closet' on 19 February 1712, and '2 Stands to set a Bass-Viol on to make it sound louder in playing on it' on 29 December 1716. He also owned at

---

[72] R. Rawson, 'From Olomouc to London: the Early Music of Gottfried Finger (c. 1655–1730)', 2 vols. (PhD diss., Royal Holloway, U. of London, 2002), ii. 159; ME: G. Finger, *The Music for Solo Viol*, ed. Rawson and P. Wagner (London, 2009), no. 12.

[73] ME: Sainte-Colombe le fils, *Tombeau pour Monsieur de Sainte-Colombe le père, précédé d'une fantasie et de quatre suites pour la viole de gambe*, ed. J. Dunford (Strasbourg, 1998).

[74] TilmouthC, 85.

[75] I am grateful to François-Pierre Goy for this information, which will be incorporated by him into a forthcoming article on the two younger Sainte-Colombes.

[76] H. D. Johnstone, 'Instruments, Strings, Wire and other Musical Miscellanea in the Account Books of Claver Morris (1659–1727)', *GSJ*, 60 (2007), 29–35; H. D. Johnstone, 'Claver Morris, an Early Eighteenth-Century English Physician and Amateur Musician *Extraordinaire*', *JRMA*, 133 (2008), 93–127.

[77] Johnstone, 'Instruments, Strings, Wire', esp. 33–5.

Ex. 2.1 Philip Falle, Passacaille in D minor, bb. 1–16

least one collection of solo gamba music: the 'Mont de Caix Pieces' purchased in August 1714 was probably a copy of *Premier livre de pièces de viole* by Louis de Caix d'Hervelois (Paris, 1708).[78] He doubtless used his viol to play the bass lines of the printed sets of sonatas, concertos and vocal music he owned.[79]

Oxford students such as Crew, Hutton, Marsh, Falle, and Morris were presumably taught music by professional musicians, from the Professor of Music downwards. Several Oxford singing-men are known to have been viol players. Francis Smith (1672–98), a chorister and then a singing-man and copyist at Christ Church, left a 'viall di Gambo' in his will.[80] Francis Withy (d. 1727), a Christ Church singing-man from June 1670, was presumably the 'Mr. Withie' who played 'a division' on the bass viol during Cosimo de Medici's visit to the Music School in May 1669.[81] Several manuscripts of bass viol music reveal contacts between

[78] RISM A/I C 38; Johnstone, 'Claver Morris', 125.

[79] Johnstone, 'Claver Morris', 121–6.

[80] Thompson, 'Some Late Sources', 284; R. Shay and R. Thompson, *Purcell Manuscripts: the Principal Musical Sources* (Cambridge, 2000), 313–14. For his hand, see *Christ Church Library Music Catalogue*, comp. J. Milsom (http://library.chch.ox.ac.uk/music/).

[81] J. D. Shute, 'Anthony a Wood and his Manuscript Wood D 19(4) at the Bodleian Library, Oxford: an Annotated Transcription' (PhD diss., International Institute for Advanced Studies, Clayton, MO, 1979), ii. 110. For Withy, see *VdGSIM*, ii. 10–12.

him and Oxford students. Early in his career he copied a set of Simpson divisions on a leaf inserted into GB-Ob, MS Mus. Sch. c.71, an appendix to a copy of Simpson's 1667 *Division-Viol* otherwise copied by William Noble (d. 1681). Noble, a Merton student from 1667 and a chaplain at Christ Church from 1677, included pieces by John and Francis Withy, as well as Jenkins, Butler, Poole, and others.[82]

On 4 December 1687 Francis Withy recorded on the cover of GB-Ob, MS Mus. Sch. c.61 that it was 'The gift of his loving Scoller / Hen: Knight A: B: è Coll Wadh[am]'. Henry Knight (b. 1662) studied at Wadham between 1682 and 1689, becoming rector of West Knighton in Dorset in 1690 and a canon of Hereford Cathedral in 1695.[83] The manuscript, labelled 'Divitions for ye Bass Violl', includes pieces from the traditional repertory by Simpson, Peter Young and Withy himself, as well as violin and recorder music attributed to Matteis, Colista, Robert King, Finger, and Corelli that could have been played on the gamba using the octave-transposing convention.[84] The last piece in the main sequence is a violin version of a Finger sonata published for recorder in 1701.[85] Francis also contributed some Jenkins duets for two bass viols and other pieces to US-U, q763 P699c, manuscript additions to a copy of Playford's *Cantica sacra* (1674),[86] and copied Benjamin Hely's sonatas and pieces by Marais in GB-Ob, MS Mus. Sch. E.428. US-NYp, MS JOG 72–50 is not in his hand, though it contains dances for solo bass viol by 'Ed. Withie' and 'F.W.' on pp. 37–43.[87]

It is difficult to know to what extent Oxford's singing-men were involved in its secular musical life. If Withy's copies of Hely were made from the autograph parts that arrived in Oxford after the composer's death in 1699 (Ch. 1), it suggests that he was still active as a viol player in the early eighteenth century. But he was not a member of the music club that met at the Mermaid Tavern around 1690, or its successor, active a quarter of a century later.[88] Nevertheless,

---

[82] *Alumni Oxonienses: the Members of the University of Oxford, 1500–1714*, comp. J. Foster (Oxford, 1888; repr. 1968), 1073; *VdGSIM*, ii. 155–8, where it is asserted wrongly that Noble was a singing-man at Christ Church and that it is bound up with a copy of Simpson's *Compendium of Practical Music*. For John Withy, see *VdGSIM*, ii. 10–12.

[83] Foster, *Alumni Oxonienses*, 861.

[84] *VdGSIM*, ii. 138–43; ME: F. Withy, *Divisions for Solo Viol*, ed. P. Connelly (Sydney, 1998).

[85] Rawson, 'From Olomouc to London', ii. 209, R1109.

[86] *VdGSIM*, ii. 12

[87] Information from Robert Rawson and John Cunningham. See also Rawson, 'From Olomouc to London', ii. 376. For Edward Withy, see *VdGSIM*, ii. 10–11.

[88] M. Crum, 'An Oxford Music Club, 1690–1719', *Bodleian Library Record*, 9 (1974), 83–99.

the music owned by the later group, including vocal music by Carissimi, Bassani, Henry and Daniel Purcell, Pepusch, and Galliard, trio sonatas by Corelli, Bonporti, Pez, Bononcini, and Haym, and concertos by Albinoni, Dall'Abaco, and Vivaldi, would have needed string bass instruments – more likely at that period to have been viols rather than violoncellos, assuming that the players were amateurs.

❧ Cambridge

CAMBRIDGE, like Oxford, had a 'public professor of music', established in 1684 for Nicholas Staggins, though it did not have an established and endowed music school with regular music meetings, nor, it seems, the equivalent of less formal meetings such as those organised in Oxford.[89] Nevertheless, in 1653 the poet and Cambridge graduate Nicholas Hooke published an extravagant tribute to the viol player John Lillie, 'Musick-Master in Cambridge', as a leading figure in the town's musical life.[90] This was not just local pride: in 1656 Sir Peter Leycester of Tabley House in Cheshire listed 'Mr. Lilly for the sixe=stringe treble' among 'the most excellent in curious handling of the Instruments of moderne English Musicians'.[91]

Thomas Mace (1612/13–?1706) was another prominent Cambridge viol player. He became a singing man at Trinity College in 1635 and remained in Cambridge for the rest of his long life. His *Musick's Monument* is mostly concerned with the lute, though the section on the viol includes three lyra-viol pieces (with treble and bass parts in staff notation for the first),[92] and there are also manuscript lyra-viol pieces by him. He described himself in a 1690 advertisement as 'a Deaf Person Teacheth MUSICK to *Perfection*' and explained that 'by reason of his great Age, v. 77. is come to Town' to sell his 'whole Stock of *Rich Musical Furniture*'.[93] The instruments were a chamber organ, 'a pair of fair, large-siz'd *Consort Viols*, chiefly fitted for That, or *Consort* Use; *and 'tis great pity they should be parted*', two

[89] C. F. Abdy Williams, *A Short Historical Account of the Degrees in Music at Oxford and Cambridge* (London, 1894), 37–8, 130, 156.

[90] Scholes, P., *The Puritans and Music in England and New England* (Oxford, 1934; repr. 1969), 175–6. For Lillie, see *BDECM*, ii. 725–6.

[91] Chester, Cheshire Record Office, MS DLT/B33, fol. 84v; see E. Segerman, 'A 1656 Tabley MS: on Viol Players, Cittern and Gittern', *FOMRHI Quarterly*, 46 (January 1987), 34–5, comm. 774.

[92] T. Mace, *Musick's Monument* (London, 1676; repr. 1968), 251–64.

[93] T. Mace, *An Advertisement to all Lovers of the Best Sort of Musick* ([London], 1690); CC: GB-Lbl, Harley MS 5936, fol. 129v, no. 384. There is a transcription in BurneyH, ii. 377–8.

harpsichords (one 'a *Pedal-Harpsicon*', as described in *Musick's Monument*),[94] a '*Dyphone*' (a strange combination of '*Theorbo* and *French Lute*', also described in *Musick's Monument*),[95] and 'several other *Theorbo's, Lutes* and *Viols*, very good'. Mace advertised unsold copies of *Musick's Monument* as well as his music library: 'Great Store of *Choice Collections* of the Works of the *most Famous Master-Composers*, that have lived in these last 100 Years, as Latin, English, Italian and some French'. While he was in London he offered to teach 'The *Theorbo*, the *French Lute*, and the *Viol*, in all their Excellent Ways and Uses; as also *Composition*, together with the *Knack* of procuring *Invention* to Young Composers'.

Francis North (1637–85) was a probable pupil of Lillie or Mace. He was at St John's College between 1653 and 1655, and according to his brother Roger 'began his use of Musick' there, 'learning to play on the base violl', and 'becoming 'one of the neatest violists of his time'.[96] The clergyman, ecclesiastical scholar and collector John Covel or Colvill (1638–1722), undergraduate, fellow and eventually master of Christ's College, was also presumably a gamba player since he owned GB-Ob, Printed Book, Mus. 184.c.8.[97] It is a copy of Simpson's 1659 *Division-Violist* with a manuscript appendix that includes divisions by the royalist journalist and press censor Roger L'Estrange (1616–1704), a fellow viol player and Cambridge man from an East Anglian family, as well as three autograph pieces by Jenkins, apparently written in old age.[98] Letters written by Matthew Hutton and Thomas Ford of Buckingham to Covel in 1699–1700 concern a piece by Carissimi that Hutton had promised Covel while visiting Cambridge.[99]

Covel's music book is of interest because it was used well into the eighteenth century. When his library was auctioned in 1724 it was apparently purchased by one Richard Ramsbotham, who signed and dated it that year. Ramsbotham added a sequence of music in the treble clef, including the parts of 'Six Sonatas for 2 Viols Compos'd by M[r] Christian Schickhardt being his first Opera' copied successively (pp. 146R–134R). He was clearly copying violin music (he wrote the labels

---

94   Mace, *Musick's Monument*, 235–6.

95   Ibid., 203–6.

96   *Roger North on Music*, ed. Wilson, 34.

97   For Covel, see *Cambridge under Queen Anne, Illustrated by Memoir of Ambrose Bonwicke and Diaries of Francis Burman and Zacharias Conrad von Uffenbach*, ed. J. E. B. Mayor (Cambridge, 1911), 147–52, 470–3.

98   See A. Ashbee, 'Bodleian Library, Printed Book, Mus. 184.c.8 Revisited', *The Viol*, 2 (Spring 2006), 18–21. For L'Estrange, see esp. Ashbee, '"My Fiddle is a Bass Viol": Music in the Life of Sir Roger L'Estrange', in *Sir Roger L'Estrange and the Making of Restoration Culture*, ed. A. Dunan-Page and B. Lynch (Aldershot, 2008), 149–66.

99   Willetts, 'Music from the Circle of Anthony Wood', 73, 75, pl. xxiii (c).

'Violino Primo' and 'Violino Secondo' above some of the sonatas), though he may have done so in order to play them on the bass viol using the octave-transposing convention; he presumably purchased the book because it was largely a collection of viol music. The sonatas do not come from J. C. Schickhardt's op. 1 (for recorder and continuo), and do not correspond to any known works by him.[100]

John Gostling (1650–1733) studied at St John's College between 1668 and 1675/6, was ordained in 1675, and became a minor canon at Canterbury Cathedral later that year; posts in the Chapel Royal and St Paul's Cathedral followed.[101] He was a notable bass singer, written for by Purcell, Blow and others, though he also 'played on the viol da gamba, and loved not the instrument more than Purcell hated it'.[102] We should probably be sceptical about Purcell hating the gamba, since he probably learned it as a boy in the Chapel Royal, drew on the English viol tradition for his early consort music, used it in his trio sonatas, and wrote at least one piece with gamba obbligato (Ch. 1); the anecdote seems designed to 'explain' Purcell's catch 'in Commendation of the *Viol*', 'Of all the instruments that are' z263.[103] Hawkins thought that Purcell set it 'to vex Mr. Gostling' and called it a 'mock eulogium', but if so it is extremely gentle satire, imitating the wide leaps of gamba music in the second line and a bowed-out trill in the third (Ex. 2.2).

Evidence of Gostling's interest in viol consort music is provided by the library of his son William, sold after his death in 1777; Hawkins, who prepared the catalogue, stated that it was founded on his father's collection.[104] It contains some seventeenth-century manuscripts, such as 'Fantasies, MS. Fol. 5 Books complete, by Dering, Gibbons, Lupo, &c. &c' (I/11), 'Coperario's Phantazia's, MS. 2 Books – Ditto, 24, in his own Hand-writing' (II/7), 'Lock's Fantasias, and Lature's Minuets, MS. – Lawes's Royal Concert, &c. &c.' (II/15), 'Coperario's Fantazias, MS. – Lawes, &c. Anthems and Lessons' (II/31), and three copies of Simpson's *Division-Viol* (II/24, 26, 27). Most of the manuscripts cannot be identified today, but 'Jenkins's, Purcell's, &c. &c. Sonatas and Overtures, with Kirchers extolled

[100] For Schickhardt's works, see D. Lasocki, 'Johann Christian Schickhardt (*c.* 1681–1762): a Contribution to his Biography and a Catalogue of his Works', in *Tijdschrift van de Vereniging voor Nederlandse muziekgeschiedenis*, 27 (1977), 28–55.

[101] For John Gostling, see esp. R. Ford, 'Minor Canons at Canterbury Cathedral: the Gostlings and their Colleagues', 3 vols. (PhD diss., U. of California, Berkeley, 1984), 158–324; *BDECM*, i. 498–502.

[102] HawkinsH, ii. 747.

[103] ME: H. Purcell, *Works*, 22A: *Catches*, ed. I. Spink (London, 2000), 16–17, no. 23.

[104] Langford, *A Catalogue of the Scarce, Valuable and Curious Collection of Music, Manuscript and Printed, of the Reverend and Learned William Gostling* (26, 27/5/1777); CC: GB-Lbl, Hirsch IV.1083. See also Ford, 'Minor Canons at Canterbury Cathedral', esp. 459–93, 960–1. For William Gostling, see Ford, 'Minor Canons at Canterbury Cathedral', esp. 325–459.

Ex. 2.2 Henry Purcell, 'Of all the instruments that are', z263

Sonata, MS.' (II/13) is now US-NHub, Osborn MS 515. It contains consort music by Lawes, Jenkins (including two otherwise unknown sets for treble, two lyra viols and bass and for treble and two basses), Dietrich Becker (most of *Musicalische Frühlings-Früchte*, 1668), Henry Purcell (including autographs of some otherwise unknown overtures and dances), Daniel Purcell, and others.[105] There were still three part-books in 1848, though only the bass survives today.[106] It has Kent connections: one copyist also contributed to US-NH, Filmer 7 (from the collection of the Filmer family of East Sutton in Kent), and another was Robert Wren, organist of Canterbury Cathedral 1675–91.[107] It was probably used by Gostling and his friends in late seventeenth-century Canterbury.

A later Cambridge viol player, the theologian and historian Conyers Middleton (1683–1750), suggests that there was still tuition available there around 1700: he studied at Trinity College from 1699, became a fellow in 1705, was ordained in 1708, and became university librarian in 1721. However, when Zacharias Conrad von Uffenbach visited Cambridge in 1710 he recorded that there were 'no professional musicians' at the weekly music club at Christ's College, 'but simply bachelors, masters and doctors of music, who perform'; he thought the music 'both vocal and instrumental' very poor.[108] There are references to Middleton's love of music in the writings of his friends and acquaintances. John Nichols associated it with the period of his celebrated conflict with Richard Bentley (master of Trinity College and professor of divinity), when 'his attention was more devoted to musick than to study'.[109] Middleton was among those Cambridge academics created doctors of divinity during George I's visit in 1717; Bentley had attempted to extract a fee for the privilege, sparking off a row that lasted nearly a decade. Nichols added: 'Dr. Bentley, who was no great friend to musick, gave Dr. Middleton the disgraceful epithet of "fiddling Conyers," from his playing not unfrequently upon the violin.' According to the antiquary William Cole, Middleton's third marriage in 1747 to Ann Wilkins revived his musical interests:

---

[105] See R. Ford, 'Osborn MS 515: a Guardbook of Restoration Instrumental Music', *Fontes artis musicae*, 30 (1983), 174–84. For the Henry Purcell pieces, see esp. Shay and Thompson, *Purcell Manuscripts*, 292–4. ME: H. Purcell, *Works*, 31: *Fantazias and Miscellaneous Instrumental Music*, ed. T. Dart, rev. M. Tilmouth, A. Browning, and P. Holman (London, 2/1990), xiv–xv.

[106] Holman, *Henry Purcell*, 63.

[107] For Wren, see W. Shaw, *The Succession of Organists of the Chapel Royal and the Cathedrals of England and Wales from c. 1538* (Oxford, 1991), 47; Ford, 'Osborn MS 515', 175.

[108] *Cambridge under Queen Anne*, ed. Mayor, 133.

[109] J. Nichols, *Literary Anecdotes of the Eighteenth Century*, 9 vols. (London, 1812–15; repr. 1966), v. 405–23, at 406.

few people played better than herself on the harpsichord, a talent that catched Dr Middleton's attentions as much, or more perhaps, than anything else; for he was immoderately fond of music, and was himself a performer on the violin; and there were few weeks passed that he had not a general concert at his house, and every evening a private one, where himself and wife and niece did not perform.[110]

Horace Walpole, a friend from student days, recalled that Middleton played on 'the bass viol'.[111]

◈ *The Inns of Court and Continental Universities*

OXFORD and Cambridge were restricted to Anglicans in the eighteenth century, so the families of dissenters had to send their children to universities elsewhere. Thus Dudley Ryder (1691–1756), the grandson of a nonconformist minister, went to Edinburgh and Leiden before starting legal studies at the Middle Temple in 1713; he eventually became Chief Justice of the King's Bench. He is best known for his student diary, started in June 1715 and kept up for more than a year.[112] We learn from it that he played the viol and the 'flute' (probably still the recorder). He used his instruments to amuse himself in his room when he did not feel like studying, and occasionally made music with friends. Much of what he played was probably quite simple – on 22 August 1715 he played 'two or three tunes on the viol' – though he also accompanied vocal music: he 'played over one anthem and sung with it to the bass' in a session with his cousin Joseph Billio on 29 August, and 'Played upon my viol and sung some of my Italian songs' on 10 September; he realised that his sight-singing skills were weak, needing 'some other music to guide my voice and ear'.

At the time Ryder was having regular lessons with 'Mr. Cynelum', his 'viol master' – presumably another sighting of the London Sainte-Colombe. Sainte-Colombe clearly had a good effect on his playing. On 22 July 1715, shortly after his first lesson, he wrote that his friend Jeremiah Burroughs had 'much more command of the viol than I have, [and] plays with more freedom and ease', while after a lesson on 18 October he complained of the 'great difficulty' he had drawing 'a soft and fine note' – still a familiar problem today. Nevertheless, by

---

[110] *The Yale Edition of Horace Walpole's Correspondence*, 15: *Horace Walpole's Correspondence with Sir David Dalrymple, Conyers Middleton ...*, ed. W. S. Lewis, C. H. Bennett and A. G. Hoover (London, 1952), 291–315, at 310.

[111] Ibid., 293.

[112] I. Woodfield, 'Dudley Ryder, 1715–1716: Extracts from the Diary of a Student Viol Player', *JVdGSA*, 21 (1984), 64–8.

19 April 1716 he wrote after a lesson: 'I was never so well pleased with my own performance as today. I am in hopes I shall be able to play delicately upon it and touch it finely', and on 19 October he 'played upon my viol; pleased myself very much'. In the later stages he became keen to improve his general musical education. On 7 March 1716 he 'played upon my viol endevouring to learn to play over the several keys and voluntaries upon each of them, which will give me a much greater relish of music and make more fit to play lessons', while on 25 April he 'Read some of the book in which the grounds of the bass viol is taught and the method of playing divisions and composing' – evidently a copy of Simpson's *Division-Viol*. He had also begun to take part in more ambitious music making. On 27 March he took part in impromptu performances of 'French opera songs' (including an excerpt from Lully's *Psyché*) with a French singer, two recorders and bass viol (played by an unnamed silk weaver), and on 20 August he played 'some music set for two viols' with Burroughs. Interestingly, the viol is the only bass instrument ever mentioned: there is no sign of lutes or keyboards.

Ryder may have started the viol while he was in the Netherlands, as Peregrine Hyde Osborne did, and the same is probably true of Gabriel James Maturin (1700–46). Maturin was the son and grandson of Huguenot ministers, was born in Utrecht, and subsequently moved with his family to Ireland. He studied at Trinity College, Dublin between 1718 and 1725, was subsequently ordained in the Church of Ireland, and was elected Dean of St Patrick's Cathedral, Dublin in November 1745, succeeding Jonathan Swift.[113] As a governor and secretary of the board of Mercer's Hospital and a member of the Charitable Musical Society, Maturin was involved with the charity concerts Handel gave in Dublin, including the first performance of *Messiah* on 13 April 1742.[114] The Charitable Musical Society grew out of a music club founded in Dublin in about 1710. It built the Great Music Hall in Fishamble Street (where *Messiah* was performed), and used it to give public concerts. Brian Boydell suggested that the society also continued to 'hold convivial musical evenings in the more private and intimate surroundings of the Bull's head Tavern'.[115] It was there, presumably, that Maturin

---

[113] *Alumni Dublinienses: a Register of the Students, Graduates, Professors, and Provosts of Trinity College in the University of Dublin (1593–1860)*, ed. G. D. Burtchaell and T. U. Sadleir (Dublin, 2/1935), 563; *Clergy of Dublin and Glendalough: Biographical Succession Lists*, comp. J. B. Leslie, rev. W. J. R. Wallace (Belfast, 2001), 881 (Kerry Houston and Triona O'Hanlon).

[114] See esp. H. Townsend, *An Account of the Visit of Handel to Dublin, with Incidental Notices of his Life and Character* (Dublin, 1852), 29–71, 112–17, esp. 66; B. Boydell, *A Dublin Musical Calendar, 1700–1760* (Dublin, 1988), 74–86.

[115] Boydell, *A Dublin Musical Calendar*, esp. 267–9.

played the 'base viol' mentioned in the advertisement for the sale of his effects in 1747.[116]

There were other viol players in London's legal circles. Thomas Edwards (d. 1757), later a poet and literary editor, was studying at Lincoln's Inn when he promised a Revd William Jones on 22 November 1723 to send 'the Base Viol ... as soon as I can have it fitted up to my liking'.[117] He wrote in a subsequent undated letter:

> I believe musical Instruments when they fall into the hands of the ignorant suffer as much as the Roman Empire did by the inundation of the Goths & Vandals. I have done my best towards recovering the Viol which I have here sent from its barbarity & if it is polish'd enough to be acceptable to you it will answer my expectations. I have a great love for music though I cannot touch any instrument and therefore am glad that this if it be worth your acceptance has now a Master that will make so good a Use of it.

It is not clear what he had done to recover the viol from barbarity, or how he was able to do so without playing it himself, though the references to the Roman Empire and the Goths and Vandals suggest that it was a gamba – an instrument perceived to be in decline.

Most of our information about John Immyns (*c*. 1700–1764) comes from Hawkins.[118] He was 'an attorney by profession', was a member of the Academy of Ancient Music, and founded the Madrigal Society in 1741; he is best known today as an antiquarian (Ch. 9). He 'had a cracked counter-tenor voice, and played upon the flute, the viol da gamba, the violin, and the harpsichord, but on none of them well'. He had been 'a great beau' in his younger days, but was 'guilty of some indiscretions, which proved an effectual bar to success in his profession, and reduced him to the necessity of becoming a clerk to an attorney in the city'. Attorneys were on the lowest rung of the legal ladder: they practiced in common law courts and did not need a university education. Hawkins, who had been one in his youth, described them as 'Men of low extraction, domestic servants, and clerks to eminent lawyers' whose 'broken fortunes drive, or a confidence in their abilities tempts to seek a maintenance in it'.[119] They could join the Inns of Chancery, which (like the four Inns of Court, to which they were attached)

---

[116] *The Dublin Journal*, 6–10/1/1747 (John Cunningham). See Boydell, *A Dublin Musical Calendar*, 109.

[117] GB-Ob, MS 1007 (David Hunter).

[118] HawkinsH, ii. 886–7.

[119] P. Scholes, *The Life and Activities of Sir John Hawkins, Musician, Magistrate, and Friend of Johnson* (London, 1953), 4.

would have provided opportunities for young people of slender means to receive musical instruction. Immyns 'lived some years in extreme poverty' until a friend obtained him the post of lutenist of the Chapel Royal, succeeding John Shore (d. 1752).[120] Hawkins added that he learned the lute, tablature and figured bass from *Musick's Monument*.

This throws light on the activities of Edward Ferrar (1671–1730), another musical attorney. Edward was the grandson of John Ferrar, the founder with his brother Nicholas of the religious household at Little Gidding in Huntingdonshire, famous today from T. S. Eliot's *Four Quartets*. Two of his elder brothers, Thomas, rector of Little Gidding and two nearby parishes, and Basil, a grocer in Stamford, were involved in a pioneering music club in Stamford in the 1690s, and all three seem to have been involved in collecting or copying a music collection that formed part of the Ferrar family papers, bequeathed to Magdalene College, Cambridge in 1797; it was mostly transferred to GB-Cfm around 1915.[121] Edward seems to have been the copyist of most of the gamba music, much of it in MU. MS 647. He also probably assembled the collection of prints, including *Aires & Symphonys for ye Bass Viol* (MU. 1172); the unique bass part of *Select Lessons for the Bass Viol of Two Parts, Collected by our Best Viollist out of the Works of that Great Master Giovanni Schenk* (MU. 882), a selection printed by Walsh in 1703 from Schenck's op. 6;[122] and William Gorton's *Choice Collection of New Ayres* (MU. 1002–3).

Edward Ferrar spent his working life as an attorney in Huntingdon, building Ferrar House, a fine redbrick house that still stands in George Street; it was enlarged by his son Edward junior, also a Huntingdon lawyer. He was often in London: letters written in 1701, 1702 and 1703 find him at the Bolt and Tun Inn off Fleet Street, and he wrote from that address as late as 24 November 1716.[123] It was in London, presumably, that he acquired much of his music, and, perhaps, where he learned the viol; he may have been a pupil of Benjamin Hely in London in

[120] HawkinsH, ii. 733. For Immyns in the Chapel Royal, see D. Burrows, *Handel and the English Chapel Royal* (Oxford, 2005), 570.

[121] B. White, '"A Pretty Knot of Musical Friends": the Ferrar Brothers and a Stamford Music Club in the 1690s', in *Music in the British Provinces 1690–1914*, ed. R. Cowgill and P. Holman (Aldershot, 2007), 9–44; P. Holman, 'Continuity and Change in English Bass Viol Music: the Case of Fitzwilliam MU. MS 647', *VGSJ*, 1 (2007), 20–50. See also 'Introduction / Finding List', in *The Ferrar Papers 1590–1790 in Magdalene College, Cambridge*, ed. D. Ransome [CD-ROM edition] (Wakefield, 1992).

[122] RISM A/I S 1449, 1455. See also W. C. Smith, *A Bibliography of the Musical Works Published by John Walsh during the Years 1695–1720* (Oxford, 2/1968), 40–1, no. 136.

[123] *The Ferrar Papers*, nos. 1634, 1635, 1637, 1647–9, 1653, 1913.

1690s (Ch. 1). To judge from MU. MS 647, Edward mostly played solo music on his viol, much of it in arrangements, including tunes from Purcell's theatre music, movements from Matteis's *Ayrs for the Violin*, popular tunes from D'Urfey's *Pills to Purge Melancholy*, and, in the latest layer, several Handel minuets probably taken from publications of 1728 and 1729 – suggesting that he was still active shortly before his death.

There is also ensemble music in the collection, including the 1703 Walsh reprint of William Williams's trio sonatas (MU. 524–7), and manuscripts of theatre suites by John Eccles, John Lenton and ?Thomas Tollett (MU. MSS 640, 642 and 646), though they may have been used by Basil, Thomas and the Stamford music club rather than by Edward. Edward does not seem to have been a member of the Stamford club: he does not feature in most of their letters concerning music. Huntingdon, about thirty miles from Stamford, was presumably too far to attend regular meetings. Thomas complained in an undated letter of (probably) February 1694 that 'We are in extreme want of a Bass Viol', telling his correspondent, the Revd Henry Bedell of Southwick in Northamptonshire: 'if you can procure one for us you will much oblige the whole Consort'.[124] For Edward Ferrar, like Dudley Ryder and doubtless many others, the viol was essentially an instrument for solitary amusement. In his fondness for arrangements, borrowing music from fashionable genres such as Italian opera and theatre music, violin music and popular song, he was a man of his time.

❧ Artisans and Tradesmen

THE third category of gamba-playing amateurs is the smallest and most interesting: it was unusual at the time for artisans or tradesmen to become sufficiently educated and engaged in art music to take up a complex and relatively expensive instrument. Yet it did happen. A striking example is the coal merchant and concert promoter Thomas Britton (1644–1714). He was of humble origins and came to London from his native Northamptonshire to become apprenticed to a small-coal merchant in Clerkenwell; he had started his business there by 1677.[125] It is not clear how Britton became interested in music, came to take up the viol, or start his famous concerts, though the journalist Ned Ward wrote that his music club 'was at first begun, or at least confirmed by *Sir Roger-le-Strange*, many Years before his Knighthood' – L'Estrange was knighted in

---

[124] White, 'A Pretty Knot of Musical Friends', 32–3.

[125] See esp. *The Remains of Thomas Hearne, Reliquiae Hearnianae*, comp. J. Bliss, ed. J. Buchanan-Brown (London and Fontwell, 1966), 165–7; C. A. Price, 'The Small Coal Cult', *MT*, 119 (1978), 1032–4.

1685.[126] He added that L'Estrange was 'a very musical Gentleman, and had a tolerable Perfection of the Base-Viol, a very fashionable Instrument of those Days', and that he and 'other ingenious Gentlemen, who were lovers of the *Muses*' frequented his concerts mainly because of 'the unexpected Genius to Books and Musick that they happened to find in their smutty Acquaintance, and the profound Regard that he had in general to all Manner of Literature'. Britton presumably prospered sufficiently to afford to pay for musical instruction – according to Ward he was 'Master enough of Musick to play his Part tolerably well, upon several instruments' – and he assembled a notable collection of music and instruments.

Hawkins wrote that Britton's concert room was above his coal store in Clerkenwell, that among the performers were J. C. Pepusch (corroborated by Pepusch's D major trio sonata 'called Smalcoal' (Cook 2:014), GB-Lbl, Add. MS 64965, fols. 32v–34),[127] Handel, the violinist and recorder player John Banister junior, the organist Philip Hart, and the violinist Obadiah Shuttleworth; Britton 'frequently played the viol da gamba in his own concert'.[128] His music library, 'mostly pricked by himself', according to Thomas Hearne, was auctioned after his death 'for near an hundred pounds'.[129] It included a vast amount of instrumental music of all types, including some lots of early seventeenth-century consort music such as 'Five books of Pavans, Ayres, &c. neatly bound' (32), '2 sets of fancies of 3 and 4 parts by Ferrabosco, Lupo, and other excellent authors.' (59), and '6 sets ditto [of books] for [?to] the organ by Bird, Bull, Gibbons, &c.' (127).[130] He also owned music with solo gamba parts, including two copies of Simpson's *Division-Violist* (42, 43), '12 Sonatas by Fiorenzo a Kempis for a violin, and viol da gamba and bass' (54), 'Hely's Sonatas for 3 viols, and ditto by several authors' (94), 'A great collection of divisions on grounds' (lot 128), and 'Simpson's Months and Seasons' (160), the virtuosic sets of fantasias and fantasia suites for treble, two bass viols and continuo. The twenty-seven instruments, 'sold for fourscore pounds' according to Hearne,[131] included eleven violins, two piccolo violins, two violas, and two bass violins, but no complete sets of viols. 'A fine viol by Mr. Baker of Oxford'

[126] E. Ward, 'The Small-Coal-Man's Musick Club', *A Compleat and Humorous Account of all the Remarkable Clubs and Societies in the Cities of London and Westminster* (London, 7/1756), 299–306, at 300–1; CC: *ECCO*, ESTC T117498.

[127] D. F. Cook, 'The Life and Works of Johann Christoph Pepusch (1667–1752), with Special Reference to his Dramatic Works and Cantatas', 2 vols. (PhD diss., King's College, U. of London, 1982), ii. 92.

[128] HawkinsH, ii. 788–92.

[129] *The Remains of Thomas Hearne*, comp. Bliss, ed. Buchanan-Brown, 166.

[130] The catalogue is lost, though there is a seemingly complete transcription in HawkinsH, ii. 792–3. See also Coral, 'Music in English Auction Sales', esp. 57–9.

[131] *The Remains of Thomas Hearne*, comp. Bliss, ed. Buchanan-Brown, 166.

(20), 'Another excellent one, bellied by Mr. Norman' (21), and 'Another, said to be the neatest that Jay ever made' (22) – were presumably basses. If Britton performed his viol consort music it was presumably with violins playing the upper parts.

Another Midlands viol player who made his fortune in London was the apothecary and botanist James Sherard (1666–1738).[132] Sherard was born at Bushby near Leicester and was apprenticed in 1682 to Charles Watts, curator of the Apothecaries' Garden in Chelsea (now the Physic Garden). He quickly established himself after setting up his own business in London, becoming a fellow of the Royal Society in 1706, and was able to retire as an apothecary before he was sixty. His later years were mostly spent studying botany and developing his famous botanic gardens at Eltham in Kent; botany was the life-long interest of his elder brother William (1659–1728). As executor of William's will James was involved in the negotiations that led to the endowment of the Sherardian chair of botany at Oxford. As a reward the university made him a doctor of medicine in 1731, and the following year he became a fellow of the Royal Society of Physicians.

Until recently James was mostly known to musicians for his two sets of Corellian trio sonatas opp. 1 and 2, published by Roger in Amsterdam in 1701 and (probably) 1716.[133] Op. 1 was dedicated to Wriothesley Russell, second Duke of Bedford, who went on the grand tour between 1697 and 1699, accompanied by William for part of the time.[134] James seems to have been drawn into the musical circle at Southampton House, Russell's London residence; he mentioned in the dedication that the duke had done him 'the Honour to hear them perform'd', presumably with his household musicians Nicola Cosimi (violin) and Nicola Haym (violoncello). Hawkins tells us that James 'played finely on the violin',[135] so he may have been the other violinist, though his music library, now in the Music School collection of GB-Ob, suggests that he also played the gamba.

The provenance and full extent of Sherard's library has yet to be established, though it was surprisingly cosmopolitan for an English amateur – especially someone who apparently had not ventured abroad by the time most of it was

---

[132] For Sherard, see esp. M. Tilmouth, 'James Sherard, an English Amateur Composer', *ML*, 47 (1966), 313–22.

[133] Ibid., 316–18. Op. 2 is dated *c.* 1711 in *GMO*, though its plate number, 398, suggests that it was published in 1716; see R. Rasch, '"La famoso mano di Monsieur Roger": Antonio Vivaldi and his Dutch Publishers', *Informazioni e studi Vivaldiani*, 17 (1996), 89–135, at 96–8.

[134] G. S. Thomson, *The Russells in Bloomsbury, 1669–1771* (London, 1940), 82–93; Tilmouth, 'James Sherard', 315–16.

[135] HawkinsH, ii. 806.

assembled.[136] It includes sets of trio sonatas evidently copied in London by Sher-ard himself and others, including MSS Mus. Sch. D.252 (his op. 2 with autograph revisions and corrections), D.254 (Purcell, Blow, Legrenzi, Bononcini, and other Italian composers), D.256 (Lonati and Colista), and D.255 (Corelli's op. 2 with a bass part labelled 'Bass de viol' instead of Corelli's *violone*).[137] There are also many prints of Italian trio sonatas and other instrumental ensemble music ranging in date from 1629 to 1692, and manuscripts of more recent vocal and instrumen-tal music, much of it from Rome, apparently collected by William during Rus-sell's grand tour. James wrote in the dedication to his op. 1 that 'by my Brother's attendance on *your Grace* abroad, I was furnish'd with Books, and other Materi-alls, which gave me the first tast and acquaintance with the *Italian Musick*'.

Less expected are several related groups of German manuscripts, including sacred music and a five-part sonata by Samuel Capricornus, apparently copied in the Stuttgart area, sacred music and instrumental ensemble music from Saxony by J. P. Krieger, Kuhnau, Schelle, and Rosenmüller, and sacred music and bass viol music apparently from Lübeck, some copied by Jacob Pagendarm (1646–1706), cantor at the Marienkirche from 1679.[138] Margaret Crum suggested that Sherard acquired them either from his brother (the grand tour took in Germany) or from J. W. Franck, who settled in London around 1690; the collection includes a piece by Franck.[139] However, Peter Wollny argues that the collection was assem-bled rather later, between 1690 and 1710.[140] One of the Lübeck manuscripts, MS Mus. Sch. D.249, nos. 18–23, fols. 104–133v, contains a set of six sonatas by gamba and continuo by Schenck (versions of op. 2, nos. 2 and 4), Johann Martin Radeck, David Adam (or Arnold) Baudringer, Buxtehude (BuxWV268 in D major), and

[136] Identifications of items from Sherard's library are made in the 'Revised Descrip-tions', GB-Ob, Music Reading Room, MUS.AC.4, and in the typescript of Margaret Crum's unpublished lecture, 'James Sherard and the Oxford Music School Collection', given to the Oxford Bibliographical Society in the early 1980s (Peter Ward-Jones and Harry Johnstone).

[137] Shay and Thompson, *Purcell Manuscripts*, 114–17; S. Mangsen, 'The Dissemina-tion of Pre-Corellian Duo and Trio Sonatas in Manuscript and Printed Sources: a Preliminary Report', in *The Dissemination of Music: Studies in the History of Music Publishing*, ed. H. Lenneberg (Lausanne, 1994), 71–105, at 96–7.

[138] M. Crum, 'Music from St Thomas's, Leipzig, in the Music School Collection at Oxford', in *Festschrift Rudolf Elvers zum 60. Geburtstag*, ed. E. Herttrich and H. Schneider (Tutzing, 1985), 97–101; P. Wollny, 'A Collection of Seventeenth-Century Vocal Music at the Bodleian Library', *Schütz-Jahrbuch*, 15 (1993), 77–108. For Pagendarm, see esp. K. J. Snyder, *Dieterich Buxtehude, Organist in Lübeck* (New York, 1987), 88–9, 91.

[139] Crum, 'Music from St Thomas's, Leipzig', 100–1.

[140] Wollny, 'A Collection of Seventeenth-Century Vocal Music', 87–8.

anonymous (D minor, also possibly by Buxtehude), while another, D.253, has four suites for two bass viols by Peter Grecke.[141] Baudringer and Grecke worked with Buxtehude in Lübeck while Radeck was a Copenhagen organist. Sherard's ownership is shown by his annotation 'Viola di gamba Soli' on D.249, fol. 119v, and versions in his hand of the D major and E major Grecke suites in D.253.

There are also at least eighteen gamba works by Gottfried Finger in MSS Mus. Sch. C.93, D.228 and D.249, all apparently either autograph or in Sherard's hand (Ch. 1). In one case, the A major/Bb major sonata for *scordatura* bass viol and continuo RI144, the gamba part (D.228, no. 20, fols. 103v–104) is autograph while Sherard copied both parts (D.249, no. 29, fols. 153–156v). In another, the D major Sonata or suite R176 for two bass viols (with a missing continuo part), the two viol parts were started by the composer and continued by Sherard (D.249, no. 12, fols. 66–69v), demonstrating that they were working together.[142] Also, Sherard wrote 'Mr. Finger' on Mus. Sch. D.253, fol. 26v, the cover of one of the Grecke suites, perhaps indicating the source of the manuscript. All in all, it looks as if Finger was Sherard's viol teacher in the 1690s and supplied him with copies of his own music. Sherard seems to have modelled his mature music hand on Finger's, making them difficult to distinguish. Perhaps Finger supplied Sherard with the rest of his German manuscripts, either before he left London in 1701 or through an intermediary later.

It is well known that Daniel Defoe (?1660–1731) was interested in music, though it may come as a surprise that he was a viol player. He came from a nonconformist family in London, was educated at the dissenting academy in Newington Green, and was engaged in various business ventures before becoming a writer. The evidence of his viol-playing comes in two publications. In *Augusta triumphans* (1728), which proposed the establishment of a music academy based on Christ's Hospital, he wrote: 'I have been a Lover of the Science [music] from my Infancy, and in my younger days was accounted no despicable Performer on the Viol and Lute, then much in Vogue'.[143] Much the same thing was said in a

---

[141] ME: *Three Stylus Phantasticus Sonatas for Bass Viol and Bc, by Baudringer, Radeck and Anon.*, ed. S. Heinrich (Oxford, 2005); D. Buxtehude, *Violadagamba Solo: Sonata D-Dur für Viola da Gamba und Basso Continuo BuxWV268*, ed. L. and G. von Zadow (Heidelberg, 2005); *Lübecker Violadagamba Solo: Sonate D-Moll für Viola da Gamba und Basso Continuo*, ed. L. and G. von Zadow (Heidelberg, 2006); P. Grecke, *Two Suites for Two Bass Viols*, ed. D. Beecher (Hannacroix, NY, 1998). See also Snyder, *Dieterich Buxtehude*, 300, 371.

[142] A page of the first viol part, fol. 66, is illustrated in Rawson, 'From Olomouc to London', 40.

[143] B. Trowell, 'Daniel Defoe's Plan for a Music Academy at Christ's Hospital, with some Notes on his Attitudes to Music', in *Source Materials and the Interpretation*

letter to *The Weekly Journal* for 18 December 1725. It is anonymous, but Elizabeth Gibson has convincingly attributed it to Defoe:

> I am an Old Stager in this Art, and tho' I have the Dissatisfaction of seeing the Viol, to which I have serv'd a thirty Years Apprenticeship; excluded our modern [Musick], yet I am so obstinate to think that it has its Charms, and so far from approving of this Way of confining Musick to two or three Instruments, that, I think, a certain Master deserves Thanks of the musical World for introducing, in one of his late Operas, the Welsh Harp, which, for many Reasons, merits great Encouragement, giving to the Performer a peculiar Grace; and, as it is compleat, so in Harmony to none inferior.[144]

The late opera was Handel's *Giulio Cesare* (1724), which has parts for gamba, theorbo and harp in Act II (Ch. 3). If Defoe really had played the viol for thirty years by 1725, then he started it in the middle of the 1690s, when he was beginning to make his name as a writer. Nothing has come to light of his own musical activities at that time or later.[145]

The most unexpected viol player is the clock maker John Harrison (1693–1776), famous today for making timekeepers accurate enough to enable longitude to be established at sea. He was the son of a carpenter employed at Nostell Priory in Yorkshire, and moved as a child to Barrow upon Humber, where his father's employer, Sir Rowland Winn, had another estate. Asides in Harrison's 'An Account of the Discovery of the Scale of Musick' (1775) suggest that his musical education came from the parish church choir at Barrow; he mentioned 'the Experience of 20 Years' leading a psalmody choir.[146] The Cambridge mathematician Robert Smith wrote in 1749 that Harrison had used a monochord to adjust the frets on his 'base viol',[147] and Harrison referred to his viol ('the King of Instruments') a number of times in his own rather confused account of the system.[148] It had six strings, was fretted, and he used it to demonstrate perfect tuning: 'But I may here notify, or certify, that an Organist, who upon hearing me play some Tunes upon my Viol, owned that it spoke to Perfection itself', and again: 'Now here it may be proper to notify, that no Beatings are to be heard from

of Music: a Memorial Volume to Thurston Dart, ed. I. Bent (London, 1981), 403–27, at 407.

144 Gibson, *The Royal Academy of Music*, 388–9.

145 For a survey, see Trowell, 'Daniel Defoe's Plan', 414–24.

146 J. Harrison, *A Description Concerning such Mechanism as will Afford a Nice or True Mensuration of Time* (London, 1775), 67–108, at 85; CC: *ECCO*, ESTC N006209. See also Kassler, *The Science of Music in Britain*, i. 453–6.

147 Kassler, *The Science of Music in Britain*, i. 454.

148 Harrison, *A Description*, 78, 92–5, 96.

a Viol when truly fretted, or rightly in Order, no, nor, if you please, from two Viols, playing slowly a Psalm-Tune and its Bass'. It is not clear how his system worked on the viol, nor for that matter when or where he first encountered the instrument.

Nathanael St André (1679/80–1776), surgeon and anatomist of Swiss origin, is probably the most notorious gamba player discussed in this book. He is mainly known today for his role in the affair of the imposter Mary Toft, who supposedly gave birth to rabbits at Guildford in 1726, and for eloping with the wife of his friend Samuel Molyneux, MP for Exeter, on the night of Molyneux's death. A posthumous biography stated that he 'was early interested in music, for he played upon some musical instrument as soon as he was old enough to handle one, to entertain his benefactors', and added: 'Whether anatomy, surgery, knowledge of music, or his performance on the Viol de Gambo, on which he was the greatest master, got him the intimacy with Mr. Molyneux, is not easy to determine'.[149] St André mentioned 'my Printed and Manuscript Musick together with all my Musical Instruments' in his will.[150] His biography also mentions that his sister taught French 'at Chelsea boarding-school'. It is not known whether they were related to the St André who provided the choreography for Shadwell's *Psyche* (1675),[151] though Nathanael was also a dancing master and is depicted as one with a violin under his arm in *Cunicularii, or The Wise Men of Godalmin in Consultation*, an etching attributed to Hogarth satirising the Toft affair.[152]

❧ *Female Viol Players*

IT has been asserted that the gamba was a male instrument at the time,[153] but this is not so. It was the only single-line instrument considered suitable for upper-class women: its soft and plaintive voice fitted in with contemporary notions of female reticence, it did not involve contorting the face or placing phallic objects in the mouth, as wind instruments did, and it could be played

---

[149] *The Gentleman's Magazine*, 51 (July 1781), 320–2, at 320.

[150] GB-Lna, PROB 11/1019, fols. 94v–98, at 95v–96.

[151] *BDA*, xiii. 171–2.

[152] F. Haslam, *From Hogarth to Rowlandson: Medicine in Art in Eighteenth-Century Britain* (Liverpool, 1996), 28–51. The etching is not accepted as genuine in recent Hogarth scholarship, see J. Barlow, *The Enraged Musician: Hogarth's Musical Imagery* (Aldershot, 2005), x.

[153] S. McVeigh, *Concert Life in London from Mozart to Haydn* (Cambridge, 1993), 87; M. Rosenthal, *The Art of Thomas Gainsborough* (New Haven, CT, 1999), 167. See A. Otterstedt, *The Viol: History of an Instrument*, trans. H. Reiners (Kassel, 2002), esp. 84–9.

without placing the body in an ungraceful posture, as was required by the violin. Thus John Essex in 1722:

> The *Harpsicord*, *Spinnet*, *Lute* and *Base Violin*, are Instruments most agree-able to the L A D I E S: There are some others that really are unbecoming the Fair Sex; as the *Flute*, *Violin* and *Hautboy*; the last of which is too Man-like, and would look indecent in a Woman's Mouth; and the *Flute* is very improper, as taking away too much of the Juices, which are otherwise more necessarily employ'd, to promote the Appetite, and assist Digestion.[154]

Essex must have been thinking of the bass viol rather than the bass violin, which was played exclusively by men in the eighteenth century and by professionals until the 1730s. The exception that proves the rule is the Miss Marshall from Nottingham, who played a five-string violoncello in 1774 (Ch. 5), though an old woman plays one in a female trio-sonata group in Mercier's painting *Hearing* (1743–6).[155]

An objection to the viol as a female instrument was that it normally required the legs to be parted. The author of the Burwell Lute Tutor (*c.* 1660–72) claimed that it 'intangleth one in spreading the Armes and opening the Legges which doth not become man much lesse woaman'.[156] Ned Ward was thinking of the same problem when he wrote (tongue-in-cheek) that it was 'now hug'd only at Boarding-Schools, between the Knees of young Ladies, lest their Virgin Modesty otherwise should cause their Legs to grow so close together, that whenever they marry, their Bridegrooms should be puzzled to perform the nuptial Ceremony'.[157] However, the voluminous skirts of the period preserved modesty, and it was occasionally played 'side-saddle'. More gamba-playing women will be discussed in Chapter 7, and in 1889 Edward Payne stated that it was 'a favourite instrument with ladies in the last century'; he added: 'It is really a much more suitable instru-ment for ladies than the violoncello, and it is possible that in the course of time it will be revived for their use.'[158] Just over a year later Hélène Dolmetsch began playing it in public (Ch. 9).

Female gamba players sometimes figure in Restoration literature. In Shadwell's

---

[154] J. Essex, *The Young Ladies Conduct, or Rules for Education* (London, 1722), 84–5; CC: *ECCO*, ESTC T116429 (Andrew Woolley).

[155] Ingamells and Raines, 'A Catalogue of the Paintings, Drawings and Etchings of Philip Mercier', 62, pl. 5d. For female violoncellists, see esp. E. Cowling, *The Cello* (London, 1975), 79–180.

[156] M. Spring, *The Lute in Britain: a History of the Instrument and its Music* (Oxford, 2001), 421.

[157] Ward, 'The Small-Coal-Man's Musick Club', 300.

[158] E. J. Payne, 'The Viola da Gamba', *PMA*, 15 (1888–9), 91–107, at 99.

play *Epsom-Wells* (1673) Mrs Jilt was able to play 'six Lessons on the Viol *de Gambo*' before she went to London,[159] while in Vanbrugh's *The Relapse* (1697) Hoyden's education is described as follows: 'the Parson of the Parish teaches her to Play on the Base-Viol, the Clerk to sing, her Nurse to Dress, and her Father to Dance'.[160] In *The Levellers, a Dialogue between two Young Ladies, Concerning Matrimony* (1703), Politica, a tradesman's daughter, 'learned to dance and sing, to play on the Bass-Viol, Virginals, Spinnet and Guitair' at boarding school.[161] Real female players included Susanna Perwich,[162] Samuel Pepys's wife Elizabeth, his maid Mary Mercer, and an acquaintance, Sarah Jaggard.[163] Female players after 1700 are rarer, but they include Cristina Steffkins (Ch. 1), and (presumably) a certain Ann Owen, who copied Simpson's *Division-Viol* (1665) on paper made in Queen Anne's reign.[164] The subject of Aaron Hill's poem 'To Mrs. L - - -R, *playing on a Bass-Viol*' also cannot be precisely identified, though she probably belonged to the Westmoreland Lowther family.[165] Hill wrote a manuscript poem, 'To MRS. LOWTHER', in a volume of plays once owned by 'E. Lowther', dating it 'York ye 23^d of April. *1730*'.[166] Two of his published letters to Mrs Lowther are dated 20 February and 26 September 1731; 'The Reverend Mr. William Lowther' and 'Mrs. Lowther, of Scotland-Yard' subscribed to the collection.[167] Hill refers to her playing chords – PROUD of its charming *pow'r*, your tuneful *bow* / Floats o'er the *chords* majestically *slow*' – and singing to her own accompaniment: 'YOUR voice, soft rising, thro' the lengthen'd *notes*, / The marry'd harmony, united, floats; / Two charms, so join'd, that they compose but one; / Like heat and brightness, from the self-same sun'.

[159] T. Shadwell, *Epsom-Wells, a Comedy* (London, 1673), 41; CC: *EEBO*, Wing s2843.

[160] J. Vanbrugh, *The Relapse, or Virtue in Danger, being the Sequel of The Fool in Fashion, a Comedy* (London, 1697), 18; CC: *EEBO*, Wing v57.

[161] I have been unable to locate a copy, though it was reprinted in *The Harleian Miscellany, or A Collection of Scarce, Curious, and Entertaining Pamphlets and Tracts, as well in Manuscript as in Print, Found in the late Earl of Oxford's Library*, 8 vols. (London, 1744–6), v. 416–33, at 420; CC: GB-Lbl, 185.a.9.

[162] Scholes, *The Puritans and Music*, 160–2.

[163] S. Pepys, *The Diary*, ed. R. Latham and W. Matthews, 11 vols., v: *1664* (London, 1971), 53–4, 282; vii: *1666* (London, 1972), 377.

[164] R. Charteris, 'A Newly Discovered Manuscript Copy of Christopher Simpson's *The Division-Viol*', *Chelys*, 23 (1994), 47–53.

[165] A. Hill, *Works*, 4 vols. (London, 1753), iii. 32–3; CC: *ECCO*, ESTC T107059.

[166] A. E. Case, 'Aaron Hill and Thomson's *Sophonisba*', *Modern Language Notes*, 42 (1927), 175–6.

[167] Hill, *Works*, i. 56–8, 79–81.

❧ Scotland

MANY female viol players were Scottish, perhaps because the musical culture north of the border was more conservative than in England – where the harpsichord was increasingly the main female instrument. Women did not have access to most of the milieux where men encountered art music and learned instruments, so they were more likely than them to come from upper-class families, able to afford tuition at home. Thus Grisell Baillie (1692–1759) was the daughter of the landowner and politician George Baillie of Mellerstain House in Berwickshire.[168] The household accounts of her mother, Lady Grisell, record that the Edinburgh Sainte-Colombe (rendered as 'Sinckolum' and 'St. Culume') taught her teenage daughter the viol for six months in 1707, and had her viol mended; she was taught singing by the Polish-Jewish lutenist and composer James Kremberg and the harpsichord by Henry Crumden.[169] She may have played the viol as an adult: her harpsichord teacher in London between 1719 and 1721 was Pietro Giuseppe Sandoni, the author of two gamba works (Ch. 3).

There may have been viol players among the four daughters of William Ker, second Marquess of Lothian, of Newbattle Abbey in Midlothian. A Newbattle household account book for 1708 records two guineas paid 'to the viol master for two months', while an inventory of Newbattle taken in May 1764 includes 'In My Lady's Garrett … an old harpsichord and case, a viologambo, and organ'.[170] The most likely viol players were the two younger daughters, Lady Elizabeth and Lady Mary; by 1708 their elder sisters, Lady Ann and Lady Jean, were already married and had left home. As in England, some girls received their musical education in boarding schools. Sir Hugh Campbell, 15th Thane of Cawdor and Laird of Islay, wrote from Elgin to his agent in Edinburgh on 13 December 1677 about his daughter: 'Iff I fynde Maggie ane extraordinar player on the virginellis she sall have an pair of the best harpsecordis that Ingland can afford, and therefor lett hir tak much panis. I do not fancy the viola da gamboe, the siter or kittarr is mor

---

[168] See D. Johnson, *Music and Society in Lowland Scotland in the Eighteenth Century* (London, 1972), 26–7, 30–1; Goodwill, 'The Musical Involvement of the Landed Classes, 27.

[169] Household Book of Lady Grisell Baillie, i. 180, 181, transcript from photocopies of the originals at Mellerstain House, deposited in the library of the National Museums of Scotland, Edinburgh (Anthony Hicks). See also I. Woodfield, 'The Younger Sainte-Colombe in Edinburgh', *Chelys*, 14 (1985), 43–4; Goodwill, 'The Musical Involvement of the Landed Classes', 112–13, 123.

[170] C. McCart, 'The Kers and the Maules: Music in the Lives of Two Seventeenth-Century Scottish Aristocratic Families', 2 vols. (BA diss., Colchester Institute, 1988), i. 22–3.

proper.'[171] Nevertheless, in 1679 a Mr Chambers was paid £18 Scots a quarter to teach Margaret 'the violl de gambo'; £66 13s. 4d. was spent on 'a pair of virginalls' and £2 14s. on 'a musick book to Mrs. Margrat'.

Scottish manuscripts including viol music sometimes reveal the names of female owners. One containing English mid-seventeenth-century lyra-viol music, GB-Eu, Reid Library, Mus.m.1, has the names 'I.F. 1671' on the binding and 'magdlen Cockburn Iohn' on the inside front cover.[172] The tablature seems to have been written by the person, possibly the English violinist Jeffery or Jafery Banister, who also copied manuscripts from Newbattle Abbey and from Panmure House in Angus, the seat of the Maule family.[173] Another late seventeenth-century Newbattle Abbey manuscript, now lost but reportedly with the name 'W. Ker' on the flyleaf, contained a mixture of Scots and English tunes in tablature, though it is not clear whether it was intended for lute or viol, and the inclusion of tunes with titles such as 'I long for her virginitie' and 'Dance naked' suggests that it was not copied for a young girl.[174] Yet another manuscript with lyra-viol music, GB-En, Dep. 314/24, seems to have been copied partly by Lady Margaret Cochrane and her sister Helen, daughters of William, Lord Cochrane, son of the first Earl of Dundonald; Lady Helen married John Gordon, 16th Earl of Sutherland in 1680, and the manuscript has remained in the family's possession.[175]

Other missing Scottish lyra-viol manuscripts include one discovered at Scone Palace in 1937 but apparently lost in World War II,[176] and two owned by the Paisley antiquarian Andrew Blaikie in the 1820s.[177] Both Blaikie manuscripts were reportedly in the same hand, possibly that of the Glasgow musician Andrew

---

[171] *The Book of the Thanes of Cawdor: a Series of Papers Selected from the Charter Room at Cawdor, 1236–1742*, ed. C. Innes (Edinburgh, 1859), 338, 351.

[172] E. Stell, 'Sources of Scottish Instrumental Music, 1603–1707', 2 vols. (PhD diss., U. of Glasgow, 1999), 71–9, 391–8; W. Edwards, 'The Musical Sources', in *Defining Strains: the Musical Life of Scots in the Seventeenth Century*, ed. J. Porter (Oxford, 2007), 47–71, at 60–61. I am grateful to John Cunningham for providing me with a copy.

[173] McCart, 'The Kers and the Maules', esp. 53–6; P. Holman, *Four and Twenty Fiddlers: the Violin at the English Court, 1540–90* (Oxford, 2/1995), 364–6.

[174] Edwards, 'The Musical Sources', 60.

[175] Stell, 'Sources of Scottish Instrumental Music', 194–200, 456–9; Edwards, 'The Musical Sources', 65.

[176] F. Traficante, 'Music for Lyra Viol: Manuscript Sources', *Chelys*, 8 (1978–9), 4–22, at 22; Stell, 'Sources of Scottish Instrumental Music', 127–30, 421–2; Edwards, 'The Musical Sources', 56.

[177] Traficante, 'Music for Lyra Viol', 13; Stell, 'Sources of Scottish Instrumental Music', 38–46, 379–84; Edwards, 'The Musical Sources', 65–6.

Adam,[178] and contained almost the same repertory. One, dated Glasgow 1683, was owned by Lady Katherine Boyd (b. c. 1675), daughter of William, first earl of Kilmarnock. Forty pieces from the latter, dated 1692, survive in a copy made by the Dundee collector Andrew Wighton, now GB-DU, Mus. 10455. The Leyden manuscript, GB-NTu, Bell-White MS 46 (GB-En, Adv.5.2.19 is an 1843–4 copy), also has lyra-viol music copied by Andrew Adam, in the 1690s.[179] Its original binding was apparently lettered 'Pour la viole' on the spine, suggesting a French owner or copyist. These manuscripts suggest that lyra-viol music was copied in Scotland a little later than in England (Ch. 1).

We are on more certain ground with Margaret Sinkler's manuscript, GB-En, MS 3296 (formerly Glen 143(i)).[180] It was also copied by Andrew Adam and is dated 31 October 1710. It consists of tunes written in the treble clef which seem to be principally for violin: the chart entitled 'how to term your Stopps upon the treble viol according to the Gam ut or Scale or Musick' (fol. ii^v) gives first-position finger positions for an instrument tuned g–d'–a'–e'' – a late instance of 'treble viol' being used to mean the violin.[181] But another chart, entitled 'the Gam ut on the viol de gambo the consort way of playing' (fol. iii^v), gives the notes available on each string for the bass viol in ordinary tuning. Upper-class women at the time would not have played the violin, so if Margaret Sinkler played the tunes in her manuscript it was probably down the octave on the gamba. Sinkler (1688–1756) seems to have been the daughter of Henry St Clair of Herdmanston near Haddington in East Lothian; she married Sir William Baird of Newbyth in East Lothian in 1711.[182]

Among these upper-class women it comes as a surprise to encounter a viol player lower down the social scale. On 30 January 1710 Jean Chein of Huntly in Aberdeenshire offered her services as a governess to 'the much Honoured the Lady THUNDERTON' – most likely Margaret Dunbar of Thunderton House in

---

[178] Suggested by Stell, 'Sources of Scottish Instrumental Music', 43.

[179] Traficante, 'Music for Lyra Viol', 13; Stell, 'Sources of Scottish Instrumental Music', 113–23, 410–19; Edwards, 'The Musical Sources', 66; J. Robinson, 'John Leyden's Lyra Viol Manuscript in Newcastle University Library and George Farquhar Graham's Copy in the National Library of Scotland', *VdGSJ*, ii (2008), 17–57. For Adam, see esp. J. Porter, 'The Margaret Sinkler Music Book, 1710', *Review of Scottish Culture*, 16 (2003–4), 1–18, at 9.

[180] Stell, 'Sources of Scottish Instrumental Music', 42–3, 169–71; Porter, 'The Margaret Sinkler Music Book'; Edwards, 'Seventeenth-Century Scotland', 66. ME: *The Margaret Sinkler Music Book*, ed. Porter (forthcoming).

[181] For earlier English instances, see esp. Holman, *Four and Twenty Fiddlers*, 124, 136–8.

[182] Porter, 'The Margaret Sinkler Music Book', 1–3.

Elgin.[183] She claimed to 'play on the Treble and Gambo, Viol, Virginelles and Manicords, which I can do, but on no other' – that is treble and bass viols, virginals and clavichord. The last known female Scottish viol player is Anna Leith of Whitehaugh in Aberdeenshire (*c.* 1686–1738), who married William Forbes of Tolquhon in 1706. Her son, John Forbes Leith, wrote on 26 April 1779 to the poet and philosopher James Beattie that his mother 'play'd upon the Virginal and Viol d' Gambo' but that 'Family troubles untun'd her so that I knew naught of her Skill till she surpriz'd me with it in 1737 at London'.[184] He added that 'Her turn for Musick was good, and hereditary', and mentioned four family music books, two of which had belonged to his grandfather and were 'for the Lute or Guittar' (i.e. in tablature), and a third that had belonged to her. It is not clear whether that book was also in tablature, or whether she surprised her son by playing the harpsichord or the gamba.

James Maule (1658/9–1723), later fourth earl of Panmure, was an important male Scottish viol player.[185] James was in France with his younger brother Harie or Harry (1659–1734) between 1677 and 1680. While they were there they acquired a collection of vocal and instrumental music, listed in 'Ane Catollogue of Books left at Ed[inbu]r[gh] A[u]gustt 1685'.[186] It includes three or four books of solo viol music by Sainte-Colombe senior, two of which survive (GB-En, MSS 9468, 9469),[187] and three (GB-En, MSS 9465–9467) containing music by Marin Marais, including pre-publication versions of viol parts from his *Pièces de viole*, i–iii (1686 and 1689, 1701, 1711), and some not otherwise known, seemingly mostly in the composer's hand.[188] It has been said that Harie was the viol player because

183 E. Dunbar Dunbar, *Social Life in Former Days, chiefly in the Province of Moray* (Edinburgh, 1865), 15. See also 'Royal Dunbar Lineage', *Dunbar Surname DNA Project* (www.dunbardna.com).

184 H. M. Shire, 'Court Song in Scotland after 1603: Aberdeenshire, ii: the Forbes-Leith Music Books, 1611–1779', *Edinburgh Bibliographical Society Transactions*, 3/3 (1956), 165–8, at 166 (David Johnson).

185 Goodwill, 'The Musical Involvement of the Landed Classes', 24.

186 McCart, 'The Kers and the Maules', 32–4; Goodwill, 'The Musical Involvement of the Landed Classes', 161–3; P. Cadell, 'French Music in the Collection of the Earls of Panmure', in *Defining Strains*, ed. Porter, 127–37.

187 Sainte-Colombe, *Recueil de pièces pour basse de viole seule (c. 1680): facsimilés des manuscrits 9469 et 9468, National Library of Scotland, Edinburgh, Manuscrits Panmure*, intro. F.-P. Goy (Geneva, 2003).

188 S. Cheney, 'Early Autograph Manuscripts of Marin Marais', *EM*, 38 (2010), 59–72. ME: M. Marais, *The Instrumental Works*, ed. J. Hsu, ii: *Pièces de viole, second livre (1701)* (New York, 1986), 255–74; vii: *La gamme et autres morceaux de simphonie pour le violon, la viole et claveçin (1723); Unpublished Pieces from the Panmure Manuscripts* (New York, 2002), xv–xvi, 85–135, 141–4, 151–4.

in October 1680 he paid the carriage on a chest of four viols sent from Paris to Leith,[189] and a set of part-books (GB-En, MSS 9455–7) containing music for two trebles and bass by Jenkins, Christopher Simpson and others has his signature on fol. 1v of the bass book.[190] However, James wrote in his third-person autobiography that he played 'on the Bass viol de Gambo, at which he was thought a good proficient, being with the best master he was reckoned on[e] of his best scholars'.[191] The 'best master' was presumably Sainte-Colombe, so James would have been a fellow-pupil with Marais. Again, there is no evidence that he continued to play the viol in later life, though in April 1714 'Ane Bass viol w[i]t[h] a case' was in the 'big closet' at the Maules' lodgings in Edinburgh.[192]

A source of information about male viol players in Edinburgh is a document entitled 'The Order of the Instrumental Music for the Feast of St Cecilia, 22d November 1695' giving the names of the performers and the pieces performed. The document, compiled by James Christie, the 'preses' or president of the concert, is lost but was published in a diplomatic transcription by William Tytler (1711–92) together with his valuable if occasionally inaccurate commentary.[193] Tytler was an early member of the Edinburgh Musical Society, where he would have encountered many of the individuals mentioned. His article has been taken at face value by historians,[194] though I have argued that it cannot date from as early as 1695.[195] The pieces included 'Barrett's Trumpet Sonata', scored for trumpet, oboe and strings, and 'Pepulsh for 2 flutes and 2 violins' and 'Pepulsh, 2 violins and 2 haut.', both with continuo. There is a sonata by John Barrett for trumpet, oboe and strings, the overture of the suite for Baker's play *Tunbridge Walks, or The Yeomen of Kent* (1703); the string parts were published in that year,[196] but the sonata survives complete in GB-Lbl, Add. MS 49599, fols. 1–8v. Pepusch did

[189] McCart, 'The Kers and the Maules', 26; Cadell, 'French Music in the Collection of the Earls of Panmure', 135.

[190] Stell, 'Sources of Scottish Instrumental Music', 150–3; C. McCart, 'The Panmure Manuscripts: a New Look at an Old Source of Christopher Simpson's Consort Music', *Chelys*, 18 (1989), 18–29, at 19–20.

[191] Goodwill, 'The Musical Involvement of the Landed Classes', 144.

[192] Ibid., 56.

[193] W. Tytler, 'On the Fashionable Amusements and Entertainments in Edinburgh in the Last Century, with a Plan of a Grand Concert of Music on St Cecilia's Day, 1695', *Transactions of the Society of the Antiquaries of Scotland*, 1 (1792), 499–510; CC: *ECCO*, ESTC T145138. For Tytler, see *BMB*, 422, where his surname is given wrongly as 'Tyler'.

[194] For instance, R. Chambers, *Domestic Annals of Scotland from the Revolution to the Rebellion of 1745* (Edinburgh, 1861), 139–40; Johnson, *Music and Society*, 11–12.

[195] P. Holman, 'An Early Edinburgh Concert', *EMP*, 13 (January 2004), 9–17.

[196] C. A. Price, *Music in the Restoration Theatre* (Ann Arbor, MI, 1979), 227–8, 240.

not arrive in England until 1697, and his pieces for four treble instruments and continuo are presumably among those published in his op. 8 (c. 1717–18);[197] what seems to be a pre-publication version of no. 6 (Cook 3:006), scored specifically for two recorders, two violins and continuo, is in GB-Lbl, Add. MS 64965, fols. 53–56, a scorebook apparently copied by a Pepusch pupil around 1710.[198] One of the participants, David Wemyss (1678–1720), is listed by Tytler as 'Lord Elcho', which means that the concert must taken place before 28 June 1705, when he became Earl of Wemyss.[199] If the Barrett sonata was the one composed for *Tunbridge Walks* in 1703, then it must have been given on 22 November 1703 or 1704.

The document gives seven names in the bass section of the orchestra, four 'professors or masters of music', Henry Crumden, 'Mr Sinkolm' or 'St Columb' (i.e. Sainte-Colombe), Daniel Thomson, and James McClachlan, and three 'gentlemen', James Christie, Robert Gordon, and John Middleton. Tytler stated that one of the seven, Henry Crumden, played the harpsichord, and that the other six played a mixture of 'viol de Gambos' and 'violincellos' – by which he probably meant bass violins; the violoncello seems to have been unknown in Scotland until Lorenzo Bocchi arrived in Edinburgh in 1720 (Ch. 3). We might expect that the professionals played violin-family instruments (though Sainte-Colombe's presumed father and brother were gamba players), and that the amateurs played viols; Tytler wrote of James Christie: 'I remember in my youth to have heard play. His instrument, I think was the viol di Gambo, on which he was an excellent solo performer.' Two of the professionals also doubled on other instruments: Daniel Thomson was the trumpeter in the Barrett sonata and two other pieces and only played the bass once, in a Torelli sonata for four violins and continuo. James McClachlan, presumably a relative of the John McLachlan or McLaughlan (d. 1702) who wrote fiddle settings of Scots tunes around 1700, also played the violin in several pieces.[200]

An Edinburgh musician conspicuous by his absence in the document is John Beck, active in Edinburgh in the 1690s and the main contributor to the Balcarres

---

[197] J. C. Pepusch, *VI Concerts à 2 flûtes à bec, 2 flûtes traversières, haubois ou violins & basse continue*, op. 8 (Amsterdam, c. 1717–18; repr. 1993); RISM A/I P 1260; ME: ed. D. Lasocki (London, 1974). The publication date can be estimated from the plate number, 434; see Rasch, 'La famoso mano di Monsieur Roger', 101. See also Cook, 'The Life and Works of Johann Christoph Pepusch', ii. 107–10, 286.

[198] ME: J. C. Pepusch, *Quintett in F Dur*, ed. T. Dart (London, 1959), published before the sole surviving copy of op. 8 came to light in Sweden. For the MS, see Cook, 'The Life and Works of Johann Christoph Pepusch', ii. 255–7; *BLIC*.

[199] I am grateful to François-Pierre Goy for pointing this out.

[200] Spring, *The Lute in Britain*, 479. See also M. Spring, 'The Balcarres Lute Book', *Lute News*, 87 (October 2008), 7–14, at 10–11.

lute manuscript (*c.* 1701–5).[201] He was presumably a lutenist, though he may also have played the viol, assuming that he was the author of 'for 3 bass viols by Mr Beck', GB-Lbl, Add. MS 64965, fol. 21, consisting of a single statement of the Italian *Ruggiero* ground bass after a short prelude (Ex. 2.3). It was perhaps intended to serve as the basis for improvised divisions of the sort that Christopher Simpson recommended in his *Division-Viol*. Perhaps Beck had died or had left Edinburgh by the time the St Cecilia concert was put on. There is not much evidence of later Scottish gamba players, though a poem, 'LYROCLASTES; / OR, / An elegy on a BASS VIOL, broke by a short-sighted gentleman, who sat down upon it', was published in Edinburgh in 1760.[202] It is not clear who owned the instrument, sat on it, or wrote the poem, though a reference to its 'soul-enchanting song, / Sweet though sonorous, delicate though strong' suggests that it was a gamba. The poem must date from after 1745, for there is a reference to the rebellion of that year. James Watt made at least one gamba in Glasgow around 1760 (Ch. 4), and a large late eighteenth-century collection of Scots fiddle music, GB-En, MS 3346, compiled in Edinburgh by John Brysson, gives a 'gamut' or tuning for the 'violdigambo'.[203]

❧ *Conclusions*

T^HE fifty years from 1660 to 1710 was a period of enormous change in England, in music as in the rest of the arts and society in general. The decline of viol consorts and consort music went hand in hand with the decline of traditional court and country-house culture. Amateur musicians, taking their cue from London professionals, turned to the violin and the recorder, and to a more varied repertory of imported instrumental ensemble music, including Italian and German sonatas and works written in similar idioms in England. This did not mean that they forsook the bass viol. It was still needed to play bass lines because the bass violin and the violoncello were restricted to professionals until the 1730s. The traditional repertory of divisions continued in circulation, perhaps sustained by the continued availability of *The Division-Viol*, and it was supplemented by solo music in staff notation (replacing lyra-viol music in tablature) and by imported sets of solo music. As late as *c.* 1724 the London bookseller John Brotherton included a section of 'Sonatas and Airs for One, Two, or Three Viols'

---

[201] For Beck, see esp. Spring, 'The Balcarres Lute Book', 10. Stell, 'Sources of Scottish Instrumental Music', 28, suggests that he was Johann Hector Beck, recorded in Frankfurt-am-Main between 1650 and 1670, though there is no evidence for this.

[202] *A Collection of Original Poems by the Rev. Mr Blacklock and other Scotch Gentlemen* (Edinburgh, 1760), 215–17; CC: *ECCO*, ESTC T116769.

[203] Information from David Johnson.

Ex. 2.3 John Beck, 'for 3 bass viols' in A major

in a catalogue of prints imported from Michel-Charles Le Cène in Amsterdam, consisting of five sets by Schenck, three by Marais, two by Caix d'Hervelois and Jacob Riehmann, and single sets by Kühnel, Snep, Hacquart, and others.[204] However, arrangements were increasingly popular, and the octave-transposing treble clef allowed bass viol players access to any music written for soprano voices or instruments.

These changes were closely associated with changes to the bass viol's role in society. While its old aristocratic associations continued in France and Germany, not many upper-class Englishmen are known to have played it after about 1700. Most amateur viol players were members of the professions, and probably encountered it where they received their education: Oxford, Cambridge and the Inns of Court in London. There were even a few players further down the social scale, such as the coal merchant Thomas Britton and the clock maker John Harrison. Many ordinary players would have been involved in the music clubs that were developing in London and provincial towns at the time, though the viol's solo repertory also enabled them to use it for solitary diversion. Some players lived into the 1740s and 50s and beyond, though these is little evidence of amateur viol playing after about 1730. There were some female players at this period, and a surprising proportion of them were in Scotland, probably because of its conservative musical culture, though the viol does not seem to have been cultivated there any longer than in England.

[204] J. Brotherton, *An Account of Printed Musick, for Violins, Hautboys, Flutes and other Instruments, by Several Masters* (London, *c.* 1724), [19]; CC: *ECCO*, ESTC T146301.

CHAPTER 3

'Per la Viola da Gamba': Immigrants in Early Eighteenth-Century London

E NGLISH musical culture changed decisively with the establishment of an Italian opera company in London.[1] The process began in 1705 with the opening of the Queen's (later King's) Theatre in the Haymarket, built by John Vanbrugh for the production of operas. In the event, the first Italian-style opera was Thomas Clayton's *Arsinoe*, put on by Vanbrugh's rival Christopher Rich at Drury Lane on 16 January 1705. The first Italian opera was Jakob Greber's *Gli amori d'Ergasto*, which opened the Queen's Theatre on 9 April. Over the next two years the two theatres underwent a bewildering series of changes of management and artistic policy, which was only resolved at the end of 1707 when the Lord Chamberlain decreed that the Queen's Theatre should put on operas and Drury Lane plays. The opera company failed at the end of the 1717 season and was replaced in 1720 by the Royal Academy of Music.[2] The Haymarket Theatre (and its successor built on the same site after the 1789 fire) remained the home of Italian opera in London until 1867.[3]

The Queen's Theatre orchestra in its first phase was twenty-five to thirty strong, a mixture of native Englishmen and immigrants from Italy, France, Germany, and elsewhere.[4] The bass section seems to have consisted of one or two double basses, three bassoons and three to five instruments variously described as 'Violoncelli', 'Bass Viols', or just 'Bases'. The musicians concerned are unlikely

---

[1] See esp. C. A. Price, 'The Critical Decade for English Music Drama, 1700–1710', *Harvard Library Bulletin*, 26 (1978), 38–76; *Vice Chamberlain Coke's Theatrical Papers, 1706–1715*, ed. J. Milhous and R. D. Hume (Carbondale and Edwardsville, IL, 1982); W. Dean and J. M. Knapp, *Handel's Operas, 1704–1726* (Oxford, 1987), 140–67.

[2] E. Gibson, *The Royal Academy of Music, 1719–1728: the Institution and its Directors* (New York, 1989); Dean and Knapp, *Handel's Operas, 1704–1726*, 298–323.

[3] See esp. D. Nalbach, *The King's Theatre, 1704–1867* (London, 1972).

[4] See the lists in A. Nicoll, *A History of English Drama, 1660–1900*, ii: *Early Eighteenth Century Drama* (Cambridge, 3/1961), 278–29; *Vice Chamberlain Coke's Theatrical Papers*, ed. Milhous and Hume, 30–3, 38–9, 68–9, 78–9, 118–19, 127, 133, 151, 158–60, 179–80, 191–2.

to have played the violoncello on some occasions and the gamba on others, and it is also unlikely that they would have used gambas instead of violoncellos in the bass section of an Italian opera orchestra.[5] It is clear that the players concerned, including Nicola Haym, James Paisible, François Goodsens, and Giovanni Schiavonetti or Zanetti, were cellists or bass violin players first and foremost, and that these are more examples of 'bass viol' used to mean violin-family instruments. Nevertheless, it is possible that several of them did play the gamba outside the orchestra, and this may also be true of some Italian cellists who subsequently joined it, such as Filippo Amadei and Giovanni Bononcini.

This may seem surprising, since these Italians were representatives of modernity at a time when the gamba was rapidly losing ground among English musicians. But recent research suggests that the viol was more common in Italy at the time than was once thought.[6] There are many surviving viols by or attributed to contemporary Italian makers, including Gennaro and Giuseppe Gagliano, Matteo Gofriller, Giovanni Grancino, Giuseppe Guarneri (father of 'del Gesù'), Francesco and Vincenzo Rugeri, and Antonio Stradivari.[7] There are also references to the use of the gamba in Italy, and some music has survived. For instance, a Florentine court inventory of 1700 shows that two instruments described as *violetta all'inglese da gamba* were actually six-string English instruments.[8] In 1704 Vivaldi's salary at the Pietà in Venice was increased to allow for his teaching *viole all'inglese*, and five of his works have parts labelled *viola all'inglese*, *violetta all'inglese* or *violoncello all'inglese*; two recent studies have concluded that his *all'inglese* instruments were ordinary viols.[9] Other contemporary composers who wrote for the gamba in Italy include Alessandro Scarlatti (the cantata 'Già

---

5   In trying to understand the meaning of 'bass viol' in this context I am indebted to J. A. Sadie, 'Handel: in Pursuit of the Viol', *Chelys*, 14 (1985), 3–24; L. Lindgren, 'Italian Violoncellists and some Violoncello Solos Published in Eighteenth-Century Britain', in *Music in Eighteenth-Century Britain*, ed. D. W. Jones (Aldershot, 2000), 121–57.

6   V. Ghielmi, 'An Eighteenth-Century Italian Treatise and other Clues to the History of the Viola da Gamba in Italy', in *The Italian Viola da Gamba: Proceedings of the International Symposium on the Italian Viola da Gamba, Magnano, Italy, 29 April – 1 May 2000*, ed. S. Orlando (Solignac, 2002), 73–85.

7   T. G. MacCracken, 'Italian Instruments in a List of Extant Viols Made before 1900', in *The Italian Viola da Gamba*, ed. Orlando, 127–44; M. Herzog, 'Stradivari's Viols', *GSJ*, 57 (2004), 183–94.

8   Ghielmi, 'An Eighteenth-Century Italian Treatise', 81–2.

9   Ibid., 80–1, 84; M. Talbot, 'Vivaldi and the English Viol', *EM*, 30 (2002), 381–94. For an alternative argument, that the *violoncello inglese* was a viola d'amore-like instrument with sympathetic strings, see B. Hoffmann, 'Il violoncello all'inglese', *Studi Vivaldiani*, 4 (2004), 43–51.

sepolto è fra l'onda') and the young Handel (the cantata 'Tra le fiamme', HWV170 (1707), the oratorio *La Resurrezione*, HWV47 (1708), and the Sonata in C for gamba and obbligato harpsichord).[10] Thus we should not be surprised to find gamba players among the many Italian musicians who migrated to England at the time.

ᔆᗎ *Nicola Haym and François Goodsens*

O F the cellists in the Haymarket Theatre orchestra between 1707 and 1710, two, Haym and Goodsens, need to be discussed as possible gamba players. Nicola Haym (1678–1729) seems to have been first Italian cellist in England. He was the son of a Roman instrument maker and was a professional cellist in the city from at least 1694.[11] He arrived in London in March 1701 in the retinue of Wriothesley Russell, Marquess of Tavistock, soon to be the second Duke of Bedford.[12] Haym became 'Master of his Chamber Musick', and worked subsequently for Charles Montague, Baron Halifax, and James Brydges, Earl of Carnarvon, later Duke of Chandos. In 1706 he began a career in the theatre, initially at Drury Lane (he arranged Bononcini's *Camilla*, produced there on 30 March) and then at the Haymarket Theatre. He also wrote or revised the texts of operas produced by the company, including Handel's *Teseo* (1713). From 1720 he was one of the two principal violoncellos in the orchestra of the Royal Academy of Music,[13] becoming its secretary in 1722.

Most sources give Haym as a cellist. The Modenese diplomat Giuseppe Riva mentioned him as 'a Roman and a violoncellist' in a letter of 7 September 1725,[14] while an obituary described him as being 'deservedly famous for divinely touching the *Violoncello*, or *Four-string Base*, in which he was not equal'd by more than two or three Persons in Europe'.[15] However, in his contract with Christopher Rich, drawn up on 14 January 1706 to cover his work on *Camilla*, he agreed 'to play his part upon yᵉ Bass Violl' in performances of the opera and in 'subscription Musick or other Extraordinary

---

[10] Sadie, 'Handel: In Pursuit of the Viol', 5–11. For the sonata, see Ch. 9, fn. 139.

[11] For Haym, see esp. L. Lindgren, 'The Accomplishments of the Learned and Ingenious Nicola Francesco Haym (1678–1729)', *Studi musicali*, 16 (1987), 247–380; N. F. Haym, *Complete Sonatas*, ed. Lindgren, RRMBE, 117, 2 vols. (Middleton, WI, 2002), i: vii–xii; Lindgren, 'Italian Violoncellists', 137–8.

[12] G. S. Thomson, *The Russells in Bloomsbury, 1669–1771* (London, 1940), esp. 121–31.

[13] J. Milhous and R. D. Hume, 'New Light on Handel and the Royal Academy of Music in 1720', *Theatre Journal*, 35 (1983), 149–67, at 159.

[14] O. E. Deutsch, *Handel: a Documentary Biography* (London, 1955), 185–6.

[15] Lindgren, 'The Accomplishments of the Learned and Ingenious Nicola Francesco Haym', 247.

Musick'.[16] The Countess of Carnarvon wrote to the Dowager Duchess of Bedford on 5 November 1715 'to know upon w[ha]t terms Mr Hyems yt [that] plays upon the Base Viol served the Duke of Bedford'.[17] Haym was employed at Cannons as composer, violoncellist and *violone* player; when Brydges dismissed him on 4 April 1718 he mentioned hiring 'another Bass in your stead'.[18]

All of these references are probably to violin-family instruments, though the gamba was certainly played at Cannons. The 1720 catalogue of instruments belonging to Brydges, compiled by J. C. Pepusch, includes 'A Bass viol made by Henn: Jay in Southwark 1613 with a Case to it', and 'A Bass viol made by Barrack Norman 1702'.[19] The Jaye was 'at London in Albemarle Street' while the Norman was subsequently 'found at Cannons'. These instruments were clearly viols: Jaye is not known to have made violin-family instruments (Norman made both types),[20] and Pepusch's list also includes 'A Violincello or Bass Violin by M^r. Mears' – probably Richard Meares junior rather than his father and namesake, who mostly made bass viols.[21] This is important because it shows us that Pepusch was still using 'bass viol' to mean the gamba; it will help us to understand the instrumentation of his own works. However, it does not support the case for Haym as a gamba player, for there was at least one other person employed at Cannons who played the viol, as we shall see. We saw in Chapter 1 that Haym's *violone* is likely to have been a bass violin rather than a large member of the viol family. The bass parts of his *Dodeci sonate a trè*, op. 1 (Amsterdam, 1703) and *Sonate a trè*, op. 2 (Amsterdam, 1704) are labelled 'Violone o leuto', while, significantly, the obbligato parts in op. 2, nos. 10 and 11 are labelled 'violoncello'.[22] Haym presumably used the bass violin for bass parts and the smaller violoncello for playing solos.

The case of Francis, Francisco or François Goodsens (d. 1741) is also ambiguous. A 'Signor Francisco' appeared in public concerts in London in the spring of 1703, and on 26 October that year 'Mr *Francisco* upon the *Bass-Viol*' was one of

---

[16] GB-Lna, LC7/3, fols. 86, 87; facs.: G. Bononcini, *Camilla, Royal College of Music, MS 779*, intro. L. Lindgren, MLE, series E, vol. 1 (London, 1990), app. 1–5, at 3–4.

[17] G. Beeks, 'Handel and Music for the Earl of Carnarvon', in *Bach, Handel, Scarlatti: Tercentenary Essays*, ed. P. Williams (Cambridge, 1985), 1–20, at 3.

[18] Ibid., 8, 12.

[19] *The British Violin: the Catalogue of the 1998 Exhibition '400 Years of Violin and Bow Making in the British Isles'*, ed. J. Milnes (Oxford, 2000), 34.

[20] B. Hebbert, 'A Catalogue of Surviving Instruments by, or Ascribed to, Barak Norman', *GSJ*, 54 (2001), 285–329.

[21] See esp. B. Hebbert, 'Three Generations of the Meares Family in the London Music Trade, 1638–1749' (MMus diss., U. of Leeds, 2001), 79–91.

[22] ME: Haym, *Complete Sonatas*, ed. Lindgren, ii. 43–53.

three musicians employed at the Lincoln's Inn Theatre said to be 'as Celebrated as any now living'.[23] He was presumably the 'Francisco' who was a cellist in the Haymarket Theatre orchestra from 1707, and the 'Francesco' listed as 'Violoncello' in J. S. Cousser's commonplace book.[24] Despite the Italian form of his first name, he was a French Huguenot: his name was given as François when his eldest recorded child, Judith Cecile, was baptised in the Huguenot church in Westminster on 9 December 1708.[25] He was sworn in as a royal musician on 27 October 1711, and on 8 March 1712 his post was confirmed and defined: he was given £40 a year to play the bass violin in the Chapel Royal, with the note 'he hath in consert with ye Organ performed upon ye Base Violin in Our Royall Chappells to Our Satisfaction'.[26]

As part of his duties he presumably used GB-Lbl, R.M.27.a.10, from the early eighteenth-century set of Chapel Royal part-books, now R.M.27.a.1–15. The front cover is stamped 'VIOLONCELLO / CHAPEL ROYAL', and the book contains bass parts for services and anthems ranging from Tallis and Byrd to Croft and Weldon; it was begun c. 1713.[27] Goodsens was effectively given a new post (he replaced William Gorton, employed as a violinist), so the references to him as 'Violist' in Chapel Royal records for 1717, 1721, 1727, 1728, and 1742 (a document appointing Peter Gillier as his successor) are not directly connected with the Restoration practice of using viols to support the bass of the choir.[28] Rather, they seem to be more examples of the developing vernacular use of 'viol' to mean the violoncello, and this conclusion is reinforced by occasional references to bass violins in the Chapel. For instance, in 1726 it was ordered that the 'Lutenist & Base Violin's' were to attend 'on all Sundays; and at other times, when any of the Royal Family shall be present', and Goodsens was paid for a 'Case to Violoncello' in February 1735.[29] Thus I am not convinced by the suggestion that payments for the repair of 'the Great and small Viol used in the Chapple' in 1721 and 1725, and one in 1727 for the repair of 'the Double Bass and Bass Violin used in the Chap-

---

[23] Lindgren, 'Italian Violoncellists', 138.

[24] *Vice Chamberlain Coke's Theatrical Papers*, ed. Milhous and Hume, 30–3, 38, 69, 79, 119, 127, 133, 151, 158, 159, 179, 192; US-NHub, Osborn Music MS 16, p. 411 (Samantha Owens).

[25] *IGI* (Olive Baldwin and Thelma Wilson).

[26] *RECM*, ii. 108, 131; v. 102. See also *BDECM*, i. 495.

[27] M. Laurie, 'The Chapel Royal Part-Books', in *Music and Bibliography: Essays in Honour of Alec Hyatt King*, ed. O. Neighbour (London, 1980), 28–50, at 38.

[28] *The Cheque Books of the Chapel Royal*, ed. A. Ashbee and J. Harley, 2 vols. (Aldershot, 2000), i. 51, 147, 196, 208; ii. 29.

[29] Ibid., ii. 21; D. Burrows, *Handel and the English Chapel Royal* (Oxford, 2005), 475.

ple', mark a change of instrument.[30] Johann Mattheson, who was well informed about English music as the secretary of the English resident in Hamburg, wrote in 1713 that the Chapel Royal and St Paul's choirs were accompanied by 'the organ and sometimes a violoncello or theorbo' ('der Orgel und erwan einem *Violoncello* oder einer *Theorbe*').[31] At present there is no hard evidence that Goodsens played the viol.

❧ *Henry Eccles and Pietro Chaboud*

HOWEVER, two other members of the Haymarket Theatre orchestra in its early days can be identified as gamba players. References to 'Mr Igl' and 'Gall:-Echel' in late 1710 appear to be to the violinist Henry Eccles.[32] Eccles gave a benefit concert at Stationers' Hall on 15 May 1713 in which he played 'a Sonata on the Violin, and a single Piece on the Bass-Viol'.[33] The concert was said to be 'For the Entertainment of his Excellency the Duke d'Aumont, Embassador extraordinary from France', and Eccles was described as 'Musician to his Grace'. He is listed as 'Violin. V. da gamba' in Cousser's commonplace book – confirming that 'bass viol' really does mean the gamba in this case.[34] He seems to have worked subsequently in Paris, publishing sets of violin sonatas there in 1720 and 1723. No. 11 from the 1720 set has become popular in arrangements for various instruments, though Eccles stole its second movement from Bonporti, and many of the other movements in the collection are by Giuseppe Valentini.[35]

Pietro Chaboud was principally a wind player. He was appointed 'sonatore di fagotto e serpente' at San Petronio in Bologna from 1 December 1679, and served to 30 April 1685 as one of the two trombonists; around 1690 he presented a petition to be allowed to serve there again, presumably after an absence.[36] He played the transverse flute in later London concerts, so he was presumably the unnamed 'Bolognese the traverse' who was paid on 23 May 1702 for a private concert for the Duke of Bedford.[37] He was a bassoonist in the Haymarket Theatre orchestra from

[30] Burrows, *Handel and the English Chapel Royal*, 475.

[31] J. Mattheson, *Das neu-eröffnete Orchestre, oder Universelle und gründliche Anleitung* (Hamburg, 1713; repr. 2004), 297 (Tim Crawford).

[32] *Vice Chamberlain Coke's Theatrical Players*, ed. Milhous and Hume, 158, 159, 161.

[33] *DC*, 12/5/1713.

[34] US-NHub, Osborn Music MS 16, p. 418 (Samantha Owens).

[35] W.B Squire, 'Henry Eccles's Borrowings', *MT*, 64 (1923), 790.

[36] Lindgren, 'Italian Violoncellists', 138–9; M. Vanscheeuwijck, *The Capella Musicale of San Petronio in Bologna under Giovanni Paolo Colonna (1674–95): History, Organization, Repertoire* (Brussels, 2003), 282–5.

[37] Thomson, *The Russells in Bloomsbury*, 130.

1707, and he is mentioned as being in the service of the Duke of Ormond in two letters written by Haym to the Vice Chamberlain in 1708.[38] He also played the bassoon in concerts given 'att ye Duthess of Shrewsburys at Kensenton' in, probably, the 1712–13 season, and was presumably the 'M^r. Pietro' who was among the basses in the orchestra for the Lord Mayor's Day, 1714.[39]

The first evidence that Chaboud played the gamba comes from the German diarist Zacharias Conrad von Uffenbach, who attended a benefit concert for François Goodsens on 14 June 1710 at the Great Room in Peter's Court off St Martin's Lane.[40] He reported that it was directed by Pepusch and that there were about sixteen performers, including the soprano Marguérite de l'Epine, Pepusch's future wife.[41] One piece particularly caught his attention:

> The instrumental music was very beautiful. Pepusch, who directed everything and played the thorough-bass, excelled all the others. But the best of all was a most charming 'Concert' played by Pepusch with a 'Flöte' [recorder] and 'Viol di gamba'. The person who played the recorder is a Frenchman named Paisible, who has no equal … the other, who played the gamba, also incomparably, is an Italian named Signor Pietro, who has a large salary from the Duke of Ormond. He certainly performed miracles. When the concert was over he wanted to play a solo on the transverse or German flute, however the ladies got up, and when they went away all the music stopped, which had lasted in all only two hours. I could have listened with great pleasure all night.

This passage is important because it suggests that the 'bass viol' that Chaboud was repeatedly described as playing in advertisements for London concerts really was a gamba. Phrases such as 'several solos on the Base-Viol and German Flute' played by 'Signor Pietro' are mentioned in advertisements for concerts on 25 April 1715, 27 March 1717 and 18 February 1719; on 7 May 1719 he played 'A Solo on the Bass Viol').[42] A benefit for 'Signior Pietro' at Merchant Taylor's Hall on 29

[38] *Vice Chamberlain Coke's Theatrical Papers*, ed. Milhous and Hume, 31, 33, 80–81, 114.

[39] Ibid., 191–2; D. Burrows, 'Handel's London Theatre Orchestra', *EM*, 13 (1985), 349–57, at 353, 355, where the entry is mistranscribed as 'Mr Pictio'.

[40] TilmouthC, 76.

[41] Trans. adapted from D. F. Cook, 'The Life and Works of Johann Christoph Pepusch (1667–1752), with Special Reference to his Dramatic Works and Cantatas', 2 vols. (PhD diss., King's College, U. of London, 1982), i. 28–30 [Cook]; D. Lasocki, 'Professional Recorder Players in England, 1540–1740', 2 vols. (PhD diss., U. of Iowa, 1983), i. 438–9, 458.

[42] *DC*, 23/4/1715; *DC*, 23, 27/3/1717; *DC*, 16–18/2/1719; *DC*, 6, 7/5/1719.

April 1719 included 'A Solo on the Bass Viol and German Flute by Signor Petro and Signor Pipo', which could mean that Filippo Amadei (see below) played a solo on the gamba while Chaboud played one on the flute, or that they played together in a trio sonata, or even that Chaboud played solos on the flute and the gamba accompanied by Amadei on the violoncello.[43]

Julie Anne Sadie suggested that the bass parts of the two sets of *Solos for a German Flute, a Hoboy or Violin with a Thorough Bass for the Harpsicord or Bass Violin, being all Choice Pieces by the Greatest Authors and Fitted to the German Flute by Sig[r]. Pietro Chaboud* (1723; repr. 1985) were intended for a gamba rather than a violoncello or bass violin, for the part never goes down to *C* (below the range of the six-string bass viol in *D*) even in the two *C* major sonatas, Set 1, nos. 2 and 5.[44] However, most of them seem to be transposed versions of violin sonatas, by Pietro Castrucci, Geminiani, Bigaglia and/or Vivaldi, and others,[45] so the avoidance of *C* may have more to do with the transpositions needed to bring the upper parts into suitable ranges for the flute. In any case, gamba players could easily have tuned the bottom string down to *C*, as they often do today. This evidently happened with the bass parts of Pepusch's violin sonatas – see below.

The 7 May 1719 concert is the last hard evidence of Chaboud's presence in London. His name appears once in the accounts of the Cannons household, for Lady Day 1718, but there is no receipt or signature, and there is no sign that he served there after that date, though parts marked 'German flute' or 'traversa' in several anthems Haym wrote for Cannons in 1716 suggest that he had worked there.[46] 'Pietro' was one of the bassoons in three preliminary lists for the orchestra of the Royal Academy of Music, drawn up before or during a meeting on 15 February 1720.[47] Whether he actually served in the orchestra when it started performing on 2 April 1720 is not known. The 1723 publication does not necessarily

43 *DC*, 24/4/1719.

44 Sadie, 'Handel: in Pursuit of the Viol', 15. See W. C. Smith and C. Humphries, *A Bibliography of the Musical Works Published by the Firm of John Walsh during the Years 1721–1766* (London, 1968), 78–9, nos. 350, 351. It was advertised in *DC*, 22/5/1723.

45 See F. M. Sardelli, *Vivaldi's Music for Flute and Recorder*, trans. M. Talbot (Aldershot, 2007), 66–70.

46 Beeks, 'Handel and Music for the Earl of Carnarvon', 8. Haym's autograph of the anthems, GB-Lbl, Add. MS 62561, is dated 29/9/1716.

47 Milhous and Hume, 'New Light on Handel', 158–61. They point out that the Duke of Portland, a director of the Royal Academy, changed the position of Chaboud's name in the third document, but his intention was apparently to move him from the fourth to the second rank of salaries, not to change his instrument from bassoon to violoncello, as they assert. There is no other evidence that Chaboud played the violoncello.

mean that he was still in London or even alive then: Walsh and Hare published several posthumous collections by William Babell (d. 1723).[48]

Chaboud was clearly an outstanding performer, and he is important for several reasons. He was apparently the first Baroque flute player in London, and therefore probably played the 'Flute D. Almayne' solo in John Eccles's *Judgement of Paris* (1701),[49] and the 'Flute allemande' part in the overture to James Kremberg's 'New-framed Entertainment', GB-Lcm, MS 2231, fol. 1, probably written soon after. He is also the first Italian known to have played the gamba in London. As such, he may have been responsible for some of the Italianate gamba music that was composed, arranged or published there at the time. We should start with the piece Chaboud played with Paisible and Pepusch in 1710. Uffenbach used the French word *concert* for it, by which he probably meant something akin to the English word 'consort', just meaning a mixed ensemble.[50] It was probably a trio sonata for recorder, viola da gamba and harpsichord continuo, a variant of the German type of trio sonata for violin, gamba and continuo (Ch. 1). As it happens, Pepusch's Sonata in G major (Cook 2:021) for recorder, gamba and continuo fits the bill exactly. It exists in two sources. In the score-book GB-Lbl, Add. MS 64965, fols. 68v–73, it is entitled 'Sonata / Fluto / Viola / di gamba / e / Basso / del Sig^r Pepusch', while in D-Dl, Mus. 2160-Q-2 it is entitled 'No: 2 Trio / Flauto Violino e Basson / Partitura solo / Del Sig^r Pepusch' and the gamba part is an octave higher.[51] It is also listed in the 1762 Breitkopf catalogue as 'del Sgr. Pepusch, *a Viol. D. G. Fl. e B.*'[52] The GB-Lbl version is clearly the original. The manuscript is close in time and place to the composer: it was apparently copied around 1710 by one of Pepusch's pupils and contains seventeen pieces and two treatises attributed to him.

Cook 2:021 is also much more extended and virtuosic than Pepusch's other two sonatas with similar scorings, in D minor (Cook 2:023) for flute or violin, 'viola' and continuo, and in E minor (Cook 2:027) for flute or violin, violin or

---

[48] Smith and Humphries, *A Bibliography of ... John Walsh during the Years 1721 to 1766*, 27–9, nos. 107, 109, 113.

[49] J. Eccles, *The Judgement of Paris* (London, 1702); facs., intro. R. Platt, MLE, series C, vol. 1 (Tunbridge Wells, 1984), 28–31.

[50] P. Holman, *Four and Twenty Fiddlers: the Violin at the English Court, 1540–1690* (Oxford, 2/1995), 132. See also several papers in *From Renaissance to Baroque: Change in Instruments and Instrumental Music in the Seventeenth Century*, ed. J. Wainwright and Holman (Aldershot, 2005).

[51] Cook, 'The Life and Works of Johann Christoph Pepusch', ii. 95, 222, 255–7; ME: J. C. Pepusch, *Sonata in G*, ed. B. Clark (Dundee, 2005).

[52] *The Breitkopf Thematic Catalogue: the Six Parts and Sixteen Supplements, 1762–1787*, ed. B. S. Brook (New York, 1966), 80.

Ex. 3.1 J. C. Pepusch, Sonata in G major, Cook 2:021, 4th movement, bb. 27–38

gamba and continuo.[53] Cook 2:023 is said to be for 'Flauto Traversa' in the source, D-ROu, Mus. Saec. XVII-37³, though the part does not go below *f'* and is suitable for the treble recorder. The flute part of Cook 2:027 goes down to *e'* several times and therefore must be for the transverse instrument. The second parts of the three sonatas are similar in range (*d* or *e* to *c"* or *d"*) and function (they are essentially second treble parts down an octave, never doubling the bass), though the one in Cook 2:021 is much more demanding than the others, and in the minuet-like last movement there is some idiomatic writing for the gamba using the open *a* and *d'* strings, nicely differentiated from the recorder writing (Ex. 3.1). Cook 2:021 was surely written for professionals such as Paisible and Chaboud, while the others look as if they were written for amateurs, with relatively simple second parts in a neutral style, equally suitable for gamba, viola – or for that matter, violin up the octave.

53 Cook, 'The Life and Works of Johann Christoph Pepusch', ii. 96, 98, 223, 225, 226; ME: J. C. Pepusch, *Triosonate D-moll*, ed. H. Ruf, Hortus Musicus, 161 (Kassel, 1959); J. C. Pepusch, *Triosonate E moll*, ed. Ruf, Antiqua, 87 (Mainz, 1965).

Three other Pepusch works have solo gamba parts: the Sonata in G minor (Cook 2:040) for two violins, gamba and continuo, D-Dl, Mus. 2160-Q-5, and two sonatas for violin, gamba and continuo, in B minor (Cook 2:029), GB-Lcm, MS 1198 (1), and A minor (Cook 2:030), D-Dl, Mus. 2160-Q-3.[54] Another, in G major 'del Sigr. PEPUSCH, a V. da G. 2 Violini con Cembalo', was advertised by Breitkopf in 1766 but seems to be lost.[55] Also, a sonata for flute, gamba and continuo, which could be one of the ones already discussed or another work, was included in Pepusch's lost op. 7 trio sonatas, published by Jeanne Roger in Amsterdam around 1717.[56] The 1737 catalogue of Michel-Charles Le Cène (Roger's successor) listed op. 7 just as 'X. Sonate de Pepusch opera settima à une flute Traversiére ou Hautbois, un violon & basse continue', but a more precise description in the 1759 sale catalogue of the stock of Nicolas Selhof, bookseller at The Hague, describes no. 9 as for 'Flute Traversiere, une Viole de Gambe & Basse Continue'.[57]

We also need to consider Pepusch's use of the label 'bass viol' on continuo parts. Some manuscript scores of his sets of violin sonatas have title-pages that specify the instrument,[58] such as 'Two Setts of Sonatas / Composed / For a Violin & a Base Viol or Harpsichord. / The First / For M[r] Slater / The other for M[r] Butler / BY / M[r] John Christ. Pepusch' (GB-Lbl, Add. MS 31531), or 'Sixteen Solos or Sonatas / FOR / A Violin, a Base Viol, or Harpsichord / Composed / For Madam Greggs of Durham / By / John Christop[r] Pepusch' (GB-Lbl, Add. MS 31532). They were written by the same individual, probably a professional copyist working for the composer. Given the evidence of Pepusch's list of the Cannons instruments, it is likely that 'bass viol' means the gamba, despite the fact that the bass parts of the sonatas regularly go down to C rather than D. In this respect Pepusch was behind the times: the Walsh and Hare publication of his XXIV Solos for a Violin (c. 1707–8), including some of the sonatas in the manuscript sets, labels the bass

54 Cook, 'The Life and Works of Johann Christoph Pepusch', ii. 99, 104, 222–3, 252.

55 The Breitkopf Thematic Catalogue, ed. Brook, 239.

56 Its date can be estimated from the plate number, 429; see R. Rasch, '"La famoso mano di Monsieur Roger": Antonio Vivaldi and his Dutch Publishers', Informazioni e studi vivaldiani, 17 (1996), 89–135, at 101.

57 Catalogue des livres de musique, imprimés à Amsterdam, chez Michel Charles Le Cène (Amsterdam, 1737), 33, repr. in F. Lesure, Bibliographie des éditions musicales publiées par Estienne Roger et Michel-Charles le Cène (Amsterdam, 1696–1743) (Paris, 1969); Catalogue d'une très belle bibliothèque de livres ... deslaissez par feu monsieur Nicolas Selhof (The Hague, 1759), facs., intro. A. H. King (Amsterdam, 1973), 146, lot 1043.

58 Cook, 'The Life and Works of Johann Christoph Pepusch', ii. 16–58, 66–75, 219–20, 242–4, 265–8.

'HARPSICORD or BASS VIOLIN'.[59] English publications began to specify the bass violin and the violoncello as continuo instruments shortly after 1700 (Ch. 1).

Chaboud may also be connected with an oblong quarto of fourteen pages, published by Walsh and Hare with the following title:

> AIRES & SYMPHONYS for ye Bass VIOL / being / A Choice Collection of ye most favorite Song tunes, Aires & Symphonys / out of the late Operas, Curiously contriv'd & fitted to the Bass Viol by the best Masters. / also some excellent Lessons made purpose for y^t Instrument, / as Almands, Corants, Sarabands & Jiggs. / the whole fairly engraven and carefully Corrected.[60]

The first section, pp. 1–8, consists of solo bass viol arrangements of fifteen numbers from six operas produced at the Haymarket Theatre, ranging from Bononcini's *Camilla* to Mancini's *Hydaspes*, the latter first performed on 23 March 1710. The arrangements were probably made from the collections published by Walsh of songs from the operas, such as *Songs in the New Opera Call'd Hydaspes, as they are Perform'd at the Queen's Theatre*.[61] It was advertised on 30 May 1710 and includes the four arias included in *Aires & Symphonys*. *Aires & Symphonys* was presumably published soon after.

The arrangements of Italian opera arias in *Aires & Symphonys* are unimpressive at first sight: they mostly consist of the top line of the instrumental passages or the vocal line, with a few chords added to make them idiomatic for the bass viol. But they are surprisingly effective, and are of interest because they are in the octave-transposing treble clef, first used in *The Compleat Violist* (1699) (Ch. 2), and because several of them include Italianate florid ornamentation. The most interesting is 'Ungrateful cruel maid' from Conti's *Clotilda* (1709), which includes two rapid runs up to melody notes and a fine example of a cadential flourish (Ex. 3.2). In *Songs in the New Opera Call'd Clotilda* (1709), p. 4, this aria, originally 'Hor sì m'insegna il ciel', is said to have been sung by 'Sign^r. Nicolini' – the castrato Nicola Grimaldi.[62] Thus the arrangement may be an attempt

[59] RISM A/I P 1264; CC: GB-Lbl, e.15.b. See also Cook, 'The Life and Works of Johann Christoph Pepusch', ii. 277–8; W. C. Smith, *A Bibliography of the Musical Works Published by John Walsh during the Years 1695–1720* (London, 2/1968), 82–3, no. 264a; R. L. Hardie, '"Curiously Fitted and Contriv'd": Production Strategies Employed by John Walsh from 1695 to 1712, with a Descriptive Catalogue of his Instrumental Publications' (PhD diss., U. of Western Ontario, 2000), 322–5.

[60] CC: GB-Lbl, c.63. See Smith, *A Bibliography of ... John Walsh during the Years 1695–1720*, 114, no. 378; Hardie, 'Curiously Fitted and Contriv'd', 355.

[61] D. Hunter, *Opera and Song Books Published in England, 1703–1726: a Descriptive Bibliography* (London, 1997), 188–9, no. 69.

[62] Ibid., 155–6, no. 53.

Ex. 3.2 'Ungrateful cruel maid' from Conti's *Clotilda*,
?arranged by Pietro Chaboud, bb. 9–14

to reproduce the effect of Grimaldi's singing, made by someone in the orbit of the Haymarket Theatre; the ornaments are not in the parent publication. The title-page of *Aires & Symphonys* states that the arrangements were made 'by the best Masters', but I suspect that the plural was used to imbue the collection with as much authority as possible and should not be taken literally. Chaboud is the prime suspect as arranger, being the only person in the opera company at the time known to have played the gamba.

The rest of the collection, the 'excellent Lessons made purpose', consists of two groups of dance music. The first (pp. 8–12), notated like the aria arrangements in treble and bass clefs, consists of two-, three- and four-movement suites in G major, Bb major, A minor, C major and D major. They are fairly simple in style, with textures similar to the aria arrangements, and with several Italianate *moto perpetuo* jigs. They could be by Chaboud himself. The second group, in alto and bass clefs, consists of four-movement suites in D major and D minor followed by two movements in A minor and singletons in G minor and G major. These are more complex: there are more chords and the Allemand and Corant from the D major suite use the common device of suggesting the presence of several parts by alternating rapidly between the top and the bottom of the gamba (Ex. 3.3). The second A minor piece, entitled 'A Farewell', belongs to the contemporary English genre of short elegiac instrumental pieces used to commemorate musicians or public figures.[63] It suggests that the composer was an Englishman, as do several other movements, including a Purcellian jig in D minor and a 'Brisk Aire' in G major with some Scotch snaps.

The other relevant collection is a set of gamba arrangements of Corelli's op. 5 violin sonatas. Two of them, nos. 6 and 11, were published in an untitled English edition engraved by the London engraver and music seller Thomas Cross ('T. Cross Sculp.' appears at the end of each sonata). Three of the five known examples

[63] M. Tilmouth, 'Farewell', *GMO*.

Ex. 3.3 Anonymous, Allemand in D major, bb. 9–17

are bound in with copies of Christopher Simpson's *Chelys / The Division-Viol* (1712), the third edition of *The Division-Violist*, published by Richard Meares junior.[64] Meares probably commissioned Cross to engrave the two sonatas so that he could offer customers a bonus of up-to-date gamba music. However to complicate things F-Pn, Vm⁷ 6308 contains all the op. 5 sonatas in gamba arrangements, including nos. 6 and 11 in essentially the same versions.[65] In both sources the violin part is down the octave in alto and bass clefs, and no. 1 in D major, no. 6 in A major, and no. 11 in E major are also transposed down a tone, into C major, G major, and D major respectively, while no. 5 in G minor is transposed down a fourth, into D minor. The arranger adapted the violin multiple stopping to make it suitable for the gamba, supplying some six-note chords (Ex. 3.4). No. 12, the 'La folia' variations, is given in Vm⁷ 6308 as originally notated by Corelli, perhaps because the arranger thought it was more or less playable as it stood – if so, it is an another early example of the transposing treble clef used for gamba music.

There have been several attempts to work out who made these arrangements. The manuscript's location in Paris might suggest that they were the work of a French musician, but Hazelle Miloradovitch pointed out that they

---

[64] GB-Lam, Spencer Collection, A/2/Simpson; GB-Lbl, Hirsch.I.536; GB-Lbl, g.299. In addition, GB-Lbl, K1.i.11.(2), the only copy listed in RISM A/1 C 3842, is bound with Simpson's *The Division-Violist* (London, 1659). A fifth unbound copy, formerly in Robert Spencer's collection, is repr., intro. G. Dodd, VdGS Music, 136 (London, 1980).

[65] Facs.: A. Corelli, *Sonatas for Viol and Basso Continuo, Paris, Bibliothèque Nationale, MS VM⁷ 6308*, intro. H. Miloradovitch (Peer, 1989). See also H. Miloradovitch, 'Eighteenth-Century Manuscript Transcriptions for Viols of Music by Corelli and Marais in the Bibliothèque Nationale, Paris: Sonatas and *Pièces de Viole*', *Chelys*, 12 (1983), 47–73.

Ex. 3.4 Arcangelo Corelli, Sonata in G minor, op. 5, no. 5,
?arranged in D minor by Pietro Chaboud, Allegro, bb. 96–104

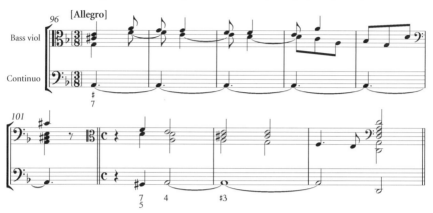

were apparently made for a six- rather than a seven-string viol, and that they lack the bowing and fingering instructions common in French viol music.[66] She put forward Johann Schenck or Conrad Höffler as possible arrangers, but also mentioned Gottfried Finger, a suggestion made by Christopher Hogwood in a 1981 BBC radio broadcast. However, Finger left England in 1701 for good, while Schenck and Höffler never came to London, so far as is known. Also, the Paris manuscript looks as if it was copied by an Italian. It is in the oblong quarto format favoured at the time by Italian musicians for solo sonatas and cantatas rather than the upright folio format that was more common in Germany. The handwriting of the titles and the tempo markings is Italianate, as is the style of the braces, the clefs and the shape of the notes, the stems, and the beams, while the manuscript's 'Dutch' paper (with a fleur-de-lys watermark and IV countermark) would have been readily available in London in the early eighteenth century.[67] The simplest explanation is that the set of arrangements was made in London by Chaboud or another Italian gamba player, that Cross engraved two sonatas from it, and that the original manuscript or a copy subsequently found its way to Paris.

There is another early use of the transposing treble clef in the piece entitled 'viola da Carlo Marini' in GB-Lbl, Add. MS 64965, fols. 24v–25. It is a version of the finale of the Sonata in E major, no. 11 of *Sonate a violino solo con suo basso continuo*, op. 8 (Venice, 1705) by the Bergamo composer Carlo Antonio Marino or Marini.[68] Marino seemingly never visited England, but Roger's reprint of

---

[66] Miloradovitch, 'Eighteenth-Century Manuscript Transcriptions for Viols', 51–3.

[67] Information from François-Pierre Goy and Robert Thompson.

[68] RISM a/i m 697.

op. 8 would have been easily accessible,[69] and two of his other collections were advertised in London in 1706.[70] The arrangement was made by transposing the piece down a tone to D major, making the top note a written $c\sharp'''$ rather than $d\sharp'''$. The intention was presumably to make the solo part suitable for a 'viola', and the treble clef (implying octave transposition) suggests it was *da gamba* rather than *da braccio*. I know of no evidence that viola players in England used octave-transposing notation; their few solo parts are written in C clefs. Thus the 'Tenor Viola' part in Pepusch's Sonata in G major (Cook 2:020), GB-Lbl, Add. MS 64965, fols. 65v–68v, is in a mixture of soprano (C1) and mezzo-soprano (C2) clefs.

❧ David Boswillibald and John Walther

THE next gamba-playing member of the Haymarket Theatre orchestra was David Boswillibald (d. 1729). His name gave English writers a good deal of trouble. The west-country doctor Claver Morris called him 'Baswilwaldt',[71] while he is given in Chapel Royal documents for 1721, 1722, 1724 and 1726 as 'Possenwolt David', 'David Williwald', 'David Beswilliwald', and 'David Beswllibald'.[72] He was presumably related to the singer George Jacob Bößwillibald, who is recorded as a singer at the Ansbach court in 1703 (as a boy), and between 1705 and 1723 as an adult.[73] Georg Jacob sang in an opera in Berlin in 1708,[74] and came to London in 1716: he sang in two operas at the Haymarket Theatre that spring and gave a benefit concert at Hickford's Room on 9 June, when he was described as 'Signor Giorgio Giacomo Beswillibald, Servant to His Serene Highness the Margrave of

[69] RISM A/I M 698; CC: GB-Lbl, f.132.d. See F. Lesure, *Bibliographie des éditions musicales*, 74. It was also offered for sale in J. Brotherton, *An Account of Printed Musick for Violins, Hautboys, Flutes and other Instruments, by Several Masters* (London, c. 1724), [10]; CC: *ECCO*, ESTC T146301. There is a contemporary Italian arrangement in D major for 'viola' of Marino's Sonata in A major, op. 8, no. 6, A-Wn, EM.67.Mus.; ME: C. Marino, *Sonata in D for Viola and Cembalo*, ed. K. Stierhof (Vienna, 1973).

[70] TilmouthC, 65, 66.

[71] H. D. Johnstone, 'Claver Morris, an Early Eighteenth-Century English Physician and Amateur Musician *Extraordinaire*', *JRMA*, 133 (2008), 93–127, at 108–9.

[72] Burrows, *Handel and the English Chapel Royal*, 602, 608, 609.

[73] H. H. F. K. Mersmann, *Christian Ludwig Boxberg und seine Oper "Sardanapalus" Ansbach 1698, mit Beiträgen zur Ansbacher Musikgeschichte* (Berlin, 1916), 50, 51; G. Schmidt, *Die Musik am Hofe der Markgrafen von Brandenburg-Ansbach vom ausgehenden Mittelalter bis 1806* (Kassel, 1956), 73, 74, 76 (Samantha Owens).

[74] J. G. Walther, *Musicalisches Lexicon, oder Musicalische Bibliotec* (Leipzig, 1732), 99; CC: GB-Lbl, M.R.Ref.2.a.

Brandenburgh Anspach, Brother to Her Royal Highness the Princess of Wales'.[75] I have preferred the form 'Boswillibald', used in the baptism record of David's daughter Elizabeth at Salehurst in Sussex on 17 April 1729, and in his will, proved on 29 June 1729.[76]

Boswillibald was principally a double bass player. He was one of two 'Double Basses' in the list of players for the 1714 Lord Mayor's day concert (the earliest record of him);[77] one of two 'Counterbases' in the 1720 list of the Royal Academy orchestra;[78] one of two double bass players in Chapel Royal documents relating to performances of orchestral Te Deums; and was given as 'M^r. David. Contrabasso / Bösewilibald' in J. S. Cousser's commonplace book.[79] He was one of four musicians chosen by Francesco Geminiani in June 1725 to assist the Philo-musicae et architecturae societas Apollini, a musical Masonic lodge in London.[80] It was involved in the publication of Geminiani's concerto transcriptions of Corelli's op. 5 sonatas, and owned sonatas and concertos by Albicastro, Albinoni, Bianchi, and Marino, so it is likely that Geminiani (violin) and the other three, Gaetano Scarpettini (violin), Francesco Barsanti (?viola), and Charles Pardini (violoncello), led the sections of an amateur string orchestra and played the concertino parts in concertos. Boswillibald was presumably hired to play double bass – an instrument not normally played by amateurs. Finally, he was one of two 'Double Basses' in the orchestra for the 1727 Lord Mayor's day concert, when it was said that 'The Performers are all from the Opera and both Theatres and the Musick Composed by Mr Hendell &c'.[81]

We have one description of Boswillibald playing the gamba: on 1 October 1718 Claver Morris recorded that, in a session of music-making in his house in Wells, 'Mr Walter and Mr Baswilwaldt play'd Schenk's Sonatas for 2 Viols, which were very excellent; they all 'sate up 'till past 2'.[82] Schenck's only sonatas for two viols (as opposed to solos with continuo) are in *Le nymphe di Rheno*, op. 8 (Amsterdam, 1702). Boswillibald's duet partner was a colleague in the Italian opera orchestra, the violinist John Walther, Walter or Walters. He appears in its lists from late 1707 until 1712 or 1713, placed in the second violins in those that give a breakdown of

---

75 *DC*, 1/6/1716. See also *LS*, ii/1, 368, 387, 398, 406.

76 *IGI*; GB-Lna, PROB 11/630, fol. 130.

77 Burrows, 'Handel's London Theatre Orchestra', 353, 355.

78 Milhous and Hume, 'New Light on Handel', 158–60.

79 US-NHub, Osborn Music MS 16, p. 414 (Samantha Owens).

80 A. G. Pink, 'The Musical Culture of Freemasonry in Early Eighteenth-Century London' (PhD diss., Goldsmith's, U. of London, 2007), 98–125, 312–23.

81 Burrows, 'Handel's London Theatre Orchestra', 354, 355.

82 Johnstone, 'Claver Morris', 109.

the orchestra, was one of the violins in the orchestra assembled for the 1714 Lord Mayor's Day concert, and was among the violins in two of the 1720 lists of the projected Royal Academy orchestra.[83] In the third the Duke of Portland marked him 'out of town', and there is no trace of him after that. Like Boswillibald, he was probably German: he used the form 'John Walther' on an opera orchestra receipt rather than the English forms Walter or Walters.[84] There is no other evidence that he played the gamba.

⁛ *Angelo Zannoni and Filippo Amadei*

THE Venetian singer Angelo Zannoni appeared in London about the same time as Boswillibald. He made his debut ('lately arriv'd from Italy') at the King's Theatre on 30 December 1714 as Argante in Handel's *Rinaldo*, appeared in the pasticcios *Lucio Vero* and *Arminio*, and performed in two benefit concerts before, presumably, returning to Italy at the end of the season.[85] In the first concert, his benefit at the Great Room in James Street on 9 May 1715, he sang and played 'several Solo's on the Base-Viol'. In the second, at the same venue on 16 May, he is just advertised as singing, though the concert, 'For the Benefit of a Lady under Misfortune', was described as 'a Consort of Vocal and Instrumental Musick'. We might question whether his 'bass viol' really was a gamba were it not for the fact that he apparently played the solo viol part in Vivaldi's opera *L'incoronazione di Dario*, put on in Venice in January 1717.[86] He sang the character of Niceno, the supposed composer of a *cantata in scena* with a *viola all'inglese* obbligato performed on stage towards the end of Act I.

Pippo or Filippo Amadei worked in Rome from at least 1685 until 5 February 1715, when he departed for England with the violinists Pietro and Prospero Castrucci in the retinue of Richard Boyle, Earl of Burlington, who was returning from the Grand Tour.[87] He quickly established himself in England. Music by him was performed in Christopher Bullock's play *A Woman's Revenge* at Lincoln's Inn

---

[83] *Vice Chamberlain Coke's Theatrical Papers*, ed. Milhous and Hume, esp. 30–1, 151, 158, 159, 192; Milhous and Hume, 'New Light on Handel', 158–60; Burrows, 'Handel's London Theatre Orchestra', 353, 355.

[84] *Vice Chamberlain Coke's Theatrical Papers*, ed. Milhous and Hume, 187.

[85] *DC*, 30, 31/12/1714; *DC*, 9, 16/5/1715; *LS*, ii/1, 336, 345, 349, 355, 356; Dean and Knapp, *Handel's Operas, 1704–1726*, 161, 184.

[86] Talbot, 'Vivaldi and the English Viol', 390–2.

[87] Gibson, *The Royal Academy of Music*, 62–9; Lindgren, 'Italian Violoncellists', 140. See also J. Clark, 'Lord Burlington is Here', in *Lord Burlington: Architecture, Art and Life*, ed. T. Barnard and Clark (London, 1995), 251–310.

Fields in November 1718.[88] Pietro Rolli mentioned in a letter of 13 July 1719 that he was in the service of the Prince of Wales with the harpsichordist Pietro Sandoni,[89] and he was still in Burlington's household in April 1720.[90] He was the first violoncello in the projected Royal Academy orchestra in 1720;[91] he arranged the pasticcio *Arsace*, first performed at the King's Theatre on 1 February 1721; and around the same time composed Act I of *Muzio Scevola* in conjunction with Bononcini (Act II) and Handel (Act III); it was first performed at the King's Theatre on 15 April 1721.[92] He probably left England to return to Rome in or shortly after 1723: he is last heard of playing in a Corelli concerto at Drury Lane on 20 March 1723,[93] though he was still mentioned in a roll-call of distinguished musicians in the verse pamphlet *The Session of Musicians*, published in May 1724.[94]

Amadei was a cellist first and foremost. In *The Session of Musicians* he is referred to as 'Signor *P – po* with his four-string'd Bass', while Johann Mattheson, in a discussion of *Muzio Scevola*, referred to him in January 1723 as '*Mattei* (who under the name of *Pipo*, i.e. *Filippo*, plays the *violoncello* in London)'.[95] Nevertheless, some references suggest that he also played the gamba. One is a red herring: it is sometimes said that he played a bass viol concerto at Drury Lane on 14 March 1722, but the actual words in the advertisement are: 'A Concerto on the Bass Violin, composed and performed by Sig. Pippo'.[96] A letter written by the painter Edward Gouge from Rome in June 1707 mentions 'Pipo, that famous bas violist' playing in weekly concerts at the house of an English resident, though, as have seen, references of this sort cannot be assumed to mean the gamba.[97]

However, a third instance is more promising. Amadei seems to have acquired a 'bass viol' while he was in Paris with Burlington during their trip from Rome to London in the spring of 1715. In Burlington's account book there is a payment of 10 sols for 'Porteridge for a Bass Viol' on 7 April 1715, followed by another on 1 May for £1 18s. 3d. 'for 3 Trunks one Base Viol Case & Other Bagage', and a third the next day for expenses 'getting Sen[r] Pepo's things that were taken by y[e]

[88]   *LS*, ii/2, 513.

[89]   Gibson, *The Royal Academy of Music*, 114; trans. in Deutsch, *Handel*, 92–3.

[90]   Gibson, *The Royal Academy of Music*, 67.

[91]   Milhous and Hume, 'New Light on Handel', 158–60.

[92]   Gibson, *The Royal Academy of Music*, 138–43; Dean and Knapp, *Handel's Operas, 1704–1726*, 368–84.

[93]   R. Maunder, *The Scoring of Baroque Concertos* (Woodbridge, 2004), 127–8.

[94]   Deutsch, *Handel*, 168.

[95]   Deutsch, *Handel*, 146.

[96]   Maunder, *The Scoring of Baroque Concertos*, 127.

[97]   Gibson, *The Royal Academy of Music*, 58.

Custom House Officers'.[98] The instrument was seemingly impounded by customs at Dover with some of his other possessions, and a fee was paid to redeem them. If it was a French instrument then it was probably a gamba: Amadei is unlikely to have purchased a violoncello in France when he would have had access to fine instruments in Italy. Paris was one of the main centres for the production of gambas, with makers such as Nicolas Bertrand, Guillaume Barbey and Claude Pierray.

❧ *Giovanni Bononcini*

GIOVANNI Bononcini was also brought to England by the Earl of Burlington, who apparently encountered him in Rome during his second Italian trip in the summer of 1719. Bononcini arrived in London in October 1720, initially to work for the Royal Academy, though in 1724 his association with known Jacobites and the opposition to him generated by the pro-Handel faction among the Academy's directors and supporters caused him to consider moving to Paris; on 14 May he accepted an offer from the Duchess of Marlborough of £500 a year to direct private performances of his music. He left England permanently in 1732 following the scandal created by his attempt to pass off a madrigal by Antonio Lotti as his own at the Academy of Ancient Music.[99]

He was initially recruited by the Royal Academy to play in its orchestra and to compose operas for the company: on 30 November 1719 the directors resolved that 'Seignr Bona Cini be writ to, To know his Terms for composing & performing in the Orchester'.[100] However, he does not appear in the lists of the orchestra drawn up in February 1720, and it appears from an advertisement the following year that he rationed his appearances as a performer:

Any Lady of Gentlemen may have the Opera of CRISPO rehears'd at their Apartments, by all the best Performers, who will engage 20 Persons or more to subscribe to Signor Bononcini's Cantata's; but it is humbly desired no one may be invited who is not already a Subscriber, or does not promise to subscribe to the said Cantata's. N. B. Crispo is the best Composition of Bononcini, and is never to be perform'd but in this manner, for his own Benefit; and where ever 30 Subscriptions are procured, Bononcini will play

[98] Chatsworth House archives, Burlington, Misc. Box 2 (Jane Clark).

[99] L. Lindgren, 'The Three Great Noises "Fatal to the Interests of Bononcini"', *MQ*, 61 (1975), 560–83. For Bononcini in England, see esp. Dean and Knapp, *Handel's Operas, 1704–1726*, 306–14.

[100] Milhous and Hume, 'New Light on Handel', 152.

on the Violoncelli, which he never does but where he proposes a particular Advantage to himself.[101]

A couple of weeks earlier John Hervey, first Earl of Bristol, had been the host for one of these chamber opera performances. An entry in his account book for 5 June reads: 'Gave ye two Castruchis & Weiber ye lutenist, to each 2 guineas, for playing to Bononcini & Senezini & Mrs. Robinson, when Crispo was performed at my house, £6..6..0.'[102] Unless there were other musicians present who were paid separately, it looks as if *Crispo* was performed for Hervey in a version for two sopranos (Anastasia Robinson and Senesino), two violins (Pietro and Prospero Castrucci), lute (John Francis Weber; see Ch. 4), and violoncello (Bononcini). It did not appear on the stage of the King's Theatre until 10 January 1722.[103]

Bononcini's reluctance to perform in public may account for the lack of direct evidence that he played the gamba. But circumstantial evidence is provided by obbligatos for two gambas in two of his stage works, *Il fiore delle eroine* (Vienna, 1704) and *Il ritorno di Giulio Cesare vincitore della Mauritania* (Vienna, 1704 or 1705),[104] as well as two works with gamba parts attributed to just to 'Bononcini': a cantata for soprano, gamba and continuo, 'Sono amante', in the Bokemeyer collection at D-B,[105] and '*Bononcini*, 1 Suonate da Camera a quattro, 1 Violini 2 Viola da Gamba è Basso Continuo' in the stock of Nicolas Selhof.[106] It has also been suggested that the G major 'Sonatta à Violon[c]ello Solo, del sig^r Bononcin' in an Italian manuscript now in Vienna is actually for gamba because of 'several chords which can only be played on that instrument'.[107] The problem with ascribing these 'Bononcini' pieces to Giovanni is that his cellist brother Antonio may also have been a gamba player: there are parts for two gambas in his oratorio *Il trinfo della grazia, overo La Conversione di Maddalena* (Vienna,

---

[101]   DP, 23/6/1721.

[102]   *The Diary of John Hervey, First Earl of Bristol, with Extracts from his Book of Expenses, 1688 to 1742*, ed. S. H. A. Hervey (Wells, 1894), 158.

[103]   *LS*, ii/2, 657; Gibson, *The Royal Academy of Music*, 153.

[104]   ME: M. Strümper, 'Die Viola da gamba am Österreichischen Kaiserhof: Untersuchungen zur Instrumenten- und Werkgeschichte der Wiener Hofmusikkapelle im 17. und 18. Jahrhundert' (PhD diss., U. of Vienna, 2001); CD-ROM version (Vienna, 2002).

[105]   Ghielmi, 'An Eighteenth-Century Italian Treatise', 80.

[106]   *Catalogue d'une très belle bibliothèque*, intro. King, 216, lot 2326.

[107]   A-Wn, Mus. MS E.M.23; ME: A. Bononcini, *Complete Sonatas for Violoncello and Basso Continuo*, ed. L. Lindgren, RRMBE, 77 (Madison, WI, 1996), 149–52; B. Wissick, notes to *Antonio and Giovanni Bononcini: Sonatas and Cantatas*, Wissick, S. Sanford, C. Liddell, A. Lawrence-King, T. Chancey, Centaur 2630 (2003); information from Mark Caudle.

1707).[108] However, Selhof at The Hague is more likely to have stocked a quartet by Giovanni, who worked in London, than Antonio, who seemingly never came near the Netherlands. Selhof also owned two manuscripts of violoncello sonatas ascribed specifically to 'Giovanni Bononcini'.[109]

❧ Lorenzo Bocchi

THE Italian cellist and composer Lorenzo Bocchi was probably a gamba player by virtue of the fact that there are two sonatas for gamba and continuo in his collection *A Musicall Entertainment for a Chamber* (Dublin, 1724; Edinburgh, 2/1726; repr. *c.* 1990), no. 11 in D minor and no. 12 in F major; the instrument is described as a 'SIX STRING BASS' on the title-page.[110] Bocchi arrived in Edinburgh in July 1720 in the company of the Scottish tenor Alexander Gordon, who had sung in Naples in the 1717–18 season, was in Lucca in 1719, was in London by late November that year, and sang for the Royal Academy in London in the spring of 1720; he may have accompanied Gordon from Italy. They evidently arrived in Edinburgh to put on public concerts, but Gordon soon moved to London and a new career as an antiquarian, and Bocchi can be traced in Edinburgh mainly through his collaborations with the writer and publisher Allan Ramsay senior, including two wedding entertainments put on there in 1720 and 1723, a Scots cantata published in *A Musicall Entertainment*, and possibly the ballad opera version of Ramsay's play *The Gentle Shepherd* (1729). He moved to Dublin sometime between February 1723 and August 1724. While he was there he contributed to several of the early publications of John and William Neale, including important collections of Scottish and Irish tunes, and was involved in the earliest-known Dublin concerts. He returned to Edinburgh sometime between 27 July 1725 and 22 February 1726, and is last heard of performing there on 20 July 1729 with the young violinist Matthew Dubourg.

Bocchi was an attractive and reasonably fluent composer, writing in a post-Corelli idiom with some references to Vivaldi and Handel. He also developed an interest in the vernacular music of the British Isles. Neale's publication *A Colection of the most Celebrated Irish Tunes* (Dublin, ?1724; repr. 1986) begins with his setting of the Irish tune 'Pléaráca na Ruarcach' 'improved with diferent divitions after yᵉ Italian maner'; the title-page states it was '*As performed at the*

[108] ME: Strümper, 'Die Viola da gamba am Österreichischen Kaiserhof'.

[109] *Catalogue d'une très belle bibliothèque*, intro. King, 209, lots 2152, 2153.

[110] RISM A/I B 3232, 3233. See esp. P. Holman, 'A Little Light on Lorenzo Bocchi: an Italian in Edinburgh and Dublin', in *Music in the British Provinces, 1690–1914*, ed. R. Cowgill and Holman (Aldershot, 2007), 61–86.

Ex. 3.5 Lorenzo Bocchi, Sonata no. 12 in F major,
'English Aire Improv'd after an Italian Manner', bb. 1–17

Subscription Consort *by Senior Loranzo Bocchi*'. It consists of a solo line in the treble clef, presumably played by Bocchi down the octave on the violoncello or gamba, with a treble-clef 'Chorus' part, probably for a violin or violins, and an unfigured bass. The second movement of Bocchi's Sonata no. 12, labelled 'English Aire Improv'd after an Italian Manner', does similar things with the popular tune 'The Parson among the Peas', treating it as the theme of an Italianate sonata movement with imitations and sequential passages (Ex. 3.5).[111] The third movement of this sonata, a minuet 'In Imitation of a french Horn', borrows its rhythmic patterns from the 'Minuet for the French Horn' from Handel's Water Music, HWV348/7. Sonata no. 11 is a suite-like three-movement work consisting of a prelude with dotted notes and roulades in the manner of French overtures, a courante-like movement, and a minuet. Bocchi's sonatas are no masterpieces, but the writing is effective enough, and nos. 11 and 12 are of interest as the last gamba solos published in Britain before the modern revival.

[111] Sources of the tune are listed in F. B. Zimmerman, *Henry Purcell, 1659–1695: an Analytical Catalogue of his Music* (London, 1963), D137.

❦ *Handel*

W E can now discuss the gamba pieces Handel wrote in London around
1724. *Giulio Cesare in Egitto*, HWV17, his setting of Haym's libretto written in the summer and autumn of 1723 and first produced at the King's Theatre
on 20 February 1724, contains a gamba part in Act II, Scene 2.[112] The scene is (in
the parallel English translation) 'A Garden of Cedars, with prospect of Mount
Parnassus, on which is seated the Palace of Virtue'. Caesar enters and 'A Symphony of various Instruments' begins, to which he responds in a short recitative.
'Parnassus opens' during a second sinfonia and 'Virtue [Cleopatra in disguise]
appears sitting on a Throne, attended by the Nine Muses'. She sings the famous
seduction song 'V'adoro pupille', after which 'Caesar runs towards Cleopatra,
Parnassus shuts, and the Scene is as before'.

The Parnassus scene is famous for its rich and complex instrumentation. An
on-stage band, consisting (in the final version) of oboe, two violins, viola, gamba,
theorbo, harp, bassoon, and violoncello, is accompanied by muted strings in the
pit. It is significant that the number of musicians on stage apparently comes to
nine, for the music the group plays represents the Concert of the Muses, frequently
portrayed in Renaissance and Baroque art. Some manuscripts give 'bassons' and
'violoncelli' in the plural, but Handel and his contemporaries occasionally used
plural forms of such words while apparently meaning single instruments – as in
the statement just quoted that Bononcini 'will play on the Violoncelli'.[113] The nine
instrumentalists could have represented the Muses on stage, though Dean and
Knapp suggest that they were hidden while extras mimed.[114]

Handel used the three exotic instruments, gamba, theorbo and harp, to evoke
the luxurious atmosphere of Cleopatra's court, and perhaps also to represent
ancient stringed instruments such as the lyre, kithara and barbiton. We know
today that European stringed instruments were not bowed before the eleventh
century, but that was not established in the eighteenth century.[115] Charles Burney
wrote about an '*Etruscan Lyre*, with seven strings' depicted on a vase in the collection of Sir William Hamilton, British ambassador in Naples:

[112] N. F. Haym, *Giulio Cesare in Egitto, Drama* (London, 1724), 36–9; CC: *ECCO*,
ESTC T072410. See esp. Dean and Knapp, *Handel's Operas, 1704–1726*, 484, 490–1,
513–14.

[113] Maunder, *The Scoring of Baroque Concertos*, 240, cites an instance in Handel's
op. 3, no. 6 where the marking 'Bassons' in the autograph was rendered as
'Basson Solo' in the printed parts.

[114] Dean and Knapp, *Handel's Operas, 1704–1726*, 490.

[115] W. Bachmann, *The Origins of Bowing and the Development of Bowed Instruments
up to the Thirteenth Century* (London, 1969), esp. 1–23.

The lower part of the instrument has much the appearance of an old Base-Viol, and it is not difficult to discover in it more than the embryo of the whole Violin family. The strings lie round, as if intended to be played with a *bow*; and even the cross lines on the tail-piece are such as we frequently see on the tail-pieces of old Viols.[116]

Handel's music for the scene exists in three versions.[117] The first is in the autograph score, GB-Lbl, R.M.20.b.3, fols. 76–79v, the second in J. C. Smith's score, GB-Lbl, R.M.19.c.6, fols. 64v–69, while the third, presumably that performed in 1724, is in a number of sources, including Smith's second score, D-Hs, MA/1019, fols. 67v–71v, and GB-Lbl, R.M.19.c.7, fols. 56v–61.[118] In the autograph the first sinfonia is scored just for 'Hautb.', 'Viola da gamba', 'Harpa', and 'Teorba'. The harp plays the melody and bass, doubled in the treble by the oboe and in the bass by the theorbo, while the gamba plays a viola-like inner part in the tenor clef (Ex. 3.6). The second sinfonia starts with the same instruments, but the theorbo and the gamba play an arpeggiated demisemiquaver figure in unison decorating the bass in a mixture of tenor and bass clefs; the 'Orchestra' (four-part strings 'senza Cembalo') joins in only for the last eight bars (Ex. 3.7). In the aria the singer is mainly accompanied by the bass, marked 'Viola da Gamba Harpa e Teorba', with punctuating orchestral chords between the phrases. In this version there were only four instruments on stage: oboe, gamba, harp and theorbo.

In the second version the first sinfonia is the same as in the autograph, except that the bass part previously given to the theorbo is assigned to 'Bassi' and the theorbo is added to the bass line of the harp part. The second sinfonia is also the same as in the autograph, but the aria has been revised so that the voice is accompanied more or less continuously by a nine-piece on-stage band, consisting of 'Viol: e Hautb. 1°', 'Viol: 2', 'viola', 'viola da gamba', 'Teorba', 'Harpa', and 'Bassons e violoncell:'; the orchestra, with the bass now marked 'Cembalo', adds punctuating chords as before. The harp and theorbo continue to play continuo from the bass line, but the gamba has a new part that changes function, at various times playing chords, doubling the second violin, providing a tenor part when the viola is silent, adding a fifth part to the string chords, and doubling the bass. It is notated in a mixture of tenor and bass clefs.

In the final version Handel turned his attention to the sinfonias. He rewrote them using the nine-piece on-stage band, giving the three exotic instruments

---

[116] BurneyH, i. 386.

[117] ME of the first and third versions: G. F. Handel, *Giulio Cesare in Egitto*, ed. W. Dean and S. Fuller (Oxford, 1998), 102–9, 328–36.

[118] For the musical sources, see ibid., 366–9; Dean and Knapp, *Handel's Operas, 1704–1726*, 508–26.

Ex. 3.6 G. F. Handel, *Giulio Cesare in Egitto*, HWV17, Act II, Scene 2,
first version, first sinfonia

more sophisticated and idiomatic things to do (Ex. 3.8). He replaced the rather
unpromising demisemiquaver idea with separate, more sophisticated parts. The
gamba now has a multi-functional role as in the aria, though with more multiple stopping; the chords sometimes provide a continuo realisation of the bass
line and sometimes provide extra inner parts. He returned the theorbo to the
bass line in the second sinfonia, but subtly elaborated its part with repeated
notes so that it supports the gamba and can easily be distinguished from the
other bass instruments. Similarly, he elaborated the harp part so that the listener
can easily distinguish it from the other treble and bass instruments. The next
step, which so far as we know he did not take, would have been to revise the

Ex. 3.7 G. F. Handel, *Giulio Cesare in Egitto*, HWV17, Act II, Scene 2, first version, second sinfonia, bb. 1–8

Ex. 3.8 G. F. Handel, *Giulio Cesare in Egitto*, HWV17, Act II, Scene 2,
third version, first sinfonia

gamba, harp and theorbo parts of the aria along the same lines. The three versions provide us with a fascinating insight into Handel's working methods, and show him devising ever more subtle ways to use the exotic instruments. However, even his most sophisticated gamba writing is strangely old-fashioned in that it combines several functions instead of just acting as a soloist in the tenor register.

The modern solo role for the gamba is demonstrated by the other work Handel wrote for it around 1724. Actually, 'wrote' is the wrong word, for all he did was copy out the first bar of his G minor sonata, HWV364, at the foot of the first page of the autograph of the violin version, GB-Cfm, MU. MS 261, p. 21, putting the solo part down an octave in the alto clef and annotating it 'Per la Viola da Gamba'.[119] It was presumably an instruction for a copyist to write out the whole piece in that form. The resulting work is playable on the bass viol, as recordings have demonstrated, though it is not particularly idiomatic.[120] Mark Caudle has found that Handel's D major violin sonata, HWV371 (c. 1750), works rather better when treated in the same way. By the 1720s the treble clef was well established among gamba players, so they could have played any of his solo or trio sonatas without having to make or obtain a transcription.[121]

However, gamba players continued to arrange Handel, witness the set of seven arias in NL-DHa, K-XIX-1 taken from *Radamisto* (1720), *Muzio Scevola* (1721), *Floridante* (1721), *Lotario* (1729), and *Atalanta* (1736), and arranged for 'Flauto Picolo' in *d″* (using transposing notation), gamba, and continuo.[122] The original violin parts are given to the recorder, while the gamba has the vocal line in the treble clef but changes to the bass line in the bass clef for the ritornelli. The arranger was probably working in the Netherlands: in England the recorder part would have been labelled 'sixth flute' or the equivalent in other languages. Richard King

---

[119] See esp. T. Best, 'Handel's Chamber Music: Sources, Chronology and Authenticity', *EM*, 13 (1985), 476–99, at 479, 485; ME arr. for gamba: G. F. Handel, *Sonata in G-Moll*, ed. G. and L. von Zadow, intro. P. Holman (Heidelberg, 2009).

[120] For instance, *The Noble Bass Viol: English Music from Purcell to Handel for Three Bass Viols and Continuo*, M. Caudle, The Parley of Instruments, Hyperion CDA67088 (1999). For a similar opinion, see R. G. King, 'Handel and the Viola da Gamba', in *A Viola da Gamba Miscellany*, ed. S. Orlando (Limoges, 2005), 63–79, at 71–72.

[121] *The Noble Bass Viol* includes a performance of Handel's Trio Sonata in G minor, HWV393, with the violin parts played down an octave on two bass viols; ME in this form: G. F. Handel, *Sonata G-Moll für 2 Violen da Gamba oder andere Streichinstrumente (Violinen, Violen, Violoncelli) und Basso Continuo* HWV393, ed. G. and L von Zadow, intro. P. Holman (Heidelberg, 2007).

[122] See King, 'Handel and the Viola da Gamba', 75–9. I am grateful to Richard King for providing me with transcriptions.

Ex. 3.9 Francesco Guerini, Sonata in A major, op. 1, no. 4, Andante, bb. 1–8

suggests that he was someone working for Handel's pupil Princess Anne, daughter of George II, who married in 1734 Willem IV, Prince of Orange,[123] and that the intended gamba player was Jan Frederick Riehman, a relative of the oboist and composer Jacob Riehman, also a gamba player.[124] Jan Frederick studied in London in 1734–5 with one of the Castrucci brothers, and composed a lost collection, *Suites de préludes pour la basse de viole* (1727).[125] Another collection probably written with him in mind is Francesco Guerini's *VI sonate a violino con viola da gamba o cembalo*, op. 1 (Amsterdam, c. 1739).[126] Guerini, a Neapolitan violinist, had been in England in 1730 (which probably explains why he dedicated his op. 1 to Elizabeth Russell, Countess of Essex), and became a colleague of Jan Frederick at Willem IV's court.[127] The role of the gamba varies from playing a simple bass line to being virtually an equal partner with the violin, with demanding passagework and some chords in sixths and thirds (Ex. 3.9). The music is in a simple but effective *galant* style.

Who played Handel's English gamba parts? We can presume that the player in

[123] R. G. King, 'Handel's Travels in the Netherlands in 1750', *ML*, 72 (1991), 372–86, esp. 378–80.

[124] For Riehman, see R. G. King, 'The Riehman Family of Court Musicians and Composers', *Tijdschrift van de Vereniging voor Nederlandse Muziekgeschiedenis*, 44 (1994), 36–50.

[125] Ibid., 43–44, 46.

[126] CC: GB-LEbc, Special Collections, Music, E-8.1 GUE; ME (of the Paris reprint): ed. C. Contadin and M. Pelliciari (Albese con Cassano, 2003).

[127] *The Daily Journal*, 11, 14, 15/4/1730; R. Rasch, 'The Italian Presence in the Musical Life of the Dutch Republic', in *The Eighteenth-Century Diaspora of Italian Music and Musicians*, ed. R. Strohm (Turnhout, 2001), 177–210, at 186, 190–1.

Giulio Cesare was a member of the Royal Academy orchestra. Of those discussed, two, Haym and Goodsens, can probably be eliminated because there is no hard evidence that they played the gamba, and Goodsens does not appear in the 1720 lists of the orchestra. There are stronger grounds for believing that Chaboud, Walther and Amadei played the gamba, though there is no evidence that they were still in England or even alive in 1724. Bononcini was in London in 1724, but is unlikely to have played in *Giulio Cesare*, partly because he rationed his appearances as a performer and partly because he and Handel were the focus of rival and mutually antagonistic factions in the opera company and among the public at large. Handel may even have known that Bononcini had used gambas in *Il ritorno di Giulio Cesare* and decided to show that he too could write effectively for the instrument in an opera about the same historical figure. Bocchi was in Dublin in 1724. Another candidate not yet discussed, the German-Italian cellist Fortunato Chelleri, came to England just too late: it was said to be 'the first Time of his appearing on the English Stage' when he played 'a Solo on the Bass-Viol' at the Lincoln's Inn Fields Theatre on 4 April 1725.[128] He returned to London the following year, though there is no other evidence of him playing the gamba. Once again, a single uncorroborated reference to the 'bass viol' needs to be treated with caution.

This leaves David Boswillibald. He played the gamba, was in London at the right time, and was seemingly a member of the Royal Academy orchestra; he was certainly a follower of Handel, subscribing to multiple copies of the John Cluer scores of *Rodelinda* (1725), *Scipione* (1726), *Alessandro* (1726), and *Admeto* (1727).[129] Handel may have written the gamba part for him in *Guilio Cesare* partly because he was a double bass player rather than a cellist. The evidence (the 1720 Royal Academy lists, the 1727 list of the Lord Mayor's day orchestra, and descriptions of the opera orchestra in 1728 and 1733) suggests that it was his practice to have two double basses with between two and four violoncellos.[130] Thus, with two cellists in the on-stage band, one playing the gamba, the violoncello section of the pit orchestra might have been seriously depleted. Overall, Handel does not seem to have taken much interest in the gamba, though for what it is worth, a German instrument of about 1700 said to be 'Formerly the property of Handel

---

[128] *DC*, 12/4/1725. See also Lindgren, 'Italian Cellists', 141–2.

[129] D. Hunter and R. M. Mason, 'Supporting Handel through Subscription to Publications: the Lists of *Rodelinda* and *Faramondo* Compared', *Notes*, 2nd series, 56 (1999), 27–93, at 50.

[130] Dean and Knapp, *Handel's Operas, 1704–1726*, 33–4; Burrows, 'Handel's London Theatre Orchestra', 354, 355; M. W. Stahura, 'Handel and the Orchestra', in *The Cambridge Companion to Handel*, ed. D. Burrows (Cambridge, 1997), 238–48, esp. 240–3.

and presented by him to Mr. Bernard Granville' was exhibited at the Music Loan Exhibition of 1904 alongside a portrait of a 'Gentleman playing the Viola da Gamba. Supposed to be a portrait of Handel'.[131] Incidentally, the handsome title-page of the Cluer score of *Giulio Cesare*, using a design derived from an engraving by Bernard Picart published in Paris in 1708, features a couple in Spanish costume playing the harpsichord and gamba; it was not used for the other Cluer editions of Handel's operas, so it was presumably chosen to remind buyers of the use of the instrument in the opera (Plate 3).[132]

🐚 *New Sources*

HANDEL'S 1724 gamba parts seemed an anomaly when nothing comparable was known from the same period in England. That has now changed with the discovery of new pieces that come from the circle of Italian musicians in London. The source closest to Handel is probably a manuscript now in GB-Lhh, no. 1998.127. It was partly copied by hands also found in music manuscripts once owned by the Baillie family of Mellerstain House in Berwickshire, now in GB-Er, and consists largely of solo cantatas with string accompaniment by the harpsichordist Pietro Giuseppe Sandoni (1685–1748), though there is also a copy of Handel's cantata 'Crudel tiranno amor', HWV97, as well as some English songs and ornamented voice parts of Italian arias.[133] Sandoni is best known today from his connections with Handel: he was sent by Handel to Venice in 1722 to recruit the soprano Francesca Cuzzoni, and married her in 1725.

The piece in question, 'Lascio il core in quest'amplesso' (fols. 64–71) is entitled 'Cantata a voce sola con due viole e teorba di Pier Giuseppe Sandoni'. It is clear from the writing of this charming piece that the obbligato parts are for gambas: they are in the treble clef (to be read an octave lower) and the second part goes below the range of the viola several times in the last aria (Ex. 3.10). The same piece was printed in Sandoni's *Cantate da camera e sonate per il*

---

131   *An Illustrated Catalogue of the Music Loan Exhibition held ... by the Worshipful Company of Musicians at Fishmongers' Hall, June and July 1904* (London, 1909), 152, 229; see also *A Special Loan Exhibition of Musical Instruments, Manuscripts, Books, Portraits, and other Mementoes of Music and Musicians* (London, 1904), 103, 122, nos. 1096, 1254. The gamba had been offered for sale in 1844; see *The Liverpool Mercury*, 13/9/1844, and in 1858 (wrongly described as a viola d'amore), see Puttick and Simpson, *Catalogue of the Very Important and Interesting Musical Collections of a Distinguished Amateur, with Selections from various Libraries* (29, 30/1/1858), lot 186.

132   For the title-page, see *Handel: a Celebration of his Life and Times, 1685–1759*, ed. J. Simon (London, 1985), 131.

133   Information from Anthony Hicks.

Ex. 3.10 P. G. Sandoni, 'Lascio il core in quest'amplesso', bb. 1–17

cembalo (*c.* 1727; repr. 1983), pp. 23–33, but with the obbligato parts unlabelled and in the treble and tenor clefs respectively. It looks as if Sandoni originally scored the cantata with two gambas and theorbo, but published it in a version with the more mainstream combination of soprano, violin, cello and continuo. Immediately after it in the manuscript (fol. 71v) there is an anonymous, untitled chromatic contrapuntal piece that could also be for gamba (Ex. 3.11). It is for a solo instrument (written in the alto clef with the range *a–d"*) and bass, and is seemingly a fast movement from a sonata. The connection between Sandoni, the gamba and the Baillie family can easily be explained: there are payments to Sandoni in Lady Grisell Baillie's Household Book for teaching her daughter Grisie the harpsichord between 1719 and 1721; the family had moved to London in

Ex. 3.11 Anonymous, Sonata movement in D major, bb. 1–12

1714.[134] Much earlier, when she was a child in Scotland in 1707, Grisie was taught the viol by the French musician Sainte-Colombe junior (Ch. 2). There is nothing in the Household Book to suggest that she was still playing the gamba around 1720, though Sandoni's cantata is perhaps evidence that she was, and that there was another gamba player in her circle – perhaps one of the Italian gamba-playing cellists already discussed.

There is another gamba work by Sandoni: a simple but effective three-movement C major sonata 'del Sʳ. G. Sandoni', consisting of a binary prelude, an 'Allemanda' and a 'Menuetto'. It is the first of a set of six early eighteenth-century gamba sonatas in the late eighteenth-century Williamson Manuscript, GB-Lu, Special Collections, MS 944/2/1–3 (Ch. 8).[135] Several sonatas in the set are arrangements. No. 2 in B♭ major was assembled from two violin sonatas in Angelo Michele Besseghi's *Sonate da camera*, op. 1 (Amsterdam, *c.* 1710), one of

134 Household Book of Lady Grisell Baillie, ii. 5, 29, 54, transcript from photocopies of the originals at Mellerstain House, deposited in the library of the National Museums of Scotland, Edinburgh (Anthony Hicks).

135 P. Holman, 'A New Source of Bass Viol Music from Eighteenth-Century England', *EM*, 31 (2003), 81–99.

Ex. 3.12 Anonymous, Sonata in D major,
no. 5 from the Williamson Manuscript, Vivace, bb. 18–23

the Roger publications offered for sale in London in 1724.[136] No. 4 in G minor was assembled from two of Francesco Barsanti's op. 1 recorder sonatas (1724; repr. 1727).[137] No. 3 in B minor also seems to be a compilation. The first and third movements, a duple-time contrapuntal Allegro and a jig-like Allegro, are unidentified, but the middle movement is the D major minuet from Handel's Water Music, HWV349/13, transposed into A major – which makes a comfortable range for the gamba but an uncomfortable key relationship with the outer movements.

Nos. 5 in D major and 6 in G major are unidentified, but are closer to bass viol duets than conventional solo sonatas. The bass sometimes echoes the solo part, moves in sixths and thirds with it, and crosses it to become the top part. This does not necessarily mean that they are by the same composer. No. 5 is an unusual and effective work with three triple-time movements, an extended 3/8 Vivace using a neat mixture of rondo and binary patterns, a Corellian Sarabanda with a walking bass, and a simple Menuetto (Ex. 3.12). No. 6 is in a simpler, more old-fashioned style and is more clumsily composed. It is in five movements (a duple-time Largo followed by an Allemanda, a Corrente, a Sarabanda, and a gavotte-like Vivace), and relies heavily on sequences rising and falling by step, with a Purcellian turn of phrase on occasion.

The set was seemingly arranged and compiled by a gamba player in England around 1730. The latest identifiable music is the Handel minuet in no. 3, which was probably arranged from the two-part version, HWV546 (published in a Walsh collection of minuets in 1729), rather than the orchestral version in the Water Music.[138] HWV546 and the minuet from no. 3 are both in A major and have crotchets in bars 3 and 7 of the second section instead of the fanfare-like quavers familiar from the orchestral version (Ex. 3.13). The copyist of the Williamson Manuscript, working in the 1770s or 1780s, probably found the sonatas more or

136   RISM A/I B 2465; CC: GB-Lbl, f.246.c.(3). See Lesure, *Bibliographie des éditions musicales*, 60; Brotherton, *An Account of Printed Musick*, [10].

137   RISM A/I B 1052, 1053. See Smith and Humphries, *A Bibliography of … John Walsh during the Years 1721 to 1766*, 35, nos. 141–4.

138   ME: G. F. Handel, *Einzeln überlieferte Instrumentalwerke II*, ed. T. Best, Hallische Händel-Ausgabe, IV/19 (Kassel, 1988), no. 80.

Ex. 3.13 G. F. Handel, Minuet in A major, HWV546, comparing (a) the version in the
Williamson Manuscript and (b) the two-part version published by Walsh

less in their present form, for it is unlikely that anyone by then would have both-
ered to arrange music by so obscure and old-fashioned a composer as Angelo
Michele Besseghi (1670–1744), a Bolognese violinist who worked in France. A
curious feature of the arrangements is that the movements by Barsanti (and in
one case Besseghi) were shortened as well as transposed down to suit the viol,
perhaps because the arranger found Barsanti's unusually well-developed movements too long (Ex. 3.14).

The third new source is a manuscript of Italian cantatas, GB-Cfm, MU. MS 46.
On fol. 1 it is entitled (misleadingly) 'Libro, delle Cantate:- / Dell. / Sig^r: Giou:
Bononcini.', and is mostly the work of a prolific copyist of Italian music apparently

Ex. 3.14 Francesco Barsanti, Sonata in C minor, op. 1, no. 4, Gavotta, bb. 32–44, comparing (a) the version published in 1724 and (b) the version in the Williamson Manuscript

working in London *c.* 1705–7.[139] The manuscript contains transcriptions of eleven of the *Cantate da cammera a voce sola*, op. 1 (Rome, 1700) by the Roman organist

[139] L. Lindgren, 'J. S. Cousser, Copyist of the Cantata Manuscript in the Truman Presidential Library, and other Cantata Copyists of 1697–1707, who Prepared the Way for Italian Opera in London', in *Et facciam dolci canti: studi in onore di Agostino Zino in occasione del suo 65° compleanno*, ed. B. M. Antolini, T. M. Gialdroni, and A. Pugliesi, 2 vols. (Lucca, 2003), 737–82, esp. 741–3, 764–6 (Samantha Owens).

Tommaso Bernardo Gaffi.[140] Five of them, 'La dove anzi ò vetusto' (fols. 13–21v; 1700, no. 1), 'Qual ogetto si palesa' (fols. 22–32; 1700, no. 2), 'Lungi dal ben' (fols. 50–55v; 1700, no. 6), 'Vendicatemi ò cieli' (fols. 61–68v; 1700, no. 8), and 'Nò che creder mai più' (fols. 87–96v; 1700, no. 12), have the unlabelled obbligato parts allocated to 'Viol di Gamba'; Gaffi just mentioned 'Violino', 'Tenore' (i.e. viola) and 'Violone' (bass violin) in the preface. A sixth cantata, 'Dove sei, dove t'ascondi' (fols. 97–101v), is a version of the fourth of Francesco Gasparini's *Cantate da camera a voce sola*, op. 1 (Rome, 1695; repr. 1984), with the unlabelled obbligato part also assigned to 'Viol di Gamba'.[141] The manuscript also contains cantatas for voice and continuo by Gasparini, Aldrovandini and Mancini, and a cantata with oboe obbligato by Lotti. Gaffi's cantatas are attractive works and deserve to be taken up by gamba players. Since the copyist seems to have been a German working in the circle of Italian musicians in London, an obvious suspect is David Boswillibald, though he would have had to have arrived in England rather earlier than his first known appearance in 1714, and Mu. MS 46 could just have been copied for a gamba-playing client. Boswillibald seems to have remained in England until his death in 1729, so Sandoni could have written his gamba sonata for him, though the set of sonatas in the Williamson manuscript was probably assembled a few years after that, in the early 1730s.

❧ *Saint-Hélène*

THE only known professional gamba player in England in the 1730s apart from Jan Frederick Rhieman was the French musician Jean-François Saint-Hélène. On 10 May 1732 a benefit concert at Hickford's Room for Anna Maria De Fesch and Saint-Hélène included 'a Solo, composed and perform'd by Mr. St. Helene, on the Bass Viol, another on the Violoncello, it being the first Time of his performing in publick'.[142] The concert also included 'Church Musick for six or eight Voices' by Anna Maria's husband, Willem De Fesch; she sang some Italian songs and he played a violin concerto. This was also their London debut: until the previous year Willem had been *kapelmeester* at Antwerp Cathedral. The mention of 'Violoncello' as well as 'Bass Viol' makes it clear that the latter was a gamba, and Saint-Hélène is known to have composed gamba music, now lost. The sale catalogue of Selhof's stock included two manuscripts described as '*St. Helene*, Pieces a Viola da Gamba Solo col Basso Continuo'; they were probably the same as 'Sant Hellene Suites de Pieces par Accords pour la Bassa de Violla 2 Livres' that

---

[140] RISM A/I G 99; CC: GB-Lbl, κ.2.h.16.

[141] RISM A/I G 463.

[142] *DP*, 10/5/1732.

had belonged to the Amsterdam publisher Michel-Charles Le Cène (d. 1743).[143] Saint-Hélène is listed in J. S. Cousser's address book as 'St. Helen. exc[ellent] Viol: da Gambist. lives in Abbé-Street, at Mr. Duffis'.[144] This is presumably the Abbey Street in central Dublin rather than the one in Bermondsey south of the Thames; Cousser worked in London from 1704 to 1707 but in Dublin from 1707 to his death in 1727. Saint-Hélène was also at the University of Leiden on 22 March 1741, when he was described as 'Gallus' and 'Musicus'.[145]

However, Saint-Hélène must have been in London at least once before his supposed debut in 1732. His *XII Solos for a Violin, with a Thorough Bass for the Harpsicord* were 'Printed for the Author and Sold by him at his Lodgings over against ye Pay Office near ye South Sea house in Broad street, and at M^r. Bressans Musical Instrument Maker at ye Green door in Sommerset house yard in ye Strand'.[146] The print is undated, but *BLIC* plausibly dates it 1721. Ten movements from the *XII Solos* were reprinted in the anthology *Medulla musicae* (*c.* 1727), published by Cluer and collected by 'R. M. Philomusicus' – probably the music seller Richard Meares; the GB-Lbl copy of *XII Solos* has 'And Rich. Meares St Paulls' added in ink to the bottom of the title-page.[147] The *XII Solos* are attractive works written in a mixture of French and Italian idioms; with a few adjustments to the violin chords they could easily be played down the octave on the gamba. Saint-Hélène was apparently the last person to play the gamba in public in London until Abel appeared in the spring of 1759.

❧ *Conclusion*

T HE establishment of an Italian opera house in London with an orchestra made up largely of immigrants gave the gamba a new lease of life. In the process its old varied and multi-faceted solo repertory was replaced by Italian or Italianate sonatas, cantatas and arias, often arranged for gamba. The gamba also ceased to be used to play bass parts, and its professional players began to use it as

---

[143] *Catalogue d'une très belle bibliothèque*, intro. King, 209, lots 2170, 2171; R. Rasch, 'I manoscritti musicali nel lascito di Michel-Charles Le Cène (1743)', in *Intorno a Locatelli: studi in occasione del tricentenario della nascita di Pietro Antonio Locatelli (1695–1764)*, ed. A. Dunning (Lucca, 1995), 1039–1070, at 1060, 1066 (Bettina Hoffmann).

[144] US-NHub, Osborn Music MS 16, p. 8 (Samantha Owens).

[145] R. Eitner, *Biographisch-Bibliographisches Quellen-Lexicon der Musiker und Musikgelehrten christlicher Zeitrechnung bis Mitte des neunzehnten Jahrhunderts*, 10 vols. (Leipzig, 1902; repr. 1958), viii. 386.

[146] RISM A/I s 369; CC: GB-Lbl, h.3855.

[147] CC: GB-Lbl, c.25.

a 'novelty' solo alternative to their main orchestral instruments, the violoncello, the double bass or the bassoon. This change went hand-in-hand with a change in the way its music was notated. Instead of being written in the bass and alto clefs, it was increasingly written in the treble clef, to be read an octave lower. Thus gamba players now had access to any instrumental or vocal music written in the treble clef, in the process reducing the amount of music specially written for them.

London was not the only place where these changes occurred. Vienna also had Italian gamba-playing cellists, and the change to a repertory based on Italianate sonatas and concertos can be observed in Germany – for example in Telemann and J. S. Bach. German composers also mostly treated it as a solo instrument in the tenor range, though in Bach's sacred music the older multi-faceted role is still found, the instrument sometimes playing an independent tenor part, some-times decorating the bass, and sometimes just doubling it.[148] In Bach's three gamba sonatas it usually plays a solo part independent of the bass, though in the third movement of the D major, BWV1028, it reverts to playing the bass during a harpsichord solo, and a manuscript of Bach's sonatas for violin and harpsichord, BWV1014–19, copied in 1725 by Johann Heinrich Bach, has the rubric 'col Basso per Viola da Gamba accompagnato se piace'.[149] By the middle of the century the gamba had become essentially a solo instrument, witness Leopold Mozart's statement that it 'serves mostly for playing an upper part' ('dienet meistentheils zu eine Oberstimme').[150]

The German repertory also relied increasingly on arrangements. Examples are Bach's gamba sonatas, which may all be versions of conventional trio sonatas, Ludwig Christian Hesse's arrangements of French operas by Rameau and others for one and two gambas,[151] a Berlin manuscript of arrangements, also prob-ably by Hesse, of violin sonatas by Corelli, G. B. Somis, Senaillé, Boismortier, Mascitti, Leclair, Montenari, and Franz Benda,[152] or two sonatas from William Corbett's *Six Sonatas for Two Flutes and a Bass*, op. 2 (1705) arranged for two gambas and bass in a manuscript from the Stuttgart court collection now at

[148] L. Dreyfus, *Bach's Continuo Group: Players and Practices in his Vocal Works* (Cambridge MA, 1987), 166–9, 253–6.

[149] Ibid., 255.

[150] J. Webster, 'Violoncello and Double Bass in the Chamber Music of Haydn and his Contemporaries, 1750–1780', *JAMS*, 29 (1976), 413–38, at 416.

[151] M. O'Loghlin, *Frederick the Great and his Musicians: the Viola da Gamba Music of the Berlin School* (Aldershot, 2008), 129–30, 134–6.

[152] ME: *Königliche Gambenduos für zwei Bassgamben*, ed. L. and G. von Zadow, 5 vols. (Heidelberg, 2002).

Rostock.[153] However, it was in London that the gamba was identified most completely with modernity – with the fashionable world of Italian opera and the cosmopolitan virtuosi that played in the opera orchestra. It was a remarkable transformation for an instrument that had long been an important symbol of England's musical heritage. It is also a fascinating example of the way that the roles and cultural meanings of an instrument can change as society and musical life changes leaving the instrument itself largely unchanged. To borrow terminology from information technology, the software changes while the hardware remains the same.

[153] ME: W. Corbett, *Zwei Sonaten für zwei Bass-Gamben und Bass*, ed. M. Jappe (Stuttgart, 2003), made without knowledge of op. 2; see W. Corbett, *Sechs Sonaten für zwei Altblockflöten und Basso Continuo*, ed. P. Rubardt (Leipzig, 1969), nos. 1 and 2.

CHAPTER 4

'Awake my Cetra, Harp and Lute':
John Frederick Hintz and
the Cult of Exotic Instruments

MUSICAL history is largely concerned with composers and their compositions. Leaf through any general music dictionary and it soon becomes
clear that most of the space is taken up with biographies of composers, histories of musical genres, accounts of music in particular places, and so on. But
the music business also depends on many ancillary trades: copyists, publishers,
printers, instrument makers, repairers, keyboard tuners, and latterly promot-
ers, managers, agents, journalists, and critics. This chapter uses a case-study of
an instrument maker working in mid-eighteenth-century London to place the
gamba in the context of the cult of exotic instruments at the time, and to inves-
tigate the role the cult played in musical and cultural changes in England in the
second half of the eighteenth century.

John Frederick Hintz appears in some dictionaries of violin makers, even
though he does not seem to have made violins, and that most of the information
(repeated parrot-fashion from dictionary to dictionary) is incorrect. The following is typical:

> HINDS, FREDERICK. / Worked in London, 1740–1776. Made admirably
> modelled viol-da-gambas, some since converted into 'cellos. Rash and pet-
> ulant critics have occasionally called-down his varnish, but their censure
> is entirely wrong. Also produced a few violins that meet the eye very agree-
> ably indeed, and super-added to this is an invitingly mellow, though not
> large, tone. Guitars and zithers bear his name. / F. Hinds, Maker / Ryder's
> Court, Leicester Fields / 17 London 76.[1]

Hintz (the form 'Hinds' does not appear in any contemporary source) set up shop
as an instrument maker in 1752, not 1740, and he died in 1772, so he cannot have
made an instrument in 1776. Viols and English guitars survive by him, and he

---

[1] W. Henley, *Universal Dictionary of Violin and Bow Makers* (Brighton, 2/1973), 575.
See also B. W. Harvey, *The Violin Family and its Makers in the British Isles: an
Illustrated History and Directory* (Oxford, 1995), 354.

claimed to make a number of other exotic types. Violins were part of his stock-in-trade at his death, though he never claimed to make them.

Most attention has been devoted to Hintz's viols. Seven are known at present: (1) a seven-string bass dated 1760 (London, Victoria and Albert Museum);[2] four medium-size instruments (with a body-length of about 57 cm), often described as tenors: (2) 1762 (Copenhagen);[3] (3) 1762 (private collection, USA) (Plate 4);[4] (4) 1763 (Ann Arbor), now a violoncello;[5] (5) ?1764 (Edinburgh);[6] and two small alto-size instruments (with a body-length of about 44 cm): (6) undated (private collection, USA) (Plate 5),[7] and (7) undated (unknown private collection).[8] An eighth viol was listed in an 1893 catalogue as 'VIOL DE GAMBA, by F. HINDS, Ryder's Court, Leicester Fields, London, 1776 (six strings), ¾ size, original and very perfect condition, original label, with case fitted with mahogany / [£]15'.[9] As can be seen, its label seems to be the one quoted by Henley, though it is hard to know whether it was just misread, was a forgery, or was added posthumously

---

[2] 37–1870; see A. Baines, *Victoria and Albert Museum, Catalogue of Musical Instruments*, ii: *Non-Keyboard Instruments* (London, 1968), 5, no. 1/6, illus. fig. 5. See also G. Thibault, J. Jenkins, and J. Bran-Ricci, *Eighteenth-Century Musical Instruments: France and Britain* (London, 1973), 44, no. 24.

[3] DE-Km, Claudius 267/59; see G. Skjerne, *Carl Claudius' Samling af Gamle Musikinstrumenter* (Copenhagen, 1931), 214, 216, illus. at 217. It has a second label of James and John Simpson, music sellers in Sweeting's Alley *c.* 1767–95; see C. Humphries and W. C. Smith, *Music Publishing in the British Isles* (Oxford, 2/1970), 292, 382.

[4] Sold at Sotheby's, 8/11/2005, lot 354, and illus. in the catalogue. I am grateful to Thomas MacCracken for information about this and other Hintz viols.

[5] Ann Arbor, University of Michigan, Stearns Collection, 1313; see A. A. Stanley, *Catalogue of the Stearns Collection of Musical Instruments* (Ann Arbor, MI, 1918), 194; B. M. Smith, 'Two Hundred Forty-One European Chordophones in the Stearns Collection of Musical Instruments', 3 vols. (PhD diss., U. of Michigan, 1977), 698–700, illus. 701–2.

[6] Edinburgh University, Collection of Historic Musical Instruments, 949, see *Historic Musical Instruments in the Edinburgh University Collection*, ed. A. Myers, ii/C/1: *Viols and Violins* (Edinburgh, 1995), 37–8. The handwritten label appears to read '1734', though it is 'difficult to read and may be wrong'; 1764 is most likely.

[7] Sold at Sotheby's on 25/11/1976, lot 305, and illus. in the catalogue; subsequently in the collection of Howard Mayer Brown and at US-Cn.

[8] Formerly in the collections of Dietrich Kessler and Denis Nesbitt; sold at Sotheby's on 14/6/1990, lot 290, and illus. in the catalogue. See also *Made for Music: an Exhibition to Mark the 40th Anniversary of the Galpin Society* (London, 1986), no. 4; J. Montagu, 'Salerooms', *EM*, 19 (1991), 103–5, at 103.

[9] Withers, *Catalogue of Ancient Instruments &c.* (London, 1893), 29; CC: William Waterhouse collection (Thomas MacCracken, Michael Fleming).

by a successor; the instrument is not known today. Little research has been done into Hintz's English guitars, though there are a number in museums, and several have passed through the salerooms in recent years.[10] Most are undated, though there are two from 1757, his earliest instruments known today.[11] Two Hintz guitars have shallow lute-shaped bodies, an alternative to the conventional shape, one of which, dated 1761, is highly decorated.[12]

Hintz's instrument-making career can also be traced through advertisements of various types. There are two undated trade cards with a common text but different decorative designs (Plates 6, 7).[13] The earliest-known newspaper advertisement, in *The London Evening Post* for 6 August 1754, has a similar text, beginning 'FREDERICK HINTZ / *At the Golden Guittar, in Little Newport Street, facing Newport Market,* / MAKES and Sells all Sorts of the completest Guittars; as also the AEolian Harp, an Instrument play'd by the Wind', and followed by the verse beginning 'Sweet heavenly harp!' The same verse appears in *The Public Advertiser* for 17 December 1755, but prefaced by expanded advertising copy: 'FREDERICK HINTZ, at the Golden Guittar, the Corner of Ryder's Court, Leicester-Fields is

---

[10] One was sold at Phillips on 17/1/1985; see J. Montagu, 'Salerooms', *EM*, 13 (1985), 566–8, at 566. Another (or possibly the same one) was sold by Gardiner Houlgate in Bath on 29/5/1992; see J. Montagu, 'Salerooms', *EM*, 20 (1992), 659–60. A fine undated example sold at Bonhams on 23/6/2009, lot 30, is now in a private collection in the USA.

[11] One, known as 'Sarah Wesley's guitar', was restored by Arthur Robb and is at John Wesley's Chapel, Bristol (www.art-robb.co.uk). The other is Edinburgh University, Collection of Historic Musical Instruments, 1066; see *Historic Musical Instruments in the Edinburgh University Collection*, ed. A. Myers, ii/B/2: *Lutes, Citterns and Guitars* (Edinburgh, 2/2003), 19–20. There are undated English guitars by Hintz in the same collection, 310 and 1116; see ibid., 20–1; and in Oxford, Ashmolean Museum, Hill Collection, no. 37; see D. D. Boyden, *Catalogue of the Hill Collection of Musical Instruments in the Ashmolean Museum, Oxford* (Oxford, 1969), 42–3, pl. 37; J. Whiteley, *Stringed Instruments: Viols, Violins, Citterns, and Guitars in the Ashmolean Museum* (Oxford, 2008), 98–9.

[12] GB-Lml, 61.199/12; Vermillion SD, National Music Museum, Arne B. Larson Collection, NMM 1286 (www.usd.edu/smm/Pluckedstrings.html#1286); see L. Graf, 'John Frederick Hintz, Eighteenth-Century Moravian Instrument Maker, and the Use of the Cittern in Moravian Worship', *Journal of Moravian History*, 5 (2008), 7–39, at 17–19. For other lute-shaped English guitars, see for instance A. Baines, *European and American Musical Instruments* (London, 1966), 43, illus. 251, 252; Baines, *Victoria and Albert Museum: Non-Keyboard Instruments*, 53–4, nos. 11/16 and 11/17, illus. fig. 75; Thibault, Jenkins and Bran-Ricci, *Eighteenth-Century Musical Instruments*, 96, no. 56.

[13] London, Tony Bingham Collection, formerly in the Hill Collection (Ben Hebbert).

the Original Maker of that Instrument, call'd The Guittar or Zittern, who has for many Years made and taught that Instrument, and has lately made a great Improvement on it, so that it may in a Moment be set to any Instrument or Voice. He teaches after c[o]mmon Notes in the best and easiest Manner: he also makes the AEolian Harp, an Instrument play'd by the Wind'.

The next advertisement is in *The Public Ledger*, 18 June 1761:

> FREDERICK HINTZ, / Original Guittar Maker, / WHO makes the compleat-est GUITTARS of all Sorts and Prices, and a new and delightful Instrument, called the Trumpet Marine, it is played with a bow, in Sound and Loudness similar to a Trumpet, it keeps long in Tune, and may be learned with the utmost Ease and Facility; upon the Water, or in a Garden in the Country, it is delectable to the Ear, and may be played in a Concert. He also makes the AEolian Harp, an Instrument played by the Wind, on which he has made an Improvement to play Tunes on, with an additional String, by which all the Strings of the Guittar can be tuned by it. Made and Sold Wholesale or Retail, at his Musical Warehouse, in Little Newport Street, the Corner of Ryders Court, Leicester-Fields, where the best Strings for the Guittar are to be had, and Guittars lent out on reasonable terms.

Then comes an entry in a 1763 trade directory:

> Hintz, Frederick. *The Corner of Ryder's-court, Leicester-fields.* Guittar-maker to her Majesty and the Royal Family; makes Guittars, Mandolins, Viols de l'Amour, Viols de Gamba, Dulcimers, Solitaires, Lutes, Harps, Cymbals, the Trumpet-marine, and the AEolian Harp.[14]

Followed by *The Public Advertiser*, 8 February 1766:

> THE favourite Instrument the MANDOLIN, taught by a reputable Master. For further Particulars please to enquire or to send a Line directed for P.B. at Mr. Hint's, Guittar-maker to his Majesty, the Corner of Riders Court, Leicester Fields, and they shall be punctually waited on. / Good Mandolins to be had at the abovementioned Place; likewise all Kind of Instruments and Music.

And the same newspaper, 17 March 1766:

> FREDERICK HINTZ, Guittar-Maker to Her Majesty and all the Royal

---

[14] T. Mortimer, *The Universal Director, or The Noble and Gentleman's True Guide to the Masters and Professors of the Liberal and Polite Arts and Sciences, and of the Mechanic Arts, Manufacturers, and Trades, Established in London and West-minster, and their Environs* (London, 1763), ii. 51; CC: ECCO, T013191. See also 'An Eighteenth-Century Directory of London Musicians', *GSJ*, 2 (1949), 27–31, at 30.

Family, at his Musical Instrument Warehouse, the Corner of Ryder's Court, Leicester Fields, humbly acquaints the Ladies, &c. that he has, after many Years Study and Application in endeavouring to bring this favourite Instrument the Guittar (being the first Inventor) still to a greater Perfection in regard to tuning and keeping the same in Tune, which has always been a principal Defect as well as inconvenient, has now found out, on a Principal entirely new, several Methods, whereby it is much easier and exacter tuned, and also remains much longer in Tune than by any Method hitherto known; which compleat Improvement has met with universal Esteem and Approbation. He has now by him a great Variety finished, in the neatest Taste; where those Ladies who chuse to change their's, or have them altered to this new Improvement, may depend on having them done to the greatest Perfection. Where likewise may be had Spanish Guittars, Mandolins, and all other Sorts of Musical Instruments, with great choice of the newest and best Musick on the most reasonable Rates. / N.B. Where also may be had the best Strings for Guittars, Violins, Mandolins, &c.[15]

After Hintz's death on 24 February 1772 an auction was announced of his stock-in-trade, initially in *The Morning Chronicle*, 31 July:

To be SOLD by AUCTION, / By Mr. ELDERTON, / on the Premises, / On Thursday, August 13, and the following day, THE Genuine STOCK in TRADE / Household Furniture, Linen, China, and Pictures of Mr. Hintz, the corner of Riders-court, Newport-street, Musical Instrument-maker, deceased, consisting of Guittars, Lutes, Mandolins, Harps, Harpsichords, Spinnets, Clarrichords, Forte Pianos, Eolian Harps, German Harps, Dulcimers, Psalteries, Violins, Tenors, Bass Viols, Viol de Gambols, Trumpet Moriens, German Flutes, &c. It is allowed that the late Mr. Hintz, was one of the first Guittar-makers in Europe; and that his instruments in general were very excellent.[16]

An advertisement in the same newspaper on 11 August announced a postponement until 20 August 'on account of some of the said instruments being not quite finished'.

Hintz also acted as a music seller and publisher. He was one of those advertised in October 1761 as selling John Jones's *Lessons for the Harpsichord ... Volume II* ('Miss Hintz' appears in the subscription list),[17] and the Adelph Hummel edition

[15] Repeated in *MC*, 22/3/1766; *MC*, 9/5/1766.

[16] Repeated in *MC*, 3, 5, 7, 10, 13–15, 17–20/8/1766.

[17] Humphries and Smith, *Music Publishing in the British Isles*, 370; RISM A/I J 637; CC: GB-Lbl, R.M.16.a.12.(3).

of Anton Filtz's *Five Trios and One Quartetti for a German Flute or Violin, Violon-cello Obligato and a Bass* (*c.* 1765).[18] He also published two collections of English guitar music in the early 1760s:

> *A Choice Collection of* / Psalm and Hymn Tunes / *set for the* / CETRA or GUITTAR / by / *Frederick Hintz* / *And sold at his Music Shop the Corner of Ryder's Court Leicester Fields, London.* / Awake my CETRA, Harp and Lute, / No longer let your Strings be mute; / And I my tuneful Part to take, / Will with the early Dawn awake.[19]

> *A Choice Collection of* / AIRS, MINUETS, MARCHES, / SONGS and COUNTRY DANCES &c. / *By several Eminent Authors* / Adapted for the / GUITTAR / *As also a Book of Psalm & Hymn Tunes.* / [rule] / LONDON Printed and sold by *Fred: Hintz* at his Music Warehouse in little / Newport Street the corner of Ryders Court Leicester Fields where the best Guittars / are made, also Trumpet Marine and OEolion Harps.[20]

The title-page of the first claims that Hintz 'set' (arranged) the psalm and hymn tunes for the English guitar, while in the second minuets on pp. 2, 5 and 12 are attributed to him and the minuet on p. 8 has 'Variations by F. H.' Thus, as well as making instruments, publishing music and running a music shop, he taught the English guitar and arranged and composed for it.

Hintz's activities pose a number of obvious questions. Why did he make small viols at a time when the only member of the family still in use was the bass, the viola da gamba? Can his claim to be the English guitar's 'Original Maker' (1755 advertisement) or 'first Inventor' (March 1766 advertisement) be taken seriously? And why did he seemingly confine himself to making exotic instruments? For answers we must turn to Hintz's life.

❧ *Life*

A GOOD deal is now known about Hintz thanks to scholars in two different fields: furniture history and the early history of the Unitas Fratrum or Moravian Brethren – the Protestant church whose members emigrated under the threat of persecution from Moravia to Saxony in the early eighteenth century,

---

[18] RISM A/I F 790; CC: GB-Lbl, R.M.17.c.6.(3).

[19] RISM A/I H 5637; CC: GB-En, Cwn 544 (Nicholas Temperley). Another edition, RISM A/I H 5636, has the imprint 'London *Printed by* R: BREMNER *in the* STRAND'; CC: GB-Lbl, A.861. See also N. Temperley, *The Hymn Tune Index: a Census of English-Language Hymn Tunes in Printed Sources from 1535 to 1820,* 4 vols. (Oxford, 1998), i. 255, where H 5637 is dated *c.* 1763 and H 5636 1765.

[20] CC: GB-Lbl, a.(76).w.1.

and went on to found settlements in Britain, North and South America, the
Caribbean, the Far East, and elsewhere.[21] It turns out that he had three separate
careers, as a furniture maker, as a Moravian 'labourer' or evangelist, and as an
instrument maker and music seller.[22]

He was born in 1711 at Greifenhagen near Stettin in Pomerania (now Szczecin
in Poland). Nothing is known of his early life, though he presumably learned
furniture making in Germany, possibly in Moravian circles; he set up in business
in London, witness an advertisement in *The Daily Post* on 22 May 1738:

> To be SOLD, / At the Porcupine in Newport-street, near / Leicester-Fields, /
> A Choice Parcel of Desk and Book-Cases of Mohogony, Tea-Tables, Tea-
> Cheets [i.e. chests] and Tea-Boards, &c. all curiously made and inlaid with
> fine Figures of Brass and Mother of Pearl. They will be sold at a very reason-
> able Rate, the Maker, FREDERICK HINTZ, designing soon to go abroad.

Hintz is not known to have signed or labelled any furniture, though the phrase
'all curiously made and inlaid with fine Figures of Brass and Mother of Pearl'
has been used to attribute to him pieces with these features, including a bureau
cabinet at Temple Newsam House near Leeds,[23] and a tea table in the Victoria and
Albert Museum.[24] The inlaid decoration on these pieces is similar to that on his
1761 English guitar, confirming that the furniture and the musical instruments
were made by a single person.

Hintz sold up in 1738 because he was returning to Germany. He took ship
from London on 13 June 1738 in a party that included John Wesley, and he married Anna Rosina Demuth, a Moravian deaconess, at Marienborn on 7 May 1739.[25]
He spent most of his time at the Moravian settlements at Marienborn and Herrnhaag (near Frankfurt am Main), working partly as a cabinet maker.[26] His wife

---

[21] See esp. J. E. Hutton, *A History of the Moravian Church* (London, 2/1909); C. J.
Podmore, *The Moravian Church in England, 1728–1760* (Oxford, 1998); J. C. S.
Mason, *The Moravian Church and the Missionary Awakening in England, 1760–
1800* (London, 2001).

[22] For Hintz, see esp. L. Boynton, 'The Moravian Brotherhood and the Migration
of Furniture Makers in the Eighteenth Century', *Furniture History*, 29 (1993),
45–58; J. Lomax, '"Guittar-Maker to her Majesty and the Royal Family": John
Frederick Hintz (1711–1772)', *Moravian History Magazine*, 22 (2002), 2–10; L. Graf,
'Moravians in London: a Case Study in Furniture-Making, *c.* 1735–65', *Furniture
History*, 40 (2004), 1–52; L. Graf, 'John Frederick Hintz', esp. 9.

[23] Lomax, 'Guittar-maker to her Majesty', 2, 8–10.

[24] Graf, 'Moravians in London', 14–15.

[25] C. J. Podmore, 'The Fetter Lane Society, 1738', *Proceedings of the Wesley Historical Society*, 46/5 (May 1988), 125–53, at 142; Graf, 'John Frederick Hintz', 12.

[26] Graf, 'John Frederick Hintz', 11–12.

died in June 1745, and later that year he briefly visited England, where he was in contact with the Bedford congregation.[27] In November 1746 he returned to Germany for his second wedding: he married a fellow Moravian, Ann Williams from Derbyshire, at Marienborn on 19 April 1747; they became Moravian acolytes at Herrnhaag on 4 June.[28] Soon after their return to England they moved to the Moravian settlement at Fulneck near Leeds, where the first of their five children was born.[29]

Hintz and his family returned to London at the end of 1749, and not long after he ceased to be a Moravian evangelist. The circumstances are set out in Ann's obituary, written on the day of her death, 15 April 1764:

> His being advised to return afterwards to his trade seeming heavy to them, by degrees their connexion with the Congregation diminished more & more. The Br. & Sr. [Brothers and Sisters] also were not satisfied with her, but grieved to observe in her too much of a worldly manner & look, & an unsuitable affectation of gentility. Indeed she did not come much among us for many years while she was still able, & yet would be purposing & speaking of doing it. In her confinement thro' sickness for the last 2 years, she often bewailed her mis-spent time, & longed & begged to recover the thread again, & possess once more the grace which she had neglected.[30]

Hintz had already turned to musical instrument making while in Yorkshire. On 14 March 1748 the London congregation asked him to make a harpsichord to replace their chapel organ, which was in store while repairs were carried out to the building, and on 17 October he promised the Fulneck community that he would 'get the Harpsichord ready' – presumably a different instrument.[31] He clearly made harpsichords: they were part of his stock-in-trade, and 'a neat Harpsichord by Hintz' was auctioned in London in January 1773.[32] 'A large Double Harpsichord with Two Setts of beautiful keys, made of snake-wood, with Four Stops and in exceeding fine condition' was advertised in *The Leeds Mercury* on 10 September 1776 as the work of 'Christian Frederick Hinte', an otherwise unknown maker.[33] This is perhaps a garbled reference to an instrument Hintz made in Yorkshire in the 1740s.

---

[27] Ibid., 12.

[28] Ibid., 12–13.

[29] Ibid., 13–14.

[30] Ibid., 38.

[31] Ibid., 11.

[32] *DA*, 11, 13, 15, 17, 18/1/1773.

[33] D. H. Boalch, *Makers of the Harpsichord and Clavichord, 1440–1840*, rev. C. Mould (Oxford, 3/1995), 91.

Hintz opened his music shop shortly after he returned to London with assistance from the Moravian community. On 12 September 1751 it was noted that 'Br Hintz cannot get thro in his business'; on 18 September it was requested that 'If anyone who has credit by anyone who sells mahogany wood it might be serviceable to Br. Hinz'; on 14 January 1752 the question was raised whether his plan to set up in business was approved; and on 24 February it was noted that he had opened his shop in Newport Street, and 'some of his Bills were brought into the conference'.[34] The bills, presumably, were his trade cards. However, he continued to deal in, if not make, furniture: on 23 August 1753 he supplied tables, chairs and mirrors to a fellow Moravian, Charles Henry de Larisch, and he is described as a furniture maker in Moravian records until 1764.[35]

Despite being described as 'in no close connexion' with the Moravians in 1764, he remained in contact with them, was given a Moravian funeral, and was buried in their cemetery in Chelsea.[36] The circumstances are recounted in the international Moravian chronicle for 1772:

> On April 25th our well-known brother, Friedrich Hinz, departed this life after suffering from the effects of a stroke for quite some time. We visited him and found him blessed and aware of his sins. At one point he expressed himself in a very heartfelt manner: the God of the Brethren is my God; and although I have been guilty in many things, I have nonetheless been forgiven, and on this day you will find your poor Hinz with our dear Saviour. His son implored that the soul-departed body of his father be buried on our God's Acre, and we could not refuse him such a thing. At the burial Br. Latrobe delivered a very fitting sermon full of beneficial advice and admonition.[37]

Brother Latrobe was Benjamin La Trobe, the Provincial Helper or leader of the Moravians in Britain at the time and the father of the Moravian missionary, writer and composer Christian Ignatius La Trobe.

&. *Hintz and Moravian Music*

Hintz's Moravian activities throw new light on his instrument making. Music was central to Moravian life and worship.[38] Count Zinzendorf, the

34 Graf, 'John Frederick Hintz', 15.

35 Graf, 'Moravians in London', 15.

36 Boynton, 'The Moravian Brotherhood', 52–3.

37 Graf, 'John Frederick Hintz', 39; trans. Lanie Graf.

38 See esp. H. H. Hall, 'Moravian Music Education in America, *c.* 1750 to *c.* 1830, *Journal of Research in Music Education*, 29 (1981), 225–34; A. Wehrend,

Moravian leader, thought that every aspect of daily life could be offered up to God, and that hymns were the best way of expressing worship. He encouraged the development of hymn singing, and was a prolific hymn writer himself. As well as using music in services, the Moravians encouraged it in education and for recreation. Their attitude to music was summed up by Christian Ignatius La Trobe:

> All that learn this science in their schools, are taught to consider the practice thereof, whether vocal or instrumental, as leading to the same grand point, in which all other parts of learning ought to center, namely, in the service of the LORD, and the promotion of his glory on earth.[39]

A striking feature of Moravian music was the cultivation of plucked instruments among its female members, following the authority of Luther's translation of the Bible, where, for instance, David soothes Saul with *Saitenspiel* – string playing. Paintings by Johann Valentin Haidt show Zinzendorf's daughters Henriette Benigna Justine and Marie Agnes playing what appear to be cittern-like instruments akin to English guitars.[40] There are many references to instruments called 'Cither', 'Cyttern', 'Zitter' or 'Zittern' being played in the diaries recording the activities of the various 'choirs' (Moravian communities were segregated according to age, sex and marital status) in the settlement at Bethlehem, Pennsylvania between 1749 and 1756; most of them come from the Single Sisters' Diary – i.e. they feature unmarried girls.[41] A letter written there on 16 August 1787 by a girl of twelve gives us a good idea of the musical activities: 'Here I am taught music, both vocal and instrumental; I play the guitar twice a day – am taught the spinnet and forte-piano; – and sometimes I play the organ … After we are in bed, one of the ladies, with her guitar and voice, serenades us to sleep.'[42] A manuscript book at Bethlehem contains chorales and other pieces set in tablature for a

---

Musikanschauung, Musikpraxis, Kantatenkompositionen in der Herrnhuter Brüdergemeine: ihre musikalische und theologische Bedeutung für das Gemeinleben von 1727 bis 1760 (Frankfurt am Main, 1995); *The Music of the Moravian Church in America*, ed. N. R. Knouse (Rochester, NY, 2008).

[39] C. I. La Trobe, *Hymn-Tunes Sung in the Church of the United Brethren* (London, 1806), iii; CC: author's collection.

[40] Illus. in A. Michel, 'Quellen zur Geschichte der Zister in Sachsen vom 16. bis 19. Jahrhundert', *Gitarre und Zister: Bauweise, Spieltechnik und Geschichte bis 1800. 22. Musikinstrumentenbau-Symposium Michaelstein, 16. bis 18. November 2001*, ed. M. Lustig (Blankenburg, 2004), 87–120, at 113–14, 116–17. See also Graf, 'John Frederick Hintz', 24, 25.

[41] Bethlehem PA, Moravian Archives, SS1 (Lanie Graf). See also Graf, 'John Frederick Hintz', 22–38.

[42] Hall, 'Moravian Music Education in America', 230.

six-course plucked instrument.[43] It was owned by Johann Andreas Hübner, who taught there from 1780 to 1790.

This is the context for understanding Hintz's claim to have invented the English guitar. Is it possible? The instrument had a tremendous vogue in Britain in the second half of the eighteenth century, particularly among upper-class women.[44] Hintz addressed his March 1766 advertisement to 'the Ladies, &c.' and claimed to be 'Guitar-Maker to Her Majesty and all the Royal Family' – which makes it possible that the large guitar shown in Francis Cotes's painting *Princess Louisa and Princess Caroline* (1767) was made by him.[45] With nine or ten metal strings tuned in six courses to a C major chord, the English guitar was easy to play: most of its music was simple, was usually in C major and was notated on a single stave in the treble clef. It also made the player look elegant. The fashionable gamba and English guitar player Ann Ford wrote that 'the Attitude this Instrument [the English guitar] almost naturally throws the Performer in, is very graceful', forming the 'Line of Beauty' described in William Hogarth's *Analysis of Beauty*;[46] it is illustrated by Gainsborough's famous painting of her (Ch. 7). By contrast, wind instruments distorted the face; playing violin-family instruments involved undignified and ungraceful postures, placing the instrument under the chin or between the legs; and keyboard instruments usually had to be played facing partially or wholly away from a potential audience.

Moreover, the English guitar is clearly related to existing German instruments such as the Hamburg bell-cittern or *cithrinchen* and the Thuringian *wald-cittern*.[47] Hintz would have known instruments of this sort from his years in Saxony, and it is possible that he introduced a modified version to Britain. The earliest-known dated English guitar appears to be one by Remerus Liessem dated

43 P. M. Fox, 'Music in Moravian Boarding Schools through the Early Nineteenth Century', in *The Music of the Moravian Church in America*, ed. Knouse, 212–27, at 219.

44 For the English guitar, see esp. P. Coggin, '"This Easy and Agreable Instrument": a History of the English Guittar', *EM*, 15 (1987), 204–18; S. Walsh, 'Is the English Guitar a Guitar or a Cittern?', *FoMRHI Quarterly*, 47 (April 1987), 43–7, comm. 798; R. MacKillop, 'The Guitar, Cittern and Guittar in Scotland: an Historical Introduction up to 1800', in *Gitarre und Zister*, ed. Lustig, 121–53; G. Doc Rossi, 'Citterns and Guitars in Colonial America', in *Gitarre und Zister*, ed. Lustig, 155–68.

45 The Royal Collection, RCIN 404334 (www.royalcollection.org.uk/eGallery).

46 A. Ford, *Lessons and Instructions for Playing on the Guitar* (London, ?1761), 4; CC: GB-Lbl, i.160.c.

47 See esp. A. Michel, 'Zistern in der traditionellen Musik Sachsens und Thüringens', *Studia instrumentorum musicae popularis*, 10 (Stockholm, 1992), 81–90; A. Michel, 'Quellen zur Geschichte der Zister', in *Gitarre und Zister*, ed. Lustig.

1756,[48] though there are references to others with earlier dates, including one dated 1750 attributed to Benjamin Banks of Salisbury,[49] one by J. C. Elschleger with an unclear date that may be 1753,[50] and one, unknown today, that was supposedly made by Hintz in London in 1740.[51] 1740 seems impossibly early for an English guitar, and he was seemingly in Germany in that year. However, there are early descriptions of Moravians in London playing citterns or guitars. Carl Notbeck played 'very sweetly on his little cithren in soft tones' during a Moravian service on 24 November 1747, and on 2 May 1751 Hintz himself sang the last two verses of the chorale 'O sacred head now wounded' 'gently touching the Guitar' as John Senft, his friend and spiritual mentor, lay dying.[52] What is certainly true is that German citterns of the time often had ten wire strings, like the English guitar, and that most of the Guitar makers in London were German. In addition to Hintz, Liessem, and Elschleger, they include Michael Rauche and Johann Zumpe – the last better known as a piano maker.

Hintz was one of the most prominent and respected English guitar makers. After his death the advertisements for his stock-in-trade stated: 'It is allowed that the late Mr. Hintz, was one of the first Guittar-makers in Europe; and that his instruments in general were very excellent'. In his March 1766 advertisement he claimed to have developed an improvement 'whereby it is much easier and exacter tuned, and remains much longer in Tune than by any Method hitherto known; which compleat Improvement has met with universal Approbation'. This seems to refer to the change from conventional wooden pegs to a system whereby the strings are attached to metal levers adjustable with a little key similar to that

[48] Baines, *Victoria and Albert Museum: Non-Keyboard Instruments*, 48, no. 11/1, illus. fig. 71. For Liessem, see Harvey, *The Violin Family and its Makers in the British Isles*, 362. See also J. Tyler, 'English Guitar Makers in Eighteenth-Century Britain: a Directory', *FoMRHI Quarterly*, 113 (August 2009), 11–18, comm. 1876; T. Takeuchi, 'Additions to Comm. 1876: some more English Guitars', *FoMRHI Quarterly*, 114 (November 2009), 5, comm. 1884.

[49] *An Illustrated Catalogue of the Music Loan Exhibition held … by the Worshipful Company of Musicians at Fishmongers' Hall, June and July 1904* (London, 1909), 138, where, like the 1757 Hintz guitar at Bristol, it is said to have belonged to Sarah Wesley. It is dated 1757 in the catalogue produced for the exhibition, *A Special Loan Exhibition of Musical Instruments, Manuscripts, Books, Portraits, and other Mementoes of Music and Musicians* (London, 1904), 113, no. 1181. It is probably the instrument illus. in A. W. Cooper, *Benjamin Banks, 1727–1795, the Salisbury Violin Maker* (Salisbury, 2/1995), 49.

[50] E. Wells and C. Nobbs, *Royal College of Music Museum of Instruments Catalogue*, iii: *European Stringed Instruments* (London, 2007), 94, RCM 21.

[51] *An Illustrated Catalogue of the Music Loan Exhibition*, 138. It is undated in *A Special Loan Exhibition of Musical Instruments*, 113, no. 1178.

[52] Graf, 'John Frederick Hintz', 26, 33.

used to wind up a pocket watch – hence the term 'watch-key mechanism'. Hintz was not the only person who used it or claimed to have invented it. A 1767 guitar by Rauche has a seemingly original one,[53] and in the 1780s John Preston engraved 'PRESTON INVENTOR' on the ones he made; examples are an undated instrument by Hintz with a replacement head and two by Preston himself.[54] No one patented it.[55]

I suggest that Hintz started to make cittern-like instruments in England to cater for the demand from the developing English Moravian communities. He played and taught the English guitar, and his *Choice Collection of Psalm and Hymn Tunes*, one of the few psalmody publications with English guitar accompaniment, appears to be a Moravian hymn book: it contains English translations of German chorales, including 'Now let us praise the Lord' (p. 7), a version of 'Nun danket alle Gott'. Eight of its hymns were also published in the first English Moravian hymn book with music, James Hutton's *The Tunes for the Hymns in the Collection with Several Translations from the Moravian Hymn-Book* (c. 1744),[56] while the texts of eight others are found in word-books of Moravian hymns.[57] However, as his business developed and he distanced himself from the community, Hintz doubtless began to make guitars for the general market – including members of the aristocracy and the royal family. On 29 March 1757 he received £3 7s. for a guitar ordered by the Duke of Bedford for Lady Caroline Russell.[58]

If so, what of Hintz's viols? The conventional description of the small ones as altos or tenors carries the implication that they were intended for viol consorts, or at least were used to play the inner parts of ensemble music. However, we have seen that the bass viol was the only member of the family in use in eighteenth-century England, and was essentially a solo instrument after about 1720. Some contemporary antiquarians collected manuscripts of consort music, though there is no sign that they played them on viols (Ch. 9). My alternative

---

[53] Wells and Nobbs, *Royal College of Music: European Stringed Instruments*, 95, RCM 333.

[54] Baines, *Victoria and Albert Museum: Non-Keyboard Instrument*, 50, no. 11/5, illus. fig. 72; Wells and Nobbs, *Royal College of Music: European Stringed Instruments*, 97, 98, RCM 161, 331.

[55] B. Woodcroft, *Patents for Inventions: Abridgments of Specifications relating to Music and Musical Instruments, A.D. 1694–1866* (London, 2/1871; repr. 1984).

[56] Temperley, *The Hymn Tune Index*, esp. i. 176–7.

[57] *A Collection of Hymns with Several Translations from the Hymn-Book of the Moravian Brethren*, 2 vols. (London, 3/1746); CC: *ECCO*, ESTC T053105. *A Collection of Hymns of the Children of God in all Ages … Designed Chiefly for the Use of the Congregations in Union with the Brethren's Church*, 2 vols. (London, 1754); CC: *ECCO*, ESTC T053156.

[58] G. S. Thomson, *The Russells in Bloomsbury, 1669–1771* (London, 1940), 205.

explanation is that Hintz's small viols were made for children – just as today children are started off on half- or three-quarter-size violoncellos. Again, his original impetus may have been to make them for Moravians, though in time it is possible that he developed a relationship with Charles Frederick Abel or one of the other professional gamba players in London, supplying instruments to his pupils. Such an arrangement is suggested by the fact that he never promoted his viols in newspaper advertisements. Perhaps his very small examples, nos. 6 and 7, were made for young girls; it was the only bowed instrument considered socially acceptable for upper-class women to play at the time (Ch. 7). Interestingly, the alto-size instrument no. 6 had possibly original metal frets when sold in 1976 (Plate 5), raising the possibility that it had originally been equipped with metal strings – presumably to allow it to be tuned as a bass viol without having to be fitted with unfeasibly thick strings.

❧ The Cult of Exotic Instruments

HINTZ advertised eleven types of instrument in 1763: the gamba, English guitar, mandolin, viola d'amore, dulcimer, solitaire, lute, harp, cymbal, trumpet marine, and Aeolian harp. Gambas, English guitars, mandolins, dulcimers, lutes, harps, trumpet marines, and Aeolian harps were in his stock-in-trade, as well as psalteries and German harps, violins, 'Tenors' (i.e. violas), German flutes, and four types of keyboard instrument: harpsichords, spinets, 'Claricords' (clavichords), and 'Forte Pianos'). He also advertised 'Spanish Guittars' on 17 May 1766. There are two striking features of these lists. First, all the instruments advertised in 1763 can be described as exotic – that is, they were not used in orchestras at the time, nor were they among those solo instruments generally played by amateurs. A more typical stock was advertised by Robert Bremner in about 1765.[59] He had some of the same exotica as Hintz: 'Viol de Gambo's', mandolins, trumpet marines, 'Guitars several sorts', 'Dulcemores' 'Aeolean Harps', and 'Welch Harps'. However, he also sold the normal orchestral instruments: violins, violas, violoncellos, double basses, flutes, oboes, clarinets, bassoons, trumpets, horns, and kettle drums, as well as four types of keyboard instrument: harpsichords, spinets, clavichords, and 'Lyrichords' – the large *Geigenwerk* or bowed keyboard instrument developed by Roger Plenius.[60]

[59] E. Halfpenny, 'An Eighteenth-Century Trade List of Musical Instruments', *GSJ*, 17 (1964), 99–102.

[60] See E. Halfpenny, 'The Lyrichord', *GSJ*, 3 (1950), 46–9; C. W. Simons, 'Sostenante Piano', 1: 'Bows', *GMO*. For Plenius, see esp. Boalch, *Makers of the Harpsichord and Clavichord*, rev. Mould, 147–8.

Second, most of these exotic instruments, though unusual in England, were still current in German-speaking areas of Europe. There was, of course, a strong viol-making tradition in England up to about 1720, and lightly constructed English instruments continued to prized at home and abroad: Thomas Gainsborough owned three gambas by Henry Jaye and two by Barak Norman (Ch. 7), and of twenty-one gambas seemingly attributed to particular makers in the 1759 sale catalogue of the stock of Nicolas Selhof, bookseller at The Hague, ten seem to be by Englishmen.[61] However, Hintz's viols are closer to the heavily built violoncello-like instruments made by German viol makers, and features of the design and craft techniques 'reveal a maker trained in Central Europe, and moreover someone more familiar with plucked than bowed instruments', according to William Monical, who restored no. 6 in the 1980s.[62]

Similarly, clavichords had been used all over Europe in the Renaissance, but were largely confined to Germany and Scandinavia by the eighteenth century. Nevertheless, Hintz and Bremner stocked them, and there is evidence that German immigrants made them in London. On 9 June 1733 'a Clavichord made by Wilbrook' was advertised for sale in London.[63] John Wilbrook, one of Herman Tabel's workmen, may have been German, perhaps related to Hermann Willenbrock, clavichord and harpsichord maker in Hanover.[64] In 1763 Frederick Neubauer was described as 'Maker of double-basset and treble-key'd Harpsichords, with six stops, and of Piano-fortes, Lyrichords, Classichords, etc.', and the following year included the 'Clarichord' in a list of keyboard instruments he sold.[65] There are also scattered references to the use of the clavichord in England. On 27 March 1756 Mrs Delany mentioned that her daughter Mary was 'now practising the clavicord', while on 9 October 1773 Burkat Shudi sold 'brass wire for a clafcord'.[66] A 'clarichord' was included in London auctions in December 1757, May 1763, March 1767 (a 'four-stop clarichord'), June 1775, June 1779, and June 1786 – the last in the sale of the effects of the composer John Stanley.[67] There is a mid-eighteenth-century English clavichord by Peter Hicks in the Victoria and

[61] *Catalogue d'une très belle bibliothèque de livres ... deslaissez par feu monsieur Nicolas Selhof* (The Hague, 1759), facs., intro. A. H. King (Amsterdam, 1973), 253.

[62] Thomas MacCracken, personal communication.

[63] *The Country Journal, or The Craftsman*, 9/6/1733.

[64] Boalch, *Makers of the Harpsichord and Clavichord*, rev. Mould, 208, 682–3.

[65] T. Mortimer, *The Universal Director*, 51; GZ, 7/1/1764.

[66] *The Autobiography and Correspondence of Mary Granville, Mrs. Delany*, ed. A. Hall, 3 vols. (London, 1861), iii. 414; Boalch, *Makers of the Harpsichord and Clavichord*, rev. Mould, 175.

[67] *PA*, 27/12/1757; *GZ*, 5, 6, 9, 11/5/1763; *GZ*, 6, 11, 12/3/1767; *MP*, 2/6/1775; *MP*, 23/6/1779; *GZ*, 20, 21/6/1786.

Albert Museum,[68] and the instrument by Ugo Annibale Traeri (Modena, 1726) at Maidstone supposedly belonged to Handel and seems to have been in England since the eighteenth century.[69]

The viola d'amore seems to have been invented in south Germany or Austria in the late seventeenth century, and that area remained the centre of its cultivation.[70] Among those who wrote for it were Ariosti, Fux and Albrechtsberger (Vienna), Biber (Salzburg), Pez (Stuttgart), Graupner (Darmstadt), and Carl Stamitz and Toeschi (Mannheim).[71] Most of those who played it in London came from German-speaking areas. Ariosti made his London debut on 12 July 1716 in 'a new Symphony … in which he performs upon a New Instrument call'd Viola D'Amour'; he published a set of lessons for viola d'amore and continuo in 1724.[72] John Joseph Grosman or Grossman played 'a Solo on the Viol d'Amour' in London concerts on 13 April 1743, 6 April 1752 and 11 January 1753, and a viola d'amore concerto at the Salisbury Festival on 9 September 1748.[73]

Carl Stamitz played viola d'amore solos and concertos during his stay in London between 1777 and 1780.[74] According to the diarist and amateur musician John Marsh Stamitz played concertos at the Salisbury Festival in September 1777 on 'a kind of fretted tenor called a viol d'amore, with 6. strings'.[75] In one concert it was so hot that:

[68] R. Russell, *Victoria and Albert Museum, Catalogue of Musical Instruments*, i: *Keyboard Instruments* (London, 1968), 56–7, no. 27, fig. 27; Boalch, *Makers of the Harpsichord and Clavichord*, rev. Mould, 89, 385.

[69] Boalch, *Makers of the Harpsichord and Clavichord*, rev. Mould, 660; B. Brauchli, *The Clavichord* (Cambridge, 1998; repr. 2005), 137–9.

[70] See esp. H. Danks, *The Viola d'Amore* (Halesowen, 1976); M. Rônez, 'Aperçus sur la viole d'amour en Allemagne du Sud vers 1700', in *Amour et sympathie* (Limoges, 1995), 223–71.

[71] M. and D. Jappe, *Viola d'amore Bibliographie* (Winterthur, 1997).

[72] *DC*, 10, 11/7/1716. The lessons were included with six cantatas in an untitled print, RISM A/I A 1420, facs.: A. Ariosti, *Cantates and a Collection of Lessons for the Viol d'Amore* (London, 1724; repr. 1980), 34–47. See also D. D. Boyden, 'Ariosti's Lessons for Viola' d'Amore', *MQ*, 32 (1946), 545–63; L. Lindgren, 'Ariosti's London Years', 1716–1729', *ML*, 62 (1981), 331–51.

[73] *DA*, 5/4/1743; *GA*, 13/3/1752; *PA*, 9/1/1753; E. Chevill, 'Music Societies and Musical Life in Old Foundation Cathedral Cities, 1700–1760' (PhD diss., King's College, U. of London, 1993), 245–6. For Grossman, see B. Matthews, *The Royal Society of Musicians of Great Britain, List of Members, 1738–1984* (London, 1985), 64; *BDA*, vi. 432.

[74] For instance, *PA*, 26–28/5/1777; *PA*, 6/4/1778; *PA*, 30/4/1779; *PA*, 4/5/1780. See also *BDA*, xiv. 233–4.

[75] *The John Marsh Journals: the Life and Times of a Gentleman Composer (1752–1828)*, ed. B. Robins (Stuyvesant, NY, 1998), 167.

poor Stamitz was this even'g much plagued w'th his viol d'amore & was continually interrupted by the strings breaking, w'ch terribly disconcerted & irritated him; which was probably further increas'd by his having the misfortune of a moist hand, to counteract which he had it seems a quantity of hair powder or flour in one of his coat pockets, in which he occasionally immers'd his fingers, to absorb the moisture.[76]

Nevertheless, the instrument was not just made or played by Germans. Richard Meares junior advertised 'Viols d'Amour' on a trade card printed around 1718,[77] and Ben Hebbert has argued that a fragmentary instrument made by Meares around 1725, now at Brigham Young University, was originally a viola d'amore.[78] Other non-German players in eighteenth-century Britain include William Corbett,[79] Giovanni Battista Marella (listed as 'Teacher of the Guittar and Viol d'amour'),[80] Giuseppe Passerini (who taught 'Viol d'amour' and 'Viola Angelica', among other instruments),[81] and François-Hippolyte Barthélemon.[82] It was also played by Moravians, notably by Christian Renatus von Zinzendorf, who died in London on 28 May 1752.[83]

The marine trumpet or *tromba marina*, the greatly elongated one-stringed bowed instrument played in harmonics in imitation of the natural trumpet, was also associated with German-speaking Europe. Of the 180-odd surviving instruments, most are in German, Swiss or central European museums and seem to have been made in those areas.[84] Many came from convents and were used as substitute trumpets – which would have been unseemly for nuns to play. The origin of the name *tromba marina* or 'trumpet marine' is obscure, and the

---

[76] Ibid., 168.

[77] Repr. in *The British Violin: the Catalogue of the 1998 Exhibition '400 Years of Violin and Bow Making in the British Isles'*, ed. J. Milnes (Oxford, 2000), 17.

[78] B. Hebbert, 'Three Generations of the Meares Family in the London Music Trade, 1638–1749' (MMus diss., U. of Leeds, 2001), 43, 46–8, 86–7.

[79] *BDECM*, i. 299–302.

[80] *St James's Chronicle*, 19/5/1763. See also B. Boydell, *A Dublin Musical Calendar, 1700–1760* (Dublin, 1988), esp. 284; S. McVeigh, 'Italian Violinists in Eighteenth-Century London', in *The Eighteenth-Century Diaspora of Italian Music and Musicians*, ed. R. Strohm (Turnhout, 2001), 139–76, at 170.

[81] *PA*, 27/2/1753; *The London Chronicle*, 24/7/1760; J. Burchell, *Polite or Commercial Concerts? Concert Management and Orchestral Repertoire in Edinburgh, Bath, Oxford, Manchester, and Newcastle, 1730–1799* (New York, 1996), esp. 83–4.

[82] *PA*, 8/2/1764; *PA*, 3/3/1768; *PA*, 4/5/1776.

[83] Wehrend, *Musikanschauung, Musikpraxis*, 50 (Lanie Graf).

[84] Listed in C. Adkins and A. Dickinson, *A Trumpet by any other Name: a History of the Trumpet Marine*, 2 vols. (Buren, 1991).

stories that connect it with sailors and its use as a foghorn seem to be fanciful. There were no nuns or convents in London, and Hintz's 1761 advertisement suggests that he was hoping to sell his marine trumpets to amateurs as recreational instruments 'upon the Water, or in a Garden in the Country'; the phrase 'and may be played in a Concert' suggests a possible role for them in amateur orchestral societies as substitute trumpets. No English instruments seem to survive, even though Hintz made them, Richard Meares junior advertised them on his trade card of *c.* 1718, and dictionary and encyclopaedia articles imply that there were examples available to be examined.[85] The only contemporary English reference to an instrument seems to be the 'curious Trumpet Marine' advertised for sale at Boston, Lincolnshire in January 1737.[86]

Hintz sold several other instruments that were probably thought of as German. The lute, one of the most popular solo instruments throughout Europe in the seventeenth century, fell rapidly out of use in Italy, France and England after 1700, leaving German-speaking areas as the main centre of its cultivation. Most eighteenth-century lute and theorbo makers were German or Austrian, including J. C. Hofmann (Leipzig), J. H. Goldt and Joachim Tielke (Hamburg), Mattias Griesser (Innsbruck), and Michael Rauche (London).[87] Lute composers after about 1720 include J. S. Bach, Telemann, Silvius Leopold Weiss, Lauffensteiner, Falckenhagen, Kropfgans, Baron, Hagen, Kohaut, Haydn, and Friedrich Wilhelm Rust.

A few English eighteenth-century amateurs played lute-family instruments, though most professional lutenists in London after about 1720 were German or had Germanic names.[88] John Francis Weber (d. 1751) played the lute, theorbo and mandolin in London from the early 1720s.[89] In his will he stated that he was from Genoa, though his name suggests that he was of German extraction. J. S. Cousser

---

[85] For instance, 'A New Musical Dictionary', W. Tans'ur, *The Elements of Musick Display'd* (London, 1772; repr. n.d.), v. 190–226, at 223; *Encylopaedia Britannica, or A Dictionary of Arts, Sciences and Miscellaneous Literature*, ed. C. Macfarquhar and G. Gleig, 18 vols. (Edinburgh, 3/1797), xviii. 593; 'Trumpet Marine', in *The Cyclopaedia, or Universal Dictionary of Arts, Sciences, and Literature*, ed. A. Rees, 39 vols. (London, 1819).

[86] *The London Evening Post*, 20/1/1737.

[87] For instruments by these makers, see for instance Baines, *European and American Musical Instruments*, 29–30, illus. 185, 187, 189, 190, 194; Baines, *Victoria and Albert Museum: Non-Keyboard Instruments*, 31–2, nos. 7/6, 7/7, illus. figs. 43, 44.

[88] See esp. P. Holman, 'The Lute Family in Britain in the Eighteenth and Nineteenth Centuries', *Lute News*, 84 (December 2007), 7–21.

[89] For Weber, see esp. P. E. Daub, 'Music at the Court of George II (r. 1727–1760)' (PhD diss., Cornell U., 1985), 69–70, 358; Holman, 'The Lute Family in Britain in the Eighteenth and Nineteenth Centuries', 10, 20.

listed him as 'Webber. Theorbista à Londra' in his commonplace book,[90] and he was probably the 'Sig[nor] Viebar' or 'Vebar' who played his own 'Solo on the Arch-Lute' at Drury Lane on 14 March 1722.[91] The Mr Senel who played a lute solo and two concertos in concerts put on by Charles Barbandt in March and April 1756 was perhaps the same as or was related to the Bohemian 'Senal oder Senel' who played the 'Violino-Harmonika' or nail-violin.[92] Rudolf Straube, a pupil of J. S. Bach in Leipzig in the 1730s, is first heard of in a concert in Bath on 1 January 1759, when he played 'several Lessons upon the Arch-Lute and Guittar in a Singular and Masterly Manner'.[93] He settled in London and is best known today for his connections with Gainsborough (Ch. 7). The Mr Weise or Weiss who appeared in London concerts in the spring of 1773, causing confusion with the flute player Carl Weiss in the process, was probably Johann Adolphus Faustinus Weiss from Dresden, the son of Silvius Leopold Weiss.[94]

The dulcimer, the trapeze-shaped box fitted with courses of metal strings and struck with hammers, was also mainly made and played in the Alpine regions in the seventeenth and eighteenth centuries.[95] Its German name is *Hackbrett*, with the diminutives *Brettl* in Austria and *Hachbrattli* in Switzerland, and in 1723 the Italian writer Filippo Bonanni called it 'Salterio Tedesco'.[96] It was usually called 'dulcimer' in English and was used in eighteenth-century England. It is depicted in a drawing attributed to Marcellus Laroon, *The Beggar's Opera Burlesqued*, and in a print derived from it.[97] Tans'ur defined it as 'A wire Instrument struck with two small Pieces of Cane'.[98] The dulcimer had down-to-earth associations as in more recent times, hence its use in variety turns, such as that performed by the

[90] US-NHub, Osborn Music MS 16, p. 62 (Samantha Owens).

[91] *DP*, 12, 13/3/1722; *DC*, 13/3/1722.

[92] *PA*, 18/3/1756; *PA*, 25/3/1756; *PA*, 1/4/1756; E. L. Gerber, *Historisch-biographisches Lexicon der Tonkünstler*, 2 vols. (Leipzig, 1790–2; repr. Graz, 1977), ii. col. 501.

[93] K. E. James, 'Concert Life in Eighteenth-Century Bath' (PhD thesis, Royal Holloway, U. of London, 1987), 990. For Straube, see esp. *J. S. Bach*, Oxford Composer Companions, ed. M. Boyd (Oxford, 1999), 470.

[94] *PA*, 17/2/1773; *PA*, 19/4/1773; *PA*, 6/5/1773. In *PA*, 6/5/1773 'MR. WEISS, German Flute Player' pointed out that 'many Mistakes have arisen from a Gentleman of the same Name … that Gentlemen's Instrument is the Lute'.

[95] See esp. B. Geiser, *Das Hackbrett in der Schweiz* (Visp, 1973); J. H. van der Meer, Geiser and K.-H. Schickhaus, *Das Hackbrett, ein alpenländisches Musikinstrument* (Herisau, 1975).

[96] P. Bonnani, *Gabinetto armonico* (Rome, 2/1723); facs. as *The Showcase of Musical Instruments*, intro. F. L. Harrison and J. Rimmer (New York, 1964), no. 64.

[97] Illus. J. Barlow, *The Enraged Musician: Hogarth's Musical Imagery* (Aldershot, 2005), 88–9.

[98] Tans'ur, 'A New Musical Dictionary', 196.

magician, painter and freak Matthias Buchinger or Buckinger, described at his first London appearance as 'A German born without Hands, Feet, or Thighs' who plays 'upon the Dulcimer, as well as any Musician'; his bizarre act was seen at various times and places in London between 1717 and 1731.[99] Later in the century the act of one Hermon Boaz included standing 'with his naked head on the pointed teeth of a woolcomber's comb', using his feet to play 'a tune on a dulcimer, which is placed against the ceiling for that purpose'.[100] In July 1773 a reward was offered for two servants who absconded with 'a Violin and a Dulcimer', pointing out 'it is supposed that they make Use of the said Instruments about the Town to make a Livelihood', while in September 1785 it was reported that 'an aged man, who has for some years gained a subsistence by playing a dulcimer in the public houses in the neighbourhood of Clerkenwell', had been robbed in the street.[101]

Nevertheless, Georg Noëlli or Noel, the Dutch-Jewish musician who studied at Dresden with Pantaleon Hebenstreit, came to England in or before 1748 and stayed at least until 1769, playing dulcimer-like instruments variously called the 'German cymbal', the 'cymbalo' and the 'pantaleon' in concerts.[102] In York on 8 September 1748 he played 'several Grand Lessons composed by Handel, Festing, Arne &c. on the CYMBALO'.[103] He is shown playing a small dulcimer in the etching by Sir Abraham Hume after Thomas Orde that seemingly represents some of those who played in a concert at Christ's College, Cambridge on 8 June 1767 (Plate 8).[104] The concert included a 'Concerto Panthaleone', a 'Solo Panthaleone', a 'Cantata accompanied by the Panthaleone Obligato', and 'Overture Mr. Noel'. He advertised in January 1769 that that he intended to perform every day except Fridays and Sundays at his apartments behind the Royal Exchange on his 'curious and inimitable PANTALEONE, an instrument which derives its name from the inventor, and consists of two hundred and seventy-six Roman strings, of different Magnitude, which contain five octaves compleat'.[105]

It is less clear what Hintz meant by the solitaire. It was not advertised by Bremner nor defined by Tans'ur, and the *OED* does not give the word any musical

---

99 For instance, *DC*, 10/10/1717; *DA*, 9/2/1731.

100 *The General Evening Post*, 26/12/1771.

101 *DA*, 28/7/1773; *The Whitehall Evening Post*, 29/9/1785.

102 For Noel, see *BDA*, xi. 38–9; T. Fawcett, *Music in Eighteenth-Century Norwich and Norfolk* (Norwich, 1979), 12, 44.

103 Chevill, 'Music Societies and Musical Life', 266.

104 See C. Hogwood, 'A Note on the Frontispiece: *A Concert in Cambridge*', in *Music in Eighteenth-Century England: Essays in Memory of Charles Cudworth*, ed. C. Hogwood and R. Luckett (Cambridge, 1983), xv–xviii.

105 *GZ*, 2/1/1769.

meanings. However, an obvious possibility is that it was a psaltery – an instrument similar to the dulcimer but plucked with a quill.[106] Hintz advertised 'Solitaires' in 1763, though there were also 'Psalteries' in his stock, and one of his trade cards depicts a trapeze-shaped psaltery- or dulcimer-like instrument. The psaltery was less common than the dulcimer, being largely confined to Spain and Italy, though it too was played in eighteenth-century England. A Signor Caruso accompanied a song 'on the SALTERO, which was never perform'd in any Concert before' during a performance of Hasse's *Dido* at the King's Theatre on 26 April 1748, and played concertos on the violoncello and 'Saltero' at the Salisbury Festival on 9 August that year, when he was described as the 'only Master' of it in London.[107] Ann Ford also seems to have played it in her private concerts in the late 1750s (Ch. 7).

Juan Bautista (Baptista) Pla (*c.* 1720–after 1773), the Catalan oboe virtuoso who travelled around Europe with his brother and fellow-oboist José in the 1740s and 50s, is recorded as playing the 'psalterion' or 'salterio' in London concerts in 1753 and 1769.[108] Giambattista Dall'Olio's 'Avvertimenti pei suonatori di salterio' (1770) discusses 'the improvement introduced by the Spanish Plà', which enabled the player 'to play easily in keys requiring flats'; it includes a diagram of the 'Salterio riformata dal PLA'.[109] Two psalteries made by Dall'Olio in Bologna in 1764 and 1780 survive in the Museo Civico, Modena.[110] An English keyboard manuscript from the 1760s or 1770s includes short scores of two three-movement pieces in a simple post-Vivaldi style entitled 'Concerto per Salterio'. They are both in D major, and were thus presumably not intended for Pla's improved psaltery. The slow movement of the second one shows the style of writing; the bass is probably an accompaniment rather than the lowest line of the solo (Ex. 4.1).[111] Finally, Victor Gonetti taught 'The Harpsichord, Spanish Guitar, Apollo's Harp, Harmonic Glasses, Psaltery, and Singing, in the most elegant stile, on moderate

[106] See esp. N. van Ree Bernard, *The Psaltery* (Buren, 1989); B. Kenyon de Pascual, 'The Spanish Eighteenth-Century *Salterio* and some Comments on its Italian Counterpart', *Musique–Images–Instruments*, 3 (1997), 32–62.

[107] *GA*, 26/4/1748; Chevill, 'Music Societies and Musical Life', 244–5.

[108] B. Kenyon de Pascual, 'Juan Bautista Pla and José Pla: Two Neglected Oboe Virtuosi of the Eighteenth Century', *EM*, 18 (1990), 109–12, at 110. See also M. Haakenson, 'Two Spanish Brothers Revisited: Recent Research surrounding the Life and Instrumental Music of Juan Bautista Pla and José Pla', *EM*, 35 (2007), 83–96.

[109] Trans. van Ree Bernard, *The Psaltery*, 64, 65, 80–82.

[110] Kenyon de Pascual, 'The Spanish Eighteenth-Century *Salterio*', 56.

[111] In the possession of Tim Crawford; I am grateful to him for allowing me access to it.

Ex. 4.1 Anonymous, 'Concerto per Salterio' in D major, Largo

terms', and played them in London concerts in the late 1770s and 1780s; the Apollo's Harp was his own invention.[112]

What Hintz meant by 'Cymbals' is not immediately clear. It was presumably not the brass percussion instrument, since Hintz specialised in wooden stringed instruments. Nor was it a dulcimer, since he advertised both types in 1763. It was probably a hurdy-gurdy, as illustrated on both of his trade cards. *Vielle*, the contemporary French term, was translated as 'Cymbal' in a French-English dictionary of 1688,[113] and in 1772 Tans'ur gave 'A Wire, or Gut Instrument play'd by Keys, and a Friction wheel' as the first of his two meanings for the word, the other being the brass instrument.[114] The hurdy-gurdy was a common street instrument in eighteenth- and nineteenth-century Britain. John Baptist Malchair heard a Piedmontese girl playing the tune 'La Rochelle' on 'a Cymbal' in an Oxford Street

---

[112]　For instance, *GZ*, 31/5/1779; *MH*, 19/4/1782; *PA*, 13/6/1783; *MC*, 17/4/1785.

[113]　G. Strahle, *An Early Music Dictionary: Musical Terms from British Sources, 1500–1740* (Cambridge, 1995), 406.

[114]　Tans'ur, 'A New Musical Dictionary', 194.

Illus. 4.1 Old Sarah, the well-known hurdy-gurdy player,
Henry Mayhew, *London Labour and the London Poor* (London, 1861–2)

on 22 December 1784.[115] When gathering material for his *London Labour and the London Poor* in the middle of the nineteenth century, Henry Mayhew interviewed 'THE WELL-KNOWN HURDY-GURDY PLAYER', 'Old Sarah' (b. 1786).[116] She told him: 'It took me just five months to learn the – cymbal, if you please – the hurdy-gurdy ain't it's right name' (Illus. 4.1). Hurdy-gurdies were even heard occasionally in concerts. At Ruckholt House on 24 April 1749 a Mr Barrow, 'who has given the greatest satisfaction to Masters and others who have heard him, and is allowed the greatest Performer they ever heard, is also engag'd every Morning and Afternoon to play on his double Cymbal'.[117]

[115] S. Wollenberg, 'John Baptist Malchair of Oxford and his Collection of "National Music"', in *Music in the British Provinces, 1690–1914*, ed. R. Cowgill and P. Holman (Aldershot, 2007), 151–61, at 157.

[116] H. Mayhew, *London Labour and the London Poor*, 4 vols. (London, 1861–2; repr. New York, 1968), iii. facing 151, 159–61.

[117] *GA*, 13–15, 18–20/4/1749.

It is not immediately obvious what type of harp Hintz sold. Bremner specifically advertised 'Welch Harps' in his catalogue – that is, the triple harp regularly played in London concerts by Welsh musicians until the 1780s – but Hintz may have been offering his customers something different. We think of the eighteenth-century pedal harp as a French instrument, but in fact the single-action pedal mechanism was invented in Germany around 1720 or earlier, and Paris did not become the centre for harp playing and manufacture until the Austrian princess Marie-Antoinette, a harpist herself, came to Paris in 1770. The pedal harp was popularised in London concerts by the Welshman Edward Jones starting in the 1775 season, when he was described as 'Professor on the Improved Welch or Pedal Harp'.[118] However, the London instrument maker and dealer Organist Vietor advertised pedal harps as early as 1766, when he offered 'a fine Welch Harp, with seven Pendals'; later advertisements mention 'two well-tuned perfect David's, or German, Harps with seven Pedals', 'Two David's harps, one with seven pedalls, the other with movements, for the sharps and flats', and 'A Large German Harp, with 7 pedals'.[119] Thus the plain 'Harps' in Hintz's stock were presumably the Welsh triple type, while 'German Harps' may have been early pedal instruments; a south-German example dated 1755 survives at Nuremburg.[120]

Of the remaining instruments advertised by Hintz, two, the mandolin and the Spanish guitar, came from the south. The mandolin, the four-course wire-strung instrument tuned like a violin (as opposed to the older six-course gut-strung *mandolino*), was becoming fashionable in Britain in the 1760s, thanks to the advocacy of Gabriele Leoni (Leone) and Giovanni Battista Gervasio. Leoni played mandolin solos in London concerts in 1763 and 1766,[121] and was also active in Paris, where he published some collections of mandolin music; his *Méthode raisonnée pour passer du violon à la mandoline* (Paris, 1768) was published in London as *A Complete Introduction to the Art of Playing the Mandoline* (1789).[122]

---

[118] For instance, *PA*, 21/3/1775; *PA*, 26/4/1775.

[119] *PA*, 2/5/66; *GZ*, 16/5/68; *GZ*, 14/2/69; *GZ*, 22/3/70.

[120] Illus. J. H. van der Meer, *Musikinstrumente von der Antike bis zur Gegenwart* (Munich, 1983), 125.

[121] *PA*, 13/4/1763; *PA*, 20/3/1766; *PA*, 11/4/1766; S. McVeigh, *Concert Life in London from Mozart to Haydn* (Cambridge, 1993), 246.

[122] For Leoni, see esp. J. Tyler and P. Sparks, *The Early Mandolin* (Oxford, 1989), esp. 87–8, 90–2, 94–5, 148–50, 152, 156; C. Price, J. Milhous and R. D. Hume, *The Impresario's Ten Commandments: Continental Recruitment for Italian Opera in London, 1763–64* (London, 1992), passim; P. Holman, 'Ann Ford Revisited', *ECM*, 1 (2004), 157–81, at 165, 168. *A Complete Introduction* is dated 1785 in Tyler and Sparks, *The Early Mandolin*, 156, but was entered at Stationers' Hall on 16/11/1789; see *Music Entries at Stationers' Hall, 1710–1818*, comp. M. Kassler (Aldershot, 2004), 138.

Gervasio was in Britain between at least 1768 and 1776, described himself as 'Master of the MANDOLINE to their Royal Highnesses the Daughters of the King of France', and played the mandolin in London concerts in 1768, 1770 and 1771 as well as working in Dublin, Oxford and Bath.[123] The gut-strung Spanish guitar was rare in England at the time: the old five-course instrument had long been replaced by the English guitar, and the new type is generally thought not to have arrived until Giacomo Merchi played in London in 1766.[124] However, Leoni played the Spanish guitar in the private concerts given by Ann Ford around 1759, and Ford herself plays one in a preliminary drawing for Gainsborough's painting of her (Ch. 7).[125] Hintz offered the services of a 'reputable Master' to teach the mandolin on 8 February 1766 and advertised Spanish guitars and mandolins a few weeks later, on 17 March. He was certainly up to the minute.

One instrument sold by Hintz remains to be discussed: the Aeolian harp. It is a device for harnessing the wind to activate strings stretched over a wooden box rather a conventional musical instrument.[126] The idea supposedly goes back to Classical times, though it only became common in mid-eighteenth-century England. In 1748 the poet James Thomson described it in two poems, 'The Castle of Indolence' and an 'Ode on Æolus's Harp', stating in a footnote appended to the latter that 'AEolus's Harp is a musical instrument, which plays with the wind, invented by Mr. Oswald'; the Scottish music publisher and composer advertised examples for sale in October 1751.[127] Whether James Oswald really did invent the Aeolian harp (or re-invent it: it was described in print several times in the seventeenth century) is disputed.[128] His pupil William Jones of Nayland advanced his cause while Charles Burney was sceptical.[129] Oswald did not patent it (there are no

---

[123] PA, 3/3/1768; PA, 21/1/1769; PA, 15/1/1770; PA, 27/4/1770; PA, 27/3/1771. For Gervasio, see esp. James, 'Concert Life in Eighteenth-Century Bath', 626; Tyler and Sparks, *The Early Mandolin*, passim; B. Boydell, *Rotunda Music in Eighteenth-Century Dublin* (Dublin, 1992), 92, 187, 192.

[124] J. Tyler and P. Sparks, *The Guitar and its Music from the Renaissance to the Classical Era* (Oxford, 2002), 206–8. For Merchi, see James, 'Concert Life in Eighteenth-Century Bath', 812–14; Tyler and Sparks, *The Guitar and its Music*, passim.

[125] Sudbury, Gainsborough's House, illus. Holman, 'Ann Ford Revisited', 163.

[126] See esp. *Aeolian Harp*, ed. S. Bonner, 4 vols. (Duxford, 1968–74); T. L. Hankins and R. J. Silverman, *Instruments and the Imagination* (Princeton, NJ, 1995; repr. 1999), 86–112.

[127] *Aeolian Harp*, ed. Bonner, iii. 15–19; Hankins and Silverman, *Instruments and the Imagination*, 91–2.

[128] Hankins and Silverman, *Instruments and the Imagination*, 89–90.

[129] *Aeolian Harp*, ed. Bonner, iii. 30–2; Hankins and Silverman, *Instruments and the Imagination*, 93–5.

relevant patents before 1862),[130] and several models were available. Other music sellers who sold them besides Hintz include Longman and Broderip (a model designed by William Jones),[131] and Bremner.[132] An English example from about 1780 is a long rectangular box with ten gut strings stretched over it, similar in shape to those depicted on Hintz's trade cards.[133] In 1761 Hintz advertised 'an Improvement to play Tunes on, with an additional String', presumably accompanied by chords from the wind-activated strings.

Why did Hintz sell so many exotic instruments of German origin? With his Moravian connections he would have been in a good position to develop contacts with potential suppliers among instrument makers in Germany. However, there were also deeper forces at work. German musical culture, conservative in some respects, allowed the survival of Renaissance and Baroque instruments such as the lute, the cittern, the viola d'amore, the gamba, and the *tromba marina*. But there was also a strain of innovation and inventiveness in Germany that produced, for instance, the first pedal harps; that weird and wonderful type of dulcimer, the pantaleon; exotic types of oboe such as the oboe d'amore and oboe da caccia; and the rapid and inventive development of the piano by makers in Germany in the 1740s and the 1750s, and then in England by German immigrants in the 1760s and 1770s. It is significant that the piano was largely developed in Germany rather than in Italy, where it had been invented.

It has long been recognised that German musicians flooded into London in the 1750s and 1760s, eager to get away from their war-ravaged homeland and attracted by Britain's growing wealth and the stability of its political and social institutions (Ch. 5).[134] This had the effect of changing the orientation of English music from a culture dominated by Italians and the genres they cultivated, such as opera, the cantata, the solo sonata and the *concerto grosso*, to one focused on the more modern genres of instrumental music developed in Germany, such as the symphony, the string quartet, the keyboard concerto, and the accompanied sonata. In London the most glamorous shop-window for the new musical culture was the concert series run by J. C. Bach and Abel, as Charles Burney recognised:

---

[130] Woodcroft, *Patents for Inventions*, 359–60.

[131] Hankins and Silverman, *Instruments and the Imagination*, 94.

[132] Halfpenny, 'An Eighteenth-Century Trade List', 100.

[133] Illus. in Thibault, Jenkins and Bran-Ricci, *Eighteenth-Century Musical Instruments*, 107, no. 66. See also Baines, *European and American Musical Instruments*, illus. 381, 382.

[134] See esp. A. Jarvis, 'The Community of German Migrant Musicians in London c. 1750–c. 1850', 2 vols. (Master of Studies in Local and Regional History diss., U. of Cambridge, 2003).

Content with our former possessions and habits, we went on in the tranquil
enjoyment of the productions of Corelli, Geminiani, and Handel, at our
national theatres, concerts and public gardens, till the arrival of Giardini,
Bach, and Abel; who soon created schisms, and at length, with the assistance of [J. C.] Fischer, brought about a total revolution in our musical
taste.[135]

The role played by German keyboard makers in London in this process has long
been recognised, but Hintz and his fellow-makers of stringed instruments also
made an important contribution.

🐚 New Instruments

EVERY age has its novel instruments (copies of old instruments might be
thought to be the novelties of our own time), though it seems that there was
a crescendo of interest in them in mid-eighteenth-century Britain, reaching a
strange fortissimo in the 1760s and 70s. In addition to those plucked or ham-
mered instruments already discussed one might mention the bell harp, a combination of psaltery and Aeolian harp made by John Simcock of Bath and others;[136]
the colascione and colascioncino, two- or three-stringed long-necked folk-lutes
from the Mediterranean tuned a fourth apart, played in London by the Colla
brothers and Giacomo Merchi;[137] the 'Merchino-Moderno', played by Merchi in
Bath in 1768, which may or may not be the same as the 'Liutino Moderno' he
played in London the following year;[138] the pandola, played by Nicolaes Cloes in
London in 1753 and in Dublin the following year, when it was described as a 'new
Instrument';[139] and the syron or arch-cittern, another German import, at least
one of which was made in London, by Remerus Liessem in 1757.[140]

---

[135] BurneyH, ii. 1015. See also McVeigh, *Concert Life in London*, esp. 120–8.

[136] Baines, *European and American Musical Instruments*, 62, illus. 376, 377; Baines,
       Victoria and Albert Museum: Non-Keyboard Instruments, 73–4, no. 15/7, illus. fig.
       100; Thibault, Jenkins and Bran-Ricci, *Eighteenth-Century Musical Instruments*,
       113–14, nos. 68, 69.

[137] *PA*, 5/5/1753; *PA*, 18/2/1766; James, 'Concert Life in Eighteenth-Century Bath',
       812–14; Tyler and Sparks, *The Early Mandolin*, esp. 138–9.

[138] *PA*, 27/4/1769; James, 'Concert Life in Eighteenth-Century Bath', 813. For Merchi,
       see esp. Tyler and Sparks, *The Early Mandolin*, 86, 89, 139.

[139] *PA*, 22/3/1753; Boydell, *A Dublin Musical Calendar*, 203, 275. See also Tyler and
       Sparks, *The Early Mandolin*, 30, 64.

[140] Boston, Museum of Fine Arts, 17.1749 (www.mfa.org/collections).

Novel bowed instruments include the 'Viol D'Venere of 22 Strings', played and presumably invented by William Corbett;[141] the *violetta marina*, 'a viola with sympathetic strings' according to Burney, specified in Handel's *Orlando* (1732) and played by its inventor, Pietro Castrucci with his brother Prospero;[142] the *viola angelica*, played and taught by Giuseppe Passerini;[143] the Ipolito, 'a new instrument of five strings, invented by Mr. Hipolitus Barthelemon, and made by Mr. Merlin', which perhaps combined the tunings of the violin and the viola;[144] the cither viol or sultana, a variant of the viola d'amore without sympathetic strings but with wire bowed strings, developed by Thomas Perry of Dublin in the 1760s;[145] Carl Stamitz's 'new-invented Instrument, called the Violetton', played by him in London in 1778;[146] the pentachord, a type of five-string violoncello invented by Sir Edward Walpole and promoted by Abel (Ch. 5); John Marsh's basso viola, a viola-cello hybrid made for him by Benjamin Banks;[147] and the baryton, played by Andreas Lidel in London in the 1770s (Ch. 8), and possibly by a Mr Ferrant, who played a 'paridon' in Norwich on 28 August 1745, claiming it was the only one in the country.[148]

Why all this interest in novel and exotic instruments? For professionals such as Barthélemon, Merchi, Cloes, or Lidel, a powerful incentive to take up, or even invent, a novel instrument must have been to carve out a distinctive niche for themselves in London's crowded and highly competitive concert world. At this period professional music making was still largely a service offered to the fashionable *beau monde*, which placed a premium on novelty – hence the large proportion of advertisements that attach the adjective 'new' to performers, instruments or particular pieces. Most professionals used novel instruments as an added attraction to be deployed in solos or concertos, using their main instrument for their normal orchestral activities. Abel reversed the normal pattern, making the gamba his main instrument, and reserving the violoncello for playing in orchestras and ensembles and the harpsichord for teaching and

[141] *BDECM*, i. 301.

[142] BurneyH, ii. 698; Jappe, *Viola d'amore Bibliographie*, 106.

[143] *PA*, 11/3/1760; *London Chronicle*, 24/7/1760.

[144] *MP*, 6/3/1778. See also *John Joseph Merlin, the Ingenious Mechanick*, ed. A. French (London, 1985), 87.

[145] Baines, *European and American Musical Instruments*, 22, illus. 134, 135; Baines, *Victoria and Albert Museum: Non-Keyboard Instruments*, 12–14, nos. 2/8, 2/9, illus. fig. 16; Thibault, Jenkins and Bran-Ricci, *Eighteenth-Century Musical Instruments*, 50–2, nos. 27, 28; *The British Violin*, ed. Milnes, 68–9.

[146] *PA*, 6/4/1778.

[147] *The John Marsh Journals*, ed. Robins, esp. 160–1, 775.

[148] Fawcett, *Music in Eighteenth-Century Norwich and Norfolk*, 44.

directing (Ch. 5). Professionals also had to be able to play any exotic instruments their aristocratic pupils wished to learn, which was presumably why
Straube turned to the English guitar in England; why Gonetti played the mandolin, the English guitar, the psaltery, and the musical glasses; and why Frederic Theodor Schumann played the musical glasses and the English guitar
as well as the flute and the harpsichord – which were presumably his main
instruments.[149]

❧ John Joseph Merlin, Charles Clagget and James Watt

TOWARDS the end of the century the craze for exotic instruments began to
subside, as the pianoforte and the genres of instrumental music using it –
the piano sonata, the piano trio and the other types of accompanied sonata –
came to dominate amateur music making. There was still a good deal of experiment and innovation in instrument making, but it was increasingly concerned
with applying Enlightenment principles of systematic and rational enquiry to
existing instruments. The trend was particularly marked in England, where the
developing industrial revolution involved the improvement of machines and
instruments of all types. The Royal Society had long been a forum for the discussion of new developments, in the arts as well as the sciences, and occasionally concerned itself with music and musical instruments.[150] Thus the Oxford
academic Thomas Salmon showed in 1705 how unequal temperament could be
applied to viols, using divided frets and moveable fingerboards where required
(Ch. 2). Salmon had developed his system some years earlier: on 21 March 1689
the viol maker Richard Meares advertised that he would use it to 'fret lutes,
viols, etc.'[151] A few eighteenth-century patent applications were devoted to new
types, such as Adam Walker's celestina (1772), John Joseph Merlin's compound
harpsichord-piano (1774), or John Lawrence Geib's 'new musical instrument'
that combined 'the pianoforte, clavicord, or spinett' (1792),[152] though most were
devoted to improving existing instruments. Some were attempts to improve
harpsichords, such as William Barton's proposal for quills of 'silver, brass, steel,
& other sorts of metall' (1730), Burkat Shudi's for the Venetian swell (1769),

149   Holman, 'Ann Ford Revisited', 174.

150   L. Miller and A. Cohen, *Music in the Royal Society of London, 1660–1806* (Detroit,
      MI, 1987), esp. 18–22; P. Gouk, *Music, Science and Natural Magic in Seventeenth-
      Century England* (New Haven, CT, 1999), esp. 205–7.

151   TilmouthC, 8.

152   Woodcroft, *Patents for Inventions*, 8–10, 18–19, 26–7. See also *John Joseph Merlin,
      the Ingenious Mechanick*, 97–102.

or Thomas Haxby's for a pedal to produce stop changes on a single-manual instrument (1770).[153]

Merlin (1735–1803) was more inventor, mechanic and showman than dedicated musical instrument maker.[154] He came from Huy in modern Belgium and spent some years in Paris working as a mechanic before coming to England in 1760. His early years in London were spent working on automata at Cox's Museum in Spring Gardens, but after he set up on his own in 1773 he diversified into mathematical instruments and inventions, such as clocks and watches, weighing machines and scales, various types of wheelchair, the dutch oven, the roller skate, and various musical instruments. He is remembered today for supposedly playing the violin on roller skates at an assembly at Carlisle House, 'when, not having provided the means of retardating his velocity, or commanding its direction, he impelled himself against a mirror, of more than five hundred pounds' value, dashed it to atoms, broke his instrument to pieces, and wounded himselff most severely'.[155]

A catalogue, *Merlin's Mechanical Exhibition* (1787–9), includes a barrel mechanism to convert a harpsichord into an automatic instrument (no. 15); kettle drums tuned by a single screw (no. 16); 'A superb Patent *Double Bass Piano-Forte Harpsichord*, which has twenty different Stops' (no. 24), one of three types of harpsichord-piano; '*New Violins*, made equal to the best Cremonas, with new-invented Pegs, and Tail-pieces which prevent the strings from slipping' (no. 28); and, most interesting for the present study, '*Bass Viols*, equal in Tone to the best Cremonas, having the new-invented Pegs and Tail-pieces, and which upon trial will be found of great Utility' (no. 29).[156] A later catalogue, *Morning and Evening Amusements at Merlin's Mechanical Museum* (1803), lists some of the same instruments, but also includes the 'VOCAL-HARP', describing it as:

> the body of a *Welch* Harp, strung with catgut, and laid on one side; forming an instrument somewhat similar to a Harpsichord. It has a regular set of keys, by playing on which the most melodious and pleasing sounds may be

---

153   *John Joseph Merlin, the Ingenious Mechanick*, 2, 6–7. See also E. R. Ripin, 'Expressive Devices Applied to the Eighteenth-Century Harpsichord', *The Organ Yearbook*, 1 (1970), 65–80.

154   For Merlin, see esp. P. Scholes, *The Great Doctor Burney*, 2 vols. (Oxford, 1948; repr. 1971), ii: 202–9; *John Joseph Merlin, the Ingenious Mechanick*, 11–16; Boalch, *Makers of the Harpsichord and Clavichord*, rev. Mould, 128–30, 505; *The British Violin*, ed. Milnes, 50–2, 256–7.

155   T. Busby, *Concert Room and Orchestra Anecdotes of Music and Musicians, Ancient and Modern*, 3 vols. (London, 1825), ii. 137. See also *John Joseph Merlin, the Ingenious Mechanick*, 83.

156   Facs.: *John Joseph Merlin, the Ingenious Mechanick*, 138–9.

obtained, alternately resembling Violins, Violoncellos, Tenors, Flageolets, Eolian Harps, and a full Organ.[157]

It is difficult to know whether Merlin's 'bass viols' were really gambas or whether this is yet another example of the vernacular use of the term to mean the violoncello, though he used both terms in his catalogues, and he moved in the same circles as Abel, Gainsborough and Sir Edward Walpole, all gamba players.[158]

The Irish violinist Charles Clagget makes an interesting comparison with Merlin. Until he was over forty he was just a professional musician, often working with his younger brother Walter, a cellist and gamba player (Ch. 8). They came from Waterford and are first heard of in Canterbury in June 1747, when they were said to be twelve and ten respectively – which suggests that they were born around 1735 and 1737 respectively, about five years earlier than is conventionally said.[159] Charles is subsequently recorded in Devises and Bath (1751–2), Newcastle (1758–60), Edinburgh (1760), Bath (1760), Dublin (1763–9), Liverpool (1771–3), and Manchester (1773–5), before apparently settling in London in 1776.[160] He seems to have remained there, with visits to Bath (1792–4) and Norwich (1795).[161] He was declared bankrupt in April 1793, and disappears from view after 20 November 1795, when a sale of his instruments was held; he probably died around then.[162]

Charles may have developed interests in inventing and improving musical instruments as a result of meeting the inventor and steam engine pioneer James Watt (1736–1819). Watt seems to have started repairing musical instruments in

[157] Facs.: ibid., 140–2.

[158] For Merlin and Gainsborough, see ibid., esp. 29–32.

[159] *The Kentish Post*, 20/5–3/6/1747 (Joan Jeffery). However, Walter stated that he was 42 when he joined the Society (later Royal Society) of Musicians) on 1/2/1784; see *BDA*, iii. 291. See also J. C. Kassler, *The Science of Music in Britain, 1714–1830: a Catalogue of Writings, Lectures and Inventions*, 2 vols. (New York, 1979), i. 191–9.

[160] *BDA*, iii. 290–1; Kassler, *The Science of Music in Britain*, 191–2; James, 'Concert Life in Eighteenth-Century Bath', 544; Boydell, *Rotunda Music in Eighteenth-Century Dublin*, 52, 68, 77–80, 84–5, 179–83; Burchell, *Polite or Commercial Concerts?*, 124; R. Southey, *Music-Making in North-East England during the Eighteenth Century* (Aldershot, 2006), 26, 43, 170, 181, 205.

[161] James, 'Concert Life in Eighteenth-Century Bath', 543–5; Fawcett, *Music in Eighteenth-Century Norwich and Norfolk*, 50, 71. It is often said that Charles or Walter ran the Apollo Gardens in St. George's Fields, but Charles stated in *The Times*, 12/8/1790 that 'to prevent future mistakes, he takes this method of informing the Public, that he never was engaged in those Gardens, nor in any other public place in London. The Christian name of the Proprietor of those Gardens, i[s] CRISPUS'. For Crispus Claggett (who seems to have been unrelated), see *BDA*, iii. 292.

[162] *The New London Magazine*, 4 (1793), 197; *The Times*, 10/11/1795.

Glasow in 1758 while he was in partnership with the merchant and architect John Craig, and before long was making and selling them, despite the fact that he 'had an absolute deficiency of any musical ear'.[163] Nevertheless, his nineteenth-century biographer thought he had a genius for repairing them:

> Succeeding beyond expectation in his first attempts in that novel line, it is wonderful how many dumb flutes and gouty harps, dislocated violins and fractured guitars, nervous viol-di-gambas, histerical mandolins, and thorough-basses suffering from hoarseness, came thenceforward to be cured by him of their complaints, and restored to health and harmony.[164]

Watt and his associates are known to have made flutes: tools needed for their manufacture survive in his reconstructed workshop in the Science Museum in London, including a stamp 'T LOT' that was clearly intended to give the false impression that instruments so stamped were the work of the Paris maker Thomas Lot.[165] Watt also made at least one organ, in 1761,[166] and was involved in making stringed instruments.

This is where Charles Clagget came in. He probably met Watt when he was in Scotland in 1760, and seems to have acted as his agent in Dublin from 1763. Between 19 July 1761 and April 1764 he purchased instruments from Watt worth a total of £164 4s. 6d.[167] They were mostly guitars (presumably of the English type) made by Watt's employee Robert Allan, though the first purchase included a gamba, perhaps intended for his brother Walter (Ch. 8). Charles had been in partnership with the Dublin instrument maker William Gibson,[168] though the arrangement had broken down, and he wrote to Watt on 30 September 1765 suggesting a partnership in Dublin; he pointed out that Watt would have little competition there and offered to explain all the improvements Gibson had made to guitars.[169] Watt's reply is lost, though the proposed partnership came to nothing, and he soon changed from instrument making to chemical, civil and mechanical engineering; he moved to Birmingham in 1774 and went into partnership with

---

[163]   J. P. Muirhead, *The Life of James Watt, with Selections from his Correspondence* (London, 1858), 46. See also R. L. Hills, *James Watt*, 3 vols. (Ashbourne, 2002–6), esp. i. 111–15; M. Wright, 'James Watt, Musical Instrument Maker', *GSJ*, 55 (2002), 104–29.

[164]   Muirhead, *The Life of James Watt*, 48.

[165]   Wright, 'James Watt', 112–25.

[166]   Hills, *James Watt*, 113–14.

[167]   Ibid., 113.

[168]   J. Teahan, 'A List of Irish Instrument Makers', *GSJ*, 16 (1963), 28–32, at 28, 29.

[169]   Hills, *James Watt*, 1113; Wright, 'James Watt', 111.

Matthew Boulton.[170] Nevertheless, Clagget remained in contact with him for many years. A document drawn up by him, 'Descriptions of a Lute', survives in the Boulton and Watt Collection in Birmingham.[171] He included the lute among the instruments taught in the 'Academy' he advertised in *The Times* on 12 August 1790.

Furthermore, a box of components survives in Watt's workshop at the Science Museum relating to Clagget's first invention, 'Improvements on the violin and other instruments played on finger boards', patented on 7 December 1776.[172] A version of it applied to the violoncello was described with diagrams in *A New and Complete Tutor for the Violoncello* (1785).[173] Clagget wrote to Watt in 1788 requesting help to establish a further patent for this invention.[174] The idea was to divide the fingerboard into two interlocking pieces, one of which could be lowered to enable the other to serve as raised frets to guide the fingers of beginners. When such guidance was no longer needed the moveable piece could be raised to form a smooth fingerboard. The patent also mentions several other devices, including one for the 'guitar or other similar instruments' that used a sliding fingerboard to effect transposition. Watt or one of his associates made up a batch of ebony pieces for the interlocking fingerboards, though Michael Wright has pointed out that they are unfinished and crudely made. He suggests that they were made some time before Clagget was granted the patent. Even had the divided fingerboard worked satisfactorily, one wonders whether it would have been commercially viable: a simpler alternative, tying gut frets onto violin necks, had been used since the seventeenth century. Nevertheless, it is interesting for the possibility that it might have been inspired by Walter Clagget's fretted gamba.

Clagget's later inventions mostly concerned keyboard and brass instruments. They were outlined in a patent granted on 15 August 1788 and in later publications, notably *Clagget's Musical Museum* (1790), a catalogue similar to those produced by Merlin, and *Musical Phaenomena Founded on Unaswerable Facts* (1793), the first (and apparently only) booklet of a projected series describing his inventions.[175] In 1793 Clagget again wrote to Watt requesting help with two of these inventions, a new type of piano and a mechanical organ.[176] The most important

[170]   Hills, *James Watt*, esp. 120–41.

[171]   Wright, 'James Watt', 111.

[172]   Woodcraft, *Patents for Inventions*, 11–12; Wright, 'James Watt', 125–7.

[173]   B. Neece, 'The Cello in Britain: a Technical and Social History', *GSJ*, 56 (2003), 77–115, at 110–11.

[174]   Hills, *James Watt*, 113.

[175]   Woodcraft, *Patents for Inventions*, 21–3; Kassler, *The Science of Music in Britain,* i. 194–8.

[176]   Hills, *James Watt*, 113.

were chromatic trumpets and horns (which combined two natural instruments a semitone apart), the teliochordon (a keyboard instrument with as many as thirty-nine notes to the octave), and the aiuton or ever-tuned organ (a combination of celesta and *geigenwerck* using a revolving band of seal-skin to excite tuned steel bars).

Clagget promoted his new instruments diligently in these pamphlets, in advertisements, in concerts and demonstrations, and by collecting celebrity endorsements (including an enthusiastic one from Haydn),[177] though none of his innovations caught on and no examples seem to survive. Hand-stopping, introduced to England by Giovanni Punto in the 1770s (Ch. 5), had already made the horn chromatic, while English trumpeters soon found that the slide trumpet, first described by John Hyde in 1799, offered a more practical way of making the trumpet chromatic; Reginald Morley-Pegge and Art Brownlow are both sceptical about the practicality of Clagget's chromatic brass instruments.[178] The writer Capel Lofft mentioned the aiuton's 'clearness, purity, and fullnesss of tone' and its 'beauty of swell and diminution', but thought it 'deficient in practical utility'.[179] Nevertheless, Clagget's relationship with James Watt is a fascinating 'might have been'. Had Watt gone into partnership with him in 1765, moved to Dublin, and devoted himself to musical instrument making, the subsequent development of musical instruments, let alone science, manufacturing, civil engineering, mining, and public transport, would doubtless have been rather different.

---

[177] H. C. R. Landon, *Haydn: Chronicle and Works*, iii: *Haydn in England, 1791–1795* (London, 1976), 159.

[178] R. Morley-Pegge, *The French Horn* (London, 2/1973; repr. 1978), 26–30; A. Brownlow, *The Last Trumpet: a History of the English Slide Trumpet* (Stuyvesant, NY, 1996), 17, 20, 22–5.

[179] *The Monthly Magazine*, 30 (1810), 411.

CHAPTER 5

'A Solo on the Viola da Gamba': Charles Frederick Abel as a Performer

WHEN Carl Friedrich (Charles Frederick) Abel made his debut at the Great Room in Dean Street, Soho on 5 April 1759 he was apparently the first gamba player to appear in public in London for more than twenty-five years – since Jean-François Sainte-Hélène played at Hickford's Room in nearby Panton Street on 10 May 1732 (Ch. 3).[1] Abel belonged to a dynasty of gamba players. His grandfather, the organist and viol player Clamor Heinrich (1634–96), worked at Celle, Hanover, and Bremen, and published several collections of instrumental music, including *Dritter Theil musicalischer Blumen* (Frankfurt am Main, 1677), consisting of suites for violin, *scordatura* bass viol and continuo; his sonata 'sopra CucCuc' for violin, bass viol and continuo is in several English sources.[2] His father, Christian Ferdinand (1682–1761), worked at the Cöthen court as a violinist and gamba player from 1714 to 1737, and was probably the person for whom J. S. Bach wrote gamba parts in the sixth Brandenburg concerto and the Cöthen revision of 'Mein Herze schwimmt im Blut', BWV199.[3]

---

[1] Abel anglicised his Christian names for his English publications and in official documents, such as those relating to his lawsuit against Longman, Lukey and Co., GB-Lna, C12/71/6 (1773), or the letters patent for his denization, GB-Lna, C97/611497 (11/5/1775) (Ann van Allen-Russell).

[2] RISM A/I A 50. E. Albertyn, 'The Hanover Orchestral Repertory, 1672–1714: Significant Source Discoveries', *EM*, 33 (2005), 449–71, at 456–8; R. Carter, 'Clamor Heinrich Abel's *Dritter Theil musicalischer Blumen*, 1677: a Lost Source of Lyra Consort Music', *VdGSJ*, 3 (2009), 55–82. For the sonata, see M. Caudle, 'The English Repertory for Violin, Bass Viol and Continuo', *Chelys*, 6 (1975–6), 69–75, at 70–1.

[3] See esp. F. Flassig, *Die solistische Gambenmusik in Deutschland im 18. Jahrhundert* (Göttingen, 1998), 105–15; C. Wolff, *Johann Sebastian Bach, the Learned Musician* (Oxford, 2000), 193–6, 199–200.

&. *Early Life*

CARL Friedrich Abel was born in Cöthen on 22 December 1723, the fourth child of Carl Ferdinand.[4] Presumably his father taught him initially, and he seems to have studied with J. S. Bach in Leipzig, though there is no documentary evidence of his presence at the Thomasschule.[5] According to Charles Burney he was 'a disciple of Sebastian Bach', while Ernst Ludwig Gerber thought that he was 'probably the pupil of the great Sebastian Bach' ('wahrscheinlich den Unterricht des großen Sebast. Bach').[6] In Leipzig Abel would have come into contact with Bach's youngest son, Johann Christian, his future business partner in London, and the lutenist and harpsichordist Rudolf Straube, a Bach pupil from 1733 to 1747 who also settled in London (Ch. 7). J. S. Bach's three sonatas for gamba and harpsichord are now dated 1736–41, and therefore could have been written for Abel, and Abel may have played one of the gamba parts in the late version of the St Matthew Passion, probably performed in 1742.[7]

Abel was still in Leipzig on 13 October 1743 when he played in a concert put on by the newly founded Grosses Concert:

> All [the other] soloists received applause, but especially Monsieur Abel, playing the viola da gamba. His performances in a trio and in a solo fantasy was greatly admired, so that on the following day he gave a command performance, solo, for his Royal Majesty [August III, King of Poland; Friedrich August II, Elector of Saxony]. As a result he was fortunate enough to be appointed, by the grace of the King, to the [Dresden] royal chapel.[8]

Abel was *Violgambist* at the Dresden court from 1745, initially at 180 thalers a year and at 280 thalers from 1746.[9] He is listed separately from the cellists, though he

---

4 For Abel's biography, see esp. W. Knape, *Karl Friedrich Abel: Leben und Werke eines frühklassischen Komponisten* (Bremen, 1973); M. Charters, 'Abel in London', *MT*, 114 (1973), 1224–6; *MGG2*, *Personenteil*, i. cols. 31–35.

5 B. F. Richter, 'Stadtpfeifer und Alumnen der Thomasschule in Leipzig zu Bachs Zeit', *Bach Jahrbuch*, 4 (1907), 32–78, esp. 68–76; Knape, *Karl Friedrich Abel*, 30.

6 BurneyH, ii. 1018; E. L. Gerber, *Neues historisch-biographisches Lexicon der Tonkünstler*, 3 vols. (Leipzig, 1812–14; repr. Graz, 1969), i. cols. 4–8, at 4.

7 See esp. C. Wolff, 'Bach's Leipzig Chamber Music', *Bach: Essays on his Life and Music* (Cambridge, MA, 1991), 223–38, at 228, 234; *J. S. Bach*, ed. M. Boyd, Oxford Composer Companions (Oxford, 1999), 186–7, 360–1; D. R. Melamed, *Hearing Bach's Passions* (New York, 2005), esp. 135–6.

8 H. Gärtner, trans. R. G. Pauly, *John Christian Bach: Mozart's Friend and Mentor* (Portland, OR, 1994), 39–40.

9 *Königl. Polnischer und Churfürstl. Sächsischer Hof- und Staats-Calender* (Leipzig, 1745–56) (Janice Stockigt); M. Fürstenau, *Zur Geschichte der Musik und*

may have played the violoncello in orchestral pieces, as he seems to have done in London. No gamba works by him are known from this period, with the possible exception of his early B♭ violoncello concerto, WKO 52 (Ch. 6), though there is an aria for soprano, gamba obbligato and strings, 'L'augeletto in placi stretto', by Johann Adolf Hasse, the Dresden *Kapellmeister.*[10]

According to Burney, Abel was forced to leave Dresden because of the turmoil created by the Seven Year's War (Frederick the Great invaded Saxony at the end of August 1756 and occupied Dresden soon after):

> At length finding that the oeconomy to which that court was reduced by the horrors of war rendered his subsistence scanty and precarious, he quitted the service in 1758, and departed from the capital of Saxony with only three dollars in his pocket. He travelled on foot to the next little German province, where he found his talents were not only honoured but rewarded. This success, however, only raised his ambition, and excited a stronger desire to try his fortune elsewhere; he went therefore soon to another court, and still on to a third, remaining only at each long enough to acquire a sufficient sum to defray his expenses to a new scene of action; when, at length, he arrived in England, 1759, where his worth was soon discovered and rewarded.[11]

Burney probably received this information at first hand, but it does not entirely accord with the facts. Abel seems to have left Dresden in 1755 rather than 1758: he is last listed in the Dresden court calendar for 1756, though he does not appear in a list of the musical establishment printed in that year by Friedrich Wilhelm Marpurg, so he probably left during the previous year.[12] Also, Ernst Ludwig Gerber gave 'a dispute' ('Ein Zwist') with Hasse as the reason for Abel's departure in his first biography of the composer, though he later changed it to conform to Burney's version of events.[13] Perhaps Abel did not tell Burney the whole truth because he did not want to be thought difficult to work with in London's

---

des Theaters am Hofe zu Dresden, 2 vols. (Dresden, 1861–2; repr. Leipzig, 1971), ii. 240, 295. For the Dresden court orchestra, see esp. O. Landmann, 'The Dresden Hofkapelle during the Lifetime of Johann Sebastian Bach', *EM*, 17 (1989), 17–30.

[10] M. Cyr, 'Carl Friedrich Abel's Solos: a Musical Offering to Gainsborough?', *MT*, 128 (1987), 317–21, at 319–20.

[11] BurneyH, ii. 1018–19.

[12] F. W. Marpurg, *Historische-kritische Beyträge zur Aufnahme der Musik*, 5 vols. (Berlin, 1754–60), ii. 475–7.

[13] E. L. Gerber, *Historisch-biographisches Lexicon der Tonkünstler*, 2 vols. (Leipzig, 1790–92; repr. Graz, 1977), i. cols. 4–5; Gerber, *Neues historisch-biographisches Lexicon*, i. cols. 4–5.

competitive concert scene. We do not know where he went after Dresden, though Goethe mentioned him among the artists and virtuosi who visited his family home in Frankfurt am Main while he was child.[14] He may also have stopped off in Mannheim and Paris before crossing the Channel, presumably in the winter of 1758–9.

Abel was one of the many Germans involved in the music trade who came to England at this period, many of them doubtless because of the war. A number of instrument makers settled in London in the late 1750s and early 1760s (Ch. 4), and among the musicians who made the journey were the organist and violinist Karl Friedrich Baumgarten (1758); Rudolf Straube (1759); Johann Schmeling and his violinist daughter Gertrud Elisabeth, later the singer Mrs Mara (1759); and possibly the organist George Berg (late 1750s). William Herschel came to England at the beginning of the war as a Hanoverian army bandsman, though he returned to Germany with his regiment, and was present when the army was defeated at the Battle of Hastenbeck on 26 July 1757; he returned to England by way of Hamburg soon after. At the time Britain was seen as a haven of peace and prosperity, even by those such as Abel and Straube who came from states on the opposing side.[15]

✿ First Years in England

ABEL was at the centre of London's concert life for nearly thirty years, from 1759 until his death on 20 June 1787, with the exception of several years spent in Germany in the early 1780s. His debut, a benefit concert on 5 April 1759 at the Great Room in Dean Street, was clearly designed to show off the range of his talents. The preliminary advertisements stated that 'Mr. Abel will perform several Pieces upon the Viola Digamba, a Concerto on the Harpsichord, and a Piece upon an Instrument newly invented in England, called the Pentachord', though there were changes nearer the day: on 2 April his gamba pieces were identified as 'a Solo and a Concerto on the Viola Digamba', and the day before the concert the wording changed to 'a Solo and a Concerto on the Harpsichord and a Piece composed on Purpose for an Instrument newly invented in England, called the Pentachord, all composed by himself'.[16] It is unclear whether these changes were real or just confusions in the advertising. Abel gave another benefit concert in the same room on 25 April 1760, and soon began to appear in the benefits of his

---

[14] Knape, *Karl Friedrich Abel*, 35, 38–40.

[15] For a useful recent survey, see F. McLynn, *1759: the Year Britain Became Master of the World* (London, 2004).

[16] *PA*, 27, 31/3/1759; *PA*, 2, 4, 5/4/1759.

colleagues, such as the one given there on 28 January 1761 to raise money to have the castrato Giusto Ferdinando Tenducci released from a debtors' prison, or the one at the King's Theatre in the Haymarket on 12 March 1761 in aid of the Society (later Royal Society) of Musicians; he joined the Society on 1 March.[17]

At that period the London concert season was quite short, starting in January or February and ending in May, when the aristocracy left London for their country estates. In the summer and autumn leading musicians took the opportunity to tour the provinces. Thus on 28 May 1759 John Courtney of Beverley reported that in a concert at Trinity College, Cambridge 'the principal instrumental Parts were perform'd by the Finest Players in England vizd. Sigr. [Felice] Giardini – First Violin. [Joseph] Tacet – German Flute. [John] Vincent – Hautboy. [John] Gordon – Violoncello. Abel – Violino di Gamba, or 6 string Bass'.[18] Abel was clearly already moving in the best musical circles, and that October he appeared at the Salisbury Festival, one of the most prominent provincial musical organisations. *The Salisbury Journal* hinted coyly beforehand that 'an excellent Performer on the VIOL GAMBO, is expected on this Occasion whose Name at present, we are not at Liberty to mention'.[19] The next week it revealed that 'Mr. ABEL, one of the finest Players in Europe upon the VIOL DE GAMBO, will oblige the Company with a Solo upon that Instrument'.[20] After the concerts, on 3 and 4 October, it reported that 'Signior Abel performed the principal violoncello' in the orchestra as well as entertaining 'the company each night with a Solo on the Viol de Gambo, which exceeded anything of the kind that was ever heard'.[21] There were performances of Handel's *Joshua* and *Samson* as well as a festival service with anthems and a Jubilate 'Selected from the choicest Compositions of the best *Italian Masters*'.

Abel made his Bath debut on 4 February 1760 at Wiltshire's Assembly Rooms with a benefit concert that included two gamba solos and two harpsichord pieces as well as overtures by Handel, a cantata by Arne, a song by Boyce, and two of his own 'overtures' or symphonies.[22] At this stage he was clearly trying to

---

[17] *PA*, 25/4/1760; *PA*, 16, 17/1/1761; *PA*, 9–12/3/1761; B. Matthews, *The Royal Society of Musicians of Great Britain, List of Members, 1738–1984* (London, 1985), 13.

[18] GB-HU, DDX/60 (David Hunter).

[19] *The Salisbury Journal*, 17/9/1759; B. Matthews, 'Abel in Salisbury', *MT*, 115 (1974), 217.

[20] *The Salisbury Journal*, 24/9/1759.

[21] Ibid., 8/10/1759.

[22] K. E. James, 'Concert Life in Eighteenth-Century Bath' (PhD diss., Royal Holloway, U. of London, 1987), 439; J. Burchell, *Polite or Commercial Concerts? Concert Management and Orchestral Repertoire in Edinburgh, Bath, Oxford, Manchester, and Newcastle, 1730–1799* (New York, 1996), 131, 166; *Music and*

ingratiate himself with the English public by performing music by native composers, though he and J. C. Bach were later thought of as the leaders of a faction in London musical life that promoted modern Continental music at their expense.[23] He was expected to play 'many choice pieces on the violdegambo and the harpsicord' at a benefit concert in Edinburgh in July 1760, though it was postponed.[24] He returned to Bath with Giardini in October 1761 and they appeared together at Wiltshire's Rooms on 11 November.[25] Bach, Abel and Giardini were among the 'occasional and superior aids' who were 'induced every season to visit Bath', according to the painter Ozias Humphry;[26] at this period the Bath season was essentially an extension of the London cultural scene. Most virtuosi at the time concentrated on just one or two instruments, so Abel was unusual in that he played at least four in his first concerts in England: gamba, violoncello, harpsichord, and pentachord. In addition, in his 1763 London benefit, given on 3 March at the Great Room in Spring Gardens, he promised unidentified 'new Instruments, never heard in public before', and music he had composed for them.[27]

As its name indicates, the pentachord was a five-string violoncello. Its inventor was Sir Edward Walpole (Ch. 7): his younger brother Horace stated that he 'invented a most touching instrument, which, from the number of strings, he called a *pentachord*'.[28] James Cervetto wrote in the dedication to his *Six Solos for the Violoncello and a Bass*, op. 3 (1777) that Sir Edward was 'the sole Inventor of the Pentachord' and added: 'I know not a more fit Instrument to Accompany the Voice, and the Tone of which is not equalled by any Other Instrument.'[29] The pentachord was rare: the only other person known to have used it in London concerts was Alexander Reinagle, who played it three times in 1782–3; on the second occasion, one of the Wesley family concerts, he played

Theatre in Handel's World: the Family Papers of James Harris, 1732–1780, ed. D. Burrows and R. Dunhill (Oxford, 2002), 345; S. Sloman, *Gainsborough in Bath* (New Haven, CT, 2002), 101, 235.

[23] For instance, J. Hawkins, 'Memoirs of Dr. William Boyce', in *Cathedral Music*, ed. W. Boyce (London, 2/1788), ix.

[24] Burchell, *Polite or Commercial Concerts*, 98.

[25] James, 'Concert Life in Eighteenth-Century Bath', 439; Sloman, *Gainsborough in Bath*, 101, 235.

[26] James, 'Concert Life in Eighteenth-Century Bath', 439.

[27] PA, 3/3/1763.

[28] *The Yale Edition of Horace Walpole's Correspondence*, 29: *Horace Walpole's Correspondence with William Mason I*, ed. W. S. Lewis, G. Cronin jr. and C. H. Bennett (London, 1955), 196.

[29] RISM A/I C 1735; CC: GB-Lbl, G.511.(1).

a trio with his younger brother Hugh (violoncello), its composer, and Samuel Wesley (violin).[30] However, a Miss Marshall aged fourteen from Nottingham played a 'five-stringed Violoncello' in concerts in York and Newcastle in 1774, on one occasion playing a duet for two of them with Mr Marshall, presumably her father.[31]

A pentachord made in about 1775 is still in existence, though it is now an ordinary four-string violoncello. It is stamped 'I. Merlin London' (the inventor and instrument maker John Joseph Merlin; Ch. 4), though it is said to have been made by John Carter, an associate of William Forster.[32] An accompanying letter written by a later owner, the artist John Cawse, records that its tuning was 'the same as the Violoncello Viz. C G D A & the fifth or treble string is tuned a 4th above the A to the note D & Precludes the necesity of shifting that is required in Passages above the 3ᵈ Position in violoncello Playing'. As Cawse implied, the main function of five-string violoncellos was to make high-lying solos easier. It is likely, for instance, that the obbligato part in 'But oh, sad virgin' from Handel's *L'Allegro, il Penseroso ed il Moderato*, HWV55/22 (1740), was written for one, though probably with the top string tuned to e'' rather than d''; it is cruelly difficult on an ordinary violoncello.[33] Abel presumably played the pentachord as a tribute to Sir Edward Walpole, a probable patron and pupil, but it also suggests that he was less accomplished on the violoncello than on the gamba, and used the pentachord to avoid high positions. There is no record of him playing solos on any type of violoncello after 1760.

Abel is also not known to have played harpsichord solos in public after 1760, and this was also probably because his keyboard technique was too limited to compete with London's established keyboard virtuosos. He was listed in 1763 as 'Composer of Music and Teacher on the Harpsichord',[34] and is shown

---

[30] *PA*, 17/5/1782; *PA*, 10/4/1782; A. McLamore, '"By the Will and Order of Providence": the Wesley Family Concerts, 1779–1787', *RMARC*, 37 (2004), 71–220, at 84, 134. For the Reinagle family, see esp. A. McClenny Krauss, 'Alexander Reinagle, his Family Background and Early Professional Career', *American Music*, 4 (1986), 425–56.

[31] *York Courant*, 11/1/1774; *The Newcastle Courant*, 12, 19/3/1774 (Roz Southey). See also *BDA*, x. 103–4.

[32] Illus. *John Joseph Merlin, the Ingenious Mechanick*, ed. A. French (London, 1985), 107–9; *The British Violin: the Catalogue of the 1998 Exhibition '400 Years of Violin and Bow Making in the British Isles'*, ed. J. Milnes (Oxford, 2000), 256–7. For Carter and Forster, see *The British Violin*, ed. Milnes, 44, 74–76.

[33] I am grateful to Mark Caudle and Charles Medlam for advice on this point.

[34] T. Mortimer, *The Universal Director, or The Noble and Gentleman's True Guide to the Masters and Professors of the Liberal and Polite Arts and Sciences, and of the Mechanic Arts, Manufacturers, and Trades, Established in London and*

at a harpsichord in Charles Robineau's 1780 painting in the Royal Collection.[35] William Jackson wrote that:

> Abel, in point of Execution, pretended to nothing on the Harpsichord; (Piano-fortes did not then exist) but his *creeping* over the Keys shewed great Knowledge of Combination and Succession of Chords. He had a Trick of keeping one Note as a Centre, round which he would wander through a Variety of Passages and Harmonies, not understood by the common Ear indeed, but affording much Gratification to the learned Professor.[36]

Charles Burney agreed: 'On the harpsichord, though he had not a great hand for lessons, he used to modulate, in arpeggio, with infinite variety and knowledge'; we shall see that Burney also used 'modulate' to describe Abel's improvisations on the gamba.[37] Concentrating on the gamba made sense for Abel. It allowed him to carve out a distinctive niche in London's concert life, where there was little danger of competition from younger and more fashionable players – a perennial problem for virtuosos on more popular instruments.[38]

Before leaving this subject we should dispose of the persistent idea that Abel played the horn. It only seems to go back as far as Carl Ferdinand Pohl's pioneering account of the visits of Mozart and Haydn to London, which lists him as performing 'auf dem Waldhorn'.[39] Pohl gave no evidence for his assertion, though it has been suggested that it arose out of Abel's 'admiration for a keyboard sonata by Ferdinand [*recte* Charles Frederick] Horn' – presumably the second of Horn's *Six Sonatas for the Piano Forte or Harpsichord, with an Accompanyment for a Violin & Violoncello*, op. 1 (London, 1786).[40] According to Charlotte Papendiek it 'particularly attracted the notice of Abel', being 'chromatic, the melody of the

Westminster, and their Environ (London, 1763), 31; CC: *ECCO*, T013191. See also 'An Eighteenth-Century Directory of London Musicians', *GSJ*, 2 (1949), 27–31, at 27.

35   Illus. S. J. Wynn, 'Karl Friedrich Abel: Some Contemporary Impressions', *JVdGSA*, 10 (1973), 4–10, at 4.

36   A. Asfour and P. Williamson, 'William Jackson of Exeter: New Documents', *Gainsborough's House Review* (1996–7), 39–152, at 66.

37   BurneyH, ii. 1020.

38   For a case study of this problem among violinists in the 1780s, see I. Woodfield, *Salomon and the Burneys: Private Patronage and a Public Career* (Aldershot, 2003).

39   C. F. Pohl, *Mozart und Haydn in London*, 2 vols. (Vienna, 1867), i. 155. The idea was still current in the 1970s; see C. F. Abel, *Six Selected Symphonies*, ed. S. M. Helm (Madison, WI, 1977), viii.

40   W. Knape *et al.*, 'Abel: (4) Carl Friedrich Abel', *GMO*; RISM A/1 H 7422.

adagio pretty, and the whole sonata of a superior cast'.[41] More likely, Pohl simply misunderstood concert advertisements, such as the one for William Yates's benefit concert at Hickford's Rooms on 5 March 1764 that included a 'Horn Piece, Mr. Abel'.[42] The work in question was probably an orchestral piece by Abel with solo horn writing; there is no evidence that he played in the concert.

ᥡ *Promoting Concerts*

IT was not long before Abel became involved in running and promoting a concert series. Evidence has recently come to light that he was organising concerts for the society hostess Theresa Cornelys at Carlisle House in Soho Square as early as the 1761 season.[43] A few years later, at the beginning of the 1765 season, he went into partnership with J. C. Bach (who had arrived in London from Milan in 1762), starting the Bach–Abel concerts; their first few seasons were at Carlisle House. Thomas Gainsborough's first portrait of Abel dates from around then, and may have been painted to mark the moment when he and Bach caught the attention of polite society and established themselves at the head of the German faction of their profession (Frontispiece).[44] In 1768 they moved to Almack's Assembly Rooms in King St, St James's, but returned to Carlisle House for the 1774 season. From 1775 they were at the newly built Hanover Square Rooms.

Abel was one of the greatest gamba virtuosos of his time, so it is not surprising that his primary role in London concerts was to play solos on the instrument. Advertisements for more than sixty concerts include the phrase 'A Solo on the Viola da Gamba by Mr. Abel', and it became so familiar that it was used as the title of John Nixon's caricature 'A Solo on the Viola di Gamba / Mr Abel.', issued as an etching in July 1787 to mark the musician's death (Plate 9).[45] It is likely that

[41] C. L. H. Papendiek, *Court and Private Life in the Time of Queen Charlotte, being the Journals of Mrs. Papendiek, Assistant-Keeper of the Wardrobe and Reader to her Majesty*, ed. A. Delves Broughton, 2 vols. (London, 1887), i. 255.

[42] *PA*, 5/3/1764.

[43] J. Summers, *The Empress of Taste: the Life and Adventures of Teresa Cornelys, Queen of Masquerades and Casanova's Lover* (London, 2003), esp. 120–1.

[44] London, National Portrait Gallery, no. 5947. See esp. E. Waterhouse, *Gainsborough* (London, 2/1966), 51, no. 3; M. Rosenthal, *The Art of Thomas Gainsborough* (New Haven, CT, 1999), 40–2; Sloman, *Gainsborough in Bath*, 100–1.

[45] London, National Portrait Gallery, no. 5178. The etching is illus. J. H. Mee, *The Oldest Music Room in Europe: a Record of Eighteenth-Century Enterprise at Oxford* (London, 1911), facing 32. See also *Catalogue of Political and Personal*

he also played gamba solos in the many cases when the advertisements use less specific phrases such as 'a Concert of / Vocal and Instrumental MUSIC. / With Solos by Sig. Bach, Sig. Abel and Mr. Fisher', or merely: 'Mess. Bach, Abel, Fischer, Cirri and Barthelemon, will perform several Pieces of their Composition'.[46] In several cases we know from eyewitness accounts that he played gamba solos where evidence from advertisements is lacking. The advertisements for the benefit put on by Bach and Abel at the Great Room in Spring Gardens on 29 February 1764 (their first-known public collaboration) merely mention that Abel would play 'several new Pieces of Instrumental Music', though Elizabeth Harris wrote that 'Abel play'd two solos on his Viol di Gambo delightfull'.[47]

Such evidence is particularly valuable for the main Bach–Abel concerts, since advertisements almost never contain details of the performers or the pieces to be performed, their purpose being to remind their exclusive clientele of the event, not to bring in an audience. It is the advertisements for one-off benefits that usually give a list of individual pieces and details of the principal performers, though Abel revealed an unusual amount about his plans for the 1782 season soon after Bach's death on 1 January. At that moment he was presumably concerned to reassure his subscribers that the death of his partner would not affect the quality of what was on offer:

> MR. ABEL takes the Liberty of acquainting the Nobility and Gentry, Subscribers to his CONCERTS for the ensuing Season, That it is his Intention to vary the Subjects of Performance every Night; for which Purpose he has at considerable Expence and Trouble collected the newest Compositions of the first Masters in Europe, viz. of Hayden, Boccherini, Dietten [?Dittersdorf], Cambini, Stamitz, and others; and he intends humbly to offer, in the Course of the Season, some new Works of his own, composed expressly for the Purpose. / That having engaged what he presumes to think the best Band of Instrumental Performers in Europe, and three capital Singers, he flatters himself he shall meet with the same Encouragement and Approbation he and his late worthy Colleague enjoyed for many Years past. / N. B. An Order of Concert will be delivered every Night of the Music to be Performed.[48]

Satires Preserved in the Department of Prints and Drawings in the British Museum, 11 vols. (London, 1870–1954), vi. 991, no. 8264.

[46] *PA,* 9/3/1769; *PA,* 22/5/1769.

[47] *PA,* 25, 27–9/2/1764; *Music and Theatre in Handel's World,* ed. Burrows and Dunhill, 415.

[48] *PA,* 5, 6, 16/2/1782.

No 'orders of concert' seem to survive, and it was not until the Earl of Abingdon reorganised the concerts for the 1783 season, following Abel's departure for Germany, that it became customary to advertise complete programmes.[49]

🎝 'A Solo on the Viola da Gamba'

WHAT was meant by the formula 'A Solo on the Viola da Gamba by Mr. Abel'? The word 'solo' was sometimes applied to pieces played on keyboards and other instruments such as the harp and the lute that were able to provide their own harmony and therefore did not need to be accompanied. For instance, J. C. Bach played a 'Solo on the Piano Forte' in a concert at the Thatched House in St James's Street on 2 June 1768, while Edward Jones regularly played a 'Solo on the Pedal Harp' in concerts during the 1770s – for instance, in the intervals of oratorios at Covent Garden on 10, 15 and 27 March 1776.[50] However, it was more commonly applied to pieces for instruments that needed to be accompanied, while the words 'sonata' or 'lesson' were more often applied to keyboard music. In his *New Tutor for the Violin* (c. 1790) François-Hippolyte Barthélemon, a prominent colleague and follower of Abel, defined 'Solo' as 'a Piece of Music for one Instrument whilst the Bass accompanies'.[51] Burney agreed: 'SOLO, in *Italian Music*, used substantively, implies a composition for a single instrument, with a quiet and subdued accompaniment, to display the talents of a great performer; as a solo for a violin, German flute, or violoncello'.[52]

The problem with understanding 'solo' as it applied to the gamba is that, like the mandolin, the English guitar or the baryton, its role was ambiguous: it could serve as a melody instrument, accompanied by a bass instrument, but it could also be played unaccompanied, using multiple stops to provide its own accompaniment. This ambiguity is reflected in Abel's surviving solo gamba music, which divides into sonatas with continuo or bass accompaniment and unaccompanied pieces. They are strikingly different in form, idiom and style. The sonatas with bass, in two or three movements, are in the *galant* style and are concerned with graceful melody and elegant proportion rather than virtuosity, while the

[49] S. McVeigh, 'The Professional Concert and Rival Subscription Series in London, 1783–1793', *RMARC*, 22 (1989), 1–135.

[50] *PA*, 27/5/1768; *PA*, 6, 15, 26/3/1776.

[51] S. McVeigh, *The Violinist in London's Concert Life, 1750–1784: Felice Giardini and his Contemporaries* (New York, 1989), 132.

[52] C. Burney, 'Solo', in *The Cyclopaedia, or Universal Dictionary of Arts, Sciences, and Literature*, ed. A. Rees, 39 vols. (London, 1819). For Burney's contributions to Rees's *Cyclopaedia*, see J. C. Kassler, *The Science of Music in Britain, 1714–1830: a Catalogue of Writings, Lectures and Inventions*, 2 vols. (New York, 1979), ii. 1200–1204.

unaccompanied pieces are just grouped by key, and are much more ambitious and serious, often mixing elements of the Baroque style with more modern idioms. They also use multiple stops to a much greater extent than the solos.

Abel used the two types for different purposes. Assessments of his public persona repeatedly emphasise simplicity and feeling rather than virtuosity. In a letter of 18 July 1773 Thomas Gainsborough thought that while the oboist J. C. Fischer had a genius for 'dexterity, quickness, &c', Abel excelled at 'feeling upon the instrument'.[53] W. T. Parke recalled that on 5 February 1785 Abel 'performed a solo on the viol di gamba with his accustomed elegance and sensibility'.[54] Henry Bate thought that his 'powers on the *Viol de Gambo*, were particularly great; – no person ever touched that instrument with sweeter effect and taste!'[55] Charles Burney published a warm and perceptive tribute to Abel in the last volume of his *History of Music*:

> His performance on the viol da gamba was in every particular complete and perfect. He had a hand which no difficulties could embarrass; a taste the most refined and delicate; and a judgment so correct and certain as never to let a single note escape him without meaning. His compositions were easy and elegantly simple, for he used to say, "I do not chuse to be always struggling with difficulties, and playing with all my might. I make my pieces difficult whenever I please, according to my disposition and that of my audience." Yet in nothing was he so superior to himself, and to other musicians, as in writing and playing an *adagio*; in which the most pleasing, yet learned modulation; the richest harmony; and the most elegant and polished melody were all expressed with such feeling, taste, and science, that no musical production or performance with which I was then acquainted seemed to approach nearer perfection.[56]

The essential point is that, though Abel 'had a hand which no difficulties could embarrass', he did not always choose to do play difficult music: 'I make my pieces difficult whenever I please, according to my disposition and that of my audience.' I take this to mean that he played difficult, recherché music to his friends in private, but played in a simpler and more approachable manner in public. Even in his most elaborate solos, such as the two 'Prussian sonatas', virtuosity is not the

---

53 *The Letters of Thomas Gainsborough*, ed. J. Hayes (New Haven, CT, 2001), 117–18.

54 W. T. Parke, *Musical Memoirs*, 2 vols. (London, 1830), i. 53. However, the programme for that concert does not include a gamba solo by Abel, see McVeigh, 'The Professional Concert', 57.

55 *MH*, 21/6/1787.

56 BurneyH, ii. 1019. A footnote states: 'This was written in 1779'.

main concern. They would have been ideal vehicles for the display of sensibility, taste and feeling, and they could still have been understood and enjoyed at first hearing. I argue in Chapter 6 that Abel must have written dozens if not hundreds of solos for his own use in concerts, but that they are nearly all lost.

Abel adopted a rather different style in private. Burney wrote that 'when he was in spirits and fancy, I have heard him modulate in private on his six-string base with such practical readiness and depth of science, as astonished the late Lord Kelly and Bach, as much as myself'.[57] Bate particularly mentioned his private performances: 'Those were the happy judges who heard him play by the fireside, when he took his flight into fine airs, double stops and arpeggios, and put his twelve o'clock *light* and *shade* into every note!'[58] The implication is that Abel's private performances were more remarkable and memorable than his public ones, partly because, as Bate suggested in the same article, the gamba was too soft to be heard properly in public concerts:

> His fine execution on the *Viol de Gamba*, very few people had an opportunity of forming any judgement on, in public rooms, from the extreme tenderness of the strings, and the reason perhaps of his Adagios being most attended to and admired, was, that slow music invites more silence, than noisy Allegro.

William Jackson made a similar point: 'His Performance on the Viol de Gamba in a Room was pleasing as well as masterly, but the Instrument had a thin nosy [nasal] Effect in a Concert', and made an interesting and rare criticism of Abel's performing style: 'His Custom (when performing on the Viol da Gamba) of accelerating the Movement in the last two or three Bars always produced a bad Effect'.[59]

The most remarkable description of Abel's private performances comes from an obituary:

> justly admired as he was at his publick Performances, it was a few only of his intimate Friends in private who were Witnesses of his most wonderful musical Powers, to come at which, a Bottle or two of good Burgundy before him, and his Viol di Gambo within his Reach, were necessary. In that Situation his Friends would introduce the Subject of the human Passions, and Abel, not very capable of expressing *in English his own sentiments*, would catch up his Viol Di Gambo, and tell the Story of Lefevre thereon, till he brought Tears into the Eyes of his Hearers, and not lay it down, till he

[57] BurneyH, ii. 1020.

[58] *MH*, 23/6/1787.

[59] 'William Jackson of Exeter: New Documents', ed. Asfour and Williamson, 66.

had made his Friend Gainsborough dance a Hornpipe on the Bottom of a Pewter Quart Pot.[60]

A correspondent in the same newspaper, who thought Abel 'unquestionably the greatest musician this century produced', wrote that 'those *only* who have heard him in private … knew the extent of his astonishing power of tuning their [his listeners'] souls to his Viol di Gamba': 'I have been one of those *machines* he has so played upon, as to have been, as I thought, near death; the pegs of life seemed stretched beyond their bearings; and I sincerely believe he perceived it, and let me down again by degrees.[61] Significantly, he added: 'his play at such moments was not compositions, but given subjects, such as love, war, rage, or fandangoes'.

These passages suggest that Abel's improvisations were often programmatic, and were effectively a musical discourse on the nature of emotion in the arts, a topic made fashionable by works such as William Collins's ode 'The Passions' (1746), William Hogarth's *Analysis of Beauty* (1753), Charles Avison's *Essay on Musical Expression* (1753), and Edmund Burke's *Philosophical Enquiry into the Origin of our Ideas of the Sublime and Beautiful* (1757). The choice of 'the Story of Lefevre', the famous touching deathbed scene of Lieutenant Le Fever in Laurence Sterne's *Tristram Shandy*, is significant, for Sterne was extremely musical, prob-ably played the gamba, and is known to have attended the Bach–Abel concerts (Ch. 7). Both were regarded in their own fields as exponents of sensibility – the cult of sincere and direct emotion that was at its height in the 1760s. As another obituary put it, 'The death of Abel occasions a great loss to the musical world. Sensibility is the prevailing and beautiful characteristic of his compositions. – He was the *Sterne* of *Music*. – The one *wrote*, and the other *composed* to the *soul*.'[62]

Once Abel's career in London was established he settled into a pattern in which his main contribution to a concert was a single viola da gamba solo. After attending a Bach–Abel concert on 12 May 1779 and finding Abel absent, a disap-pointed John Marsh wrote that the composer 'usually played a piece upon the viol da gamba immediately after the 1st. overture'.[63] He added: 'This happen'd as I was inform'd from his then being on his annual jaunt to Paris to procure some of the best *claret*.' In fact, Abel's solo did not always come immediately after the opening item. There are forty complete surviving concert programmes that include Abel playing a gamba solo. An analysis reveals that his solo was the second item of the first act eight times, but the fourth item in the first act seven

---

[60] *St James's Chronicle*, 28–30/6/1787.

[61] *St James's Chronicle*, 6/4/1790.

[62] *DUR*, 23/6/1787.

[63] *The John Marsh Journals: the Life and Times of a Gentleman Composer (1752–1828)*, ed. B. Robins (Stuyvesant, NY, 1998), 197.

times, the third item nine times, and the third item in the second act eleven times – an option favoured by the Professional Concert in 1785–7. On one day, 19 May 1775, he was able to play in two simultaneous concerts: he contributed to a benefit for Caterina Galli and Giovanni Salpietro at Hickford's Room in Brewer Street, but he also played a 'Solo on the Viol de Gamby' as the fourth item of Act I for Eligio Celestino's benefit at Carlisle House in Soho Square.[64] The concerts began at 7 pm and 7.30 pm respectively, though luckily the venues were quite close.

How would Abel's gamba solos have been accompanied? There has been an assumption in modern times that the bass line would have been played on a second viol – as in a recent edition.[65] However, Abel seems to have been the only gamba player in the concerts he contributed to, and by the middle of the century the instrument was used to play solo or concertante parts in the alto or tenor register rather than bass lines. Its music was nearly always notated in the octave transposing treble or alto clefs rather than the bass clef. It is likely that Abel's solos were normally accompanied just by a violoncello. In nearly all cases the bass line is unfigured, and in one of the autographs several pieces are specifically labelled 'Viola da Gamba & violoncello' (Ch. 6). By the 1770s it was becoming common to omit the harpsichord in pieces of this sort – those by Andreas Lidel are also for 'Viola da Gamba e Violoncello' (Ch. 8) – though publications still usually provided a figured bass.

🎵 Solos by other Composers

So far I have assumed that Abel always played his own solos in concerts, but that is not necessarily so. It is significant that several of his London colleagues wrote gamba music even though they themselves are not known to have played the instrument. There are four sonatas for viola da gamba and obbligato harpsichord by J. C. Bach (Ch. 6), though they have obbligato keyboard parts and are therefore unlikely to have been advertised as 'a solo on the viola da gamba'. The Bohemian violinist and viola player Antonín Kammel mentioned six lost solos 'for the Viola da gamba, which start in a very decorative way' in a list of new compositions he included in a letter to his patron, Count Waldstein, on 20 October 1766.[66] Kammel (d. 1784) was an associate of

[64] *PA*, 19/5/1775.

[65] C. F. Abel, *Six Sonatas for Two Violas da Gamba from the Countess of Pembroke's Music Book*, ed. B. Capleton, 2 vols. (West Malvern, 1997).

[66] M. Freemanová and E. Mikanová, '"My Honourable Lord and Father …": Eighteenth-Century English Musical Life through Bohemian Eyes', *EM*, 31 (2003), 210–31, at 216.

Ex. 5.1 W. A. Mozart, theme of a lost solo in F major for viola da gamba or violoncello

Bach and Abel from his arrival in London in 1765. Pietro Pompeo Sales visited London in 1776, worked with Abel, and wrote a song with gamba obbligato (Ch. 8).

The young Mozart may also have written gamba music for Abel. Leopold Mozart, in a list of works written by his son between the ages of seven and twelve, included 'für die Viola da Gamba' under the heading 'Verschiedene Solo'.[67] It (or one of them) could be the solo in F major whose incipit survives in a thematic catalogue formerly in the Breitkopf and Härtel archives in Leipzig (Ex. 5.1). It has been suggested that the intended performer was Joseph Wenzel von Fürstenberg at Donaueschingen (Leopold's list includes violoncello solos written for the prince) or Maximilian III Joseph, Elector of Bavaria, an accomplished gamba player.[68] The Mozarts were in Donaueschingen for twelve days in October 1766, and at the Elector's court in Munich for most of the following month.[69] However, Abel is a much stronger contender, for Wolfgang's contacts with him lasted more than a year. The Mozarts were members of the Bach–Abel circle during their stay in London from April 1764 to July 1765, and while they was there Wolfgang copied out a score of Abel's Symphony in Eb, WKO 18, published in 1767 as op. 7, no. 6; it was long thought to be Mozart's Symphony no. 3.[70] Wolfgang also marked Abel's death in 1787 by basing the finale of his A major violin sonata, K526, on the finale of Abel's A major sonata op. 5, no. 5, WKO 121, for harpsichord, violin or flute and violoncello.[71]

There is little sign that Abel was interested in earlier gamba music, though the sale of his effects on 12 December 1787 included 'concertos by Rameau' (I/12).[72]

---

[67] N. Zaslaw, 'Leopold Mozart's List of his Son's Works', in *Music in the Classic Period: Essays in Honor of Barry S. Brook*, ed. A. Atlas (New York, 1985), 323–58, esp. 328, 344–7.

[68] Zaslaw, 'Leopold Mozart's List of his Son's Works', 344–5; Flassig, *Die solistische Gambenmusik in Deutschland*, 184–6, 285.

[69] O. E. Deutsch, *Mozart: a Documentary Biography*, trans. E. Blom, P. Branscombe, and J. Noble (London, 1965; repr. 1990), 66–7.

[70] WKO, pp. 21, 30; Knape, *Karl Friedrich Abel*, 58–9; N. Zaslaw, *Mozart's Symphonies: Context, Performance Practice, Reception* (Oxford, 1989; repr. 1991), 26, 28.

[71] WKO, p. 197; Zaslaw, *Mozart's Symphonies*, 28.

[72] S. Roe, 'The Sale Catalogue of Carl Friedrich Abel (1787)', in *Music and the Book Trade from the Sixteenth to the Twentieth Century*, ed. R. Myers, M. Harris, and G. Mandelbrote (London, 2008), 105–43, at 131.

Ex. 5.2   (a) C. F. Abel, Andante in D major, WKO 191, bb. 1–4 compared with
(b) Louis de Caix d'Hervelois, Musette in D major, bb. 1–3

This was probably the English edition of Rameau's *Pieces de clavecin en concerts* (Paris, 1741), published by Walsh as *Five Concertos for the Harpsicord … Accompanied with a Violin or German Flute or Two Violins or Viola* (1750; repr. New York, 1986).[73] Copies of printed *pièces de viole* by Louis de Caix d'Hervelois supposedly annotated by Abel existed in the nineteenth century (Ch. 8), and there is a remarkable similarity between the opening of the Musette in D major from Caix d'Hervelois's *Troisième œuvre* (Paris, 1731; repr. 1974), pp. 14–15, and Abel's unaccompanied Andante, WKO 191, in the same key (Ex. 5.2, a, b).[74] Abel's knowledge of French gamba music was presumably acquired during his visits to Paris. It was reported in May 1782 that Abel 'is gone to Paris, according to his annual Custom, for a Couple of Months. His patron there is one of the *Fermieres Generales*, who is passionately fond of the Viol di Gamba, and who allows Abel for his two Months Performance on it *Two Hundred Guineas* a Month, a Gratification equal to that which Abel receives from our *Queen*!'[75] The Monsieur Monnet in Paris who purchased a gamba from Abel in November 1771 was presumably another patron or pupil.[76]

&. *Concertos*

ABEL did not just play solos in London concerts; on a number of occasions he played concertos. He was advertised as playing 'a Concerto on the Viola Digamba' prior to his London debut, and subsequently played them during Jommelli's oratorio *La Betulia liberata* at the King's Theatre in the Haymarket on

73 RISM A/I R 193.

74 RISM A/I C 43 (Richard Sutcliffe).

75 *PA*, 18/5/1782.

76 US-NHub, Osborn Manuscript Files A, no. 11 (David Hunter).

25 February 1768, during Handel's *Acis and Galatea* at the King's Theatre on 15 March 1775, in a concert at the Pantheon on 16 March 1780, and at a private concert at the Duke of Queensberry's in January 1785.[77] There are also advertisements where the instrument is not specified, such as the 'Concertos by Mess. Abel, Bach, Fisher, Kammell, and Weise' played in a concert at Almack's Great Room on 20 April 1769, or the 'Concerto[s] by Mess. Bach, Abel, and Fisher' in a concert in the same room four days later.[78] In the case of Charlotte Papendiek's anecdote about Abel playing a concerto while drunk, it is clear that he was playing a bowed instrument – it was tuned by someone else and handed to him – and she would surely have mentioned the fact had it not been the gamba:

> The same season [1782], on the occasion of the Musical Fund entertainment, his particular friends dined with him in order to conduct him to the theatre in safety. In that they succeeded, but not in keeping him from indulging in his supposed necessitous error. He was led on to the stage between two persons, and his instrument was given to him ready tuned. He played almost better than ever, and when his concerto was finished they dropped the curtain, for he could not rise from his seat to bow.[79]

One does not like to spoil a good story, but the advertisement for the Society of Musicians' benefit on 25 January 1782 does not mention Abel as a performer, though one of his concertos for oboe, violin and violoncello was performed.[80] However, it is interesting that the location was the King's Theatre in the Haymarket, the location of several of his known concerto performances, for in a theatre he could have played on stage accompanied by the orchestra in the pit, enabling his instrument to be heard more clearly than in a conventional concert room. This practice was evidently not confined to gamba concertos: John Marsh wrote that a benefit concert for the Society of Musicians at the Haymarket Theatre on 10 February 1774 'was all perform'd in the common orchestra [i.e., the pit], except those that played solo concertos, who mounted the stage just above by themselves'.[81]

---

77 *PA*, 29/1/1768; *PA*, 15/3/1775; *PA*, 16/3/1780; *DUR*, 11/1/1785.

78 *PA*, 20, 24/4/1769.

79 Papendiek, *Court and Private Life*, ii. 154.

80 *PA*, 25/1/1782.

81 *The John Marsh Journals*, ed. Robins, 118–19. For this practice, see J. Spitzer and N. Zaslaw, *The Birth of the Orchestra: History of an Institution, 1650–1815* (Oxford, 2004), 357–8, and the items cited in fn. 31; R. Maunder, *The Scoring of Baroque Concertos* (Woodbridge, 2004), 120, 126–7.

With the discovery of the sale catalogue of Abel's possessions we now have hard evidence that he composed gamba concertos, for it includes 'Mr. Abel's last solos and concertos, for the viola de gambo' (I/34).[82] Unfortunately, none of them (with the possible exception of WKO 52) appear to have survived, but if an anecdote is to be believed, at least one circulated outside Abel's immediate circle:

> An amusing story of his ready wit is the following: one evening, when taking a walk with Lord Kelly in a suburb of London, they heard sounds of music issuing from a tavern, and on approaching the place, recognised it as a gamba concerto by Abel, which was being murdered by the tavern musician. "I wonder who that is," said Lord Kelly. "Who else could it be but Cain?" was Abel's reply.[83]

❧ *Chamber Music and Private Concerts*

ABEL also played the gamba in chamber ensembles, an activity not mentioned in concert advertisements, though Elizabeth Harris wrote to her son James that the Bach–Abel concert on 6 March 1765 included 'a most delightfull quartetto between Abel, Bartolemon, Tacett & Ciri'.[84] François-Hippolyte Barthélemon was a violinist, Joseph Tacet a flute player, and Giovanni Battista Cirri a cellist, so the work in question was presumably a quartet for flute, violin, viola da gamba and cello; Abel is known to have written at least ten works for that combination, one of which survives, the Quartet in G major, WKO 227 (Ch. 6). J. C. Bach's Quintet in F major, B77 was published in *Three Favorite Quartetts and One Quintett for the Harpsichord, Violin, Flute, Hautboy, Tenor and Violoncello* (1785), though the viola part is labelled 'VIOLA da GAMBO'.[85] Also, Bach's B♭ major string quartet, B60, published in Paris in 1776, exists in several versions with variant scorings, including one in B-Br, II 4103 (5) Mus.

---

[82] Roe, 'The Sale Catalogue of Carl Friedrich Abel', 131.

[83] E. S. J. van der Straeten, *The History of the Violoncello, the Viol da Gamba, their Precursors and Collateral Instruments* (London, 1914; repr. 1971), 89. I have been unable to find a contemporary English source for this anecdote, though *Musikalischer Almanach*, ed. J. F. Reichardt (Berlin, 1796), part ix, no. 1, has a version of it concerning the performance of an Abel symphony at Vauxhall Gardens.

[84] *Music and Theatre in Handel's World*, ed. Burrows and Dunhill, 441.

[85] RISM A/I B 317; CC: GB-Lbl, h.32.c. ME: J. C. Bach, *The Collected Works*, 41: *Music for Five and Six Instruments*, ed. E. Warburton (New York, 1986), 171–93. See also D. McCulloch, 'Mrs Papendiek and the London Bach', *MT*, 123 (1982), 26–9; Bach, *The Collected Works*, 48/1: *Thematic Catalogue*, comp. Warburton (New York, 1999), 58, where it is suggested that B77 was composed 'during the last year or two of [Bach's] life'.

Fétis 3054 attributed (wrongly) to Haydn and scored for oboe, violin, gamba and violoncello.[86]

Chamber works of this sort would mostly have been performed in private concerts at court and in the houses of the aristocracy. These events were not advertised, and we only get a few glimpses of them from descriptions in newspapers, diaries, letters and memoirs. Burney, for instance, wrote that the Duke of York was 'one of [Abel's] first and best patrons', while it was stated that Abel's death 'makes an other vacancy in the establishment of the Duke of Cumberland' – apparently the only evidence for the post.[87] W. T. Parke described musical parties given by the duke in September 1789 at the Royal Lodge in Windsor Great Park, including 'our usual quartets and quintets', and morning concerts given twice a week during the winter concert season at his London residence, Cumberland House; the duke died in 1790.[88]

Abel certainly played in chamber ensembles as a member of Queen Charlotte's household. A group called the 'Queen's Chamber Band' was listed from 1775 in the annual editions of *The Court and City Register* alongside the larger Queen's Band, though it probably had an informal existence earlier, since Bach and Abel began to advertise themselves as 'Chamber Musician to the Queen' in 1764.[89] According to Charlotte Papendiek, writing about court life in 1774, Bach had a house at Richmond, 'where my father [Frederick Albert, George III's hairdresser] visited him, and cultivated a lasting friendship. These practices led to private quartett parties twice a week, assisted by Abel, the celebrated viol-di-gamba player; [Wilhelm] Cramer, the violinist; and Fis[c]her, the oboe player'.[90] She explained that Bach and Abel took it in turns to provide new music, and recalled one occasion, apparently in 1776:

> Bach had totally forgotten that it was his turn, so after dinner he sat down and wrote an enchanting first movement of a quintett in three flats. He sent off for two copyists, who wrote down the parts from score over his shoulders, while he wrote the harmony, after having composed the melody.

[86] ME: J. Haydn, *Divertissement pour hautbois, violon, viola da gamba et basse*, ed. A. Dolmetsch (London, 1930); J. C. Bach, *The Collected Works*, 40: *Music for Four Instruments*, ed. D. J. Keahey (New York, 1990), 363–82.

[87] BurneyH, ii. 1019; *The World*, 25/6/1787.

[88] Parke, *Musical Memoirs*, i. 121–2; ii. 187–90.

[89] C. S. Terry, *John Christian Bach*, rev. H. C. R. Landon (London, 2/1967), 151–2; Charters, 'Abel in London', 1225; McVeigh, *The Violinist in London's Concert Life*, 37–8; McVeigh, *Concert Life in London from Mozart to Haydn* (Cambridge, 1993), 49–52.

[90] Papendiek, *Court and Private Life*, i. 65.

The quintet is ranked among the best of his compositions, and the melody is sweetly soothing.[91]

Terry suggested that the piece in question was the E♭ quintet, B73, no. 4 of Bach's *Six Quintettos for a Flute, Hautboy, Violin, Tenor and Bass*, op. 11 (1774).[92] If so, Bach would have been writing out from memory rather than composing from scratch.

By 1774–5, when *The Court and City Register* first listed the Queen's Chamber Band, Cramer and Fischer had been replaced respectively by Frederick Nicolai and Redmond Simpson; the four-man group remained the same until 1782, when the flute player Charles Papendiek (Charlotte's brother-in-law) replaced Bach.[93] However, it did not always consist of the four official members. Papendiek presumably took part in pieces that required his instrument, such as Bach's op. 11, no. 4, before he formally joined the group. On 24 January 1775 James Harris reported that the players in a concert at the Queen's House were 'Bach, Abel, Cramer, & Nicolai – they played sonata's & trio's – Abel played a viol de gamba solo, & Bach a harpsicord concerto'; at the end the queen sang an aria from Handel's *Ottone*.[94] George III's equerry Robert Fulke Greville recorded that on 12 and 14 August 1781 Fischer, Bach, Abel and Crosdill played in concerts in the music room at Windsor Castle.[95]

There are also descriptions of the queen's musical establishment in German sources. In 1783 C. F. Cramer stated that Abel, as director, played the keyboard in concerts ('Directeur. Herr Carl Fried. Abel, spielt bey Concerten den Flügel'), but was a soloist on the gamba ('ausser diesem aber ist er Solo Spieler auf der Viola da Gamba') – implying that he directed larger groups from the keyboard. After describing the main Queen's Band, he listed seven individuals, 'Abel, [J. S.] Schröter, Cramer, Nicolai, Papendick, Fischer und Crosdill', who were required to play for the queen twice a week, evidently in the chamber

---

[91] Ibid., i. 75–7.

[92] Terry, *John Christian Bach*, 152, 302; Bach, *Thematic Catalogue*, comp. Warburton, 55–7; ME: Bach, *Music for Five and Six Instruments*, ed. Warburton, 81–101. The flute quartet in E♭ B53, op. 8, no. 3 (1772), is suggested as an alternative in McCulloch, 'Mrs Papendiek and the London Bach', 29.

[93] *The Court and City Register, or Gentleman's Complete Annual Calendar for the Year 1775* (London, 1774), 86; CC: *ECCO*, T126631. I have been unable to find a copy of the 1782 volume, but see McVeigh, *The Violinist in London's Concert Life*, 37–8. See also Papendiek, *Court and Private Life*, i. 244; ii. 198, 200, 210, 228, 244–5, 265–6.

[94] *Music and Theatre in Handel's World*, ed. Burrows and Dunhill, 796.

[95] *The Diaries of Colonel the Hon. Robert Fulke Greville, Equerry to his Majesty King George III*, ed. F. McKno Bladon (London, 1930), 26, 30.

band.[96] J. F. Reichardt, who visited London in 1785, wrote in 1793 that Abel 'was a gamba player and also played the bass in the queen's regular small chamber concerts, but more usually the alto part on the gamba'.[97] ('Er war *Gambist* und spielte bei den gewöhnlichen kleinen Kammerkoncerten der Königinn auch den Bass, gewöhnlicher aber den *Alt* auf der Gambe.') Three years later Reichardt was more specific: Abel's role was 'to play the viola part on the gamba, but sometimes also to accompany [at] the keyboard' ('Abel die Bratsche auf der Gambe zu spielen, zuweilen auch wohl den Flügel zu accompagniren').[98] This was echoed by Gerber: Abel's role was to 'play the viola part on his gamba, and to accompany occasionally at the keyboard in Bach's absence' ('die Bratsche auf seiner Gambe zu spielen, und nur dann und wann, in Bachs Abwesenheit, auf dem Flügel zu accompagniren').[99]

These statements generally support the eyewitness descriptions and the musical evidence. In the 1781 concerts described by Fulke Greville the group seems to have consisted of Fischer (oboe), Abel (gamba), Crosdill (violoncello), and Bach (keyboard); there are no surviving works for that combination by Bach or Abel. However, in 1774 and 1775 Abel's regular colleagues seem to have been Fischer or Simpson (oboe), Cramer or Nicolai (violin) and Bach (keyboard), so it is likely that Abel played the bass. Works by Bach for keyboard, oboe, violin and violoncello were played in London concerts in 1779 and 1781. They do not survive in their original form, though Richard Maunder has argued that one of them was the original version of the Sextet in C major, B78, for the same combination with two horns.[100] In the 1775 concert described by James Harris, the other players were Cramer and Nicolai (violins) and Bach (keyboard), so Abel probably played the bass when he was not playing his gamba solo; the concerto mentioned was presumably scored for harpsichord, two violins and bass, as in Bach's op. 1 (1763) and op. 7 (1770). The evidence discussed earlier suggests that Abel's gamba solos

[96] C. F. Cramer, *Magazin der Musik*, i/2 (Hamburg, 1783), 1037–9.

[97] J. F. Reichardt, 'Berichtigungen und Zusätze zum Gerberschen Lexicon der Tonkünstler', in *Studien für Tonkünstler und Musikfreunde … furs Jahr 1792*, ed. Reichardt and F. L. A. Kunzen, ii (Berlin, 1793), 3; repr. in *Ernst Ludwig Gerber: Ergänzungen, Berichtigungen, Nachträge*, ed. O. Wessely (Graz, 1969), 5–16, at 5. For Reichardt in London, see S. McVeigh, *Concert Life in London*, 95, 127, 151, 209, 221.

[98] *Musikalischer Almanach*, ed. Reichardt, part iv.

[99] Gerber, *Neues Historisch-Biographisches Lexicon*, i. col. 5.

[100] Bach, *Thematic Catalogue*, comp. Warburton, 59; ME of B78: Bach, *Music for Five and Six Instruments*, ed. Warburton, 195–229. See also S. Roe, 'The Sextet in C major, by J. C. or J. C. F. Bach?', in *Haydn, Mozart and Beethoven: Studies in the Music of the Classical Period: Essays in Honour of Alan Tyson*, ed. S. Brandenburg (Oxford, 1998), 13–19.

were normally accompanied by a violoncello, though when he played solos in these chamber concerts, as on 24 January 1775, he must have been accompanied just by Bach on the keyboard, unless there was a cellist present who is not mentioned in the descriptions or one of the other players changed to the violoncello. The scoring of Bach's op. 11 quintets – flute, oboe, violin, viola, and continuo – more or less conforms to the list of players given by C. F. Cramer: Papendiek (flute), Fischer (oboe), Cramer or Nicolai (violin), Abel (viola part on the gamba), Crosdill (violoncello), and Schröter (keyboard). Bach's Quintet in F, B77, already discussed, was among several works advertised in 1785 as having been 'originally composed' for Queen Charlotte.[101]

🎵 *Abel as a Cellist*

THIS raises the question: when Abel played bass lines did he use the gamba or the violoncello? We have seen that he played violoncello and pentachord solos in his first two years in Britain, and led the violoncellos in the 1759 Salisbury Festival. A remark made in a letter from Henry Hoare junior to James Harris junior on 22 May 1770 contains a hint that Abel played the violoncello in orchestras: 'I have been very happy in repeatedly meeting your father close to the Abel violincello at Almacks, whose taste for musick is as pure as elegant'; Bach and Abel directed benefits at Almack's Assembly Rooms on 17 and 18 May.[102] James Bretherton's engraved caricature 'CONCERTO SPIRITUALE', dated 23 March 1773, shows Abel playing a conventional four-string violoncello in the company of J. C. Fischer and the Bohemian horn player Jan Václav Stich alias Giovanni Punto; the print does not identify the musicians, but some copies have their names added in ink or pencil (Illus. 5.1)[103] Fischer had been a close associate of Bach and Abel ever since he arrived in London in 1768, while Punto played in a number of London concerts with them in the 1772 and 1773 seasons, including a benefit for Fischer at the Theatre Royal in the Haymarket on 25 March 1773, two days after the print was published.[104]

---

[101]   Bach, *Ten Chamber Works*, ed. Warburton, viii.

[102]   *Music and Theatre in Handel's World*, ed. Burrows and Dunhill, 591; *PA*, 17, 18/5/1770.

[103]   Abel and Fischer are identified on a copy in my possession, while all three are identified on one discussed in H. D. Johnstone, 'Treasure Trove at Gloucester: a Grangerized Copy of the 1895 Edition of Daniel Lysons' History of the Three Choirs Festival', *RMARC*, 31 (1998), 1–90, at 15; see also *Catalogue of Political and Personal Satires*, v: 157, no. 5217.

[104]   *PA*, 25/3/1773.

Illus. 5.1 James Bretherton, *Concerto Spirituale* (1773)

Several of Abel's reported pupils or followers, including James Cervetto, John Crosdill and Johann Georg Christoph Schetky, were professional cellists (Ch. 8), and the sale catalogue of his effects includes a batch of solo violoncello music, which he probably used for teaching: 'Solos for the Violoncello by Eiffert', '6 Solos by Cervetto, jun.', '6 ditto by Flackton', and '8 duets by Paxton' (I/5).[105] They can be identified as Philip Peter Eiffert's *Six Solos for a Violoncello with a Thorough Bass for the Harpsichord* (1761); James Cervetto's *Six Solos for the Violoncello with a Thorough Bass for the Harpsicord*, op. 1 (1768), or the *Six Solos*, op. 3 already discussed; William Flackton's *Six Solos, Three for a Violoncello and Three for a Tenor, Accompanied either by a Violoncello or Harpsichord*, op. 2 (1770); and Stephen Paxton's *Eight Duetts for a Violin and Violoncello or Two Violoncellos*, op. 2 (*c.* 1777).[106] Abel's virtuosic D major duet for two violoncellos, wko 228 was

[105] Roe, 'The Sale Catalogue of Carl Friedrich Abel', 130.

[106] Eiffert: RISM A/I E 581, 582; CC: Gb-Lbl, g.511.f.(3). Cervetto, op. 1: RISM A/I C 1731, 1732: CC: GB-Lbl, h.204.i.(1). Flackton: RISM A/I F 1110; CC: GB-Lbl, g.24.(2). Paxton, RISM A/I P 1074; CC: GB-Lbl, g.500.(1).

written for Cervetto and Crosdill, who performed it several times in 1778 and 1779, and his later solo and obbligato violoncello parts may all have been written for others.[107] He may have even have stopped playing the instrument altogether towards the end of his life: he does not appear among the violoncellos in a list of the orchestra for the 1787 season of the Professional Concert.[108]

Thus, once Abel was established in England, he only ever played gamba solos in public, though he presumably directed ensembles from the harpsichord. It was the practice in England at the time for orchestras to be directed by the first violin and the keyboard in tandem,[109] and Bach and Abel took turns to direct their concerts.[110] Abel probably played the violoncello in orchestras when Bach was directing concerts, and in chamber music when no other cellist was available, though he seems more commonly to have taken part in quartets and quintets by playing the viola parts on the gamba.

❧ Abel in Germany

ABEL left England at the end of the 1782 concert season, following Bach's death. It is often said that he went to visit his brothers in Germany,[111] though a letter dated 29 January 1782 from Charles Pratt, first Earl Camden, to the Foreign Secretary, Thomas Robinson, second Baron Grantham, shows that the real reason was to escape his creditors.[112] Pratt wrote that Abel 'is at present abroad, & afraid to return with[ou]t a protection that he has compounded with all his Creditors except one who is obstinate & stands out'. Pratt added that he had 'a friendship for Abel who taught one of my daughters' (Ch. 7), and made it clear that the 'protection' (a safe-conduct) would be provided by Count von Brühl, the Saxon ambassador in London. An article published in 1784, probably written by Samuel Arnold, stated that 'the Town grew tired of them [the Bach–Abel concerts], and

---

[107] *PA*, 1/5/1778; *PA*, 4/3/1779; *PA*, 8/4/1779. It was published as C. F. Abel, *A Duetto for Two Violoncellos as Performed at the Hanover Square Concert by Messrs. Crosdill & Cervetto* (London, 1788; repr. Heidelberg, 2008); RISM A/I A 142; ME: ed. G. and L von Zadow, intro. P. Holman (Heidelberg, 2008). It was entered at Stationers' Hall on 25/3/1788, see *Music Entries at Stationers' Hall, 1710–1785*, comp. M. Kassler (Aldershot, 2004), 105.

[108] McVeigh, 'The Professional Concert', 57.

[109] McVeigh, *Concert Life in London*, 216–19; Spitzer and Zaslaw, *The Birth of the Orchestra*, 387–93.

[110] McVeigh, *Concert Life in London*, 14–15.

[111] For instance, Charters, 'Abel in London', 1226; *BDA*, i. 5.

[112] GB-BEcr, L30/14/320/2.

the proprietors were obliged to withdraw themselves, with the loss of a great sum of money'; Bach reportedly died with debts of £4,000.[113] William Jackson wrote in 1802 that 'Bach and Abel, for some Years carried on a Concert in Partnership, which, from the Number of Subscribers, and the Terms of Subscription, ought to have been a lucrative Undertaking, but it was not so'.[114]

We know little about Abel's journey, though he apparently started in Paris, for the 18 May 1782 report already quoted stated that 'Abel is gone to Paris, according to his annual Custom, for a Couple of Months'. The next sighting comes in an article published on 24 January 1783 but apparently written in the summer or early autumn of 1782.[115] It reveals that he had been in Potsdam, where the Crown Prince Friedrich Wilhelm (later King Friedrich Wilhelm II) presented him with 'a beautiful box and 100 Louis d'or' ('einer schönen Dose und 100 Louisd'or'). The box must be the 'exceeding curious gold box with Chinese figures, mounted with brilliant diamonds, present from the King of Prussia' in Abel's sale (II/74).[116] In 1796 Reichardt merely wrote that Abel was at 'various courts and places' ('verschiedenen Höfen und Orten'), though he included an anecdote about his drinking, incidentally revealing that he stayed some weeks in Potsdam before going to Berlin.[117]

Abel also went to Ludwigslust, south of Schwerin, where his brother Leopold August was a court violinist. The 1783 article states that Abel played 'three solos at the court with the most powerful expression', describing his tone as 'extraordinarily beautiful and pure, and his performance highly touching. His *adagio* moved one to tears' ('Er spielt bey Hofe 3 Solos mit dem mächtigsten Ausdruck. Sein Ton ist äusserst schön und rein, und sein Vortrag aufs höchste rührend. Sein Adagio erweichte bis zu Thränen'). Some of the Berlin manuscripts of Abel's music are presumably souvenirs of his 1782 visit. They will be discussed in Chapter 6, but we should note here that they include scores of three sonatas for gamba and bass and two for violoncello and bass, as well as parts of the cello concertos, WKO 52 and 60, and a score of the D major concerto for oboe, violin, violoncello and orchestra, WKO 43. Some of them were presumably written for Friedrich

---

[113] *The European Magazine*, 5 (5/1784), 366; Terry, *John Christian Bach*, 96, 143, 167; McVeigh, 'The Professional Concert', 1. For Arnold's role in *The European Magazine*, see S. McVeigh, 'London Newspapers 1750 to 1800: a Checklist and Guide for Musicologists', *A Handbook for Studies in Eighteenth-Century English Music*, 6 (Oxford, 1996), whole vol., at 18.

[114] 'William Jackson of Exeter: New Documents', ed. Asfour and Williamson, 66.

[115] Cramer, *Magazin der Musik*, i/1 (1783), 179.

[116] Roe, 'The Sale Catalogue of Carl Friedrich Abel', 133.

[117] *Musikalischer Almanach*, ed. Reichardt, part iv; part ix, no. 5.

Wilhelm, a gamba player as well as a cellist,[118] and in one case there is evidence that this is so: 'The last concerto which Mr. Abel composed, designed for the present King of Prussia' was in the sale of Abel's effects (I/37).[119] This was probably WKO 60, by far the more modern of his two surviving violoncello concertos. However, not all of these pieces were necessarily written for Berlin: one of Abel's concertos for oboe, violin and violoncello had been composed by September 1777, when John Marsh heard it at the Salisbury Festival.[120]

Abel apparently intended to return to England in the autumn of 1782: the 1783 article mentions that he had to be back in London by the end of November, and that people in Hamburg would probably not be able to hear him during his hasty journey. In fact, the journey was much more leisurely than that, for Abel seems not to have appeared in London for another two years; presumably the 'protection' mentioned in Pratt's letter was not immediately granted. It is likely that he did visit Hamburg at some point during those years to see his elder brother Ernst Heinrich, an artist. No fewer than seventeen portraits by Ernst Heinrich were in the sale of his effects (II/22–25), including one of Giardini – which suggests that the artist worked for a time in London; he was eventually granted the administration of his brother's estate.[121] The first evidence of Abel's return to England is the report of 11 January 1785, already mentioned, that he had 'lately' performed a gamba concerto at the Duke of Queensberry's, though the previous week, on 6 January, a 'New Rondo' composed 'by Mr. Abel for Mr. Tenducci accompanied on the oboe and pianoforte' was performed in Bath.[122]

❧ Abel's Instruments

IN November 1783, while Abel was still in Germany, a gamba of 1718 by Joachim Tielke was offered for sale in Hamburg by 'the widow of a deceased distinguished merchant and great music lover' ('der Wittwe eines verstorbenen

---

[118] M. O'Loghlin, *Frederick the Great and his Musicians: the Viola da Gamba Music of the Berlin School* (Aldershot, 2008), esp. 121–43.

[119] Roe, 'The Sale Catalogue of Carl Friedrich Abel', 131.

[120] *The John Marsh Journals*, ed. Robins, 168.

[121] Roe, 'The Sale Catalogue of Carl Friedrich Abel', 135; GB-Lna, PROB 6/163, fol. 214 (25/9/1787).

[122] James, 'Concert Life in Eighteenth-Century Bath', 440. It may be *A Favourite Rondeau*; RISM A/I AA 142a, published by George Goulding; Goulding established himself as a London music publisher *c.* 1786, see C. Humphries and W. C. Smith, *Music Publishing in the British Isles* (Oxford, 2/1970), 159.

angesehenen Kaufmanns und großen Musicfreundes').[123] According to the detailed description:

> The back and the sides are made from brown [Brazilian] king's-wood, with very artificially worked figures of ivory, so cleanly inlaid that one must duly admire it. The front is made from choice pine. Its neck as well as the finger-board are veneered with tortoiseshell; on it are also beautifully worked with figures and floral motifs inlaid with mother of pearl. The pegs are finely made of ivory. The head is made of ivory, beautifully carved in the shape of an angel. Its bow, made earlier by Meyer, is of brown Pernambuco wood. The case containing this instrument is really spacious, lined on the inside with baize and covered outside with brown leather.

> der Boden sowohl, als der Rand umher, sind von braunen Königsholz, mit sehr künstlich ausgearbeiteten Figuren von Elfenbein so sauber eingelegt, daß man es billig bewundern muß. Der Deckel darauf ist von dem ausgesuchtesten Tennenholz. Der Hals daran, wie auch Grifbret und Saitenbret sind mit Schildpatt fournirt; darauf sind wieder herrlich ausgearbeitete Figuren und Blumenwerk von Perlmutter eingelegt. Die Wirbel daran sind von Elfenbein künstlich gemacht. Der Kopf oben an ist von Elfenbein in Engelgestalt ganz prächtig gearbeitet. Der Bogen dabey ist von braunen Fernambouckholz, ehedem von Meyer gemacht. Das Futteral, worinn dieses Instrument liegt, ist ganz compendiös, inwendig mit Boye ausgefüttert, auswendig mit braunem Leder überzogen.

This instrument is relevant in the present context because Günter Hellwig identified it with the highly decorated Tielke bass viol in the Victoria and Albert Museum.[124] It is now undated, does not have a bow or a case, and has a later scroll and machine heads rather than the original pegs and head, though it does have 'very artificially worked figures of ivory' on the back and the sides, as well as ivory, tortoiseshell and mother of pearl decoration on the neck. It was certainly in England by 1835, when it was owned by John Cawse, a follower of Abel (Ch. 8), and an obvious possibility is that Abel acquired it in Hamburg and brought it to England. Perhaps it was the instrument described in Abel's sale as an 'exceeding valuable and fine-toned Viol de Gamba' and a 'capital viol de gamba, in a mahogany case, his best instrument' (I/44), though the case of the Hamburg instrument

---

[123] Cramer, *Magazin der Musik*, i/2 (1783), 1009–30, at 1029.

[124] G. Hellwig, *Joachim Tielke: ein Hamburger Lauten- und Violenmacher der Barockzeit* (Frankfurt am Main, 1980), 321–6, no. 135; A. Baines, *Victoria and Albert Museum, Catalogue of Musical Instruments*, ii: *Non-Keyboard Instruments* (London, 1968), 6–7, no. 1/10, illus. fig. 7.

was covered in leather. The claim in the advertisement that 'the greatest virtuoso, even an Abel, could not wish for a finer instrument' ('der größeste Virtuos, selbst ein Abel, sich kein besseres Instrument wünschen könnte') might have been made in the knowledge that he was a potential customer. Two other gambas are mentioned in his sale catalogue, one without any details (I/45) and the other as part of a job lot: 'Four mahogany music stands, an old viol de gamba, and a lute' (I/40).

Several gambas are shown in pictures of Abel. The first is the Gainsborough painting from about 1765, already mentioned (Frontispiece). This is a puzzle for two reasons. It is a seven-string instrument with Germanic characteristics, such as a gilded rosette and distinctive sound holes, while the one in the preparatory drawing has 'f' holes, a different-shaped scroll, and does not appear to have a rosette (Plate 10.[125] Also, the rosette and the sound holes suggest that it is the same instrument as the one hanging up at the back of Gainsborough's portrait of Ann Ford, painted in Bath in 1760 (Ch. 7). A possible explanation is that Gainsborough depicted one of Abel's gambas in the drawing, perhaps made in the composer's London house, but finished the painting in his Bath studio using a German instrument from his own collection or one that belonged to Ann Ford. The second and more famous Gainsborough portrait,[126] painted in 1777, shows yet another instrument: a six-string gamba also with Germanic features, such as the shape of the sound-holes and the way they extend deep into the body – characteristic of an instrument-making tradition based on the violin family rather than on viols (Plate 11).[127] Abel's apparent liking for German gambas makes sense. Their heavy, violin-influenced construction gives them a loud, focused sound, closer to the violoncello than to earlier English and French gambas – the main alternatives. German instruments would have been more suitable than other types for performing in large, noisy rooms, for competing with other instruments in chamber ensembles, and for playing concertos.

ॐ *Last Years*

AFTER his return in the winter of 1784–5 Abel became an elder statesman in London's concert scene. He was a director and composer for the Professional Concert at Hanover Square, but he was also principal composer for Salomon's

---

[125] London, National Portrait Gallery, no. 5081.

[126] San Marino, CA, Henry E. Huntington Art Gallery, inv. 25/19. See esp. Waterhouse, *Gainsborough*, 51, no. 1; Rosenthal, *The Art of Thomas Gainsborough*, 89, 92.

[127] Ben Hebbert, private communication.

rival series at the Pantheon in Oxford Street.[128] He provided new overtures or symphonies for the first seven Hanover Square concerts, while symphonies or overtures by him were performed in each of the first four Pantheon concerts,[129] and his concertos for violin, oboe, cello and orchestra were played in the second Hanover Square Concert and the first Pantheon concert; on both occasions they was said to be new.[130] The concertos were either WKO 42 and 43, already mentioned, or others now lost.[131] The symphonies were probably the five late works WKO 37–41.[132] 'Symphonies by Abel, his last work, unpublished' was an item in Abel's sale (I/38),[133] and two days later, on 14 December, *DUR* reported: 'We are happy to hear, that the last symphonies, concertantes, and favourite concertos for the violoncello, by the late celebrated Mr. Abel, are not likely to be buried in oblivion; as the manuscript copies have been purchased, and will most likely be published'. Unfortunately, the publications never materialised. He seems to have continued to compose until almost the end of his life, though he markedly reduced his public performances after his return from Germany. He only played gamba solos in three of the twelve Hanover Square concerts in the 1785 season, and in four out of twelve in both the 1786 and 1787 seasons.[134] Nevertheless, he played a solo at his last appearance, in a benefit concert for Mrs Billington at the Hanover Square Rooms on 21 May 1787; he died on 20 June and was buried St Marylebone Church four days later.[135]

❧ *Conclusions and Contexts*

A BEL'S career was distinctive in several respects. He was by far the most important London musician of his time who was a virtuoso on an unusual or exotic instrument, though he played the violoncello in orchestras and ensembles. He was able to limit his solo performances to the gamba partly because he was its supreme exponent, though things were undoubtedly made easier for him by the fashion for exotic instruments that developed in London in the 1750s, an aspect of a general change from a musical culture dominated by Italians and vocal music to one dominated by Germans and instrumental music (Ch. 4). He

---

[128] McVeigh, 'The Professional Concert', 39, 40, 45.

[129] Ibid., 40–2, 45–6.

[130] Ibid., 41, 45.

[131] WKO, pp. 63, 67–8.

[132] WKO, pp. 55–61.

[133] Roe, 'The Sale Catalogue of Carl Friedrich Abel', 131.

[134] McVeigh, 'The Professional Concert', 40–4, 50–4, 57–61.

[135] *PA*, 21/5/1787; London, Metropolitan Archives, P89/MRY1/314.

was one of the many German musicians at the time who emigrated from Germany to England, in the process exchanging the life of a courtier for a more modern freelance career. He represents modernity in that he seems to have composed almost nothing but instrumental music, and, strange as it might seem, his espousal of the gamba also represents modernity. He was linked to Sterne as an apostle of sensibility; the idea that the gamba was particularly associated with that fashionable cult will be pursued in Chapter 7. By the 1760s the gamba was coming by default to be thought of as a German instrument, and thus as part of the Germanic musical culture that was developing in London. Most of Abel's gamba-playing rivals, such as Ludwig Christian Hesse, Andreas Lidel, Franz Xaver Hammer, and Joseph Fiala, also came from German-speaking areas of Europe.

CHAPTER 6

'Composed to the Soul':
Abel's Viola da Gamba Music

WITH eighty-six surviving works featuring the gamba in solo or obbligato roles, Charles Frederick Abel is by far the most prolific composer for the instrument after the Baroque period.[1] We have twenty-nine pieces for unaccompanied gamba (plus four short cadenza-like passages); forty-four solos or sonatas and two separate minuets for gamba and bass; four duets for gamba and violoncello; two incomplete trios for flute, gamba and bass; a gamba part possibly from a sonata with obbligato harpsichord; a quartet for flute, violin, gamba and violoncello; two quartets for gamba, violin, viola and violoncello; and an aria with gamba obbligato. Yet much is lost, and what survives is not necessarily representative of the corpus of gamba music he composed over his working lifetime.

Virtually none of Abel's surviving gamba music seems to have been written before he came to England in the winter of 1758–9 at the age of thirty-five. He played a trio and a fantasy on the gamba in a Leipzig concert in 1743, probably of his own composition (Ch. 5), and was employed at the Dresden court for about a decade as a gamba player, where he would have needed a good deal of solo material; it was the custom at the time for virtuosi to write their own solos provided that they were competent to do so. Abel was an established composer before he came to England: the 1761 Breitkopf catalogue lists flute solos and concertos by 'Abel, Music[ien] de la Chamb[re] du Roy de Polo[g]n[e]', indicating that they were written while he was at Dresden.[2]

The only possible surviving gamba work written at that time is the Concerto in B♭, WKO 52. It survives in a set of parts, D-B, Mus. MS 252/10, with the solo part labelled 'Violoncello Concertato',[3] and it also exists as a flute concerto, WKO 51,

---

[1] See the lists in F. Flassig, *Die soloistische Gambenmusik in Deutschland im 18. Jahrhundert* (Göttingen, 1998), 238–308; B. Hoffmann, *Catalogo della musica solistica e cameristica per viola da gamba* (Lucca, 2001). WKO is a thematic catalogue of Abel's works, now rather out of date.

[2] S. M. Helm, 'Carl F. Abel Symphonist: a Biographical, Stylistic and Bibliographical Study' (PhD diss., U. of Michigan, 1953), 6, 310, 313.

[3] ME: C. F. Abel, *Kompositionen*, ed. W. Knape, 16 vols. (Cuxhaven, 1958–74), ix: 91–110; C. F. Abel, *Konzert B-dur für Violoncello (Gambe), Streicher und Continuo*, ed. H. Lomnitzer (Wolfenbüttel, 1961).

Ex. 6.1 C. F. Abel, (a) solo part of Flute Concerto in C major, WKO 51 compared with (b) solo part of Violoncello Concerto in B♭ major, WKO 52, 1st movement, b. 130

with the outer movements a tone higher, in C major, but with the Adagio a third higher in G major.[4] The flute version is clearly the arrangement: Abel preferred the subdominant key to the dominant for slow movements; some of the solo figuration seems more suitable for a stringed instrument than the flute; and one passage was seemingly rewritten to keep it within the range of the flute (Ex. 6.1). WKO 52 is clearly an early work. It is scored just with four-part strings and continuo, like Abel's other early concertos; his three later concertos, for violoncello in C major, WKO 60, and for oboe, violin and violoncello in B♭ major and D major, WKO 42, 43,[5] have horns and oboes in the accompanying group, as do all the symphonies and overtures he published in England. Also, it is written in that nervous, rather unmelodious style cultivated in northern Germany in the 1740s and 50s, typified here by shooting scales in the ritornelli of the outer movements, triplet passagework in the solo sections, and melodic lines in the slow movement decorated with appoggiaturas and Lombard rhythms. The elegant, melodious *galant* style Abel cultivated in England is conspicuous by its absence.

The solo writing in WKO 52 is strikingly different from Abel's later solo violoncello parts in WKO 42, 43, and 60, as well as Abel's Duet in D major, WKO 228 for two violoncellos (Ch. 5). Their solo parts descend repeatedly to the bass register, with a good deal of cello-like passagework and some four-note chords. By contrast, the solo part of WKO 52 is simpler and stays in the alto/tenor register (going only down to *A*), as in Abel's gamba solos. For this reason it has been suggested it that it was originally written for the gamba, though the solo writing does not have any distinctively viol-like features.[6] Abel must have composed gamba concertos in London: he played them in concerts on a number of occasions (Ch. 5), and 'Mr. Abel's last solos and concertos, for the viola de gambo' was in the sale of his effects (I/37).[7]

---

4 ME: Abel *Kompositionen*, ed. Knape, ix. 77–90.

5 ME: ibid., viii. 1–48, 51–113; x, supp. 1.

6 Abel, *Konzert B-dur*, ed. Lomnitzer, Preface.

7 S. Roe, 'The Sale Catalogue of Carl Friedrich Abel (1787)', in *Music and the Book Trade from the Sixteenth to the Twentieth Century*, ed. R. Myers, M. Harris, and

Much must also be lost in other genres. Abel seems to have used the gamba to play viola parts in Queen Charlotte's chamber band and elsewhere, and in 1794 the London booksellers Evan and Thomas Williams offered for sale 'TEN Quartettos, in score, for a Viola da Gamba, Flute, Violin, and Violoncello in Abel's handwriting', as well as 'Twenty-four Trios, in score, for a Viola da Gamba, Violin, and Violoncello, by Abel, and in his own hand-writing'.[8] Of these, we only have the Quartet in G major, WKO 227, though others may survive as conventional quartets and trios, as we shall see. He must also have composed many more gamba sonatas than survive today. He was at the centre of London's concert life for twenty-five years, and is known to have participated in more than 400 public concerts during that time. He was advertised playing 'A Solo on the Viola da Gamba' more than sixty times, though many advertisements do not say exactly what his role was, those for the Bach–Abel concerts never list particular pieces, and doubtless many appearances went unrecorded. In addition, his appearances in London concerts might well have been equalled by those in private concerts at court and in the houses of the aristocracy, and in provincial concerts outside the London concert season. He would doubtless have repeated pieces on occasion, but the increasing desire for novelty in London's concert life would probably have limited his ability to do so.[9]

We shall see that most of Abel's surviving sonatas come from manuscripts owned by a single amateur player, the Countess of Pembroke. The autograph collections of solo sonatas he would have needed for his own use are all lost, as are those owned by his other pupils and followers. It is hard to believe that he played pieces as simple and undemanding as most of those in the Countess of Pembroke's manuscripts; we must assume that he composed dozens if not hundreds of others on a much higher musical and technical level, similar in their demands to the two 'Prussian' sonatas or the unaccompanied pieces in the Drexel manuscript. Some of these missing sonatas were listed in the 1794 advertisement: 'Eighteen Solos, in manuscript, by Abel, for the Viola da Gamba, written by himself, with the appoggiaturas and graces to the adagios, as he played them', and 'Ten Solos, in manuscript, by Abel, of his latest compositions, and which he played himself at the Hanover-square Concerts'. They do not correspond to manuscripts known today, though the ten solos may have been included in the lot 'Mr. Abel's last solos and concertos, for the viola de gambo' in the sale catalogue of his effects.

G. Mandelbrote (London, 2008), 105–43, at 131.

[8] MH, 3/4/1794.

[9] See esp. S. McVeigh, *Concert Life in London from Mozart to Haydn* (Cambridge, 1993), 92–100.

🙢 *The Drexel Manuscript*

THE one manuscript of Abel's gamba music that was seemingly compiled for his own use is US-NYp, Drexel MS 5871.[10] It is an oblong large quarto in a modern binding, but with an autograph decorative cartouche pasted onto the first flyleaf (Plate 12), the remains of the original binding. It was later signed 'Jos^ph. / Coggins / April / 8th. 1801' – that is, the London organist, oboist and clarinettist Joseph Coggins (1786–1866).[11] Identical inscriptions on flyleaves at each end, 'To / E. F. Rimbault Esqre. (L.L.D.F.S.A.) / In memoriam – / Kindness shown to the aged & afflicted Widow / Mrs. H. Coggins / Falm^o. [?Falmouth] 10.5.66.', suggest that it was a keepsake given by Coggins's widow to the antiquarian Edward Rimbault. At the sale of Rimbault's library in 1877 it found its way with many other items into the collection of the American tycoon Joseph W. Drexel; Drexel's collection forms the nucleus of the Music Division of US-NYp.[12] At that stage it was still in its original binding, described in the sale catalogue as 'old red morocco, g[ilt] e[dged] paper label on side with autograph of C. F. Abel'. Coggins was too young to have purchased it at Abel's sale in 1787, though his teacher John Wall Callcott could have done so; 8 April 1801 was probably the date Coggins acquired it.

The manuscript consists of single type of paper (fleur-de-lys watermark, 'G R' (George Rex) initials, and a Whatman countermark), but has two main sequences of music copied at different times. Abel copied solo gamba pieces on pp. 1–25, and then a second individual, probably Coggins, added scores of Corelli's trio sonatas op. 1, nos. 1–12, and op. 3, nos. 1–5 (pp. 26–111). The rest of the pages are unused, with the exception of a remarkable anonymous 'Solo per il Cembalo' added to the reversed end of the volume (pp. 132–134R). Mary Cyr attributed it to J. C. Bach because it begins with an idea strikingly similar to the opening of J. S. Bach's Fantasia in C minor, BWV906, though in the major rather than the minor.[13] In a similar vein, J. C. Bach's Sonata in B♭ major, B2, for violin and keyboard, op. 10,

---

[10] Facs.: C. F. Abel, *27 Pieces for the Viola da Gamba: New York Public Library, MS Drexel 5871*, intro. W. Knape (Peer, 1993). I am grateful to John Cunningham for examining the manuscript for me.

[11] For Coggins, see B. Matthews, *The Royal Society of Musicians of Great Britain, List of Members, 1738–1984* (London, 1985), 38.

[12] Sotheby, Wilkinson and Hodge, *Catalogue of the Music Library of Edward Francis Rimbault, LL.D.* (31/7–7/8/1877; repr. 1975), lot 1361.

[13] M. Cyr, 'Carl Friedrich Abel's Solos: a Musical Offering to Gainsborough?', *MT*, 128 (1987), 317–21, at 320–1. It is not listed in J. C. Bach, *The Collected Works*, 48/1: *Thematic Catalogue*, comp. E. Warburton (New York, 1999) [B], or in WKO.

no. 1 refers to the Praeludium of his father's Partita in B♭, BWV825.[14] However, the solo could equally be by Abel: it is in his hand, and he could easily have encountered BWV906 when he was in Leipzig.

The gamba pieces in Drexel MS 5871 are almost entirely autograph. Other examples of his elegant hand are in both of the Countess of Pembroke's collections of his gamba solos, discussed below; the score of his String Quartet in E major, op. 15, no. 1, WKO 73 (Utrecht, Universiteitsbibliotheek);[15] sheets with cadenzas tipped into the parts of his C major cello concerto, WKO 60 (D-B, KH M20); and the oboe parts of his Symphony in C major, WKO 38 (D-B, KH M9).[16] Unfortunately Walter Knape, who catalogued Abel's music and its sources in the 1960s, is not a reliable guide to his hand, failing to recognise genuine examples and wrongly claiming copies made by others as autographs.[17] A systematic search would doubtless bring new autographs to light.

Abel notated gamba music in the treble clef (expecting it to be played an octave lower), occasionally changing to the bass clef for low notes. He used a distinctive form of treble clef, often with dots either side of the *g'* line of the stave, and a bass clef with the tail swept round and underneath like the @ sign of an e-mail address (Plate 13). He wrote the notes rapidly and boldly, forming the note-heads and stems with single strokes of the pen, and not bothering to join the beams to the note stems. He seems to have written the Drexel manuscript for his own use: it has omissions and corrections; and he did not worry about too much about spacing, often leaving gaps at the end of lines or extending the staves by hand into the margin. Mary Cyr asserted that the 'presence of a few fingerings and the generally neat appearance' suggest that Abel 'intended it to be studied by another player,[18] though he copied it less carefully than some of the autographs owned by the Countess of Pembroke. Some of the fingerings were seemingly added by another hand, probably the individual who added crosses in red crayon and pencil at various points, perhaps to indicate dubious places, those difficult to read, or those that needed practising.

The contents also suggest that Abel compiled the manuscript for his own use. While his sonatas or solos with bass mostly consist of two and three contrasted

---

[14] Noted in C. S. Terry, *John Christian Bach*, rev. H. C. R. Landon (London, 2/1967), 188. See also J. C. Bach, *Thematic Catalogue*, comp. Warburton, 27.

[15] Illus. WKO, p. 118.

[16] S. Roe, 'The Sale Catalogue of Carl Friedrich Abel', 119–20.

[17] See Abel, *Kompositionen*, ed. Knape, vii. 157; viii. 50; ix. 60, 76; x, supp. 2, v, vi; WKO, pp. 14, 62, 82, for reproductions of hands identified as autograph (wrongly, in my opinion). WKO, p. 119 describes the manuscript of op. 15, no. 1 as a 'probably an autograph' ('wahrscheinlich Autograph').

[18] Cyr, 'Carl Friedrich Abel's Solos', 320.

Ex. 6.2 C. F. Abel, Flourish in D major, US-NYp, Drexel MS 5871, p. 8 (not in WKO)

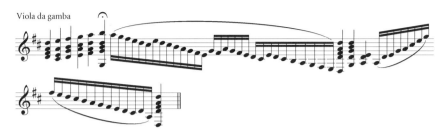

movements, using the patterns Fast–Minuet or Fast–Slow–Minuet, these pieces are in a single sequence, apparently grouped just by key: seventeen pieces in D major (pp. 1–17) are followed by five in D minor (pp. 18–22), a singleton in D major (p. 23), and a pair in A major (pp. 24–5). They do not seem to be in meaningful multi-movement sequences, though they have been grouped into conventional sonatas in several modern editions.[19] The D minor group, for instance, comprises an arpeggiated prelude, a minuet, two duple-time fast movements, and an Adagio, while the pair of A major pieces are both fast, Allegretto and Allegro. There are also four short flourishes (pp. 8, 13, 17) that seem designed to be slotted into the cadential points of complete movements (Ex. 6.2). They do not belong to any of the pieces in the Drexel manuscript, so they may have been intended as cadenzas for other works, possibly lost concertos.

The Drexel pieces are strikingly different in style from Abel's sonatas with bass. They are much more technically demanding, with frequent multiple stops or strings of sixths and thirds, wide-ranging arpeggiated passages, dramatic leaps across the whole instrument, virtuoso passages extending up to a written a''', and richly ornamented slow movements with Italianate florid ornamentation. They are also more varied in style. As we might expect, there are a number of pieces labelled 'Tempo di Minuet' or using minuet patterns and rhythms. Some of them are quite extended and complex, with demanding passagework. One piece, WKO 203, 204 (p. 17), has two variations, while two, WKO 200 (p. 14) and WKO 202 (p. 16), use the *rondeau* pattern. In some of them, such as the Andante, WKO 191 (p. 6), and the little untitled piece WKO 199 (p. 13), there is a piquant tension between the melancholy and private spirit of the music and the rhythms and the phraseology of the formal, public dance. Another piece that uses a conventional modern idiom to excellent effect is the charming jig-like Allegro, WKO 212 (p. 25), a miniature rondo evoking a peasant dance.

---

[19] For instance, C. F. Abel, *6 Sonate per la viola da gamba*, ed. C. Denti (Bologna, 2002); C. F. Abel, *Six Sonatas for Unaccompanied Viola da Gamba*, ed. M. Charters (Ottawa, 1982).

Ex. 6.3   C. F. Abel, Prelude in D minor, WKO 205, bb. 1–12

However, a surprising number of pieces use elements of the Baroque style. Some just lack the contrasts we expect in *galant* music. Charles Burney wrote that J. C. Bach 'seems to have been the first composer who observed the law of *contrast*, as a *principle*',[20] and Abel used the same approach in his published instrumental music. So it would have struck his contemporaries as remarkable when, as with the Allegros WKO 186 (p. 1) and WKO 198 (pp. 12–13), he wrote binary movements using the sort of patterns of continuous semiquavers in scales, arpeggios and broken-chords we associate with J. S. Bach's unaccompanied string music. The D minor piece, WKO 205 (p. 18), belongs to the related genre of arpeggio prelude, in which the pattern to be used is indicated here and there, leaving most of the music notated in block chords (Ex. 6.3). With the interest focused almost solely on the harmony it is not surprising that Abel used unusually complex and rapid progressions of the type we associate with Baroque music. Burney probably had pieces of this sort in mind when he wrote that Abel 'used to modulate, in arpeggio, with infinite variety and knowledge' on the harpsichord, and that 'when he was in spirits and fancy, I have heard him modulate in private on his six-string base with such with such practical readiness and depth of science, as astonished the late Lord Kelly and Bach, as much as myself'.[21]

Several D minor pieces in the Drexel manuscript also use elements of the Baroque style, of which the most remarkable is the Adagio, WKO 209. With its florid ornamentation, richly chordal idiom and chromatic harmonic style, it inhabits the tragic world of the gamba solos in J. S. Bach's passions or some of C. P. E. Bach's music in the *Empfindsamkeit* or sensibility style. There is a particularly memorable moment when the opening idea returns only to dissolve immediately into an extravagant welter of cadenza-like arpeggios (Ex. 6.4). Music like this is so unusual in Abel's output that it must have had some special significance, signalled by the use of the minor mode: of the 108 pieces in his main published instrumental collections, opp. 1–18, only one, the E minor flute sonata, op. 6, no. 3, is not in the major. Furthermore, there are hardly any minor slow movements

---

[20] BurneyH, ii. 866.

[21] BurneyH, ii. 1020.

Ex. 6.4 C. F. Abel, Adagio in D minor, wko 209, bb. 31–40

Viola da gamba

within the major-mode works: in the many works with two movements both are in the tonic, while in those with three nearly all the central slow movements are in related major keys rather than in the relative or tonic minor. Abel was not the only composer at this period to associate the minor with old music and with passionate personal expression: one thinks of J. C. Bach's C minor keyboard sonata, op. 5, no. 6, with its elaborate fugue, or Mozart's Adagio and Fugue in C minor, K546.

In Abel's case, pieces such as wko 209 – or, for that matter, two other elaborately ornamented movements in a similar style, wko 187 (p. 2) and the Adagio, wko 189 (p. 4) – seem to be prime examples of the sort of music he played in private. Henry Bate described him playing 'fine airs, double stops and arpeggios' by the fireside, and another obituarist wrote: 'justly admired as he was at his publick Performances, it was a few only of his intimate Friends in private who were Witnesses of his most wonderful musical Powers, to come at which, a Bottle or two of good Burgundy before him, and his Viol di Gambo within his Reach, were necessary'.[22] The writer added the interesting observation: 'In that Situation his Friends would introduce the Subject of the human Passions', and 'not very capable of expressing *in English his own sentiments*', Abel would take part in the discussion by 'telling the story' on the gamba of Lieutenant Le Fever in Laurence Sterne's *Tristram Shandy*. Sterne had a similar attitude: Pierre Dubois has argued that music in *Tristram Shandy* 'comes in when words reveal themselves unequal to their task of expressing ideas or feeling'.[23] Another contemporary witness, who had also clearly heard Abel's private performances, wrote that his 'play at such moment was not compositions, but given subjects, such as love, war, rage, or fandangoes'.[24]

We have no idea whether these programmatic improvisations were ever written

[22] *MH*, 23/6/1787; *St James's Chronicle*, 28–30/6/1787.

[23] P. Dubois, 'Sterne et la musique, ou l'harmonie impossible', *Anglophonia*, 11 (2002), 263–76, at 263.

[24] *St James's Chronicle*, 6/4/1790.

down. But many of them are likely to have been musical expressions of sensibility, given that another obituarist wrote of Abel that 'Sensibility is the prevailing and beautiful characteristic of his compositions. – He was the *Sterne* of *Music*. – The one *wrote*, and the other *composed* to the *soul*'.[25] I shall have more to say about Abel, Sterne and the sensibility movement in Chapter 7, though it is worth noting here that *Empfindsamkeit* was its equivalent in northern Germany;[26] that C. P. E. Bach was its musical embodiment; that Bach and Abel presumably knew each other and had similar musical backgrounds; and that these pieces bring us as close as we are likely to get to the music Abel played in his private performances, and to an English equivalent of Bach's programmatic instrumental works such as the Rondo in E minor, 'Abschied von meinem Silbermannischen Claviere', H272, (1781), the Trio Sonata in C minor, 'Sanguineus und Melancholicus', H579 (1749), or the fantasia from the Sonata in C minor, H75 (1753), which attracted texts derived from Hamlet's soliloquy and the last words of Socrates.[27] Unfortunately, we do not know what the seemingly programmatic pieces in the Drexel manuscript were intended to represent.

The most self-consciously Baroque piece in the Drexel manuscript is WKO 196 (pp. 10–11), the D major 'Fuga'. Its starting point is not, as we might expect, the fugues in J. S. Bach's unaccompanied violin and violoncello music, or more generally Abel's musical upbringing in Leipzig. Instead, he chose the subject from the fugue in Corelli's Concerto Grosso in D major, op. 6, no. 1. His fugue is densely argued and beautifully worked out, in two and three parts, with real answers, a stretto at the end, and an ingenious semiquaver passage that sounds like a free episode to the casual listener but in fact conceals two statements of the subject (Ex. 6.5). His choice of subject is interesting because Corelli's concertos were largely kept in the repertory in eighteenth-century England by those who favoured the 'ancient' Baroque style and were opposed to the *galant* style popularised by Bach and Abel.[28] Thus all twelve of Corelli's op. 6 concertos and eight of his sonatas in Geminiani's concerto arrangements were in the repertory of

[25] *DUR*, 23/6/1787.

[26] See esp. D. Heartz and B. A. Brown, 'Empfindsamkeit', *GMO*; R. Taruskin, *The Oxford History of Western Music*, 6 vols., ii: *The Seventeenth and Eighteenth Centuries* (Oxford, 2005), 409–18.

[27] See esp. E. E. Helm, 'The "Hamlet" Fantasia and the Literary Element in C. P. E. Bach's Music', *MQ*, 58 (1972), 277–96; H.-G. Ottenburg, *C. P. E. Bach*, trans. P. J. Whitmore (Oxford, 1987), 58–60, 78–85, 168. For C. P. E. Bach's works, see Helm, *Thematic Catalogue of the Works of Carl Philipp Emanuel Bach* (New Haven, CT, 1989) [H].

[28] See esp. W. Weber, *The Rise of Musical Classics in Eighteenth-Century England: a Study in Canon, Ritual, and Ideology* (Oxford, 1992), 77–89; P. Allsop, *Arcangelo Corelli: 'New Orpheus of Our Times'* (Oxford, 1999), 188–99.

Ex. 6.5 C. F. Abel, Fuga in D major, WKO 196, bb. 23–6

Viola da gamba

the Concerts of Ancient Music; individual works from these sets were played 100 times in its concerts between its inception in 1776 and 1790.[29]

A clue to understanding the choice of subject comes in a letter to a journal in 1800 which claimed that Abel 'composed a *fugue* purposely for his friend Gainsborough to practise on the viol-di-gamba'.[30] Thomas Gainsborough was certainly interested in old music (Ch. 7), and may have suggested the subject – assuming of course that WKO 196 is the piece referred to. I also wonder whether Abel composed it as a kind of private joke, intended to remind his friends that his musical interests and sympathies were far wider than might have been suspected from his public persona. Bach and Abel were regarded with animosity by the more extreme members of the ancient music faction: Hawkins wrote that 'the style they introduced was void of the chief excellencies of music, it was coarse and artless; their basses had no melody, but were tediously monotonous, and to the eye resembled a row of pins'. However, Hawkins was aware that they had 'two styles of composition, the one for their own private delight, the other for the gratification of the many'.[31] The pieces in the Drexel manuscript are rare and fascinating examples of the first type. Interestingly, the sale of Abel's effects included a printed 'score of the 12 concertos composed by Corelli' (I/14).[32]

🙋 *The Pembroke Manuscript*

GB-Lbl, Add. MS 31697, the best-known collection of Abel's gamba music, is associated with Elizabeth Herbert, Countess of Pembroke (Ch. 7). The statement on its title-page (fol. 2), that it was 'formerly the Music Book of the Countess of Pembroke', has encouraged the idea that it is a single manuscript, but in fact it is a scrapbook into which seven separate items were pasted, the first

---

[29] Weber, *The Rise of Musical Classics*, 179, 255.

[30] *The Monthly Mirror*, 9 (1800), 146–7.

[31] J. Hawkins, 'Memoirs of Dr. William Boyce', *Cathedral Music*, ed. W. Boyce (London, 2/1788), ix.

[32] S. Roe, 'The Sale Catalogue of Carl Friedrich Abel', 131.

five of which are Abel autographs. Item 1 (fols. 3–6v) consists of four sheets of paper (probably originally two folded sheets) containing the Sonata in G major for gamba and bass, wko 152. The other four contain unaccompanied pieces. Item 2, a fragment glued onto fol. 6v, has the Minuet in G major, wko 153. Item 3 (fol. 7), another fragment, has the Minuet in D major, wko 154. Item 4 (fols. 8–9v) consists of two sheets (probably originally a single folded sheet) containing the Sonata in G major, wko 155. The fragment Item 5 (fol. 9v), glued to the back of Item 4, has an Adagio in G major, related to the first movement of wko 155. The only piece not in Abel's autograph is a solo gamba arrangement of the aria 'In diesen heil'gen hallen' from Act II of Mozart's *Die Zauberflöte* added to the blank fourth side of Item 1 (fol. 6v) by an unidentified individual (Hand B).

The rest of the scrapbook consists of two separate manuscripts (Item 6, fols. 10–44v, and Item 7, fols. 45–83v), each containing sequences of fifteen sonatas with bass, wko 151a, 156–69 and 170–85; Item 6 also contains two separate minuets in C major and D major for gamba and bass (fols. 37, 39), omitted in WKO. Both manuscripts have title-pages, the second now partly obliterated and stating wrongly that it contains fourteen sonatas. They were copied by the same individual, Hand C, who seems to have worked directly from Abel's lost autographs, imitating the composer's characteristic treble clef, with dots either side of the g' line, and his habit of omitting clefs after the first system of a movement. He was probably working for the Countess of Pembroke, whose signature appears on fol. 45, the original front cover of Item 7; samples of her hand (e.g. GB-Lbl, Add. MS 32991, fol. 374) confirm that it is her handwriting. The binder glued that page onto a leaf of the scrapbook to hold it in place, cutting out a window so that the signature remained visible.

Other items in the collection are connected with the countess. An unidentified individual (Hand D) annotated several of the autographs, adding the statement 'Composed for the Lady Pembroke / The original Manuscript' to Item 4, the unaccompanied sonata, wko 155. Another individual (Hand E), with rounded and spidery handwriting, added 'The Table or Finger Board of the VIOLA da GAMBA.', a chart of finger positions glued to the inside front cover, fol. 1v. He also drew the collection's title-page (fol. 2), heading it 'SONATAS & SOLOS, / formerly the Music Book of the Countess of the Pembroke / FOR THE VIOLA DA GAMBA / C F ABEL' and adding 'by Cheeseman. Engraver & Violist 1835.' – revealing that he was the artist and amateur gamba player Thomas Cheeseman (Ch. 8). He was a member of Abel's social circle as a young man, though he probably acquired the contents of Add. MS 31697 much later, after the countess's death in 1831. At that stage it was apparently a bundle of separate manuscripts. A first version of the title-page, over which fol. 2 was pasted, can partly be read: 'THIRTY ONE SONATAS &C. / COMPOSED [illegible] *Abel* / FOR THE V[IOLA DA] GAMBA'.

Ex. 6.6 W. A. Mozart, 'In diesen heil'gen hallen' from *Die Zauberflöte*,
arranged for solo viola da gamba, bb. 18–25

Viola da gamba

This suggests that Cheeseman originally bound Items 6 and 7 together, adding
Items 1–5 at the front in 1835; the later history of the collection will be discussed
in Chapter 8.

✿ Unaccompanied Pieces

T HE only piece in the collection not by Abel is the arrangement of Mozart's
'In diesen heil'gen hallen' (fol. 6v).[33] It must have been added long after Abel's
lifetime, for *Die Zauberflöte* was not written until 1791, and the first appearance
of the aria in an English publication seems to be in Thomas Attwood's opera *The
Mariners* (1793), set to the words 'Why swells my wavy burnish'd grain'.[34] The
gamba arrangement shares some melodic corruptions and a variant ending with
this and other early English editions of the aria. One, published around 1800 by
Monzani and Cimador, may have been the direct model, for it is in G major, the
key of the arrangement; Mozart's original is in E major (Ex. 6.6).[35] The arrangement is grateful to play and surprisingly sonorous; it was presumably made by a
gamba player around 1800.

The most significant unaccompanied piece is WKO 155, entitled 'SONATA /
viola da Gamba Solo / Senzza Basso / di C. F. Abel'. It consists of three concise
binary movements: Adagio (the tempo mark was cropped by the binder except
for the loop of the letter 'g', but the variant version on fol. 9v is clearly marked
'Adagio'), Allegro and Minuet. The Slow–Fast–Fast pattern is unusual for Abel,
and may provide a clue to its date: Abel's three-movement gamba solos with bass
sometimes end with a minuet, but in them the slow movement is always placed
second. However, Slow–Fast–Fast patterns are used in the two 'Prussian' sonatas,
probably composed in 1782 (see below), so it may be that WKO 155 was written after
his return to London in the winter of 1784–5. Hand D's annotation 'Composed for

33 ME: F. X. Hammer, *Three Pieces for Unaccompanied Viola da Gamba* / W. A.
Mozart, 'In diesen heil'gen Hallen', *Anonymous Arrangement for Unaccompanied
Viola da Gamba*, ed. D. J. Rhodes, VdGS Music Edition, 194 (n.p., 2003).

34 T. Attwood, *The Mariners, a Musical Entertainment in Two Acts* (London, 1793),
28–9; CC: GB-Lbl, D.280.(3).

35 W. A. Mozart, *Within these Sacred Bowers, Canzoneta* (London, ?1800); CC:
GB-Lbl, G.290.0.4.

Ex. 6.7 C. F. Abel, (a) Adagio in G major, GB-Lbl, Add. MS 31697, fol. 9v (not in WKO), compared with (b) Sonata in G major, WKO 155, 1st movement, bb. 9–16

the Lady Pembroke' seems plausible, given that the sonata is significantly simpler and easier to play than most of the pieces in the Drexel manuscript, and that Abel provided a number of fingerings for the second and third movements – to be distinguished from those added lightly in pencil by a later hand.

The Adagio in Item 5 was ignored by Knape, presumably because it is related to WKO 155/1. However, the differences between them are of interest. They are both the same length and cover similar ground, though the amount of decoration varies and the second section of WKO 155/1 begins with a continuous eight-bar phrase rather than the two four-bar phrases of the separate piece, which is more logical and musically satisfying (Ex. 6.7). Also, Abel is more precise about the notation of appogiaturas in WKO 155/1, all of which suggests that it is the final version and the separate piece a first draft. It seems that Item 5 (fol. 9v) and Item 2 (the bottom half of fol. 6v containing the G major minuet, WKO 153) originally formed a single ten-stave sheet. They are both written on rather stained grey-brown paper, and the cropped remains of 'T[empo] d[i] m[enue]t', presumably the original title of WKO 153, can just be made out at the bottom of Item 5. It seems that Abel cut the sheet in two himself because the substitute title 'Tempo di Menuet' of WKO 153 seems to be in his hand. It is not clear why he did this, nor whether these loose sheets belonged to the Countess of Pembroke or were added to the collection at a later stage.

Abel seems to have copied Item 3 (fol. 7) onto another half-sheet of the same ten-stave paper. It contains a minuet for solo gamba, WKO 154 in D major, that is of particular interest because it is related to the 'Tempo di Minuet', WKO 201, in the Drexel manuscript (p. 15). Their relationship is closer than is immediately apparent from their openings: the second idea of WKO 154 is similar to the first idea

Ex. 6.8 C. F. Abel, (a) Tempo Minuetto, WKO 154, bb. 5–15, compared with
(b) Tempo di Minuet WKO 201, bb. 17–27

of the second section of WKO 201, and both pieces feature drone effects exploit-
ing the open *a* string, doubtless intended to imitate bagpipes or hurdy-gurdies
(Ex. 6.8). They are both fine pieces, but WKO 201, consisting of two sections of sixteen and forty-four bars, is more developed and sophisticated than WKO 154, with
sections of twenty and twenty-four bars. Also, it has complex figuration requiring a higher level of virtuosity, and an elaborate structure combining elements of
the *da capo* aria and the binary pattern. Thus WKO 154 is probably a preliminary
study for WKO 201, throwing more valuable light on Abel's working methods.

❧ *Solos with Bass*

IN all, there are thirty-one solos with bass by Abel in Add. MS 31697: the Sonata
in G major, WKO 152, in the autograph Item 1, and two sets of fifteen in the
non-autograph Items 6 and 7.[36] All the music in Items 6 and 7 was copied by
the same individual (Hand C), though the titles in Item 6 ('Sonata 1[mo]', 'Sonata
2[do]', and so on) were apparently added by Thomas Cheeseman, and Hand D

---

[36] ME: C. F. Abel, *Kompositionen*, xvi. 133–9, 142–206; C. F. Abel, *Sonatas for the
Viola da Gamba*, ed. G. Houle, 3 vols. (Albany, CA, 2/2005).

apparently added similar titles to Sonata nos. 13 and 15 of Item 7 (fols. 77v, 81v), wrongly labelling the latter '14'. Hand D also seems to have added fingerings to the first few bars of Sonata no. 1 of Set 6 (fol. 10v), while someone else, possibly Cheeseman, added figures to the bass of WKO 156, Sonata no. 2 of Set 6, thereby showing that at least one early owner or user thought that these pieces should be accompanied by a continuo instrument. All the other bass parts are unfigured; when Abel played solos in public concerts he was probably accompanied just by a violoncello (Ch. 5).

The two sets of sonatas are broadly similar in style. They are all in C major, G major, D major or A major, are all relatively easy, and are genial works in the *galant* style, in two, three, or (in one case) four movements. Nevertheless, there are some differences between the two sets. Item 6 consists of two-movement works except for nos. 1, 11, 12, and 15, WKO 151a, 165, 166, 169, which have three, and no. 14, WKO 168, which has four. In the two-movement sonatas a duple-time Allegro or Moderato is followed by a minuet in the same key, while a slow movement in the home key or the subdominant is added to the three-movement sonatas, mostly in the middle, though WKO 169 has the unusual sequence Allegro–Minuetto–Allegretto. WKO 168 has two minuets, in the subdominant and the home key respectively.

Item 7 consists of three-movement sonatas except for the two-movement works nos. 12 and 15, WKO 181, 184; WKO 181 has a minuet with two variations making it seem as substantial as a three-movement sonata. We might think that this means that the first set was composed earlier than the second, particularly since we are familiar with the mature Viennese sonatas of Haydn, Mozart and Beethoven, where the three-movement type predominates.[37] However Abel, like J. C. Bach, wrote two-movement sonatas throughout his career, and apparently chose the pattern partly according to genre. His accompanied sonatas opp. 2 (1760), 5 (1764), 13 (1777), and 18 (1784) are mostly two-movement works, as are his sonatas op. 9 (1772) for violin, violoncello and continuo, while all of his string quartets opp. 8 (1769), 12 (1775), and 15 (1780) have three movements, as do his string trios op. 16 (1783).

The two-movement pattern was associated in England with light, didactic works, so it is significant that the simplest and easiest works are in Item 6, and the most complex and technically demanding ones at the end of Item 7. Indeed, it looks as if the sets were arranged to introduce technical difficulties one by one. Item 6, nos. 2 and 3, WKO 156, 157, are short and easy works, using simple patterns of largely stepwise crotchets and quavers. Triplet sextuplets under a single bow are introduced in the first movement of no. 4, WKO 158, arpeggio patterns first

---

[37] See esp. W. S. Newman, *The Sonata in the Classic Era* (New York, 2/1972), 133–4.

occur in the minuet of no. 6, WKO 160, while the minuet of no. 7, WKO 161, runs up to a written d''', the highest note required in the two sets. The minuet of no. 8, WKO 162, is the first to have extended passagework in semiquavers, while no. 9, WKO 163, is the first in A major, the most extreme home key in the two sets, and has some double stops in the minuet. The first movement of no. 11, WKO 165, is the first to be dominated by semiquaver patterns, and the first with a slow movement, introducing simple Italianate ornamentation. There is little development after this until near the end of Item 7. The first movement of Item 7, no. 12 in D major, WKO 181, is virtually in continuous semiquavers, using a less demanding version of the figuration in the unaccompanied Allegro in the same key, WKO 186, Drexel MS 5871, p. 1. In the slow movements of nos. 13 and 14, WKO 182, 183, the Italianate ornamentation approaches the complexity of that found in some of the pieces in the Drexel manuscript.

The one work outside this didactic scheme is the Sonata in C major, WKO 151a. It comes at the beginning of Item 6, though it is one of the more developed and demanding works, with a passage going up to written c''' in the first movement and some florid ornamentation in the second. It is also of interest in that there are several places in its minuet where the bass has two-note chords in thirds. Brian Capleton asserted that the chords were 'typical gamba writing', but in fact they are also easily playable on the violoncello.[38] It also seems to be the only sonata in the two sets that exists elsewhere: in D-B, M1905.247, a score copied by the Braunschweig cellist and gamba player Johannes Klingenberg (1852–1905) with the solo part notated in the treble clef, and D-B, Mus. MS 263 (2) (listed by Knape as WKO 151), an arrangement from the same period with the solo part mostly in the bass clef and the bass realised for keyboard.[39] A number of small differences show that the Berlin manuscripts do not derive from Add. MS 31697; they were probably copied from a now-lost late eighteenth-century manuscript similar to those that preserve Abel's 'Prussian' sonatas. Another complication is that the Berlin manuscript of the Quartet in G major, WKO 227 (discussed below), has yet another version of WKO 151a's slow movement.

One piece in Add. MS 31697 remains to be discussed: the Sonata in G major, WKO 152, in the autograph Item 1. Its three movements are no longer than many in Items 6 and 7, though the solo part is consistently more demanding: it runs up to d''' several times in the first movement, and there is a nice balance between

---

[38] B. Capleton, 'Carl Friedrich Abel and the Viola da Gamba: a Study of Lbl, Add. [MS] 31697 and its Context' (MMus diss., London, Royal College of Music, 1994), 51–3. I am grateful to Mark Caudle for advice on this point.

[39] For Klingenberg, see M. O'Loghlin, *Frederick the Great and his Musicians: the Viola da Gamba Music of the Berlin School* (Aldershot, 2008), esp. 68. I am grateful to Günter von Zadow for information about these and other Berlin MSS.

Ex. 6.9 C. F. Abel, Sonata in G major, WKO 152, Allegro, bb. 1–10

tuneful ideas in the *galant* style and passagework in semiquavers. The Adagio is elaborately decorated, while the last movement is not a minuet but a 2/4 *moto perpetuo* Allegro in continuous semiquaver patterns of scales and arpeggios, doubtless intended to be played very fast as a display piece (Ex. 6.9). WKO 152 is important because it is the only solo in Add. MS 31697 that looks as if was composed by Abel for his own use in public concerts, though the presence of some original fingerings (there are also many later fingerings) probably indicate that he copied it for the Countess of Pembroke. The annotator, Hand C, did not specifically state that it was written for her, though it may be intended to be included in the statement that the collection was 'formerly the Music Book of the Countess of Pembroke'. If she did play it, it was presumably after she had mastered the two sets of sonatas in Items 6 and 7.

🎜 *The other Pembroke Manuscript*

ANOTHER part-autograph manuscript of Abel's gamba solos that belonged to the Countess of Pembroke exists in a private collection, and is at present inaccessible. It seems to have been unknown to scholars until 26 May 1994, when it was sold at Sotheby's,[40] though it was sold by Puttick and Simpson on 27 November 1882, lot 508, when it was described as 'Abel (C. F.) Fourteen Duets for Viol da Gamba and Violoncello, *written for his pupil, Lord Pembroke. In the Autograph of Abel and unpublished, and has Autograph of Lady Elizabeth Pembroke on fly-leaf, half calf*'.[41] The amateur gamba player Edward Payne purchased it for £2 6s., and it was presumably it was acquired it after Payne's death in 1905 by the

---

[40] Sotheby's, 26/5/1994, lot 97 (Stephen Roe).

[41] Puttick and Simpson, *Catalogue of the Extensive Library of a Distinguished Musician* (17/11/1882); CC: GB-Lbl, S.C.P.210.(10).

violin maker Arthur Frederick Hill (1860–1939); it was sold by Hill's widow at Sotheby's on 17 June 1947.[42] At that sale it was described as 'Ten Sonatas for the Viol da Gamba and Bass, and Four Duets for the Viola da Gamba and Violoncello, MANUSCRIPT *on paper*, 65 pp., 14 *staves to a page*, g. e. [gilt edges], *by Riviere / 4to / 18ᵗʰ Century*'.

The 1994 catalogue also mentions the signature, 'Eliz: Pembroke', and tells us that the manuscript is a folio volume of sixty-six pages consisting of seven systems per page on fourteen-stave paper, and that it contains fourteen pieces. It is discussed as if it was a single manuscript, though most of the pieces are said to have 'separate title-pages', and the one illustrated is similar to the title-pages for Items 1 and 4 of Add. MS 31697, which suggests that it is a collection of separate manuscripts bound together, though seemingly with a uniform appearance. The 1994 catalogue also states that the pieces were copied by two hands. It identifies the main one as Abel's autograph, and the page illustrated shows this to be the case (Plate 14). The other hand, not illustrated nor described, copied three sonatas (nos. 8–10) in the middle of the manuscript, though it is not clear whether he used the same paper as the autographs.

The pieces divide into two types: nos. 3–10, 13 and 14 are labelled 'Sonata' and seem to be conventional solos with a simple bass accompaniment, as with the piece illustrated. The other four, nos. 1, 2, 11 and 12, are called 'Duetto', and three of them are specifically 'per la Viola da Gamba & violoncello', so it is likely that in them the two instruments have a more equal relationship. It is unfortunate that they are not illustrated, for there is nothing else like them in Abel's gamba music. Perhaps they were written for the Earl and Countess of Pembroke to play together. If so, then they were probably written in the 1770s, when they were both at Wilton and Henry was active as a cellist (Ch. 7). We can learn a little more about the pieces from the 1994 catalogue. One has two movements and the rest three, mostly using the Fast–Slow–Minuet pattern. It is interesting that several are in relatively extreme keys: no. 3 is in E major and no. 4 in E♭ major, while nos. 5–7 are in B♭ major and no. 8 is in F major. Flat keys are not so easy on the viol as C, G, D and A major, used repeatedly in Add. MS 31697. The movement illustrated in the catalogue, the Adagio from no. 3, has some elaborate ornamentation and ends with a written-out cadenza. This may mean that Abel wrote it and the other sonatas with bass for his own use, though some autograph fingerings suggests that he made the copy for the countess. It may be an accident of

⁴² Sotheby's, 17/6/1947, lot 241. For Hill, see B. W. Harvey, *The Violin Family and its Makers in the British Isles: an Illustrated Guide and Directory* (Oxford, 1995), 190, 195–6; *The British Violin: the Catalogue of the 1998 Exhibition '400 Years of Violin and Bow Making in the British Isles'*, ed. J. Milnes (Oxford, 2000), 88–9.

survival that nearly all of Abel's gamba sonatas come from manuscripts owned by the Countess, though it suggests a long and fruitful musical relationship.

℘ *Six Easy Sonnatas*

T HE only publication of Abel's gamba music is a mystery. It is normally said to have been issued by J. J. Hummel of Amsterdam in 1772.[43] However, it has an English title, '*Six / EASY SONNATAS / for the* HARPSICHORD / or for / A VIOLA DA GAMBA / *VIOLIN* or *GERMAN FLUTE / with a /* Thorough – Bass Accompaniment / *Composed by* / C. F. ABEL', and the only evidence of Hummel's involvement is a printed label stuck on the title-page of the only known copy, D-Dl, Mus. 3122-R-2; it reads: 'A AMSTERDAM / *Chez J: J: HUMMEL Marchand / de la Musique / Prix f 2,, 10.*[44] The date apparently comes from an entry in the Breitkopf thematic catalogue for 1772 which lists the sonatas in the harpsichord section with the title 'VI. Sonate di C. F. ABEL. *Amsterdam.*[45] This apparently refers to Hummel's own edition: 'Six SONATINES pour le Clavecin / ou le / Violon e Basse Continue à l'usage des Commencants', with the plate number 302.[46] It was advertised on 14 and 15 September 1773; is listed in the harpsichord section of his 1773 catalogue as '*Abel*, 6 Sonatines'; and appeared in subsequent catalogues until 1802.[47] *Six Easy Sonnatas* was presumably printed in London, perhaps for Abel himself. He initially issued some of his collections, later assigning them to Robert Bremner, his main London publisher. However, no Bremner edition of *Six Easy Sonnatas* is known, and it lacks the imprint found on the title-pages of his other self-published collections, such as 'Printed for the Author & Sold at his House N⁰,, 201, Oxford Street, Sold also by R. Bremner in the Strand', used on *Six Sonatas for a Violin, a Violoncello, & Base, with a Thorough Base for the Harpsichord*, op. 9 (1772).[48]

There is little doubt that the *Six Easy Sonnatas*, WKO 141–6, are gamba works, despite the wording of the title-page. Abel's practice of notating gamba music

---

43   For instance, in WKO, p. 225. The edition is not recorded in RISM A/I.

44   Facs., intro. M. O'Loghlin (Heidelberg, 2005); ME: C. F. Abel, *Six Easy Sonnatas*, 2 vols., ed. L. and G. von Zadow, intro. O'Loghlin (Heidelberg, 2005).

45   *The Breitkopf Thematic Catalogue: the Six Parts and Sixteen Supplements, 1762–1787*, ed. B. S. Brook (New York, 1966), 471.

46   WKO, p. 225, where a copy at D-B, Mus. O 9755 is mentioned. It is not recorded in RISM A/I.

47   C. Johannson, *J. J. & B. Hummel Music-Publishing and Thematic Catalogues*, 3 vols. (Stockholm, 1972), i. 30; ii. F.10, F.50.

48   RISM A/I A 125; ME: C. F. Abel, *Kompositionen*, ed. Knape, xiii–xiv (Cuxhaven, 1969), 49–95.

in the octave-transposing treble clef made it possible to offer alternative scorings without having to provide alternative parts. There were some upper-class amateurs playing the gamba in the early 1770s (Ch. 7), though presumably not enough of them to justify aiming a publication at them exclusively. Nevertheless, the sonatas are similar in their style, idiom and technical demands to the more developed works in Add. MS 31697: they have three movements in the Fast–Slow–Minuet pattern, and similar types of figuration, with occasional two- or three-note chords mostly at cadences. The keys chosen for nos. 1–5 – C major, A major, D major, and G major – are also the most common ones in Add. MS 31697, though no. 6 in E minor, WKO 146, is one of only two gamba sonatas by Abel in the minor. Interestingly, it seems to demonstrate that by the early 1770s Abel was aware of the later Berlin style – as distinct from the post-Baroque north German idiom he used in his youth. Bach and Abel were the leaders of the German musical community in London, and regularly employed and promoted visiting virtuosi, so they would have been aware of the latest trends in the German-speaking world. Berlin composers tended to use minor keys more than their contemporaries elsewhere, and developed a musical language that exploited the expressive potential of angular melodic lines and unexpected harmonic twists and turns, often spiced up with appoggiaturas and other unprepared dissonances. The style is admirably demonstrated by the opening of WKO 146/1 (Ex. 6.10).

One movement, WKO 144/1 (the Allegro of Sonata no. 4 in G major) is closely related to WKO 178/1 (Add. MS 31697, Item 7, no. 9), giving us an interesting glimpse of Abel's working methods. Such movements are laid out in the standard binary pattern, though they use elements of the ritornello technique familiar from contemporary concertos and arias: the appearances of the main theme, in the tonic at the beginning, in the dominant after the double bar, and in the tonic in the middle of the second section, are interspersed with sequential passagework making the necessary modulations. The main themes of the two movements have similar melodic and harmonic outlines (Ex. 6.11), though the one in WKO 178/1 is a regular eight-bar phrase, while its counterpart in WKO 144/1 is elided with the beginning of the passagework, making an attractively irregular ten-bar phrase. The passagework itself is completely different: in the last section of WKO 178/1 Abel uses simple arpeggios, while in WKO 144/1 he increases the momentum by inserting a passage of triplet quavers and makes an effective climax by repeating the semiquaver runs from near the end of its first section. A complication is that the triplet-quaver passage is remarkably similar to one near the end of WKO 158/1 (Add. MS 31697, Item 6, no. 4) (Ex. 6.12). These connections may just be the result of habitually thinking along the same lines, though they confirm that *Six Easy Sonnatas* is a primarily a collection of gamba music.

Ex. 6.10 C. F. Abel, Sonata in E minor, WKO 146, Moderato, bb. 1–14

Ex. 6.11 C. F. Abel, (a) Sonata in G major, WKO 178, Allegro, bb. 1–8,
compared with (b) Sonata in G major, WKO 144, Allegro, bb. 1–10

Ex. 6.12 C. F. Abel, (a) Sonata in D major, WKO 158, Moderato, bb. 31–5,
compared with (b) Sonata in G major, WKO 144, Allegro, bb. 33–7

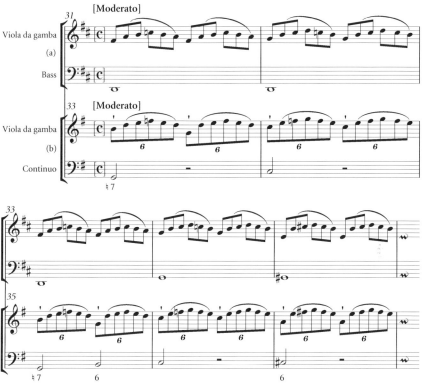

𝆕 *The 'Prussian' Sonatas*

Two Abel gamba sonatas survive only in Berlin manuscripts: the G major, WKO 149, in D-B, KHM 25b, and the E minor, WKO 150, in KHM 25a.[49] Knape asserted that they are autograph, but that is not so.[50] They are the work of a typical professional German copyist of the period, concerned with the visual appearance of his work, displaying formalistic and decorative features, and following tradition by making the first page of each manuscript a formal 'title-page' with an incipit of the work's first movement. This is at variance with Abel's own practice, as is the use of the formal title 'Sigʳ Abel'; he signed his work 'C. F. Abel'. A similar hand, also wrongly claimed as autograph by Knape, copied Abel's two violoncello sonatas, in D-B, KHM 24 (WKO 147) and KHM 25 (WKO 148).[51]

---

49 WKO, p. 233; ME: C. F. Abel, *Zwei Berliner Sonaten für Viola da Gamba und Bass*, ed. G. and L. von Zadow, intro. M. O'Loghlin (Heidelberg, 2006).

50 WKO, p. 233.

51 ME: C. F. Abel, *Zwei Berliner Sonaten für Violoncello und Bass*, ed. G. and L. von Zadow, intro. M. O'Loghlin (Heidelberg, 2007).

Fred Flassig and Michael O'Loghlin labelled WKO 149 and 150 Abel's 'Prussian' sonatas, presumably by analogy with C. P. E. Bach's six 'Prussian' keyboard sonatas H24–29, dedicated to Frederick the Great.[52] They argued that Abel wrote them during his visit to Berlin and nearby Potsdam in 1782. Frederick the Great's nephew, the Crown Prince Frederick William II (1744–97), played the gamba in his youth and later turned to the violoncello, prompting Mozart, Boccherini, Beethoven, Dittersdorf, Duport, and others to dedicate music with prominent violoncello solos to him.[53] Abel dedicated his string quartets op. 15 (1781), WKO 73–8 to the prince, and gave the violoncello prominent parts in a few movements, though there is no evidence that he planned the set with his visit to Berlin in mind.[54] Frederick William seems to have largely given up playing the gamba by the 1780s, so it is unlikely that the solo parts of WKO 149 and 150 were intended for him, though O'Loghlin wondered whether he might have accompanied Abel on the gamba.[55] It is significant that the bass part of WKO 149 goes down to *AA* and *BB*, notes below the range of the violoncello but playable on the seven-string bass viol. It is just labelled 'Basso' and is not figured; there is no sign that Abel intended a continuo instrument.

An important feature of WKO 149 and 150 is the use of what O'Loghlin christened the 'Berlin Sonata Schema', the practice of writing sonatas in a three-movement pattern of increasing speed, starting with a slow movement. WKO 149 consists of an Adagio and two Allegros, the last in 2/4 and therefore presumably the fastest, though marked 'ma non Presto'. WKO 150 uses the pattern Siciliano–Allegro–Presto, the last also in 2/4. O'Loghlin sees Abel's use of these 2/4 movements instead of his customary minuets as a concession to Berlin taste.[56] Abel also used a melodic and harmonic idiom influenced by Berlin composers. O'Loghlin draws attention to an unusual amount of unprepared dissonance in the first movement of the G major sonata, often involving false relations and angular leaps, and a remarkable passage involving chromatic lines in contrary motion towards the end of both sections of the following Allegro – a characteristic Berlin feature that

---

[52] Flassig, *Die soloistische Gambenmusik in Deutschland*, 199–200; O'Loghlin, *Frederick the Great and his Musicians*, 1; Helm, *Thematic Catalogue of the Works of Carl Philipp Emanuel Bach*, 10–12, 266.

[53] See esp. M. Parker, 'Soloistic Chamber Music at the Court of Friedrich Wilhelm II: 1786–1797' (PhD diss., Indiana U., 1994); O'Loghlin, *Frederick the Great and his Musicians*, esp. 14–15, 126–9, 132–3.

[54] ME: C. F. Abel, *Kompositionen*, ed. Knape, xii (Cuxhaven, 1964). See Parker, 'Soloistic Chamber Music at the Court of Friedrich Wilhelm II', 356–62.

[55] O'Loghlin, *Frederick the Great and his Musicians*, esp. 14–15, 126–30. See also Flassig, *Die soloistische Gambenmusik in Deutschland*, esp. 138–44, 162–7, 272–3.

[56] O'Loghlin, *Frederick the Great and his Musicians*, 198–204.

Ex. 6.13 C. F. Abel, Sonata in G major, wko 149, Allegro, bb. 21–8

Ex. 6.14 C. F. Abel, Sonata in E minor, wko 150, Allegro, bb. 15–27

O'Loghlin calls the 'small dark cloud' (Ex. 6.13). Another harmonic cloud can be heard in the first Allegro of the E minor sonata. No sooner has the music moved to the relative major than it plunges into its tonic minor – far removed from the home key (Ex. 6.14). This fine movement uses a highly inflected idiom throughout, with augmented and diminished chords in the harmony and outlined in the melodic lines. O'Loghlin also points out that the fermata at the end of the Siciliano, wko 150/1, was a device 'often used to add an element of significance to the opening slow movement of Berlin School sonatas'. The sonatas are not particularly virtuosic, though they are more serious and substantial than those in English sources, and give us a tantalising glimpse of those he must have written for his own use in London.

✿ Trios and Accompanied Sonatas

ABEL wrote two works for flute, gamba and continuo. They survive in a publication for violin, violoncello and continuo, and are incomplete: no copy of the violin part survives. The evidence comes mainly from documents relating to a lawsuit initiated by Abel in 1773 against the publishers James Longman and Charles Lukey. The background to the case is as follows. A 1710 act 'for the encouragement of learning' gave authors exclusive publication rights for fourteen years (renewable for another fourteen years provided the author was still alive), though it was unclear whether it applied to music.[57] Composers sometimes resorted to obtaining a crown privilege for their works, also for fourteen years; Abel was granted his on 15 April 1760.[58] There was also the possibility, hotly contested, that books were copyright at common law. To try to resolve the issue, Bach and Abel started a campaign against Longman and Lukey in the spring of 1773 citing works published without their consent. Bach's case, initiated on 18 March, concerned 'a new Lesson for the Harpsichord or Piano Forte' and 'a new Sonata for the Harpsichord or Piano Forte with Accompanim[en]t'. Bach described the latter as a 'musical composition for the Harpsichord called a Sonata together with an accompanyment for the Viol da Gamba', though Longman and Lukey changed the scoring in the publication to 'a Flute or Fiddle and violoncello'.[59]

Abel's case, initiated on 7 May, concerned '*Les Suites des trios Primieres /* TRIOS / *Pour le /* VIOLON, VIOLONCELLO, / et / BASSO. / *Composées /* par / CHARLES FREDERICK ABEL. / [rule] / LONDON / Printed & Sold by LONGMAN, LUKEY, & Cº. No. 26. Cheapside'.[60] It was a sequel to another Longman–Lukey publication, *Three Trios for a Violin, Violoncello, and Bass Figur'd for the Organ or Harpsicord* (?1772),[61] and both were reprints of publications by Markordt in Amsterdam. The model for the latter was *Troi[s] trios pour le violon, violoncello, et basso* (Amsterdam, ?1772),[62] but unfortunately the model for *Les suites des trios*

---

57 See esp. J. Small, 'J. C. Bach Goes to Law', *MT*, 126 (1985), 526–9; D. Hunter, 'Music Copyright in Britain to 1800', *ML*, 67 (1986), 269–82; R. J. Rabin and S. Zohn, 'Arne, Handel, Walsh and Music as Intellectual Property: Two Eighteenth-Century Lawsuits', *JRMA*, 120 (1995), 112–45.

58 GB-Lna, SP 44/374 (Ann van Allen-Russell).

59 Small, 'J. C. Bach Foes to Law', 527.

60 RISM A/I A 130; CC: GB-Ckc, Rowe O/P A-bl, violoncello and bass parts only. There is another copy of the violoncello part at AUS-NLwm (Nancy Hadden).

61 RISM A/I A 128; CC: GB-Lbl, h.5.c.(1).

62 RISM A/I A 129; CC: GB-Cu, MR.320.a.75.304–306.

primieres does not survive, though it was mentioned in Longman and Lukey's answer of 30 November 1773:

> these Defendants Jointly and severally answering say that they respectively have not nor have they ever heard nor do they or either of them believe that the said Complainant, Charles Frederick Abel, ever published the said Three Trios or either of them himself, and they these Defendants severally admit that the said three Trios entitled as follows: *Les Suite de Trios pur le Violen Violencello et Basso*, were on or about the middle of the year 1772 engraved and printed by one Markordt of Amsterdam, who sent the same to them these Defendants in England and these Defendants sold the same in England.[63]

It is not clear why Abel's initial bill of complaint was concerned only with the second Longman–Lukey publication since they both potentially infringed Abel's copyright. *Three Trios* (and Markodt's model, *Troi[s] trios*) are reprints of Abel's op. 9, nos. 1, 6 and 4, while the third of *Les suites des trios primieres* is a variant of op. 9, no. 5. However, the first two sonatas of *Les suites des trios primieres* are otherwise unknown,[64] and are presumably those referred to in Abel's bill of complaint: 'about 10 years ago your orator composed and wrote two other musical works or compositions called Trios each being composed for a Flute, Viol di gamba and a Bass'. Abel added that Longman and Lukey had obtained copies of them 'by undue means'; had published them at a large profit; had pretended they were not by Abel; and had even denied that his compositions were protected by a privilege. Longman and Lukey defended themselves by pointing out that they had obtained the sonatas from Markordt, and that it had been standard practice for English publishers to reprint foreign editions. The case dragged on to 1777, and its outcome is unclear, though Bach's was settled out of court in 1774.[65] Without the violin or flute part it is difficult to assess the two sonatas. However, Abel's bill of complaint tells us that it they were written 'about 10 years ago', that is, around 1762. They are in F major and G major, and are in three movements, the last a minuet as so often in Abel. Their violoncello parts are in the tenor clef, with a small range (*e*–*bb'* and *d*–*b'* respectively), and would be eminently suitable for the gamba. But that is also true of the op. 9 sonatas: their violoncello parts all have small ranges, without chords. It is possible that some or

[63] GB-Lna, c12/71/6 (Ann van Allen Russell). The words 'the middle of the year 1772' are unclear.

[64] WKO, pp. 137–8 wrongly implies that they are reprints of sonatas from op. 9.

[65] Small, 'J. C. Bach Goes to Law', 528–9.

all of them were originally written for violin, gamba and bass; we have seen that an autograph score of twenty-four trios for that combination existed in 1794.

Mention of Bach's 'Sonata together with an accompanyment for the Viol da Gamba' brings us to the subject of accompanied sonatas, and calls for a brief digression. The publication described in the documents relating to Bach's lawsuit is lost, though the work apparently survives as 'Sonata / a / Piano Forte / e / Viola da Gamba / di / G C Bach', fols. 14–17v of a manuscript now in an inaccessible private collection.[66] According to the sale catalogue, it was copied by a scribal hand, though with an autograph title-page. Its second movement was published, seemingly by Longman and Lukey, as 'A FAVORITE RONDÒ / FOR THE HARPSICHORD OR FORTE PIANO WITH AN / ACCOMPANYMENT FOR A TENOR / COMPOSED BY SIG^R. BACH'.[67] The first movement is a version of the first movement of op. 10, no. 5, B6, for keyboard and violin, while the rondo is an abbreviated version of the 'Tempo di Menuetto' from the F major oboe concerto, B80.

The same manuscript contains a 'Sonata di Cembalo, e / Viola da Gamba / Obligata Bach' (fols. 23–27), a version of op. 10, no. 1 in B♭ major, B2; and a transcription of op. 10, no. 3 in G major, B4 (fols. 31–4). The latter was copied in separate parts, entitled respectively 'Sonata / Cembalo' and 'Sonata / Viola da Gamba', by the young Muzio Clementi, who had been in England since 1767 or 1768 and seems to have begun his London career in 1774. A fourth J. C. Bach accompanied sonata, a gamba version of B15 in F major for keyboard and violin, published as op. 16, no. 6 (1779), survives in a manuscript now at US-AUS, Finney 8 (9), and is therefore available for study.[68] The gamba version seems the earlier and less sophisticated of the two, though some of the variants can be explained by the need to cater for a tenor-range instrument more suitable for chords than the violin. These arrangements were presumably made for Abel, though it is easy to imagine him playing accompanied sonatas on the gamba extempore by reading the violin parts down the octave and adapting them where necessary.

The gamba part of a work attributed to Abel may come from an otherwise unknown accompanied sonata similar to those by J. C. Bach. It survives in GB-Lu, Special Collections, MS 944/2/1–3, pp. 30–1, of the first part-book, is entitled

---

[66] Sold at Sotheby's, 29/5/1992, lot 463 (Stephen Roe).

[67] CC: GB-Lbbc; facs.: J. C. Bach, *The Collected Works*, 48/3: *Music Supplement*, ed. E. Warburton (New York, 1999), 595–7.

[68] ME: J. C. Bach, *The Collected Works*, 38: *Music for Two Instruments*, ed. D. J. Keahey (New York, 1991), 331–7; J. C. Bach, *The Collected Works, Music Supplement*, ed. Warburton, 587–91.

Ex. 6.15 C. F. Abel, Sonata or Solo in C major, GB-Lu, Special Collections, MS 944/2/1–3, pp. 30–1 (not in WKO), first movement, bb. 1–4

'F. Abel per il Viol di Gambo', and was copied immediately after the solo parts of a set of six gamba sonatas from about 1730 (Ch. 3, 8). It is in C major and consists of three movements, untitled but presumably intended to be Allegro, Adagio or Andante, and Minuet. At first sight it appears to be the solo part of a sonata for gamba and bass, though there is no bass line for it in the bass part-book, and its tessitura is rather lower (notated in alto and bass clefs) than the solo parts of Abel sonatas. There is also no display passagework, and it spends much of the time seemingly just playing the bass or an inner accompaniment part. An obvious possibility is that it is the gamba part of a sonata with obbligato keyboard, which would explain why the main theme of the first movement seems designed to fit in thirds and sixths with another part – probably the right hand of the keyboard (Ex. 6.15). It does not come from any of Abel's published sets of accompanied sonatas.

✄ *The Quartet in G major*

As already mentioned, the Quartet in G major, WKO 227, for flute, violin, gamba and violoncello is a probable survivor from the set of ten quartets offered for sale in London in 1794. It exists in several versions. It was first published by the late Edgar Hunt from a set of parts in his possession.[69] This version is in two movements, Allegro moderato and an Allegretto in *rondeau* form. According to a note in the edition, the tenor part is labelled 'Violetta' in the work's title but 'Viola da gamba' on the part itself, and is notated in the treble clef. This makes it likely that the manuscript comes from the late eighteenth or early nineteenth centuries (it would probably been notated in the tenor or alto clef had it been written in more recent times), though some wrong notes and missing accidentals suggest that it is not autograph. The second source, a set of parts in the hand of

[69] ME: C. F. Abel, *Quartet in G for Flute, Violin, Viola (da gamba) and Violoncello*, ed. E. Hunt (London, 1951).

Johannes Klingenberg, D-B, Mus. MS 253/10, is scored specifically for flute, violin, gamba and violoncello.[70] A number of variants show that Hunt's manuscript was not Klingenberg's source.

The Klingenberg version also has a slow movement, a Cantabile in 3/4 scored for gamba solo with violin and violoncello accompaniment. It is another version of the middle movement of the G major solo sonata, WKO 151, which Klingenberg also copied. He described it as an insertion ('Einlage'), and it looks as if it is his own arrangement. There are several versions of the violin and violoncello parts, as if he was experimenting with them, and several dubious features, including chords in the violin and violoncello parts, anachronistic expression marks such as *mf* (almost unknown in eighteenth-century music), a 'hairpin' crescendo, and the modern type of accent mark. The movement has four more bars at the end than in WKO 151, which functions rather like the keyboard postludes of nineteenth-century songs. Significantly, there is a similar postlude in the version of WKO 151/2 in D-B, Mus. MS 263(2), the late nineteenth-century arrangement with a realised keyboard part. Klingenberg presumably had access to an eighteenth-century manuscript of WKO 227, the same or similar to the one offered for sale in Hamburg on 25 February 1783 as 'Abel, I Quatuor. Viola da Gamba Fl. Violin & Violoncel G dur'.[71] It is likely that this version had only two movements, and that Klingenberg assembled and arranged the three-movement version himself.

To complicate matters further, there are several other versions of WKO 227's outer movements. Both are included in a conventional flute quartet in CZ-Pnm, XXII A 7, the first of a set of seven quartets or divertimenti by Abel, five of which are variants of his string quartets op. 12 (1775).[72] This version has a different slow movement, in common time rather than 3/4. Furthermore, the Allegretto of WKO 227 is also found as the finale of Abel's String Quartet in G major, op. 12, no. 6, WKO 72/3.[73] The two-movement version of WKO 227 is an attractive piece, though it needs a critical edition that reconciles the two main sources properly, and it must be admitted that there is nothing particularly distinctive or idiomatic about its gamba part. It serves mainly to show that the viola parts of conventional chamber music by Abel, J. C. Bach and their circle can legitimately serve as repertory for gamba players today. Several chamber pieces by J. C. Bach exist with similar alternative scorings (Ch. 5).

---

[70] ME: C. F. Abel, *Quartet no. 3 for Flute, Violin, Viola da Gamba and Cello*, ed. R. Whelden (Albany, CA, 2003).

[71] C. F. Cramer, *Magazin der Musik*, i/1 (Hamburg, 1783), 283.

[72] RISM A/II: 550.255.644, 645; 550.255.647–651. They are not listed in WKO.

[73] ME: C. F. Abel, *Kompositionen*, ed. Knape, xii. 155–9.

❧ The Lambach Quartets

WITH this in mind, it comes as a surprise to encounter versions of two of Abel quartets in which the gamba replaces the first violin rather than the viola. They survive in manuscripts at A-LA, and are contemporary arrangements of no. 2 in B♭ major, WKO 62, and no. 5 in A major, WKO 65, of *Six Quartettos for Two Violins, a Tenor and Violoncello Obligati*, op. 8 (1768).[74] The arrangements were made by copying out the first violin part, and putting it down the octave in the alto clef. The use of the alto clef is at variance with Abel's practice, and the manuscript title-page describes WKO 62 as 'Quartetto N. 3', suggesting that they were not copied directly from the print. The arrangements were probably made without Abel's knowledge or approval; perhaps the copyist just used his own initiative, knowing that the composer was a famous gamba player. Nevertheless, they make attractive additions to the repertory. We might think that the gamba, playing the first violin part down the octave, would be obscured by the second violin and viola, though the example of contemporary bassoon quartets shows that a tenor-range instrument with a distinctive timbre can easily compete with a higher-pitched accompaniment.

❧ 'Frena le belle lagrime'

ABEL wrote only one important vocal work, the aria 'Frena le belle lagrime', scored for soprano, viola da gamba obbligato, strings, and continuo.[75] It was written for the pasticcio *Sifare*, put on at the King's Theatre in London for a single performance on 5 March 1767 as a benefit for the castrato Tommaso Guardacci; Guardacci, playing the title role, sang the aria in Act II, Scene 5.[76] Advertisements for the production stated that the aria would be 'Accompanied by Mr. ABEL, on the Viola de Gamba'; his contribution was singled out in brief report in *Lloyd's Evening Post*: 'The music in this Opera is very pleasing; in which was introduced a Cantabile Song, accompanied by Mr. Abel on the Viola

---

74 CC: DK-Kk, U110-SC 110 mu 6606-0834; ME: C. F. Abel, *Kompositionen*, ed. Knape, xi. 13–28a, 52–62.

75 ME: C. F. Abel, *'Frena le belle lagrime': an Aria for Soprano, Obbligato Viola da Gamba, Strings and Continuo*, ed. W. Hunt (London, 1989). It is not listed in WKO.

76 *Sifare, an Opera, as Perform'd at the King's Theatre in the Hay-Market for the Benefit of Signor Guardacci, Musician to his Royal Highness the Grand Duke of Tuscany* (London, 1767); CC: GB-Lbl, 907.i.10.(9). See also Terry, *John Christian Bach*, rev. Landon, 108–9.

de Gambo. Mr. Abel's delicate performance on this instrument is beyong [*sic*] description'.[77] Welcker published a full score in *The Favourite Songs in the Opera Sifari*, advertised from 11 May 1767.[78]

It is strange that Burney thought that the aria was 'laboured, and had not the effect that might be expected from the united powers of two such complete musicians',[79] for it is one of Abel's finest achievements. It is a large-scale *da capo* aria in the modern Italian operatic style that Burney favoured and constantly promoted in his writings. Abel set the A section (in the published translation 'Stop, oh stop the starting tears; / My soul, my rapture! / If I but see you weep, / My fortitude forsakes me.') in a suitably plaintive style, with the gamba echoing, supporting and engaging in dialogue with the voice, the two gently supported by pulsating muted strings.[80] He followed tradition by setting the second stanza ('Alas! Wake not within my breast / A new crowd of soft affections, / Full enough, I feel already / Are the throbs that love has caus'd'.) to music in contrasted style – in the relative minor, with pizzicato strings, and with a suitably agitated gamba part in semiquaver arpeggios (Ex. 6.16). It is a good example of the tendency in eighteenth-century *opera seria* to use obbligato instruments to convey much of the emotional force of an aria, leaving the voice free to enunciate the text. At this period the structure and musical idiom of the *da capo* aria was closely connected to the concerto. Thus Abel's aria gives us a precious glimpse of what his lost mature gamba concertos might have been like, and it is a powerful demonstration of the ways Abel used the gamba to express musical sensibility.

❧ *Conclusion*

WE have more gamba music by Abel than any of his contemporaries, and probably more than anyone else in the eighteenth century with the possible exception of Telemann. Yet what survives is probably only a small proportion of his output, and it is not representative: we have many of his easy teaching pieces but only a handful of the sort of solos with bass he would have played in public concerts. But even in the simplest piece Abel's craftsmanship is always impeccable, and we have the Drexel manuscript and pieces such as the two 'Prussian' sonatas and 'Frena le belle lagrime' to remind us that he was capable of deeper things. Nevertheless, Burney reported Abel's words: 'I do not chuse to

---

[77] *PA*, 2, 4, 5/3/1767; *Lloyd's Evening Post*, 9/3/1767.

[78] CC: GB-Lbl, G.206k.(2.); *PA*, 11/5/1767.

[79] BurneyH, ii. 874.

[80] Trans. from *Sifare, an Opera*, 25.

Ex. 6.16 C. F. Abel, 'Frena le belle lagrime' from *Sifare*, bb. 101–12

be always struggling with difficulties, and playing with all my might. I make my pieces difficult whenever I please, according to my disposition and that of my audience.'[81] His simple and tuneful gamba music is a telling illustration of that philosophy.

[81] BurneyH, ii. 1019.

CHAPTER 7

'The Heart of Sensibility':
Writers, Artists and Aristocrats

WE have seen that Charles Frederick Abel was described as 'the *Sterne* of *Music*', thereby linking him to Laurence Sterne (1713–68), the author of *The Life and Opinions of Tristram Shandy, Gentleman* (1759–67) and *A Sentimental Journey through France and Italy* (1768). This was not hyperbole: there is a description of Abel improvising on the gamba using as a subject the famous deathbed scene of Lieutenant Le Fever in *Tristram Shandy*, bringing 'Tears into the Eyes of his Hearers' (Ch. 6), and in a spurious letter about sensibility Sterne is made to say that 'there is an amiable kind of *cullibility*, which is as superior to the slow precaution of worldly wisdom, as the sound of *Abel's Viol di Gamba*, to the braying of an ass on the other side of my paling'.[1] This chapter will examine the gamba as an emblem of sensibility, and Abel's role in inspiring a revival of the instrument in the 1760s and 1770s among writers, artists and aristocrats.

❧ *Laurence Sterne*

IT is appropriate to start with Sterne, since he was extremely musical, seems to have been an admirer of Abel, and may have played the gamba.[2] Like other eighteenth-century clergymen, he probably learned music at university; he was at Jesus College, Cambridge from 1733 to 1737, where he would doubtless have encountered Conyers Middleton, the University Librarian and a bass viol player (Ch. 2). Sterne remembered in his memoirs that 'Books, painting, fiddling, and shooting' were his amusements when he was an obscure Yorkshire clergyman in the 1740s and 50s.[3] He borrowed sonatas by Albicastro and Carlo Marino and concertos by Vivaldi from York Minster Library in

[1] *Original Letters of the late Reverend Mr. Laurence Sterne* (London, 1788), 109–14, at 111; CC: *ECCO*, T014810. It is not accepted as genuine; see *Letters of Laurence Sterne*, ed. L. P. Curtis (Oxford, 1935), 251–2.

[2] P. Holman, 'Laurence Sterne as a Musician', *VdGSJ*, 2 (2008), 58–66. See also esp. A. H. Cash, *Laurence Sterne: the Early and Middle Years* (London, 1975); A. H. Cash, *Laurence Sterne: the Later Years* (London, 1986); I. C. Ross, *Laurence Sterne, a Life* (Oxford, 2001).

[3] *Letters of Laurence Sterne*, ed. Curtis, 4.

1752.[4] An anecdote told to William Hazlitt by a Dr Marriott has him leaving his daughter Lydia in the middle of an epileptic fit because he was 'engaged to play the first fiddle at York that night' – probably in the music club that met at the George in Coney Street.[5] According to another anecdote relating to this period, he 'performed on the bass-viol to his friends; and his wife, who "had a fine voice and a good taste in music," sometimes contributed to the entertainment by accompanying her husband on his favourite instrument'.[6]

If anything, Sterne's interest in music increased around 1760, when he was involved with the singer Catherine Fourmantel,[7] and his fame as the author of *Tristram Shandy* began to give him access to society concerts, such as the one in May 1760 in which the Duke of York played the violin, or the Bach–Abel concert on 14 January 1767 which he described as 'the best assembly, and the best Concert I ever had the honour to be at'.[8] The latter was directed by J. C. Bach and presumably featured a gamba solo by Abel.[9] After Sterne's death in London on 18 March 1768 a 'Bass viol' found in his effects was disposed of for six guineas.[10] Once again, we cannot assume that 'bass viol' in this sort of context means the gamba, particularly since Sterne may have been a cellist: in 1757 he sold a copy of Salvatore Lanzetti's *vi Solos for Two Violoncellos with a Thorough Bass* (1737) to the Staffordshire landowner Samuel Hellier, who inscribed it 'Lanzetti's Solos bought of the so much celebrated Mr Sterne, Prebendary of York and author of Tristram Shandy & Garricks Sermons &c'.[11] However, it is often said in the literature that

[4] D. Griffiths, *A Catalogue of the Printed Music Published before 1850 in York Minster Library* (York, 1977), xv. The collections were apparently H. Albicastro, *Sonate da camera à tre*, op. 8 (Amsterdam, 1704/5); C. A. Marino, *Sonate à tre*, op. 7 (Amsterdam, 1706); *Vivaldi's most Celebrated Concertos in all their Parts* (London, 1715); and *The Second Part of Vivaldi's most Celebrated Concertos in all their Parts* (London, 1717), the last two the Walsh edition of *L'estro armonico*, op. 3 (Amsterdam, 1712); RISM A/I A 694, M 695, V 2204, V 2206; Griffiths, *A Catalogue*, nos. 4, 221, 304, 305.

[5] *The Monthly Repository of Theology and General Literature*, iii (1808), 376–7; D. Griffiths, *A Musical Place of the First Quality: a History of Institutional Music Making in York c. 1550–1990* (York, [1990]), 105.

[6] Given without a source in W. L. Cross, *The Life and Times of Laurence Sterne* (New Haven, CT, 3/1929), 67.

[7] See Cash, *Laurence Sterne, the Later Years*, 47–52.

[8] *Letters of Laurence Sterne*, ed. Curtis, 110–12, 296.

[9] *PA*, 13/1/1767.

[10] *Letters of Laurence Sterne*, ed. Curtis, 441.

[11] I. Ledsham, *A Catalogue of the Shaw-Hellier Collection in the Music Library, Barber Institute of Fine Arts, the University of Birmingham* (Aldershot, 1999), 155. See also L. Lindgren, 'Italian Violoncellists and some Violoncello Solos

Sterne was a gamba player, and he had connections with at least one of the female players discussed later: Margaret Georgiana, Countess Spencer. In 1761 Sterne dedicated the Story of Le Fever in Book 6 of *Tristram Shandy* to her, and stayed with her and her husband at Wimbledon Park.[12]

Sensibility, in the specialised sense applicable to Sterne and the eighteenth-century novel, is defined by the *OED* as the 'Capacity for refined emotion; delicate sensitiveness of taste; also, readiness to feel compassion for suffering, and to be moved by the pathetic in literature or art.'[13] One of its chief characteristics was the direct, sincere and lively expression of emotion associated with the writings of Jean Jacques Rousseau, particularly his novel *Julie, ou la nouvelle Héloïse* (1761). It can be a seen as a middle-class challenge to formal and cynical aristocratic manners, though, as we shall see, some aristocratic women espoused it as a means of asserting themselves and their female concerns in a male-dominated society. For similar reasons it had attractions for unconventional male aristocrats such as Sir Edward Walpole and John, Viscount Bateman, who had strong artistic interests and only a marginal role in politics and high society. Apart from Rousseau, Sterne was the writer most associated with the sensibility cult. Modern critics have tended to tended to emphasise the scandalous and satirical elements in *Tristram Shandy*, though his contemporaries preferred the pathetic and sentimental episodes, collected with similar material from *A Sentimental Journey* and *The Sermons of Mr. Yorick* (1760) in the wildly popular compendium *The Beauties of Sterne, including all his Pathetic Tales and most Distinguished Observations on Life, Selected for the Heart of Sensibility* (1782).[14]

❧ Ann Ford

S TERNE'S untimely death from tuberculosis was a story that might have appealed to 'the heart of sensibility', though the person who embodied the cult most completely was Ann Ford (1737–1824).[15] She came to prominence

Published in Eighteenth-Century Britain', in *Music in Eighteenth-Century Britain*, ed. D. W. Jones (Aldershot, 2000), 121–57, at 150–51.

[12] Cash, *Laurence Sterne, the Later Years*, 108–9; Ross, *Laurence Sterne*, 268–9.

[13] See esp. J. M. Todd, *Sensibility, an Introduction* (London, 1986); J. Mullan, *Sentiment and Sociability: the Language of Feeling in the Eighteenth Century* (Oxford, 1988); P. Langford, *A Polite and Commercial People: England, 1727–1783* (Oxford, 1989), 461–87.

[14] Ross, *Laurence Sterne*, 418–19, 469.

[15] See esp. 'Mrs. Thicknesse', *Public Characters of 1806* (London, 1806), 84–137; M. Rosenthal, 'Thomas Gainsborough's Ann Ford', *The Art Bulletin*, 80 (1998), 649–65; P. Holman, 'Ann Ford Revisited', *ECM*, 1 (2004), 157–81.

in the early 1760s for four main reasons. She was the subject of one of Thomas Gainsborough's most arresting portraits, probably painted in the summer of 1760 (Plate 15).[16] Her entanglement with the Earl of Jersey, made public by a pamphlet war in 1761, enabled her to portray herself as an innocent and virtuous woman at the mercy of an unscrupulous aristocrat, in the mould of the sentimental heroines in Richardson's novels *Pamela* and *Clarissa*.[17] Her attempts to promote public concerts initially attracted a good deal of attention, partly because it was unusual for an upper-middle-class female to perform in public, and because her father (a prominent solicitor) disapproved, and created a scandal by calling out the Bow Street Runners in an attempt to disrupt her first concert, on 18 March 1760.[18] Most important, however, was her affected style of performance. The poet William Whitehead wrote on 16 November 1758 that 'She has a glorious voice, & infinitely more affectation than any Lady you know. You would be desperately in love with her in half an hour, & languish & die over her singing as much as she does herself'.[19] In her first concert she reportedly 'displayed such exquisite sensibility' while singing 'Return, O God of hosts' from Handel's *Samson* that 'many of her friends actually burst into tears'.[20]

Ann Ford had many talents: she was a linguist, an artist, the author of several published works including an autobiographical novel, *The School of Fashion* (1800), and was admired for her acting and dancing.[21] However, her chief interest was music, and her first and main instrument was the viola da gamba. Her husband, the soldier, writer and adventurer Philip Thicknesse (1719–92), wrote in his pioneering account of Thomas Gainsborough that her 'fingers from a child had been accustomed' to playing the gamba,[22] which means that learned the instrument in the 1740s, at a time when it was at a low ebb in England. She was depicted in a lost painting by Nathaniel Hone in 'the character of a muse

---

[16] Cincinatti, Cincinatti Art Museum, no. 1927.396, bequest of Mary M. Emery. See E. Waterhouse, *Gainsborough* (London, 2/1966), 92, no. 660; M. Rosenthal, *The Art of Thomas Gainsborough* (New Haven, CT, 1999), 167–73; S. Sloman, *Gainsborough in Bath* (New Haven, CT, 2002), esp. 73–5, 193.

[17] See Holman, 'Ann Ford Revisited', esp. 169–72.

[18] Ibid., 171, 179.

[19] Volume of Whitehead letters, Stanton Harcourt Manor, Oxfordshire (Susan Sloman). I am grateful to the Hon. Mrs Gascoigne for permission to quote from the letter.

[20] 'Mrs. Thicknesse', 95–6.

[21] Holman, 'Ann Ford Revisited', esp. 160, 168–9.

[22] P. Thicknesse, *A Sketch of the Life and Paintings of Thomas Gainsborough, Esq.* (London, 1788), 26; CC: *ECCO*, T85246. For Thicknesse, see esp. P. Gosse, *Dr. Viper, the Querulous Life of Philip Thicknesse* (London, 1952).

playing on a lyre, sweeping the strings of the viol di gamba, and *expressing*, if not uttering, melody', while a gamba hangs on the wall in Gainsborough's painting of her, and she is playing the instrument in a drawing by Susanna Duncombe (Plate 16).[23]

Ann began her concert activities with a private series on Sundays; they presumably took place between October 1758 (when the castrato Giusto Ferdinando Tenducci, one of the performers, arrived in England) and March 1760 (when she began her public concerts).[24] There are two lists of 'occasional performers' in her biography, published in 1806. Apart from Tenducci, there were eight 'PROFESSORS': John Burton (harpsichord), Charles Froude or Frowd (violin), Joseph or Thomas Baildon (voice), 'Leoni', probably Gabriele Leoni (Spanish guitar), Stephen Paxton (violoncello), Thomas Arne (harpsichord), and Giuseppe Passerini (viola d'amore).[25] The 'AMATEURS' were Thomas Erskine, sixth Earl of Kelly (violin), the Countess of Tankerville (flute), Lord Dudley and Ward (voice), Lord Bateman ('viol di gamba'), Sir Charles Bingham (flute), the Marchioness of Rockingham (voice, who 'never sang but once'), and Philip Thicknesse ('theorb, or lute'). Ann herself is just given as playing 'the viol di gamba' with an otherwise unknown 'Saltero' listed immediately below her as playing 'Spanish guitar, archlute, and the piano-forte'. Bruce Alan Brown has suggested convincingly that this is an error, that 'Saltero' is actually an instrument rather than a person, and that she should also be credited with playing four more instruments: the psaltery (Ch. 4), Spanish guitar, archlute, and pianoforte.[26]

Ann certainly played many different instruments. In a preliminary drawing for Gainsborough's painting of her she holds a Spanish guitar,[27] while the author of her biography mentions that Gainsborough 'employed his pencil on her portrait; on which occasion she was represented tuning her harp, and leaning on her own compositions'.[28] When Philip Thicknesse put his Bath house up for sale in March 1775 the contents were auctioned, including 'a fine Milanese fiddle, a treble [i.e. triple] Welch harp, a guitar, and other musical instruments'.[29] She is shown with English guitars in the Gainsborough painting, in a drawing by Giovanni Battista Cipriani, and in a cartoon in one of the Ann Ford-Earl of

[23] London, Tate Gallery, T04273.

[24] 'Mrs. Thicknesse', 89–90.

[25] Holman, 'Ann Ford Revisited', 164–5, 167, 168.

[26] B. A. Brown, 'Ann Ford and the Salterio', *ECM*, 2 (2005), 377.

[27] Sudbury, Gainsborough's House, illus. in Holman, 'Ann Ford Revisited', 163.

[28] 'Mrs. Thicknesse', 88. A painting conforming to this description and said to be of Ann Ford is in a private collection (Mike Parker).

[29] W. T. Whitley, *Thomas Gainsborough* (London, 1915), 102–3.

Illus. 7.1 Ann Ford, 'All ye that pass by, to Jesus draw nigh',
Lessons and Instructions for Playing on the Guitar (London, ?1761)

Jersey pamphlets.[30] The last appears to show a guitar with a shallow lute-like body.

More information is found in the advertisements for her public concerts. Those for her 1760 subscription series at the Little Theatre in the Haymarket show that she played a solo on the gamba in each programme, and that she planned 'to accompany a Song, ('Oh Liberty, thou choicest treasure') on the Viol de Gambo' on 22 April. In addition, she played a concerto on the 'Guittar' (i.e. the English guitar) on 25 March, a 'Lesson and Song accompanied with the Guittar' on 8 April, a 'Lesson on the Guittar, and (by particular Desire) the 104th Psalm' on 14 April, and 'a Lesson on the Guittar, and … a Hymn set by herself' on 22 April.[31] The hymn was presumably 'All ye that pass by, to Jesus draw nigh', printed in an appendix to her treatise *Lessons and Instructions for Playing on the Guitar* (?1761) (Illus. 7.1).[32] Ann reportedly set it to make amends for laughing when the Methodist leader Selina Hastings, Countess of Huntingdon, 'drawled out or rather sung a long methodistical grace, with strange intonations, and so uncommon a cadence' at a dinner party; Ann's biographer added that it was 'still

30 Illus. Holman, 'Ann Ford Revisited', 162, 172.

31 Ibid., 179–80.

32 CC: GB-Lbl, i.160.c.

used in the chapels of this persuasion' – that is, in the Countess of Huntingdon's Connexion.[33]

Ann's first season of concerts made her £1,500,[34] so it is not surprising that she decided to put on another series in 1761.[35] She started by advertising a subscription concert on 23 January, though the subscriptions clearly did not come in as anticipated, for by 19 January she was warning that it would be 'the last Time of her appearing in Public'. In that concert she played a gamba solo, a lesson on the English guitar, and sang the 104th Psalm, accompanying herself 'on the Arch Lute'. In fact, it was not quite her last public appearance: from 15 October to 7 November 1761 she advertised that she would be available 'every Day between the Hours of One and Three' at Cox's Auction Room (near Spring Gardens on the eastern side of St James's Park) to sing 'a few English Airs, and accompanying herself on the Musical Glasses'; she would '(if desired) play a Solo on the Viol di Gambo, and a Lesson on the Guittar'. The musical glasses were a new accomplishment: in her published instructions for them, advertised on 2 November 1761, she stated it was 'not above four Weeks since I first heard them, and little more than a Fortnight since I made my first Attempt to play'.[36]

Ann's performances in the autumn of 1761 were a sad come-down from her successes the previous year. Cox's Auction Room was a much more obscure venue than the Little Theatre in the Haymarket, and Count Friedrich von Kielmansegge, a German visitor who heard her on the last day, implied that there was only one other performer, a violoncellist:

> In the morning of the 7th of November I went to hear Miss Four's [Ford's] concert. She is a pupil of Schumann, and has performed here for some time on musical glasses. She plays entire concerts with one finger, on a row of tuned wine-glasses, and is accompanied by a violoncello; she sings well, and has a good voice, accompanying herself on the *viola di Gamba* and guitar, and gives her audience a varied entertainment.[37]

By contrast, in 1760 there was an orchestra and distinguished soloists including the oboist Redmond Simpson, the bassoonist John Miller, and the violinist Thomas Pinto.

---

[33] 'Mrs. Thicknesse', 90–1.

[34] Holman, 'Ann Ford Revisited', 170.

[35] Ibid., 180.

[36] A. Ford, *Instructions for Playing on the Musical Glasses* (London, 1761), 3; CC: GB-Lbl, b.5, photographs of the apparently unique copy, US-CAh, Mus 372.2F.

[37] F. von Kielmansegge, *Diary of a Journey to England in the Years 1761–1762*, trans. S. P. Kielmansegg (London, 1902), 147–8.

Part of the problem was that, as Simon McVeigh has pointed out, the years 1761 to 1764 'saw a spate of daily exhibition performances given by young ladies and by self-publicising teachers', several of them, like her, playing 'novelty' instruments such as the musical glasses and the English guitar.[38] The musical glasses (wine glasses in a wooden frame tuned with water) were especially popular: other players included a Miss Lloyd (Ann's successor at Cox's Auction Room); Frederic Theodor Schumann (Ann's teacher); Marianne Davies (an exponent of Benjamin Franklin's glass harmonica; see below); and a Mr Drybutter (who offered 'Ten Tunes to each Set of Company' for only a shilling per person at his house in Pall Mall in late November and early December 1761).[39] Schumann was clearly competing aggressively with his pupil: from 27 October he offered to play 'every Day upon the GLASSES, between the Hours of One and Three' at his house in Bury Street, Piccadilly.[40] On 7 November, the day she gave up for good, he wrote in triumph: 'AS Mr. SCHUMAN's Performances on the MUSICAL GLASSES have given so great Satisfaction to the Public, he now begs Leave to return his grateful Thanks for the Encouragement he has met with'.[41] No wonder she called it a day.

The rest of Ann's long life can be briefly summarised. After her last London performance she accompanied Philip Thicknesse and his second wife, Lady Elizabeth, to Suffolk; at the time Philip was Governor of Languard Fort near Felixstowe. She was there when Lady Elizabeth died in childbirth on 30 March 1762. She became Thicknesse's third wife on 27 August 1762, and they subsequently moved to Welwyn in Hertfordshire, and then to a farm she had inherited in Monmouthshire. In 1766 they visited France, settling in Bath on their return. In 1775 they embarked on a year's journey through France and Spain, followed in 1782–3 by a similar trip to the Netherlands. In 1789 they moved from Bath to Sandgate near Hythe in Kent, and in 1791 they went on another trip to France. In 1792 they decided to settle in Italy, but Philip died suddenly on 19 November near Boulogne. Ann was subsequently imprisoned by the revolutionary authorities, narrowly escaping the guillotine. She was released in July 1794 and returned to London, where she lived quietly until her death on 20 January 1824.

Ann seemingly performed in public only once after her marriage, in aid of the Bath Casualty Charity as part of morning service at the Margaret Chapel in Bath on 12 December 1787. Between the first and second lessons she sang an

---

[38] S. McVeigh, *Concert Life in London from Mozart to Haydn* (Cambridge, 1993), 91.

[39] *PA*, 27, 30/11/1761; *PA*, 4/12/1761.

[40] *PA*, 27, 29, 30/10/1761; *PA*, 2, 4, 6/11/1761.

[41] *PA*, 7/11/1761; also *PA*, 11, 13, 16/11/1761.

anthem by John Weldon with organ accompaniment, probably taken from his *Divine Harmony* (1716), and after the prayers she sang her own setting of 'All ye that pass by' accompanying herself on the gamba.[42] Three pieces printed in *DUR* during 1787 make it clear that she was still a fine performer. On 10 February it reported: 'That Lady is an elegant, delicate, powerful, and learned performer on several instruments. Her vocal powers have seldom been equalled'. It continued on 29 June (nine days after Abel's death): 'By the death of Abel there is now but one capital *Viol Di Gambo* player in England, and that is a Lady, whose adagios, if not so highly dressed with graces, are not inferior, in point of sentiment and delicacy of touch, to that great master'. On 3 July it added: 'The best performer on the *Viol di Gamba* now in England, or perhaps in Europe, is Mrs. Thicknesse. She was second only to Abel, as a general player. In more particular points, she was his equal.' On 10 February she was also praised as a composer: 'her compositions possess a happy union of taste and science. Her sonatas for the Viol da Gamba, with accompaniments for the harpsichord, &c. would do honour to Abel.' The 3 July report went further: 'This accomplished lady has also composed for that instrument, and her compositions possess a degree of science, taste, and delicacy, which the best of Mr. Abel's productions never excelled.' Unfortunately, her gamba sonatas have not survived.

Ann Ford would have attracted attention had she been a model of propriety in her private life. Her attempts to earn her living by performing in public were remarkable for a woman of her time and social situation, though they were apparently driven by short-term expedience rather than proto-feminist convictions: once she was married and financially secure she conformed to the social norms of the day and essentially restricted herself to performing in private. Also, her decision to promote public concerts and to appear in them as an instrumentalist was not as daring as has been made out. Other women in similar circumstances include Marianne Davies (flute, glass harmonica, and keyboard); a Miss Carter (voice and harpsichord); and female violinists such as Elizabeth Plunkett, Maddalena Sirmen, Gertrud Elisabeth Mara née Schmeling, Hannah Taylor, and Louisa Gautherot.[43]

Simon McVeigh and Michael Rosenthal argued that Ann challenged the norms of the time by playing the gamba, claiming that it was a 'male' instrument.[44] We might think it was considered unsuitable for women because it

---

[42] 'Mrs. Thicknesse', 131; Holman, 'Ann Ford Revisited', 175–6.

[43] Holman, 'Ann Ford Revisited', 177. See also G. P. Ogden, 'Growth of Violin Playing by Women', *Violin Times*, 6 (4/1899), 106–8; F. G. E[dwards], 'Lady Violinists', *MT*, 47 (1906), 662–8, 735–40; McVeigh, *Concert Life in London*, 85–7.

[44] McVeigh, *Concert Life in London*, 87; Rosenthal, *The Art of Thomas Gainsborough*, 167.

normally required the legs to be parted, though the Duncombe drawing shows
Ann playing it 'side-saddle'. However, there is no evidence for this. Some female
gamba players in Britain and continental Europe have already been discussed
(Ch. 1), and more will be encountered later in this chapter. Ann was not even the
first woman to play it in public in London: Sarah Ottey, 'a young Gentlewoman',
played violin, harpsichord and 'Bass Viol' solos at Stationers' Hall on 9 March
1720 and at the Lincoln's Inn Fields Theatre on 2 May 1721 and 27 February 1723.[45]
There is a gamba in Nathaniel Hone's portrait of the singer, harpsichordist and
composer Elisabetta de Gambarini (1731–65), used as the frontispiece of her *Lessons for the Harpsichord, Intermix'd with Italian and English Songs*, op. 2 (1748)
(Plate 17), which suggests that she played it, unless its presence was just a pun on
her name.[46] Elisabetta could well have been Ann Ford's teacher. To judge from
the subscription lists of *Lessons for the Harpsichord* and her op. 1, *Six Sets of Lessons for the Harpsichord* (1748),[47] they moved in similar upper-class circles; Elisabetta's parents were Italian aristocrats. Gambarini was only seven years older
than Ann, though by the late 1740s (when Ann probably took up the gamba) she
was already singing for Handel, publishing her compositions, and playing the
harpsichord and organ in public concerts.

However, Ann was distinctive in that she concentrated on exotic instruments.
As a performer on the gamba, English and Spanish guitars, archlute, triple harp,
psaltery, musical glasses, and pianoforte, she exemplifies the fashion for exotic
instruments as much as the instrument maker John Frederick Hintz (Ch. 4). In
the late 1750s the pianoforte was still rare enough in England to be thought of as
exotic; production did not begin in London until the 1760s.[48] She also appears to
have encouraged other performers in her private concerts to play exotica: Philip
Thicknesse played the lute and theorbo; John, Viscount Bateman the gamba; and
Giuseppe Passerini the viola d'amore rather than his main instrument, the violin.
At the time such obsolete instruments were a fashionable novelty, chiming to
some extent with the current pre-Romantic enthusiasm for the past in all artistic
fields, including music. However, the revival of old music played on old instruments did not get under way until the 1830s and 40s (Ch. 9), and it is more likely
that Ann concentrated on them because they were suitable vehicles for her displays of sensibility. With an affected style of performance, moving her audiences

---

45 *DP*, 5/3/1720; *DC*, 2/5/1721; *DC*, 8, 17, 27/2/1723; see E[dwards], 'Lady Violinists',
     662.

46 CC: GB-Lbl, R.M.15.h.18. For Gambarini, see A. F. G. Noble, 'A Contextual Study
     of the Life and Published Keyboard Works of Elisabetta de Gambarini' (PhD
     diss., U. of Southampton, 2000).

47 CC: GB-Lbl, R.M.15.h.17.

48 See esp. M. Cole, *The Pianoforte in the Classical Era* (Oxford, 1998), 43–51.

to tears, she exemplified the display of direct and sincere emotion and artless self-absorption that was central to the cult. The gamba and the other instruments she played – soft, refined, plaintive and exotic – imply a Rousseauesque rejection of brilliance, virtuosity and the musical mainstream. Significantly, she seems to have avoided playing the harpsichord, the main vehicle for female virtuosity at the time.

Of course, this stance laid Ann open to ridicule. At the end of Act I of Charles Colman senior's afterpiece *The Musical Lady*, first performed at Drury Lane on 6 March 1762, the protagonist Sophy appears with her 'Viol-di-Gambo', and sings a 'little Venetian ballad-tune'.[49] She does not play it but hands it to her household musician Rosin, who accompanies her; Jane Pope, the actress portraying Sophy, presumably did not play the gamba. Sophy also has a set of musical glasses delivered and asks her servant to 'lay the Guittar and the Viol d'amour on the Harpsichord', saying 'I shall make use of them both'. The play satirises Ann as an eligible heiress (she was still single when it was put on); for her interest in exotic instruments; for her passion for Italian music (Ann published 'A Little Italian Ballad after the Manner of Venetian' in her treatises); and for her affected style of performance. In similar vein, Thomas Gainsborough wrote to James Unwin on 1 March 1764 about the education of his daughters as artists: 'I don't mean to make them only Miss Fords in the Art, to be partly admired & partly laugh'd at at every Tea Table; but in case of an Accident that they may do something for Bread.'[50] As Ann doubtless discovered when her concerts lost their fashionable appeal, exquisite sensibility could easily seem like amateurish affectation.

❧ *Female Aristocrats*

THE gamba had a more straightforward appeal for most aristocratic women: it had long been associated with princes and the aristocracy; its plaintive voice fitted in with contemporary notions of female reticence; it was the only bowed instrument that was socially acceptable for them to play; and it was not an orchestral instrument, so they avoided demeaning associations with professional musical life. The most interesting and important of Ann Ford's gamba-playing contemporaries was Elizabeth Herbert, Countess of Pembroke; they were both

---

[49] C. Colman, *The Musical Lady, a Farce as it is Acted at the Theatre-Royal in Drury-Lane* (London, 1762), 15–16; CC: *ECCO*, T041649 (Richard Sutcliffe). See *The London Stage 1660–1800*, 5 parts, 4: *1747–1776*, ed. G. W. Stone jr. (Carbondale, IL, 1962), 921.

[50] *The Letters of Thomas Gainsborough*, ed. J. Hayes (New Haven, CT, 2001), 25–8, at 26.

born in 1737. We encountered Elizabeth in Chapter 6 as the owner of most of the surviving sources of Abel's gamba music. She was presumably a pupil of Abel, though there is no direct evidence of this, and information about her musical activities is surprisingly difficult to come by.

She was born Lady Elizabeth Spencer, second daughter of Charles, third Duke of Marlborough. When she was eighteen, in 1756, she married the soldier Henry Herbert, tenth Earl of Pembroke (1734–94), and settled down with him at Wilton House near Salisbury – the probable scene of much viol playing more than a century earlier, when the third and fourth Earls of Pembroke were patrons of John Coprario and William Lawes.[51] The marriage had its ups and downs. Henry caused a scandal in 1762 by eloping to the Netherlands with the daughter of a lord of the Admiralty, though he was reconciled with Elizabeth the next year. He continued to have affairs, and in 1767 Elizabeth joined her brother, Lord Robert Spencer, in Paris. Henry and Elizabeth were reconciled again in 1770, though in November 1782 she became Lady of the Bedchamber to Queen Charlotte and subsequently settled at Pembroke Lodge in Richmond Park. Henry spent much of his later life abroad, and died at Wilton in 1794. Elizabeth will be familiar from Alan Bennett's play *The Madness of George III* and the ensuing film *The Madness of King George*, where she features as the object of the king's deluded affections during his bouts of madness. In the film she was portrayed as being much younger than she was in the late 1780s, and, improbably, as a seductive court intriguer.[52] She lived to a great age, dying in 1831.

Henry may have been an incorrigible rake (Horace Walpole was 'not surprised at any extravagance in his Lordship's morals'),[53] but he was not stupid: he rose rapidly through the army and published an influential book on equestrianism that went through four editions. He also shared an interest in music with Elizabeth and their son George Augustus. His main instrument was the violoncello: he supposedly imported a Stradivarius violoncello from Italy, commissioned Benjamin Banks of Salisbury to make one using wood from a cedar of Lebanon at

[51] See esp. *Henry, Elizabeth and George (1734–80): Letters and Diaries of Henry, Tenth Earl of Pembroke and his Circle*, ed. S. Herbert (London, 1939); *Pembroke Papers (1780–1794): Letter and Diaries of Henry, Tenth Earl of Pembroke and his Circle*, ed. S. Herbert (London, 1950); T. Lever, *The Herberts of Wilton* (London, 1967), 169–203.

[52] For the circumstances of her portrayal in the film, see A. Bennett, *Untold Stories* (London, 2005), 337, where he relates a Pembroke family anecdote about her 'glacial private parts', as he puts it in the index.

[53] *The Yale Edition of Horace Walpole's Correspondence*, 25: *Horace Walpole's Correspondence with Sir Horace Mann and Sir Horace Mann the Younger IX*, ed. W. S. Lewis *et al.* (London, 1971), 497.

Wilton, and was the dedicatee of James Cervetto's op. 1 violoncello solos.[54] There are autograph bills for lessons from Cervetto in 1772, 1773, 1776, and 1777, and from John Crosdill in 1777.[55] Elizabeth played the harpsichord and the gamba, and probably the English guitar as well: she was the dedicatee of a set of English guitar sonatas by Pasqualino di Marzis.[56]

There is a fascinating insight into Henry's musical interests and connections in GB-Ob, Tenbury MS 745, a manuscript labelled 'Pembroke 1777' containing two sequences of pieces in every key using no fewer than eight clefs.[57] The first consists of solos for violin and bass attributed to Cramer, Giardini, Gaetano Chiabrano (who taught Henry in Turin in 1769),[58] Corelli, Tartini, Locatelli, Handel, and others, while the second consists of duets for violin and cello by Schwindl, Giardini, Costanzi, Gehot, Campioni, Lidarti, and Demachi. Writing to George's tutor, William Coxe, on 23 March 1779, Henry made it clear that he commissioned the manuscript as part of George's musical education (hence the arcane clefs and keys), and that he had played the pieces over 'carefully with Giardini, Cramer, Bach, Abel, Crosdill, Cervetto, & Gehot, who have examined & corrected them carefully'.[59]

Henry patronised prominent members of London's immigrant musical community, including the violinist Giuseppe Soderini in the 1760s and early 1780s.[60] Elizabeth Harris described Felice Giardini playing after a dinner at Wilton on 19 November 1772, while on 9 September 1777 John Marsh mentioned that the Flemish violinist Joseph Gehot was 'frequently staying' there.[61] Chiabrano, Cramer and Giardini appear in Wilton House accounts for 1770 and 1771, while the vio-

---

54 W. Sandys and S. A. Forster, *The History of the Violin* (London, 1864), 227, 362; J. Cervetto, *Six Solos for the Violoncello with a Thorough Bass for the Harpsicord*, op. 1 (London, 1768); RISM A/1 C 1731; CC: GB-Lbl, h.204.i.(1).

55 Chippenham, Wiltshire and Swindon History Centre, 2057/A6/15; 2057/A6/21.

56 P. di Marzis, *Six Sonatas for the Cetra or Kitara, with a Thorough Bass* (London, c. 1760); RISM A/1 P 997; CC: GB-Lbl, e.376. The date in *BLIC*, c. 1750, is too early for the English guitar (Ch. 4). For di Marzis, see Lindgren, 'Italian Violoncellists', 143.

57 See E. H. Fellowes, *The Catalogue of Manuscripts in the Library of St. Michael's College, Tenbury* (Paris, 1934), 149.

58 *Henry Elizabeth and George*, ed. Herbert, 157.

59 Ibid., 156–7.

60 *Pembroke Papers*, ed. Herbert, 136; *The John Marsh Journals: the Life and Times of a Gentleman Composer (1752–1828)*, ed. B. Robins (Stuyvesant, NY, 1998), 240; *Music and Theatre in Handel's World: the Family Papers of James Harris, 1732–1780*, ed. D. Burrows and R. Dunhill (Oxford, 2002), 694–5.

61 *The John Marsh Journals*, ed. Robins, 165.

linist Antonio Lolli was paid in 1773 and 1774.[62] A bill listing music William Napier sold to Henry in 1776–7 includes sets of violoncello solos by Stephen Paxton (op. 1); accompanied sonatas by Cecilia Maria Barthélemon and Hüllmandel (op. 3); duets by Asplmayr (probably op. 3); trios by Campioni and Sacchini (op. 1); quartets by J. C. Bach, Abel and Giardini, Boccherini (op. 10), and Schetky (op. 6); 'concerto symphonies' by Davaux (op. 7); and keyboard concertos by J. C. Bach (probably op. 13).[63] Elizabeth must have been able to read the treble clef to play Abel's gamba sonatas, so she might have played violin parts from these collections, though, like Abel, she may also have played viola parts on the gamba.

There seem to be only two pieces of evidence (apart from her manuscripts) that Elizabeth was a gamba player. Elizabeth Harris wrote to her son on 13 November 1774 about an all-female production in Salisbury of Mallet's play *Elvira* and Garrick's *Florizel and Perdita*.[64] She quoted a note sent by Henry to her husband, James Harris: 'I can snuff candles; I can scrape on the violoncello[;] if either of those sciences will entitle me to a place in your theatre I will perform gratis[.] P S My wife says she can thrum the harpsecord or viol de gamba'. On 11 July 1780 Sir William Hamilton, British Resident in Naples, told George Augustus that he had 'left off the fiddle' and had 'taken to the Tenor' – i.e. the viola.[65] He went on: 'I should think some of Abel's Musick for the Viol di Gamba wou'd do well on the Tenor', and asked him for copies of 'any old solos or pieces of his Musick ... out of Lady Pembroke's books' to be sent to him with her permission.

Elizabeth may have come into contact with Abel at the Salisbury Festival as early as 1759 (Ch. 5), though the main period of musical activity at Wilton seems to have been between 1770, when she came back from Paris, and 1782, when she entered the queen's service. It is possible, of course, that she learned the gamba from Elisabetta de Gambarini rather than Abel (Gambarini's father Charles published a description of the Wilton pictures in 1731),[66] or from someone in Paris in the late 1760s. If the latter, then the two non-autograph sequences of solos, GB-Lbl, Add. MS 31697, Items 6 and 7, which are apparently graded pieces for a beginner, could date from the early 1770s; they might be the 'old solos or pieces' referred to by Hamilton. They were probably copied by one of the resident musicians at Wilton, such as Ciabrano, Soderini or Gehot. Elizabeth's other manuscripts of

---

[62] Chippenham, Wiltshire and Swindon History Centre, 2057/A5/4; 2057/A6/7.

[63] Chippenham, Wiltshire and Swindon History Centre, 2057/A6/21.

[64] *Music and Theatre in Handel's World*, ed. Burrows and Dunhill, 778.

[65] *Henry, Elizabeth and George*, ed. Herbert, 494–5.

[66] C. Gambarini, *A Description of the Earl of Pembroke's Pictures* (Westminster, 1731); CC: GB-Lbl, c.193.a.256.

Abel's gamba music contain rather more difficult music and may therefore be a little later.

Several of Elizabeth's relatives also seem to have played the gamba. Margaret Georgiana, Countess Spencer (1737–1814) was her first cousin by marriage and her exact contemporary: she was the daughter of the diplomat Stephen Poyntz and married John Spencer, later first Earl Spencer, in 1755.[67] John was the younger brother of Charles Spencer, Elizabeth's father, who became third Duke of Marlborough in 1733. Her married life, at Althorp in Northamptonshire, at Wimbledon Park, and at Spencer House in London, was a happy contrast to Elizabeth's at Wilton. She is best known today as the mother of the Whig society hostess Georgiana Cavendish, Duchess of Devonshire, though she was a remarkable woman in her own right. Mrs Delany described her shortly before her marriage as 'well educated, a most sensible, generous, delicate mind, and I think a very agreeable person', while the antiquarian Cardinal Albani, who met her in Rome in 1764, described her as the most accomplished woman he had ever met.[68]

Early in their marriage the Spencers were glamorous and fashionable members of society, though she continued to be interested in more serious things. She was an accomplished linguist, dabbled in art, botany and poetry, and included leading intellectuals in her social circle, including Garrick, Rousseau and Sterne. Interestingly, given the connections between the gamba and sensibility, Betty Rizzo sees her as an example of the way genteel women in the second half of the century used it as 'a badge of superiority': 'sensibility, with its concomitant benevolence (or altruism), was not only the superior moral position but also the only admissible superiority for the submissive gender'.[69] This came to the fore after her husband's death in 1783, when she retired to Holywell House in St Albans. As a widow she was best known for her determined and formidably well-organised charitable activities.

As a musician, Margaret Georgiana seems to have been a gamba player first and foremost, though she was painted by Pompeo Batoni in 1764 with an English guitar,[70] and Giardini dedicated to her his *Six Trios for the Guittar, Violin and Piano Forte; or Harp, Violin and Violoncello,* op. 18 (1775).[71] Like Ann Ford, she may have been taught the gamba by Elisabetta de Gambarini: her mother-in-law,

---

[67] For Margaret Georgiana, see esp. J. Friedman, *Spencer House: Chronicle of a Great London Mansion* (London, 1993), esp. 51–63, 198–203.

[68] *The Autobiography and Correspondence of Mary Granville, Mrs. Delany,* ed. A. Hall, 3 vols. (London, 1861), iii. 340; Friedman, *Spencer House,* 55.

[69] B. Rizzo, *Companions without Vows: Relationships among Eighteenth-Century British Women* (Athens, GA, 1994), 240, also 255–66.

[70] For the painting, see Friedman, *Spencer House,* 50–1.

[71] RISM A/I G 1955; CC: GB-LEbc, Brotherton Collection, Music GIA.

yet another Georgiana (1716–80) and the wife of the Hon. John Spencer, was a subscriber to Gambarini's op. 2. To judge from bills among the Althorp papers, Margaret Georgiana was active as a gamba player in the 1770s: there are payments to George Gardom on 12 March 1772 for 'Puting A Viol da Gamba in Order', and for a set of strings on 15 July; on 12 October he was paid for putting the same instrument or another one in order and for another set of strings; on 14 January 1775 a J. Barrett was paid 7s. 6d. for a 'Bow for the Viola da Gamba'[72] In a letter to Margaret Georgiana dated 29 December 1779 her friend Caroline Howe wrote: 'I should like to be hearing one of y^r. new pieces of musick upon y^r Viol de gamba. Did you surprise Ld Spencer?'[73]

The Althorp accounts also list music purchased, some from Robert Bremner, including sets of accompanied sonatas by J. C. Bach (op. 10), Boccherini (op. 3), Schobert (opp. 5, 8 and 9), and Vento (books 4 and 5); a set of trios by Kammel, and his notturnos (op. 6) for two violins and bass; quartets by Haydn (opp. 1 and 2); quintets by J. C. Bach (op. 11); overtures or symphonies by Abel (opp. 7 and 10); and two collections listed as 'Ables Sonatas for the harpsicord' and 'Able Sonatas'.[74] Obvious possibilities are Abel's accompanied sonatas opp. 2 (1760) or 5 (1764), or the *Six Easy Sonnatas for the Harpsichord or for a Viola da Gamba, Violin or German Flute* (Ch. 6). Like their Herbert cousins, the Spencers mostly favoured chamber music by up-to-date German and Italian composers, though they also purchased James Nares's six keyboard fugues (1772) and a set of accompanied sonatas by John Garth. Margaret Georgiana also probably used the treble clef to read gamba solos and violin parts and the alto clef to read viola parts.

The other Spencer by marriage who may have played the gamba was Lavinia, Viscountess Althorp (1762–1831). She was the eldest daughter of Charles Bingham, first Earl of Lucan, and in 1781 she married Margaret Georgiana's only son, George John Spencer, Viscount Althorp. Lavinia was a strong-willed and cultured woman like her mother-in-law, though nothing is known of her musical activities at present except that she was the dedicatee of Tommaso Giordani's *Three Sonatas for the Piano-forte or Harpsichord with Obligato Accompaniments for the Flute or Violin and Viola de Gamba or Tenor*, op. 30 (1782).[75] Giordani (c. 1730–1806) spent the 1770s working for the Italian opera house in London,

---

[72] GB-Lbl, Add. MS 75755. I am grateful to Ian Woodfield for drawing the Althorp Papers to my attention.

[73] GB-Lbl, Add. MS 75614.

[74] GB-Lbl, Add. MS 75755.

[75] RISM A/I G 2286; CC: GB-Lbl, g.272.v.(6), keyboard part only. It has been completed with photographs of the other parts from the unique complete copy, sold at Christie's in 1979 and now in a private collection. ME of no. 3: ed. U. Drüner (Adliswil, 1982).

contributing music to operas and probably playing the harpsichord.[76] In the 1780 and 1781 seasons he seems to have taken part in the concert series at the Pantheon,[77] though it was probably the failure of his comic opera *Il bacio* after three performances in April 1782 that prompted him in 1783 to return to Dublin, where his family had settled in the 1760s. Giordani's involvement with the Haymarket Theatre and the Pantheon concerts makes it unlikely that his op. 30 trios were written with Abel in mind. The Italian operatic community mostly managed to keep German musicians out of the Haymarket Theatre, and the Pantheon concerts were started in 1774 to compete with the Bach–Abel concerts with 'a blatantly anti-German stance … featuring Italian and English music'.[78] There are no known gamba players among Giordani's professional colleagues, so it is likely that he wrote the sonatas for his dedicatee – who presumably paid for the publication.

Giordani seems 'always to have been near the bottom of the pecking-order of the King's Theatre composers',[79] and was accused at the time of stealing passages from J. C. Bach and others.[80] So it is surprising and pleasing to find that his op. 30 sonatas are substantial works, with a sophisticated relationship between the instruments. The keyboard sometimes plays a figured bass, sometimes has a concerto-like part, and sometimes joins in equal dialogue with the other instruments, which have more interesting and demanding parts than in conventional keyboard concertos or accompanied sonatas; Giordani was an important innovator in this respect.[81] In op. 30 flute and gamba are the first options on the title-page, and the top part is labelled 'Flute' when it is cued in the keyboard part. The lower obbligato part is sometimes cued as 'Tenor' in the keyboard part, though its part has 'VIOLA' – i.e. viola da gamba – as a running title at the top of each page. In range, clef and musical idiom it suits both instruments equally well. It is surprising that gamba players have largely ignored these sonatas, since their *galant* musical idiom – stolen or otherwise – is most attractive (Ex. 7.1).

We saw in Chapter 5 that Charles Pratt, first Earl Camden wrote to the Foreign Secretary on 29 December 1782 about Abel's financial difficulties, mentioning

[76] C. Price, J. Milhous and R. D. Hume, *Italian Opera in late Eighteenth-Century London*, i: *The King's Theatre, Haymarket, 1778–1791* (Oxford, 1995), esp. 278, 280, 282–3.

[77] See esp. McVeigh, *Concert Life in London*, 15, 17; *GZ*, 24/1/1780.

[78] McVeigh, *Concert Life in London*, 15.

[79] Price, Milhous and Hume, *Italian Opera in late Eighteenth-Century London*, i: 280.

[80] *ABC Dario Musico* (Bath, 1780), 24–5; CC: *ECCO*, T019051.

[81] See T. Giordani, *Three Quintets for Keyboard and Strings*, ed. N. Temperley, RRMCE, 25 (Madison, WI, 1987), vii, ix.

Ex. 7.1 Tommaso Giordani, Sonata in B♭ major, op. 30, no. 3,
Larghetto sostenuto, bb. 46–62

Ex. 7.1 *continued*

that 'I among others have a friendship for Abel who taught one of my daughters'.[82]
The daughter in question was presumably the one that the doctor, poet and sati-
rist John Wolcot *alias* Peter Pindar praised in verse in 1787, incidentally showing
that Abel's name was pronounced in the English fashion:

> There too the rare *Viol-di-Gamba* PRATT,
> Whose Fingers fair, the Strings so nicely pat,
> And Bow, that brings out Sounds unknown at Babel –
> Though not so sweet as those of Mr. ABEL.
>
> Dear Maid! the daughter of that PRINCE of PRATTS,
> Who Music *cons*, as well as Law; and swears
> The Girl shall *scrub* no Soul's but Handel's Airs,
> To whom he thinks our great Composers, Cats.

---

[82] Bedford, Bedfordshire and Luton Archives and Record Service, L30/14/320/2. For
Pratt, see H. S. Eeles, *Lord Chancellor Camden and his Family* (London, 1934).

> *Id est*, SACCHINI, HAYDN, BACH, and GLUCK,
> And Twenty more, who never had the Luck
> To please the nicer ears of *some crown'd* FOLK:[83]

Pratt had four daughters, of whom only Elizabeth (d. 1826) seems to have been unmarried in 1787, and was therefore still a maid and a Pratt. The verses imply that her father was an obstinate Handelian, insisting that she played nothing but Handel on her gamba. The 'nicer ears' presumably belonged to George III, another Handel fanatic. Elizabeth was evidently a fine player: it was reported in 1789 that 'A daughter of the Earl of CAMDEN performs, with great taste, on the *Viol de Gamba*. This is the only Lady, in this country who has attempted any performance on this instrument – and with justice we may say she excels, as she accompanies and plays well in *Quartetts*'.[84]

&. *Male Aristocrats*

IT was socially acceptable for upper-class men to play violin-family instruments at this period – it enabled them to participate in domestic ensemble music and in amateur orchestras – so their reasons for playing the gamba were less obvious and more diverse than their female counterparts. It must often have been simply a way of appearing distinctive and discerning to their friends. This may be so in the case of Edward (later Sir Edward) Walpole (1706–84), the inventor of the pentachord (Ch. 5).[85] He had held court posts and was a Member of Parliament, though he only had a marginal position in public life, partly because of his consuming interests in music and the fine arts, and partly because of his unconventional private life: he lived openly with a former milliner, Dorothy Clements (d. 1738), and then with her sister Jane, and was falsely accused of sodomy in 1750.[86]

He is glimpsed mostly through the writings of his younger brother Horace. On 25 May 1745 Horace recommended a trip to Edward's house in Englefield Green in Surrey, praised Edward's 'pretty children', and mentioned that he

---

[83] P. Pindar, *Ode upon Ode, or A Peep at St James's, or New-Year's Day, or What You Will* (London, 1787), 36–7; CC: ECCO, N010878.

[84] *MP*, 24/2/1789.

[85] For Walpole, see *The Gentleman's Magazine*, 54/1 (1/1784), 74; *The Last Journals of Horace Walpole during the Reign of George III from 1771–1783*, ed. A. F. Steuart, 2 vols. (London, 1910), i. esp. vii–viii; W. S. Lewis, *Rescuing Horace Walpole* (New Haven, CT, 1978), 34–42.

[86] For the case, see esp. N. M. Goldsmith, *The Worst of Crimes: Homosexuality and the Law in Eighteenth-Century London* (Aldershot, 1998), 109–96.

'plays extremely well on the bass-viol, and has generally other musical people with him'.[87] According to Horace, Edward was a favourite of Frederick, Prince of Wales, and was 'constantly a performer at his private concerts' at Leicester House.[88] Frederick insulted him at one concert by asking him if he was 'a fiddler by profession', at which 'Sir Edward started with rage, and, running to the bell, rung it violently, and a page entering, bade him take away a bass viol and call his servants'. The dispute, which was about political allegiance, was soon resolved, and Edward later presented the prince with 'a valuable Cremonese violoncello'. We might wonder whether Edward's 'bass viol' really was a gamba were not it for the fact that Horace, who was certainly knowledgeable enough to distinguish between the two instruments, seems to have done so on this occasion. Also, Abel gave Edward's pentachord its first public outing in 1759, and was therefore probably his teacher and the recipient of his patronage. In a touching tribute Horace mentioned Edward's 'great natural eloquence, wit, humour even to admirable mimicry, uncommon sensibility, large generosity and charity', adding that 'he drew well, but seldom' and 'was a profound musician' who chiefly shone in 'pathetic melancholy'.[89] Once again, the gamba is associated with sensibility and pathos.

Benjamin Franklin (1706–90), inventor, scientist, writer and American patriot, was of humble origins but moved in English high society during his periods in London from 1757 to 1762 and from 1764 to 1775 as the agent of Pennsylvania and (latterly) other American colonies. As a musician is he best known for inventing the *armonica* or glass harmonica, a mechanised version of the musical glasses in which glass bowls were fixed in a nested sequence on a spindle, enabling their rims be played much like a keyboard when turned by a treadle; in its final form the required moisture was provided by keeping the glasses dipped in a shallow trough of water.[90] Franklin also owned and presumably played several other exotic instruments. His son-in-law Richard Bache wrote to him on 14 July 1778 listing some of the musical instruments stolen from his house during the British occupation of Philadelphia: 'a welch harp, bell harp, the set of tuned bells which were in a box, Viol de Gambo, all the spare Armonicas Glasses and one or two of the spare cases. Your armonica is safe'.[91]

[87] *The Yale Edition of Horace Walpole's Correspondence, 9: Horace Walpole's Correspondence with George Montagu I*, ed. W. S. Lewis and R. S. Brown jr. (London, 1941), 14.

[88] *The Last Journals of Horace Walpole*, ed. Steuart, i. 104–6.

[89] Lewis, *Rescuing Horace Walpole*, 35.

[90] A. H. King, 'Musical Glasses [Armonica; Harmonica; Glass Harmonica]', *GMO*.

[91] *The Papers of Benjamin Franklin, 27: July 1 through October 31, 1778*, ed. C. A. Lopez *et al.* (New Haven, CT, 1988), 88–92, at 89.

On 5 December 1789 Franklin asked his friend Benjamin Vaughan in London to:

> procure for me one of those little Books that teach to tune and play upon the Instrument called *Viol de Gambo*; which is about the Size of a Bass Viol, but is not the same, this having *Six Strings*. Send with the Book a Bow proper for the Instrument, and a Set of Strings. I suppose they may be had at any Music Shop.[92]

The only printed 'little book' of this sort, *The Compleat Violist* (1699), was presumably long out of print, though basic information could have been obtained from general instruction books such as William Tans'ur's *The Elements of Musick Display'd* (1772) (Ch. 2). Franklin owned a gamba by 1778, so it is likely that the requests were for someone else. It is not known when and where he first encountered the gamba, though he was acquainted with Margaret Georgiana Spencer and her husband while he was in London in the early 1770s.[93] Incidentally, by describing the gamba as 'about the Size of a Bass Viol but ... not the same', Franklin provided more evidence that 'bass viol' commonly meant the violoncello.

We have seen that John, second Viscount Bateman (1721–1802) played the gamba in Ann Ford's private concerts. He too had Spencer blood in his veins: his father William married Anne Spencer in 1720, so he was first cousin to Elizabeth, Countess of Pembroke, and first cousin by marriage to Margaret Georgiana, Countess Spencer. He was described (possibly by Philip Thicknesse) as 'one of the most accomplished noblemen of the age; his good sense and liberal education; taught him to know the world early in life; and his good spirits and great fortune, enable him to make a proper use of both'.[94] He was a friend of Thicknesse, subscribing to five copies of his 1777 travel book.[95] In a letter of 1 June 1773 written from Bateman's London house in Park Lane, Thicknesse mentioned 'taking a string from a Viol Di Gambo', probably for Bateman.[96] Thicknesse may have played the gamba himself: an etching of his cottage near Languard Fort made

---

[92] Unpublished letter, see *The Papers of Benjamin Franklin* (www.franklinpapers. org).

[93] *The Papers of Benjamin Franklin, 19: January 1 through December 31, 1772*, ed. W. B. Willcox *et al.* (New Haven, CT, 1975), 275, 447. See also *The Papers of Benjamin Franklin, 34: November 16, 1780, through April 30, 1781*, ed. B. B. Oberg *et al.* (New Haven, CT, 1998), 253–4.

[94] P. Thicknesse (attrib.), *Sketches and Characters of the most Eminent and Singular Persons now Living, by Several Hands* (Bristol, 1770), 34; CC: *ECCO*, T064122.

[95] P. Thicknesse, *A Year's Journey through France and Part of Spain*, 2 vols. (Bath, 1777), [iii]; CC: *ECCO*, T085368. See also Gosse, *Dr. Viper*, esp. 148–62.

[96] US-SM, MS TH 74, quoted by permission (Susan Sloman).

by Thomas Gainsborough in 1753–4 has a border decorated with various musical instruments, including a bass viol, suggesting that he took it up long before he met Ann (Plate 18).[97]

Bateman was also a patron of Gainsborough, though sometimes with some reluctance, according to Thicknesse.[98] Gainsborough visited Bateman several times at his country estate, Shobdon Court in Herefordshire, and Bateman commissioned from him a small portrait and a landscape.[99] Thicknesse later claimed to have urged Bateman to 'give him [Gainsborough] countenance and make him known', thus ensuring his subsequent success in London.[100] Another friend and patron of Gainsborough, the amateur artist Coplestone Warre Bampfylde (1720–91) of Hestercombe near Taunton, owned 'A Viola da Gamba by J. C. Hoffmann of Leipsig' among a number of stringed instruments, including a Stradivarius violin.[101] Little is known of his musical activities.

❧ Thomas Gainsborough and Musical Artists

THIS brings us to Gainsborough's musical interests, and more generally to late eighteenth-century gamba-playing artists. In addition to the features that attracted members of the *bon ton*, artists were inspired by the gamba's elegant shape and by its frequent appearances in sixteenth- and seventeenth-century paintings. The first was apparently the Welsh painter Thomas Jones (1742–1803). According to his memoirs, Jones 'began learning to play on the violdigamba' in March 1766, soon after his pupilage with Richard Wilson expired and he set up on his own.[102] Unfortunately, his teacher, 'who was a foreigner, after having put me to the expence of ten or twelve Guineas for the Instrument, Entrance &c disappeared, which put an end to that piece of Business'. There are no further refer-

---

[97] I am grateful to Susan Sloman for drawing this etching to my attention.

[98] R. R. Wark, 'Thicknesse and Gainsborough: some New Documents', *The Art Bulletin*, 40 (1958), 331–4.

[99] Waterhouse, *Gainsborough*, 53, 114, nos. 48, 912; Rosenthal, *The Art of Thomas Gainsborough*, 80, 81, 202, 203.

[100] Sloman, *Gainsborough in Bath*, 225, fn. 41; Thicknesse, *A Sketch of the Life and Paintings of Thomas Gainsborough*, 32.

[101] Christie, *A Catalogue of a Valuable Collection of Engravings and Etchings in Portfolios, Books and Books of Prints, Formed by the late C. W. Bampfylde, Esq.* (7, 8/7/1820), 6, lot 1/107 (Susan Sloman, Philip White). For Bampfylde, see Sloman, *Gainsborough in Bath*, esp. 128–30, 132.

[102] 'Memoirs of Thomas Jones, Penkerrig, Radnorshire, 1803', ed. A. P. Oppé, *Walpole Society*, 32 (1951), whole vol., at 11. For Jones, see esp. *Thomas Jones (1742–1803): an Artist Rediscovered*, ed. A. Sumner and G. Smith (New Haven CT, 2003).

ences to the gamba in Jones's memoirs, though the elder Thomas Shaw of Bath taught him the violoncello at North Aston in Oxfordshire in March 1773.[103]

Gainsborough probably met Abel when the composer made his Bath debut in February 1760 (Ch. 5), and subscribed to his op. 2 sonatas.[104] However, there is no evidence of Gainsborough playing the gamba until his famous letter to the musician, writer and artist William Jackson, in which he mentioned that 'My Friend Abel has been to visit me, but he made but a short stay, being obliged to go to Paris for a Month or six weeks, after which He has promised to come again.'[105] Later in the letter Gainsborough exclaimed: 'I'm sick of Portraits and wish very much to take my Viol de Gam and walk off to some sweet Village where I can paint Landskips and enjoy the fag End of Life in quietness & ease', and added: 'My Comfort is, I have 5 Viol's da Gamba, 3 Jayes and two Barak Normans'. The letter is just headed 'Bath June 4th', though it may have been written in 1769.[106] Abel figures a few times in Gainsborough's later letters. Writing to the artist Giovanni Battista Cipriani on 14 February 1774, he mentioned 'a Tune … that Abel wrote for me', presumably for the gamba, that he had left in Giardini's house.[107] In a letter to David Garrick, written on 24 or 25 March 1774 and known only in extracts, someone or something was 'shut up in a Viol da Gambo-case … to be lost in the harmony of Abel's sweet-sounding Instrument'.[108]

The other important contemporary evidence of Gainsborough's interest in the gamba is a letter from Philip Thicknesse to John Cooke dated 4 August 1774:

> Mrs. Thicknesse has quarreled with Gainsborough – this has vexed me, yet I think she had some cause, – he fell in love with her viol de gambo (& it certainly is the finest in the world) – he more than once *said to me* he would give an hundred guineas for it: I persuaded her to give it to him: & she did upon condition he painted my picture at full length. When he had got my face in & my body sketched, with my dog, *Boy*, he, instead of finishing it, set it by, to paint Fis[c]her the Hautboy player, at full length: & painted him in Scarlet, laced, like a Colonel of the Guards: – now Mrs. Thicknesse who happened to see Fischer in a *laced, coat finished* (a picture *not to be paid for.*) & mine in plain *ked kigg, it turned her sick*: so without saying anything

[103] 'Memoirs of Thomas Jones', ed. Oppé, 27.

[104] Sloman, *Gainsborough in Bath*, 101, 235, fn. 18.

[105] *The Letters of Thomas Gainsborough*, ed. Hayes, 67–8.

[106] Implied by its placing between a letter to Joshua Kirby dated 5 December 1768, ibid., 61, and one to Jackson dated 'Feb: 6th', said by Hayes to be 'probably 1770', ibid., 70.

[107] Ibid., 123–4.

[108] Ibid., 125.

to me, she wrote him a saucy [letter], & he sent the Viol back. However he and I are as we were, and I have insisted upon it, that he finishes the picture very well, & sends it to Mrs. Thicknesse, because I asked him where he could find a woman who had *such an instrument* to show herself to advantage upon, who would have given it up, for the picture of an old superanuated invalid soldier – & that I should answer the Question – no where but in the Crescent at Bath. He is ashamed, for he shall *never* have the viol now, & I don't care a farthing about the picture: – yet I have been vexed about this business …[109]

A much longer version of this story in Thicknesse's biography of Gainsborough adds the information that the viol in question was 'made in the year 1612, of exquisite workmanship, and mellifluous tone', and was 'certainly worth an hundred guineas'.[110] After the death of Thicknesse's daughter the instrument was 'sold to M^r. Brodrep' – presumably the London music and musical instrument seller Francis Broderip. Perhaps it was one of the three instruments by Henry Jaye that Gainsborough mentioned in his letter to Jackson, though no Jaye viol dated 1612 is known today.[111]

As often with Thicknesse, there is another side to the story. In 1829 the writer Allan Cunningham recorded a different version of the incident, 'communicated to me by a lady who had it from Mrs. Gainsborough herself':

The painter (according to this account) put an hundred guineas privately into the hands of Mrs. Thicknesse, for the viol-di-gamba; her husband, who might not be aware of what passed, renewed his wish for his portrait; and obtained what he conceived to be a promise that it should be painted. This double benefaction was, however, more than Gainsborough had contemplated: he commenced the portrait, but there it stopped; and after a time, resenting some injurious expressions from the lips of the governor [Thicknesse], the artist sent him the picture, rough and unfinished as it was, and returned also the viol-di-gamba.[112]

---

[109] Wark, 'Thicknesse and Gainsborough', 333. For Gainsborough's painting of J. C. Fischer, see esp. Waterhouse, *Gainsborough*, 67, no. 252; Sloman, *Gainsborough in Bath*, 104–5.

[110] P. Thicknesse, *A Sketch of the Life and Paintings of Thomas Gainsborough*, 20–31, at 21.

[111] M. Fleming, T. MacCracken and K. Martius, 'Provisional List of Extant Viols by Henry Jaye', *Jaye Project* (http://www.vdgs.org.uk/information-JayeProject.html).

[112] A. Cunningham, *The Lives of the most Eminent British Painters, Sculptors, and Architects*, 6 vols. (London, 1829–33), i. 332–3.

The most famous account of Gainsborough's gamba playing is in Jackson's 'Character of Gainsborough', published in 1798.[113] Jackson began by stating that 'Gainsborough's profession was painting, and music was his amusement – yet, there were times when music seemed to be his employment, and painting his diversion'. He then introduced his main theme: that Gainsborough became obsessed with a succession of instruments belonging to famous performers, naively believing that by purchasing the instrument he would also acquire the vendor's skill. Jackson began his account of these crazes with Giardini:

> When I first knew him he lived at Bath, where Giardini had been exhibiting his *then* unrivalled powers on the violin. His excellent performance made Gainsborough enamoured of that instrument; and conceiving, like the Servant-maid in the Spectator, that the music lay in the fiddle, he was frantic until he possessed the *very* instrument which had given him so much pleasure – but seemed much surprised that the music of it remained behind with Giardini![114]

Gainsborough established himself in Bath in 1758 and painted Giardini in the early 1760s, so this episode, if it ever took place, presumably occurred about then.[115]

According to Jackson, Gainsborough next became obsessed with Abel's gamba:

> He had scarcely recovered this shock (for it was a great one to *him*) when he heard Abel on the viol-di-gamba. The violin was hung on the willow – Abel's viol-di-gamba was purchased, and the house resounded with melodious thirds and fifths from "morn to dewy eve!" Many an Adagio and many a Minuet were begun, but none completed – this was wonderful, as it was Abel's *own* instrument, and therefore *ought* to have produced Abel's own music![116]

Jackson went on to describe similar infatuations with Fischer's oboe and a triple harp (it was 'not a pedal-harp') owned by an unnamed musician, before 'another visit from Abel brought him back to the viol-di-gamba'. 'This, and occasionally a

---

[113] W. Jackson, *The Four Ages, together with Essays on Various Subjects* (London, 1798), 147–61; CC: *ECCO*, T135509.

[114] Jackson, *The Four Ages*, 148.

[115] For Gainsborough's portrait of Giardini, see Waterhouse, *Gainsborough*, 70, no. 311.

[116] Jackson, *The Four Ages*, 148–9.

little flirtation with the fiddle, continued some years', though Jackson mentioned a later infatuation with John Crosdill's violoncello.[117]

This is all very entertaining, but others thought more highly of Gainsborough's musical prowess, and Jackson's anecdotes are sometimes contradicted by other evidence. In a letter to James Unwin on 7 November 1765 Gainsborough mentioned 'a little Fiddle that Giardini pick'd up here at Bath, which nobody would think well of, because there was nobody who knew how to bring out the tone of, and which (though somewhat undersized) in his Hands produced the finest Music in the World', showing that he was quite able to distinguish between the quality of an instrument and its player.[118] The connoisseur and amateur artist Sir George Howland Beaumont remembered in 1824 that Gainsborough once 'offered any picture he had to a friend of mine for a fiddle', even though his friend was 'a very indifferent performer', yet Gainsborough saw 'it was an excellent fiddle & very rationally thought it would enable him to make the best use of his own skill'.[119]

Jackson wrote that Gainsborough 'hated the harpsichord and the piano-forte',[120] though the artist owned a Shudi and Broadwood harpsichord: the firm's accounts for 5 March 1774 read: 'Mr. Dashwood and Gardine [Giardini] bought a harp[sichor]d, no. 708, for Mr. Gainsborough, painter in the Circle, Bath.'[121] The fencing master Henry Angelo, whose father was a friend of Gainsborough, wrote that the painter 'could modulate to a certain degree on a keyed instrument, and used frequently to chaunt any rhodomontade that was uppermost, accompanying himself with the chords on my mother's *piano-forte*'; Angelo described him reading through old music, including 'Purcell's chaunt', 'a specimen of old Bird', and 'a touch of [James] Kent and old Henry Lawes', much to J. C. Bach's amusement.[122] He also quoted part of Jackson's essay, though he judged it 'somewhat of a caricature', pointing out that Gainsborough could 'accompany a slow movement of the harpsichord, both on the fiddle and the flute, with taste and feeling'.[123] In

[117] Ibid., 149–51.

[118] *The Letters of Thomas Gainsborough*, ed. Hayes, 36–7.

[119] *The Letters of Thomas Gainsborough*, ed. M. Woodall ([Ipswich], 2/1963), 181, 183, where it is wrongly dated 11/11/1829. The original letter, at Birmingham Museum and Art Gallery, is dated 11/11/1824 (Susan Sloman).

[120] Jackson, *The Four Ages*, 160.

[121] D. H. Boalch, *Makers of the Harpsichord and Clavichord, 1440–1840*, rev. C. Mould (Oxford, 3/1995), 621. See also W. Dale, *Tschudi the Harpsichord Maker* (London, 1913), 67–9.

[122] *Reminiscences of Henry Angelo, with Memoirs of his late Father and Friends*, 2 vols. (London, 1828), i. 184–5.

[123] Ibid., i. 186–8.

another late anecdote Gainsborough is pictured taking 'his fiddle, or his viol de gamba' to 'strum Matthew Locke's music for *Macbeth*, whilst he accompanied with his mellifluous voice part of the witches' song, and repeated over and over "dance to the hopper of the mill"'.[124] Gainsborough was clearly interested in old music, though he was not to know that the famous *Macbeth* music was actually written by Richard Leveridge rather than Locke.[125]

Jackson made his most controversial statement in his summing up: 'In this manner he frittered away his musical talents; and though possessed of ear, taste, and genius, he never had application enough to learn his notes. He scorned to take the first step, the second was of course out of his reach; and the summit became unattainable'.[126] However, in a letter dated 3 March 1800 'Arbitrator' described Jackson's anecdotes as 'a series of improbable tales', and went on to make a very different assessment of Gainsborough's musical abilities:

> Your present correspondent has, more than once, seen Gainsborough *playing from notes*; but not content with his own oracular testimony, he has applied to several musicians of eminence, who had a personal knowledge of that artist, and they unite in opposing Mr. Jackson's statement: nay, one of them assures me, that Abel composed a *fugue* purposely for his friend Gainsborough to practise on the viol-di-gamba: – And could this be done without having learned his notes?
>
> I am told, that the above celebrated artist, and musician, who had once been convivial associates, were, of late years, estranged from each other, and I therefore impute to a *lapsus memoriae*, what I cannot suppose to have arisen from intentional misrepresentation.[127]

Gainsborough must have been a fine player if the fugue in question was Abel's in D major, WKO 196, for unaccompanied gamba (Ch. 6). The suggestion that he and Jackson 'were of late years estranged from one another' is interesting, for we have only one rather formal letter from Gainsborough to Jackson after 20 January 1773,[128] and one gets the feeling that something was biting Jackson, even if it was only the need to feel more confident about his mediocre talents as a painter by

---

[124] [W. H. Pyne], 'The Greater and Lesser Stars of Old Pall Mall, Chapter I', *Fraser's Magazine for Town and Country* (11/1840), 547–59, at 551.

[125] R. Fiske, 'The *Macbeth* Music', *ML*, 45 (1964), 114–25. The phrase 'dance to the hopper of the mill' is a misremembered version of 'to which we dance in some old mill upon the hopper stone or wheel' in 'Let's have a dance upon the heath'.

[126] Jackson, *The Four Ages*, 154.

[127] *The Monthly Mirror*, 9 (1800), 146–7.

[128] *The Letters of Thomas Gainsborough*, ed. Hayes, 110–11, 140.

denigrating Gainsborough's as a musician.[129] The painter and diarist Joseph Farington, writing after Jackson's death in 1803, thought that the composer became embittered because of his relatively low status in the musical world:

> As a musician Jackson had talents which enabled him to produce some very popular compositions, but he was not sufficiently scientific to enable him to be able to take a lead in London with Dr. Arne & others: this & other circumstances it is believed affected his temper. – [Ozias] Humphrey was acquainted [with] him 30 years ago, at which period He was very pleasant[.][130]

Jackson admitted to Humphry in 1778 that his friendship with Gainsborough had 'suffered some abatement', though he mentioned several visits to the painter's London house in a letter of October 1783.[131] Jackson's fine song with gamba obbligato, 'When fond, you Damon's charms recite', published in his *Twelve Songs*, op. 16 (1793), may be a souvenir of this period.[132]

In many ways, the Revd Henry Bate (later Sir Henry Bate Dudley) is a more reliable witness than Jackson. He was a close friend of Gainsborough, and was one of his most prominent public supporters as editor and proprietor of *The Morning Herald*.[133] He was also a friend of Abel (Ch. 5) and was the recipient of Gainsborough's impassioned response to the composer's death, written a few hours after the event.[134] Thus it is significant that his assessment of Gainsborough the musician agrees with 'Arbitrator' rather than Jackson:

> He touched that instrument [the viola da gamba] with the most exquisite skill, truth, and expression; and in an adagio movement, or largo, his richness of tone, expression, and feeling brought him very near indeed to Abel's standard. Let a musician who has heard him, speak, and he will con-

---

[129] For Jackson as a painter, see J. Hayes, 'William Jackson of Exeter: Organist, Composer and Amateur Artist', *The Connoisseur*, 173 (1970), 17–24; A. Asfour and P. Williamson, *William Jackson of Exeter (1730–1803)* (Sudbury, 1997).

[130] *The Diary of Joseph Farington*, 16 vols., vi: *April 1803-December 1804*, ed. K. Garlick and A. Macintyre (New Haven, CT, 1979), 2114, entry for 24/8/1803.

[131] A. Asfour and P. Williamson, 'William Jackson of Exeter: New Documents', *Gainsborough's House Review* (1996–7), 39–152, at 113–15, 135, fn. 3.

[132] RISM A/I J 190–192; CC: GB-Lbl, G.362.(4); ME: ed. D. J. Rhodes, VdGS Music, 192 (n.p., 2003). It was entered at Stationers' Hall on 25/1/1793; see *Music Entries at Stationers' Hall, 1710–1818*, comp. M. Kassler (Aldershot, 2004), 190.

[133] See esp. Rosenthal, *The Art of Thomas Gainsborough*, 96–8. For *MH*, see S. McVeigh, 'London Newspapers 1750 to 1800: a Checklist and Guide for Musicologists', in *A Handbook for Studies in Eighteenth-Century Music*, 6 (Oxford, 1996), whole vol., esp. 4–8, 32–33.

[134] *The Letters of Thomas Gainsborough*, ed. Hayes, 164. Bate quoted from the letter in *MH*, 21/6/1787.

fess this. Dr. [John] Walcot, who is an excellent musical critic, after hearing Gainsborough about two years since, in an adjoining room, play a minuet of Vanhall's, and an allegro air, exclaimed, 'That must be Abel, for by God, no man besides can so touch an instrument!' Mr. Abel certainly presented Gainsborough with a viol de gamba, but this was in return for two valuable landscapes and several beautiful drawings. This instrument was worth little, but at Mr. Abel's death the instrument which Mr. Gainsborough seriously admired he purchased, and paid forty guineas for; and at the same sale the presents from the genius of the pencil to the musician sold for about £200, though they consisted only a part of his liberal gifts.[135]

There are several points of interest here. It shows that Gainsborough maintained his interest in the gamba until the last years of his life, and that he was accomplished enough to be mistaken for Abel. Some sets of instrumental music by the Bohemian composer Johann Baptist Vanhal were republished in London, though there are no surviving original gamba works by him; the minuet in question was presumably an arrangement.[136] Most important, it gives us more information about gambas owned by Gainsborough. The one he 'seriously admired' and purchased for 40 guineas was probably the 'capital viol de gamba, in a mahogany case, his best instrument' in Abel's sale (I/44). I argued in Chapter 5 that it was the Tielke gamba offered for sale in Hamburg in 1783, now in the Victoria and Albert Museum; its later history is explored in Chapter 8.

We can learn more about Gainsborough's musical possessions from Jackson's essay. It includes an anecdote about Gainsborough's purchase of a lute and a book of lute lessons from an unnamed 'German professor', prefaced by the comment that 'upon seeing a Theorbo in a picture of Vandyke's; he concluded (perhaps, because it was finely painted) that the Theorbo must be a fine instrument'.[137] Gainsborough was fascinated by the proportions and craftsmanship of stringed instruments. Jackson wrote that he had 'as much pleasure in looking at a violin as in hearing it', and added: 'I have seen him for many minutes surveying, in silence, the perfections of an instrument, from the just proportion of the model, and beauty of the workmanship.'[138] Gainsborough found the German professor in a garret 'at dinner upon a roasted apple, and smok-

[135]   *MH*, 25/8/1788, quoted from Whitley, *Thomas Gainsborough*, 362 (Susan Sloman).

[136]   See esp. *Themen-Verzeichnis der Kompositionen von Johann Baptiste Vanhal*, comp. A. Weinmann (Vienna, 1988); P. R. Bryan, *Johann Wanhal, Viennese Symphonist: his Life, his Symphonies and his Musical Environment* (Stuyvesant, NY, 1997).

[137]   Jackson, *The Four Ages*, 151.

[138]   Ibid., 160.

ing a pipe'.[139] The conversation between the two, which eventually resulted in the artist buying the lute and the lute book and securing the promise of lessons, features a picturesque attempt to render a German accent, as in *'May lude ish wert much monnay! it ish wert ten guinea'* or *'Ah, py cot, I can never part wit my poog!'*

It is clear that the professor was the German lutenist and harpsichordist Rudolf Straube (Ch. 4). A manuscript version of the story in Straube's lute manuscript, GB-Lbl, Add. MS 31698, fols. 43–43v, is headed 'Gainsborough the Artist & Rodolph Straube'; it contains some variants, including different spellings of Straube's German accent, suggesting that it was not just copied from Jackson. John Marsh, who visited Straube on 13 February 1777 in a vain attempt to buy a lute for a friend, Mr Chafy, reported that the garret was in Pimlico, and found that Straube had only one lute 'which he play'd & wo'd not part with (at least for a second hand price) & as he gave me little or no hope of meeting with one elsewhere I at length gave over the search'.[140] Straube was also presumably the unnamed German lutenist described by Jackson as playing an air with twenty-four variations, 'every strain of which he most punctually repeated!'[141] The Revd John Chafy (1719–82), vicar of Great Bricett in Suffolk, was painted playing the violoncello by Gainsborough around 1750–2 shortly before he moved to Alveston in Wiltshire.[142] He built himself a house in the Close at Salisbury, and was involved in Salisbury musical life (where he came into contact with Marsh) playing the violoncello and English guitar.[143]

Corroboration that Gainsborough did purchase Straube's lute is provided by items in the sale catalogue of his effects, auctioned on 2 July 1792: 'A lute' (87), 'Ditto [i.e. another lute], a very fine tone' (88), and 'An Amatus [Amati] violin and a tenor in a case' (89).[144] An unfinished portrait by Gainsborough of his daughter Margaret shows her playing a large lute or theorbo

139 Ibid., 151–4.

140 *The John Marsh Journals*, ed. Robins, 158.

141 Jackson, 'A Proper Length Necessary for Musical and Literary Productions', *The Four Ages*, 415–19, at 417.

142 London, Tate Gallery, T03895 (http:www.tate.org.uk); Rosenthal, *The Art of Thomas Gainsborough*, 183–4.

143 *The John Marsh Diaries*, ed. Robins, esp. 145, 147, 148, 153–6, 159, 161, 180, 188, 214, 218, 223, 224.

144 Christie, *A Catalogue of the Remainder of the Capital Collection of Pictures, Drawings, etc. of that Ingenious and Esteemed Artist, Mr. Gainsborough, Dec.* (2/6/1792); CC: New York, Frick Art Library, quoted with permission (Susan Sloman).

(Plate 19),[145] while a further sale of Gainsborough's effects on 11 May 1799 included 'A Spanish guitar, curiously inlaid' (114) and 'A lute ditto [i.e. curiously inlaid]' (115).[146] The lute was sold for £2 10s. to 'Hopner' – that is the painter John Hoppner (1758–1810). Hoppner was another musical artist: he had been a choirboy in the Chapel Royal and painted Haydn for the Prince of Wales in 1791–2.[147] The instruments in question may be the thirteen-course lutes by J. C. Hofmann (1725) and Michael Rauche (1762).[148] Hofmann, like Straube, was from Leipzig, while the Rauche lute is beautifully decorated with ebony and ivory – fitting the description of the 'curiously inlaid' lute. Rauche published all three of Straube's English publications, two of which are for English guitar,[149] and an English guitar is depicted on the back of the upper peg-box of the Rauche lute. Gainsborough's gambas did not feature in these sales, and must have been disposed of separately.

The connection between artists and the gamba did not cease with Gainsborough: we shall see in the next chapter that Thomas Cheeseman and John Cawse played it, and owned a cache of old instruments and music, including Add. MS 31698, the only known item from Gainsborough's music library. It is sometimes said that the tenor viol ascribed to Richard Blunt, now in the Ashmolean Museum in Oxford, once belonged to the painter John Constable (1776–1837), though the instrument was attributed variously to John Shaw, William Baker, Richard Blake and Richard Blanke in the twentieth century,[150] and there seems to be no hard evidence that the painter ever owned a viol; no instruments appear in the catalogue

[145] Illus. Whitley, *Thomas Gainsborough*, facing 122, where it is identified as Mary Gainsborough and is said to be 'in the collection of Mr. Adolf Hirsch'. Its present whereabouts are unknown and it is now thought to be a portrait of Margaret Gainsborough; see Waterhouse, *Gainsborough*, 68, no. 281.

[146] Christie, *A Catalogue of the Remainder of the Capital and Valuable Books of Genuine Sketches, Studies and Designs after Nature, Books of Prints, Architecture, Musical Instruments, and two Laymen, of the late Celebrated Artist, Thos Gainsborough, Esq. Dec.* (11/5/1799); CC: Christie's, quoted with permission.

[147] For Hoppner, see esp. J. H. Wilson, 'The Life and Work of John Hoppner (1758–1810)' (PhD diss., U. of London, 1992).

[148] London, Horniman Museum, no. 1975.506, formerly in the Dolmetsch collection (Matthew Spring); GB-Lv, no. 9–1871; see A. Baines, *Victoria and Albert Museum, Catalogue of Musical Instruments*, ii: *Non-Keyboard Instruments* (London, 1968), 31, figs. 43, 43A, 44.

[149] R. Straube, *Lessons for Two Guittars with a Thorough Bass* (London, c. 1765); CC: GB-Lbl, e.108.ff.(2); R. Straube, *Three Sonatas for the Guittar, with Accompanyments for the Harpsichord or Violoncello* (London, 1768; repr. 1979); R. Straube, *The Mecklenburgh Gavotte, with Six Variations for the Harpsichord, Pianoforte* (London, ?1768); CC: GB-Lbl, e.374.b.

[150] For instance, J. Whitely, *Stringed Instruments: Viols, Violins, Citterns, and Guitars in the Ashmolean Museum* (Oxford, 2008), 12–13. However, see M.

of his household effects, sold in 1838.[151] However, he was certainly musical: lot 147 of the 1838 sale was 'A music stool', and he is said to have owned a small viola of 1682 by William Baker of Oxford,[152] as well as a violoncello with the label 'Made by / JOHN DUNTHORNE. / East-Bergholt Suffolk / March 11th 1803'.[153] Dunthorne (1770–1844), Constable's friend, fellow artist and early mentor, wrote to him on 21 March 1802 about 'a violoncello which I have nearly finished'.[154] It may be that this instrument was referred to as a 'bass viol' by Constable's family or in the early literature, giving rise to the legend that he owned a real viol.

❧ *Conclusion*

FUTURE research will doubtless bring more viola da gamba players to light among England's late eighteenth-century aristocrats, artists and writers, though a pattern has now emerged. One or two of them may have played the gamba before Abel arrived in London in 1759, perhaps taught by Elisabetta de Gambarini, though the majority ware apparently inspired to take it up by Abel's example, and some of them may have been his pupils. They must have chosen it for the same reasons as attracted aristocrats and distinguished people to the gamba in other parts of Europe: it had historic aristocratic associations; it had never been a regular member of the orchestra; it marked the player out as someone with distinctive taste; and it was the only bowed instrument that was socially acceptable for upper-class women to play. Most important, its low, plaintive and refined voice became strongly associated with the English sensibility cult around 1760. Artists saw gambas (and other exotic instruments) in sixteenth- and seventeenth-century paintings they admired, and were attracted by their complex shape and beautiful craftsmanship. We shall see in the next chapter how professional musicians responded to Abel's example, and how his influence lasted far into the nineteenth century.

Fleming, 'The Identities of the Viols in the Ashmolean Museum', *VdGSJ*, 3 (2009), 117–30, esp. 119–20.

[151] Foster, *A Catalogue of Household Furniture, Books, Pictures, Prints, &c., by Order of the Administrator of the late John Constable, Esq. R. A.* (22/12/1838); CC: GB-Lv.

[152] *The British Violin: the Catalogue of the 1998 Exhibition '400 Years of Violin and Bow Making in the British Isles'*, ed. J. Milnes (Oxford, 2000), 23.

[153] Ipswich, Christchurch Mansion, 1941-20A; see B. Neece, 'The Cello in Britain: a Technical and Social History', *GSJ*, 56 (2003), 77–115, at 99–100.

[154] *John Constable's Correspondence*, 6 vols., 2: *Early Friends and Maria Bicknell (Mrs. Constable)*, Suffolk Records Society, 6 (Ipswich, 1964), 30.

CHAPTER 8

'The Art of Playing it has never
Died Out in this Country':
Abel's Competitors, Followers and Successors

O N 4 March 1889 Edward Payne, lecturing on the viola da gamba to the
Musical Association in London, stated: 'I could prove, if it were necessary,
that the art of playing it has never died out in this country, but that the traditions
of the instrument have survived in a constant succession of amateur players'.[1]
This assertion will come as a surprise to those brought up with the myth that
the gamba needed reviving in the late nineteenth century, and that Arnold Dolmetsch was the person who accomplished the task in Britain.[2] Yet Payne knew
what he was talking about, and was not the sort of person to make wild, unverifi-
able claims. He was a lawyer, honorary recorder of his native High Wycombe, and
distinguished historian of America and the colonies. As a musician, he played
the violin, the gamba and the lute, and was an acknowledged expert on early
stringed instruments, contributing many articles to *Grove 1*, including 'Violin'.
His obituary singled out his concern for historical accuracy: 'it must be allowed
that there was nothing careless or slipshod about his mode of reaching his results.
He accepted no mere gossip or idle tradition such as readily accumulate about
famous workers in all careers'.[3]

This chapter and the next will substantiate Payne's statement from two contrasted perspectives. This one examines Abel's influence on his colleagues, com-
petitors and successors, and traces his legacy in nineteenth-century Britain. For
much of that time players continued to treat the gamba as an exotic but essentially contemporary instrument, and played modern or relatively recent music on
it. Chapter 9 discusses the gamba's role in the developing early music movement,

---

[1] E. J. Payne, 'The Viola da Gamba' *PMA*, 15 (1888–9), 91–107, at 93. For Payne, see
J. Catch, 'Edward John Payne, Victorian Gambist', *GSJ*, 50 (1997), 127–35; J. Catch,
'A Buckinghamshire Polymath: Edward John Payne', *Records of Buckingham-
shire*, 32 (1990), 120–9.

[2] Payne's statement is contested in J. B. Rutledge, 'Late Nineteenth-Century Viol
Revivals', *EM*, 19 (1991), 409–18, at 409. See also the correspondence in *EM*, 20
(1992), 525–6.

[3] *MT*, 46 (1905), 114–15.

the emphasis there being on a decisive break with tradition and the self-conscious revival of old music played on old instruments. These two attitudes existed side-by-side for much of the century and can sometimes be found expressed in the activities of a single individual. Thus Edward Payne stands at the end of a tradition inherited from Abel, but was also involved in early music revivals of the 1880s.

❧ *Abel's Competitors*

ABEL'S presence in England had as profound an effect on his fellow professionals as it had on amateurs (Ch. 7). The gamba does not seem to have been played in public in London between Saint-Hélène's appearance on 10 May 1732 and Abel's debut on 5 April 1759. However, there may have eight or more professional gamba players working in England at various times between 1759 and Abel's death in 1787. Of the eight, four are unnamed: (1) the person – presumably a member of the Drury Lane orchestra – who took the part of Rosin in Colman's play *The Musical Lady* in March 1762, which involved playing the gamba on stage (Ch. 7); (2) the foreigner who took the painter Thomas Jones's money for some gamba lessons in March 1765 and then disappeared (Ch. 7); (3) the person who appeared in a concert at Cooper's Hall in King St, Bristol on 17 January 1771: the programme included 'A Song by Miss Marshall, accompanied by the Piano Forte and Viol de Gambo' and 'A favourite Lesson on the Harpsichord by Miss Marshall, accompanied by the Viol de Gambo';[4] and (4) the copyist of the Williamson Manuscript.

Of these, (2) will probably remain unidentified; Abel was a foreign gamba player but would surely have been mentioned by name by Jones, and he did not disappear in 1765. (3) may have been the Mr Marshall who also appeared in the concert. Miss Marshall, from Nottingham, was eleven years old, so he was presumably her father; she was presumably the person who played a five-string violoncello in York and Newcastle in 1774 (Ch. 5). Ann Thicknesse née Ford was living nearby in Bath at the time, though she would surely not have been allowed to appear incognito – least of all by her publicity-seeking husband.

However, (1) is readily identifiable. The violinist and inventor Charles Clagget purchased a gamba from James Watt in July 1761, probably for his violoncellist brother Walter (Ch. 4). They were both in Newcastle in 1758–9, moving to Scotland late in 1759: they gave a joint concert in St Mary's Chapel in Edinburgh on 25 March 1760, and Bremner published a set of their violin duets in Edinburgh around then, stating on the title-page that 'This Work may likewise be had of

---

4 *The Bristol Journal*, 12/1/1771 (Ian Woodfield, Jonathan Barry).

the Authors'.[5] Soon after Walter moved to London: he played violoncello solos in concerts at the Haymarket Theatre on 26 February 1761 and the George Tavern in Westminster on 30 March 1762, and on 13 April 1762 put on a benefit concert at the George Tavern which included 'Lesson on the Viola da Gambo by Mr. Claget', 'Solo on the Violoncello by Mr. Claget', and '(by particular desire) the Second of Stanley's Concertos' – presumably John Stanley's op. 2, no. 2, with its eloquent violoncello solo.[6] Later in that year Walter wrote music for *The Witches, or Harlequin Cherokee*, put on 23 November at Drury Lane.[7] The actor James Dance *alias* Love, who devised *The Witches*, had been manager of the Canongate Theatre in Edinburgh while the Claggets were there, which is probably why Walter was chosen to write its music. Walter is the obvious person to have played Rosin in *The Musical Lady*.

Like his brother, Walter was a versatile musician and led a varied life. In Bath in October 1758 he described himself as 'Musician and Dancing-master' who taught the 'Violin, Violoncello, Guitar, German-Flute' as well as tuning harpsichords and spinets, and listed his instruments as 'Violin, Violoncello, Tennor [viola], Double Bass, Oboe, German flute, Clarinet &c.' when he joined the Society (later Royal Society) of Musicians on 4 April 1784.[8] He had returned to his native Ireland by the summer of 1766, when he joined his brother in the Rotunda orchestra in Dublin, and he remained there for some years.[9] His second period in London is obscure because of confusions between him, his brother and the Crispus Clagget who ran the ill-fated Apollo Gardens, though it probably lasted from

5   *The Edinburgh Evening Courant*, 25/3/1760; *Six Duetts for Two Violins Intended to Improve and Entertain Practitioners, by Messrs. Claget* (Edinburgh, ?1760); CC: GB-Lbl, h.210.a.(4). For the Claggets in Newcastle, see R. Southey, 'Competition and Collaboration: Concert Promotion in Newcastle and Durham, 1752–1772', in *Concert Life in Eighteenth-Century Britain*, ed. S. Wollenburg and S. McVeigh (Aldershot, 2004), 55–70, at 67–8; R. Southey, *Music-Making in North-East England during the Eighteenth Century* (Aldershot, 2006), 26, 43, 170, 205.

6   *PA*, 26/2/1761; *PA*, 30/3/1762; *PA*, 13/4/1762.

7   W. Clagget, *The Comic Tunes in The Witches, or Harlequin Cherokee, as they are Perform'd at the Theatre Royal in Drury Lane, Set for the Violin, German Flute, or Harpsichord* (London, 1762), RISM A/I C 2545; CC: GB-Lbl, C.152. See also *The London Stage, 1660–1800*, 5 parts, 4: *1747–1776*, ed. G. W. Stone jr. (Carbondale, IL, 1962), esp. 964; R. Fiske, *English Theatre Music in the Eighteenth Century* (Oxford, 2/1986), 407.

8   R. D. Leppert, 'Music Teachers of Upper-Class Amateur Musicians in Eighteenth-Century England', in *Music in the Classic Period: Essays in Honor of Barry S. Brook*, ed. A. W. Atlas (New York, 1985), 133–58, at 140–41; B. Matthews, *The Royal Society of Musicians of Great Britain, List of Members, 1738–1984* (London, 1985), 36–7.

9   B. Boydell, *Rotunda Music in Eighteenth-Century Dublin* (Dublin, 1992), 77.

1784 until 1790, when he resigned from the Royal Society of Musicians, presumably because he was leaving the capital. He is recorded in Newcastle from spring 1791: his son William was buried at St Andrew's church on 1 March, and a benefit concert in the city on 22 March included 'Violoncello solo, by Mr. CLAGGET, from LONDON'.[10] He remained in Newcastle until his death on 27 January 1797; he was buried in St Nicholas's church the following day, and a benefit concert for his 'widow and five young children' was advertised for 1 February, when he was described as joining 'the most amiable and inoffensive disposition' to 'ingenuity in his profession'.[11]

The only other reference to Walter as a gamba player is in an advertisement for concerts in June 1766 at the concert hall in Fishamble Street, Dublin – the room where *Messiah* was first performed.[12] 'Messrs. Claget' promised to accompany the singers on 'Guitars, Italian and Spanish, the Viola-di-Gamba, the German Flute and the Musical Glasses', and Walter advertised 'Several Sets of Musical Glasses' for sale, giving his address as 'near the Bank in Mary's Abbey'. He had encountered musical glasses in London in February 1763, when he was advertised as accompanying a Mr. Largeau in daily performances at the Swan and Hoop Tavern near the Royal Exchange.[13] Walter mostly wrote attractive but unenterprising solos and duets for violoncellos or violins, often incorporating popular tunes. No gamba music by him survives, though two collections of violoncello solos he published at the time he was playing the gamba might have provided him with suitable material, and could do so today.[14]

Our fourth unidentified gamba player is the copyist of the Williamson Manuscript, three part-books now in GB-Lu, Special Collections, MS 944/2/1–3.[15] It contains a set of six early eighteenth-century gamba sonatas apparently arranged and compiled by a gamba player in London around 1730, including a seemingly original gamba sonata by Pietro Giuseppe Sandoni and arrangements of music by Barsanti, Handel and Angelo Michele Besseghi (Ch. 3). But the part-books

---

[10] Information from Roz Southey; *The Newcastle Courant*, 19/3/1791.

[11] Information from Roz Southey; *Newcastle Chronicle*, 28/1/1797.

[12] Boydell, *Rotunda Music in Eighteenth-Century Dublin*, 79.

[13] PA, 10/2/1763.

[14] *Six Solos for Two Violoncellos* (London, ?1761); RISM A/I C 2552; CC: GB-Lbl, g.305.a; *Six Solos and Six Scots Airs, with Variations for the Violin or Violoncello with a Thorough Bass for the Harpsichord*, op. 2 (London, 1762); RISM A/I C 2547; CC: g.502.(2). The former is dated *c.* 1763 in *BLIC*, but is probably the same as the 'Six Solos for a Violoncello, by Mr. Clagett' advertised among 'NEW MUSICK' in *The Kentish Post*, 26–30/9/1761 (Joan Jeffery).

[15] P. Holman, 'A New Source of Bass Viol Music from Eighteenth-Century England', *EM*, 31 (2003), 81–99.

were copied much later: they also contain seven trio sonatas by the Bavarian composer Maximilian Humble, six of which were published in London as his op. 1 (1768); an anonymous string trio labelled 'S^r. Bach. R' (perhaps meaning that it had been revised or corrected – *rivedúto* – by J. C. Bach); and the gamba part of an otherwise-unknown piece by Abel (Ch. 6). The collection seems to have been owned in turn by John Williamson senior (1740–1815), a Canterbury surgeon; his son John (1790–1828), also a Canterbury surgeon; the organist Stephen Elvey (1805–60); and his brother Sir George (1816–93); it was donated to London University in 1925. John Marsh mentioned John Williamson senior a number of his times in his diary as a steward of the Canterbury orchestra in the 1780s and as a participant in other musical events; he described him as 'a very steady & good performer (as far as his execution went) upon the fiddle[,] tenor or violoncello'.[16]

The most interesting of these encounters came on 21 September 1786, when Marsh described a musical tea party that included Williamson and the cellist and composer Stephen Paxton (1734–87), who was visiting Canterbury.[17] Paxton was a violoncellist first and foremost, but he also played the gamba. In an undated letter of 1810–13 to the Methodist minister Adam Clarke, the Catholic bluestocking Mary Freeman Shepherd discussed the conversion of the composer Samuel Wesley to Catholicism in 1784, mentioning that she heard of the event from 'Mr. Payton', the 'famous viol-de-gamba performer'.[18] Another letter, written by Shepherd to Samuel Wesley himself in the 1790s, shows that 'Payton' was a slip of the pen: she meant to write 'Paxton'.[19] The 1810–13 letter was written long after the event, though it is clear that Shepherd knew Paxton (a fellow Catholic) in the 1780s, so there is no reason to doubt her testimony. It becomes more credible when we remember that Paxton played the violoncello in Ann Ford's private concerts in the late 1750s, when he would have come into contact with Ann and other gamba players.

Paxton was born in Durham but was based in London from 1756, and would therefore have been well placed to acquire the music in the Williamson manuscript. However, a comparison between the literary hand in the manuscript and

---

[16] *The John Marsh Journals: the Life and Times of a Gentleman Composer (1752–1828)*, ed. B. Robins (Stuyvesant, NY, 1998), 299.

[17] Ibid., 384–6. For Paxton, see esp. B. Crosby, 'Stephen and other Paxtons: an Investigation into the Identities and Careers of a Family of Eighteenth-Century Musicians', *ML*, 81 (2000), 41–64.

[18] M. Kassler and P. Olleson, *Samuel Wesley (1766–1837): a Source Book* (Aldershot, 2001), 544.

[19] Ibid., 532.

an autograph letter of 1775 shows that he was not the copyist.[20] Another possibility is John Williamson senior, though the only example of his hand that has so far come to light is the signature on his will, which is too small a sample to decide the issue.[21] We might question whether an amateur musician would have had such an elegant and practised hand as the manuscript's copyist. On balance, it is more likely that it is the work of yet another professional gamba player working in London in the 1770s or 1780s. Paxton has a similar profile as an instrumental composer to Walter Clagget: his five collections of violoncello solos or duets for violin and violoncello, published between 1771 (op. 1) and 1786 (op. 6), are mostly in a simple, accessible style, often incorporating popular tunes.[22] There does not seem to be any surviving gamba music by him, though some of his violoncello solos might be adapted for the gamba or his violin parts be read on the instrument down the octave.

This is the place to mention the portrait of a gamba player by an unknown artist, now in the Caldwell Collection.[23] The clothes and the style of the painting suggest that it was painted in England in the early 1760s, and the six-string gamba has a female head similar to those on several Barak Norman instruments.[24] The relaxed but assured pose suggests that the subject was a professional. It is unlikely to be a portrait of Abel, as has been suggested, since the sitter is much thinner than Abel was even in the 1760s (as in Gainsborough's first portrait, painted around 1765; Ch. 5), and has a rather different face structure. Walter Clagget and Stephen Paxton are more promising candidates: they were in their late twenties in the early 1760s, and were thus about the right age.

❧ Andreas Lidel

MOST of those discussed so far were probably prompted to take up the gamba by Abel's example. However, that may not so in Paxton's case, since he had further encounters with the instrument in the 1770s when he played in concerts

---

[20] Crosby, 'Stephen and other Paxtons', 52

[21] Maidstone, Centre for Kentish Studies, PB4 1/11 (Ian Davies, Paul Pollak).

[22] RISM A/I P 1072–8, 1080. One of them, S. Paxton, *Six Easy Solos for a Violoncello or Bassoon, in which are Introduced some Favourite Scots &c. Airs*, op. 3 (London, 1778), has a ME: ed. N. Pyron (London, 1986).

[23] For the Caldwell Collection, see J. Caldwell, 'Antique Viols and Related Instruments from the Caldwell Collection', *JVdGSA*, 11 (1974), 60–89.

[24] B. Hebbert, 'A Catalogue of Surviving Instruments by, or Ascribed to, Barak Norman', *GSJ*, 54 (2001), 285–329, at 329. I am grateful to Ben Hebbert, Susan Sloman, Teri Noel Towe, and Thomas MacCracken for helping me to assess the painting.

with the Austrian baryton and gamba player Andreas Lidel or Lidl.[25] Nothing is known about Lidel's early life except that it was reported in 1776 that he was 'one of the pupils of the celebrated Haydn' ('l'un des éleves du celebre Hayden'), and in 1782 it was said that he came from Vienna.[26] He entered the service of Prince Nikolaus Esterházy on 1 August 1769, and was provided on 23 July 1770 with four books of eight-stave paper to write baryton pieces for the prince; in January 1772 he was listed as 'Paritonista'.[27] He presumably taught the prince the baryton and played parts written for it by Haydn, Tomasini and other Esterházy composers as well as his own music.[28] He left Esterházy service on 15 May 1774, and played in Augsburg on 23 and 25 October that year.[29] He was in Paris in 1775, living in 'rue Dauphine, aux Armes de l'Empire', and reportedly played for Baron de Bagge and in other private concerts before returning to Germany.[30] He presumably travelled to England in the winter of 1775–6: his first-known London appearance was on 9 February 1776.

Lidel was active in England for more than four years: he is last heard of on 30 March 1780, when he played a duet for violin and baryton with Samuel Wesley in a Wesley family concert.[31] During that time he appeared at least twenty times in London and twice in Oxford – at the Holywell Music Room on 14 and 18 November 1776.[32] However, he gave his address as 'Nº. 29 Great Castle Street, Cavendish Square' on the title-page of his op. 8 (1781), and his op. 9 was presumably published after that, though by William Forster rather than the

---

[25] The title-pages of his English publications, most of which were self-published, all use the form 'Lidel', while his grandson was consistently known as 'Joseph Lidel'.

[26] *Almanach musical* (Paris, 1775–83; repr. Geneva, 1972), ii. 32; *Musikalischer Almanach auf das Jahr 1782* (Berlin, 1782), 105.

[27] H. Unverricht, *Geschichte des Streichtrios* (Tutzing, 1969), 145; H. C. R. Landon, *Haydn: Chronicle and Works*, i: *Haydn at Eszterháza, 1766–1790* (London, 1978), 74, 91, 162.

[28] See esp. E. Fruchtman, 'The Baryton Trios of Tomasini, Burgksteiner, and Neumann', 2 vols. (PhD diss., U. of North Carolina, Chapel Hill, 1960); Landon, *Haydn at Eszterháza*, esp. 158–60, 349–59.

[29] Landon, *Haydn at Eszterháza*, 74; F. Flassig, *Die solistische Gambenmusik in Deutschland im 18. Jahrhundert* (Göttingen, 1998), 219–20. Flassig quotes C. D. F. Schubart's statement that Lidel played in Augsburg in 1776, though this is unlikely, given that he was in England by 9/2/1776, and seemingly remained there for the rest of the year.

[30] *Almanach musical*, ii. 31–2, 139.

[31] A. McLamore, '"By the Will and Order of Providence": the Wesley Family Concerts, 1779–1787', *RMARC*, 37 (2004), 71–220, at 122.

[32] R. Hughes, 'Haydn at Oxford: 1773–1791', *ML*, 20 (1939), 242–9, at 243–4.

composer.[33] Thus he may have left England in or soon after 1781, possibly to return to Paris: his op. 11 was published there (his op. 10 is not known),[34] and we shall see that three sets of manuscript pieces with gamba parts survive in Paris. Also, Fétis stated that he was in Berlin in 1784,[35] and the Berlin and Amsterdam publisher Hummel issued some of his collections, including two that may not be reprints of London editions.[36]

According to Burney, Lidel 'died of a consumption in London, at about thirty years of age, in 1788', though he must have been rather older than that to have been taken on at Eszterháza in 1769; he was probably born around 1750.[37] Also, he seems to have died long before 1788, for 'A fine toned baritton, the favorite instrument of that late excellent performer, Mr. A. Lidel' was sold on 14 February that year as part of the effects of the collector Joseph Gulston (I/81).[38] If Gulston acquired the baryton after Lidel's death, as seems likely, it must have been before his own death on 16 July 1786, and possibly long before since he was in serious financial difficulty at the end of his life and was forced to sell his books in 1784 and his prints in 1786. Thus Lidel may have died in the early 1780s soon after he ceased to give London concerts; he is listed as 'M. Lidl, en Angleterre' in the 1779 volume of the *Almanach musical*, but is absent when lists of performers reappear in the 1782 volume.[39]

The fact that a London-based collector acquired Lidel's baryton suggests that he died there, though his grandson Joseph, a prominent mid-nineteenth-century cellist who spent his working life in Britain, was born in Bavaria. We shall see that Joseph possessed at least two instruments owned by his grandfather. Gulston was musical and his sale included 'A capital fine toned base viol and case'

---

[33] A. Lidel, *A Third Sett of Six Duettos for Two Violins or Violin and Violoncello*, op. 8 (London, 1781); RISM A/I L 2386; CC: GB-Lbl, g.426.b; A. Lidel, *Six Solos for a Violin and Bass*, op. 9 (London, ?1781); RISM A/I L 2387; CC: GB-Lbl, g.1780. aa.(1). *BLIC* dates the latter *c.* 1780.

[34] A. Lidel, *Six quatuors pour une flutte, un violon, alto et basse*, op. 11 (Paris, n.d.); RISM A/I L 2388.

[35] F. J. Fétis, *Biographie universelle des musiciens*, 10 vols. (Paris, 1860–80), v. 299.

[36] RISM A/I LL 2383a, 2385a. I have been unable to consult the unique copies of these editions, at RUS-Mrg.

[37] C. Burney, 'Lidl', in *The Cyclopaedia, or Universal Dictionary of Arts, Sciences, and Literature*, ed. A. Rees, 39 vols. (London, 1819); see also BurneyH, ii. 1020.

[38] Greenwood, *A Catalogue of the Large and very Valuable Collection of Ancient and Modern Music, by all the Great and Favourite Masters, Musical Instruments … and other Effects of Joseph Gulston, Esq., Deceased* (14–16/2/1788); CC: ECCO, T182881.

[39] *Almanach musical*, v (1779), 181. There was no 1780 volume, and there is no list of performers in ibid., vi (1781).

(I/74) and 'An excellent small viol de Gamba' (I/77), as well as violins, violas and a violoncello, two flutes, three Spanish guitars, 'a capital French Pedal Harp, by Cusseneau' (I/76), and harpsichords by Shudi and Tabel (I/75, 84).[40] There is no obvious gamba music among the sixty-nine lots of music, though there are several collections by Abel as well as 'Twenty volumes, by Lidel, Uttini, Astorga, &c.' (I/19). A more detailed catalogue, in GB-Lbl, Add. MS 24357, shows how comprehensive Gulston's music library was, though again it does not contain any obvious gamba music. His viols and baryton may just have been rare and beautiful objects to be collected rather than played.

Lidel's main instrument was the baryton, the variant of the gamba with a second rank of metal strings which sound in sympathy with the six or seven gut strings and can be plucked behind the neck by the thumb of the left hand.[41] He seems to have played a number of different barytons during his career, and to have had a hand in developing its stringing. He reportedly played one of his own invention in Paris in 1775 with seven bowed strings and twelve metal strings tuned chromatically, while in 1782 he was credited with increasing the metal strings to twenty-seven;[42] the largest number on a surviving instrument is twenty-five.[43] A report of Lidel's first known appearance in London, in a concert directed by François-Hippolyte Barthélemon at the Casino in Great Marlborough Street on 9 February 1776, stated that he played on 'a new instrument never exhibited before in public in this kingdom, somewhat resembling a viola di Gamba, but with the accompanyment of sixteen additional strings'; the writer added that on 'this affecting instrument' Lidel 'contrived to unite in it almost every species of musical expression, from the delicate pathos of the viol d'amour to the sprightly and articulate tinglings of the harp'.[44] In 1798 Charles Burney called him 'Seventeen-string Jack', implying the use of an instrument with six gut strings and eleven metal strings or seven gut strings and ten metal strings:

The plan of self-accompaniment on the *viol de gamba* was carried to a considerable degree of perfection a few years ago, by the late exquisite

---

[40] Lot I/75, 'an exceeding good harpsichord in a mahogany case', is described as 'a capital Harpsichord by Bur. Shudi' in Greenwood's advertisement, *DUR*, 19/1/1788.

[41] E. Fruchtman, 'The Baryton: its History and Music Re-Examined', *Acta Musicologica*, 34 (1962), 2–17; P. Jacquier, 'Le baryton á cordes: une méthode de recherche en lutherie', *Amour et sympathie* (Limoges, 1995), 101–71; C. A. Gartrell, *A History of the Baryton and its Music, King of Instruments, Instrument of Kings* (Lanham, MD, 2009).

[42] *Almanach musical*, ii. 31–2; *Musikalischer Almanach fur das Jahr 1782*, 105.

[43] Gartrell, *A History of the Baryton and its Music*, 132.

[44] *MP*, 12/2/1776.

performer, M. L I D L, nick-named *Seventeen-string Jack*; who, with infinite pains and difficulty, thumbed a base, *pizzicato*, with his thumb on strings placed behind the neck of his instrument, while the bow and his fingers acted as usual on the strings over the finger-board: but the execution of this Herculean labour in a concert, while two or three violoncellos and a harpsichord lie idle, is useless toil and ingenuity.[45]

The former option was used on the Tielke baryton owned by Lidel and described by his grandson in 1849, as we shall see. However, both the 1750 J. J. Stadlmann instrument owned by Nikolaus Esterházy and the 1660 Stainer once at Eisenstadt have or had ten metal strings, and the 1732 D. A. Stadelmann reputedly owned by Haydn has fourteen.[46] There was clearly no standardisation in the design and construction of barytons.

Lidel is always given in advertisements as playing the baryton, except for two occasions when the gamba is mentioned. Interestingly, in one of those, his second London appearance on 15 February 1776, the programme was changed: advertisements on 12 February mention him playing a gamba solo while later ones list a baryton solo.[47] Perhaps he became aware of Abel's position in London's concert life and thought better of challenging him on his own instrument. In addition to baryton solos, which he played quite frequently, Lidel played duets for violin and baryton three times: with Franz Lamotte on 23 May 1776 at Carlisle House, with Lamotte again in his own benefit concert at the New Rooms in Tottenham Street on 28 May 1777, and with Thomas Linley junior in his benefit concert the following year, on 5 May 1778.[48] On one occasion a duet for viola d'amore and baryton with François-Hippolyte Barthélemon was advertised, though the concert, a benefit for Mary Barthélemon at the Casino in Great Marlborough Street, was repeatedly postponed and may not have taken place.[49] On another occasion, his benefit concert on 20 April 1779 at the Tottenham Street Rooms, Lidel played a baryton concerto, and he planned to play a concerto for violin and baryton with Lamotte on 23 May 1776, though it was replaced by a duet.[50]

[45] Unsigned review in *The Monthly Review*, 27 (10/1798), 189–94, at 193. A contemporary annotation ascribes it to 'D[r]. B[urne]y' in the CC, *British Periodicals* (http://britishperiodicals.chadwyck.co.uk); there is a similar passage in Burney, 'Lidl', in *The Cyclopaedia*, ed. Rees.

[46] Gartrell, *A History of the Baryton and its Music*, 139–41; L. Somfai, *Joseph Haydn, his Life in Contemporary Pictures* (London, 1969), 36, 37.

[47] *GZ*, 12/2/1776; *MP*, 12/2/1776; *PA*, 12–15/2/1776.

[48] *PA*, 23/5/1776; *PA*, 28/5/1777; *PA*, 5/5/1778.

[49] *PA*, 29/4/1776; *PA*, 6, 7/5/1776.

[50] *PA*, 23/5/1776; *PA*, 20/4/1779.

None of Lidel's baryton music has survived in its original form, though some pieces may exist in arrangements. It is significant that his concerts featured duets for violin or viola d'amore and baryton because he was famous for his published string duets. The first set, op. 3 (1778), is for violin and viola or violoncello, while op. 6 (?1780–1) consists of three duets for violin and viola and three for violin and violoncello;[51] op. 8 is for two violins or violin and violoncello. The first set was particularly popular, and was reprinted at least five times, in Paris and The Hague as well as in London.[52] On 21 May 1778 John Marsh played one from op. 3 in a concert in Salisbury, remarking that 'it seem'd to please so much that Mr [James] Harris frequently afterwards put one down on the bill'; on 2 August 1781 Marsh again played one in a Salisbury concert, with the violinist Giuseppe Soderini.[53] As late as 1864 Lidel was remembered for his '"Duetts for Violin and Tenor," and other music where the viola is brought prominently forward'.[54] It is easy to imagine that the lower parts of some of these duets were originally for baryton, or were adapted by Lidel for it in performance. An indication that this is so is provided by the Rondo of op. 3, no. 5, which also appears in his Sonata no. 2 for gamba and bass (Ex. 8.1).

In two cases it seems that printed works by Lidel were performed in different versions in London concerts. A 'Quintetto, entirely new, for a Flute, Violin, two Tenors, Violoncello Obligato' was played by 'Master Weichsel, Mess. Decamp, Reinagle, Kammell, Lidel' in Lidel's benefit concert at the Tottenham Street Rooms on 20 April 1779.[55] Benefit concerts were often used by performers as showcases for new compositions, so the piece was almost certainly one of Lidel's op. 5 quintets,[56] for 'Master Weichel' (the young Charles Weichsel or Weichsell) was a violinist, George Louis Decamp a flautist, and Antonín Kammel a violinist and viola player, while the brothers Alexander and Hugh Reinagle were both cellists. Thus Lidel presumably played one of the viola parts on the gamba or the baryton. Incidentally, evidence that Lidel, like Abel, also played the violoncello is provided by a vignette on the title-page of the Hummel edition of the

---

[51] A. Lidel, *Six Duettos for the Violin and Tenor, with a Separate Part for the Violoncello, to be Play'd Occasionally instead of the Tenor*, op. 3 (London, 1778); RISM A/I L 2372; CC: GB-Lbl, g.421.(13); A. Lidel, *A Second Sett of Six Duettos, Three for Violin and Tenor, and Three for Violin and Violoncello*, op. 6 (London, ?1780–1); RISM A/I L 2383; CC: GB-Lbl, g.421.(12).

[52] RISM A/I L 2373–7.

[53] *The John Marsh Journals*, ed. Robins, 180, 240.

[54] W. Sandys and S. A. Forster, *The History of the Violin* (London, 1864), 131.

[55] *PA*, 20/4/1779.

[56] A. Lidel, *Three Quintettos for a Flute, Violin, Two Tenors and Violoncello Obligato*, op. 5 (London, ?1779); RISM A/I L 2380; CC: GB-Lbl, g.398.k.(2).

Ex. 8.1 Andreas Lidel, (a) Duet in G major, op. 3, no. 5, Rondo, compared with (b) Sonata no. 2 in C major for viola da gamba and violoncello, Rondeau, bb. 1–8

op. 5 quintets – assuming that it was intended to be a portrait of the composer (Plate 20).[57]

The other case, the only known occasion when Lidel encroached on Abel's territory by playing the gamba in a London concert, is particularly interesting. A 'Trio, entirely new, for a Violin, Viola da Gamba and Violoncello' played by 'Mess [Thomas] Linley, [Stephen] Paxton and Lidel' and 'composed by Lidel' formed part of his benefit concert at the New Tottenham Street Rooms on 5 May 1778.[58] It was one of two occasions when Paxton is known to have appeared with Lidel (the other was in a benefit concert at Hickford's Room on 30 May 1777, when Lidel played the baryton),[59] and it provides us with more evidence that Paxton came into contact with the gamba and gamba players.

This advertisement is important because it provides evidence for the dating of

57 RISM A/I L 2382; CC: DK-Kk, Gieddes Samling V, 10 mu 6208.0378 (http://img. kb.dk/ma/giedde/gso5-10bm.pdf).

58 PA, 5/5/1778.

59 PA, 30/5/1777.

one of Lidel's six trios for violin, gamba and violoncello. They survive in manuscript parts in F-Pn, Vm⁷ 6300 along with parts of Lidel's eight divertimenti for viola, gamba and bass (Vm⁷ 6301), and two versions in score of six sonatas for gamba and violoncello (Vm⁷ 6298).[60] According to a F-Pn catalogue compiled in 1803, the trios 'were arranged by the author for Mr Dogny, while the original manuscript [was] purchased at his sale [presumably the sale of his effects after death] in 1797' ('ont eté ar[r]angé par l'auteur p[ou]r M[onsieu]r Dogny. Cep[andant] le man[u]sc[rit] original [etait] acheté à sa vente en 1797').[61] Nothing is known of Dogny, though he was probably a French pupil or patron of Lidel. The trios, the divertimenti and one of the copies of the solo sonatas are all in the same hand. It is unlikely to be autograph, as has been suggested,[62] given the number of errors and ambiguities in the texts. Also, Lidel is named as 'And: Lidl', but he consistently used the monogram 'Lidelmppia' (presumably meaning 'Lidel, m[anu] p[ro]p[r]ia' – Lidel's own hand) when authenticating copies of his London publications.[63]

A further complication is that the Paris trios are variants of Lidel's *Six Trios*, op. 1 (1776).[64] In the print, as with most works of this sort, the first treble has most of the melodic material and the demanding passagework. In the manuscript version the gamba mostly takes the second violin part down the octave in the outer movements, though the parts are occasionally swapped around to give it more interesting material, and it takes the upper part in all the slow movements. The passagework also differs in places, and is sometimes more elaborate in the manuscript version (Ex. 8.2). All in all, it looks as if the manuscript trios were arranged from op. 1 by Lidel for Dogny in the early 1780s. We are fortunate to have the Paris manuscripts of Lidel's gamba music, but a glimpse of what is lost is provided by a 1794 advertisement by the London booksellers Evan and Thomas Williams which included 'Six Concertos, Nine Trios, Twenty-three

---

[60] ME: A. Lidel, *Three Sonatas for Viola da Gamba and Violoncello*, ed. D. Beecher (Hannacroix NY, 1997); A. Lidel, *Six Sonatas for Viola da Gamba and 'Cello*, ed. H. Miloradovitch (Albany, CA, 1998); A. Lidel, *String Trios for Violin, Viola da Gamba and 'Cello*, ed. D. Beecher, 2 vols. (Hannacroix, NY, 1999); there is currently no ME of the divertimenti. See also Flassig, *Die solistische Gambenmusik in Deutschland*, 219–24.

[61] Lidel, *Six Sonatas for Viola da Gamba and 'Cello*, ed. Miloradovitch, i.

[62] Ibid.; Flassig, *Die solistische Gambenmusik in Deutschland*, 221.

[63] For Haydn's use of the same formula, see Somfai, *Joseph Haydn, his Life in Contemporary Pictures*, xviii, xix.

[64] A. Lidel, *Six Trios for a Violin (or Flauto), Violino Secondo and Violoncello Obligato* (London, 1776); RISM A/I L 2367; CC: GB-Lbl, g.409.(8); R.M.26.c.1.(6). Lidel, *String Trios*, ed. Beecher, does not take into account the op. 1 version.

Ex. 8.2 Andreas Lidel, (a) Trio in C major, Andante, bb. 1–6, comparing (a) the version published as op. 1, no. 1 with (b) the manuscript version in F-Pn, Vm7 6300

Duets, and Twelve Solos, for the Viola da Gamba, by Lidl, many of them in his hand-writing'.[65]

Hubert Unverricht suggested (without knowing the manuscript versions) that Lidel's op. 1 and his *Six Sonatas*, op. 4 (1778) are arrangements of baryton trios originally written for Nikolaus Esterházy.[66] This could be so, and the three Paris

---

[65] *MH*, 3/4/1794.

[66] Unverricht, *Geschichte des Streichtrios*, 145; A. Lidel, *Six Sonatas for Violin, Tenor, & Violoncello*, op. 4 (London, 1778); RISM A/I L 2378; CC: GB-Lbl, g.416.(1).

collections are also clearly related to the Austrian baryton repertory. The trios and divertimenti are similar in scoring and idiom to the two main types of baryton trio: for baryton, viola and bass, and baryton, violin and bass. Haydn mostly used the viola for his 126 authentic trios (Hob XI:1–126), as did Anton Neumann and Joseph Purksteiner or Burgksteiner, though all but four of the trios by the violinist Alois Luigi Tomasini are with violin.[67] Haydn also wrote trios, quintets and octets with baryton, as well as at least twenty-five duets for two barytons or baryton and bass.[68] Those known or thought to have been with violoncello are lost, though they were probably similar in style and texture to Lidel's gamba sonatas. Lidel's divertimenti, like Haydn's baryton trios, are cast in three short movements, often including a minuet as the second or third, and are relatively modest in their technical demands, with most of the interest concentrated in the gamba parts. The trios are more ambitious, with generally longer movements and considerable demands made on all three players.

As we might expect, the six solos have the most demanding gamba parts, though the movements are relatively brief and the violoncello parts are simple accompaniments with virtually no solo material. Naturally, Lidel's gamba parts do not have any indications for plucking metal strings, but that is also true of Tomasini's baryton parts and some of Haydn's. Evidence that the sonatas are early works, written before he came to London, is provided by the first and third movements of no. 1 in D major, which were reworked and expanded by the cellist and gamba player Franz Xaver Hammer (1741–1817).[69] Hammer worked alongside Lidel in Esterházy service between his arrival in 1771 and Lidel's departure in 1774, which is probably when he acquired a copy of Lidel's sonata, suggesting in turn that it (and perhaps the whole set) dates from that period. Lidel is one of the most attractive late gamba composers, with a sure sense of musical architecture, a virtuoso string player's ability to write effectively and gratefully for his instrument, and a Haydnesque pithiness and wit. Gamba players have already begun to explore the manuscript collections, and there is also no reason why they (and baryton players) should not follow the composer's example and find excellent new repertory in his printed works, such as the three sets of duets and the op. 5 quintets.

[67] For the repertory, see esp. Fruchtmann, 'The Baryton Trios'; Unverricht, *Geschichte des Streichtrios*, 137–74; Landon, *Haydn at Eszterháza*, 349–59; Gartrell, *A History of the Baryton and its Music*, 65–83.

[68] See A. van Hoboken, *Joseph Haydn: Thematisch-bibliographisches Werkverzeichnis*, i: *Instrumentalwerke* [Hob] (Mainz, 1957), 659–65.

[69] ME: F. X. Hammer, *Five Sonatas for Viola da Gamba, Violoncello or Basso and Harpsichord*, ed. D. J. Rhodes (Albany, CA, 2004), 14–20.

&. *Pietro Pompeo Sales*

PIETRO Pompeo Sales or Salis (1729–97), an Italian composer who worked mostly for the Augsburg prince-bishops, is sometimes said to have played the gamba in London concerts, presumably because one of the items in a benefit concert for his wife Franziska at the Hanover Square Rooms on 26 April 1776 was 'Song, Signora Salis, with the Viola da Gamba Obligato, Signor Salis'.[70] However, there is no other record of him playing the gamba or any other stringed instrument; he was presumably a keyboard player since he wrote concertos and chamber music with obbligato harpsichord. The sentence appears to mean that Sales was the song's composer rather than the gamba player. There are other instances of potentially confusing wording in advertisements, including one for John Crosdill's benefit on 19 April 1776: 'Song, Signora Salis, with Violoncello Obligato, Bach'.[71] Here J. C. Bach was clearly the composer, and the violoncello was presumably played by Crosdill, one of London's leading cellists. Abel must have played the gamba obbligato on 26 April: Franziska Sales sang in a concert at Abel's house on 2 March 1776,[72] and he appeared in all six of the London concerts that featured her as well as one at the Holywell Music Room in Oxford on 20 May.[73] The sonata for *gambetta* and obbligato harpsichord attributed to Sales in a manuscript at D-ZL could have been written for Abel, though one of his employers, the Elector Clemens Wenzeslaus of Saxony, also played the viol.[74] The meaning of the word *gambetta* is not entirely clear, though if it refers to some sort of treble viol then it could be just a local adaptation of a work originally written for an ordinary gamba. The *gambetta* part is written in the treble clef, the clef that Sales would presumably have used when writing for Abel. His song with gamba obbligato has not been identified.

&. *Professional Players after Abel*

THE often-encountered idea that Abel was the last gamba player goes back to the obituaries written after his death. One newspaper asserted that 'the

---

[70] C. F. Pohl, *Mozart und Haydn in London*, 2 vols. (Vienna, 1867), ii. 374; *PA*, 26/4/1776.

[71] *PA*, 19/4/1776.

[72] *Music and Theatre in Handel's World: the Family Papers of James Harris, 1732–1780*, ed. D. Burrows and R. Dunhill (Oxford, 2002), 883.

[73] J. H. Mee, *The Oldest Music Room in Europe: a Record of Eighteenth-Century Enterprise at Oxford* (London, 1911), 25–6.

[74] Flassig, *Die solistische Gambenmusik in Deutschland*, 203–17. ME: *Nebauer and Sales: Sonatas for Gambetta and Keyboard*, ed. S. Heinrich (Oxford, 2004), 14–24.

instrument is now lost'; another thought that it is 'not an instrument in general use, and will perhaps die with him'; while Burney wrote that 'The instrument is now as dead as this great musician, and seems to have departed this life at the same time'.[75] However, there were gamba players active in German-speaking parts of Europe after 1787, including Franz Xaver Hammer and Joseph Fiala (1748–1816), and Abel was not even the last professional player in Britain in the continuous tradition, as we shall see. The persistent notion that a gamba was placed in Abel's coffin (he was buried at St Marylebone Church on 24 June 1787) only seems to go back to a semi-fictional story published in German in 1866,[76] though it is still current today.[77] We saw in Chapter 5 that three of his instruments were sold after his death.

Several of Abel's pupils and followers may have played the gamba. A 'viol di gamba' was in the 1795 auction of property seized from the violinist Wilhelm Cramer (1746–99), presumably for the payment of debts (II/156).[78] Cramer had been a long-standing colleague of Abel, and was listed by Burney as one of those who 'may be ranked of his school':

> His manner of playing an *adagio* soon became the model of all our young performers on bowed-instruments: Barthelemon, Cervetto, Cramer, and Crosdil, who may be ranked of his school, were more sparing of notes in a cantabile than, during youth, their great facility of execution would have stimulated them to, if Abel's discretion, taste, and pathetic manner of expressing, I had almost said of *breathing*, a few notes, had not kept them in order.[79]

It is not clear whether Burney meant that the four musicians actually received lessons from Abel, or whether they were just influenced by his playing. If the

---

[75] *The World*, 25/6/1787; *MP*, 22/6/1787, quoted in BurneyH, ii. 1019–20; C. Burney, 'Violoncello', in *The Cyclopaedia*, ed. Rees.

[76] London, Metropolitan Archives, P89/MRY1/314; *PA*, 28/6/1787; E. Polko, 'The Last Viola da Gamba Player', in *Musical Tales, Phantasms and Sketches*, 2 vols., ii (London, 1877), 51–73, at 73. It was trans. M. P. Maudslay from Polko, *Musikalische Märchen, Phantasien und Skizzen*, 2 vols., ii (Leipzig, 1866).

[77] For instance, M. Cyr, 'Carl Friedrich Abel's Solos: a Musical Offering to Gainsborough?', *MT*, 128 (1987), 317–21, at 321; A. Otterstedt, *The Viol: History of an Instrument*, trans. H. Reiners (Kassel, 2002), 94.

[78] Boulton, *A Catalogue of the Neat and Genuine Household Furniture, and other Effects of a Gentleman, Well Known in the Musical World* (17, 18/6/1795); CC: GB-Lbl, 1479.bb.16. The Sheriff of Middlesex added the annotation on p. 15: 'the Goods and Chattels in this Catalogue … were seized by me at the property of William Cramer'.

[79] BurneyH, ii. 1020.

former, then it is more likely that Cramer and Barthélemon (1741–1808) were taught the gamba by Abel than James Cervetto (1748–1837) or John Crosdill (d. 1825), since Cramer and Barthélemon were violinists and therefore might have thought it worth while learning the gamba to receive the maximum benefit from Abel's instruction.[80] Cervetto and Crosdill could have received lessons on the violoncello, and this is implied in a nineteenth-century passage about Johann Georg Christoph Schetky (1737–1824): 'The violoncello being his favourite instrument, he took some lessons from Abel (the celebrated performer on the viol da gamba), under whom he soon became a proficient.'[81] This probably happened early in 1772, between Schetky's arrival in London and his appointment as principal violoncello of the Edinburgh Musical Society. The Earl of Kelly, its Deputy Governor, asked Abel's advice about the appointment in a letter dated 11 February 1772.[82]

❧ *Johan Arnold Dahmen*

T H E distinction of being the last professional gamba player in Britain in the continuous tradition seems to belong to the cellist Johan Arnold Dahmen. He came from a family of Dutch professional musicians, was baptised in The Hague on 9 March 1766, the son of Wilhelm, and is recorded as 'bassist' at the Utrecht Collegium Musicum in 1787.[83] He seems to have come to London in the winter of 1790–1 with his elder brother Peter, a violinist, who made his first known appearance on 18 March 1791 in J. P. Salomon's second subscription concert.[84] Johan Arnold is not known to have played in London that year, though on 19 November *The Cambridge Chronicle and Journal* reported:

> We understand that the celebrated musical composers Mr. Haydn and Mr. Salomon, came here last week to hear a private performance on the Violin and Violoncello by Messrs. Dahmen, who are lately arrived from Germany. They expressed the highest approbriation of the superior skill and abilities of these performers, and immediately engaged them for their concerts

[80] M. Charters, 'Abel in London', *MT*, 114 (1973), 1124–6, at 1225, asserts that Abel taught Barthélemon the viol without providing any evidence.

[81] Sandys and Forster, *The History of the Violin*, 184.

[82] D. Johnson, *Music and Society in Lowland Scotland in the Eighteenth Century* (London, 1972), 74.

[83] J. C. M. van Riemsdijk, *Het Stads-musiekcollegie te Utrecht (Collegium Musicum Ultrajectinum), 1631–1881* (Utrecht, 1881), 46.

[84] H. C. R. Landon, *Haydn: Chronicle and Works*, iii: *Haydn in England, 1791–1795* (London, 1976), 60; S. McVeigh, 'The Professional Concert and Rival Subscription Series in London, 1783–1793', *RMARC*, 22 (1989), 1–135, at 98.

in Hanover Square. We are glad to hear that Messrs. Dahmen will have a public concert in Cambridge before they leave this part of the country.[85]

The concert was on 30 November in the 'Town-Hall' (the Guildhall), and included 'Concerto Violin – P. Dahmen', 'Concerto Violoncello – Dahmen', and 'Duetto, Violino & Violoncello – Dahmen', as well as a Haydn symphony. Deutsch suggested that Haydn attended the concert and that the symphony was from his first London set. The newspaper report is not entirely accurate. Peter was already working for Salomon, though the private performance might have been an audition for his brother: Johan Arnold duly appeared in a list of 'Principal Instrumental Performers' for Salomon's 1792 season, and in the third concert on 2 March he made 'his First Appearance in this Country' playing a Pleyel concerto.[86]

GMO states that Johan Arnold died in 1794, but that is not so. He played in Salomon's orchestra until the end of the 1796 season (his brother disappeared after the 1795 season), though he seems to have dropped out of London concerts until a benefit concert at the King's Theatre on 28 January 1799;[87] he was reportedly in Germany in 1796–7.[88] His annual benefit concerts were seemingly discontinued in 1803, perhaps because of ill health.[89] In 1806 Charles Edward Horn deputised when 'poor Dahmen, the second violoncello, was taken ill of the Opera House', though Dahmen was well enough to appear with Angelica Catalani at Corri's Rooms in Edinburgh on 26 and 28 September 1807 and at the Theatre Royal, Newcastle, on 15 October, playing a violoncello concerto on each occasion.[90] In a later concert on the tour, in Glasgow on 9 October, it was reported that he 'was struck with the palsy so severely that he cannot be moved'.[91] He advertised a concert at Hanover Square Rooms on 31 March 1808, 'being in some degree recovered from his late serious indisposition', though no further details are known.[92] He seems to have died in the spring of 1813: an advertisement for a benefit concert at the King's Theatre on 20 May for his wife and nine children mentions his 'long and

---

[85] O. E. Deutsch, 'Haydn in Cambridge', *The Cambridge Review*, 62 (1940–1), 312, 314.

[86] Landon, *Haydn in England*, 131, 139; McVeigh, 'The Professional Concert', 109.

[87] *MH*, 26/12/1798; *The Times*, 26/1/1799.

[88] E. S. J. van der Straeten, *The History of the Violoncello, the Viol da Gamba, their Precursors and Collateral Instruments* (London, 1914; repr. 1971), 95, given without a source.

[89] *The Times*, 24/2/1800; 23/2/1801; 22/2/1802; 24/3/1803.

[90] *Charles Edward Horn's Memoirs of his Father and Himself*, ed. M. Kassler (Aldershot, 2003), 32; *The Caledonian Mercury*, 26, 28/9/1807; *The Newcastle Courant*, 10/10/1807.

[91] *MC*, 16/10/1807.

[92] *MC*, 21/3/1808.

painful illness, which commenced while pursuing his professional labours in the North of England, and from which he never recovered'.[93] The concert featured a piano concerto played by 'Miss Dahmen (only eleven years of age)', an item repeated in concerts in Edinburgh and Leeds in 1814.[94]

Dahmen was a prolific composer. His publications go up to op. 45, though many seem to be lost, and some of the collections of flute music attributed to him are apparently by a flute-playing namesake in Amsterdam.[95] Also, two London publications were given op. 6,[96] three were given op. 35 (one of which just seems to be the op. 45 quartets misnumbered),[97] and there are at least five collections without opus numbers, including a remarkable collection of sacred songs with string quartet or piano.[98] As we might expect, Dahmen published a good deal of music for his main instrument: there are at least six surviving printed sets of solos, duets and trios with violoncello solos. On several occasions he was advertised as playing his own violoncello concerto, for instance in Salomon's concert in the Hanover Square Rooms on 17 March 1796 or his benefit at the King's Theatre in the Haymarket on 28 January 1799.[99]

We know that Dahmen played the gamba partly from the Leicester stocking

[93] *The Times*, 18/5/1813. The *IGI* records his marriage to Eliza Sophia Fruinn at St Anne, Soho on 24/5/1795, and the births and baptisms of two daughters: Eliza Frances, born on 23/2/1808 and christened at St Pancras Old Church on 11/4/1808, and Caroline Louise Lane, born on 1/2/1811 and christened at St Andrew Undershaft on 25/6/1813. A son, John Arnold, married Mary Ann Hubert on 22/6/1833 at Isleworth, and died on 25/2/1860; see *The Era*, 4/3/1860.

[94] *The Caledonian Mercury*, 22/1/1814; *The Leeds Mercury*, 5/3/1814.

[95] See R. de Reede, 'Niederländische Flötisten und Flötisten in der Niederlanden, 1700–1900', *Tibia*, 24 (1999), 345–55, 433–41, at 433–6.

[96] J. A. Dahmen, *Three Trios for a Violoncello Obligato with Accompaniments for a Violin & Bass*, op. 6 (London, c. 1798); RISM A/1 D 9; CC: GB-Ckc, Rw.19.207–9.2; J. A. Dahmen, *Six Canzonets with Accompaniment for the Harp or Piano Forte*, op. 6 (London, c. 1805); CC: GB-Lbl, G.805.m.(19).

[97] J. A. Dahmen, *Three Quartetts for Two Violins, Tenor, and Bass* (London, WM 1808), op. 35; CC: GB-Lbl, R.M.f.8.(2); J. A. Dahmen, *Three Solos for the Violoncello with an Accompaniment for a Bass*, op. 35 (London, WM 1808); CC: g.24.c.(5); J. A. Dahmen, *Three Trios, for Two Violins & a Violoncello*, op. 35 (London, WM 1810); CC: g.417c.(4).

[98] J. A. Dahmen, *Eleven Sacred Songs and Two Choruses in Score, the Words Taken Chiefly from the Psalms* (London, WM 1807); CC: GB-Lbl, G. 599; collection of William Davies. Three songs from the collection are recorded on *Vital Spark of Heav'nly Flame: Music of Death and Resurrection from English Parish Churches and Chapels, 1760–1840*, Psalmody, The Parley of Instruments / Peter Holman, Hyperion, CDA67020 (1998; rec. 1997).

[99] *MP*, 17/3/1796; *The Times*, 26/1/1799.

manufacturer and amateur musician William Gardiner (1769–1853), who described him playing it in two concerts at a Huddersfield music meeting.[100] In the second concert he 'played two solos upon the viol di Gamba, which had a sweet effect. I think his instrument had six strings, from which he drew the most delicate tones, more like the viol d'amour than the violoncello; but its greatest excellence was shown in the arpeggios, for which it is especially adapted'. There are also advertisements for three London concerts in which Dahmen played the instrument in a trio of his own composition: 'Trio, two French Horns and Viola da Gamba, Messrs. Leander and Mr. Dahmen; [composed by] Dahmen' featured in his 1799 benefit, and similar wording was used for a subscription concert at Willis's Rooms on 14 March 1800, and his benefit on 24 February 1801.[101] The brothers Lewis Henry and Vincent Thomas Leander were the leading horn players in London at the time, though David Rhodes wondered whether Dahmen might have written the trio for his horn-playing brothers Herman and Wilhelm;[102] they visited London, and Herman supposedly died as a British soldier in the Peninsular War.

Unfortunately, the piece (assuming it was a single piece) is lost, so we do not know how the strange combination of instruments was deployed and exploited. However, a surprising number of chamber pieces by late eighteenth-century German composers combine the gamba with horns. C. D. F. Schubart wrote in 1806 that the gamba 'suffers no heavy accompaniment, since it mostly accompanies itself. A violin, two horns and a bassoon are here the best accompaniment'.[103] An example is the Trio in D major for flute, gamba and horn by the Mannheim cellist and composer Peter Ritter (1763–1846).[104] Gamba music by Dahmen may also be hidden in his published violoncello pieces, as with Abel's trios for flute, gamba and continuo and Lidel's for violin, gamba and violoncello. Possible suspects include his *Three Trios*, opp. 6, 8, and 9,[105] and *Three Solos for the Violoncello*, op. 35. Like Lidel, Dahmen was a follower of Haydn. The small proportion

[100]   W. Gardiner, *Music and Friends, or Pleasant Recollections of a Dilettante*, 3 vols. (London, 1838), i. 401, 403.

[101]   *The Times*, 14/3/1800; 23/2/1801.

[102]   D. J. Rhodes, 'The Viola da Gamba, its Repertory and Practitioners in the late Eighteenth Century', *Chelys*, 31 (2003), 36–63, at 58.

[103]   Ibid., 37–8.

[104]   Ibid., 38–9.

[105]   J. A. Dahmen, *Three Trios for a Violin, Tenor and Violoncello*, op. 8 (London, ?1798); CC: GB-Lbl, h.17.b; J. A. Dahmen, *Three Trios for Flute, Tenor and Violoncello*, op. 9 (London, 1803); CC: GB-Lbl, g.222.(9). The latter was entered at Stationers' Hall on 9/7/1803, see *Music Entries at Stationers' Hall, 1710–1818*, comp. M. Kassler (Aldershot, 2004), 507.

of his output that has been explored in modern times suggests that it would repay a more detailed study.

🕭 The 'Constant Succession' of Amateurs

WITH Dahmen's death the eighteenth-century tradition of professional gamba playing seems to have ended in Britain, though it continued with Payne's 'constant succession of amateur players'. The first was the engraver and painter Thomas Cheeseman or Cheesman. He was probably the individual baptised at East Peckham in Kent on 14 May 1760, the son of John and Sarah.[106] He was apprenticed to the Italian engraver Francesco Bartolozzi between about 1775 and 1788, and he enrolled as a student at the Royal Academy in 1790. A painting of him around 1777 has been attributed to Bartolozzi,[107] and he published a sonnet in Bartolozzi's memory in 1831.[108] He established himself as an engraver in the 1790s, published *Rudiments of Drawing the Human Figure from Cipriani, Guido, Poussin, Rubens* (1816), and painted some miniatures in the 1820s. Between 1830 and 1834 he was employed by the Society of Dilettanti to make drawings of all the sculptures in the British Museum. It is sometimes said that he died in 1834, but he was still alive the following year, as we shall see.

The most important source of information about Cheeseman comes from the writings of his cousins the Strickland sisters, notably an article about him published by Susanna Moodie née Strickland in Toronto in 1863, and the 1887 biography of the popular biographer Agnes Strickland by her sister Jane Margaret; yet another literary sister was Catharine Parr Traill née Strickland.[109] The Strickland sisters grew up at Reydon Hall near Bungay in Suffolk, though Catharine and Susanna emigrated to Canada with their husbands in 1832 and 1834. They were both famous in later life as pioneer Canadian writers: Catharine made her name with *The Backwoods of Canada* (1836), a collection of letters to

[106] *IGI*; see also *Allgemeines Lexicon der Bildenden Künste von der Antike bis zur Gegenwart*, ed. U. Thieme and F. Becker, 37 vols. (Leipzig, 1912; repr. 1951), vi. 448–9; D. Alexander, 'Thomas Cheesman', *The Dictionary of Art*, ed. J. Turner, 34 vols. (London, 1996), vi. 528.

[107] National Portrait Gallery, NPG 780.

[108] *The Royal Lady's Magazine and Archives of the Court of St. James's*, 1 (1831), 281.

[109] S. Moodie, 'My Cousin Tom: a Sketch from Life', *The British American Magazine*, 1 (5/1863), 12–20; J. M. Strickland, *Life of Agnes Strickland* (Edinburgh, 1887). For the Stricklands, see esp. U. Pope-Hennessy, *Agnes Strickland: Biographer of the Queens of England, 1796–1874* (London, 1940); *Susanna Moodie: Letters of a Lifetime*, ed. C. Ballstadt, E. Hopkins, and M. Peterman (Toronto, 1985); C. Gray, *Sisters in the Wilderness: the Lives of Susanna Moodie and Catharine Parr Traill* (Toronto, 1999).

her family back home, and Susanna with the autobiographical *Roughing it in the Bush* (1852).

Cheeseman and the Stricklands seem to have had the greatest contact in the 1820s, before Susanna and Catharine married and emigrated and when they were trying to establish themselves in London literary society; he painted miniatures of Susanna, Catharine and Agnes at that period.[110] Jane Margaret wrote that Cheeseman 'generally passed the summer months at Reydon, where he was a very welcome and beloved guest', and they often went to stay at 71 Newman Street, his London home between 1802 and 1829.[111] Susanna stated that he never married, having been disappointed in love as a young man; that he lived with his niece Eliza; that the house in Newman Street was dirty, with the floor of his studio 'strewed with dirty music and dirty old books'; and that he was a Catholic 'though born of Protestant parents'. Nevertheless, he was cultured: he was 'an antiquarian, among his other accomplishments', who 'had imbibed a great dislike to everything English' during his 'long residence with the Italians' – presumably Bartolozzi and other members of the Italian community in London. 'I verily believe', she continued, that 'he thought in Italian; and being an exquisite musician, both on the viol to Gomba [*sic*] and the violin, never played any but Italian music.' Jane Margaret added that his library was 'stored with rare books in many languages, and portfolios filled with choice prints and fine drawings'.

Susanna Moodie gives us a valuable if romanticised portrait of Cheeseman, though she was wide of the mark when stating that he 'never played any but Italian music'. In his 1889 lecture Edward Payne showed off his 1611 Henry Jaye bass viol,[112] stating: 'I have reason to think that it is the identical instrument

---

[110] The miniatures of Susanna and Catharine are illus. in *Susanna Moodie: Letters of a Lifetime*, ed. Ballstadt, Hopkins and Peterman, 7, 8; and at www.collections-canada.gc.ca/moodie-traill/027013-200-e.html.

[111] Strickland, *Life of Agnes Strickland*, 15–17; *Exeter Working Papers in British Book Trade History: The London Book Trades, 1775–1800, a Preliminary Checklist of Names* (http://bookhistory.blogspot.com/2007/01/london-1775-1800-c.html).

[112] Payne, 'The Viola da Gamba', 93, where it is said to be by 'Henry Key'. It was exhibited by Payne in the Music Loan Exhibition in London in 1904, see *A Special Loan Exhibition of Musical Instruments, Manuscripts, Books, Portraits, and other Mementoes of Music and Musicians* (London, 1904), 103, no. 1091; *An Illustrated Catalogue of the Music Loan Exhibition held … by the Worshipful Company of Musicians at Fishmongers' Hall, June and July 1904* (London, 1909), 151. It later belonged to Francis Galpin, see 'Dotted Crotchet' [F. G. Edwards], 'Private Musical Collections, ii: the Rev. F. W. Galpin's Musical Instruments', *MT*, 47 (1906), 521–9, at 526; F. W. Galpin, *Old English Instruments of Music: their History and Character*, rev. T. Dart (London, 4/1965), pl. 17. It is now at NL-DHgm, Ec 1954-0009; see M. Fleming, T. MacCracken, and K. Martius, 'Provisional

which was used by Thomas Cheesman, the engraver and miniature painter, and which was given by his representatives in 1842, together with Abel's copy of "De Caix," to Mr. Cawse, the artist.' Payne gave some details of the copies of Caix d'Hervelois: 'A copy of the "Suites" of the latter, which once belonged to Abel, and has many of his notes and fingerings, and which afterwards passed through the hands of the amateur violists Cheesman and Cawse, lies on the table.' And again: 'I have also a great curiosity in the shape of De Caix's works, with Abel's alterations and fingering. There are two volumes – one was bought in London, and the other seems to have been in Germany for nearly a century.'[113] No copy of the various collections of *Pièces de viole* by Caix d'Hervelois with manuscript annotations has come to light, though they presumably included copies of the *Second livre* (Paris, 1719), from which Payne took three illustrations for his lecture (Ch. 9), and the *Troisième œuvre* (Paris, 1731), which includes a musette that evidently inspired one of Abel's unaccompanied pieces (Ch. 5).

As a pupil of Bartolozzi in the late 1770s and early 1780s, Cheeseman would have come into contact with Abel. Bartolozzi engraved G. B. Cipriani's design for a ticket for the Bach–Abel concerts and Carlini's 1782 portrait of J. C. Bach, and Henry Angelo mentioned all four as frequent guests of his father Domenico, a fashionable fencing master:

> Well do I remember the delightful evenings which for years were frequent under my paternal roof, when they [Bach and Abel], with Bartolozzi and Cipriani, formed a little friendly party, and amused themselves with drawing, music, and conversation, until long after midnight.[114]

They were also fellow Masons: Cipriani joined the Lodge of the Nine Muses on 23 January 1777, Bartolozzi on 13 February 1777, Abel on 13 February 1778, and Bach on 15 June 1778.[115] Cheeseman was probably a pupil of Abel and might therefore have received the Caix d'Hervelois volume directly from him; it is not listed in the sale catalogue of Abel's effects (Ch. 5).

List of Extant Viols by Henry Jaye', *Jaye Project* (http://www.vdgs.org.uk/information-JayeProject.html).

[113] Payne, 'The Viola da Gamba', 100, 106; see also 93–4. I have been unable to trace these volumes. For gamba music by Caix d'Hervelois, see RISM A/I c 38–40, 43, 45, 46.

[114] *Reminiscences of Henry Angelo, with Memoirs of his late Father and Friends*, 2 vols. (London, 1828), i. 17–20.

[115] S. McVeigh, 'Freemasonry and Musical Life in London in the late Eighteenth Century', in *Music in Eighteenth-Century Britain*, ed. D. W. Jones (Aldershot, 2000), 72–100, at 94.

Cheeseman owned other musical memorabilia. John Cawse's letter accompanying the Merlin-Carter pentachord states that 'it was some years in the Possession of Mr Cheeseman the Engraver' (Ch. 5). Cheeseman owned, probably assembled, and dated 1835 the part-autograph collection of Abel's gamba music, GB-Lbl, Add. MS 31697 (Ch. 6). He also contributed to GB-Lbl, Add. MS 31698, the part-autograph collection of Rudolf Straube's lute music: he drew a diagram entitled 'a View of yᵉ Theorboe Fingerboard' (fol. 6), as well as untitled fingerboard charts (fols. 41, 42v); the latter are for a six-stringed instrument tuned D–G–c–e–a–d' – i.e. a gamba rather than a lute or theorbo. Cheeseman presumably acquired the constituent parts of Add. MS 31697 after the Countess of Pembroke's death in 1831.[116] He probably died in 1842, the year, according to Payne, that 'his representatives' (presumably his executors) gave the Jaye viol and Abel's copy of Caix d'Hervelois to John Cawse.

John Cawse was a more prominent artist than Cheeseman, though for some reason it is Cheeseman who tends to be found in art dictionaries. He was probably the individual christened at St Mary, Whitechapel on 27 Jan 1779, son of Charles Woodroffe Cawse and his wife Mary.[117] Charles Woodroffe was described as 'Staymaker and dealer in Whale Fins' in his will, made on 28 March 1784 and proved on 7 July.[118] From his two treatises on painting we learn that John was a pupil of John Opie, and was a picture restorer; the second book includes a section on cleaning and restoring.[119] He exhibited at the British Institution, the Royal Academy and elsewhere, and was also a book illustrator, contributing to the novels of Captain Marryat, Fenimore Cooper and others. He died on 19 January 1862.[120]

Cawse had strong connections with the musical and theatrical world, and painted, among others, Joseph Grimaldi (1807),[121] Sir George Smart,[122] the cellist Charles Jane Ashley,[123] and Carl Maria von Weber (1826). Two versions

---

[116]   No music is mentioned in her will, GB-Lna, PROB 11/1785 (26/5/1831).

[117]   *IGI*. For Cawse, see *Allgemeines Lexicon*, ed. Thieme and Becker, vi. 238.

[118]   GB-Lna, PROB 11/1119.

[119]   J. Cawse, *Introduction to the Art of Painting in Oil Colours* (London, 1822); CC: GB-Lbl, 7870.bb.65; id, *The Art of Painting Portraits, Landscapes, Animals, Draperies, Satins &c. in Oil Colours* (London, 1840); CC: GB-Lbl, 786.i.29.

[120]   *The Gentleman's Magazine*, 212 (2/1862), 242.

[121]   London, National Portrait Gallery, no. 827.

[122]   GB-Lfom (Colin Coleman). It was exhibited in the 1904 Music Loan Exhibition, see *A Special Loan Exhibition*, 123, no. 1279; *An Illustrated Catalogue*, 233. A mezzotint by E. Stalker is in London, National Portrait Gallery, no. D4251.

[123]   Exhibited by Arthur F. Hill in the 1904 Music Loan Exhibition, see *A Special Loan Exhibition*, 121, no. 1223; *An Illustrated Catalogue*, 227.

of his painting of Weber survive,[124] and 'a very interesting drawing of Weber's head, taken after death by John Cawse' was sold in July 1907.[125] Weber arrived in London on 5 March 1826, and stayed with Sir George Smart at his house in Great Portland Street, dying there during the night of 4–5 June. Cawse's wife and his daughters Mary and Harriet were all singers. Charles Dibdin junior recalled that Cawse helped to paint the scenery for the 1813 season at Sadler's Wells and listed his wife ('a very pretty singer') as a member of its company in 1808, adding that she was 'Mother of the two Misses Cawse, of Covent Garden Theatre, pupils of Sir George Smart'.[126] Smart assisted Weber during the Covent Garden production of *Oberon*, in which Harriet Cawse played Puck.[127] Henry Phillips recalled that the daughters 'both had beautiful voices; the eldest, Mary Cawse, having a high soprano, and the other, Harriet, a mezzo-soprano of great beauty and expression'.[128] Mary died in 1850, but Harriet came out of retirement to sing at the Little Theatre in the Haymarket in 1851, and enjoyed 'a comfortable and peaceful old age'.[129]

Cawse must have been interested in the gamba before he inherited items from Cheeseman: a lyra viol manuscript has the inscription 'The Gift of Mr John Webb. / July the 18[th -] 1828 – to / JCawse' on the inside front cover.[130] He clearly understood what it was: he added on a flyleaf: 'Corantos, Sarabands, Fantazias, Almaynes, Pavins, Thumps, & / Airs, by John Jenkins, Will[m]. Lawes, and Symon Ives, all Set for the / Viola da Gamba / or / Bass Viol / in / Tablature Notation', though he may not have realised that most of the pieces are the third part of lyra viol trios: the original leather binding is stamped 'TERTIVS' on the front. The donor was presumably the poet, antiquary and clergyman John Webb (1770–1869), Rector of Tretire with Michaelchurch in Herefordshire. He had an interest in music, adapting Méhul's oratorio *Joseph* and part of Haydn's *The Seasons*, and

[124] GB-Lcm, repr. J. Warrack, *Carl Maria von Weber* (Cambridge, 1968), facing 240; GB-Lfom, exhibited at the 1904 Music Loan Exhibition, see *A Special Loan Exhibition*, 123, no. 1284; *An Illustrated Catalogue*, 233.

[125] *MT*, 48 (1907), 530.

[126] *Professional & Literary Memoirs of Charles Dibdin the Younger, Dramatist and Upward of Thirty Years Manager of Minor Theatres*, ed. G. Speaight (London, 1956), 97, 106. See also 'X', 'From my Study', *MT*, 34 (1893), 75–8, at 75, quoting a letter from Arthur Cawse Edmunds, the son of Cawse's daughter Mary.

[127] Warrack, *Carl Maria von Weber*, 344–5. See also *Leaves from the Journals of Sir George Smart*, ed. H. B. and C. L. E. Cox (London, 1907), esp. 248–9.

[128] H. Phillips, *Musical and Personal Recollections during Half a Century*, 2 vols. (London, 1864), i. 168.

[129] 'X', 'From my Study', 75; *MW*, 29 (31/5/1851), 348–9.

[130] GB-HAdolmetsch, MS II.B.3 (Jeanne Dolmetsch); see John Cunningham, *The Consort Music of William Lawes, 1602–1645* (Woodbridge, 2010), esp. 120–2.

writing the words for Neukomm's oratorio *David*, all for the Birmingham Festival. Another item owned by Cawse but seemingly not by Cheeseman is a copy of Straube's *Due sonate a liuto solo* (Leipzig, 1746; repr. 1981); it has the signature 'J^{no} Cawse' on the title-page.[131]

Cawse also acquired the beautifully decorated Tielke bass viol now in the Victoria and Albert Museum (Ch. 5). It is inscribed 'John Cawse, 1835' in ink under the tailpiece, and has brass machine pegs by Baker of London that were probably fitted around that time. The same instrument (but with wooden pegs) seems to be depicted in Cawse's costume painting *On her Spanish Guitar she Played a Ditty which Lulled her Old Guardian to Sleep* (Plate 21),[132] and was played by Richard Hatton in a Concert of Ancient Music on 17 April 1845. He lent Hatton the instrument, and presumably showed him how to play it; he was also probably the old man who showed Henry Webb 'the fingering of the instrument' in 1862, the year of his death (Ch. 9). His collection was subsequently broken up: the Tielke gamba passed to the Victoria and Albert Museum via Simon Andrew Forster and Carl Engel (Ch. 9); the Jaye bass viol and Abel's copy of Caix d'Hervelois were later owned by Edward Payne; while the lyra viol manuscript was eventually acquired by Arnold Dolmetsch. In 1882 Payne added to the collection by purchasing at auction a part-autograph manuscript of fourteen sonatas and duets by Abel for gamba and violoncello or bass once owned by the Countess of Pembroke (Ch. 6).

Payne did not mention any other amateur gamba player after Cawse, so he was probably thinking of himself as the person who had maintained the 'constant succession' after 1862. Born in 1844, he was a teenager when Cawse died. In his lecture he referred to 'Mr. Henry Musgrave, of Lincoln's Inn and Beech Hill, Bucks, a well-known amateur violoncellist, who recently died at an advanced age' as someone who 'well remembered' Cawse's playing – which implies that he never heard him himself.[133] After studying at Oxford as a mature student he moved to London in 1874 on being called to the Bar at Lincoln's Inn. But he also referred to his 'early familiarity with the Viola da Gamba', mentioning that a copy of Playford's *Introduction to the Skill of Musick*, which gave the gamba 'a prominent place', had been 'among the favourite books of my childhood'.[134]

It is hard to know how many people played the gamba in Britain in the middle of the nineteenth century. Auguste Bertini evidently thought it worth while

---

[131]   GB-Lbl, e.374.a.

[132]   Christie, *British and Victorian Pictures* (29/5/2003), lot 249 (www.christies.com).

[133]   Payne, 'The Viola da Gamba', 93.

[134]   Ibid., 92.

to include the tuning of a seven-string 'Viola da Gamba' in his *New System for Learning and Acquiring Extraordinary Facility on all Musical Instruments* (1830; 2/1837; 3/1849), though it is not clear whether this reflected a perceived need or was just included for the sake of completeness.[135] Viols sometimes appeared in auctions, though we have no means of knowing whether they were sold and purchased by players rather than collectors. A 'viol da Gamba' was sold by Fletcher of Piccadilly on 24 June 1845 along with other instruments, including 'a viol d'amore, valuable Cremona';[136] gambas were advertised in Glasgow twice in 1849–50, and on the second occasion the instrument was described as 'a VIOL DI GAMBA about 200 years old';[137] a 'Viola di Gamba (said to be made by Rugger [?Vincenzo Rugeri], about the middle of the seventeenth century)' was advertised by 'H. Gee, Park-street, Walsall' in March 1863;[138] and Christie, Manson and Woods sold 'a curious old viol di gamba, inlaid with engraved mother o'pearl and ivory, formerly the property of Haydn' among the effects of 'the late Thomas Emmerson, Esq.' on 10 December 1869.[139] The last, the 1726 bass viol by Martin Voigt of Hamburg,[140] has been associated with Haydn several times, though without any evidence.[141] With the exception of John Frederick Hintz and James Watt (Ch. 4), no one is known to have made gambas in Britain between the early eighteenth century and the late nineteenth century.[142] There were presumably enough old instruments in circulation to cater for the few people who wanted to play it. Indeed, Edward Payne remarked in his 1889 lecture that 'specimens of all sorts are exceedingly common – I could have got fifty together this afternoon without difficulty'.[143]

---

[135] CC: GB-Lbl, 557*.e.24; see A. Myers, 'Fingering Charts for the Cimbasso and Other Instruments', *GSJ*, 39 (1986), 134–6.

[136] *The Times*, 13/6/1845.

[137] *The Glasgow Herald*, 14/5/1849; 25/2/1850.

[138] *MT*, 11 (1/3/1863), 18.

[139] *The Times*, 3/12/1869.

[140] London, Victoria and Albert Museum, no. 1298-1871; see A. Baines, *Victoria and Albert Museum, Catalogue of Musical Instruments*, ii: *Non-Keyboard Instruments* (London, 1968), 7, fig. 8.

[141] C. Engel, *A Descriptive Catalogue of the Musical Instruments in the South Kensington Museum* (London, 2/1874), 263; M. M. Scott, 'Haydn: Relics and Reminiscences in England', *ML*, 13 (1932), 126–36, at 133–4.

[142] George Saint-George (1841–1924) reportedly made gambas in London in the 1890s, see his obituary, *MT*, 65 (1/1/1924), 174; Rutledge, 'Late Nineteenth-Century Viol Revivals', 412–13.

[143] Payne, 'The Viola da Gamba', 93.

❧ *The Brousil Family*

THE gamba was not always identified with old music at the time, and was sometimes used in unexpected ways. One example, if it can be taken literally, is the 'complete band, consisting of violas di gamba, horns, trumpets, violins and a piano' mentioned in a report of the consecration of the St Alban's Place synagogue in London in September 1826.[144] Another is the Brousil family, a sextet of siblings from Prague, who toured continental Europe before coming to England.[145] Ranging in age from six to seventeen, they first appeared in London at the Gallery of Illustration, 14 Regent-Street, starting on 4 June 1856.[146] A report provides some details:

> They are the children of an honest-looking, simple-minded Bohemian, and are as engaging and interesting a group as it is possible to see. Like all Bohemian children, they have learned music with their alphabet; and their proficiency, extraordinary even in Bohemia, is here nothing less than marvellous. There are six of them – the eldest a girl of seventeen, the youngest a boy of six. The eldest seems to take a motherly care of her young brothers and sisters, and accompanies them very well on the piano. The second girl, about fourteen, already plays the violin almost as well as Teresa Milanolli; admiration of whom, it seems, induced her to make the violin her instrument. Her eldest brother, a year younger than herself, is an admirable violoncellist; the next boy plays the tenor part on the viol da gamba; and the youngest boy and girl, infants of six and seven, play the violin underparts, accompanying with the intelligence, precision, and firmness of veteran players. They perform the best solo and concerted music of the great masters, and it is impossible to listen to them without admiring delight.[147]

Early newspaper reports mention 'De Beriot's concerto no. 7', 'David's variations, partly on Masaniello', and 'some of the best compositions of Lafont, Vieuxtemps, David, Mozart, and Artot'.[148] On 18 March 1857 they played the following programme for Queen Victoria at Buckingham Palace:

144 *MC*, 23/9/1826.

145 For the family, see C. von Wurzbach, *Biographisches Lexicon des Kaiserthums Österreich*, 60 vols. (Vienna, 1856–91), ii. 161. In the 1861 census (www.ancestry.co.uk) they are shown as living at 13 Nottingham Place, St Marylebone, and the head of the household, Francis Brousil (49) is said to have been 'Ex Employee Austrian Guards'. The 1871 census lists them at 60 Burton Crescent, St Pancras.

146 *MC*, 30/5/1856; *The Times*, 31/5/1856.

147 *The Belfast News-Letter*, 11/6/1856.

148 *Lloyd's Weekly Newspaper*, 15/6/1856; *Jackson's Oxford Journal*, 30/8/1856.

Illus. 8.1 The Brousil Family, *The Illustrated London News*, 12 March 1859

No. 1. Fantasia – "Masaniello" .. .. .. Lafont.
   Violin, solo Mademoiselle Bertha 14 years of age
   Piano – Antonia   17 years
   Violin, 2d – Caecilie   6 years
   Violin, 1st M. Aloys   7 years
   Viola de Gamba – Adolphe 11 years
   Violoncello – Albin   13 years
No. 2. Reverie, violin solo .. .. .. Vieuxtemps.
No. 3. "The Bird on the Tree," sestetto .. .. Hauser.
No. 4. Duo, arranged by Bertha Brousil for Aloys, 7 years,
   and Caecilie, 6 years.
No. 5. Carnaval Bohemian, quintetto .. .. Mildner.[149]

Thus, in 1856–7 the group consisted of three violins, gamba, cello and piano, and played mostly modern salon music. The virtuosic piece by the French violinist Charles Philippe Lafont was based on themes from Auber's opera *La muette de Portici* or *Massaniello* (1828),[150] while Mildner's 'Carnaval Bohemian', also known as 'Variations on Bohemian folk songs', was written for the group by Moriz Mildner, Professor at the Prague Conservatoire.[151] 'The Bird on the Tree' was presumably by the Hungarian violinist Miska Hauser, who composed a number of

[149] *The Times*, 19/3/1857.

[150] A version for violin and piano was published as C. P. Lafont, *Grand Fantasia & Variations, on Favorite Airs in the Opera of Masaniello, for the Violin, with an Accompaniment for the Piano Forte* (London, 1836); CC: GB-Lbl, g.619.e.(3).

[151] Wurzbach, *Biographisches Lexicon*, ii. 161.

salon pieces for his instrument.[152] A second appearance at Buckingham Palace, on 31 March, included a caprice by Vieuxtemps, Hauser's Notturno, a quartet by Bertha Brousil, and Mildner's Carnaval Bohemian – evidently their *pièce de résistance*.[153] Later programmes included more serious music, by Bach, Handel, Haydn, Mozart, Beethoven, Mendelssohn, and Spohr.[154] Adolphe used a viol as a viola substitute because he was too small to manage a large instrument under his chin: 'The advantage of using the viola da Gamba in preference to the ordinary viola is, in this case, obvious – inasmuch as the viola or tenor, played in the ordinary manner, would be beyond the management of a child of twelve years of age.'[155] A photograph taken around the time they first appeared in London shows Adolphe holding what appears to be a tenor viol set up as a four-string instrument without frets (Plate 22), while another picture shows him holding a viola-shaped instrument between his knees (Illus. 8.1).[156]

The family toured Britain for a number of years, and Adolphe continued to play the gamba until at least the end of 1862,[157] though by 26 November 1863, when they appeared at Kington in Herefordshire, the group was a quartet consisting of Bertha and Cecilia (violins), 'Alonzo' or Aloys ('viol di gamba'), and Adolphe (violoncello and concertina); Aloys was then about thirteen years of age.[158] Adolphe (later known as Hans Adolf) played regularly in London chamber concerts between 1886 and 1899, and was still active in 1914, when he was dismissed from the Guildhall School of Music because of his nationality.[159] The Brousils became something of an institution, and even attracted an imitation. Members of the Greenhead family toured Britain as the Cremona Musical Union for getting on for forty years, between at least 1859 and 1896.[160] On at least one occasion they used a gamba: in two concerts at the Royal Public Rooms, Exeter in December 1866 a group of eight played piano, flute, two violins, viola, 'Viola-de-Gamba', violoncello, and 'Cornet-a-Piston'.[161] As with the Brousils, the gamba was played by a child, Master Everard Greenhead, though the programme was

---

[152] For Hauser, see *Grove 1*, iv. 669–70.

[153] *MC*, 2/4/1857.

[154] For instance, *The Derby Mercury*, 5/5/1858.

[155] *The Caledonian Mercury*, 17/5/1858.

[156] Royal Collection, RCIN 2906228 (http://www.royalcollection.org.uk/eGallery); *The Illustrated London News*, 12/3/1859.

[157] For instance, *Liverpool Mercury*, 5/12/1862.

[158] *MT*, 10 (1/1/1863), 373–4.

[159] *MW*, 64 (9/10/1886), 648; *Musical News*, 17 (1/7/1899), 17; *The Musical Herald*, 799 (1/10/1914), 360.

[160] *The Era*, 6/3/1859; 25/1/1896.

[161] *Trewman's Exeter Flying Post*, 28/11/1866.

entitled 'MORE COMIC', so it may have been more parody than tribute; they performed in exotic costumes and included comic songs in their programmes. By 1874 Everard was playing 'contra-bass' in the group.[162]

Joseph Lidel

ANOTHER person who owned and may have played old instruments, but seems to have had no interest in old music, was Joseph Lidel, the grandson of Andreas. He was born in Bavaria around 1807, and was the cellist of the Hermann string quartet, formed in Munich in 1824.[163] He toured with it across Europe, coming to England in 1826, and settled in Dublin when the quartet broke up in 1830. He is first heard of as a soloist in London in May 1838, when he was hailed as 'a most accomplished artist and clever musician'.[164] He appeared in many London concerts in the 1840s and 50s, and published numerous arrangements of popular songs and arias for violoncello and piano.[165] In the early 1850s he worked a good deal for Charles Hallé in Manchester, and conducted the Liverpool Amateur Glee and Madrigal Union.[166] He was living in London by 1861, where he died in on 25 August 1878.[167]

Lidel seems to have inherited several of his grandfather's instruments. On Thursday 22 November 1849 he gave a paper to the Society of Antiquaries in London about a Tielke baryton of 1687 in his possession:

> Mr. Lidel, of Albany Street, Regent's Park, exhibited a viol-shaped musical instrument called a *Barytone*, now disused, made by the celebrated Joachim Fielke [*sic*] in the year 1687: it was accompanied by a detailed account of the construction of the instrument. The Barytone is of a very curious and complex character. "The six cat-gut strings pass over a bridge," writes Mr. Lidel, "so constructed as to admit of the passage of the eleven wires under it, while the cat-guts pass over it and are made fast to an ebony tail-piece of the ordinary shape. The wires are made fast to an ebony bar passing obliquely under the bridge. The head-piece is very broad, and richly ornamented with open carving of classical subjects." These, together with all the other ornaments, are executed in a tasty and masterly manner; and the

---

162   *The Glasgow Herald*, 16/11/1874.

163   *Grove 1*, iv. 507.

164   *MW*, 9 (31/5/1838), 87.

165   *BLIC* lists 28 editions, arrangements and compositions by him.

166   *MT*, 5 (1/7/1853), 221.

167   *MT*, 19 (1/9/1878), 505. In the 1861 census he is shown as aged 54, of 42 Mornington Place, Marylebone, Professor of Music, born in Bavaria.

spaces between the designs are filled up with cleverly-cut open arabesques. The back is perfectly flat.

> Regarding the range of this instrument, Mr. Lidel remarks that it is "strung with six cat-gut strings for the bow, and eleven steel wires, which vibrate by sympathy with the cat-gut strings. The tone gains much in power by this arrangement,– the number of wires being sufficient to furnish constant concords with the strings in the course of the passages played on them with a bow. The amalgamation of the round tones of one set of strings, with the crisp metallic tones of the other, produces an effect of a peculiarly pleasing character; and it is well adapted to the *notturno* style of music".[168]

This published report was based on a manuscript in the Society's archives, prepared by Lidel for its secretary, John G. Ackerman.[169] It confirms that the maker's name was Tielke, not 'Fielke', and adds some information about its provenance:

> It became the property of the Duke of Tuscany who gave it to Prince Esterházy he being a fine performer on the Barytone, and a pupil of my Grandfather's (Andreas Lidel). / The Prince presented this instrument to him in token of the admiration of his great talent as a performer on the <u>Barytone.</u>

Lidel also wrote that 'the execution of the carving' on the 'headpiece' is 'very masterly', and that 'Notwithstanding the age of the Instrument they [the carvings] are still very sharp and do credit to the taste of the artist. On the back of [the] head is a Lion's face very sharp and well executed.' Lidel informed Ackerman that he wished to sell the instrument, inviting any interested member 'to treat with him as to terms'.

It is not known whether Lidel sold his baryton, and his description does not correspond to any complete Tielke known today, though a Tielke baryton neck surviving in a private collection has been identified with it.[170] It has also been identified with a 1687 Tielke apparently converted from a bass viol into a violoncello,[171] though the argument was based on the inaccurate summary of

---

168 *Proceedings of the Society of Antiquaries of London, 2: From April 1849 to April 1853* (London, 1853), 26–7.

169 Transcribed in T. M. Pamplin, 'The Baroque Baryton: the Origin and Development in the Seventeenth Century of a Solo, Self-Accompanying, Bowed and Plucked Instrument Played from Tablature' (PhD diss., Kingston U., 2000), 37–8.

170 See the discussion in ibid., 38–40.

171 London, Horniman Museum, no. 326A; see G. Hellwig, *Joachim Tielke: ein Hamburger Lauten- und Violenmacher der Barockzeit* (Frankfurt am Main, 1980), 190.

Lidel's talk published by Sandys and Forster rather than on the original documents.[172] Sandys and Forster managed to confuse it with a second instrument, a
viola d'amore: 'This instrument [the baryton] was exhibited as a viol d'amour at
the conversazione of the Musical Society of London, July 2, 1862, and Mr. Lidel
informed us that it had been given by the then Bishop of Salzburg to his grandfather.' According to Carl Engel, Lidel's viola d'amore was 'made in the year 1719,
and … formerly belonged to the Prince-Bishop of Salzburg, whose coat of arms
is gilded on the front. The back of this instrument is carved out of a solid piece of
wood.'[173] From this we can see that it is a viola d'amore attributed to the Salzburg
court luthier Andreas Ferdinand Mayr; its date is no longer visible, though it
displays the arms of Franz Anton Graf von Harrach, Prince-Bishop of Salzburg
from 1709 to 1727.[174] Thus Lidel owned at least two of his grandfather's instruments, and was interested enough to exhibit them. He may have done so in order
to encourage profitable sales, though he clearly understood in detail how the
baryton worked and should be played. It is hard to believe that, as a professional
string player, he had never tried to play it himself. Whether he also inherited a
gamba from his grandfather and played it is not known. But, as with the Brousil
family, there is no sign that he was interested in old music.

❧ The Late Nineteenth Century

By the 1880s the gamba was firmly associated with the developing early music
movement, though the older tradition of providing it with contemporary
music still lingered here and there. A case in point may be the concert given by
the Kyrle Choir in the Queen's Rooms, Glasgow on 14 April 1885. It consisted
mostly of modern choral works – Niels Gade's *Spring's Message* (the cantata
Frühlings-Botschaft, op. 35 of 1858), 'The Soul's Aspiration' by Julius Otto Grimm,
Adolf Jensen's 'Feast of Adonis' (the chorus *Adonis-Feier*, published in 1882), and
C. H. Lloyd's cantata *Hero and Leander* (1884) – though 'Two solos were played
on the viol di gamba, by Mr. Walton, a member of Mr. [W. H.] Cole's orchestra'.[175]
There is no hint that they were not contemporary pieces. Even musicians associated with the early music revival sometimes played contemporary music on
their old instruments. Carli Zoeller, a prolific composer, wrote new music for

---

[172] Sandys and Forster, *The History of the Violin*, 131.

[173] C. Engel, *A Descriptive Catalogue*, 360.

[174] London, Victoria and Albert Museum, no. 722-1878; see Baines, *Victoria and
        Albert Museum, Catalogue of Musical Instruments*, ii. 9–10, 110, fig. 10. For Mayr,
        see K. Birsak, *Salzburger Geigen und Lauten des Barock* (Salzburg, 2001), esp.
        47–54.

[175] *MT*, 26 (1/5/1885), 272.

the viola d'amore, as well as collecting old instruments and assembling a large collection of music old and modern for viola d'amore and gamba (Ch. 9). On one occasion, during a lecture to the Cremona Society on 14 March 1889, he played his own duet for viola d'amore and gamba, 'Hymn to St. Cecilia', with Edward Payne.[176]

Payne was more focused on old music than Zoeller, though a transcription in his hand of Schumann's 'Abendlied', op. 85, no. 12 (1849) is evidence of his interest in providing the gamba with a contemporary repertory (Plate 23).[177] It is headed 'Viol da Gamba' and consists of the voice part written out in the treble clef (to be read an octave lower in the eighteenth-century manner) with fingerings for the instrument. Even Arnold Dolmetsch started as a conventional violinist and composed a number of original pieces, starting with the 'introduction and scherzo for small orchestra' performed at a Royal College of Music student concert in December 1884.[178] His first London concert, at the Steinway Hall on 26 June 1889, was with a conventional string orchestra of about thirty of his pupils. They played a suite from Purcell's *Dioclesian* as well as a work of his own, described as 'four clever pieces for string band'.[179] The programme included Corelli's Sonata in F, op. 5, no. 10, for violin and continuo, though there is no mention of a harpsichord in the review.

At that stage Dolmetsch was no more engaged with old music or historical performance practice than many of his contemporaries, and he kept the two sides of his creative personality separate: his original compositions do not use old instruments, and he did not go as far as those such as Paul de Wit and Henry Saint-George who argued that old instruments should be provided with a modern repertory, thus reintegrating them into mainstream musical life.[180] Saint-George (1866–1917) wrote viola d'amore solos for his father George and gamba solos for himself,[181] and looked forward to the day when 'we shall find violists performing

[176] *MT*, 30 (1/4/1889), 233; C. Zoeller, 'The Viole d'Amour', *MS*, 36 (23/3/1889), 236–8, at 238; C. Zoeller, 'The Viole d'Amour', *MO*, 12 (4/1889), 335–7, at 337.

[177] MS in the possession of the Payne family (John Catch). Paul de Wit reportedly played the piece on the gamba in concerts in Leipzig in May 1882, see J. Boer, 'The Viola da Gamba and the Nineteenth Century', in *Viola da gamba – Baryton – Arpeggione: Festschrift Alfred Lessing, Dusseldorf 2000*, ed. B. R. Appel and Boer (Utrecht, 2003), 35–41, at 38.

[178] *MO*, 8 (1/1885), 175.

[179] *MT*, 30 (1/8/1889), 488. They were presumably those published as A. Dolmetsch, *Suite of Four Pieces* (London, 1893); CC: GB-Lbl, g.1023.(1).

[180] See Rutledge, 'Late Nineteenth-Century Viol Revivals', 409–10. For Saint-George, see *MT*, 58 (1/3/1917), 117.

[181] See, for instance, the programme reproduced in *Cremona*, 1 (1907), 79.

the *best* music of today and yesterday exactly as do the violinists', and when 'the gamba and the viola d'amore will find their way into the orchestra; not merely with experimental obbligato solos but massed as an integral part of the string foundation'.[182] The gamba and the viola d'amore acquired substantial repertories of new music during the twentieth century, though they never joined the orchestra, and Saint-George's reintegrationist programme proved to be a fantasy in an increasingly fragmented musical world. As we shall see in Chapter 9, his rival Dolmetsch soon provided a more viable model for the future by devoting himself to early music, to the revival of old instruments, and to historical performance practice.

---

[182] H. Saint-George, 'The Revival of Ancient Instruments', *MO*, 29 (3, 4/1906), 443–4, 512–13, at 513. See also Rutledge, 'Late Nineteenth-Century Viol Revivals', 410.

'Performed upon the Original Instruments for which it was Written': the Viola da Gamba and the Early Music Revival

UNTIL the eighteenth century music was essentially a fashionable novelty that hardly outlived the composers who brought it into existence. Thus Monteverdi, Schütz and other early Baroque composers were quickly forgotten after their deaths. Palestrina was remembered throughout the seventeenth and eighteenth centuries, but that was largely because his music was held up as an ideal exemplar of *stile antico* counterpoint; embodied in Fux's *Gradus ad parnassum* (Vienna, 1725), it was used as a model by generations of Austrian composers, including Haydn, Mozart and Beethoven.[1] Lully was perhaps the first composer whose music continued to be performed by later generations: his operas remained part of the repertory of the Paris opera in altered form until the late eighteenth century.[2] Corelli was probably the first whose music never entirely fell out of use, though that too was partly because it was regarded as a compositional model.[3]

ᛒ *The Early Music Revival in England*

HOWEVER, England was the place where the early music revival really began. William Weber argued that it can be traced back to the Civil War, when Anglican institutions were under threat and cathedral choirs had been

---

[1] A. Mann, *The Great Composer as Teacher and Student: Theory and Practice of Composition: Bach, Handel, Haydn, Mozart, Beethoven, Schubert* (New York, 1987; repr. 1994); J. Lester, *Compositional Theory in the Eighteenth Century* (Cambridge, MA, 1994; repr. 1996), 26–48.

[2] H. Schneider, *Die Rezeption der Opern Lullys im Frankreich des Ancien Regime*, Mainzer Studien zur Musikwissenschaft, 16 (Tutzing, 1982); W. Weber, 'Lully and the Rise of Musical Classics in the Eighteenth Century', in *Jean-Baptiste Lully: actes du colloque / Kongreßbericht Saint-Germain-en-laye – Heidelberg 1987*, ed. J. de La Gorce and H. Schneider (Laaber, 1990), 581–90.

[3] P. Allsop, *Arcangelo Corelli: 'New Orpheus of Our Times'* (Oxford, 1999), esp. 188–99.

disbanded.[4] John Barnard's *First Book of Selected Church Musick*, an anthology of cathedral music by Elizabethan and Jacobean composers, was published in 1641 on the eve of the Civil War, though it was only disseminated after the Restoration. The retrospective nature of the repertory is illustrated by James Clifford's *Divine Services and Anthems* (1663, 1664), consisting of the texts of mainly pre-Civil War works;[5] Henry Aldrich's adaptations of Palestrina and Carissimi as Anglican anthems;[6] Henry Purcell's score copies of anthems by Byrd, Tallis, Gibbons and others, largely taken from Barnard;[7] or Thomas Tudway's manuscript collection of 'ancient church music', compiled for Edward Harley, Earl of Oxford in the early eighteenth century.[8] Pre-Civil War anthems and services were initially copied after 1660 because no one had been writing church music for nearly twenty years and the repertory was in danger of being scattered and lost, though in time works by Humfrey, Blow, Purcell, and their contemporaries joined them in what gradually became a cumulative repertory. It was codified by publications, notably William Boyce's *Cathedral Music* (1760, 1768, 1773), enlarged by Samuel Arnold (1790), and John Page's *Harmonia Sacra, a Collection of Anthems in Score, Selected ... from the most Eminent Masters of the Sixteenth, Seventeenth, and Eighteenth Centuries* (1800).[9]

By the 1720s the interest in old music was beginning to expand beyond the choir-stall. The Academy of Ancient Music, founded in 1726 as the Academy of Vocal Music, focused on Renaissance polyphony but also performed Purcell's theatre works and other later works.[10] Later societies devoted at least partially to old music included the Madrigal Society, founded in 1741 and still in existence; the Glee Club, founded by Arnold in 1788, which mixed madrigals with

4   W. Weber, *The Rise of Musical Classics in Eighteenth-Century England: a Study in Canon, Ritual, and Ideology* (Oxford, 1992), esp. 23–8. See also T. Day, 'A Renaissance Revival in Eighteenth-Century England', *MQ*, 57 (1971), 575–92.

5   Weber, *The Rise of Musical Classics*, 26.

6   Ibid., 32–6; R. Shay, '"Naturalizing" Palestrina and Carissimi in late Seventeenth-Century Oxford: Henry Aldrich and his Recompositions', *ML*, 77 (1996), 368–400; ME: H. Aldrich, *Selected Anthems and Motet Recompositions*, ed. Shay, RRMBE, 85 (Madison, WI, 1998).

7   R. Shay and R. Thompson, *Purcell Manuscripts: the Principal Musical Sources* (Cambridge, 2000), 33–46.

8   Weber, *The Rise of Musical Classics*, 36–46.

9   H. D. Johnstone, 'The Genesis of Boyce's *Cathedral Music*', *ML*, 56 (1975), 26–40. The subscription proposals for *Harmonia Sacra*, dated 1/5/1797, are in *ECCO*, ESTC T002875.

10 J. Hawkins, *An Account of the Institution and Progress of the Academy of Ancient Music* (London, 1770; repr. Cambridge 1998); Weber, *The Rise of Musical Classics*, 56–74.

modern glees; and the Concentores Sodales, founded in 1798, which performed all types of old vocal music.[11] These groups mostly performed from manuscript transcriptions, made by or for collectors and antiquarians such as Henry Needler, John Travers, John Immyns, Thomas Bever, Edmund Thomas Warren, Benjamin Cooke junior, and John Stafford Smith. Publications including old secular vocal music included Warren's *A Collection of Vocal Harmony ... Composed by the Best Masters* (c. 1775), Stafford Smith's *A Collection of English Songs ... Composed about the Year 1500* (1779), Warren's *Apollonian Harmony, a Collection of Scarce & Celebrated Glees, Catches, Madrigals, Canzonets, Rounds, & Canons, Antient and Modern* (c. 1790), and Stafford Smith's *Musica antiqua: a Selection of Music of this and other Countries, from the Commencement of the Twelfth to the Beginning of the Eighteenth Century* (1812). This largely amateur and antiquarian movement was given a shop window in London's professional concert life by the Concerts of Ancient Music, founded in 1776.[12] It offered its aristocratic clientele a repertory founded on Handel, but also including Renaissance madrigals, eighteenth-century Italian vocal music, and sacred and secular vocal music by Purcell and other English composers.

The early music movement may have started as a pragmatic response to the upheavals of the Civil War, though it soon acquired a set of ideologies. Around 1700 it was associated with Tory concerns to preserve the institutions of the Church of England,[13] though later it became more diffuse and even contradictory. It was connected with attempts to define and conserve a national musical identity in the face of the rage for modern Continental music in the *galant* style, a dichotomy expressed, for instance, by the opposed outlooks and attitudes of Sir John Hawkins and Charles Burney,[14] or the contrasted repertories and audiences of the Bach–Abel concerts and the Concerts of Ancient Music.[15] But it was also part of a fashionable pre-Romantic interest in the past in many areas of British culture, expressed in such things as the revival of Gothic architecture, the mock-

---

[11] J. G. Crauford, 'The Madrigal Society', *PRMA*, 82 (1955–6), 33–46; P. Lovell, '"Ancient" Music in Eighteenth-Century England', *ML*, 60 (1979), 401–15; Weber, *The Rise of Musical Classics*, esp. 189–93.

[12] J. E. Matthew, 'The Antient Concerts, 1776–1848', *PMA*, 33 (1906–7), 55–79; Weber, *The Rise of Musical Classics*, esp. 143–97; F. M. Palmer, *Domenico Dragonetti in England (1794–1846): the Career of a Double Bass Virtuoso* (Oxford, 1997), 122–41.

[13] Weber, *The Rise of Musical Classics*, esp. 32–56.

[14] P. Scholes, *The Great Dr. Burney*, 2 vols. (London, 1948; repr. 1971), i. 289–305; R. Lonsdale, *Dr. Charles Burney, a Literary Biography* (Oxford, 1965; repr. 1986), 189–225; K. S. Grant, *Dr. Burney as Critic and Historian of Music* (Ann Arbor, MI, 1983), 283–92; Weber, *The Rise of Musical Classics*, 205–22.

[15] S. McVeigh, *Concert Life in London from Mozart to Haydn* (Cambridge, 1993), esp. 11–27.

antique poetry of James Macpherson (as 'Ossian') and Thomas Chatterton, the
Gothic novel, the trend towards historical accuracy in painting and in the theatre,
and, perhaps most important, the development of antiquarian scholarship.[16] In
music, as in other fields, Britain led the way: John Mainwaring's *Memoirs of the
Life of the late George Frederic Handel* (1760) was the first full-length biography of
a composer; the first comprehensive music histories were by Hawkins (1776) and
Burney (1776, 1782, 1789); Arnold's *The Works of Handel* (1787–97) was the first
collected edition of a composer.

ఉ *The Revival of Old Instrumental Music*

I T is important to realise that this activity was mostly concerned with vocal
music. There is little evidence of interest in early instrumental music, though
Hawkins included some keyboard pieces from GB-Lbl, Add. MS 30513 (the mid-
sixteenth-century Mulliner Book) in his *History*, and copied US-NYp, Drexel
MS 5609 from several seventeenth-century virginal books.[17] Stafford Smith, who
owned the Mulliner Book at the time, included a larger selection from it and
other virginal books in *Musica Antiqua*.[18] The nearest Stafford Smith came to
publishing consort music was two pieces by Jenkins: the two-part Air in D major
VdGS 163 (presumably taken from his copy of *New Ayres and Dialogues* (1678)
by John Banister and Thomas Low), and a two-part version of Lady Katherine
Audley's Bells VdGS 161.[19] He also owned a set of Elizabethan part-books of con-
sort music and wordless vocal music, now GB-Lbl, Add. MSS 30480–30484, and
'Corelli's Sonatas and Albinoni's Concertos, MS. in Score, with a set of Viol di
Gamba. – Sonatas, MS', the last purchased at the sale of Boyce's music library in
April 1778, lot 220.[20] The sonatas are unidentified, and there is no evidence that
Stafford Smith or Boyce owned a gamba or played the instrument.

A passage from a three-part version of Lady Katherine Audley's Bells was

[16] L. Lipking, *The Ordering of the Arts in Eighteenth-Century England* (Princeton,
NJ, 1970); P. Langford, *A Polite and Commercial People: England, 1727–1783*
(Oxford, 1989), esp. 473–6; R. Sweet, *Antiquaries: the Discovery of the Past in
Eighteenth-Century Britain* (London, 2004).

[17] HawkinsH, ii. 920–1, 924–33; V. Brookes, *British Keyboard Music to c. 1660:
Sources and Thematic Index* (Oxford, 1996), esp. 58–65; J. Flynn, 'A Reconsidera-
tion of the Mulliner Book (British Library, Add. MS 30513): Music Education in
Sixteenth-Century England' (PhD diss., Duke U., 1993), 9–13.

[18] J. Stafford Smith, *Musica antiqua* (London, 1812), 38–9, 41–3, 70–84; CC: GB-Lbl,
H.81.

[19] Stafford Smith, *Musica antiqua*, 168–9.

[20] F. L. Gramenz, 'John Stafford Smith, 1750–1836: an Early English Musicologist',
2 vols. (PhD diss., Boston U., 1987), esp. ii. 47, 126–7.

just about the only consort music Burney printed in his *History*, though he also included a few early keyboard pieces in whole or in part, and he owned some manuscripts of consort music.[21] He seems to have been the only eighteenth-century English musician to transcribe a substantial amount of consort music, though he did so because he wanted to write about it (and usually be rude about it) in his *History*, not because he wanted to perform it. GB-Lbl, Add. MSS 11585–11588 include his transcriptions of fantasias by Parsons, Tye, Bull, Ward, and du Caurroy, ricercars and canzonas by Frescobaldi, and four numbers from Thomas Morley's *First Booke of Consort Lessons* (2/1611), scored up just from his copies of the treble viol and cittern parts with an added bass.[22]

One or two antiquarians involved in the revival of old vocal music also played the gamba, though they do not seem to have brought their two interests together. There is no sign, for instance, that John Gostling and his friends used the manuscripts of viol consort music he owned (Ch. 2), or that John Immyns, founder, 'president and instructor' of the Madrigal Society, got his fellow-members to indulge in consort playing as well as madrigal singing during their meetings, despite playing the gamba according to Hawkins (Ch. 2). In 1753 a member of the Madrigal Society was paid 1s. 6d. 'for a string to his bass viol he having lent it to the Society',[23] though we cannot be sure that this instrument really was a gamba, or that it was being used in old consort music.

The antiquarian interests of the composer William Shield (1748–1829) were fostered by his friend the folk-song collector Joseph Ritson; they collaborated in *A Select Collection of English Songs* (1783) and *Scotish Songs* (1794).[24] Shield published two remarkable collections, *An Introduction to Harmony* (1800; 2/1815) and *Rudiments of Thorough Bass* (1815).[25] Despite their titles, they are advanced composition treatises, and include some old music as examples, including complete pieces or extracts by Croft, J. S. Bach, Handel, Boyce, and others. There is even a page of tablature 'engraved from Princess (afterwards Queen) Anne's lute book';

[21] BurneyH, ii. 78–9, 99–102, 324–5; White, *A Catalogue of the Valuable and very Fine Collection of Music, Printed and MS., of the late Charles Burney, Mus. D.F.R.S.* (8–15/8/1814; repr. Amsterdam, 1973), 17–19, 25.

[22] White, *Catalogue*, 15, lot 387.

[23] Crauford, 'The Madrigal Society', 37.

[24] R. Fiske, *English Theatre Music in the Eighteenth Century* (Oxford, 2/1986), 544–6; D. Harker, *Fakesong: the Manufacture of British 'Folksong', 1700 to the Present* (Milton Keynes, 1985), esp. 15–37.

[25] W. Shield, *An Introduction to Harmony* (London, 1800; 2/1815); CC: GB-Lbl, 785.l.33.(1); author's collection. W. Shield, *Rudiments of Thorough Bass* (London, 1815); CC: collection of David Wright. See also Fiske, *English Theatre Music in the Eighteenth Century*, 308, 310, 404, 546, 550–1, 557.

it is actually for five-course Baroque guitar.[26] Shield's possessions auctioned after his death in 1829 included a three-stop chamber organ (II/250), 'A Violoncello by *Barrack* Norman, in case' (II/251), 'A Viol d'Amour in case' (II/252), 'A Viol di Gamba' (II/254), and 'A Lute in case' (II/256).[27] The music in the sale included a copy of Orlando Gibbons's *Fantazies of III. Parts* (*c.* 1620) (I/23), though there is no evidence that Shield played it on his gamba, or even that he played the instrument at all.

This seems to have remained the situation until well into the nineteenth century. A number of people owned and played gambas (Ch. 8), and there was an increasing interest in manuscripts and prints of old consort music. But no one seems to have had the idea of bringing the two things together. The people who played the gamba in England in the decades either side of 1800 seem to have played contemporary music, or at least music in the eighteenth-century solo tradition. John Cawse's manuscript of seventeenth-century lyra viol music would not have been much use as a source of repertory for his gamba because it is only one part-book of a set of three containing trios; he does not seem to have owned the other two books, which are lost (Ch. 8). In 1843 Edward Rimbault published Gibbons's fantasias in score indicating that they were 'Composed for Viols' but without mentioning performance in the introduction.[28] No parts were published, only a keyboard version 'compressed from the score' by George Macfarren.[29]

Some types of old instrumental music continued to be performed in late eighteenth-century England. The Concerts of Ancient Music included items from the cumulative repertory of English string concertos founded on the concerti grossi of Corelli and Geminiani, including works by Geminiani, Handel, Giuseppe Sammartini, and Charles Avison; Avison's op. 4, no. 4 (1758) and two concer-

[26] Shield, *Rudiments of Thorough Bass*, 57. According to J. M. Ward, *Sprightly & Cheerful Musick: Notes on the Cittern, Gittern and Guitar in 16th- and 17th-Century England, LSJ*, 21 (1979–81), whole vol., at 232, the manuscript was 'presented to Wm. Shield by his friend James Smith', and is now at NL-DHgm, MS 4.E.73.

[27] Musgrave, *A Catalogue of the Music, Books, Instruments, Paintings, Engravings, &c., late the Property of William Shield Esquire (Deceased)* (22–3/6/1829); CC: GB-Lbl, 7897.d.13.(22). For Shield's library, see also C. Brown and P. Holman, 'Thomas Busby and his "FAC SIMILES OF CELEBRATED COMPOSERS"', *EMP*, 12 (August 2003), 3–12.

[28] O. Gibbons, *Fantasies in Three Parts, Composed for Viols*, ed. E. F. Rimbault (London, 1843); CC: GB-Lbl, I.431.

[29] O. Gibbons, *Fantasies in Three Parts*, arr. G. A. Macfarren (London, 1843); CC: GB-Lbl, R.M.7.c.7.

tos by Capel Bond (1766) were performed until 1812.[30] But this archaic repertory does not seem to have been performed using the instruments and the performing style of the past, and when pre-Baroque vocal pieces were performed they were usually arranged for orchestra, latterly by Henry Bishop, principal conductor from 1842 until the end of the Concerts in 1848.[31] So, when a Mediaeval song, 'L'autrier par la matinée' by Thibaut IV, King of Navarre, was sung in a concert on 29 April 1846, it was accompanied by the orchestra using Bishop's orchestration.[32]

🎵 Old Music on Old Instruments

THE idea, central to the modern early music movement, of using old instruments to play old music had its origin in Paris rather than London, with the work of François-Joseph Fétis. Fétis gave his first 'historical concert' on 8 April 1832 at the Paris Conservatoire, where he was librarian.[33] A survey of opera from Peri, Caccini and Monteverdi to Méhul, Rossini and Weber, it included instrumentalists playing 'des parties de viole, de basse de viole, de clavecin, de guitare, d'orgue et de harpe'.[34] The second concert, at the Conservatoire on 16 December 1832 (postponed from 18 November), included a 'Pièce de viole à cinque parties, par Gervaise (1556)', 'Pièce d'épinette tirée du *Virginal Book* de la reine Elisabeth' (now known as the Fitzwilliam Virginal Book), '*Concerti passegiati* pour violes, violon français, harpe, orgue et théorbe, composés par Emilio del Cavaliere', and '*La Romanesca*, fameux air de danse italien de la fin du seizième siècle'.[35] In the third concert, at the Salle Ventadour on 24 March 1833, *La Romanesca* was repeated alongside 'Un concerto de chambre pour une mandoline, un luth, une viole d'amour, une basse de viole

---

[30] O. Edwards and P. Holman, 'Capel Bond', *GMO*; N. L. Stephens, 'Charles Avison', *GMO*.

[31] M. Murata, 'Dr Burney Bought a Music Book …', *The Journal of Musicology*, 17 (1999), 76–111, at 95–107.

[32] CC of the programme: GB-Lbl, 11784.e.1. Bishop's arrangement is in GB-Lcm, MS 769, fols. 9–11v (Ann Royle).

[33] F. Niecks, 'Historical Concerts', *Monthly Musical Record*, 12 (10, 11/1882), 217–22, 242–5, esp. 219–20, 242; R. Wangermée, 'Les premiers concerts historiques à Paris', in *Mélanges Ernest Closson*, ed. C. van den Borren and A. van der Linden (Brussels, 1948), 185–96; H. Haskell, *The Early Music Revival, a History* (Mineola, NY, 2/1996), 19–21; K. Ellis, *Interpreting the Musical Past: Early Music in Nineteenth-Century France* (Oxford, 2005), esp. 22–5.

[34] *Rm*, 14/4/1832, 81–5, at 84 (Katharine Ellis).

[35] *Rm*, 3/11/1832, 318–19; *Rm*, 22/12/1832, 372–3; *Rm*, 29/12/1832, 377–9; *Rm*, 5/1/1833, 389–90 (Katharine Ellis).

et un clavecin, par Jean Strobach', played by a group including Fernando Sor (lute), Chrétien Urhan (viola d'amore), and Olive-Charlier Vaslin (bass viol).[36]

Fétis's historical concerts made a great impression in France and further afield, even though some questioned the historical accuracy of the instruments used. Aristide Farrenc wrote that the instrument Fétis called 'violone' was actually just a modern double bass,[37] while the cellist and gamba player August Tolbecque claimed in 1898 that Fétis had difficulty finding musicians capable of playing old instruments and so resorted to modernising them, 'setting up the bass viol as a cello, the viola d'amore as a viola, the pardessus de viole as a violin, the lute as a guitar, etc.' ('montant la basse de viole en *violoncello*, la viole d'amour en *alto*, le pardessus de viole en *violon*, le luth en *guitare*, etc.'); he added: 'I can vouch for the accuracy of my statement, having known the artists who took part in these concerts intimately' ('Je garantis l'exactitude de ce que j'avance, ayant connu intimement des artistes qui faisaient partie de ces concerts').[38] To be fair, Fétis wrote in 1838 that 'the performance never matched what I had in mind, and unfortunately I could not hope for better' ('l'exécution n'a jamais répondu à mes vues, et malheuresement je n'en pouvais espérer de meilleure').[39] Nevertheless, he articulated a crucial tenet of the later early music movement when he wrote that 'Art does not progress, it transforms itself' ('l'art ne progresse pas, mais qu'il se transforme') – an early challenge in musical discourse to the Enlightenment idea of progress.[40]

The first people in Britain to use obsolete instruments to play old music seem to have been the unidentified individuals who accompanied 'a sprightly and quaint ballad by HENRY LAWES' on 'the viol di gamba and harpsichord' during a concert under the direction of the harpist Nicholas Bochsa (1789–1856) at Drury Lane on 19 February 1836.[41] The song, also described as 'Lawe's ballad, "Silly heart" ', seems to have been Nicholas Lanier's strophic song 'Silly heart forbear', published in several Playford song books.[42] It was part of

an Entertainment of the most diversified and highly interesting character

---

[36] *Rm*, 30/3/1833, 65–70, at 67 (Katharine Ellis); Haskell, *The Early Music Revival*, 12.

[37] Haskell, *The Early Music*, 19–20.

[38] A. Tolbecque, *Notice historique sur les instruments à cordes et à archet* (Paris, 1898), 15–16.

[39] K. Ellis, *Music Criticism in Nineteenth-Century France: 'La Revue et Gazette musicale de Paris', 1834–1880* (Cambridge, 1995), 67.

[40] Wangermée, 'Les Premiers Concerts Historiques', 188; Haskell, *The Early Music Revival*, 19.

[41] *MP*, 20/2/1836. See also *The Times*, 20/2/1836.

[42] C. L. Day and E. B. Murrie, *English Song-Books, 1651–1702: a Bibliography* (London, 1940), 330, no. 2934.

called HISTORICAL RECORDS of VOCAL and INSTRUMENTAL MUSIC, From the Ancient Greeks down to the Present Time. Embracing specimens of the various Schools of the most celebrated Masters, presented in a chronological order, and forming a practical illustration of THE HISTORY OF MUSIC During a Period of Two Thousand Five Hundred Years.[43]

The very long programme included a specimen of ancient Greek music, Gregorian and Ambrosian chant, a troubadour song, motets and madrigals by Josquin, Palestrina, Marenzio, Giovanni Gabrieli and Gibbons, the overture and a chorus from Lully's opera *Atys*, 'Come if you dare' from Purcell's *King Arthur*, a Corelli trio sonata played by Robert Lindley (violoncello) and Domenico Dragonetti (double bass), 'an elaborate duet from a Mass, by SEBASTIAN BACH', and Tartini's 'Devil's Trill' sonata, extracts from Gluck's *Orfeo* and Rousseau's *Devin du village*, and Arne's 'Rule, Britannia'.

A second concert, on 24 February, included extracts from Handel's *Samson*, *Israel in Egypt* and *Messiah* and Haydn's *Creation*, as well as another selection of 'historical records'. A review mentioned Corelli's Trio Sonata in F major, op. 4, no. 7 (again played by Lindley and Dragonetti), Tartini's 'Devil's Trill' sonata, and Haydn's 'Farewell' Symphony,[44] though a poster for the concert owned by the late Howard Mayer Brown gives a completely different programme. According to Brown's description,

> The historical survey began with Josquin's *Stabat mater* and Gastoldi's *Il Bell'Humore* sung by five singers, and was followed by Luther's prayer *Nos verbo serva Domine* sung as a solo, an 'Anthem, in Eleven distinct Parts' by Giovanni Gabrieli performed by three singers, two cornets, viols (*sic*), and four trombones, and various other compositions.[45]

It is not clear whether the reviewer just failed to mention these pieces or whether the programme was changed at the last moment. However, Richard Charteris has pointed out that the Gabrieli 'anthem' must have been 'Surrexit Christus hodie', c66, scored for alto, tenor and bass voices, two cornetts, two violins, and four trombones with organ continuo.[46] Bochsa was clearly an important pioneer in the early music revival, though whether he used 'viols' or any old other old

---

43   *MP*, 15/2/1836.

44   *MP*, 25/2/1836.

45   H. M. Brown, 'Pedantry or Liberation? A Sketch of the Historical Performance Movement', in *Authenticity and Early Music*, ed. N. Kenyon (Oxford, 1988), 27–56, at 33, fn. 14.

46   R. Charteris, *Giovanni Gabrieli (ca.1555–1612): a Thematic Catalogue of his Music with a Guide to the Source Materials and Translations of his Vocal Texts* (Stuyvesant, NY, 1996), 118-120.

instruments (apart from the gamba and harpsichord in the Lanier song) is open to question. One of the reviewers mentioned that Bochsa had taken 'CHORON as his guide', meaning the concerts of Renaissance and Baroque music put on by Alexandre-Étienne Choron in Paris in the 1820s, though there is no sign that they used old instruments.[47] An edition of 'Surrexit Christus hodie' had been published in 1834 in the third volume of Carl von Winterfeld's *Johannes Gabrieli und sein Zeitalter*.[48]

The following year, on 19 February 1837, the pianist and composer Ignaz Moscheles (1794–1870) played some Domenico Scarlatti sonatas on a two-manual 1771 Shudi harpsichord supplied by Broadwood (the piano firm descended from Shudi),[49] repeating the performance in two other 'historical soirées' later that season.[50] It might be objected that this (and the harpsichord in Bochsa's concert) was not a true revival since harpsichords were made in London until at least 1800 and continued to be used well into the nineteenth century: the last surviving English instrument is a Kirkman of 1800, but Clementi reputedly sold them until 1802, and Carl Engel wrote in 1879 that that 'the late Mr. [Joseph] Kirkman told me that he, with his father, constructed the last harpsichord in the year 1809'.[51]

In that year Vincenzo Pucitta was advertised as 'Composer and Conductor (at the Harpsichord) of the Music' in two comic operas put on at the King's Theatre.[52] The critic Henry Robertson thought 'the restoration of the harpsichord to the orchestra' in bad taste: the 'clicking of the quills, and the whistling of the cords, render the recitative more than usually unpleasant and tedious'.[53] Nevertheless,

---

[47] Haskell, *The Early Music Revival*, 16–18.

[48] Charteris, *Giovanni Gabrieli*, 578.

[49] A. J. Hipkins, 'Harpsichord', *Grove1*, i. 688–91, at 691. The instrument, no. 639, is now in Switzerland, see D. H. Boalch, *Makers of the Harpsichord and Clavichord, 1440–1840*, rev. C. Mould (Oxford, 3/1995), 619.

[50] *MW*, 4 (24/2/1837), 155–6 (10/3/1837), 184; *MW*, 5 (24/3/1837), 28–9. See also Niecks, 'Historical Concerts', 220–1; J. Roche, 'Ignaz Moscheles, 1794–1870', *MT*, 111 (1970), 264–6. The assertion in Roche, 265, that Moscheles played J. S. Bach's D minor concerto, BWV1052, on the harpsichord in one of these concerts seems to be based on a misunderstanding of a passage in C. Moscheles, *Life of Moscheles, with Selections of his Diaries and Correspondence*, trans. A. D. Coleridge, 2 vols. (London, 1873), ii. 22–4. Moscheles played it on the piano at the Concerts of Ancient Music on 15/3/1837, see *MW*, 5 (24/3/1837), 24–5.

[51] C. Engel, 'Some Account of the Clavichord with Historical Notices', *MT*, 20 (1879), 356–9, 411–15, 468–72, at 356; A. J. Hipkins, *A Description and History of the Pianoforte and of the Older Keyboard Stringed Instruments* (London, 1896), 89; Boalch, *Makers of the Harpsichord and Clavichord*, rev. Mould, 34, 106, 457.

[52] *MC*, 10, 16, 21, 27/1/1809; *MC*, 3, 4, 6, 10, 11, 13, 17, 21/2/1809.

[53] T. Fenner, *Opera in London: Views of the Press, 1785–1830* (Carbondale and Edwardsville, IL, 1994), esp. 250, 290.

Vincent Novello was listed as harpsichordist in a prospectus circulated in October 1811 for the Pantheon's reopening as a theatre the following season,[54] and as late as 1817 *The Morning Chronicle* complained about the situation in London's minor theatres,

> where, as the proprietors are suffered [by the 1737 Licensing Act] only to give musical performances, they are obliged to have recourse to the miserable fiction of a jingling harpsichord, which pretends to accompany a still more miserable sort of a pretended recitative, by which means we have neither song nor declamation, but a wretched and unintelligible jumble of both'.[55]

Doubtless harpsichords continued to be played long after that. For instance, the London organist George Cooper (1820–76) was said to have had 'his road to the organ' as a child 'smoothed by an old harpsichord with pedals and two rows of keys, on which the lad practised at all available times'.[56] Harpsichords occasionally appear in contemporary London auctions, such as the 'excellent double-keyed Harpsichord by *Metzener,* in walnut-tree case' sold on 10 June 1820,[57] or the 'Harpsichord, by Kirkman' sold on 4 June 1828.[58]

❧ *The 1845 Concert*

THE first British revival that involved a decisive break with tradition – another feature of the later early music movement – occurred on 17 April 1845, when a Concert of Ancient Music at the Hanover Square Rooms included three pieces of supposedly Renaissance music, two of which were played by a group of 'ancient instruments'.[59] The programme was chosen by Prince Albert,

---

54 R. Cowgill and G. Dideriksen, 'Opera Orchestras in Georgian and Early Victorian London', in *The Opera Orchestra in Eighteenth- and Nineteenth-Century Europe*, ed. N.M. Jensen and F. Piperno, 2 vols. (Berlin, 2008), i. 259–321, at 297.

55 *MC*, 18/9/1817.

56 *Grove 1*, i. 398 (John Catch).

57 White, *A Catalogue of an Extensive and Valuable Collection of Music Books … part of which were the Property of the late Mr. G. E. Williams, Organist of Westminster Abbey, and several other Eminent Professors (Deceased)* (8–10/6/1820), lot 552; CC: GB-Lbl, 7897.d.13.(1). A harpsichord of 1754 by John Metzener is mentioned in Thomas Green's accounts for 1774, see *The Accounts of Thomas Green, Music Teacher and Tuner of Musical Instruments, 1742–1790*, ed. G. Sheldrick ([Ware], 1992), 46, 98.

58 Musgrave, *A Catalogue of the Valuable and Genuine Stock in Trade of a Music Seller* (3–5/6/1828), lot. 227; CC: GB-Lbl, 7897.d.13.(18).

59 J. Catch, 'Prince Albert's Early Music', *GSJ*, 42 (1989), 3–9; P. Holman, 'Early Music in Victorian England: the Case of the 1845 Concert', *Ad Parnassum*, 4/8 (2006), 81–114.

CONCERTO*.   *Emilio del Cavaliere*, A. D. 1600.

(First Time of Performance at these Concerts.)

Violino Francèse, Viola d'Amore, Viola da braccio, due *Viole da gamba,*
Chittarra, Teorbo, Arpa, Organ, and *Violone.*

And ROMANESCA, of the fifteenth century : *Violino Francèse*, due *Viole,*
due *Viole da gamba, Lute,* and *Violone.*

Messrs. LODER, H. HILL, LODER jun. HATTON, W. PHILLIPS,
Signor DE CIEBRA, Signor VENTURA, Mr. T. WRIGHT,
Mr. LUCAS, and Signor DRAGONETTI.

Illus. 9.1 Extract from the programme of the Concerts of Ancient Music,

Hanover Square Rooms, 17 April 1845

a director since 1843, so it was presumably that very modern prince who had
the revolutionary idea of bringing Fétis's ideas to London and into the fusty
world of the Concerts of Ancient Music.[60] Most of the items in the programme
were relatively recent: there were overtures by Méhul and Mozart, choruses
by Handel, Mozart, and Beethoven, and solo vocal music by Weigl, Cherubini,
Graun, Gluck, Mozart, and Handel. Arias by Cesti and Stradella were performed
in Bishop's orchestrations.[61] The two pieces played by the 'ancient instruments',
the 'CONCERTO' *Emilio del Cavalieri*, A.D. 1600' and the 'ROMANESCA, of the
fifteenth century', were the pieces, already mentioned, played in Fétis's second
historical concert (Illus. 9.1).[62] A footnote stated that the Cavalieri 'will be performed on the same description of ancient instruments as those for which it was
composed; most of them, together with the music, have been kindly forwarded
to England by M. Fétis, of the Conservatoire Royale, Brussels, for the present
Concert'.

The critics found it difficult to come to terms with the novel sounds. One
review, probably by J. W. Davison, thought that the effect of the 'singular old
instruments, rummaged for the occasion out of the dust of obscurity … was as of
a tooth comb, covered with paper, blown upon with the breath, forced through
the upper and under rows of teeth slightly compressed. Nothing could have been
more melancholy and less musical.'[63] The Welsh harpist, composer and writer John
Parry was more enthusiastic: the Cavalieri was 'charming; the parts were replete
with imitative passages, trills and flourishes – while a vein of sweet melody per-
vaded the whole', and in the Romanesca 'the melody was charmingly played by

[60] For Prince Albert's musical interests, see T. Martin, *The Life of his Royal Highness the Prince Consort*, 5 vols. (London, 1875–80), i. 485–501; N. Temperley, 'The
Prince Consort, Champion of Music', *MT*, 102 (1961), 762–4.

[61] M. Murata, 'Dr Burney Bought a Music Book …', at 90–91, 100.

[62] CC: GB-Lbl, 11784.e.1.

[63] *MW*, 20 (24/4/1845), 192.

Mr. Loder, and the accompaniments were performed on the viola da gamba, lute, and violone, in a subdued manner, which produced a delicious soothing effect'.[64] He reported that Queen Victoria 'took refreshments in the tea-room' in the interval, 'when most of the antique instruments were brought to be inspected, and Mr. Hatton played an air on the viol da gamba'.

However, Parry could not help feeling that 'the march of improvement has evidently made a great progress; for the bulky violino, viol d'amour, viol da braccio, and viol da gamba, cannot for a moment be compared with the violin, viola, and violoncello'. His ambivalence was shared by another critic, who found it difficult to take the old instruments seriously: 'Their appearance in the orchestra did not a little disturb the gravity of the assembly, for truly they presented a strange and grotesque sight'; though he admitted that they 'produced a very curious effect – something between surprise and pleasure', and he commending 'the dexterous facility with which the performers adapted themselves to their obsolete constructions'.[65] The most enthusiastic reviewer was the queen herself, though as the wife of the concert's organiser she was hardly impartial. She wrote in her journal later that night: 'It was a beautiful Concert, full of curious productions of old world music. My beloved Albert has such exquisite taste and takes such pains in collecting rare and curious, as well, as beautiful pieces of music.'[66] She thought the Cavalieri 'very curious, and the effect very pleasing', and the Romanesca 'very simple and beautiful'.

I have argued elsewhere that the Romanesca does not date from the fifteenth century, that the concerto was not written by Cavalieri (d. 1602), and that most of the instruments used were not that old.[67] The Romanesca, a folk-like tune unrelated to the sixteenth-century chord sequence, was popularised (and probably composed) by the violinist Pierre Baillot. It was played in London by a group consisting of 'Violino francèse', two violas, gamba, 'violone', and 'lute'; a score in Fétis's hand is in B-Br, MS Fétis 7328C, fols. 178–181v, and a copy from the library of the Concerts of Ancient Music is at GB-Lcm, MS 794, fols. 14–19. The 'Cavalieri' concerto, almost certainly a composition by Fétis himself, was played in London by 'Violino francèse', two violas, gamba, 'violone', harp, theorbo, and organ; Fétis's score is in B-Br, MS Fétis 7328C, fols. 205–216, and the London copy is at GB-Lcm, MS 794, fols. 1–13v. A London score, GB-Lcm, MS 1152, fols. 87–95v, of a third piece, the Strobach concerto for mandolin, viola d'amore, gamba, lute, and harpsichord, suggests that it too was considered for the 1845 concert;

[64] MP, 19/4/1845.

[65] The Illustrated London News, 6/155 (19/4/1845), 251 (Ann Royle).

[66] Catch, 'Prince Albert's Early Music', 3.

[67] Holman, 'Early Music in Victorian England', esp. 104–11.

Fétis's original is in B-Br, MS Fétis 7328C, fols. 197–202v. It was probably rejected because a harpsichord was not available, or because the lute part was too complex for the player and/or the instrument. It is almost certainly another composition by Fétis – who seems to have invented the composer, even providing an entry for him in his *Biographie universelle* and claiming that the piece had been published in Prague in 1698.[68]

The instruments are also unlikely to have come from the Renaissance. The 'Violino francèse', played by John David Loder (the leader of the Concerts) was probably one of those five-string instruments, often called 'quinton' in the trade, that combine the tunings and ranges of the violin and viola.[69] The 'violone', played by Domenico Dragonetti, seems to have been a large violoncello or bass violin. Dragonetti left it to Prince Albert in his will, describing it as 'my large Violon-cello which belonged to the celebrated English Singer [James] Bartleman' and confirming that he had played it in the 1845 concert.[70] It was exhibited in 1872 (when it was described as 'A *Basso di Camera* … Supposed to be by Domenico Montagnana of Venice, about 1725'), and again in 1885.[71] The player of the 'lute' was the guitarist and inventor Angelo Benedetto Ventura, who probably played one of his harp-lute hybrids, including the 17–19-string Harp Ventura, patented in 1828.[72] There is no evidence that the violas, harp, and organ were obsolete types.

Thus the gamba was the only instrument used with some claim to be 'antique', though it came from the early eighteenth century rather than the Renaissance. It was the Tielke instrument then owned by John Cawse and now in the Victoria and Albert Museum (Ch. 5, 7, 8). Parry reported that it was not one of the instruments lent by Fétis, and Carl Engel wrote that 'Before this instrument came into the present collection it was in the possession of Mr. Simon Andrew Forster' – Forster, a member of the instrument-making dynasty, died in 1870.[73] Sandys and

---

[68] F.-J. Fétis, 'Jean Strobach', *Biographie universelle des musiciens*, 10 vols. (Paris, 1860–80), viii. 160. See also M. Ophee, 'A History of Transcriptions of Lute Tabla-ture from 1679 to the Present', *The Lute*, 43 (2003), 1–43, at 5–7.

[69] See esp. M. Herzog, 'Is the Quinton a Viol? A Puzzle Unravelled', *EM*, 28 (2000), 8–31; J. Catch, 'Edward John Payne, Victorian Gambist', *GSJ*, 50 (1997), 127–35, at 133.

[70] Palmer, *Domenico Dragonetti in England*, 141.

[71] C. Engel, *A Descriptive Catalogue of Musical Instruments in the South Kensington Museum* (London, 2/1874), 365; *International Inventions Exhibition, London, 1885: Guide to the Loan Collection and List of Musical Instruments, Manuscripts, Books, Paintings, and Engravings*, ed. A. J. Hipkins (London, 1885), 63.

[72] S. Bonner, *Angelo Benedetto Ventura, Teacher, Inventor, & Composer: a Study in English Regency Music* (Harlow, 1971), esp. 47–52.

[73] Engel, *A Descriptive Catalogue*, 336–8. For Forster, see *BMB*, 149–50; *The British Violin: the Catalogue of the 1998 Exhibition '400 Years of Violin and Bow Making*

Forster stated in 1864 it had been purchased from 'the late Mr. John Cawse, the artist', included photographs of it in their book, and added that for the 1845 concert 'Mr. Cawse lent this viol da gamba, which was played on by Mr. Richard Hatton'.[74] The photos show that it was still equipped with frets, which suggests that Cawse and Hatton essentially used an eighteenth-century technique (Plate 24).

The programme lists 'due *Viole da gamba*', though the reviews only mention one player, Richard Hatton. The other player, the composer and cellist W. L. Phillips, apparently switched to the violoncello before the performance, presumably because he encountered difficulties finding a gamba, getting it into working order, or learning how to play it.[75] Hatton was born on 19 April 1804 and joined the Royal Society of Musicians on 2 July 1826, when he stated that he 'Performs on the Violoncello & Pianoforte, is engaged at the Theatre Royal Covent Garden as Principal Violoncello is a Single Man'.[76] As a young man he was a friend of the organist, violinist and double bass player William Joseph Castell, though Castell fled to France in the summer of 1826 owing him £26 10s.; they probably met while working at the Surrey Theatre, where Castell was chorus master and played in the orchestra.[77] Hatton resigned from the Society in 1876, presumably when he stopped performing.

The moral of the 1845 concert is that deception played a significant role in the early stages of the early music revival. Fétis perpetrated a number of other forgeries, including the song 'Pietà, signore, di me dolente', attributed to Stradella and performed in Bishop's orchestration at the Concerts of Ancient Music in London on 21 May 1845.[78] The germ of Berlioz's *L'Enfance du Christ* (1854) lay in a chorus, 'Adieu des Bergers à la Sainte Famille' ('The shepherds' farewell to the Holy

---

    in the British Isles', ed. J. Milnes (Oxford, 2000), 78.

[74] W. Sandys and S. A. Forster, *The History of the Violin* (London, 1864), 105. See also A. Baines, *Victoria and Albert Museum, Catalogue of Musical Instruments*, ii: *Non-Keyboard Instruments* (London, 1968), 6–7, no. 1/10, fig. 7.

[75] For Phillips, see esp. *MW*, 38 (31/3/1860), 207; *Grove 1*, ii. 705–6; *BMB*, 319; B. Matthews, *The Royal Society of Musicians of Great Britain, List of Members, 1738–1984* (London, 1985), 115.

[76] Matthews, *The Royal Society of Musicians*, 69.

[77] A. V. Beedell, *The Decline of the English Musician, 1788–1888: a Family of English Musicians in Ireland, England, Mauritius, and Australia* (Oxford, 1992), esp. 128–33, 154, 166, 173.

[78] Murata, 'Dr Burney Bought a Music Book …', esp. 91–3, 103. See also W. Corten, 'Fétis, transcripteur et vulgarisateur', *Revue belge de musicologie / Belgisch Tijdschrift voor Muziekwetenschap*, 50 (1996), 249–68, esp. 255–68; S. Hibberd, 'Murder in the Cathedral? Stradella, Musical Power, and Performing the Past in 1830s Paris', *ML*, 87 (2006), 551–79, esp. 554–63. Bishop's score is in GB-Lcm, MS 767, fols. 8–15v.

Family), that he wrote in 1850 and attributed to 'Pierre Ducré, master of music to the Sainte-Chapelle, 1679', claiming that he had discovered the manuscript in a cupboard there.[79] In a different vein, the antiquarian Edward Francis Rimbault is known to have invented historical evidence,[80] while Wilhelm Rust fraudulently modernised keyboard sonatas by his grandfather Friedrich Wilhelm to make it appear that they anticipated Beethoven.[81] Fritz Kreisler and Henri Casadesus come to mind as more recent recent examples of musicians who passed off their own pieces as the work of eighteenth-century composers.[82] Casadesus, like Fétis, was involved in the early music movement: he founded the Société des Instruments Anciens Casadesus with Saint-Saëns in Paris in 1901 and gave concerts on old instruments with it until 1939. Fake old music of this sort has its counterpart in the nineteenth-century copies and forgeries of early stringed instruments that still clutter museums.

The 1845 concert did not lead to a wholesale revival of old instruments in mid-nineteenth-century England (the Concerts of Ancient Music did not repeat the experiment of using them), though it marked the moment when modern ideas of historical fidelity in performance were first articulated. The 'Concerto Passegiato' was not written in the sixteenth century and may not have been performed with any genuine Renaissance instruments. Nevertheless, the intention was there: the programme proudly claimed that it would be 'performed on the same description of ancient instruments as those for which it was composed'. More than fifty years before Arnold Dolmetsch started his London concerts, the ideology that propelled and sustained the early music movement throughout the twentieth century was already in place.

[79] D. K. Holoman, *Berlioz* (London, 1989), 418–19.

[80] P. Holman, *Henry Purcell* (Oxford, 1994), 6. See also R. Andrewes, 'Edward Francis Rimbault, 1816–1876', *Fontes Artis Musicae*, 30 (1983), 30–4.

[81] M. D. Calvocoressi, 'Friedrich Rust, his Editors and his Critics', *MT*, 55 (1914), 14–16; M. D. Calvocoressi, 'The Rust Case: its Ending and its Moral', *MT*, 55 (1914), 89–91.

[82] C. L. Cudworth, 'Ye Olde Spuriosity Shoppe, or Put it in the *Anhang*', *Notes*, 12 (1954, 1955), 25–40, 533–53; W. Lebermann, 'Apokryph, Plagiat, Korruptel oder Falsifikat?', *Die Musikforschung*, 20 (1967), 413–25; Haskell, *The Early Music Revival*, esp. 50–1. For concertos attributed to J. C. Bach, C. P. E. Bach, Handel, and Boccherini that may be by Casadesus, see J. C. Bach, *The Collected Works*, 48/1: *Thematic Catalogue*, comp. E. Warburton (New York, 1999), 573, no. YC 98; E. E. Helm, *Thematic Catalogue of the Works of Carl Philipp Emanuel Bach* (New Haven, CT, 1989), 108, no. 497; A. C. Bell, *Handel Chronological Thematic Catalogue* (Darley, 1972), 396; Y. Gérard, trans. A. Mayor, *Thematic, Bibliographical and Critical Catalogue of the Works of Luigi Boccherini* (London, 1969), 546–8, no. 486. Many more pieces by Casadesus 'in the old style' are listed in H. Berck, *Viola d'amore Bibliographie* (Kassel, 1986).

🐝 *Charles Salaman, Ernst Pauer, and Henry Webb*

THE gamba does not seem to have been used in any more public early music revivals in London for more than a decade after 1845, though the fashion for old music on old instruments was beginning to catch on. On 9 January 1855 the pianist and composer Charles Salaman (1814–1901) gave a lecture at the Marylebone Institute on 'the ancient keyed stringed instruments', seemingly the first of a number of similar events he put on over the next few years.[83] On one occasion, at the Polytechnic Institution in Portman Square on 10 May 1855, he demonstrated seven instruments: 'A virginal, made for Her Majesty Queen Elizabeth (1600)'; the 1655 John Loosemore virginals (which he owned); Ruckers harpsichords of 1640 and 1651 (the latter said to have belonged to Handel); spinets of 1713 and 1724; and a 1798 double-manual harpsichord by Joseph Kirkman.[84] He played Byrd's 'Carman's Whistle' on the Loosemore virginals, Handel's 'Harmonious Blacksmith' variations on the 1651 Ruckers, and C. P. E. Bach's 'Presto in C' on the Kirkman – choices that show that he was far in advance of his time in wanting to match particular old instruments to more or less appropriate music. Queen Victoria and Prince Albert were in the audience, suggesting that their interest in old music and old instruments was not confined to the 1845 concert. Salaman was 'the chief mover' and secretary of the Musical Society (a forerunner of the Royal Musical Association), and played some pieces by Orlando Gibbons on a virginal at its first meeting in April 1858.[85] In addition to the Loosemore virginals, he owned a 1768 Kirkman harpsichord that had reportedly been selected by Charles Burney for his grandmother.[86]

Old instruments were also used by the Austrian pianist, writer and editor Ernst Pauer (1826–1905) in his 1862 concerts at Willis's Rooms. They were essentially piano recitals, though Pauer also played the same Shudi harpsichord used by Moscheles in 1837, and he included a Baroque flute and a gamba on at least one occasion. One programme included J. S. Bach's E♭ flute sonata, BWV1031, 'played

---

[83] *MW*, 33 (13/1/1855), 26. For Salaman, see esp. *MT*, 42 (1901), 530–3; *Grove1*, iii. 217–18.

[84] *MW*, 33 (12/5/1855), 300. For possible identifications of the instruments, see R. Russell, *Victoria and Albert Museum, Catalogue of Musical Instruments*, i: *Keyboard Instruments* (London, 1968), 50, nos. 7, 14, 18; W. R. Loosemore, 'A Loosemore Virginal', *MT*, 127 (1986), 255; Boalch, *Makers of the Harpsichord and Clavichord*, rev. Mould, 456–7, 492, 561, 565–6; G. O'Brien, *Ruckers: a Harpsichord and Virginal Building Tradition* (Cambridge, 2/2009), 266, 270.

[85] A. H. King, 'The Musical Institute of London and its Successors', *MT*, 117 (1976), 221–3.

[86] Boalch, *Makers of the Harpsichord and Clavichord*, rev. Mould, 437.

to perfection by Herr Pauer and Mr. R. S. Pratten'.[87] The *Musical World* critic mentioned that the pitch was a tone lower than normal, so if he was thinking of the contemporary Philharmonic pitch of $a' = 455$ then Robert Sidney Pratten would have played a Baroque flute at about $a' = 405$; a number of flutes at this pitch survive, including several from early eighteenth-century England.[88] On 15 February the programme included 'the *Sonata* in G minor, for violin and viol de gamba, by Sebastian Bach' as well as keyboard music from Chambonnières to Liszt.[89] The sonata was probably BWV1020 for violin and obbligato harpsichord, first published in 1860.[90] According to A. J. Hipkins, the gamba player, Henry Webb, 'had to obtain instruction in the fingering of the instrument from an old man of eighty-six'.[91] John Catch is surely correct to suggest that this was John Cawse, though Cawse was aged eighty-three rather than eighty-six in 1862, the year of his death.[92] Another report stated that Webb's gamba 'created great interest', and added:

> The viola da gamba has more of the tone and form of the violoncello than of the tenor [i.e. viola]. It possesses six strings. Mr. Webb had the greatest difficulty in discovering and mastering the technical characteristics of the instrument, the viola da gamba being entirely out of use at the present day. It was played upon for the last time at one of the ancient concerts when Sir Henry Bishop was the conductor, the concert taking place under the direction of the late Prince Consort.[93]

Webb was born in 1831, and is first heard of playing the second viola part of Mendelssohn's B♭ string quintet at the Hanover Square Rooms on 24 April 1851.[94] He played the viola in the Monday Popular Concerts in 1862 (to which Pauer frequently contributed), is listed as one of the principal violas of the Musical Society in 1863, played in John Ella's Musical Union in 1863 and 1865, and died on 13 February 1866 at the age of 35; he was described in his obituary as 'the eminent

---

[87] *MW*, 40 (8/2/1862), 91–2; see also *MT*, 10 (1861–3), 214–15.

[88] B. Haynes, *A History of Performing Pitch: the Story of 'A'* (Lanham, MD, 2002), esp. 124–9, 336–8, 350–1, 355–9, 432–3.

[89] *The Athenaeum*, 1791 (22/2/1862), 265.

[90] J. S. Bach, *Werke*, 9: *Kammermusik, Erster Band*, ed. W. Rust (Leipzig, 1860), 274–85.

[91] A. J. Hipkins, *Musical Instruments, Historic, Rare and Unique* (Edinburgh, 1888; repr. London, 1921), 46. See also C. F. Pohl, *Mozart und Haydn in London*, 2 vols. (Vienna, 1867), ii. 376–7.

[92] Catch, 'Prince Albert's Early Music', 6–7.

[93] *The London Review of Politics, Society, Literature, Art, and Science*, 4 (22/2/1862), 196.

[94] *MW*, 26 (26/4/1851), 260.

viola player, so well known to all the frequenters of the Monday Popular Concerts, as one of the most conscientious and painstaking artists associated with
those classical performances'.[95] He is important because he was apparently the
first professional gamba player whose main instrument was the viola rather than
the violoncello or another bass instrument. According to Hipkins, Pauer also
played the 1771 Shudi harpsichord in concerts in 1863 and 1867,[96] though he does
not seem to have repeated the experiment of using other old instruments, and in
June 1869 he played 'one of Bach's sonatas for piano and viol di gamba (the latter
obsolete instrument replaced by the violoncello of Signor [Carlo Alfredo] Piatti)'
in a concert at the Hanover Square Rooms.[97]

❧ Walter Pettit and J. S. Bach

THE most important professional gamba player at this period was the cellist
Walter Pettit. He was born in London on March 14, 1836, studied at the Royal
Academy of Music, joined the Royal Society of Musicians on 7 November 1858,
played in various London orchestras, and died on 11 December 1882.[98] Like Webb,
he played in London chamber music concerts in the early 1860s; on at least one
occasion, at St Martin's Hall on 14 March 1860, they played together, in quintets
by Georges Onslow.[99] Pettit was discussed by Edward Payne in his 1889 lecture
(Ch. 8 and below):

> I should also mention that my copy of the Paris edition of "De Caix," [Caix
> d'Hervelois] which lies on the table, belonged to Mr. Walter Pettit, an Eng-
> lish violoncellist of high merit, who was also a Viola da Gamba player, and
> whose rendering on the original instrument of some of Bach's *obbligato*
> parts is perhaps remembered by some among us.[100]

Payne is referring here to the gamba solos in J. S. Bach's passions. Bach's music

95 *MT*, 12 (1865–7), 249. See also Sandys and Forster, *The History of the Violin*, 177; C.
    Bashford, 'John Ella and the Making of the Musical Union', in *Music and British
    Culture, 1785–1914: Essays in Honour of Cyril Ehrlich*, ed. Bashford and L. Langley
    (Oxford, 2000), 193–214, at 203, fn. 30.

96 Hipkins, 'Harpsichord', *Grove 1*, i. 691.

97 *MW*, 47 (12/6/1869), 428.

98 *Grove 1*, ii. 696; Matthews, *The Royal Society of Musicians*, 114. His birth is given
    as 14/3/1835 in J. D. Brown, *Biographical Dictionary of Musicians, with a Bibliog-
    raphy of English Writings on Music* (Paisley, 1886), 469.

99 *MW*, 38 (17/3/1860), 170.

100 E. J. Payne, 'The Viola da Gamba', *PMA*, 15 (1888–9), 91–107, at 93–4; see also *MW*,
     69 (30/3/1889), 197–8.

began to make an impact in England in the early nineteenth century,[101] though things gathered pace in the 1850s, with the publication of the Bach Gesellschaft edition (started in 1851) and with performances of his major works. The St Matthew Passion was first performed in London on 6 April 1854 by William Sterndale Bennett and the Bach Society, though in a cut version that omitted 'Komm süsses Kreuz', the aria with the gamba solo.[102] It was performed in a more complete version by Joseph Barnby at Exeter Hall on 6 April 1870, and was repeated by him and others a number of times in the next few years.[103]

It seems unlikely that Pettit played the gamba solo in the St Matthew Passion in 1870, for Macfarren wrote at the time that the 'viol da Gamba' was 'an instrument now unattainable, and without a player, even if a specimen could be found', and gave a spectacularly implausible seven-string tuning: $GG–D–A–e–c'–g'–d''$.[104] He added:

> Some ingenuity is wanted to adapt the part for this obsolete instrument to present possibility, which may, perhaps, be best effected by assigning to the viola all the continuous phrases and passages, and to the basses those detached notes which are below the compass of this substitute.

However, Pettit certainly played the solo in the first English performance of the St John Passion, given by Barnby at the Hanover Square Rooms on 22 March 1872. A reviewer mentioned 'the fine performance by Mr. W. Pettit, on a genuine viol-da-gamba, of the important obligato part to the song "It is finished"' – 'Es ist volbracht'.[105] He also played in the St Matthew Passion given by Michael Costa and the Sacred Harmonic Society at Exeter Hall on 25 April 1873; a critic mentioned that 'The bright tone of the Viol da Gamba (well played by Mr. Pettit in the *obbligato* to the air, "Come, blessed cross") was exceedingly welcome', and added:

> the instrument is not, as has been asserted, a resuscitation on this occasion, for although not used in previous performances of this composition here,

[101] See esp. *The English Bach Awakening: Knowledge of J. S. Bach and his Music in England, 1750–1830*, ed. M. Kassler (Aldershot, 2004).

[102] R. Sterndale Bennett, 'Three Abridged Versions of Bach's St Matthew Passion', *ML*, 37 (1956), 336–9; I. Parrott, 'William Sterndale Bennett and the Bach Revival in Nineteenth-Century England', in *Europe, Empire, and Spectacle in Nineteenth-Century British Music*, ed. R. Cowgill and J. Rushton (Aldershot, 2006), 29–43, at 35–8.

[103] *MT*, 14 (1870–1), 459–60.

[104] G. A. Macfarren, 'Bach's Grosse Passions-Musik (St. Matthew)', *MT*, 14 (1870), 327–9, 359–61, 391–3, 423–6, at 361.

[105] *The Monthly Musical Record*, 2 (4/1872), 59. See also *MS*, 2 (30/3/1872), 169; *MT*, 15 (1871–3), 433; G. A. Macfarren, 'J. S. Bach's Music of the Passion according to the Gospel of St. John', *MT*, 15 (1872), 463–5.

it has been played by the same artist in the several recent presentations of Bach's "St. John" Passion music, and also, we believe, by Mr. Webb, at the Historical Lectures of Herr Pauer.[106]

Another report went further:

> A STATEMENT has gone the rounds of the papers to the effect that the *viol di gamba* was to be first publicly played last night in Exeter Hall, for the first time these ninety years. This is incorrect. The *viol di gamba*, admirably performed upon by Mr. Pettit, might have been heard any Friday in the Lent just part, at the Church of St. Anne, Soho; and might have been heard also at several of the Exhibition Concerts in Albert Hall, notably that of Wednesday last.[107]

The last is a reference to the free concerts accompanying the current International Exhibition in South Kensington; Barnby was the musical director and a report mentioned 'Bach's air "It is Finished", from the St. John's "Passion Music," with an obligato accompaniment on the viol da gamba'.[108]

Pettit was apparently the only professional gamba player in London in the 1870s, though the cellist John Boatwright (1838–1906) 'struck a few chords on the six-stringed viol di gamba' during a lecture on stringed instruments given by the doctor and amateur musician W. H. Stone at the Royal Institution on 26 May 1874.[109] The reporter found the gamba 'a trifle thin', though Stone 'thought the disuse of the instrument a mistake, as it might still be made to supply a want between the tenor and the 'cello'. But Boatwright was evidently not up to playing Bach on the gamba, for when Barnby performed Bach's 'Gottes Zeit ist der allerbeste Zeit', BWV106, at St Anne's Soho in March 1875 the original instruments, two recorders, two gambas and continuo, had to be replaced by 'two flutes, two first violins, two second violins, two violas, two violoncellos, two double basses, and the organ'.[110] August Manns repeated it at the Crystal Palace that October with the gamba parts played by violas and violoncellos, and additional clarinet and bassoon parts by Robert Franz.[111]

Nevertheless, by 1876 a critic was wondering whether, if 'Bach's music should

---

[106]   *MT*, 16 (1873–5), 75.

[107]   *MW*, 51 (26/4/1873), 269.

[108]   *MS*, 4 (3/5/1873), 270–1.

[109]   *MS*, 6 (30/5/1874), 350–1. For Boatwright, see Matthews, *The Royal Society of Musicians of Great Britain*, 24–5.

[110]   *MT*, 17 (1875–6), 44–5.

[111]   *The Academy*, 181 (10/1875), 441; *The Athenaeum*, 2504 (23/10/1875), 547; *MS*, 9 (23/10/1875), 271–2.

find such an acceptance with an English public as to warrant the frequent performance of his works, it becomes a question of whether a resuscitation both of the *Oboe d'Amore* and the *Viol da Gamba* would not be advisable'.[112] In 1886 Arthur Reynolds suggested that the viola d'amore and the gamba be taught 'along with the other orchestral instruments, in such institutions as the Royal Academy, Trinity College, &c.' – a recommendation that took nearly a century to be put into effect.[113] Pettit seems to have been in advance of his colleagues on the Continent in using a gamba for Bach's obbligato parts: recent surveys of German activity only cite performances of the St Matthew Passion in Krefeld on Palm Sunday 1884, in which the unnamed first cellist of the orchestra played a five-string viol, and Christian Döbereiner's performance on a seven-string viol in Munich in 1907.[114] We do not know whether Pettit played the instrument in the eighteenth-century manner, with frets and held by the knees, though Döbereiner reportedly played it 'fretless and with cello pin and overhand bow grip'.

❧ *Carli Zoeller and his Associates*

THE developing interest in Bach undoubtedly inspired English professionals to take up the obsolete instruments used in his works, though there was also interest in more obscure old music in the 1870s and 80s, as the collection of manuscripts assembled by Carli Zoeller demonstrates. Zoeller was born in Berlin on 28 March 1840, and came to England in 1873 after travelling in Germany with an Italian opera company.[115] He was a military bandmaster, serving first in the 7th (Queen's Own) Hussars and then in the 2nd Life Guards. He was a prolific composer and arranger: his compositions go up at least to op. 150 and include two operas and some orchestral pieces. More than 100 of his publications are listed in *BLIC*, including a harmony textbook, *The Art of Modulation: a Handbook* (1880), and a *New Method* for the viola d'amore (1885).[116] He died on 13 July 1889 after a

---

[112] *MT*, 17 (1876), 499.

[113] *MT*, 27 (1886), 549–50.

[114] J. B. Rutledge, 'Late Nineteenth-Century Viol Revivals', *EM*, 19 (1991), 409–18, at 415; J. Boer, 'The Viola da Gamba and the Nineteenth Century', in *Viola da gamba – Baryton – Arpeggione: Festschrift Alfred Lessing, Dusseldorf 2000*, ed. B. R. Appel and Boer (Utrecht, 2003), 35–41, at 36–7.

[115] For Zoeller, see *MT*, 30 (1889), 485; Brown, *Biographical Dictionary of Musicians*, 622.

[116] C. Zoeller, *New Method for the Viole d'Amour (the Love Viol), its Origin and History, and Art of Playing it* (London, 1885); CC: GB-Lbl, Mus. Mic.A.1, a microfilm of F-Pc, 28611. See also C. Zoeller, 'The Viole d'Amour', *MS*, 36 (23/3/1889), 236–8; *MO*, 12 (4/1889), 335–7.

fall from his horse during the Military Tournament at the Agricultural Hall in Islington.[117]

Zoeller represents a transitional stage in the early music revival. He collected old instruments, including an Eberle viola d'amore of 1730, and a Johannes Rauch viola d'amore of 1742,[118] and he clearly knew a lot about old music: his article 'Ancient Musical Literature', the fruit of original research in the British Museum and the library of the Sacred Harmonic Society (at GB-Lcm) into 'musical compositions and books written about music from the 15th, 16th, and 17th centuries', was published in twenty parts in 1879, only covering authors from Martin Agricola to Seth Calvisius.[119] However, he wrote his own viola d'amore pieces,[120] several of which were published in his *New Method* in whole or in part, and he also included in it solos from Meyerbeer's *Les Huguenots* (1836) and Carl Amand Mangold's *Tanhauser* (1846) as well as an arrangement of Mendelssohn's song without words op. 30, no. 9. He clearly regarded it as an instrument with a functioning continuous tradition, unlike 'the *Viola-da Gamba, the Lute, the Theorbe, the Spinet* and many other string- and wind-instruments' that 'by the caprice of fashion were consigned to the lumber-room, and now to be found in the curiosity shop only', as he put it in the Preface.[121] Similarly, his manuscript collection includes original nineteenth-century viola d'amore works by Johann Kràl and Eduard Zillman alongside eighteenth-century pieces by Anton Giranek, Christoph Graupner, Pietro Antonio Locatelli, Johann Pfeiffer, Carl Stamitz, Felice Turbliglio, and others.[122]

It is not clear whether Zoeller played the gamba as well as the viola d'amore,

---

[117]   *MS*, 37 (20/7/1889), 58.

[118]   The frontispiece of Zoeller's *New Method* is a drawing of the Eberle viola d'amore, said to be 'in the possession of Professor Carli Zoeller'. It was exhibited by 'Mr. Howard Head' in the 1904 Music Loan Exhibition; see *A Special Loan Exhibition of Musical Instruments, Manuscripts, Books, Portraits, and other Mementoes of Music and Musicians* (London, 1904), 105, no. 1137; *An Illustrated Catalogue of the Music Loan Exhibition held ... by the Worshipful Company of Musicians at Fishmongers' Hall, June and July 1904* (London, 1909), 151. H. Danks, *The Viola d'Amore* (Halesowen, 1976), 96, suggests that the Rauch viola d'amore is the one now at the Brussels Conservatoire, no. 1391.

[119]   C. Zoeller, 'Ancient Musical Literature', *MS*, 16 (15, 22, 29/3/1879), 158, 174, 190; *MS*, 16 (5, 12, 19, 26/4/1879), 206, 222, 238, 254; *MS*, 16 (3, 10, 17, 24, 31/5/1879), 270, 286, 302, 318, 334; *MS*, 16 (7, 14, 21, 28/6/1879), 350, 366, 382, 398; *MS*, 17 (5, 19, 26/7/1879), 2, 34, 50; *MS*, 17 (2/9/1879), 66.

[120]   Danks, *The Viola d'Amore*, 83.

[121]   Zoeller, *New Method*, 1. See also Danks, *The Viola d'Amore*, 65–6.

[122]   GB-Lbl, Add. MSS 31902, 31987, 32157, 32158, 32317, 32347. See Danks, *The Viola d'Amore*, esp. 71–82; M. and D. Jappe, *Viola d'amore Bibliographie* (Winterthur, 1997), 66–7, 113–14, 138–9, 155, 169–70, 180.

but his collection includes a good deal of eighteenth-century gamba music, mostly copied from manuscripts in German libraries. The transcriptions are in four volumes, GB-Lbl, Add. MSS 32347, 32390, 33295, and 33296, sold by Zoeller to the British Museum as part of a larger collection during the 1880s.[123] They were copied by at least five individuals, one of whom was seemingly Zoeller himself. Another signed himself 'F. Liebing Hoboist im 83. Reg.' (Add. MS 33295, fol. 68v) and 'F. Liebing hoboist im Inf. Reg. N^r. 83.' (Add. MS 33296, fol. 30v), dating the manuscripts Kassel, 25 and 24 June 1887. Nothing else is known about Liebing, and the 83rd Regiment of Foot had ceased to exist by 1887: in 1881 it was amalgamated with the 86th Regiment to form the Royal Irish (later Ulster) Rifles.

Liebing was responsible for four items in Add. MSS 33295 and 33296. Add. MS 33295, fols. 1–114v, is a complete copy of D-Kl, 4° MS Mus. 72, 1–5, a collection of five-part pavans and galliards apparently assembled by an English musician at the Kassel court soon after 1600; Liebing did not score it up but just copied the individual parts.[124] Add. MS 33296, fols. 1–58, is a copy, again made in parts, of August Kühnel's *Sonate ô partite* (Kassel, 1698) for one and two bass viols and continuo, presumably made from the unique copy at Kassel.[125] Add. MS 33296, fols. 189–221v, is a score of twelve anonymous sonatas for gamba (written in the French violin clef) and bass, copied from D-Kl, 2° MS Mus. 35.[126] They are fairly simple four-movement pieces in an attractive early eighteenth-century German idiom reminiscent of Telemann.[127] Finally, Liebing copied the parts of a mid-seventeenth-century C major 'Sonata à 3, / für / 2 Violini e Viola / da Gamba, del Sig^r Nubr.' (Add. MS 33296, fols. 222–229v) from D-Kl, 2° MS Mus. 60x, where it is attributed to 'Sigr Nub'. D-Kl attributes it to the Viennese court instrumentalist Georg Nub, though another possibility is the Johann Nebauer who dedicated a collection of dance music to Landgrave Wilhelm VI of Hesse in 1649.

Another copyist, whose work takes up most of Add. MS 32390, was French-speaking, to judge from his annotations, though he copied Berlin sources: he wrote on a flyleaf 'L'original de ces œuvres repose à la Bibliothèque royale / de Berlin'. He copied the solo part of Marin Marais's *Pièces a une et deux violes*

---

[123] Inscriptions on flyleaves: 'Purchd. Of C. Zoeller, / 14 June 1884.' (Add. MS 33247); 'Purchd of C. Zoeller, / 11 Oct. 1884' (Add. MS 32390); 'Purchased of C. Zoeller / 12 Nov. 1887.' (Add. MSS 33295, 33296).

[124] For 4° MS Mus. 72, see P. Holman, *Four and Twenty Fiddlers: the Violin at the English Court, 1540–1690* (Oxford, 2/1995), 157.

[125] B. Hoffman, *Catalogo della musica solistica e cameristica per viola da gamba* (Lucca, 2001), 111.

[126] Ibid., 192.

[127] See F. Flassig, *Die soloistische Gambenmusik in Deutschland im 18. Jahrhundert* (Göttingen, 1998), 243.

(Paris, 1686) (fols. 1–25v); pieces in score from Roland Marais's *Premier livre de pièces de viole avec la basse chifrée, en partition* (Paris, 1735) and *IIe livre de pièces de viole avec la basse chifrée, en partition* (Paris, 1738) (fols. 26–33); and the score of an anonymous C major sonata for gamba and bass (fols. 33–37). The last was presumably copied from the anonymous copy D-B, Mus. MS. 13525, but in fact it is by J. G. Graun, and survives in his autograph, D-B, SA 3627.[128] This individual also copied a score of C. P. E. Bach's Sonata in G minor, H510, for gamba and obbligato harpsichord (Add. MS 32347, fols. 1–11v), presumably from the autograph, D-B, P357.[129]

The other main copyist, seemingly Zoeller himself, copied from Darmstadt manuscripts. Add. MS 33296 contains a score of the Canon in G minor for two bass viols and continuo attributed to J. J. Fux (fols. 59–65v, from D-DS, Mus. MS 327 or 327a);[130] parts of three sonatas by Telemann for violin, gamba and continuo, in E major, TWV 42: E7 (fols. 66–77v, from D-DS, Mus. MS 1042/85), in G minor TWV 42: G11 (fols. 78–89v, from D-DS, Mus. MS 1042/89), and in G major TWV 42: G10 (fols. 90–100v, from D-DS, Mus. 1042/86); parts of Telemann's Sonata in G major, TWV 43:G12, for flute, two gambas and continuo (fols. 101–128v, from D-DS Mus. MS 1042/90); his Sonata in A minor TWV 42: A7 for flute, gamba and continuo (fols. 129–135v, from D-DS, Mus. MS 1042/87); and his Sonata in G major, TWV 42: G6 for harpsichord obbligato, gamba and continuo (fols. 136–148v, from D-DS, Mus. 1042/92 or 1045/6);[131] parts of J. C. Janitsch's Sonatas in C major and A major for gamba, violin, violoncello and continuo (fols. 149–172v) misattributed to Christoph Schaffrath (which may mean that Zoeller acquired them from Johannes Klingenberg, who made the same mistake in his own copies, D-B, Slg. Klg. 63/1, 2);[132] and parts of Johann Pfeiffer's Concerto in A minor for gamba, two violins, violoncello and continuo (fols. 173–188v), copied from the now-lost Darmstadt manuscript.[133]

---

[128] M. O'Loghlin, *Frederick the Great and his Musicians: the Viola da Gamba Music of the Berlin School* (Aldershot, 2008), 60, 215; ME from Add. MS 32390: *Anon (Berlin School c. 1760), Sonata in C major*, ed. D. A. Beecher and B. Gillingham (Ottawa, 1984).

[129] Helm, *Thematic Catalogue of the Works of Carl Philipp Emanuel Bach*, 111; O'Loghlin, *Frederick the Great and his Musicians*, esp. 175–6, 178–9, 213.

[130] Flassig, *Die solistische Gambenmusik*, 261; B. Hoffmann, *Catalogo della musica solistica e cameristica*, 78.

[131] M. Ruhnke, *Georg Philipp Telemann: Thematisch-Systematisches Verzeichnis seiner Werke. Telemann-Werkverzeichnis (TWV): Instrumentalwerke*, 3 vols. (Kassel, 1984, 1992, 1999), ii. 51, 82–3, 85–6, 99–100, 121, 170–1.

[132] O'Loghlin, *Frederick the Great and his Musicians*, esp. 180–1, 228, 230.

[133] An 1899 copy in the Klingenberg Collection at D-B is reported by Flassig, *Die solistische Gambenmusik*, 127.

Zoeller also copied pieces in Add. MS 32347 from an appendix to the periodical *Musikalische Real-Zeitung* (Speyer, 1789) illustrating a treatise on viola d'amore playing by Friedrich August Weber.[134] Two pieces in E major (fols. 12–17v) by the otherwise unknown Tommaso Carle are for violin, viola d'amore, and gamba or violoncello; three in D major by Carl Michael von Esser are effectively a sonata consisting of 'Andante zampognato', Allegro and Alla Polacca (fols. 24–27v) for viola d'amore and gamba or violoncello.[135] Unusually for the late eighteenth century, the gamba plays a simple bass line rather than an alto- or tenor-range solo part. The third piece, a Rondo Pastorale in F major (fols. 18–23v) by Johann Christian Eidenbenz, is for oboe, viola d'amore and violoncello.[136]

Zoeller probably became interested in the gamba because he encountered parts for it in viola d'amore pieces that interested him. Perhaps his manuscripts were copied for use by a group of London enthusiasts that also included Liebing, the French-speaking copyist, and Edward Payne. Some of them seem to have been used: the copy of the Marais viol part has some fingerings added in blue pencil in addition to ink ones from the original. On the other hand, the copies made by Liebing at Kassel in June 1887 were turned over almost immediately to the British Museum: Zoeller sold them on 12 November that year. How accomplished he was is open to question: he was described in as 'well known as a virtuoso on the viola d'amour' in 1886, though in 1915 Thomas Lea Southgate reported a fellow bandmaster's opinion that he was 'a bad player'.[137] Whatever the case, the Zoeller manuscripts are typical of the first stage of the gamba revival in that most of it comes from the eighteenth-century solo or chamber repertory.

❧ *The 1885 Inventions Exhibition*

A NUMBER of Continental cellists were playing the gamba by the 1880s, including August Tolbecque (1830–1919) in Niort, Jules Delsaert (1844–1900) in Paris, Édouard Jacobs (1851–1925) in Brussels, Robert Hausmann (1852–1909) in Berlin, Johannes Klingenberg (1852–1905) in Braunschweig, Paul de Wit (1852–1925) in Leipzig, and Edmund van der Straeten (1855–1934) from Düsseldorf.[138] The last studied in London and settled there in 1888, though there is no sign that

---

134 Danks, *The Viola d'Amore*, 37–48; Jappe, *Viola d'amore Bibliographie*, 193–4.

135 Jappe, *Viola d'amore Bibliographie*, 54, 57.

136 Ibid., 56.

137 Brown, *Biographical Dictionary of Musicians*, 622; T. L. Southgate, 'The Instruments with Sympathetic Strings', *PMA*, 42 (1915–16), 33–50, at 48.

138 J. B. Rutledge, 'Towards a History of the Viol in the Nineteenth Century', *EM*, 12 (1984), 328–36, at 335; A. Wenzinger, 'The Revival of the Viola da Gamba, a History', in *A Viola da Gamba Miscellany: Proceedings of the International Viola*

he was interested in early music until he published an article on the gamba in 1894.[139] Jacobs appeared in London with a group from the Brussels Conservatoire during the International Inventions Exhibition in July 1885, playing a Bach aria, a Boccherini minuet, and a Tartini sonata on the gamba accompanied on a Haas double-manual harpsichord.[140] He was clearly a fine player: *The Times* called him 'an artist of the first order'; *The Musical Times* thought that he played 'to perfection'; while the iconoclastic George Bernard Shaw characteristically used him as a stick to beat conventional cellists:

> As to the *viola da gamba*, it is not too much to say that M. Jacobs might safely challenge any violoncellist to surpass his performance upon it. The instrument he uses dates from the XVII century; no violence has been done to it to get it up to modern concert pitch; and the tone is full and pure, and very even over the whole compass of the instrument, there being none of the differences of character from string to string which are so remarkable in the violoncello. The *viola da gamba* has six strings. M. Jacobs played a sonata by Tartini admirably.[141]

Shaw went further in a second review:

> The six-stringed *viola di gamba* has actually raised the question whether it is not at least equal to the violoncello, instead of being the "nasal and ungrateful" instrument we have been taught to imagine it. But the few pieces played upon it by M. Jacobs were chosen to shew it to the greatest advantage, and certainly did not furnish an exhaustive test of its capacity.[142]

According to A. J. Hipkins, Jacobs played on a gamba 'furnished with sympathetic strings', while Mabel Dolmetsch, Arnold's third wife, claimed that Jacobs 'played his viola da gamba 'cello-wise'.[143] However, the Dolmetsch family was not above criticism at that stage: photographs of Hélène Dolmetsch, the only child from Arnold's first marriage, show her playing a bass viol with a spike (Plate 25),

    da Gamba Symposium, Utrecht 1991, ed. J. Boer and G. van Oorshot (Utrecht, 1994), 133–9, at 134.

[139] E. S. J. van der Straeten, 'The Viola da Gamba', *MO*, 17 (3, 4/1894), 361–2, 437–8.

[140] *The Times*, 3/7/1885; *MT*, 26 (1885), 477–9, at 478. For the 1885 exhibition, see *International Inventions Exhibition … Guide to the Loan Collection*, ed. Hipkins. For Jacobs, see *Baker's Biographical Dictionary of Musicians, Popular Edition*, rev. A. Remy (New York, 1900), 431.

[141] *Shaw's Music: the Complete Musical Criticism*, ed. D. H. Laurence, 3 vols. (London, 1981), i: *1876–1890*, 301–5, at 304.

[142] Ibid., 319–24, at 320.

[143] Hipkins, *Musical Instruments*, 46; M. Dolmetsch, *Personal Recollections of Arnold Dolmetsch* (London, 1957; repr. 1990), 9.

while the first Dolmetsch viol consort included instruments with sympathetic strings, as we shall see.[144]

Jacobs was not the only gamba player performing at the Inventions Exhibition. Edward Payne was on the jury that gave awards to the two music categories, 'Instruments and Appliances constructed or in use since 1800' and 'Music Engraving and Printing', and was a member of the organising committee of the associated Historic Loans Collection of instruments and documents. He exhibited three viols, the 1611 Henry Jaye bass that had belonged to Thomas Cheeseman and John Cawse, a Barak Norman bass, and a Guersan 'Quinton or Pardessus de Viole' of 1763.[145] In the accompanying concerts he 'personally demonstrated on the viola-da-gamba the capabilities of the instrument in playing several pieces, accompanied by the late Mr. A. J. Hipkins on the harpsichord'.[146]

In his 1889 lecture Payne mentioned Marcello, Abel, Rameau, Couperin, Marchand, J. S. Bach, C. P. E. Bach, Handel, Haydn, and even Schubert (the Arpeggione Sonata) as gamba composers, and played eighteenth-century solo music. He began with Abel's unaccompanied Sonata in G major, WKO155 (presumably copied from the autograph, GB-Lbl, Add. MS 31697, fols. 8–9), then played the violoncello piccolo part of 'Mein gläubiges Herze' from Bach's Cantata no. 68, claiming (wrongly) that it was intended for the gamba. He was joined by W. E. Currey in three pieces from Caix d'Hervelois's *Second livre de pièces de viole* (Paris, 1719), 'L'angelique' (pp. 29–30), 'La folète' (p. 38) and 'La villageoise' (pp. 25–6), played on two gambas. Then came an unidentified Andante 'for Baryton or Viola da Gamba' by Haydn,[147] and an arrangement of the aria 'V'adoro, pupille' from Handel's *Giulio Cesare*. He ended with two movements from the Sonata in C major for gamba and obbligato harpsichord attributed to Handel.[148]

[144] See, for instance, M. Dolmetsch, *Personal Recollections*, facing 16; M. Campbell, *Dolmetsch: the Man and his Work* (Seattle, 1975), between 48 and 49.

[145] *International Inventions Exhibition … Guide to the Loan Collection*, ed. Hipkins, 16, 33. Payne also exhibited the Jaye bass at the 1904 Music Loan exhibition; see *A Special Loan Exhibition*, 103, no. 1091; *An Illustrated Catalogue of the Music Loan Exhibition*, 151.

[146] *MT*, 46 (1905), 114–15.

[147] According to Payne, 'The Viola da Gamba', 101, it was 'Edited for violoncello and piano by Burchard (Berlin: Simrock.)'; I have been unable to identify it or the edition.

[148] A. Einstein, 'Zum 48. Bande der Händel-Ausgabe', *Sammelbände der internationalen Musikgesellschaft*, 4 (1902), 170–2, attributed it to J. M. Leffloth. For arguments that it was written by Handel in Italy, see G. Pont, 'Handel's Souvenir of Venice: the "Spurious" Sonata in C for Viola da Gamba & Harpsichord', *EMP*, 23 (March 2009), 4–18; M. Talbot, 'A Response to "Handel's Souvenir of Venice" (*EMP* 23)', *EMP*, 24 (June 2009), 31.

Payne presumably used Friedrich Grützmacher's arrangement for violoncello and piano, published in 1876; it did not appear in Chrysander's Handel edition until 1894.[149] In addition to the 1611 Jaye already mentioned, Payne exhibited gambas by Johann Ulrich Fischer (1720) and Johannes Florenus Guidantus (Bologna, 1728), while Currey exhibited his 1667 Stainer.[150] The gambas by Jaye, Fischer and Guidantus were sold after Payne's death in 1904 along with the Barak Norman bass and the Guersan quinton, a tenor viol of 1746 by Johann Joseph Seidler (?recte Elsler), a viola d'amore of 1758 by Jacob Rauch of Mannheim, and other instruments.[151]

What is striking about this stage of the revival is the lack of interest in other areas of the repertory, such as seventeenth-century English consort music, English division viol and lyra viol music, German and Austrian seventeenth-century music with gamba parts, and all types of sixteenth-century viol music. Payne did mention Christopher Simpson and the early seventeenth-century émigré composer Daniel Norcombe in his lecture (calling the latter 'a pure fountain of serious instrumental music'), but probably only because he owned a copy of the 1667 edition of *The Division-Viol*,[152] and perhaps because he owned a manuscript with many sets of divisions by Norcombe, now GB-HAdolmetsch, MS II.C.24. He took part in the revival of a Jacobean masque, *The Masque of Flowers*, at Gray's Inn on 7 July 1887, playing the gamba in a (presumably modern) string orchestra with two harpsichords, though most of its original music is lost and so was composed for the production 'in the spirit of that age' by Arthur Prendergast and H. F. Birch-Reynardson.[153] Payne seems to have seen himself as a representative of the continuous tradition – a tradition that his lecture was partly designed to describe and uphold – rather than someone who was concerned with researching

[149] Payne, 'The Viola da Gamba', 103; G. F. Handel, *Sonata für Viola da Gamba und Cembalo … für Violoncell und Pianoforte bearbeitet … von F. Grützmacher* (Leipzig, 1876); G. F. Handel, *Werke*, ed. F. Chrysander, 48: *Instrumentalmusik.* (Leipzig, 1894), 112–17.

[150] Payne, 'The Viola da Gamba', 103. Currey exhibited the Stainer in the 1904 Music Loan Exhibition, see *A Special Loan Exhibition*, 105, no. 1129; *An Illustrated Catalogue of the Music Loan Exhibition*, 152, and it was presumably the instrument exhibited in the British section of the 1892 Vienna exhibition, see R. A. Marr, *Musical History as Shown in the International Exhibition of Music and the Drama, Vienna 1892* (London, 1893), 69.

[151] Catch, 'Edward John Payne', 131–2. The Guidantus gamba is now at Vermillion, SD, National Music Museum, no. 3352 (http://www.usd.edu/nmm/). The Elsler tenor viol may be the one, formerly in the Galpin collection, that is now in the Boston Museum of Fine Arts, no. 17.1714 (www.mfa.org/artemis/collections/).

[152] Payne, 'The Viola da Gamba', 100.

[153] See *The Maske of Flowers, Celebration of the Jubilee of her Majesty*, ed. A. W. à Beckett ([London], 1887), 5, 8 (Richard Luckett).

and reviving forgotten repertories. We saw in Chapter 8 that he even copied out an arrangement of Schumann's 'Abendlied', continuing the tradition of providing the gamba with a contemporary repertory.

❧ *Mary Louisa Armitt*

THE neglect of consort music in the 1880s is understandable, given how few viol players there were in England at the time, and how little of the repertory was known, let alone available in print. In that respect, Liebing's copy of D-Kl, 4° MS Mus. 72 is highly significant, since the collection consists mostly of simple five-part pavans eminently suitable for a consort of viols. Another straw in the wind was the remarkable article 'Old English Viol Music', published in August 1888 by the writer and historian Mary Louisa Armitt (1851–1911).[154] She seems to have been the first person to realise the importance of the English consort repertory, and John Jenkins's central position in it, though a course of lectures given by John Hullah to the Royal Institution in 1865 had included Jenkins's three-part Fantasia VdGS 1, presumably played on modern instruments; Hullah stated that he had transcribed it from a manuscript 'in a contemporary handwriting, possibly that of the composer'.[155]

Hullah and Payne seem to have had a serendipitous knowledge of the gamba repertory, largely based on what old prints and manuscripts they had been able to acquire or borrow, or what music had been made available in modern editions. By contrast, Armitt conducted primary research in the Music School manuscripts in the Bodleian Library. She included four examples of Jenkins in her article: the three-part 'Antique Maske' VdGS 89 (GB-Ob, MSS Mus. Sch. D.245–7); the Almand from the Fantasia Suite in E minor for treble and two basses VdGS 8 (D.241–4 and D.261); a passage from the Fantasia of the Fantasia-Air Set for two trebles and bass VdGS, Group VII, no. 1 (F.564–7); and the first strain of the keyboard part of an air from the C major Lyra Consort VdGS 5 (C.84). Her other examples were the opening of Tomkins's three-part Fantasia no. 5 VdGS 7 (D.245–7), a wordless version of the first half of Morley's three-part canzonet 'See, see, myne owne sweet jewell'; and Davis Mell's two-part Alman in C minor VdGS 55 (E.451).[156] She described Jenkins's music as 'the fragrance of a sweet and noble

[154]   M. L. Armitt, 'Old English Viol Music', *Quarterly Musical Review*, 4 (1888), 175–92, 243–64. For Armitt, see esp. *BMB*, 12–13; E. Jay, *The Armitt Story, Ambleside* (Ambleside, 1998), xiv, 2, 4.

[155]   J. Hullah, *The Third or Transition Period of Musical History: a Course of Lectures Delivered to the Royal Institution of Great Britain* (London, 2/1876), 192–9 (Andrew Ashbee).

[156]   Armitt, 'Old English Viol Music', 189–93, 257–64.

spirit', though she doubted whether 'the English school of instrumental writing that prematurely died with him' would ever live again. Nevertheless, she asked for readers with 'the good fortune to possess old viol music in MS.' to allow her access, promising 'scored transcripts from the Bodleian collection' in return and hinting at the possibility of an 'exhaustive and critical monograph on English instrumental music', which unfortunately never materialised. By 1888 she was living far from Oxford at Hawkshead in the Lake District. There is no evidence that Armitt played the viol herself: her interest in its music seems just to have been a part of her scholarly and intellectual pursuits.

&. *Arnold Dolmetsch*

NEVERTHELESS, one wonders whether Armitt's work inspired Arnold Dolmetsch to begin the revival of the viol consort and its repertory. Dolmetsch, born in 1858 into a family of musicians and musical instrument makers in Le Mans, studied between 1879 and 1883 at the Brussels Conservatoire, where a turning point was a *concert historique* on 23 December 1879 directed by the pianist, harpsichordist and composer Louis Diémer in which Auguste Tolbecque played the gamba.[157] According to Mabel Dolmetsch his interest in old music:

> was further stimulated by contact with three musicians at the Conservatoire, [Louis] Van Wafaelghem [Waefelghem], Jakob [Édouard Jacobs] and Diémer, who (borrowing instruments from the Museum) formed a trio for the performance of eighteenth-century music on the viola d'amore, viola da gamba and harpsichord.[158]

She continued:

> His association with these three enthusiasts provided the strong incentive which started Arnold Dolmetsch on his lifelong career of musical exploration. At first his own interest centred round the honey-tongued viola d'amore, which had so fascinated him in Brussels. So he acquired a fine example by Testore, and went to the British Museum to search out some music for it. He found none; but made the startling discovery that there existed a wealth of English concerted music for viols in from two to six parts, of which he instantly appreciated the true value. Highly elated, he went straight to Sir George Grove to open up a project for the revival of this music.[159]

[157] Campbell, *Dolmetsch*, 9–10.
[158] Dolmetsch, *Personal Recollections*, 9.
[159] Ibid., 10.

What is not immediately obvious is that Dolmetsch's process of discovery took about a decade. He heard the Brussels trio in 1879, but did not move to London until 1883. He joined the newly founded Royal College of Music (of which Grove was the director) that autumn and stayed for five terms – that is, until Easter 1885; by March that year he was teaching the violin at Dulwich College.[160] It is not clear when he acquired the viola d'amore attributed to Testore, though a photograph in the Dolmetsch Collection of him holding it is dated 'c. 1888' (Plate 26).[161] He stated a number of times that his 'startling discovery' in the British Museum was made in 1889, though he did not visit its libraries until April 1890.[162] It is likely that he played the viola d'amore for several years before taking up the viol; perhaps he was inspired to take it up by Zoeller's *New Method* of 1885. He continued to play the viola d'amore for some years: there are photographs of him playing one in America in 1909.[163]

Also, it is possible that Dolmetsch was not the first person to put together a complete viol consort. On 25 November 1887 the writer and organist William Alexander Barrett (1834–91) organised a concert at the Portman Rooms in Baker Street of 'Old fashioned musick'.[164] *The Musical Times* reported that 'the rooms were made into the "counterfeit presentment" of the old Marybone Gardens 100 years back' and that 'pieces by Arne, Leveridge, Purcell, Carey, Humphries, Mozart, Webbe, Stafford Smith, Dibdin, and others were performed to the accompaniment of viols, the viola da gamba, harpsichord, &c., with the most pleasing effect'. A consort of viols would, of course, have been inappropriate for this repertory, and it is not obvious whether Barrett's group really used treble and tenor viols, though it clearly included a gamba and a harpsichord. Barrett is mainly known today as a pioneer collector of folk song, though he also had an interest in old music, publishing historical surveys of English glee and church composers and anthologies of songs by eighteenth-century English composers.

However, Dolmetsch was clearly the first person to assemble a viol consort to play sixteenth- and seventeenth-century consort music, though we can observe him feeling his way in his first few London concerts. The first, on 26 June 1889,

---

[160] Campbell, *Dolmetsch*, 15–17.

[161] Studio photograph taken by 'Barraud's, 263 Oxford Sᵗ. London' (Jeanne Dolmetsch). The instrument is illus. in *Made for Music: an Exhibition to Mark the 40th Anniversary of the Galpin Society* (London, 1986), no. 10.

[162] Campbell, *Dolmetsch*, 22, where it is suggested that Dolmetsch actually began his research at GB-Lcm, but 'quarrelled with the RCM at a later stage and therefore felt less inclined to give them credit for being his first source of discovery'.

[163] Illus. in Dolmetsch, *Personal Recollections*, facing 65; Donington, 'Arnold Dolmetsch', 237.

[164] *MT*, 28 (1887), 744. For Barrett, see esp. *MT*, 32 (1891), 659–60.

was with a modern string group (Ch. 8). He seems to have used old instruments for the first time nearly a year later, on 21 May 1890, in a miscellaneous concert given at the Princes Hall in Piccadilly by the Magpie Minstrels Madrigal Society. Henry Lawes's song 'Sweet echo' from Milton's masque *Comus* (1634) was sung by Countess Valda Gleichen, accompanied by a rather inappropriate group consisting of Arnold (viola d'amore), Hélène (viola da gamba) and Henry Bird (Broadwood harpsichord).[165] Although still a child, Hélène Dolmetsch was a talented gamba player and was already playing solos on the instrument. On 10 June at the Portman Rooms Arnold's pupils performed music by Purcell (from *The Fairy Queen*), John Stanley (a concerto), Henry Lawes ('Sweet echo' again), Christopher Simpson (divisions played by Hélène), and Handel, 'played on the harpsichords, viol d'amour, and viol da Gamba, instruments for which this particular music was written'.[166] The string group still presumably consisted of modern instruments, for the programme included two of his own pieces, 'a "Pastorale" for the violin, and his Suite for Strings' – the last repeated from his 1889 concert (Ch. 8). A critic pointed out that Hélène had played another set of divisions by Simpson on the violoncello in a concert the previous June, so she had presumably changed to the gamba during the year.[167]

On 21 November 1890 Dolmetsch provided the illustrations for a lecture given by Frederick Bridge in his capacity as Gresham Professor of Music.[168] It was apparently the first occasion since the seventeenth century that English consort music was 'Performed upon the original Instruments for which it was written', to use the formulation he chose for his public debut the following year. However, there were compromises: the instruments included 'a treble Viol with six strings, a Viola, a seven-string "Viol-d'amore" (1720), and a seven-string Viol-da-gamba (1727) furnished with sympathetic strings'.[169] The performers were Arnold, his first wife Marie, Hélène, and an unnamed pupil, with Bridge playing a Kirkman harpsichord. The programme included a fantasy and two airs by Jenkins, three dances from Locke's Consort of Four Parts, a movement from William Lawes's Royal Consort, and divisions by Simpson, the last played by Hélène 'with great skill'. Bridge played a Byrd galliard and a Bull pavan on the harpsichord, and the programme ended with two Purcell trio sonatas, played on two violins, violoncello, and harpsichord.

---

[165] CC of the programme: GB-HAdolmetsch, III.D.28/1; see also *MT*, 31 (1890), 349; Campbell, *Dolmetsch*, 30.

[166] *MS*, 38 (7/6/1890), 542; *MS*, 38 (14 /6/1890), 566; *MT*, 31 (1890), 421–2.

[167] Campbell, *Dolmetsch*, 31.

[168] CC of the programme: GB-HAdolmetsch, III.D.28/2.

[169] *MW*, 70 (29/11/1890), 948–50; *MT*, 31 (1890), 732.

By the time Dolmetsch's consort made its public debut, at the Princes Hall on 27 April 1891, there were seven players, playing six viols (the three Dolmetsches, Adeline and J. A. Milne, and W. A. Boxall), with Arnold (lute), and Ethel Davis (harpsichord); Enrichetta Kamp sang two songs.[170] The programme included viol consorts by Alfonso Ferrabosco junior, Michael East, Martin Peerson, Thomas Tomkins, and Locke, and as before Hélène played divisions by Simpson. The critical response was largely favourable, with Hélène once again singled out for praise, though there were still compromises. *The Musical Standard* pointed out that the consort pieces were 'played upon viols furnished with sympathetic strings', and *The Musical News* thought that 'The players did their best, but were not sufficiently acquainted with the peculiarities of the instruments to display them perfectly'. Clearly, there was still work to do.

﹩⸰ *Conclusion*

THE debut of the Dolmetsch viol consort in 1890–1 marks an important moment of transition in the developing British early music movement, and makes a convenient place to end this study of the viol after the 'golden age'. We can now see that Dolmetsch was not the first person in Britain to use old instruments to play old music, as his supporters and followers often claimed in the twentieth century.[171] He did not revive the viol, for there was always at least one person playing it in London throughout the nineteenth century. Nor was he the first person to revive the recorder or the lute, two other instruments associated with Dolmetsch and his followers in the early twentieth century. A recorder consort from Brussels had played at the 1885 Inventions Exhibition,[172] Edward Payne reportedly played the lute,[173] and on 18 November 1890 Francis Galpin and his wife illustrated a lecture in London by C. F. Abdy Williams with a variety of old instruments, including treble and bass viols, hurdy-gurdy, lute, theorbo, cittern, regal, spinet, recorder, shawm, and cornett.[174]

---

[170] CC of the programme: GB-HAdolmetsch, III.D.28/5. See also *MT*, 32 (1891), 358–9; *The Athenaeum*, 3314 (2/5/1891), 581; *MS*, 40 (2/5/1891), 359; *Musical News*, 1 (1/5/1891), 169.

[171] For instance, R. Donington, 'Arnold Dolmetsch', *EM*, 3 (1975), 236–9, at 236; M. Pallis, 'The Rebirth of Early Music', *EM*, 6 (1978), 41–5, at 41.

[172] *MT*, 26 (8/1885), 478.

[173] *MT*, 46 (1905), 114.

[174] *MS*, 39 (29/11/1890), 442. For Galpin, see esp. S. Godman, 'Francis William Galpin: Music Maker', *GSJ*, 12 (1959), 8–16. For instruments owned by Galpin in 1897, see W. Lynd, *A Popular Account of Ancient Musical Instruments and their Development, as Illustrated by Typical Examples in the Galpin Collection, at Hatfield, Broad Oak, Essex* (London, 1897).

But Galpin, Dolmetsch's exact contemporary, a clergyman, antiquary and amateur musician, was only at the margins of London's musical life. Dolmetsch was influential because he was a trained professional musician working in the mainstream, which allowed him to attract attention quickly and easily in the 1890s. Furthermore, he combined in a single person the various activities necessary for the development of the early music movement. He played a range of old instruments; he organised groups, devised programmes, put on concerts, collected and restored old instruments, made new instruments based on old models, and eventually established his own instrument-making workshop. Most important, he did his own research, collecting old music, editing it, and exploring historical performance practice.

Not surprisingly, some of these activities were more successful than others, though Dolmetsch provided the developing early music movement in Britain with a heady new career model. It is largely through his example that the figure of the scholar-performer, exemplified by Diana Poulton, Robert Donington, Edgar Hunt, Thurston Dart, Walter Bergmann, Robert Spencer, Gilbert Reaney, Michael Morrow, David Munrow, Christopher Hogwood, and others, came to dominate the British early music scene during the twentieth century. It is odd that Dolmetsch, a product of the Brussels Conservatoire, was the person who showed that it was possible and desirable to combine performance and research; in mainland Europe the worlds of the conservatoire and the university musicology department remained largely separate until recently. Furthermore, Dolmetsch's concentration on English sixteenth- and seventeenth-century music rather than the eighteenth-century Continental repertory was one of the reasons why early music in Britain took a rather different course in the early twentieth century from the equivalent movements in other European countries.

Bibliography

❧ Books, Articles and Theses

ABC Dario Musico (Bath, 1780)

Abdy Williams, C. F., *A Short Historical Account of the Degrees in Music at Oxford and Cambridge* (London, 1894)

Adkins, C., and A. Dickinson, *A Trumpet by any other Name: a History of the Trumpet Marine*, 2 vols. (Buren, 1991)

Aeolian Harp, ed. S. Bonner, 4 vols. (Duxford, 1968–74)

Albertyn, E., 'The Hanover Orchestral Repertory, 1672–1714: Significant Source Discoveries', *EM*, 33 (2005), 449–71

Allgemeines Lexicon der Bildenden Künste von der Antike bis zur Gegenwart, ed. U. Thieme and F. Becker, 37 vols. (Leipzig, 1912; repr. 1951)

Allsop, P., 'The Role of the Stringed Bass as a Continuo Instrument in Italian Seventeenth-Century Instrumental Music', *Chelys*, 8 (1978–9), 31–7

—— *Arcangelo Corelli: 'New Orpheus of Our Times'* (Oxford, 1999)

Alumni Dublinienses: a Register of the Students, Graduates, Professors, and Provosts of Trinity College in the University of Dublin (1593–1860), ed. G. D. Burtchaell and T. U. Sadleir (Dublin, 2/1935)

Alumni Oxonienses: the Members of the University of Oxford, 1500–1714, comp. J. Foster (Oxford, 1888; repr. 1968)

Andrewes, R., 'Edward Francis Rimbault, 1816–1876', *Fontes Artis Musicae*, 30 (1983), 30–4

Andriessen, P., *Carel Hacquart (c. 1640–1701?): een biografische bijdrage, het werk* (Brussels, 1974)

Angelo, H., *Reminiscences of Henry Angelo, with Memoirs of his late Father and Friends*, 2 vols. (London, 1828)

Armitt, M. L., 'Old English Viol Music', *Quarterly Musical Review*, 4 (1888), 175–92, 243–64

Asfour, A., and P. Williamson, 'William Jackson of Exeter: New Documents', *Gainsborough's House Review* (1996–7), 39–152

—— and —— *William Jackson of Exeter (1730–1803)* (Sudbury, 1997)

Ashbee, A., 'Music for Treble, Bass and Organ by John Jenkins', *Chelys*, 6 (1975–6), 25–42

—— *The Harmonious Musick of John Jenkins*, i: *The Fantasias for Viols* (Surbiton, 1992); ii: *Suites, Airs and Vocal Music* (forthcoming)

—— 'Bodleian Library, Printed Book, Mus. 184.c.8 Revisited', *The Viol*, 2 (Spring 2006), 18–21

—— 'Manuscripts of Consort Music in London, *c.* 1600–1625: some Observations', *VdGSJ*, 1 (2007), 1–19

—— '"My Fiddle is a Bass Viol": Music in the Life of Sir Roger L'Estrange', in *Sir Roger L'Estrange and the Making of Restoration Culture*, ed. A. Dunan-Page and B. Lynch (Aldershot, 2008), 149–66

Bachmann, W., *The Origins of Bowing and the Development of Bowed Instruments up to the Thirteenth Century* (London, 1969)

Baines, A., 'James Talbot's Manuscript (Christ Church Library, Music MS 1187); I: Wind Instruments', *GSJ*, 1 (1948), 9–26

—— *European and American Musical Instruments* (London, 1966)

—— *Victoria and Albert Museum, Catalogue of Musical Instruments*, ii: *Non-Keyboard Instruments* (London, 1968)

Baker's Biographical Dictionary of Musicians, Popular Edition, rev. A. Remy (New York, 1900)

Barlow, J. *The Enraged Musician: Hogarth's Musical Imagery* (Aldershot, 2005)

Bashford, C., 'John Ella and the Making of the Musical Union', in *Music and British Culture, 1785–1914: Essays in Honour of Cyril Ehrlich*, ed. Bashford and L. Langley (Oxford, 2000), 193–214

Beedell, A. V., *The Decline of the English Musician, 1788–1888: a Family of English Musicians in Ireland, England, Mauritius, and Australia* (Oxford, 1992)

Beeks, G., 'Handel and Music for the Earl of Carnarvon', in *Bach, Handel, Scarlatti: Tercentenary Essays*, ed. P. Williams (Cambridge, 1985), 1–20

Bell, A. C., *Handel Chronological Thematic Catalogue* (Darley, 1972)

Bellingham, B., 'The Musical Circle of Anthony Wood in Oxford during the Commonwealth and Restoration', *JVdGSA*, 19 (1982), 6–70

Bennett, A., *Untold Stories* (London, 2005)

Berck, H., *Viola d'amore Bibliographie* (Kassel, 1986)

Bergsagel, J., 'Music in Oxford in Holberg's Time', in *Hvad Fatter gjør … boghistoriske, litteraere ok musikalske essays tilegnet Erik Dal*, ed. H. Glahn *et al.* (Herning, 1982), 34–61

Best, T., 'Handel's Chamber Music: Sources, Chronology and Authenticity', *EM*, 13 (1985), 476–99

A Biographical Dictionary of Actors, Actresses, Musicians, Dancers, Managers, and other Stage Personnel in London, 1660–1800, ed. P. H. Highfill jr. *et al.*, 16 vols. (Carbondale and Edwardsville, IL, 1973–93) [*BDA*]

A Biographical Dictionary of English Court Musicians, 1485–1714, comp. A. Ashbee, D. Lasocki *et al.*, 2 vols. (Aldershot, 1998) [*BDECM*]

Birsak, K., *Salzburger Geigen und Lauten des Barock* (Salzburg, 2001)

Boalch, D. H., *Makers of the Harpsichord and Clavichord, 1440–1840*, rev. C. Mould (Oxford, 3/1995)

Boer, J., 'The Viola da Gamba and the Nineteenth Century', in *Viola da gamba – Baryton – Arpeggione: Festschrift Alfred Lessing, Dusseldorf 2000*, ed. B. R. Appel and Boer (Utrecht, 2003), 35–41

Bonnani, P., *Gabinetto armonico* (Rome, 2/1723); facs. as *The Showcase of Musical Instruments*, intro. F. L. Harrison and J. Rimmer (New York, 1964)

Bonner, S., *Angelo Benedetto Ventura, Teacher, Inventor, & Composer: a Study in English Regency Music* (Harlow, 1971)

The Book of the Thanes of Cawdor: a Series of Papers Selected from the Charter Room at Cawdor, 1236–1742, ed. C. Innes (Edinburgh, 1859)

Borsay, P., *The English Urban Renaissance: Culture and Society in the Provincial Town, 1660–1770* (Oxford, 1989)

Boulton, *A Catalogue of the Neat and Genuine Household Furniture, and other Effects of a Gentleman, Well Known in the Musical World* (17, 18/6/1795)

Boydell, B., *A Dublin Musical Calendar, 1700–1760* (Dublin, 1988)

—— *Rotunda Music in Eighteenth-Century Dublin* (Dublin, 1992)

Boyden, D. D., 'Ariosti's Lessons for Viola' d'Amore', *MQ*, 32 (1946), 545–63

—— *Catalogue of the Hill Collection of Musical Instruments in the Ashmolean Museum, Oxford* (Oxford, 1969)

Boynton, L., 'The Moravian Brotherhood and the Migration of Furniture Makers in the Eighteenth Century', *Furniture History*, 29 (1993), 45–58

Brauchli, B., *The Clavichord* (Cambridge, 1998; repr. 2005)

The Breitkopf Thematic Catalogue: the Six Parts and Sixteen Supplements, 1762–1787, ed. B. S. Brook (New York, 1966)

The British Violin: the Catalogue of the 1998 Exhibition '400 Years of Violin and Bow Making in the British Isles', ed. J. Milnes (Oxford, 2000)

Brookes, V., *British Keyboard Music to c. 1660: Sources and Thematic Index* (Oxford, 1996)

Brotherton, J., *An Account of Printed Musick, for Violins, Hautboys, Flutes and other Instruments, by Several Masters* (London, *c*. 1724)

Brown, B. A., 'Ann Ford and the Salterio', *ECM*, 2 (2005), 377

Brown, C., and P. Holman, 'Thomas Busby and his "FAC SIMILES OF CELEBRATED COMPOSERS"', *EMP*, 12 (August 2003), 3–12

Brown, H. M., 'Notes on the Viol in the Twentieth Century', *EM*, 6 (1978), 47–55

—— 'Pedantry or Liberation? A Sketch of the Historical Performance Movement', in *Authenticity and Early Music*, ed. N. Kenyon (Oxford, 1988), 27–56

Brown, J. D., *Biographical Dictionary of Musicians, with a Bibliography of English Writings on Music* (Paisley, 1886)

Brown, J. D., and S. S. Stratton, *British Musical Biography: a Dictionary of Musical Artists, Authors and Composers Born in Britain and its Colonies* (Birmingham, 1897) [*BMB*]

Brown, T., *The Compleat Musick-Master* (London, 3/1722)

Brownlow, A., *The Last Trumpet: a History of the English Slide Trumpet* (Stuyvesant, NY, 1996)

Bryan, P. R., *Johann Wanhal, Viennese Symphonist: his Life, his Symphonies and his Musical Environment* (Stuyvesant, NY, 1997)

Burchell, J., *Polite or Commercial Concerts? Concert Management and Orchestral Repertoire in Edinburgh, Bath, Oxford, Manchester, and Newcastle, 1730–1799* (New York, 1996)

Burney, C., *A General History of Music* (London, 1776–89), ed. F. Mercer (London, 1935) [BurneyH]

Burrows, D., 'Handel's London Theatre Orchestra', *EM*, 13 (1985), 349–57

—— *Handel and the English Chapel Royal* (Oxford, 2005)

Busby, T., *Concert Room and Orchestra Anecdotes of Music and Musicians, Ancient and Modern*, 3 vols. (London, 1825)

Cadell, P., 'French Music in the Collection of the Earls of Panmure', in *Defining Strains: the Musical Life of Scots in the Seventeenth Century*, ed. J. Porter (Oxford, 2007), 127–37

Caldwell, J., 'Antique Viols and Related Instruments from the Caldwell Collection', *JVdGSA*, 11 (1974), 60–89

Calendar of State Papers, Domestic Series, of the Reign of William III, 1 January – 31 December 1697, ed. W. J. Hardy (London, 1927)

Calvocoressi, M. D., 'Friedrich Rust, his Editors and his Critics', *MT*, 55 (1914), 14–16

—— 'The Rust Case: its Ending and its Moral', *MT*, 55 (1914), 89–91

Cambridge under Queen Anne, Illustrated by Memoir of Ambrose Bonwicke and Diaries of Francis Burman and Zacharias Conrad von Uffenbach, ed. J. E. B. Mayor (Cambridge, 1911)

Campbell, M., *Dolmetsch: the Man and his Work* (Seattle, 1975)

Capleton, B., 'Carl Friedrich Abel and the Viola da Gamba: a Study of Lbl, Add. [MS] 31697 and its Context' (MMus diss., London, Royal College of Music, 1994)

Carter, R., 'Clamor Heinrich Abel's *Dritter Theil musikalischer Blumen*, 1677: a Lost source of Lyra Consort Music', *VdGSJ*, 3 (2009), 55–82

Case, A. E., 'Aaron Hill and Thomson's *Sophonisba*', *Modern Language Notes*, 42 (1927), 175–6

Cash, A. H., *Laurence Sterne: the Early and Middle Years* (London, 1975)

—— *Laurence Sterne: the Later Years* (London, 1986)

Catalogue d'une très belle bibliothèque de livres … deslaissez par feu monsieur Nicolas Selhof (The Hague, 1759), facs., intro. A. H. King (Amsterdam, 1973)

Catalogue of Political and Personal Satires Preserved in the Department of Prints and Drawings in the British Museum, 11 vols. (London, 1870–1954)

Catch, J., 'Prince Albert's Early Music', *GSJ*, 42 (1989), 3–9

—— 'A Buckinghamshire Polymath: Edward John Payne', *Records of Buckinghamshire*, 32 (1990), 120–9

—— 'Edward John Payne, Victorian Gambist', *GSJ*, 50 (1997), 127–35

Caudle, M., 'The English Repertory for Violin, Bass Viol and Continuo', *Chelys*, 6 (1975–6), 69–75

Cawse, J., *Introduction to the Art of Painting in Oil Colours* (London, 1822)

—— *The Art of Painting Portraits, Landscapes, Animals, Draperies, Satins &c. in Oil Colours* (London, 1840)

Chafe, E. T., *The Church Music of Heinrich Biber* (Ann Arbor, MI, 1987)

Chambers, R., *Domestic Annals of Scotland from the Revolution to the Rebellion of 1745* (Edinburgh, 1861)

Charteris, R., 'Consort Music Manuscripts in Archbishop Marsh's Library, Dublin', *RMARC*, 13 (1976), 27–57

—— 'Matthew Hutton (1638–1711) and his Manuscripts in York Minster Library', *GSJ*, 28 (1976), 2–6

—— 'A Newly Discovered Manuscript Copy of Christopher Simpson's *The Division-Viol*', *Chelys*, 23 (1994), 47–53

—— *Giovanni Gabrieli (ca. 1555–1612): a Thematic Catalogue of his Music with a Guide to the Source Materials and Translations of his Vocal Texts* (Stuyvesant, NY, 1996)

Charters, M., 'Abel in London', *MT*, 114 (1973), 1224–6

Cheney, S., 'Early Autograph Manuscripts of Marin Marais', *EM*, 38 (2010), 59–72

The Cheque Books of the Chapel Royal, ed. A. Ashbee and J. Harley, 2 vols. (Aldershot, 2000)

Chevill, E., 'Music Societies and Musical Life in Old Foundation Cathedral Cities, 1700–1760' (PhD diss., King's College, U. of London, 1993)

Christie, *A Catalogue of the Remainder of the Capital Collection of Pictures, Drawings, etc. of that Ingenious and Esteemed Artist, Mr. Gainsborough, Dec.* (2/6/1792)

—— *A Catalogue of the Remainder of the Capital and Valuable Books of Genuine Sketches, Studies and Designs after Nature, Books of Prints, Architecture, Musical Instruments, and two Laymen, of the late Celebrated Artist, Thoˢ Gainsborough, Esq. Dec.* (11/5/1799)

—— *A Catalogue of a Valuable Collection of Engravings and Etchings in Portfolios, Books and Books of Prints, Formed by the late C. W. Bampfylde, Esq.* (7, 8/7/1820)

—— *British and Victorian Pictures* (29/5/2003) (www.christies.com)

Clark, J., 'Lord Burlington is Here', in *Lord Burlington: Architecture, Art and Life*, ed. T. Barnard and Clark (London, 1995), 251–310

Clergy of Dublin and Glendalough: Biographical Succession Lists, comp. J. B. Leslie, rev. W. J. R. Wallace (Belfast, 2001)

Coggin, P., '"This Easy and Agreable Instrument": a History of the English Guittar', *EM*, 15 (1987), 204–18

Cole, M., *The Pianoforte in the Classical Era* (Oxford, 1998)

A Collection of Hymns of the Children of God in all Ages … Designed Chiefly for the Use of the Congregations in Union with the Brethren's Church, 2 vols. (London, 1754)

A Collection of Hymns with Several Translations from the Hymn-Book of the Moravian Brethren, 2 vols. (London, 3/1746)

A Collection of Original Poems by the Rev. Mr Blacklock and other Scotch Gentlemen (Edinburgh, 1760)

Collins, P., *The 'Stylus Phantasticus' and Free Keyboard Music of the North German Baroque* (Aldershot, 2005)

Colman, C., *The Musical Lady, a Farce as it is Acted at the Theatre-Royal in Drury-Lane* (London, 1762)

Constable, J., *John Constable's Correspondence*, 6 vols., 2: *Early Friends and Maria Bicknell (Mrs. Constable)*, Suffolk Records Society, 6 (Ipswich, 1964)

Cook, D. F., 'The Life and Works of Johann Christoph Pepusch (1667–1752), with Special Reference to his Dramatic Works and Cantatas', 2 vols. (PhD diss., King's College, U. of London, 1982) [Cook]

Cooper, A. W., *Benjamin Banks, 1727–1795, the Salisbury Violin Maker* (Salisbury, 2/1995)

Coral, L., 'Music in English Auction Sales, 1676–1750' (PhD diss., U. of London, 1974)

Corten, W., 'Fétis, transcripteur et vulgarisateur', *Revue belge de musicologie/ Belgisch Tijdschrift voor Musiekwetenschap*, 50 (1996), 249–68

The Court and City Register, or Gentleman's Complete Annual Calendar for the Year 1775 (London, 1774)

Cowgill, R., and G. Dideriksen, 'Opera Orchestras in Georgian and Early Victorian London', in *The Opera Orchestra in Eighteenth- and Nineteenth-Century Europe*, ed. N. M. Jensen and F. Piperno, 2 vols. (Berlin, 2008), i. 259–321

Cowling, E., *The Cello* (London, 1975)

Cramer, C. F., *Magazin der Musik* (Hamburg, 1783–6)

Crauford, J. G., 'The Madrigal Society', *PRMA*, 82 (1955–6), 33–46

Crawford, T., 'Lord Danby, Lutenist of Quality', *The Lute*, 25/2 (1985), 53–68

—— 'Lord Danby's Lute Book: a New Source of Handel's Hamburg Music', *Göttinger Händel-Beiträge*, 2 (1986), 19–50

—— 'Constantijn Huygens and the 'Engelsche Viool', *Chelys*, 18 (1989), 41–60

Crosby, B., 'Stephen and other Paxtons: an Investigation into the Identities and Careers of a Family of Eighteenth-Century Musicians', *ML*, 81 (2000), 41–64

Cross, W. L., *The Life and Times of Laurence Sterne* (New Haven, CT, 3/1929)

Crum, M., 'Early Lists of the Oxford Music School Collection', *ML*, 48 (1967), 23–34

—— 'The Consort Music from Kirtling, Bought for the Oxford Music School from Anthony Wood, 1667', *Chelys*, 4 (1972), 3–10

—— 'An Oxford Music Club, 1690–1719', *Bodleian Library Record*, 9 (1974), 83–99

—— 'Music from St Thomas's, Leipzig, in the Music School Collection at Oxford', in *Festschrift Rudolf Elvers zum 60. Geburtstag*, ed. E. Herttrich and H. Schneider (Tutzing, 1985), 97–101

Cudworth, C. L., 'Ye Olde Spuriosity Shoppe, or Put it in the *Anhang*', *Notes*, 12 (1954, 1955), 25–40, 533–53

Cunningham, A., *The Lives of the most Eminent British Painters, Sculptors, and Architects*, 6 vols. (London, 1829–33)

Cunningham, J., *The Consort Music of William Lawes, 1602–1645* (Woodbridge, 2010)

—— and A. Woolley, 'A Little-Known Source of Restoration Lyra-Viol and Keyboard Music: Surrey History Centre, Woking, LM/1083/91/35', *RMARC*, 43 (2010), 1–22

The Cyclopaedia, or Universal Dictionary of Arts, Sciences, and Literature, ed. A. Rees, 39 vols. (London, 1819)

Cyr, M., '*Basses* and *basse continue* in the Orchestra of the Paris Opéra, 1700–1764', *EM*, 10 (1982), 155–70

—— 'Carl Friedrich Abel's Solos: a Musical Offering to Gainsborough?', *MT*, 128 (1987), 317–21

Dale, W., *Tschudi the Harpsichord Maker* (London, 1913)

Danks, H., *The Viola d'Amore* (Halesowen, 1976)

Daub, P. E., 'Music at the Court of George II (r. 1727–1760)' (PhD diss., Cornell U., 1985)

Davidson, H., *Choirs, Bands and Organs: a History of Church Music in Northamptonshire and Rutland* (Oxford, 2003)

Davidson, M., 'Samuel Pepys and the Viol', *JVdGSA*, 42 (2005), 5–18

Dawe, D., *Organists of the City of London, 1666–1850* (Padstow, 1983)

Day, C. L., and E. B. Murrie, *English Song-Books, 1651–1702: a Bibliography* (London, 1940)

Day, T., 'A Renaissance Revival in Eighteenth-Century England', *MQ*, 57 (1971), 575–92

Dean, W., and J. M. Knapp, *Handel's Operas, 1704–1726* (Oxford, 1987)

Delany, M., *The Autobiography and Correspondence of Mary Granville, Mrs. Delany*, ed. A. Hall, 3 vols. (London, 1861)

Deutsch, O. E., 'Haydn in Cambridge', *The Cambridge Review*, 62 (1940–1), 312, 314

—— *Handel: a Documentary Biography* (London, 1955)

—— *Mozart: a Documentary Biography*, trans. E. Blom, P. Branscombe, and J. Noble (London, 1965; repr. 1990)

Dibdin, C., *Professional & Literary Memoirs of Charles Dibdin the Younger, Dramatist and Upward of Thirty Years Manager of Minor Theatres*, ed. G. Speaight (London, 1956)

The Dictionary of Art, 34 vols., ed. J. Turner (London, 1996)

A Dictionary of Music and Musicians, 4 vols. ed. G. Grove (London, 1878–90) [*Grove 1*]

Dixon, G., 'Continuo Scoring in the Early Baroque: the Role of Bowed Bass Instruments', *Chelys*, 15 (1986), 38–53

Doane, J., *A Musical Directory for the Year 1794* (London, 1794; repr. 1993)

Doe, P., 'The Emergence of the In Nomine: some Notes and Queries on the Work of Tudor Church Musicians', in *Modern Musical Scholarship*, ed. E. Olleson (Stocksfield, 1980), 79–92

Dolmetsch, M., *Personal Recollections of Arnold Dolmetsch* (London, 1957; repr. 1990)

Donington, R., 'Arnold Dolmetsch', *EM*, 3 (1975), 236–9

—— 'James Talbot's Manuscript: Bowed Strings', *Chelys*, 6 (1975–6), 43–60

Dreyfus, L., *Bach's Continuo Group: Players and Practices in his Vocal Works* (Cambridge, MA, 1987)

Dubois, P., 'Sterne et la musique, ou l'harmonie impossible', *Anglophonia*, 11 (2002), 263–76

Dunbar Dunbar, E., *Social Life in Former Days, chiefly in the Province of Moray* (Edinburgh, 1865)

Edwards, F. G. ['Dotted Crotchet'], 'Private Musical Collections, ii: the Rev. F. W. Galpin's Musical Instruments', *MT*, 47 (1906), 521–9

—— 'Lady Violinists', *MT*, 47 (1906), 662–8, 735–40

Edwards, W., 'The Performance of Ensemble Music in Elizabethan England', *PRMA*, 97 (1970–1), 113–23

—— 'The Musical Sources', in *Defining Strains: the Musical Life of Scots in the Seventeenth Century*, ed. J. Porter (Oxford, 2007), 47–71

Eeles, H. S., *Lord Chancellor Camden and his Family* (London, 1934)

'An Eighteenth-Century Directory of London Musicians', *GSJ*, 2 (1949), 27–31

Einstein, A., 'Zum 48. Bande der Händel-Ausgabe', *Sammelbände der internationalen Musikgesellschaft*, 4 (1902), 170–2

Eitner, R., *Biographisch-Bibliographisches Quellen-Lexicon der Musiker und Musikgelehrten christlicher Zeitrechnung bis Mitte des neunzehnten Jahrhunderts*, 10 vols. (Leipzig, 1902; repr. 1958)

Ellis, K., *Music Criticism in Nineteenth-Century France: 'La Revue et Gazette musicale de Paris', 1834–1880* (Cambridge, 1995)

—— *Interpreting the Musical Past: Early Music in Nineteenth-Century France* (Oxford, 2005)

Encylopaedia Britannica, or a Dictionary of Arts, Sciences and Miscellaneous Literature, ed. C. Macfarquhar and G. Gleig, 18 vols. (Edinburgh, 3/1797)

Engel, C., *A Descriptive Catalogue of the Musical Instruments in the South Kensington Museum* (London, 2/1874)

—— 'Some Account of the Clavichord with Historical Notices', *MT*, 20 (1879), 356–9, 411–15, 468–72

The English Bach Awakening: Knowledge of J. S. Bach and his Music in England, 1750–1830, ed. M. Kassler (Aldershot, 2004)

Erhardt, T., 'Revisiting a Buxtehude Curiosity Once Again', *EMP*, 24 (June 2009), 16–21

Essex, J., *The Young Ladies Conduct, or Rules for Education* (London, 1722)

Examples of English Handwriting, 1150–1750, ed. H. E. P. Grieve ([Chelmsford], 1954)

Farington, J., *The Diary of Joseph Farington*, 16 vols., vi: *April 1803-December 1804*, ed. K. Garlick and A. Macintyre (New Haven, CT, 1979)

Fawcett, T., *Music in Eighteenth-Century Norwich and Norfolk* (Norwich, 1979)

Fellowes, E. H., *The Catalogue of Manuscripts in the Library of St. Michael's College, Tenbury* (Paris, 1934)

Fenner, T., *Opera in London: Views of the Press, 1785–1830* (Carbondale and Edwardsville, IL, 1994)

The Ferrar Papers, 1590–1790, in Magdalene College, Cambridge, ed. D. Ransome [CD-ROM edition] (Wakefield, 1992)

Fétis, F. J., *Biographie universelle des musiciens*, 10 vols. (Paris, 1860–80)

Field, C. D. S., 'The English Consort Suite of the Seventeenth Century' (PhD diss., U. of Oxford, 1970)

—— 'Consort Music I: up to 1660', in *The Seventeenth Century*, ed. I. Spink, The Blackwell History of Music in Britain, 3 (Oxford, 1992), 197–244

Fiske, R., 'The *Macbeth* Music', *ML*, 45 (1964), 114–25

—— *English Theatre Music in the Eighteenth Century* (Oxford, 2/1986)

Flassig, F., *Die soloistische Gambenmusik in Deutschland im 18. Jahrhundert* (Göttingen, 1998)

Fleming, M., 'Instrument Makers Named Hill and Hunt in Pepys's London', *GSJ*, 55 (2002), 382–5

—— 'The Identities of the Viols in the Ashmolean Museum', *VdGSJ*, 3 (2009), 117–30

Flood, W. H. G., 'Coleridge and Clagget', *MT*, 66 (1925), 538–9

Flynn, J., 'A Reconsideration of the Mulliner Book (British Library, Add. MS 30513): Music Education in Sixteenth-Century England' (PhD diss., Duke U., 1993)

Ford, A., *Lessons and Instructions for Playing on the Guitar* (London, ?1761)

—— *Instructions for Playing on the Musical Glasses* (London, 1761)

Ford, R., 'Osborn MS 515: a Guardbook of Restoration Instrumental Music', *Fontes artis musicae*, 30 (1983), 174–84

—— 'Minor Canons at Canterbury Cathedral: the Gostlings and their Colleagues', 3 vols. (PhD diss., U. of California, Berkeley, 1984)

Foster, *A Catalogue of Household Furniture, Books, Pictures, Prints, &c., by Order of the Administrator of the late John Constable, Esq. R. A.* (22/12/1838)

Fox, P. M., 'Music in Moravian Boarding Schools through the Early Nineteenth Century', in *The Music of the Moravian Church in America*, ed. N. R. Knouse (Rochester, NY, 2008), 212–27

Franklin, B., *The Papers of Benjamin Franklin*, 19: *January 1 through December 31, 1772*, ed. W. B. Willcox *et al.* (New Haven, CT, 1975)

—— *The Papers of Benjamin Franklin*, 27: *July 1 through October 31, 1778*, ed. C. A. Lopez *et al.* (New Haven, CT, 1988)

—— *The Papers of Benjamin Franklin*, 34: *November 16, 1780, through April 30, 1781*, ed. B. B. Oberg *et al.* (New Haven, CT, 1998)

Freemanová, M., and E. Mikanová, '"My Honourable Lord and Father …": Eighteenth-Century English Musical Life through Bohemian Eyes', *EM*, 31 (2003), 210–31

Friedman, J., *Spencer House: Chronicle of a Great London Mansion* (London, 1993)

From Renaissance to Baroque: Change in Instruments and Instrumental Music in the Seventeenth Century, ed. J. Wainwright and P. Holman (Aldershot, 2005)

Fruchtman, E., 'The Baryton Trios of Tomasini, Burgksteiner, and Neumann', 2 vols. (PhD diss., U. of North Carolina, Chapel Hill, 1960)

—— 'The Baryton: its History and Music Re-Examined', *Acta Musicologica*, 34 (1962), 2–17

Fürstenau, M., *Zur Geschichte der Musik und des Theaters am Hofe zu Dresden*, 2 vols. (Dresden, 1861–2; repr. Leipzig, 1971)

Gärtner, H., trans. R. G. Pauly, *John Christian Bach: Mozart's Friend and Mentor* (Portland, OR, 1994)

Gainsborough, English Music and the Fitzwilliam, ed. J. Huskinson (Cambridge, 1977)

Gainsborough, T., *The Letters of Thomas Gainsborough*, ed. M. Woodall ([Ipswich], 2/1963)

—— *The Letters of Thomas Gainsborough*, ed. J. Hayes (New Haven, CT, 2001)

Galpin, F. W., *Old English Instruments of Music: their History and Character*, rev. T. Dart (London, 4/1965)

Gambarini, C., *A Description of the Earl of Pembroke's Pictures* (Westminster, 1731)

Gardiner, W., *Music and Friends, or Pleasant Recollections of a Dilettante*, 3 vols. (London, 1838)

Gartrell, C. A., *A History of the Baryton and its Music, King of Instruments, Instrument of Kings* (Lanham, MD, 2009)

Geiser, B., *Das Hackbrett in der Schweiz* (Visp, 1973)

Gérard, Y., trans. A. Mayor, *Thematic, Bibliographical and Critical Catalogue of the Works of Luigi Boccherini* (London, 1969)

Gerber, E. L., *Historisch-biographisches Lexicon der Tonkünstler*, 2 vols. (Leipzig, 1790–1792; repr. Graz, 1977)

—— *Neues historisch-biographisches Lexicon der Tonkünstler*, 3 vols. (Leipzig, 1812–14; repr. Graz, 1969)

Ghielmi, V., 'An Eighteenth-Century Italian Treatise and other Clues to the History of the Viola da Gamba in Italy', in *The Italian Viola da Gamba: Proceedings of the International Symposium on the Italian Viola da Gamba, Magnano, Italy, 29 April-1 May 2000*, ed. S. Orlando (Solignac, 2002), 73–85

Gibson, E., *The Royal Academy of Music, 1719–1728: the Institution and its Directors* (New York, 1989)

Giustiniani, V., *Discorso sopra la Musica (1628)*, trans. C. MacClintock, Musicological Studies and Documents, 9 (Rome, 1962)

Glüxam, D., *Die Violinskordatur und ihre Rolle in der Geschichte des Violinspieles: unter besonderer Berücksichtigung der Quellen der erzbischöflichen Musiksammlung in Kremsier* (Tutzing, 1999)

Godman, S., 'Francis William Galpin: Music Maker', *GSJ*, 12 (1959), 8–16

Goldsmith, N. M., *The Worst of Crimes: Homosexuality and the Law in Eighteenth-Century London* (Aldershot, 1998)

Goodwill, H., 'The Musical Involvement of the Landed Classes in Eastern Scotland, 1685–1760' (PhD diss., U. of Edinburgh, 2000)

Gorton, W., *Catechetical Questions in Musick* (London, 1704)

Gosse, P., *Dr. Viper, the Querulous Life of Philip Thicknesse* (London, 1952)

Gouk, P., *Music, Science and Natural Magic in Seventeenth-Century England* (New Haven, CT, 1999)

Graf, L., 'Moravians in London: a Case Study in Furniture-Making, *c*. 1735–65', *Furniture History*, 40 (2004), 1–52

—— 'John Frederick Hintz, Eighteenth-Century Moravian Instrument Maker, and the Use of the Cittern in Moravian Worship', *Journal of Moravian History*, 5 (2008), 7–39

Gramenz, F. L., 'John Stafford Smith, 1750–1836: an Early English Musicologist', 2 vols. (PhD diss., Boston U., 1987)

Grampp, F., 'A Little-Known Collection of Canzonas Rediscovered: the *Canzoni a cinque da sonarsi con le viole da gamba* by Cherubino Waesich (Rome, 1632)', *Chelys*, 32 (2004), 21–44

Grant, K. S., *Dr. Burney as Critic and Historian of Music* (Ann Arbor, MI, 1983)

Gray, C., *Sisters in the Wilderness: the Lives of Susanna Moodie and Catharine Parr Traill* (Toronto, 1999)

Green, T., *The Accounts of Thomas Green, Music Teacher and Tuner of Musical Instruments, 1742–1790*, ed. G. Sheldrick ([Ware], 1992)

Greenwood, *A Catalogue of the Large and very Valuable Collection of Ancient and Modern Music, by all the Great and Favourite Masters, Musical Instruments … and other Effects of Joseph Gulston, Esq., Deceased* (14–16/2/1788)

Greville, R. F., *The Diaries of Colonel the Hon. Robert Fulke Greville, Equerry to his Majesty King George III*, ed. F. McKno Bladon (London, 1930)

Griffiths, D., *A Catalogue of the Printed Music Published before 1850 in York Minster Library* (York, 1977)

—— *A Musical Place of the First Quality: a History of Institutional Music Making in York c. 1550–1990* (York, [1990])

Guthrie, W., *A New Geographical, Historical, and Commercial Grammar, and Present State of the Several Kingdoms of the World* (London, 1770)

Haakenson, M., 'Two Spanish Brothers Revisited: Recent Research surrounding the Life and Instrumental Music of Juan Bautista Pla and José Pla', *EM*, 35 (2007), 83–96

Händel-Handbuch, ed. W. and M. Eisen, 4 vols. (Kassel, 1978–86) [HWV]

Halfpenny, E., 'The Lyrichord', *GSJ*, 3 (1950), 46–9

—— 'An Eighteenth-Century Trade List of Musical Instruments', *GSJ*, 17 (1964), 99–102

Hall, H. H., 'Moravian Music Education in America, *c*. 1750 to *c*. 1830, *Journal of Research in Music Education*, 29 (1981), 225–34

Handel: a Celebration of his Life and Times, 1685–1759, ed. J. Simon (London, 1985)

Hankins, T. L., and R. J. Silverman, *Instruments and the Imagination* (Princeton, NJ, 1995; repr. 1999)

Hardie, R. L., '"Curiously Fitted and Contriv'd": Production Strategies Employed by John Walsh from 1695 to 1712, with a Descriptive Catalogue of his Instrumental Publications' (PhD diss., U. of Western Ontario, 2000)

Harker, D., *Fakesong: the Manufacture of British 'Folksong', 1700 to the Present* (Milton Keynes, 1985)

The Harleian Miscellany, or A Collection of Scarce, Curious, and Entertaining Pamphlets and Tracts, as well in Manuscript as in Print, Found in the late Earl of Oxford's Library, 8 vols. (London, 1744–6)

Harman, R. A., *A Catalogue of the Printed Music and Books on Music in Durham Cathedral Library* (London, 1968)

Harrison, J., *A Description Concerning such Mechanism as will Afford a Nice or True Mensuration of Time* (London, 1775)

Harvey, B. W., *The Violin Family and its Makers in the British Isles: an Illustrated History and Directory* (Oxford, 1995)

Haskell, H., *The Early Music Revival, a History* (Mineola, NY, 2/1996)

Haslam, F., *From Hogarth to Rowlandson: Medicine in Art in Eighteenth-Century Britain* (Liverpool, 1996)

Hawkins, J., *An Account of the Institution and Progress of the Academy of Ancient Music* (London, 1770; repr. Cambridge 1998)

—— *A General History of the Science and Practice of Music* (London, 1776; 2/1853; repr. 1963) [HawkinsH]

—— 'Memoirs of Dr. William Boyce', in *Cathedral Music*, ed. W. Boyce (London, 2/1788)

Hayes, J., 'William Jackson of Exeter: Organist, Composer and Amateur Artist', *The Connoisseur*, 173 (1970), 17–24

Haym, N. F., *Giulio Cesare in Egitto, Drama*(London, 1724)

Haynes, B., *A History of Performing Pitch: the Story of 'A'* (Lanham, MD, 2002)

Hearne, T., *The Remains of Thomas Hearne, Reliquiae Hearnianae*, comp. J. Bliss, ed. J. Buchanan-Brown (London and Fontwell, 1966)

Hebbert, B., 'A Catalogue of Surviving Instruments by, or Ascribed to, Barak Norman', *GSJ*, 54 (2001), 285–329

—— 'Three Generations of the Meares Family in the London Music Trade, 1638–1749' (MMus diss., U. of Leeds, 2001)

—— 'The Richard Meares Viol in the Metropolitan Museum of Art Re-evaluated', *JVdGSA*, 20 (2003), 36–48

—— 'William Borracleffe, Nathaniel Cross, and a Clutch of Tudor Viols', *GSJ*, 51 (2003), 69–76

Hellwig, G., *Joachim Tielke: ein Hamburger Lauten- und Violenmacher der Barockzeit* (Frankfurt am Main, 1980)

Helm, E. E., 'The "Hamlet" Fantasia and the Literary Element in C. P. E. Bach's Music', *MQ*, 58 (1972), 277–96

—— *Thematic Catalogue of the Works of Carl Philipp Emanuel Bach* (New Haven, CT, 1989) [H]

Helm, S. M., 'Carl F. Abel Symphonist: a Biographical, Stylistic and Bibliographical Study' (PhD diss., U. of Michigan, 1953)

Henley, W., *Universal Dictionary of Violin and Bow Makers* (Brighton, 2/1973)

Herbert, H., *Henry, Elizabeth and George (1734–80): Letters and Diaries of Henry, Tenth Earl of Pembroke and his Circle*, ed. S. Herbert (London, 1939)

—— *Pembroke Papers (1780–1794): Letter and Diaries of Henry, Tenth Earl of Pembroke and his Circle*, ed. S. Herbert (London, 1950)

Herissone, R., *Music Theory in Seventeeth-Century England* (Oxford, 2000)

Hervey, J., *The Diary of John Hervey, First Earl of Bristol, with Extracts from his Book of Expenses, 1688 to 1742*, ed. S. H. A. Hervey (Wells, 1894)

Herzog, M., 'Is the Quinton a Viol? A Puzzle Unravelled', *EM*, 28 (2000), 8–31

—— 'Stradivari's Viols', *GSJ*, 57 (2004), 183–94

Hibberd, S., 'Murder in the Cathedral? Stradella, Musical Power, and Performing the Past in 1830s Paris', *ML*, 87 (2006), 551–79

Hill, A., *Works*, 4 vols. (London, 1753)

Hills, R. L., *James Watt*, 3 vols. (Ashbourne, 2002–6)

Hipkins, A. J., *Musical Instruments, Historic, Rare and Unique* (Edinburgh, 1888; repr. London, 1921)

—— *A Description and History of the Pianoforte and of the Older Keyboard Stringed Instruments* (London, 1896)

Historic Musical Instruments in the Edinburgh University Collection, ed. A. Myers, ii/B/2: *Lutes, Citterns and Guitars* (Edinburgh, 2/2003); ii/C/1: *Viols and Violins* (Edinburgh, 1995)

The History of the University of Oxford, iv: *Seventeenth-Century Oxford*, ed. N. Tyacke (Oxford, 1997)

Hoboken, A. van, *Joseph Haydn: Thematisch-bibliographisches Werkverzeichnis*, i: *Instrumentalwerke* (Mainz, 1957) [Hob]

Hoffmann, B., *Catalogo della musica solistica e cameristica per viola da gamba* (Lucca, 2001)

—— 'Il violoncello all'inglese', *Studi Vivaldiani*, 4 (2004), 43–51

—— 'The Nomenclature of the Viol in Italy', trans. R. Carter and J. Steedman, *VdGSJ*, 2 (2008), 1–16

Hogarth, W., *The Analysis of Beauty, Written with a View of Fixing the Fluctuating Ideas of Taste* (London, 1753)

Hogwood, C., 'A Note on the Frontispiece: *A Concert in Cambridge*', in *Music in Eighteenth-Century England: Essays in Memory of Charles Cudworth*, ed. Hogwood and R. Luckett (Cambridge, 1983), xv–xviii

Holman, P., 'Suites by Jenkins Rediscovered', *EM*, 6 (1978), 25–35

—— 'Thomas Baltzar (?1631–1663), the "Incomperable *Lubicer* on the Violin"', *Chelys*, 13 (1984), 3–38

—— *Henry Purcell* (Oxford, 1994)

—— *Four and Twenty Fiddlers: the Violin at the English Court, 1540–1690* (Oxford, 2/1995)

—— '"Evenly, Softly, and Sweetly Acchording to All": the Organ Accompaniment of English Consort Music', in *John Jenkins and his Time: Studies in English Consort Music*, ed. A. Ashbee and Holman (Oxford, 1996), 353–82

—— 'Original Sets of Parts for Restoration Concerted Music at Oxford', in *Performing the Music of Henry Purcell*, ed. M. Burden (Oxford, 1996), 9–19, 265–71

—— 'A New Source of Bass Viol Music from Eighteenth-Century England', *EM*, 31 (2003), 81–99

—— 'An Early Edinburgh Concert', *EMP*, 13 (January 2004), 9–17

—— 'Ann Ford Revisited', *ECM*, 1 (2004), 157–81

—— 'Early Music in Victorian England: the Case of the 1845 Concert', *Ad Parnassum*, 4/8 (October 2006), 81–114

—— 'Continuity and Change in English Bass Viol Music: the Case of Fitzwilliam MU. MS 647', *VGSJ*, 1 (2007), 20–50

—— 'A Little Light on Lorenzo Bocchi: an Italian in Edinburgh and Dublin', in *Music in the British Provinces, 1690–1914*, ed. R. Cowgill and Holman (Aldershot, 2007), 61–86

—— 'The Lute Family in Britain in the Eighteenth and Nineteenth Centuries', *Lute News*, 84 (December 2007), 7–21

—— 'Laurence Sterne as a Musician', *VdGSJ*, 2 (2008), 58–66

—— 'The Sale Catalogue of Gottfried Finger's Music Library: New Light on London Concert Life in the 1690s', *RMARC*, 43 (2010), 23–38

Holoman, D. K., *Berlioz* (London, 1989)

Horn, C. E., *Charles Edward Horn's Memoirs of his Father and Himself*, ed. M. Kassler (Aldershot, 2003)

Hughes, R., 'Haydn at Oxford: 1773–1791', *ML*, 20 (1939), 242–9

Hullah, J., *The Third or Transition Period of Musical History: a Course of Lectures Delivered to the Royal Institution of Great Britain* (London, 2/1876)

Humphries, C., and W. C. Smith, *Music Publishing in the British Isles* (Oxford, 2/1970)

Hunter, D., 'Music Copyright in Britain to 1800', *ML*, 67 (1986), 269–82

—— *Opera and Song Books Published in England, 1703–1726: a Descriptive Bibliography* (London, 1997)

—— 'The Irish State Music from 1716 to 1742 and Handel's Band in Dublin', *Göttinger Händel-Beiträge*, 11 (2006), 171–98

——, and R. M. Mason, 'Supporting Handel through Subscription to Publications: the Lists of *Rodelinda* and *Faramondo* Compared', *Notes*, 2nd series, 56 (1999), 27–93

Hutton, J. E., *A History of the Moravian Church* (London, 2/1909)

Illing, R., *Henry Purcell: Sonata in G minor for Violin and Continuo: an Account of its Survival from both the Historical and Technical Points of View* (Bedford Park, South Australia, 1975)

Ingamells, J., and R. Raines, 'A Catalogue of the Paintings, Drawings and Etchings of Philip Mercier', *Walpole Society*, 46 (1978), 1–70

International Inventions Exhibition, London, 1885: Guide to the Loan Collection and List of Musical Instruments, Manuscripts, Books, Paintings, and Engravings, ed. A. J. Hipkins (London, 1885)

Irving, J., 'Consort Playing in mid-Seventeenth-Century Worcester', *EM*, 12 (1984), 337–44

Jackson, W., *The Four Ages, together with Essays on Various Subjects* (London, 1798)

Jacquier, P., 'Le baryton á cordes: une méthode de recherche en lutherie', *Amour et sympathie* (Limoges, 1995), 101–71

James, K. E., 'Concert Life in Eighteenth-Century Bath' (PhD diss., Royal Holloway, U. of London, 1987)

Jappe, M., and D., *Viola d'amore Bibliographie* (Winterthur, 1997)

Jarvis, A., 'The Community of German Migrant Musicians in London *c*. 1750–*c*. 1850', 2 vols. (Master of Studies in Local and Regional History diss., U. of Cambridge, 2003)

Jay, E., *The Armitt Story, Ambleside* (Ambleside, 1998)

Jeans, S., 'The Psalterer', *GSJ*, 39 (1986), 2–20

Johannson, C., *J. J. & B. Hummel Music-Publishing and Thematic Catalogues*, 3 vols. (Stockholm, 1972)

John Joseph Merlin, the Ingenious Mechanick, ed. A. French (London, 1985)

The John Marsh Journals: the Life and Times of a Gentleman Composer (1752–1828), ed. B. Robins (Stuyvesant, NY, 1998)

Johnson, D., *Music and Society in Lowland Scotland in the Eighteenth Century* (London, 1972)

Johnstone, H. D., 'The Genesis of Boyce's *Cathedral Music*', *ML*, 56 (1975), 26–40

—— 'Treasure Trove at Gloucester: a Grangerized Copy of the 1895 Edition of Daniel Lysons' History of the Three Choirs Festival', *RMARC*, 31 (1998), 1–90

—— 'Music and Drama at the Oxford Act of 1713', in *Concert Life in Eighteenth-Century Britain*, ed. S. Wollenburg and S. McVeigh (Aldershot, 2004), 199–218

—— 'Instruments, Strings, Wire and other Musical Miscellanea in the Account Books of Claver Morris (1659–1727)', *GSJ*, 60 (2007), 29–35

—— 'Claver Morris, an Early Eighteenth-Century English Physician and Amateur Musician *Extraordinaire*', *JRMA*, 133 (2008), 93–127

Jones, T., 'Memoirs of Thomas Jones, Penkerrig, Radnorshire, 1803', ed. A. P. Oppé, *Walpole Society*, 32 (1951), whole vol.

Jones, W., *Physiological Disquisitions, or Discourses on the Natural Philosophy of the Elements* (London, 1781)

J. S. Bach, ed. M. Boyd, Oxford Composer Companions (Oxford, 1999)

Kassler, J. C., *The Science of Music in Britain, 1714–1830: a Catalogue of Writings, Lectures and Inventions*, 2 vols. (New York, 1979)

Kassler, M., and P. Olleson, *Samuel Wesley (1766–1837): a Source Book* (Aldershot, 2001)

Kenyon de Pascual, B., 'Juan Bautista Pla and José Pla: Two Neglected Oboe Virtuosi of the Eighteenth Century', *EM*, 18 (1990), 109–12

—— 'The Spanish Eighteenth-Century *Salterio* and some Comments on its Italian Counterpart', *Musique–Images–Instruments*, 3 (1997), 32–62

Kielmansegge, F. von, *Diary of a Journey to England in the Years, 1761–1762*, trans. S. P. Kielmansegg (London, 1902)

King, A. H., 'Fragments of Early Printed Music in the Bagford Collection', *ML*, 40 (1959), 269–73

—— 'The Musical Institute of London and its Successors', *MT*, 117 (1976), 221–3

King, R. G., 'Handel's Travels in the Netherlands in 1750', *ML*, 72 (1991), 372–86

——— 'The Riehman Family of Court Musicians and Composers', *Tijdschrift van de Vereniging voor Nederlandse Muziekgeschiedenis*, 44 (1994), 36–50

——— 'Handel and the Viola da Gamba', in *A Viola da Gamba Miscellany*, ed. S. Orlando (Limoges, 2005), 63–79

Klakowich, R., '"Scocca pur": Genesis of an English Ground', *JRMA*, 116 (1991), 63–77

Knape, W., *Bibliographisch-thematisches Verzeichnis der Kompositionen von Karl Friedrich Abel (1723–1787)* (Cuxhaven, 1971) [WKO]

——— *Karl Friedrich Abel: Leben und Werke eines frühklassischen Komponisten* (Bremen, 1973)

Korsten, F. J. M., *Roger North (1651–1734): Virtuoso and Essayist* (Amsterdam, 1981)

La Gorce, J., 'L'Académie Royale de Musique en 1704, d'après des documents inédits conservés dans les archives notariales', *Revue de musicologie*, 65 (1979), 160–91

Landmann, O., 'The Dresden Hofkapelle during the Lifetime of Johann Sebastian Bach', *EM*, 17 (1989), 17–30

Landon, H. C. R., *Haydn: Chronicle and Works*, iii: *Haydn in England, 1791–1795* (London, 1976)

——— *Haydn: Chronicle and Works*, i: *Haydn at Eszterháza, 1766–1790* (London, 1978)

Langford, *A Catalogue of the Scarce, Valuable and Curious Collection of Music, Manuscript and Printed, of the Reverend and Learned William Gostling* (26, 27/5/1777)

Langford, P., *A Polite and Commercial People: England, 1727–1783* (Oxford, 1989)

Lasocki, D., 'Johann Christian Schickhardt (*c.* 1681–1762): a Contribution to his Biography and a Catalogue of his Works', *Tijdschrift van de Vereniging voor Nederlandse muziekgeschiedenis*, 27 (1977), 28–55

——— 'Professional Recorder Players in England, 1540–1740', 2 vols. (PhD diss., U. of Iowa, 1983)

Laurie, M., 'The Chapel Royal Part-Books', in *Music and Bibliography: Essays in Honour of Alec Hyatt King*, ed. O. Neighbour (London, 1980), 28–50

Lebermann, W., 'Apokryph, Plagiat, Korruptel oder Falsifikat?', *Die Musikforschung*, 20 (1967), 413–25

Ledsham, I., *A Catalogue of the Shaw-Hellier Collection in the Music Library, Barber Institute of Fine Arts, the University of Birmingham* (Aldershot, 1999)

Leppert, R., 'Music Teachers of Upper-Class Amateur Musicians in Eighteenth-Century England', in *Music in the Classic Period: Essays in Honor of Barry S. Brook*, ed. A. W. Atlas (New York, 1985), 133–58

——— 'Imagery, Musical Confrontation and Cultural Difference in early Eighteenth-Century London', *EM*, 14 (1986), 323–45

Lester, J., *Compositional Theory in the Eighteenth Century* (Cambridge, MA, 1994; repr. 1996)

Lesure, F., 'L'Épitome musical de Philibert Jambe de Fer (1556)', Annales musicologiques, 6 (1958–63), 341–86

—— Bibliographie des éditions musicales publiées par Estienne Roger et Michel-Charles le Cène (Amsterdam, 1696–1743) (Paris, 1969)

Lever, T., The Herberts of Wilton (London, 1967)

Lewis, W. S., Rescuing Horace Walpole (New Haven, CT, 1978)

Lindgren, L., 'The Three Great Noises "Fatal to the Interests of Bononcini"', MQ, 61 (1975), 560–83

—— 'Ariosti's London Years, 1716–1729', ML, 62 (1981), 331–51

—— 'The Accomplishments of the Learned and Ingenious Nicola Francesco Haym (1678–1729)', Studi musicali, 16 (1987), 247–380

—— 'Italian Violoncellists and some Violoncello Solos Published in Eighteenth-Century Britain', in Music in Eighteenth-Century Britain, ed. D. W. Jones (Aldershot, 2000), 121–57

—— 'J. S. Cousser, Copyist of the Cantata Manuscript in the Truman Presidential Library, and other Cantata Copyists of 1697–1707, who Prepared the Way for Italian Opera in London', in Et facciam dolci canti: studi in onore di Agostino Zino in occasione del suo 65° compleanno, ed. B. M. Antolini, T. M. Gialdroni, and A. Pugliesi, 2 vols. (Lucca, 2003), 737–82

Lipking, L., The Ordering of the Arts in Eighteenth-Century England (Princeton, NJ, 1970)

Litterick, L., 'On Italian Instrumental Ensemble Music of the late Fifteenth Century', in Music in Medieval and Early Modern Europe: Patronage, Sources and Texts, ed. I. Fenlon (Cambridge, 1981), 117–30

Locke, J., Some Thoughts Concerning Education (London, 1693)

Locke, M., The Present Practice of Musick Vindicated (London, 1673; repr. 1974)

Lomax, J., '"Guittar-Maker to her Majesty and the Royal Family": John Frederick Hintz (1711–1772)', Moravian History Magazine, 22 (2002), 2–10

The London Stage, 1660–1800, 5 parts, 4: 1747–1776, ed. G. W. Stone jr. (Carbondale, IL, 1962)

Lonsdale, R., Dr. Charles Burney, a Literary Biography (Oxford, 1965; repr. 1986)

Loosemore, W. R., 'A Loosemore Virginal', MT, 127 (1986), 255

Lovell, P., '"Ancient" Music in Eighteenth-Century England', ML, 60 (1979), 401–15

Lynd, W., A Popular Account of Ancient Musical Instruments and their Development, as Illustrated by Typical Examples in the Galpin Collection, at Hatfield, Broad Oak, Essex (London, 1897)

McCart, C., 'The Kers and the Maules: Music in the Lives of Two Seventeenth-Century Scottish Aristocratic Families', 2 vols. (BA diss., Colchester Institute, 1988)

—— 'The Panmure Manuscripts: a New Look at an Old Source of Christopher Simpson's Consort Music', Chelys, 18 (1989), 18–29

McClenny Krauss, A., 'Alexander Reinagle, his Family Background and Early Professional Career', American Music, 4 (1986), 425–56

MacCracken, T. G., 'Italian Instruments in a List of Extant Viols Made before 1900', in *The Italian Viola da Gamba: Proceedings of the International Symposium on the Italian Viola da Gamba, Magnano, Italy, 29 April–1 May 2000*, ed. S. Orlando (Solignac, 2002), 127–44

McCulloch, D., 'Mrs Papendiek and the London Bach', *MT*, 123 (1982), 26–9

Mace, T., *Musick's Monument* (London, 1676; repr. 1968)

—— *An Advertisement to all Lovers of the Best Sort of Musick* ([London], 1690)

Macfarren, G. A., 'Bach's Grosse Passions-Musik (St. Matthew)', *MT*, 14 (1870), 327–9, 359–61, 391–3, 423–6

—— 'J. S. Bach's Music of the Passion according to the Gospel of St. John', *MT*, 15 (1872), 463–5

MacKillop, R., 'The Guitar, Cittern and Guittar in Scotland: an Historical Introduction up to 1800', in *Gitarre und Zister: Bauweise, Spieltechnik und Geschichte bis 1800. 22. Musikinstrumentenbau-Symposium Michaelstein, 16. bis 18. November 2001*, ed. M. Lustig (Blankenburg, 2004), 121–53

McLamore, A., '"By the Will and Order of Providence": the Wesley Family Concerts, 1779–1787', *RMARC*, 37 (2004), 71–220

Macleod, B. A., '"Whence Comes the Lady Tympanist?": Gender and Instrumental Musicians in America, 1853–1990', *Journal of Social History*, 27 (1993), 291–308

McLynn, F., *1759: the Year Britain Became Master of the World* (London, 2004)

McVeigh, S., 'The Professional Concert and Rival Subscription Series in London, 1783–1793', *RMARC*, 22 (1989), 1–135

—— *The Violinist in London's Concert Life, 1750–1784: Felice Giardini and his Contemporaries* (New York, 1989)

—— *Concert Life in London from Mozart to Haydn* (Cambridge, 1993)

—— 'London Newspapers 1750 to 1800: a Checklist and Guide for Musicologists', in *A Handbook for Studies in Eighteenth-Century English Music*, 6 (Oxford, 1996), whole vol.

—— 'Freemasonry and Musical Life in London in the late Eighteenth Century', in *Music in Eighteenth-Century Britain*, ed. D. W. Jones (Aldershot, 2000), 72–100

—— 'Italian Violinists in Eighteenth-Century London', in *The Eighteenth-Century Diaspora of Italian Music and Musicians*, ed. R. Strohm (Turnhout, 2001), 139–76

Made for Music: an Exhibition to Mark the 40th Anniversary of the Galpin Society (London, 1986)

Mangsen, S., 'The Dissemination of Pre-Corellian Duo and Trio Sonatas in Manuscript and Printed Sources: a Preliminary Report', in *The Dissemination of Music: Studies in the History of Music Publishing*, ed. H. Lenneberg (Lausanne, 1994), 71–105

Mann, A., *The Great Composer as Teacher and Student: Theory and Practice of Composition: Bach, Handel, Haydn, Mozart, Beethoven, Schubert* (New York, 1987; repr. 1994)

Marpurg, F. W., *Historische-kritische Beyträge zur Aufnahme der Musik*, 5 vols. (Berlin, 1754–60)

Marr, R. A., *Musical History as Shown in the International Exhibition of Music and the Drama, Vienna 1892* (London, 1893)

Marsh, J., *The John Marsh Journals: the Life and Times of a Gentleman Composer (1752–1828)*, ed. B. Robins (Stuyvesant, NY, 1998)

Marshall, A., 'The Viola da Gamba Music of Godfrey Finger', *Chelys*, 1 (1969), 16–26

Martin, T., *The Life of his Royal Highness the Prince Consort*, 5 vols. (London, 1875–80)

The Maske of Flowers, Celebration of the Jubilee of her Majesty, ed. A. W. à Beckett ([London], 1887)

Mason, J. C. S., *The Moravian Church and the Missionary Awakening in England, 1760–1800* (London, 2001)

Mattheson, J., *Das neu-eröffnete Orchestre, oder Universelle und gründliche Anleitung* (Hamburg, 1713; repr. 2004)

Matthew, J. E., 'The Antient Concerts, 1776–1848', *PMA*, 33 (1906–7), 55–79

Matthews, B., 'Abel in Salisbury', *MT*, 115 (1974), 217

—— 'The Davies Sisters, J. C. Bach and the Glass Harmonica', *ML*, 56 (1975), 150–69

—— *The Royal Society of Musicians of Great Britain, List of Members, 1738–1984* (London, 1985)

Maunder, R., *The Scoring of Baroque Concertos* (Woodbridge, 2004)

Mayhew, H., *London Labour and the London Poor*, 4 vols. (London, 1861–2; repr. New York, 1968)

Mee, J. H., *The Oldest Music Room in Europe: a Record of Eighteenth-Century Enterprise at Oxford* (London, 1911)

Meer, J. H. van der, *Musikinstrumente von der Antike bis zur Gegenwart* (Munich, 1983)

——, B. Geiser, and K.-H. Schickhaus, *Das Hackbrett, ein alpenländisches Musikinstrument* (Herisau, 1975)

Melamed, D. R., *Hearing Bach's Passions* (New York, 2005)

Mersmann, H. H. F. K., *Christian Ludwig Boxberg und seine Oper "Sardanapalus" Ansbach 1698, mit Beiträgen zur Ansbacher Musikgeschichte* (Berlin, 1916)

Michel, A.,'Zistern in der traditionellen Musik Sachsens und Thüringens', *Studia instrumentorum musicae popularis*, 10 (Stockholm, 1992), 81–90;

—— 'Quellen zur Geschichte der Zister in Sachsen vom 16. bis 19. Jahrhundert', in *Gitarre und Zister: Bauweise, Spieltechnik und Geschichte bis 1800. 22. Musikinstrumentenbau-Symposium Michaelstein, 16. bis 18. November 2001*, ed. M. Lustig (Blankenburg, 2004), 87–120

Milhous, J., and R. D. Hume, 'New Light on Handel and the Royal Academy of Music in 1720', *Theatre Journal*, 35 (1983), 149–67

Miller L., and A. Cohen, *Music in the Royal Society of London, 1660–1806* (Detroit, MI, 1987)

Miloradovitch, H., 'Eighteenth-Century Manuscript Transcriptions for Viols of Music by Corelli and Marais in the Bibliothèque Nationale, Paris: Sonatas and *Pièces de Viole*', *Chelys*, 12 (1983), 47–73

Monson, C., *Voices and Viols in England, 1600–1650: the Sources and the Music* (Ann Arbor, MI, 1982)

Montagu, J., 'Salerooms', *EM*, 13 (1985), 566–8; 19 (1991), 103–5; 20 (1992), 659–60

Moodie, S., 'My Cousin Tom: a Sketch from Life', *The British American Magazine*, 1 (5/1863), 12–20

—— *Susanna Moodie: Letters of a Lifetime*, ed. C. Ballstadt, E. Hopkins, and M. Peterman (Toronto, 1985)

Morley-Pegge, R., *The French Horn* (London, 2/1973; repr. 1978)

Mortimer, T., *The Universal Director, or The Noble and Gentleman's True Guide to the Masters and Professors of the Liberal and Polite Arts and Sciences, and of the Mechanic Arts, Manufacturers, and Trades, Established in London and Westminster, and their Environs* (London, 1763)

Morton, J., 'The Early History and Use of the G Violone', *JVdGSA*, 36 (1999), 40–66

Moscheles, C., *Life of Moscheles, with Selections of his Diaries and Correspondence*, trans. A. D. Coleridge, 2 vols. (London, 1873)

'Mrs. Thicknesse', *Public Characters of 1806* (London, 1806)

Muirhead, J. P., *The Life of James Watt, with Selections from his Correspondence* (London, 1858)

Mullan, J., *Sentiment and Sociability: the Language of Feeling in the Eighteenth Century* (Oxford, 1988)

Murata, M., 'Dr Burney Bought a Music Book…', *The Journal of Musicology*, 17 (1999), 76–111

Musgrave, *A Catalogue of the Valuable and Genuine Stock in Trade of a Music Seller* (3–5/6/1828)

—— *A Catalogue of the Music, Books, Instruments, Paintings, Engravings, &c., late the Property of William Shield Esquire (Deceased)* (22–3/6/1829)

Music and Theatre in Handel's World: the Family Papers of James Harris, 1732–1780, ed. D. Burrows and R. Dunhill (Oxford, 2002)

Music Entries at Stationers' Hall, 1710–1818, comp. M. Kassler (Aldershot, 2004)

[Music Loan Exhibition] *A Special Loan Exhibition of Musical Instruments, Manuscripts, Books, Portraits, and other Mementoes of Music and Musicians* (London, 1904)

—— *An Illustrated Catalogue of the Music Loan Exhibition held … by the Worshipful Company of Musicians at Fishmongers' Hall, June and July 1904* (London, 1909)

The Music of the Moravian Church in America, ed. N. R. Knouse (Rochester, NY, 2008)

Die Musik in Geschichte und Gegenwart: allgemeine Enzyklopädie der Musik, begründet von Friedrich Blume. Zweite, neuerarbeitete Ausgabe, ed. L. Finscher, 28 vols. (Kassel, 1994–2008) [*MGG2*]

Myers, A., 'Fingering Charts for the Cimbasso and Other Instruments', *GSJ*, 39 (1986), 134–6

Nalbach, D., *The King's Theatre, 1704–1867* (London, 1972)

Neece, B., 'The Cello in Britain: a Technical and Social History', *GSJ*, 56 (2003), 77–115

Nettl, P., 'Die Wiener Tanzkomposition in der zweiten Hälfte des siebzehnten Jahrhunderts', *Studien der Musikwissenschaft*, 8 (1921), 45–175

Newman, W. S., *The Sonata in the Baroque Era* (Chapel Hill, NC, 1959)

—— *The Sonata in the Classic Era* (New York, 2/1972)

Nichols, J., *Literary Anecdotes of the Eighteenth Century*, 9 vols. (London, 1812–15; repr. 1966)

Nicoll, A., *A History of English Drama, 1660–1900*, ii: *Early Eighteenth Century Drama* (Cambridge, 3/1961)

Niecks, F., 'Historical Concerts', *Monthly Musical Record*, 12 (10, 11/1882), 217–22, 242–5

Noble, A. F. G., 'A Contextual Study of the Life and Published Keyboard Works of Elisabetta de Gambarini' (PhD diss., U. of Southampton, 2000)

North, R., *Roger North on Music*, ed. J. Wilson (London, 1959)

O'Brien, G., *Ruckers: a Harpsichord and Virginal Building Tradition* (Cambridge, 2/2009)

Ogden, G. P., 'Growth of Violin Playing by Women', *Violin Times*, 6 (4/1899), 106–8

O'Loghlin, M., *Frederick the Great and his Musicians: the Viola da Gamba Music of the Berlin School* (Aldershot, 2008)

Ophee, M., 'A History of Transcriptions of Lute Tablature from 1679 to the Present', *The Lute*, 43 (2003), 1–43

Ottenburg, H.-G., *C. P. E. Bach*, trans. P. J. Whitmore (Oxford, 1987)

Otterstedt, A., *The Viol: History of an Instrument*, trans. H. Reiners (Kassel, 2002)

Pallis, M., 'The Rebirth of Early Music', *EM*, 6 (1978), 41–5

Palmer, F. M., *Domenico Dragonetti in England (1794–1846): the Career of a Double Bass Virtuoso* (Oxford, 1997)

Pamplin, T. M., 'The Baroque Baryton: the Origin and Development in the Seventeenth Century of a Solo, Self-Accompanying, Bowed and Plucked Instrument Played from Tablature' (PhD diss., Kingston U., 2000)

Papendiek, C. L. H., *Court and Private Life in the Time of Queen Charlotte, being the Journals of Mrs. Papendiek, Assistant-Keeper of the Wardrobe and Reader to her Majesty*, ed. A. Delves Broughton, 2 vols. (London, 1887)

Parke, W. T., *Musical Memoirs*, 2 vols. (London, 1830)

Parker, M., 'Soloistic Chamber Music at the Court of Friedrich Wilhelm II: 1786–1797' (PhD diss., Indiana U., 1994)

Parrott, I., 'William Sterndale Bennett and the Bach Revival in Nineteenth-Century England', in *Europe, Empire, and Spectacle in Nineteenth-Century British Music*, ed. R. Cowgill and J. Rushton (Aldershot, 2006), 29–43

Particular Friends: the Correspondence of Samuel Pepys and John Evelyn, ed. G. de la Bédoyère (Woodbridge, 2/2005)

Payne, E. J., 'The Viola da Gamba', *PMA*, 15 (1888–9), 91–107

Pepys., S., *The Diary*, ed. R. Latham and W. Matthews, 11 vols. (London, 1970–83)

Percival, J., *Diary of Viscount Percival afterwards First Earl of Egmont*, ed. R. A. Roberts, 3 vols., *Historical Manuscripts Commission*, 63 (London, 1920, 1923)

Philip Mercier, 1689–1760, ed. P. Ingamells and R. Raines (London, 1969)

Phillips, H., *Musical and Personal Recollections during Half a Century*, 2 vols. (London, 1864)

Pindar, P. [J. Wolcot], *Ode upon Ode, or A Peep at St James's, or New-Year's Day, or What You Will* (London, 1787)

Pink, A. G., 'The Musical Culture of Freemasonry in Early Eighteenth-Century London' (PhD diss., Goldsmith's, U. of London, 2007)

Pinto, D., *For ye Violls: the Consort and Dance Music of William Lawes* (London, 1995)

Playford, H., *A Curious Collection of Musick-Books, both Vocal and Instrumental* (London, 1690)

—— *A General Catalogue of all the Choicest Musick-Books in English, Latin, Italian and French, both Vocal and Instrumental* (London, c. 1697)

—— *A Catalogue of Vocal and Instrumental Musick, Printed and Written, being a Choice Collection of the Greatest Italian Masters, Brought over from Italy by Mr. Finger, as also several Excellent Pieces of his own Composition* (London, 1705)

Playford, J., *An Introduction to the Skill of Musick* (London, 10/1683)

Podmore, C. J., 'The Fetter Lane Society, 1738', *Proceedings of the Wesley Historical Society*, 46/5 (May 1988), 125–53

—— *The Moravian Church in England, 1728–1760* (Oxford, 1998)

Pohl, C. F., *Mozart und Haydn in London*, 2 vols. (Vienna, 1867)

Polko, E. *Musikalische Märchen, Phantasien und Skizzen*, 2 vols., ii (Leipzig, 1866); trans. M. P. Maudslay as *Musical Tales, Phantasms and Sketches*, 2 vols., ii (London, 1877)

Pollens, S., 'A Viola da Gamba Temperament Preserved by Antonio Stradivari', *ECM*, 3 (2006), 125–32

Pont, G., 'Handel's Souvenir of Venice: the "Spurious" Sonata in C for Viola da Gamba & Harpsichord', *EMP*, 23 (March 2009), 4–18

Pope-Hennessy, U., *Agnes Strickland: Biographer of the Queens of England, 1796–1874* (London, 1940)

Porter, J., 'The Margaret Sinkler Music Book, 1710', *Review of Scottish Culture*, 16 (2003–4), 1–18

Prelleur, P, *The Modern Musick-Master, or The Universal Musician* (London, 2/1731; repr. 1965)

Price, C. A., 'The Critical Decade for English Music Drama, 1700–1710', *Harvard Library Bulletin*, 26 (1978), 38–76

—— 'The Small Coal Cult', *MT*, 119 (1978), 1032–4

—— *Music in the Restoration Theatre* (Ann Arbor, MI, 1979)

——, J. Milhous, and R. D. Hume, *The Impresario's Ten Commandments: Continental Recruitment for Italian Opera in London, 1763-64* (London, 1992)

——, ——, and —— *Italian Opera in late Eighteenth-Century London*, i: *The King's Theatre, Haymarket, 1778-1791* (Oxford, 1995)

Prizer, W. F., 'Isabella d'Este and Lorenzo da Pavia, "Master Instrument Maker"', *Early Music History*, 2 (1982), 87-127

—— 'The Frottola and the Unwritten Tradition', *Studi musicali*, 15 (1986), 3-37

Puttick and Simpson, *Catalogue of the Very Important and Interesting Musical Collections of a Distinguished Amateur, with Selections from various Libraries* (29, 30/1/1858)

—— *Catalogue of the Extensive Library of a Distinguished Musician* (17/11/1882)

[Pyne, W. H.], 'The Greater and Lesser Stars of Old Pall Mall, Chapter I', *Fraser's Magazine for Town and Country* (11/1840), 547-59

Rabin, R. J., and S. Zohn, 'Arne, Handel, Walsh and Music as Intellectual Property: Two Eighteenth-Century Lawsuits', *JRMA*, 120 (1995), 112-45

Rasch, R., 'I manoscritti musicali nel lascito di Michel-Charles Le Cène (1743)', in *Intorno a Locatelli: studi in occasione del tricentenario della nascita di Pietro Antonio Locatelli (1695-1764)*, ed. A. Dunning (Lucca, 1995), 1039-70

—— '"La famoso mano di Monsieur Roger": Antonio Vivaldi and his Dutch Publishers', *Informazioni e studi Vivaldiani*, 17 (1996), 89-135

—— 'The Italian Presence in the Musical Life of the Dutch Republic', in *The Eighteenth-Century Diaspora of Italian Music and Musicians*, ed. R. Strohm (Turnhout, 2001), 177-210

Rawson, R., 'From Olomouc to London: the Early Music of Gottfried Finger (c. 1655-1730)', 2 vols. (PhD diss., Royal Holloway, U. of London, 2002) [RI]

—— 'Gottfried Finger's Christmas Pastorellas', *EM*, 33 (2005), 591-606

Records of English Court Music, comp. A. Ashbee, 9 vols. (Snodland and Aldershot, 1986-96) [*RECM*]

Ree Bernard, N. van, *The Psaltery* (Buren, 1989)

Reede, R. de, 'Niederländische Flötisten und Flötisten in der Niederlanden, 1700-1900', *Tibia*, 24 (1999), 345-55, 433-41

Reichardt, J. F., 'Berichtigungen und Zusätze zum Gerberschen Lexicon der Tonkünstler', in *Studien für Tonkünstler und Musikfreunde … furs Jahr 1792*, ed. Reichardt and F. L. A. Kunzen, ii (Berlin, 1793); repr. in *Ernst Ludwig Gerber: Ergänzungen, Berichtigungen, Nachträge*, ed. O. Wessely (Graz, 1969), 5-16

Reminiscences of Oxford by Oxford Men, 1559-1850, ed. L. M. Quiller Couch (Oxford, 1892)

Rhodes, D. J., 'The Viola da Gamba, its Repertory and Practitioners in the late Eighteenth Century', *Chelys*, 31 (2003), 36-63

Richards, J. M., 'A Study of Music for Bass Viol Written in England in the Seventeenth Century' (PhD diss., U. of Oxford, 1961)

Richter, B. F., 'Stadtpfeifer und Alumnen der Thomasschule in Leipzig zu Bachs Zeit', *Bach Jahrbuch*, 4 (1907), 32-78

Riemsdijk, J. C. M. van, *Het Stads-musiekcollegie te Utrecht (Collegium Musicum Ultrajectinum) 1631–1881* (Utrecht, 1881)

Ripin, E. R., 'Expressive Devices Applied to the Eighteenth-Century Harpsichord', *The Organ Yearbook*, 1 (1970), 65–80

Rizzo, B., *Companions without Vows: Relationships among Eighteenth-Century British Women* (Athens, GA, 1994)

Robinson, J., 'John Leyden's Lyra Viol Manuscript in Newcastle University Library and George Farquhar Graham's Copy in the National Library of Scotland', *VdGSJ*, ii (2008), 17–57

Robinson, L., 'Purcell's Fantasias: the Jewel in the Crown of English Consort Music', *EM*, 26 (1998), 357–9

Roche, J., 'Ignaz Moscheles, 1794–1870', *MT*, 111 (1970), 264–6

Roe, S., 'The Sextet in C major, by J. C. or J. C. F. Bach?', in *Haydn, Mozart and Beethoven: Studies in the Music of the Classical Period: Essays in Honour of Alan Tyson*, ed. S. Brandenburg (Oxford, 1998), 13–19

—— 'The Sale Catalogue of Carl Friedrich Abel (1787)', in *Music and the Book Trade from the Sixteenth to the Twentieth Century*, ed. R. Myers, M. Harris, and G. Mandelbrote (London, 2008), 105–43

Rônez, M., 'Aperçus sur la viola d'amour en Allemagne du Sud vers 1700', in *Amour et sympathie* (Limoges, 1995), 223–71

Rosenthal, M., 'Thomas Gainsborough's Ann Ford', *The Art Bulletin*, 80 (1998), 649–65

—— *The Art of Thomas Gainsborough* (New Haven, CT, 1999)

Ross, I. C., *Laurence Sterne, a Life* (Oxford, 2001)

Rossi, G. Doc, 'Citterns and Guitars in Colonial America', in *Gitarre und Zister: Bauweise, Spieltechnik und Geschichte bis 1800. 22. Musikinstrumentenbau-Symposium Michaelstein, 16. bis 18. November 2001*, ed. M. Lustig (Blankenburg, 2004), 155–68

Rousseau, J., *Traité de la viole* (Paris, 1687; repr. 1980)

[The Royal Society of London], *The Philosophical Transactions (from the Year 1700 to the Year 1720), Abrig'd and Dispos'd under Several Heads*, ed. H. Jones, 2 vols. (London, 2/1731)

Ruhnke, M., *Georg Philipp Telemann: Thematisch-Systematisches Verzeichnis seiner Werke. Telemann-Werkverzeichnis (TWV): Instrumentalwerke*, 3 vols. (Kassel, 1984, 1992, 1999)

Russell, R., *Victoria and Albert Museum, Catalogue of Musical Instruments*, i: *Keyboard Instruments* (London, 1968)

Rutledge, J. B., 'Towards a History of the Viol in the Nineteenth Century', *EM*, 12 (1984), 328–36

—— 'Late Nineteenth-Century Viol Revivals', *EM*, 19 (1991), 409–18

Sachs, C., *Musik und Oper am Kurbrandenburgischen Hof* (Berlin, 1910)

Sadie, J. A., 'Bowed Continuo Instruments in French Baroque Chamber Music', *PRMA*, 105 (1978–9), 37–49

—— 'Handel: in Pursuit of the Viol', *Chelys*, 14 (1985), 3–24

Saint-George, H., 'The Revival of Ancient Instruments', *MO*, 29 (3, 4/1906), 443–4, 512–13

Samuel, H., 'Johann Sigismond Cousser in London and Dublin', *ML*, 61 (1980), 158–71

—— 'Johann Sigismond Cousser Comes to London in 1704', *MT*, 122 (1981), 591–593

Sandys, W., and S. A. Forster, *The History of the Violin* (London, 1864)

Sardelli, F. M., *Vivaldi's Music for Flute and Recorder*, trans. M. Talbot (Aldershot, 2007)

Schmidt, G., *Die Musik am Hofe der Markgrafen von Brandenburg-Ansbach vom ausgehenden Mittelalter bis 1806* (Kassel, 1956)

Schneider, H., *Die Rezeption der Opern Lullys im Frankreich des Ancien Regime*, Mainzer Studien zur Musikwissenschaft, 16 (Tutzing, 1982)

Schneider, L., *Geschichte der Oper und des königlichen Opernhauses in Berlin* (Berlin, 1852)

Scholes, P., *The Puritans and Music in England and New England* (Oxford, 1934; repr. 1969)

—— *The Great Doctor Burney*, 2 vols. (Oxford, 1948; repr. 1971)

—— *The Life and Activities of Sir John Hawkins, Musician, Magistrate, and Friend of Johnson* (London, 1953)

Scott, M. M., 'Haydn: Relics and Reminiscences in England', *ML*, 13 (1932), 126–36

Segerman, E., 'A 1656 Tabley MS: on Viol Players, Cittern and Gittern', *FOMRHI Quarterly*, 46 (January 1987), 34–5, comm. 774

Sehnal, J., *Pavel Vejvanovský and the Kroměříž Music Collection: Perspectives on Seventeenth-Century Music in Moravia* (Olomouc, 2008)

Senn, W., *Musik und Theater am Hof zu Innsbruck: Geschichte der Hofkapelle vom 15. Jahrhundert bis zu deren Auflösung im Jahre 1748* (Innsbruck, 1954)

Shadwell, T., *Epsom-Wells, a Comedy* (London, 1673)

Shaw, G. B., *Shaw's Music: the Complete Musical Criticism*, ed. D. H. Laurence, 3 vols. (London, 1981)

Shaw, W., *The Succession of Organists of the Chapel Royal and the Cathedrals of England and Wales from c. 1538* (Oxford, 1991)

Shay, R., '"Naturalizing" Palestrina and Carissimi in late Seventeenth-Century Oxford: Henry Aldrich and his Recompositions', *ML*, 77 (1996), 368–400

—— and R. Thompson, *Purcell Manuscripts: the Principal Musical Sources* (Cambridge, 2000)

Shield, W., *An Introduction to Harmony* (London, 1800; 2/1815)

—— *Rudiments of Thorough Bass* (London, 1815)

Shire, H. M., 'Court Song in Scotland after 1603: Aberdeenshire, ii: the Forbes-Leith Music Books, 1611–1779', *Edinburgh Bibliographical Society Transactions*, 3/3 (1956), 165–8

Shute, J. D., 'Anthony a Wood and his Manuscript Wood D 19(4) at the Bodleian Library, Oxford: an Annotated Transcription', 2 vols. (PhD diss., International Institute for Advanced Studies, Clayton, MO, 1979)

Sifare, an Opera, as Perform'd at the King's Theatre in the Hay-Market for the Benefit of Signor Guardacci, Musician to his Royal Highness the Grand Duke of Tuscany (London, 1767)

Simpson, C., *The Division-Violist, or An Introduction to Playing upon a Ground* (London, 1659; repr. n.d.); rev. as *Chelys minuritionum artificio exornata / The Division-Viol* (London, 2/1665, 1667, 3/1712; repr. 1955)

—— *A Compendium of Practical Music* (London, 3/1678; repr. 2007)

Sittard, J., *Zur Geschichte der Musik und des Theaters am Württembergischen Hofe*, 2 vols. (Stuttgart, 1890–1; repr. 1970)

Skjerne, G., *Carl Claudius' Samling af Gamle Musikinstrumenter* (Copenhagen, 1931)

Sloman, S., *Gainsborough in Bath* (New Haven, CT, 2002)

Small, J., 'J. C. Bach Goes to Law', *MT*, 126 (1985), 526–9

Smart, G., *Leaves from the Journals of Sir George Smart*, ed. H. B. and C. L. E. Cox (London, 1907)

Smith, B. M., 'Two Hundred Forty-One European Chordophones in the Stearns Collection of Musical Instruments', 3 vols. (PhD diss., U. of Michigan, 1977)

Smith, W. C., 'Playford: some Hitherto Unnoticed Catalogues of Early Music', *MT*, 67 (1926), 636–9, 701–4

—— *A Bibliography of the Musical Works Published by John Walsh during the Years 1695–1720* (Oxford, 2/1968)

—— and C. Humphries, *A Bibliography of the Musical Works Published by the Firm of John Walsh during the Years 1721–1766* (London, 1968)

Snyder, K. J., *Dieterich Buxtehude, Organist in Lübeck* (New York, 1987)

Somfai, L., *Joseph Haydn, his Life in Contemporary Pictures* (London, 1969)

Sotheby, Wilkinson and Hodge, *Catalogue of the Music Library of Edward Francis Rimbault, LL. D.* (31/7–7/8/1877; repr. 1975)

Southey, R., 'Competition and Collaboration: Concert Promotion in Newcastle and Durham, 1752–1772', in *Concert Life in Eighteenth-Century Britain*, ed. S. Wollenburg and S. McVeigh (Aldershot, 2004), 55–70

—— *Music-Making in North-East England during the Eighteenth Century* (Aldershot, 2006)

Southgate, T. L., 'The Instruments with Sympathetic Strings', *PMA*, 42 (1915–16), 33–50

Spitzer, J., and N. Zaslaw, *The Birth of the Orchestra: History of an Institution, 1650–1815* (Oxford, 2004)

Spring, M., *The Lute in Britain: a History of the Instrument and its Music* (Oxford, 2001)

—— 'The Balcarres Lute Book', *Lute News*, 87 (October 2008), 7–14

Squire, W. B., 'Henry Eccles's Borrowings', *MT*, 64 (1923), 790

Stahura, M. W., 'Handel and the Orchestra', in *The Cambridge Companion to Handel*, ed. D. Burrows (Cambridge, 1997), 238–48

Stanley, A. A., *Catalogue of the Stearns Collection of Musical Instruments* (Ann Arbor, MI, 1918)

Steele, J., *Prosodia rationalis, or An Essay towards Establishing the Melody and Measure of Speech, to be Expressed and Perpetuated by Peculiar Symbols* (London, 1779)

Stell, E., 'Sources of Scottish Instrumental Music, 1603–1707', 2 vols. (PhD diss., U. of Glasgow, 1999)

Sterndale Bennett, R., 'Three Abridged Versions of Bach's St Matthew Passion', *ML*, 37 (1956), 336–9

Sterne, L., *Letters of Laurence Sterne*, ed. L. P. Curtis (Oxford, 1935)

—— (attrib.), *Original Letters of the late Reverend Mr. Laurence Sterne* (London, 1788)

Stiehl, C., 'Gesuch des Peter Grecke um Verleihung einer Rathsmusikantenstelle', *Monatshefte für Musik-Geschichte*, 20 (1888), 111–12

Strickland, J. M., *Life of Agnes Strickland* (Edinburgh, 1887)

Stoltzfus, I. H., 'The Lyra Viol in Consort with other Instruments' (PhD diss., Louisiana State U., 1983)

Straeten, E. S. J. van der, 'The Viola da Gamba', *MO*, 17 (3, 4/1894), 361–2, 437–8

—— *The History of the Violoncello, the Viol da Gamba, their Precursors and Collateral Instruments* (London, 1914; repr. 1971)

Strahle, G., *An Early Music Dictionary: Musical Terms from British Sources, 1500–1740* (Cambridge, 1995)

Strümper, M., 'Die Viola da gamba am Österreichischen Kaiserhof: Untersuchungen zur Instrumenten- und Werkgeschichte der Wiener Hofmusikkapelle im 17. und 18. Jahrhundert' (PhD diss., U. of Vienna, 2001); CD-ROM version (Vienna, 2002)

Summers, J., *The Empress of Taste: the Life and Adventures of Teresa Cornelys, Queen of Masquerades and Casanova's Lover* (London, 2003)

Sweet, R., *Antiquaries: the Discovery of the Past in Eighteenth-Century Britain* (London, 2004)

Takeuchi, T., 'Additions to Comm. 1876: some more English Guitars', *FoMRHI Quarterly*, 114 (November 2009), 5, comm. 1884

Talbot, M., 'Vivaldi and the English Viol', *EM*, 30 (2002), 381–94

—— 'A Response to "Handel's Souvenir of Venice" (*EMP* 23)', *EMP*, 24 (June 2009), 31

Tans'ur, W., *A New Musical Grammar, or The Harmonical Spectator* (London, 1746; repr. 2004); rev. as *A New Musical Grammar and Dictionary, or A General Introduction to the Whole Art of Musick* (London, 3/1756); rev. as *The Elements of Musick Display'd* (London, 5/1772)

Taruskin, R., *The Oxford History of Western Music*, 6 vols., ii: *The Seventeenth and Eighteenth Centuries* (Oxford, 2005)

The Tatler, ed. D. F. Bond, 3 vols. (Oxford, 1987)

Taylor, H. J., *A History of the Church known as the Moravian Church, or the Unitas Fratrum, or the Unity of the Brethren, during the Eighteenth and Nineteenth Centuries* (Bethlehem, PA, 1900; repr. New York 1971)

Taylor, T. F., *Thematic Catalog of the Works of Jeremiah Clarke* (Detroit, 1977) [T]

Teahan, J., 'A List of Irish Instrument Makers', *GSJ*, 16 (1963), 28–32

Temperley, N., 'The Prince Consort, Champion of Music', *MT*, 102 (1961), 762–4

—— *The Music of the English Parish Church*, 2 vols. (Cambridge, 1979)

—— *The Hymn Tune Index: a Census of English-Language Hymn Tunes in Printed Sources from 1535 to 1820*, 4 vols. (Oxford, 1998)

Terry, C. S., *John Christian Bach*, rev. H. C. R. Landon (London, 2/1967)

Themen-Verzeichnis der Kompositionen von Johann Baptiste Vanhal, comp. A. Weinmann (Vienna, 1988)

Thibault, G., J. Jenkins, and J. Bran-Ricci, *Eighteenth-Century Musical Instruments: France and Britain* (London, 1973)

Thicknesse, P., *A Year's Journey through France and Part of Spain*, 2 vols. (Bath, 1777)

—— *A Sketch of the Life and Paintings of Thomas Gainsborough, Esq.* (London, 1788)

—— (attrib.), *Sketches and Characters of the most Eminent and Singular Persons now Living, by Several Hands* (Bristol, 1770)

Thomas Jones (1742–1803): an Artist Rediscovered, ed. A. Sumner and G. Smith (New Haven, CT, 2003)

Thompson, R., 'A Further Look at the Consort Manuscripts in Archbishop Marsh's Library, Dublin', *Chelys*, 24 (1995), 3–18

—— 'Manuscript Music in Purcell's London', *EM*, 23 (1995), 605–18

—— 'Some Late Sources of Music by John Jenkins', in *John Jenkins and his Time: Studies in English Consort Music*, ed. A. Ashbee and P. Holman (Oxford, 1996), 271–307

Thomson, G. S., *The Russells in Bloomsbury, 1669–1771* (London, 1940)

Tilmouth, M., 'Some Improvements in Music Noted by William Turner in 1697', *GSJ*, 10 (1957), 57–9

—— 'A Calendar of References to Music in Newspapers Published in London and the Provinces (1660–1719)', *RMARC*, 1 (1960), whole vol. [TilmouthC]; 2 (1961), 1–15

—— 'Chamber Music in England, 1675–1720' (PhD diss., U. of Cambridge, 1960)

—— 'James Sherard, an English Amateur Composer', *ML*, 47 (1966), 313–22

—— 'The Beginnings of Provincial Concert Life in England', in *Music in Eighteenth-Century England: Essays in Memory of Charles Cudworth*, ed. C. Hogwood and R. Luckett (Cambridge, 1983), 1–17

Todd, J. M., *Sensibility, an Introduction* (London, 1986)

Tolbecque, A., *Notice historique sur les instruments à cordes et à archet* (Paris, 1898)

Tourin, P., *Viollist: a Comprehensive Catalogue of Historical Viole da Gamba in Public and Private Collections* (Duxbury, VT, 1979)

Townsend, H., *An Account of the Visit of Handel to Dublin, with Incidental Notices of his Life and Character* (Dublin, 1852)

Traficante, F., 'Lyra Viol Tunings: "All Ways Have Been Tryed to Do It"', *Acta musicologica*, 42 (1970), 183–205, 256

—— 'Music for Lyra Viol: Manuscript Sources', *Chelys*, 8 (1978–9), 4–22

Trowell, B., 'Daniel Defoe's Plan for a Music Academy at Christ's Hospital, with some Notes on his Attitudes to Music', in *Source Materials and the Interpretation of Music: a Memorial Volume to Thurston Dart*, ed. I. Bent (London, 1981), 403–27

Turner, W., *A Compleat History of the Most Remarkable Providences, both of Judgment and Mercy, which have Hapned in this Present Age*, 3 vols. (London, 1697)

Tyler, J., 'English Guitar Makers in Eighteenth-Century Britain: a Directory', *FoMRHI Quarterly*, 113 (August 2009), 11–18, comm. 1876

—— and P. Sparks, *The Early Mandolin* (Oxford, 1989)

—— and—— *The Guitar and its Music from the Renaissance to the Classical Era* (Oxford, 2002)

Tytler, W., 'On the Fashionable Amusements and Entertainments in Edinburgh in the Last Century, with a Plan of a Grand Concert of Music on St Cecilia's Day, 1695', *Transactions of the Society of the Antiquaries of Scotland*, 1 (1792), 499–510

Unverricht, H., *Geschichte des Streichtrios* (Tutzing, 1969)

Urquhart, M., 'Prebendary Philip Falle (1656–1742) and the Durham Bass Viol Manuscript A.27', *Chelys*, 5 (1973–4), 7–20

Vanbrugh, J., *The Relapse, or Virtue in Danger, being the Sequel of The Fool in Fashion, a Comedy* (London, 1697)

Vanscheeuwijck, M., *The Capella Musicale of San Petronio in Bologna under Giovanni Paolo Colonna (1674–95): History, Organization, Repertoire* (Brussels, 2003)

Vice Chamberlain Coke's Theatrical Papers, 1706–1715, ed. J. Milhous and R. D. Hume (Carbondale and Edwardsville, IL, 1982)

The Viola da Gamba Society Index of Manuscripts Containing Consort Music, 2 vols., comp. A. Ashbee, R. Thompson, and J. Wainwright (Aldershot, 2001, 2007) [*VdGSIM*]

The Viola da Gamba Society Thematic Index of Music for Viols, comp. G. Dodd and A. Ashbee ([York], 6/1992, 7/2002) [*VdGS*]

Wainwright, J. P., *Musical Patronage in Seventeenth-Century England: Christopher, First Baron Hatton (1605–1670)* (Aldershot, 1997)

Walden, V., *One Hundred Years of Violoncello: a History of Technique and Performance Practice, 1740–1840* (Cambridge, 1998)

Walker, D. P., and P., *German Sacred Polyphonic Vocal Music between Schütz and Bach: Sources and Critical Editions* (Warren, MI, 1992)

Walpole, H., *The Last Journals of Horace Walpole during the Reign of George III from 1771–1783*, ed. A. F. Steuart, 2 vols. (London, 1910)

—— *The Yale Edition of Horace Walpole's Correspondence, 9: Horace Walpole's Correspondence with George Montagu I*, ed. W. S. Lewis and R. S. Brown jr. (London, 1941)

—— *The Yale Edition of Horace Walpole's Correspondence, 15: Horace Walpole's Correspondence with Sir David Dalrymple, Conyers Middleton ...,* ed. W. S. Lewis, C. H. Bennett and A. G. Hoover (London, 1952)

—— *The Yale Edition of Horace Walpole's Correspondence, 25: Horace Walpole's Correspondence with Sir Horace Mann and Sir Horace Mann the Younger IX,* ed. W. S. Lewis *et al.* (London, 1971)

—— *The Yale Edition of Horace Walpole's Correspondence, 29: Horace Walpole's Correspondence with William Mason I,* ed. W. S. Lewis, G. Cronin jr. and C. H. Bennett (London, 1955)

Walsh, S., 'Is the English Guitar a Guitar or a Cittern?', *FoMRHI Quarterly,* 47 (April 1987), 43–7, comm. 798

Walther, J. G., *Musicalisches Lexicon, oder Musicalische Bibliotec* (Leipzig, 1732)

Wangermée, R., 'Les premiers concerts historiques à Paris', in *Mélanges Ernest Closson,* ed. C. van den Borren and A. van der Linden (Brussels, 1948), 185–96

Ward, E., *A Compleat and Humorous Account of all the Remarkable Clubs and Societies in the Cities of London and Westminster* (London, 7/1756)

Ward, J. M., *Sprightly & Cheerful Musick: Notes on the Cittern, Gittern and Guitar in 16th- and 17th-Century England, LSJ,* 21 (1979–81), whole vol.

Wark, R. R., 'Thicknesse and Gainsborough: some New Documents', *The Art Bulletin,* 40 (1958), 331–4

Warrack, J., *Carl Maria von Weber* (Cambridge, 1968)

Waterhouse, E., *Gainsborough* (London, 2/1966)

Weber, W., 'Lully and the Rise of Musical Classics in the Eighteenth Century', in *Jean-Baptiste Lully: actes du colloque / Kongreßbericht Saint-Germain-en-laye – Heidelberg 1987,* ed. J. de La Gorce and H. Schneider (Laaber, 1990), 581–90

—— *The Rise of Musical Classics in Eighteenth-Century England: a Study in Canon, Ritual, and Ideology* (Oxford, 1992)

Webster, J., 'Violoncello and Double Bass in the Chamber Music of Haydn and his Contemporaries, 1750–1780', *JAMS,* 29 (1976), 413–38

Wehrend, A., *Musikanschauung, Musikpraxis, Kantatenkompositionen in der Herrnhuter Brüdergemeine: ihre musikalische und theologische Bedeutung für das Gemeinleben von 1727 bis 1760* (Frankfurt am Main, 1995)

Wells, E., and C. Nobbs, *Royal College of Music Museum of Instruments Catalogue, iii: European Stringed Instruments* (London, 2007)

Wenzinger, A., 'The Revival of the Viola da Gamba, a History', in *A Viola da Gamba Miscellany: Proceedings of the International Viola da Gamba Symposium, Utrecht 1991,* ed. J. Boer and G. van Oorshot (Utrecht, 1994), 133–9

Weston, S. J., 'The Instrumentation and Music of the Church Choir-Band in Eastern England, with Particular Reference to Northamptonshire, during the late Eighteenth Century and early Nineteenth Centuries' (PhD diss., U. of Leicester, 1995)

White, *A Catalogue of the Valuable and very Fine Collection of Music, Printed and MS., of the late Charles Burney, Mus. D.F.R.S.* (8–15/8/1814; repr. Amsterdam, 1973)

—— *A Catalogue of an Extensive and Valuable Collection of Music Books ... part of which were the Property of the late Mr. G. E. Williams, Organist of Westminster Abbey, and several other Eminent Professors (Deceased)* (8–10/6/1820)

White, B., '"A Pretty Knot of Musical Friends": the Ferrar Brothers and a Stamford Music Club in the 1690s', in *Music in the British Provinces, 1690–1914*, ed. R. Cowgill and P. Holman (Aldershot, 2007), 9–44

White, B., and A. Woolley, 'Jeremiah Clarke (*c.* 1674–1707), a Tercentenary Tribute', *EMP*, 21 (November 2007), 25–36

Whiteley, J., *Stringed Instruments: Viols, Violins, Citterns, and Guitars in the Ashmolean Museum* (Oxford, 2008)

Whitley, W. T., *Thomas Gainsborough* (London, 1915)

Willetts, P. J., 'Music from the Circle of Anthony Wood at Oxford', *British Museum Quarterly*, 24 (1961), 71–5

—— 'Autograph Music by John Jenkins', *ML*, 48 (1967), 124–6

Wilson, J. H., 'The Life and Work of John Hoppner (1758–1810)' (PhD diss., U. of London, 1992)

Withers, *Catalogue of Ancient Instruments &c.* (London, 1893)

Wolff, C., *Johann Sebastian Bach, the Learned Musician* (Oxford, 2000)

Wollenberg, S., 'John Baptist Malchair of Oxford and his Collection of "National Music"', in *Music in the British Provinces, 1690–1914*, ed. R. Cowgill and P. Holman (Aldershot, 2007), 151–61

Wollny, P., 'A Collection of Seventeenth-Century Vocal Music at the Bodleian Library', *Schütz-Jahrbuch*, 15 (1993), 77–108

Woodcroft, B., *Patents for Inventions: Abridgments of Specifications relating to Music and Musical Instruments, A.D. 1694–1866* (London, 2/1871; repr. 1984)

Woodfield, I., 'Dudley Ryder, 1715–1716: Extracts from the Diary of a Student Viol Player', *JVdGSA*, 21 (1984), 64–8

—— *The Early History of the Viol* (Cambridge, 1984)

—— 'The Younger Sainte-Colombe in Edinburgh', *Chelys*, 14 (1985), 43–4

—— *Salomon and the Burneys: Private Patronage and a Public Career* (Aldershot, 2003)

Wolff, C., 'Bach's Leipzig Chamber Music', *Bach: Essays on his Life and Music* (Cambridge, MA, 1991), 223–38

—— *Johann Sebastian Bach, the Learned Musician* (Oxford, 2000)

Wright, M., 'James Watt, Musical Instrument Maker', *GSJ*, 55 (2002), 104–29

Wurzbach, C. von, *Biographisches Lexicon des Kaiserthums Österreich*, 60 vols. (Vienna, 1856–91)

Wynn, S. J., 'Karl Friedrich Abel: Some Contemporary Impressions', *JVdGSA*, 10 (1973), 4–10

'X', 'From my Study', *MT*, 34 (1893), 75–8

Zaslaw, N., 'Leopold Mozart's List of his Son's Works', in *Music in the Classic Period: Essays in Honor of Barry S. Brook*, ed. A. Atlas (New York, 1985), 323–58

—— *Mozart's Symphonies: Context, Performance Practice, Reception* (Oxford, 1989; repr. 1991)

Zimmerman, F. B., *Henry Purcell, 1659–1695: an Analytical Catalogue of his Music* (London, 1963) [Z]

Zoeller, C., 'Ancient Musical Literature', *MS*, 16 (15, 22, 29/3/1879), 158, 174, 190; *MS*, 16 (5, 12, 19, 26/4/1879), 206, 222, 238, 254; *MS*, 16 (3, 10, 17, 24, 31/5/1879), 270, 286, 302, 318, 334; *MS*, 16 (7, 14, 21, 28/6/1879), 350, 366, 382, 398; *MS*, 17 (5, 19, 26/7/1879), 2, 34, 50; *MS*, 17 (2/9/1879), 66

—— *New Method for the Viole d'Amour (the Love Viol), its Origin and History, and Art of Playing it* (London, 1885)

—— 'The Viole d'Amour', *MS*, 36 (23/3/1889), 236–8; *MO*, 12 (4/1889), 335–7

&. *Editions of Music*

Abel, C. F., *Six Easy Sonnatas for the Harpsichord or for a Viola da Gamba, Violin or German Flute* (?London, 1771; repr. Heidelberg, 2005); ME: 2 vols., ed. G. and L. von Zadow, intro. M. O'Loghlin (Heidelberg, 2005)

—— *Six Sonatas for a Violin, a Violoncello, & Base, with a Thorough Base for the Harpsichord*, op. 9 (1772); ME: *Kompositionen*, ed. W. Knape, xiii–xiv (Cuxhaven, 1969), 49–95

—— *Three Trios for a Violin, Violoncello and Bass Figur'd for the Organ or Harpsicord* (London, ?1772)

—— *Troi[s] trios pour le violon, violoncello, et basso* (Amsterdam, ?1772)

—— *Les Suites des trios primieres, trios pour le violon, violoncello, et basso* (London, ?1772)

—— *A Favourite Rondeau* (London, *c.* 1786)

—— *A Duetto for Two Violoncellos as Performed at the Hanover Square Concert by Messrs. Crosdill & Cervetto* (London, 1788; repr. Heidelberg, 2008); ME: ed. G. and L. von Zadow, intro. P. Holman (Heidelberg, 2008)

—— *Quartet in G for Flute, Violin, Viola (da gamba) and Violoncello*, ed. E. Hunt (London, 1951)

—— *Kompositionen*, ed. W. Knape, 16 vols. (Cuxhaven, 1958–74)

—— *Konzert B-dur für Violoncello (Gambe), Streicher und Continuo*, ed. H. Lomnitzer (Wolfenbüttel, 1961)

—— *Six Selected Symphonies*, ed. S. Helm (Madison, WI, 1977)

—— *Six Sonatas for Unaccompanied Viola da Gamba*, ed. M. Charters (Ottawa, 1982)

—— 'Frena le belle lagrime': an Aria for Soprano, Obbligato Viola da Gamba, Strings and Continuo, ed. W. Hunt (London, 1989)

—— *27 Pieces for the Viola da Gamba: New York Public Library, MS Drexel 5871*, intro. W. Knape (Peer, 1993)

—— *Six Sonatas for Two Violas da Gamba from the Countess of Pembroke's Music Book*, ed. B. Capleton, 2 vols. (West Malvern, 1997)

—— *6 Sonate per la viola da gamba*, ed. C. Denti (Bologna, 2002)

—— *Quartet no. 3 for Flute, Violin, Viola da Gamba and Cello*, ed. R. Whelden (Albany, CA, 2003)

—— *Sonatas for the Viola da Gamba*, ed. G. Houle, 3 vols. (Albany, CA, 2/2005)

—— *Zwei Berliner Sonaten für Viola da Gamba und Bass*, ed. G. and L. von Zadow, intro. M. O'Loghlin (Heidelberg, 2006)

—— *Zwei Berliner Sonaten für Violoncello und Bass*, ed. G. and L. von Zadow, into. M. O'Loghlin (Heidelberg, 2007)

Abel, C. H., *Dritter Theil musicalischer Blumen* (Frankfurt am Main, 1677)

Albertini, I., *Sonatinae XII Violino Solo* (Vienna and Frankfurt, 1692)

Aldrich, H., *Selected Anthems and Motet Recompositions*, ed. R. Shay, RRMBE, 85 (Madison, WI, 1998)

Ariosti, A., *Cantates and a Collection of Lessons for the Viol d'Amore* (London, 1724; repr. 1980)

Attwood, T., *The Mariners, a Musical Entertainment in Two Acts* (London, 1793)

Ayres & Symphonys for ye Bass Viol (London, 1710)

Bach, J. C., *Three Favorite Quartetts and One Quintett for the Harpsichord, Violin, Flute, Hautboy, Tenor and Violoncello* (London, 1785)

—— *The Collected Works*, 38: *Music for Two Instruments*, ed. D. J. Keahey (New York, 1991)

—— *The Collected Works*, 40: *Music for Four Instruments*, ed. D. J. Keahey (New York, 1990)

—— *The Collected Works*, 41: *Music for Five and Six Instruments*, ed. E. Warburton (New York, 1986)

—— *The Collected Works*, 48/1: *Thematic Catalogue*, comp. E. Warburton (New York, 1999) [B]

—— *The Collected Works*, 48/3: *Music Supplement*, ed. E. Warburton (New York, 1999)

Bach, J. S., *Werke*, 9: *Kammermusik, Erster Band*, ed. W. Rust (Leipzig, 1860)

Blow, J., *Anthems II: Anthems with Orchestra*, ed. B. Wood, MB, 50 (London, 1984)

—— *Venus and Adonis*, ed. B. Wood, Purcell Society Edition Companion Series, 2 (London, 2008)

Bocchi, L., *A Musicall Entertainment for a Chamber* (Dublin, 1724; Edinburgh, 2/1726; repr. c. 1990)

Bononcini, A., *Complete Sonatas for Violoncello and Basso Continuo*, ed. L. Lindgren, RRMBE, 77 (Madison, WI, 1996)

Bononcini, G., *Camilla, Royal College of Music, MS 779* [facs.], intro. L. Lindgren, MLE, series E, vol. 1 (London, 1990)

Buxtehude, D. *Violadagamba Solo: Sonata D-Dur für Viola da Gamba und Basso Continuo BuxWV268*, ed. L. and G. von Zadow (Heidelberg, 2005)

Caix d'Hervelois, L. de, *Second livre de pièces de viole* (Paris, 1719)

—— *Troisième oeuvre* (Paris, 1731; repr. 1974)

Carr, J., *Tripla Concordia, or A Choice Collection of New Airs, in Three Parts, for Treble and Basse-Violins* (London, 1677)

Cervetto, J., *Six Solos for the Violoncello with a Thorough Bass for the Harpsicord*, op. 1 (London, 1768)

—— *Six Solos for the Violoncello and a Bass*, op. 3 (London, 1777)

Chaboud., P., *Solos for a German Flute, a Hoboy or Violin with a Thorough Bass for the Harpsicord or Bass Violin, being all Choice Pieces by the Greatest Authors and Fitted to the German Flute* (London, 1723; repr. 1985)

Clagget, C. and W., *Six Duetts for Two Violins Intended to Improve and Entertain Practitioners* (Edinburgh, ?1760)

Clagget, W., *Six Solos for Two Violoncellos* (London, ?1761)

—— *The Comic Tunes in The Witches, or Harlequin Cherokee, as they are Perform'd at the Theatre Royal in Drury Lane, Set for the Violin, German Flute, or Harpsichord* (London, 1762)

—— *Six Solos and Six Scots Airs, with Variations for the Violin or Violoncello with a Thorough Bass for the Harpsichord*, op. 2 (London, 1762)

The Compleat Violist (London, 1699)

Corbett, W., *XII Sonate à tre*, op. 1 (Amsterdam, 1700; repr. 2003)

—— *Six Sonatas for Two Flutes and a Bass*, op. 2 (London, 1705); ME: *Sechs Sonaten für zwei Altblockflöten und Basso Continuo*, ed. P. Rubardt (Leipzig, 1969)

—— *Zwei Sonaten für swei Bass-Gamben und Bass* [op. 2, nos. 1 and 2], ed. M. Jappe (Stuttgart, 2003)

Corelli, A., [*Sonatas op. 5, nos. 6 and 11, Arranged for Bass Viol and Continuo*] (London, 1712; repr. 1980)

—— *Sonatas for Viol and Basso Continuo, Paris, Bibliothèque Nationale, MS VM⁷ 6308* [facs.], intro. H. Miloradovitch (Peer, 1989)

Dahmen, J. A., *Three Trios for a Violoncello Obligato with Accompaniments for a Violin & Bass*, op. 6 (London, *c.* 1798)

—— *Three Trios for a Violin, Tenor and Violoncello*, op. 8 (London, ?1798)

—— *Three Trios for Flute, Tenor and Violoncello*, op. 9 (London, 1803)

—— *Six Canzonets with Accompaniment for the Harp or Piano Forte*, op. 6 (London, *c.* 1805)

—— *Eleven Sacred Songs and Two Choruses in Score, the Words Taken Chiefly from the Psalms* (London, WM 1807)

—— *Three Quartetts for Two Violins, Tenor, and Bass* (London, WM 1808), op. 35

—— *Three Solos for the Violoncello with an Accompaniment for a Bass*, op. 35 (London, WM 1808)

—— *Three Trios, for Two Violins & a Violoncello*, op. 35 (London, WM 1810)

Dolmetsch, A., *Suite of Four Pieces* (London, 1893)

Eccles, J., *The Judgement of Paris* (London, 1702); facs., intro. R. Platt, MLE, series C, vol. 1 (Tunbridge Wells, 1984)

Eiffert, P. P., *Six Solos for a Violoncello with a Thorough Bass for the Harpsichord* (London, 1761)

Eight Divisions for a Treble Instrument, ed. S. Heinrich (Oxford, 2001)

Eight Symphonies for Bass and Treble (Violino o Treble Viol e Viola da Gamba),
ed. C. Contadin and M. Pelliciari (Albese con Cassano, 2005)

Elizabethan Consort Music: I, II, ed. P. Doe, MB, 44, 45 (London, 1979, 1988)

The Favourite Songs in the Opera Sifari (London, 1767)

Finger, G., *Sonatae XII. pro diversis instrumentis*, op. 1 (London, 1688); ME:
Three Centuries of Music in Score, ed. K. Cooper and S. T. Sommer, 8,
Chamber Music II: Trio Sonatas, Part 1 (New York, 1990), 111–81

—— *Sonata in C, opus 5, no. 10*, ed. P. Holman (London, 1980)

—— *Suite in E minor and Suite in D major for Two Bass Viols*, ed. A. Marshall
(Ottawa, 1981)

—— *Pastoralle 'Resonet in Laudibus'*, ed. K. Ruhland (Magdeburg, 2004)

—— *The Music for Solo Viol*, ed. R. Rawson and P. Wagner (London, 2009)

Flackton, W., *Six Solos, Three for a Violoncello and Three for a Tenor,
Accompanied either by a Violoncello or Harpsichord*, op. 2 (London, 1770)

Gaffi, T. B., *Cantate da camera a voce sola*, op. 1 (Rome, 1700)

Gambarini, E. de, *Six Sets of Lessons for the Harpsichord* (London, 1748)

—— *Lessons for the Harpsichord, Intermix'd with Italian and English Songs*, op. 2
(London, 1748)

Gasparini, F., *Cantate da camera a voce sola*, op. 1 (Rome, 1695; repr. 1984)

Giardini, F., *Six Trios for the Guittar, Violin and Piano Forte; or Harp, Violin
and Violoncello*, op. 18 (London, 1775)

Gibbons, O., *Fantazies of III. Parts* (London, c. 1620)

—— *Fantasies in Three Parts, Composed for Viols*, ed. E. F. Rimbault (London,
1843)

—— *Fantasies in Three Parts*, arr. G. A. Macfarren (London, 1843)

Giordani, T., *Three Sonatas for the Piano-forte or Harpsichord with Obligato
Accompaniments for the Flute or Violin and Viola de Gamba or Tenor*, op. 30
(London, 1782); ME of no. 3: ed. U. Drüner (Adliswil, 1982)

—— *Three Quintets for Keyboard and Strings*, ed. N. Temperley, RRMCE, 25
(Madison, WI, 1987)

Gorton, W., *A Choice Collection of New Ayres, Compos'd and Contriv'd for Two
Bass-Viols* London, 1701)

—— *Prelude for Solo Bass Viol*, ed. G. Dodd, VdGS Music, 87 (n.p., 1972, repr.
2005)

—— *Twelve Airs for Two Bass Viols, 1701*, ed. D. Beecher and B. Gillingham
(Ottawa, 1979)

Grabu, L., *Albion and Albanius, an Opera* (London, 1687); ME: ed. B. White,
Purcell Society Companion Series, 1 (London, 2007)

[Graun, J. G.], *Anon (Berlin School c .1760), Sonata in C major*, ed. D. A. Beecher
and B. Gillingham (Ottawa, 1984)

Grecke, P., *Two Suites for Two Bass Viols*, ed. D. Beecher (Hannacroix, NY, 1998)

Guerini, F., *VI sonate a violino con viola da gamba o cembalo*, op. 1 (Amsterdam,
c. 1739); ME: ed. C. Contadin and M. Pelliciari (Albese con Cassano, 2003)

Hacquart, C., *Chelys*, op. 3 (The Hague, 1686)

Hacquart, P., *The Complete Works for Solo Viola da Gamba*, ed. F.-P. Goy (Albany, CA, 1999)

Hammer, F. X., *Five Sonatas for Viola da Gamba, Violoncello or Basso and Harpsichord*, ed. D. J. Rhodes (Albany, CA, 2004)

Handel, G. F., *Sonata für Viola da Gamba und Cembalo … für Violoncell und Pianoforte bearbeitet … von F. Grützmacher* (Leipzig, 1876)

—— *Werke*, ed. F. Chrysander, 48: *Instrumentalmusik* (Leipzig, 1894)

—— *Einzeln überlieferte Instrumentalwerke II*, ed. T. Best, Hallische Händel-Ausgabe, IV/19 (Kassel, 1988)

—— *Giulio Cesare in Egitto*, ed. W. Dean and S. Fuller (Oxford, 1998)

—— *Sonata G-Moll für 2 Violen da Gamba oder andere Streichinstrumente (Violinen, Violen, Violoncelli) und Basso Continuo* HWV393, ed. G. and L von Zadow, intro. P. Holman (Heidelberg, 2007)

—— *Sonata in G-Moll* [HWV364a], ed. G. and L. von Zadow, intro. P. Holman (Heidelberg, 2009)

Haydn, J. [*recte* J. C. Bach], *Divertissement pour hautbois, violon, viola da gamba et basse*, ed. A. Dolmetsch (London, 1930)

Haym, N. F., *Complete Sonatas*, ed. L. Lindgren, RRMBE, 117, 2 vols. (Middleton, WI, 2002)

Hely, B., *Sonatas … for Two Bass Viols and Continuo or Three Bass Viols*, ed. I. Graham-Jones, 3 vols. (St Albans, n.d.)

—— *Two Solo Suites*, ed. I. Graham Jones (St Albans, n.d.)

Hintz, J. F., *A Choice Collection of Psalm and Hymn Tunes, Set for the Cetra or Guittar* (London, *c.* 1763; 2/*c.*1765)

—— *A Choice Collection of Airs, Minuets, Marches, Songs and Country Dances &c., by Several Eminent Authors, Adapted for the Guittar* (London, *c.* 1765)

Horn, C. F., *Six Sonatas for the Piano Forte or Harpsichord, with an Accompanyment for a Violin & Violoncello*, op. 1 (London, 1786)

Jackson, W., *Twelve Songs*, op. 16 (London, 1793)

—— 'When fond, you Damon's charms recite', op. 16, no. 7, ed. D. J. Rhodes, VdGS Music, 192 (n.p., 2003)

Jenkins, J., *Fantasia in D minor*, ed. P. Evans (London, 1958)

—— *Two Fantasia Suites for Treble Viol (Violin), Bass Viol and Organ*, ed. A. Ashbee (Albany, CA, 1991)

Königliche Gambenduos für zwei Bassgamben, ed. L. and G. von Zadow, 5 vols. (Heidelberg, 2002)

Kühnel, A., *Sonate ô partite ad una ô due viole da gamba con il basso continuo* ([Kassel], 1698; repr. 1998)

Kerll, J. K., *Ausgewählte Werke Erster Theil*, ed. A. Sandberger, Denkmäler der Tonkunst in Bayern, II/2 (Leipzig, 1901)

Lafont, C. P., *Grand Fantasia & Variations, on Favorite Airs in the Opera of Masaniello, for the Violin, with an Accompaniment for the Piano Forte* (London, 1836)

La Trobe, C. I., *Hymn-Tunes Sung in the Church of the United Brethren* (London, 1806)

Lidel, A., *Six Trios for a Violin (or Flauto), Violino Secondo and Violoncello Obligato*, op. 1 (London, 1776)

—— *Six Duettos for the Violin and Tenor, with a Separate Part for the Violoncello, to be Play'd Occasionally instead of the Tenor*, op. 3 (London, 1778)

—— *Six Sonatas for Violin, Tenor, & Violoncello*, op. 4 (London, 1778)

—— *Three Quintettos for a Flute, Violin, Two Tenors and Violoncello Obligato*, op. 5 (London, ?1779)

—— *A Second Sett of Six Duettos, Three for Violin and Tenor, and Three for Violin and Violoncello*, op. 6 (London, ?1780–1)

—— *A Third Sett of Six Duettos for Two Violins or Violin and Violoncello*, op. 8 (London, 1781)

—— *Six Solos for a Violin and Bass*, op. 9 (London, ?1781)

—— *Six quatuors pour une flutte, un violon, alto et basse*, op. 11 (Paris, n.d.)

—— *Three Sonatas for Viola da Gamba and Violoncello*, ed. D. Beecher (Hannacroix, NY, 1997)

—— *Six Sonatas for Viola da Gamba and 'Cello*, ed. H. Miloradovitch (Albany, CA, 1998)

—— *String Trios for Violin, Viola da Gamba and 'Cello*, ed. D. Beecher, 2 vols. (Hannacroix, NY, 1999)

Locke, M., *Chamber Music II*, ed. M. Tilmouth, MB, 32 (London, 1972)

—— *Anthems and Motets*, ed. P. le Huray, MB, 38 (London, 1976)

Lübecker Violadagamba Solo: Sonate D-Moll für Viola da Gamba und Basso Continuo, ed. L. and G. von Zadow (Heidelberg, 2006)

Marais, M., *The Instrumental Works*, ed. J. Hsu, ii: *Pièces de viole, second livre (1701)* (New York, 1986); vii: *La gamme et autres morceauxde simphonie pour le violon, la viole et clavecin (1723); Unpublished Pieces from the Panmure Manuscripts* (New York, 2002)

The Margaret Sinkler Music Book, ed. J. Porter (forthcoming)

Marino, C., *Sonata in D for Viola and Cembalo*, ed. K. Stierhof (Vienna, 1973)

Marzis, P. di, *Six Sonatas for the Cetra or Kitara, with a Thorough Bass* (London, c. 1760)

Medulla musicae, comp. R. M. [?Richard Meares III] (London, c. 1727)

Moss, J., *Lessons for the Basse-Viol* (London, 1671); ME: ed. T. Conner (Hannacroix, NY, 2004–5)

Mozart, W. A., *Within these Sacred Bowers, Canzoneta* (London, ?1800)

—— F. X. Hammer, *Three Pieces for Unaccompanied Viola da Gamba* / W. A. Mozart, *'In diesen heil'gen Hallen', Anonymous Arrangement for Unaccompanied Viola da Gamba*, ed. D. J. Rhodes, VdGS Music Edition, 194 (n.p., 2003)

Nineteen Divisions for Bass Viol, 2 vols., ed. S. Heinrich (Oxford, 2001)

Novell, M., *Sonate da camera, or Chamber Musick* (London, 1704)

Paxton, S., *Eight Duetts for a Violin and Violoncello or Two Violoncellos*, op. 2 (London, c. 1777)

—— *Six Easy Solos for a Violoncello or Bassoon, in which are Introduced some Favourite Scots &c. Airs*, op. 3 (London, 1778); ME: ed. N. Pyron (London, 1986)

Pepusch, J. C., *VI Concerts à 2 flûtes à bec, 2 flûtes traversières, haubois ou violins & basse continue*, op. 8 (Amsterdam, *c.* 1717–18; repr. 1993); ME: ed. D. Lasocki (London, 1974)

—— *Quintett in F Dur* [op. 8, no. 6], ed. T. Dart (London, 1959)

—— *Triosonate D-moll* [Cook 2:023], ed. H. Ruf, Hortus Musicus, 161 (Kassel, 1959)

—— *Triosonate E-moll* [Cook 2:027], ed. H. Ruf, Antiqua, 87 (Mainz, 1965)

—— *Sonata in G* [Cook 2:021], ed. B. Clark (Dundee, 2005)

Purcell, H., *Works*, 8: *Ode on St Cecilia's Day 1692*, ed. P. Dennison (Borough Green, 1978)

—— *Works*, 12: *The Fairy Queen*, ed. J. S. Shedlock, rev. A. Lewis (London, 1968)

—— *Works*, 22A: *Catches*, ed. I. Spink (London, 2000)

—— *Works*, 26: *King Arthur*, ed. D. Arundell, rev. A. M. Laurie (London, 1971)

—— *Works*, 31: *Fantazias and Miscellaneous Instrumental Music*, ed. T. Dart, rev. M. Tilmouth, A. Browning, and P. Holman (London, 2/1990)

Rameau, J.-P., *Five Concertos for the Harpsicord … Accompanied with a Violin or German Flute or Two Violins or Viola* (London, 1750; repr. New York, 1986)

Sainte-Colombe, *Recueil de pièces pour basse de viole seule (c. 1680): facsimilés des manuscrits 9469 et 9468, National Library of Scotland, Edinburgh, Manuscrits Panmure*, intro. F.-P. Goy (Geneva, 2003)

Sainte-Colombe le fils, *Tombeau pour Monsieur de Sainte-Colombe le père, précédé d'une fantasie et de quatre suites pour la viole de gambe*, ed. J. Dunford (Strasbourg, 1998)

Saint-Hélène, J.-F., *XII Solos for a Violin, with a Thorough Bass for the Harpsicord* (London, *c.* 1721)

Sales, P. P., *Nebauer and Sales: Sonatas for Gambetta and Keyboard*, ed. S. Heinrich (Oxford, 2004)

Sandoni, P. G., *Cantate da camera e sonate per il cembalo* (*c.* 1727; repr. 1983)

Schenck, J., *Select Lessons for the Bass Viol of Two Parts* (London, 1703)

Smith, J. S., *Musica antiqua* (London, 1812)

Straube, R., *Due sonate a liuto solo* (Leipzig, 1746; repr. 1981)

—— *Lessons for Two Guittars with a Thorough Bass* (London, *c.* 1765)

—— *Three Sonatas for the Guittar, with Accompanyments for the Harpsichord or Violoncello* (London, 1768; repr. 1979)

—— *The Mecklenburgh Gavotte, with Six Variations for the Harpsichord, Pianoforte* (London, ?1768)

Three Stylus Phantasticus Sonatas for Bass Viol and Bc, by Baudringer, Radeck and Anon., ed. S. Heinrich (Oxford, 2005)

Veracini, A., *Sonate da camera*, op. 3 (Modena, 1696)

Withy, F., *Divisions for Solo Viol*, ed. P. Connelly (Sydney, 1998)

Index